D0609300

SASKATCHEWAN ROUGHRIDERS

FIRST 100 YEARS

SASKATCHEWAN ROUGHRIDERS

FIRST 100 YEARS

Calder, Staseson, Folk, Hughes, Vanstone, Davis and Marce

Saskatchewan Roughriders – First 100 Years

by Robert Calder, Gord Staseson, Julie Folk, Bob Hughes, Rob Vanstone, Darrell Davis and Dan Marce

First Printing – August 2009

Published by
The Leader-Post Carrier Foundation Inc.
c/o The Leader-Post Ltd.
1964 Park Street
P.O. Box 2020
Regina, Saskatchewan Canada S4P 3G4

Library and Archives Canada Cataloguing in Publication

Saskatchewan Roughriders : the first 100 years / Robert Calder ... [et al.].

Includes bibliographical references.

ISBN 978-1-897010-61-7

1. Saskatchewan Roughriders (Football team)--History. I. Calder, Robert L., 1941-
II. Leader-Post Foundation

GV948.3.S37S28 2009 796.335'6409712445 C2009-904277-0

Cover and page design by Brian Danchuk, Brian Danchuk Design, Regina
Page formatting by Iona Glabus

Designed, Printed and Produced in Canada by:
Centax Books, a division of PrintWest Communications Ltd.
Publishing Director: Dan Marce
Publishing Coordinator: Iona Glabus
1150 Eighth Avenue, Regina, Saskatchewan, Canada S4R 1C9
(306) 525-2304 FAX: (306) 757-2439
centax@printwest.com www.centaxbooks.com

At the time of publication of this Saskatchewan Roughriders tribute book, the Leader-Post Foundation had awarded more than $250,000 in educational scholarships over its 25 years of existence. The Foundation has also donated and/or committed to a $100,000 donation to the Hospitals of Regina expansion program, earmarked for a library in the birthing area of the Regina General Hospital.

In addition to raising scholarship funds, this tribute will provide a legacy the Saskatchewan Roughrider Football Club … often referred to as Canada's Team.

The Leader-Post Foundation would also like to thank the Saskatchewan Sports Hall of Fame and Museum (SSHFM) and the Saskatchewan Lotteries Trust for their generous financial support under the terms of the Sport History Project Grant. It would also like to acknowledge the technical assistance offered by SSHFM staff and members of the SSHFM's Sport History Project Committee in preparing this publication.

Thank you for purchasing this book and for helping those we assist in their educational endeavors.

Photo Credits:

This project would not have been complete without the following who have contributed and lent their photographs for our use:

Saskatchewan Sports Hall of Fame and Museum (SSHFM)
The Leader-Post
Heenan Studios and the late Gord Heenan
Royal Studios
Solilo Studios, John, Ken and Bruce Solilo
West's Studios
The Vancouver Sun
The Vancouver Province
The StarPhoenix
The Lancaster family
The Willie Jacobs family
Joseph Dojack
Canadian Football Hall of Fame
Wyatt Photography
The Globe and Mail
Saskatchewan Archives
Sun Media Corp.
Dan Marce

ACKNOWLEDGEMENTS

At the risk of forgetting someone who contributed in whole or in part, there are many who deserve a special 'thank you' for making this tribute book to the Saskatchewan Roughriders' first 100 years so special.

First of all, to the Saskatchewan Roughrider Football Club, its Board of Directors and club management, not only for its endorsement of this centennial project but also for its full support in bringing it to fruition. Of special note: Jim Hopson and Steve Mazurak.

To the Saskatchewan Sports Hall of Fame and Museum, its Board of Directors, Sheila Kelly and Jacqueline Campbell for the financial support, guidance and providing of historical photographs that turned our authors' words into memorable images.

To the *Leader-Post*, Marty Klyne, Janice Dockham and its wonderful team of dedicated employees for its unwavering support to complete this project in the most professional manner. The hundreds of archival pictures allowed us to pay homage to our coach, player, builder, fan and volunteer heroes of the past to present this legacy with maximum impact. Specifically to Rob Vanstone, who in addition to being part of our team of authors, co-ordinated the timely contributions of historical photographs pertinent to specific storylines within the book, as well as his dedicated research and editing expertise. Also to Garnet Hendry and Dan Reban who provided the scanning and digitization of the photographs.

To Bill Dubecky and his team at Royal Studios for their equally important contributions in providing historical and pertinent pictures that 'freeze frame' memorable images of Rider heroes. Is there a more memorable picture in the minds of the Rider fans than 'The Kick'?

To all those interviewed who isolated and captured the relevance of the economic and social backdrop of times specific to events, games and league environment of the day.

To the research contributions of Ryan Whippler, Reid Lambden, Mitchell Blair, and especially those of Gordon Staseson and the venerable John Lynch.

To Grant Gayton and his team at PrintWest for their support in ensuring that this project received top priority, for a timely, high-quality product. To Wayne Standon, whose never-ending positive attitude and professionalism in providing picture scans for the optimal timing in providing historical photographs. To Iona Glabus, Publishing Assistant, who formatted, reformatted and reformatted ad nauseam, whenever a new storyline or photograph appeared. If that old saying "whatever doesn't kill you makes you stronger" is true, then Iona is a much stronger person due to the complexities of this project.

To Brian Danchuk, whose cover design and book layout provided us with a professional template to follow. In addition, Brian's guidance and expertise in all design matters are most appreciated. To not only my team of fellow authors – Bob Calder, Gordon Staseson, Julie Folk, Bob Hughes, Rob Vanstone and Darrell Davis and editor Al Driver, but also to our families, as more often than not, they were also burning the midnight oil with us as we completed this project.

Finally, to my fellow members of the Board of Directors with the Leader-Post Foundation: Chairman Jim Toth, Janice Dockham, Vern Fowke, Bill Johnson, Bill Wright, Dianne Carr and Jack Grossman. In addition, to the Sifton family, former owners of the *Leader-Post* for having the foresight to not only establish the Foundation but to assign employees Press Balmer, Jim Struthers, Joe Laxdal and Wayne Kuss to make sure it became a reality and a success. ... THANK YOU!

Dan Marce, Publisher,
Board Member of the Leader-Post Foundation

ABOUT THE AUTHORS

Robert Calder

Bob Calder, Professor of English at the University of Saskatchewan and winner of the 1989 Governor General's Literary Award for Non-Fiction, has been a Roughrider fan for fifty-five years. He is the co-author of *Rider Pride: the Story of Canada's Best-Loved Football Team (1984)*. Though he bleeds green and white whenever a Roughrider team takes to the field, he is fascinated by the colourful early history of the Club, in particular the golden age from 1910 to 1935, when the Riders dominated western football.

Gord Staseson

Gord Staseson has been involved with the Riders as a fan, volunteer and an executive member for over 75 years. He has served on the Management Committee, was Club President from 1978-81 and Chairman of CFL Board of Governors in 1982. He was a Co-founder and the Executive Producer of the 1987 Plaza of Honor, and served as the original Chair of the Selection Committee. In 1993, two years after retiring from the Plaza of Honor, he was inducted into the Plaza of Honor-builder category.

Gord has also received the Order of Canada, Saskatchewan Order of Merit and an Honorary Doctorate from the University of Regina. He was inducted into the Regina Sports Hall of Fame as a builder in seven sports in 2004.

Julie Folk

Julie Folk was born and raised in Regina, and graduated from the University of Regina with a Bachelor of Arts in Journalism. A longtime hockey player and golfer, Julie now participates in triathlons.

Julie writes, edits, proofreads, and takes photos on a freelance basis. She has worked extensively on *Inside Green*, a *Leader-Post* publication on the Saskatchewan Roughriders, and has followed the team as a fan for many years.

Bob Hughes

Bob Hughes spent 47 years in the newspaper business before retiring in May of 2008. He was probably best known as a sports columnist in Regina, covering the Saskatchewan Roughriders during the glory years of Ron Lancaster and George Reed, and beyond. Hughes covered more than 20 Grey Cup games, Stanley Cup playoffs and finals, the Olympics, the first Canadian Winter Games, Canada Summer Games, Memorial Cups, Canada Cups, Briers, the Scotties Tournament of Hearts and World Curling Championships. Hughes has co-authored or authored three other books: *Winners, A Century of Canadian Sport*, *Regina Rams–A Winning Tradition* and his most recent, *The Big Dig*, a national best-seller. Hughes is a member of the Canadian Football Hall of Fame, media section and the Regina Sports Hall of Fame. He was awarded a Canada 125 Medal by the Governor-General of Canada for his community work. Hughes is a third generation Reginan.

Rob Vanstone

Rob Vanstone is a lifelong Reginan who has been following the Saskatchewan Roughriders for nearly 40 years. He has attended two of the Roughriders' Grey Cup victories and written a book on the third. Hired by the Leader-Post in 1987, he is now the newspaper's sports editor and sports columnist, and a member of the Plaza of Honor Selection Committee.

Rob Vanstone is also the author of a tribute book to the 1966 Roughrider team, titled *West Riders Best*.

Darrell Davis

Darrell Davis was born in Regina and grew up watching his home-town football team, the Saskatchewan Roughriders. After graduating from the University of Regina, he became a sports writer with the Kindersley Clarion, the Moose Jaw Times-Herald and, in 1983, the Regina Leader-Post. He covered the CFL team for the Leader-Post from 1988 until he retired in 2008, earning enshrinement into the Canadian Football Hall of Fame's media section in 2006.

A long-time baseball coach, avid golfer and racquetball player, he is also involved with the Regina Sports Hall of Fame and has co-authored a book on the history of junior hockey's Regina Pats.

Dan Marce

Dan Marce has been a passionate supporter and seasons ticket holder of the Riders for the past 58 years. He has been a Roughrider volunteer since 1981 and worked as the Club's Director of Marketing on two separate occasions:1982-1985 and again from 1992-1993. He also served on the Roughrider Board of Directors from 1993-1999. In addition, Marce has served as the Chair of the Plaza of Honor Selection Committee from 1992-2006 and has been the Executive Producer of the Plaza of Honor Induction Ceremonies for the past 18 years.

FOREWORD

The Leader-Post Foundation has been providing scholarships and bursaries for southern Saskatchewan students for 25 years. The vast majority of the revenue for the scholarships has come from the publishing and sales of retail books. Approximately two and a half years ago, Foundation board members, Bill Wright and Dan Marce, saw the 100th anniversary of the Saskatchewan Roughriders as an opportunity to carry on the educational legacy of the Foundation by producing a tribute book to the great Roughrider tradition. They identified certain aspects of sports tribute books that seemed to be a fit and others that haven't been approached before, using these, as a guide to what they thought our fans would like.

Certainly the rich history of the club has to be chronicled and paid tribute to, but many sports franchises pay tribute to a single all-time all-star team. We felt that it was unfair to pit era against era … sizes, fitness, coaching, platooning, and many other aspects have changed the nature of not only the players, but also of the game itself. Hence, through our very football-savvy team of authors we have named era all-star teams to five eras, and where appropriate and applicable, name second-team all-stars as well. Long-time Rider fans will appreciate the many players who are honoured in this fashion.

Another interesting twist is the naming of the top 100 Riders of the first 100 years. We invited people who have followed and covered the Riders for enough years to remember the contributions of the Riders past and continue to follow the team today. Fifty-four ballots were received from those invitees who obviously put a lot of time, effort and sincerity into this survey. Readers will be interested to see the mix of old and new players, coaches and the recognition of builders who have made the Roughrider legacy.

Authors;

- (1910-1945) Bob Calder, who co-authored the tribute book *Rider Pride*, takes us through the club's formative years up to the end of the Second World War.
- (1946-1962) Gord Staseson and Julie Folk cover the post-war, pre-Ron Lancaster and George Reed era. Gord has followed and been involved with the team for over seven decades.
- (1963-1978) Bob Hughes likely could have written the Ronnie and George era in his sleep, as these were many of the years that Hughes covered the Riders in his heyday as a sports writer for the Leader-Post.
- (1979-1989) Rob Vanstone's passion for Roughrider football hit full stride during this period, long before he began covering the team for the Leader-Post. He is the newspapers' sports editor.
- (1990-Present) Darrell Davis, another long-serving member of the Leader-Post sports staff, got to cover an era with more tumultuous times than the others, but the latest years of his era are highlighted with a Grey Cup win and unparalleled fan support.
- Dan Marce has the privilege to formally recognize the achievements of the top 100 Riders of all-time. Being intimately involved with the Plaza of Honor and its inductees for the past 18 years, Dan has been fortunate enough to have met a vast number of the people named in the top 100 and has become most familiar with their careers.

How does one put together an all-star cast of authors and hope that it comes out correctly? I won't say it was easy but by recruiting a *Leader-Post* alumnus, namely Al Driver, as editor of this project was a move made to optimize the flow of this legacy book. Al's role was not only to make each era read properly but also to also ensure that six separate stories by seven different people would actually weave together in as seamless a manner as possible.

On behalf of the Leader-Post Foundation, SaskSport and our writing and editing team, we hope you enjoy reading about Canada's Team … and the Saskatchewan Roughriders' First 100 Years.

Jim Toth
Chair, the Leader-Post Foundation

TABLE OF CONTENTS

BIBLIOGRAPHY

Allan, Tony. *Football Today and Yesterday*. Winnipeg, Harlequin, 1961.

Andrews, Garry, and Calder, Bob. *Rider Pride*. Saskatoon: Western Producer, Prairie Books, 1984.

Cosentino, Frank. *Canadian Football - The Grey Cup Years*. Toronto: Musson Books, 1969.

Currie, Gordon. *100 Years of Canadian Football*. Toronto, Pagurian Press, 1968.

Kelly, Graham. *Green grit: The story of the Saskatchewan Roughriders*. HarperCollins Canada, 2001.

The *Leader-Post*

Phillips, Curt. *Saskatchewan Roughriders Player Reference, 1960-1996*. Self-published, 1997.

Saskatchewan Sports Hall of Fame

Sullivan, Jack. *The Grey Cup Story*. Don Mills, Greywood Publishing, 1971.

Vanstone, Robert: *West Riders Best - 1966 Grey Cup*, Regina, Centax Books, 2009

Yuen, Edward. *92 Years of Roughrider Football*. Regina: Self-published, 2002.

1910-1945

BY ROBERT CALDER

CHAPTER 1

Photo courtesy of SSHFM

The Saskatchewan Roughrider Football Club was born out of energy, optimism, and pride. In 1910 the city of Regina – and the newly created Province of Saskatchewan – was young, brash, and bristling with confidence. Five years earlier the Saskatchewan Act had carved 251,700 miles of desert, prairie, forest, and lakes out of the North-West Territories to create the province, with Regina as its capital. As such it was the centre of political control and police jurisdiction over an area three times larger than the British Isles and with a population of 400,000.

Regina's confidence in 1910 was based on the astonishing growth and development on the prairies in the first decade of the twentieth century.

Regina's confidence in 1910 was based on the astonishing growth and development on the prairies in the first decade of the twentieth century. The province's population in that 10 years had increased five-fold, and the effect on the cities was even more dramatic. Saskatoon went from 113 citizens in 1901 to 12,000 in 1910 while Regina's 30,000 residents were 15 times greater than those in 1900. As historian John Archer noted, "new horizons and prospects seemed limitless. The boom psychology was an urban phenomenon born of … material success and the unlimited expectation of future riches. It was fed by boundless optimism in business circles, incredible real estate promotions and the reiterated claims of a multitude of boosters."

1930 team photo – in front of the Regina exhibition grandstands (Top Photo)

Though Regina in 1910 was the capital of a frontier society preoccupied with settling and selling and building, its citizens remained well aware of the larger world of Europe, the United States and eastern Canada. Beyond news of the political, social and cultural events abroad, Reginans were interested in the sporting events of their homelands: cricket and football (ie soccer) for those from Britain, and baseball and college football for those who had come north from the United States. Prizefights and even wrestling matches (then a legitimate sport) were reported at great length in Regina's newspaper, the *Leader*.

Those who settled in the West were not merely followers of international competitions; they were also participants who quickly saw to it that their sports were transplanted and thriving in the new land. As early as 1890 cricket and baseball were played in the West, and Saskatchewan had a Cricket Shield for its provincial champions. Baseball became the dominant summer pastime, and in the early years of the new province the Western Canadian Baseball League comprised teams from Brandon, Winnipeg, Edmonton, Calgary, Medicine Hat, Lethbridge, Moose Jaw and Regina. A Saskatchewan Football (soccer) League was created, and in 1910 the Regina team was competing for the Canadian championship, in Toronto. Hockey, of course, was played everywhere, lacrosse was popular, and golfers could compete for the Saskatchewan Open Golf Title.

The Saskatchewan Roughriders might have become a rowing club rather than a football team.

In the midst of such growth and sporting activity, the reader of the Regina *Morning Leader* might have been forgiven for paying scant attention to a brief and quiet item appearing in the sports page of the September 6 edition. It noted that a meeting would be held the following Tuesday at the City Hall for the purpose of organizing a rugby club. "The original intention," the notice said, "was to make it a rowing club, but so much general interest has been created that the later plan was adopted. It is considered that a strong team can be formed in Regina and games will be played against Moose Jaw and possibly Winnipeg."

Unless the paper misprinted the item, it seems that the Saskatchewan Roughriders might have become a rowing club performing on Wascana Lake rather than a football team playing at what is now Mosaic Stadium. Regardless of this ambiguous origin, it was inevitable that football would not only find a foothold in Regina but seize its imagination and passion.

Rugby football, descended from soccer, had been played in some form in parts of North America since the middle of the nineteenth century, when regimental officers in Montreal played 15-a-side rugby. Then, on May 14, 1874 the sport took an enormous leap forward when McGill University played a team from Harvard, losing 3-0. As a result of this match, Harvard officially adopted rugby and persuaded Yale to follow its lead a year later. In 1879 the United States Intercollegiate Football Association adopted 11-man rugby, and from there the sport grew in American colleges. By the first decade of the twentieth century, professional rugby teams began to operate in the United States.

North of the border, a number of leagues, or "unions," had been created in Eastern Canada. In 1874 the Toronto Argonaut Rowing Club formed the Argonaut Football Club, adopting as its colours the blues of Oxford and Cambridge Universities. By 1875 a league comprising Toronto, Hamilton, Guelph, Stratford, St. Catharines, London and Port Hope was operating. In 1884 the Canadian Rugby Football Union was created and two years later this loose federation of several leagues sponsored the first Canadian championship game. In 1891 the CRFU became the Canadian Rugby Union, which – not always wisely or objectively – ruled Canadian football until 1967. In 1907 teams from Montreal, Toronto, Ottawa, and Hamilton broke away from their Quebec and Ontario unions and formed what was known colloquially as the "Big Four," becoming ultimately the eastern division of the Canadian Football League.

In 1909 Earl Grey, the Governor General of Canada, donated a cup for the Amateur Rugby Football Championship of Canada, and 11,000 fans gathered in Toronto to watch the Ottawa Rough Riders lose 31-7 to the University of Toronto.

In 1909 Earl Grey, the Governor General of Canada donated a cup for the Amateur Rugby Football Championship of Canada, and 11,000 fans gathered in Toronto to watch the Ottawa Rough Riders lose 31-7 to the University of Toronto. The game was played by 14 men on each side, all strictly amateurs and all of whom had to be residents of the

The 1910 Regina Rugby Club

Photo courtesy of SSHFM

city for which they played. Rather than a centre snapping the ball, play would begin with the centre "heeling" the ball back to a backfielder. Blocking was not permitted nor were tackles above the shoulders or below the knees. Lateral passes were allowed, but it would be another 20 years before anyone would see a forward pass. A score over the line was called a "try," worth four points, and a field goal from a try was worth an additional two. A field goal from a drop kick earned five points, a field goal from a free kick was worth four, while a team could get two points for a safety touch and a single for a "rouge," gained when an opposing player was unable to return the ball from his own end zone.

No one in Regina in 1910 doubted that a club could be formed that could successfully play this game. At the September 13 meeting the Regina Rugby Club was formed, and practices began two days later. Within a week the *Leader* reported optimistically that "already a splendid squad is turning out to practice and there seems to be ample material for a strong team. Many of the men are green at the game, but good coaching and chalk talks will soon remedy that." The chalk talks, necessary because not every player would be familiar with the ever-changing rules of North American football, took place every

"if you want to make the team you'll simply have to get out and show your form early in the season or some other hugger of the pigskin will hold down your job."

Friday evening. At the first such meeting, Billy Ecclestone lectured on "Football As It Ought and Ought Not To Be Played." Later talks reviewed the signals for various manoeuvres and outlined strategies for future games. Though the rugby of this era was far less complex and subtle than today's football, success often depended on knowledge of tactics and quick execution of them, and from its inception the Regina Rugby Club paid close attention to this part of the game.

In an era without radio and television, and few telephones, the most efficient way that team officials could contact players was through the pages of the morning paper. Thus the *Leader* would announce lists of players who were wanted at practice or even to report for games. Moreover, the paper often conveyed injunctions such as "the fourteen to line up in the first game will be chosen from them attending most practices from now on" or "if you want to make the team you'll simply have to get out and show your form early in the season or some other hugger of the pigskin will hold down your job." Potential players were also told that they could purchase their uniforms – in the team colours of old gold and purple – at C.W. Woods' store.

Practices were held at Railway Park each afternoon at 5.30 so that players could arrive from work in the few hours of daylight left in the prairie autumn evenings. It would be many years before the team could work out on an artificially lighted field, and as the days shortened in the late fall practices became more difficult. On more than one occasion scrimmages were held by moonlight, and as late as 1920 envious glances were cast toward Calgary, where the Tigers, preparing to meet Regina for the western title, were training with a whitewashed ball under electric lights in the Armouries.

The tradition of strong public support of the Saskatchewan Roughriders can truly be said to have begun with the Regina Rugby Club. Through the newspaper the general public was invited to the team's workouts, and soon there was a regular group of railbirds who gathered to assess the talent and to argue about the team's chances. So successful was this early public relations effort that 150 supporters accompanied the team on its first-ever game, in Moose Jaw, on October 1.

The Saskatchewan Rugby Football Union had been formed on September 22 by representatives of various Saskatchewan centres, but when Saskatoon, Weyburn, and Prince Albert were unable to field teams, league play for 1910 consisted of four games between Moose Jaw and Regina. Moose Jaw proved to be formidable, coached by Septimus "Seppi" Du Moulin, a banker by trade but also a former brilliant halfback with the powerful Hamilton Tigers, and it won the game 16-6. The Regina team argued that with a bigger line – it averaged 155 pounds – it would have won, but the *Leader* blamed the loss on the biased officiating of the referee: Seppi Du Moulin.

Though it now seems unimaginable that a club official of one team would serve as game official, it was common practice in the early days of football to have matches refereed by members of the participating clubs.

Though it now seems unimaginable that a club official of one team would serve as game official, it was common practice in the early days of football to have matches refereed by members of the participating clubs. Often the two managers would serve as referee and umpire, trading jobs halfway through the game. In a further confusion of roles, the coach of the Calgary Canucks, Joe Price, was also the sports editor of the *Calgary Herald*; and when Calgary lost the Western championship to Regina in 1915, he wrote the account of the game – and remarkably objectively.

When Regina lost to Moose Jaw three weeks later, it could have pointed to another problem common to all western clubs: its quarterback, Billy Ecclestone, was unable to play because of job commitments. Since all teams were strictly amateur, players had to balance making a living with playing for the team, and employment had to take precedence. The Regina club included farmers, lawyers, engineers, salesmen, construction workers, and even one CPR locomotive engineer, and their jobs often prevented them from attending practice or travelling to other cities.

Regina Rugby Club
EXCURSION
TO
MOOSE JAW
SATURDAY,
October 1st
Return Trip
Tickets $1.25

The Regina Rugby Club's first season was anything but auspicious. It lost all four of its games with Moose Jaw, including the provincial championship, and it was outscored 74-18 over the season. The Club officials, though, were not dismayed; the appetite for rugby had been created in the province, and plans for the 1911 season included competition against clubs from outside Saskatchewan. Though travel expenses were intimidating, the appeal of inter-provincial play was such that in Winnipeg, in October 1911, the Western Canadian Rugby Union was born. Its organizers grandly saw the WCRU doing for all the territory west of the Great Lakes what the CRU did for the east. Nine teams – two from Winnipeg, Edmonton, and Calgary, and one each from Saskatoon, Moose Jaw, and Regina – would form the Union, and the eventual Western Canadian champion would win the trophy donated by Hugo Ross. No one who experienced the amazing 2007 Roughrider season will be surprised at Regina's response to this development. "If this city can survive," observed the *Leader*, "without going entirely rugby mad, then it is a city the like of which never existed."

In 1911 the Saskatchewan Union was expanded to include a team from Saskatoon, and the Regina Rugby Club's colours were changed to blue and white, to match those of the Regina Amateur Athletic Association. It also had a new player/coach, Fred Ritter, an American who had a shrewd understanding of the game. His playing experience south of the border and dedication to fundamentals such as blocking and tackling were well blended with his tendency to use trick plays. A motivator as well as a tactician, Ritter appealed to both players and fans. Barely five feet, nine inches tall, but solidly built, he was respected for his jarring tackles and headlong rushes on punt returns. Moreover, he was able to inspire a team to perform well above its abilities. Many years later Al Ritchie, who played under Ritter, remembered his legacy: "I was exposed for the first time to a human dynamo – a man who breathed, slept, and ate football. He was our coach, our quarterback, our religion."

Fred Ritter clearly was many things – including a bit of an old-fashioned adventurer prepared to spin a tale if it enhanced his chances. For years he told Reginans that he had twice been named to the All-American football team while studying at Princeton University, and the prairie newspapers always assumed that this was true. In reality, he never did finish his freshman year at Princeton; he did complete the 1904 football season there, but then dropped out to make his fortune in the lumber trade in the emerging

Photo courtesy of Saskatchewan Archives

Fred Ritter

West. Being a "two-time All-American," then as now, opened a lot of business doors.

Under Ritter's leadership, Regina began the 1911 season with its first-ever victory, a 15-11 triumph over Moose Jaw. Its next game, in Saskatoon on September 30, was even more memorable, as indicated by the *Leader*'s headline: "RUGBY GAME AT SASKATOON ENDS IN AN UNSEEMLY RIOT LED BY POLICE. REGINA PLAYER ARRESTED AND SOAKED." The *Leader* went on:

> "In one of the most disgraceful exhibitions of lack of sportsmanship ever witnessed on a western football field, the rugby game Saturday came to an untimely close. Crowds have broken out upon the field before this the continent over, but when the crowd is led by the manager of one of the teams and a member of the police force, the thing passes the realms of the excusable. Except for a small portion of the crowd, that which instigated the riot, the whole affair came suddenly and unexpectedly. The first warning to most of those who witnessed it was the sight of a small figure running up the field with a mob of a hundred or more people in hot chase. In an instant the whole Regina team was surrounded by several hundred bloodthirsty hoodlums of Saskatoon, and for a time it looked warm for the visiting boys. Indeed, had it not been for the good services of the Mounted Police the Regina boys would certainly have had some rough usage. The city police were easily the worst of the crowd. Even the chief himself was threatening right and left to arrest players who so much as commented on the methods employed by his men. Not once did any of them make any attempt to restore order, and the threats and language they were using rather excited the crowd rather than otherwise."

With the field covered with spectators, the game was abandoned and eventually awarded to Regina. A Regina player was taken to police court and fined five dollars (a substantial sum in 1911) and costs, and then the Saskatoon team, which had not participated in the pursuit of its opponents, entertained the Regina players at dinner at the Flanagan Hotel.

As dramatic as the Saskatoon "riot" now seems, such altercations – and especially the ensuing arguments and appeals – were not uncommon in the early sporting life of western Canada. Because leagues were new and rules were in the developmental stage, without an established and respected tradition behind them, disputes were common in every sport. Moreover, the atmosphere of boosterism which prevailed everywhere in the West meant that rivalries between cities were intense. Each saw itself as the centre of the economic, political, social and cultural growth of the area, and one of the most visible signs of this pre-eminence was victory on the sporting field. Thus while today's rivalries between cities is tolerant and moderate, competition between centres in the early years of the twentieth century was certain to incite strong feelings.

Each saw itself as the centre of the economic, political, social and cultural growth of the area, and one of the most visible signs of this pre-eminence was victory on the sporting field.

The remainder of the 1911 season was less dramatic, though it ended with another dispute. Regina and Moose Jaw finished regular play with 3-1 records, and when Regina won the provincial title in a playoff game, it prepared to travel to its first interprovincial match, against the Manitoba champions, the Winnipeg Rowing Club. A day before the game was to take place, however, Winnipeg officials warned against coming because the brutally cold weather would make it very difficult to play, and so the Reginans cancelled their plans. Immediately after that, the Rowing Club claimed that the Saskatchewan champions had defaulted and they went on to play the Calgary Tigers for the first western Canadian rugby championship, losing 13-6 to the Albertans. The Regina Rugby Club was left to lick its wounds – and to be more wary in its future dealings with rival clubs.

If the 1911 season had ended with turbulence, the following one literally began like a tornado. On June 30 Regina was hit by a cyclone, and during three minutes of devastation 28 people were killed, 200 were injured, and 2,500 were made homeless. Five hundred buildings were destroyed, and when the grandstand and fence at Dominion Park were levelled, the Rugby Club lost the only grounds for major sporting events. The Regina City Council, however, found $18,000 for repairs to the Park, the club continued to play – adopting new team colours of red and black, and it won the provincial title, then called the Westman Cup.

With about 100 supporters, each of whom had paid $14.20 for a round-trip ticket, the Regina Rugby Club went to Winnipeg to play the Rowing Club, which had beaten the Calgary Tigers 4-3. In a rugged game, heightened by the bad feelings left over from the 1911 "defaulted" game, Regina won 5-0 on five single points from kicks. The city, reported the *Leader*, went rugby mad:

> "Everywhere you went about town Saturday evening people were talking football. They were talking it on the streets. They were talking it in the stores. They were talking it in the theatres. If there had been church services Saturday night some people would have been tempted to whisper football in church. In fact, on Sunday morning it was talked in one church, by the minister himself."

When the team returned to Regina on Monday morning it was met by nearly 3,000 fans and a brass band. The victorious coach was carried off the train on the shoulders of supporters, and, as the fire hall rang all its bells, 25 automobiles volunteered by citizens took the players to City Hall, where they were greeted by the Mayor. That evening the team attended a performance of *The Red Rose* at the Regina Theatre, and when the lead actress appeared in a black velvet dress with a red sash, the club colours, the house exploded in applause.

When the team returned to Regina on Monday morning it was met by nearly three thousand fans and a brass band.

Winning the Hugo Ross trophy in 1912 did more to establish football in Regina than anything else that the Rugby Club had done, but no one knew how timely the victory was. By the beginning of the 1913 season, the unbridled optimism that had marked the first dozen years of the century had waned in the face of a recession. The boom had ended: unemployment grew, seeded acreage declined, and the price of wheat became uncertain. Dollars were scarcer than before, and sports clubs had to work harder to retain their support.

Retaining that support was made easier by the appearance in Regina in September, 1913 of the powerful Hamilton Tigers. Hamilton's dominant win – by 26-4 – was indicative of the gulf between the established eastern Canadian teams and the young western ones, but the Regina performance was creditable, and it would be the last loss that the Club's supporters would have to explain for a very long time. The Regina Rugby Club would not lose another contest to any team for the next seven years.

Freddie Wilson

Photo courtesy of SSHFM

The remarkable string of victories began with an undefeated season in provincial play in 1913. The Rugby Club retained the western championship by defeating the Edmonton Eskimos 9-7 in the semi-final and, sparked by Freddie Wilson's recovery of his own punt for a touchdown in the opening five minutes, clobbering Winnipeg 29-0 in the final.

Wilson had joined the Club in 1911 at 17, and he went on to play remarkably for nearly two decades. Although he was barely 140 pounds and five feet, seven inches in height, he was a dynamo with incredible speed and an ability to launch booming kicks with either foot while on the run, often singlehandedly keeping the opposition penned in its own end. On more than one occasion he kicked the ball from midfield, raced around the line of scrimmage, and before the ball could bounce caught it on the dead run to score untouched.

With the second western title, rugby fever again hit Regina, but the Club declared that the victory belonged not only to the city but also to Saskatchewan, thus sowing the seeds for what decades later would become the "Saskatchewan Roughriders." As well, Club executives considered travelling east to challenge the Hamilton Tigers for the Grey Cup, but since the $1,000 offered by the Tigers would not begin to cover expenses, the idea was dropped in favour of waiting until financial conditions were better.

Though no one in Regina in 1913 could have known it, conditions for the Rugby Club's challenge for the Grey Cup would not improve for a decade. An economic recession which hit the Canadian West in 1913 deepened in the next two years, and in August, 1914, Canada began more than four years of the Great War. More than 42,000 Saskatchewan men and women enlisted, so many in Regina that the city actually saw its population decline. Among the earliest recruits were the Rugby Club's Clarence Dale and William Robbins and, as the war progressed, many more followed so that, as early as 1914, there were only five returning players.

The need for Canadian society to mobilize for war raised questions in rugby circles across the country about the propriety of playing football for the duration of hostilities. Some inside the sport argued that the clubs were too weakened by the loss of experienced players to be able to field competitive squads. Many outside rugby claimed that, when the country's energy should be directed toward victory in Europe, rugby might be too much of a diversion. Might not a number of able-bodied young men prefer fighting on the football field to fighting on the battlefield?

The question was hotly debated in various rugby union meetings and in newspapers across the country, and the Regina *Leader* joined others in arguing that, rather than undermining a young Canadian's desire to fight for his country, rugby actually prepared him for battle:

> "Rugby should be encouraged if for no other reason than for the number of men it has supplied for active service. The qualities it calls for make good soldiers. The fighting for the try, the spirited dashes for yards, feet, and even inches

> necessary to get the ball across the line for the coveted points – the bucking of the line – these are the qualities that carry men into the enemy's trenches."

Regardless of the validity of this argument, many members of the Regina Rugby Club made their contributions to the war effort. Among the 13,209 Saskatchewan soldiers who were wounded were six Club players: Charley Otton, Duncan Cameron, William Robbins, Roy Hamilton, Ted Porter, and N.J. "Piffles" Taylor. Among the province's 4,389 soldiers who died in Europe were 10 men who had played football in Regina: L. "Hick" Abbott, Tommy Blair, Bob Boucher, Clarence Dale, R. Legatt, Howie Longworthy, H. Pawley, Jimmy Scott, Sam Taylor, and R. "Punk" Thompson. Hick Abbott, one of Saskatchewan's most accomplished athletes and coach of the Rugby Club team in 1915, was twice wounded before being killed in the final months of the war. In recognition of his hockey skills – he was also a member of Regina's Allan Cup champions of 1914 – the Abbott Cup, awarded to the Western Canadian junior hockey champions, was named after him.

Though they unfolded against a backdrop of economic austerity and military conflict, the war years were good to the Regina Rugby Club on the field. Though the 1914 season saw the departures of Fred Ritter – to become assistant coach at Princeton – and R.L "Dinny" Hanbidge to practise law in Kerrobert – he would later become Saskatchewan's Lieutenant Governor — the following year uncovered a brilliant new quarterback in Piffles Taylor. Strong and splendidly built, he had lightning quickness, but his greatest quality was one that he shared with two superb Roughrider quarterbacks of later eras, Ron Lancaster and Kent Austin: his shrewdness in analysing the opposing team's defences. The *Leader* commented:

> "Piffles Taylor, the busy little soldier quarterback, will call the signals and the way he can fool the fellows [is] laughable. He's always raring to go and the speed with which he gets the plays away is marvelous and he has yet to be found guilty of not knowing the other fellow's weak spots and taking advantage of them."

Photo courtesy of SSHFM
Piffles Taylor

Taylor's reputation was to be earned over a number of years, and in 1915 he played only one game before leaving for the University of Toronto and eventual military service. Serving as a fighter pilot with the Royal Flying Corps, he was shot down over France and made a prisoner of war. When he was released in 1918 he returned to his home, and then, after completing his degree in Toronto, practised law in Regina. Despite the loss of an eye during the war, he returned to playing outstanding football, and on at least one dramatic occasion showed that his injury would not slow him up. In a game in Calgary in 1919, Taylor suddenly halted play while he got down on all fours and began searching the ground. It soon became obvious that a crushing tackle had jarred his glass eye loose and he was looking for it in the turf. When the missing orb was found, Taylor calmly put it back in the socket and proceeded to call signals before the horrified gaze of both friends and foes.

In later years Piffles Taylor went into business in Regina, served as alderman for five years, and was awarded the Order of the British Empire in 1946 for his contribution to Canada's Second World War effort. From his earliest contact with the Regina Rugby Club until his death in 1947, he made a sustained and vital contribution to the growth of the club and of football in general in western Canada. In 1946 he served as president of the Canadian Rugby Union, and the following year the home field of the Roughriders was given his name.

In Taylor's first year, 1915, the Regina Rugby Club won all four of its league games and then beat the Calgary Canucks 17-1 to win the western Canadian championship. In 1916 Moose Jaw withdrew from play, and Regina won both its games against Saskatoon, thereby retaining its provincial title. There was no interprovincial challenge for the Hugo Ross Trophy, however, and in 1917 the Rugby Club reluctantly suspended play for the remainder of the war.

When senior football began to be played again in 1919, the Regina Rugby Club had a bank balance of 30 cents, and so it undertook a thorough and very well organized fund-raising drive. Volunteers from the team and from such organizations as the Knights of Columbus, the Rotary Club, the Kiwanis Club canvassed the entire city in a two-day blitz with the goal being to raise $75. As the Club manager stated,

> Every man and business firm has a duty to perform towards the encouragement and promotion of the Regina Rugby Club. Honours have been won by the local rugby players year after year. The benefit from the advertising gained through the publicity given this city would be difficult to determine and cannot be fairly estimated in dollars and cents.

Whether out of civic "duty" or love of football, Reginans responded to the appeal, and more money than anyone had expected – $2,265 – was raised.

With Piffles Taylor back as quarterback, the Rugby Club demolished its opposition, defeating Moose Jaw 40-6 and 36-1, the University of Saskatchewan 45-0 and 30-0, and the Saskatoon Quakers 29-0. With a 12-0 victory over Winnipeg and a 13-1 triumph over Calgary, the Club won its sixth western title, completing an astonishing season where it had scored 205 points while allowing only eight.

The Club nevertheless again went undefeated through the 1920 season, defeating the Calgary Tigers 28-1 to retain the western title (the Winnipeg team defaulted the final).

By the 1920 season football had firmly taken hold of Regina. There were two junior clubs, the Winners Rugby Club (the junior arm of the Regina Rugby Club) and the Pats, and a juvenile club, the *Leader* Juveniles, who played against the local collegiate and Campion College. The most surprising development, however, was the emergence of a second senior club under the name of the Regina Boat Club. When Piffles Taylor and Charlie Otton joined the new team, the Regina Rugby Club suddenly had very stiff competition in its own backyard. The Club nevertheless again went undefeated through the 1920 season, defeating the Calgary Tigers 28-1 to retain the western title (the Winnipeg team defaulted the final).

The 1921 season began with the Western Rugby Football Union adopting Canadian Rugby Union rules, which meant its clubs could qualify to play for the Grey Cup. The number of players on the field was reduced from 14 to 12, and the ball was now to be put in play by a snap back rather than a heel back. The latter change meant that plays could then be initiated and carried out much more quickly and crisply than before.

The Rugby Club had a chance to try out the new rules in an exhibition game with the touring Hamilton Tigers, who had manhandled their western opposition. In an excellent game, the Tigers won 15-6, thus ending a truly remarkable string of victories for the Rugby Club. Between the previous loss to the Tigers in 1913 to then, the Club had won 32 consecutive games, outscoring its opposition 694-90. Its average of almost 23 points per game to it opponents' *three* is an astonishing statistic in any era of organized football. That record, it should be remembered, was established against teams from Edmonton, Calgary, and Winnipeg, and it brought with it seven consecutive western titles.

The 1921 season ended with the first East-West Grey Cup game, but it was not the Regina Rugby Club that represented the West. The Club had won all four of its regular season games, and it thought it had retained its provincial title when it defeated Saskatoon 10-8, but that game was declared no contest because of a disputed Regina touchdown. When Saskatoon won the replayed match 9-6, Regina lost the opportunity to defend the Hugo Ross Trophy, and the Edmonton Eskimos went to the Grey Cup game in Toronto, where they lost 23-0.

The Toronto-Edmonton Grey Cup final was the beginning of a new era in Canadian football: it had become a national sport with a national title. For the eastern football establishment, however, the emergence of competitive western teams was a threat, and the next 16 years were a period of confrontation as the West fought for equity in the committee rooms and equality on the football field. In this struggle to be taken seriously, to make the Grey Cup a truly national championship, no one did more – through its seven Grey Cup appearances between 1923 and 1934 – to make the West a legitimate contender than the Regina Rugby Club.

The summer of 1922 saw southern Saskatchewan gripped by radio fever as CKCK began its first broadcasts. Moose Jaw withdrew from the Saskatchewan league, leaving the Rugby Club and the Regina Boat Club to contend for southern honours, but the Boat Club was no threat to cross-city rivals. The Rugby Club easily won the south and then defeated the Saskatoon Quakers 7-5 to regain the provincial title. Once again, though, it lost the western playoff to the Edmonton Eskimos, this time by a score of 13-8, and it had to look on as Edmonton was again defeated – by Queen's University 13-1 – in the Grey Cup game.

Photo courtesy of Canadian Football Hall of Fame

Brian Timmis

The 1923 season was momentous for the Regina Rugby Club in a number of ways. It had to deal with the loss of Brian Timmis, who in three years with the team had earned the reputation of being the best footballer in western Canada and one of the West's best all-round athletes. A member of the famed Royal Canadian Mounted Police Scarlet Riders, he was one of many players who found their way into Club colours through being stationed in Regina. Famed for his straight-ahead style of running and fine open-field moves, he was also a superb defensive player. Timmis was famous for his refusal to wear a helmet, a habit he adopted after a game against Winnipeg. Wearing an early leather helmet, which was held in place by a thin lace under the chin, he crashed through the line and went down under a pile of players. His helmet was ripped away from his head and the leather lace bit into his neck and cut off his breathing. A fast-moving trainer rushed to the aid of the choking player, perhaps saving his life; and he never wore a helmet again, though he, after leaving Regina, played for another 15 years in Ottawa and Hamilton. Timmis became one of eastern football's greatest players, and was eventually elected to the Canadian Football Hall of Fame.

The year 1923 was memorable also because the Rugby Club appointed Tare Rennebohm as captain, thus beginning an association between the Club and Rennebohm which spanned four decades. Years after his playing days, he loved to entertain Roughrider rookies with stories of the rough battlefield football of the 1920s:

> "Just before every game, each lineman used to put a dollar in a hat. The money went to the guy who drew first blood. The opening scrimmage was always a ritual. When we lined up for the second one we looked across at our man. If we saw blood we pointed to him and claimed our hatful of dollars. Those were the days! Why, on the last play of every game, winning or losing, we went in with fists swinging. We always ended the show fightin'. The Roughrider line was feared by man and beast clear across western Canada… . Shucks nobody was mad at anybody. Those were the unwritten rules. You just didn't belong until you were blooded. Something like foxhunting except in that sport it is always the fox's blood."

Rennebohm also told of a classic gridiron feud between Regina's mammoth Bill Kerr and Saskatoon's Tiny Dickerson. In the opening game of a playoff series, Dickerson slugged Kerr in the solar plexus, causing him to throw up for the rest of the game. Swearing revenge, Kerr flattened Dickerson with a hammer blow on the third or fourth play of the next game, but the sight of the prostrate and motionless player caused him to panic. "Great Scott, Tare. I've killed him!" he exclaimed. "What'll I do now?" "Pipe down," replied Rennebohm. "Half an hour from now you'll wish you had killed him. Don't worry about him. That won't hurt him. He'll be back to give you some of your own medicine before the game is over." Dickerson did indeed arise to fight again, and the two antagonists continued to slug it out until the end of the game, after which they amiably relived the battle at a nearby bar.

Photo courtesy of SSHFM

Tare Rennebohm

Winnipeg lineman Rosie Adelman, however, wasn't treated to such an amiable post-game celebration of sportsmanship. He was once knocked out as he bent over the ball in a game in Regina, and, then, as he walked out of a Hotel Saskatchewan elevator later in the evening, he was flattened by the same player who had turned out the lights on him in the afternoon. According to the Winnipeg press, Adelman had to be carried to the train by his teammates.

During games injured players were expected, except in the most severe circumstances, to walk off the field under their own power. This practice, however, had to be abandoned in the late 1930s when Saskatchewan's Dean Griffing knocked Calgary's Jerry Searight cold with a hit that reverberated throughout the stands. In an age when medical assistance was rudimentary and stadiums did not have stretchers, there was nothing to carry the inert Searight off the field. After some moments the Calgary club solved the problem by unhinging their clubhouse door and removing its fallen gladiator on this effective, if uncomfortable stretcher.

In the 1920s injuries were treated rather simply: a player was either totally incapacitated or he played. "The hairline fractures you read about right now," Rennebohm once claimed, "didn't count in the twenties." Another Roughrider player from the 1930s, Harold Urness, recalled the devious ploys that were used to disguise injuries: Before a game, the injured leg was not visibly bandaged, but rather the other, uninjured leg was, with bamboo slats and wide white tape placed over the slats and stockings were made very visible to opposing players, so that they zeroed in on this leg, thinking that this would put the player out of the game.

In addition to the appointment of Rennebohm, 1923 saw the appointment of Alvin Horace "Al" Ritchie as manager of the Regina Rugby Club. Having moved to Regina from Ontario at the age of 21 in 1911, he soon became attracted to the intense kind of football demanded by Fred Ritter, and in 1919, following military service in Europe, he returned to Saskatchewan and resumed what would become a lifelong promotion of athletics. A full-time employee of Canada Customs, he used virtually all of his spare time and energy in coaching local teams, and each year he would arrange to take his holidays so that he could accompany his squads on their numerous playoff trips. Having spearheaded the formation of the Regina Pats junior hockey team, he coached it to national titles in 1925 and 1930. Similarly, having organized the Pats junior football club, he led it to the Canadian championship in 1928, and this feat of coaching national champions in both sports has never been equalled.

Al Ritchie

Photo courtesy of SSHFM

It was with the Regina Rugby Club that Ritchie's career was most illustriously tied in the 1920s and 1930s. Joining the Club executive in 1919, he later became treasurer and then for many years the manager. Wearing his favourite coonskin coat and biting on one of his seemingly endless supply of cigars, he became a familiar sight on football fields. As a coach he was shrewdly analytical, always willing to try adopt new techniques, and gifted at handling players. He once forbade his players from wearing gloves around Regina for two weeks so that their hands would be toughened for a playoff game in the frigid playoff conditions in Edmonton, and he once told an underperforming prima donna player that he could go back to North Dakota. "Or," he added, "you can report to the Moose Jaw Maroons, ... but who the hell wants to play in Moose Jaw?" Listening in on one of Ritchie's clubhouse talks, the *Leader* reported "quite an earful. Fight, and then some, is what the coach expects of the Riders. He reminded them that just to go along all season and win games is not all that is required. The Roughriders have a reputation all over Canada, and when the average fan goes to see them play he expects to see something smart pulled off."

He once forbade his players from wearing gloves around Regina for two weeks so that their hands would be toughened for a playoff game in the frigid playoff conditions in Edmonton,

Under Ritchie the Roughriders did indeed pull off "smart" plays, but, as Harold Urness recalled from an exhibition game against the Hamilton Tigers, he was not above improvising and using unorthodox strategy:

> "We were up against some big guns like Sprague, Timmis, Cap Fear, and others. Ritchie was not exactly a coach who had a permanent playbook around. Instead he had a lot of ideas jotted down in his many bits of paper in his pockets. As well, he tucked away in his head an assortment of trick plays which he could

Photo courtesy of SSHFM

Greg Grassick

use if the occasion was right. To prepare for Hamilton he decided on a play which he called the "S" play. In this play, Angie Mitchell would call for a direct snap to Grassick or James. Mitchell would call the signals when we came out over the ball but after a few moments he would straighten up and say, with a wave of his right hand, "Oh, Shit!" The ball was snapped on "S" and the ball carrier tucked it in and took off. That play led to the only points we scored that day."

Ritchie's devotion to the Roughriders was fierce and no medieval knight ever sought the holy grail with more passion than Ritchie pursued a Grey Cup for Regina. Moreover, he saw the day when football in western Canada would grip the imagination of every sports fan and match that of the East. Year after year he fought for national acceptance of the innovative rule changes pioneered by western clubs: the reduction of the number of players on the field from 14 to 12, the opening up of the rules of blocking, the introduction of the forward pass, and the importation of skilled, experienced players from the United States. Above all, at a time when eastern football officials and sportswriters saw the national final between East and West as a nuisance, Ritchie saw the necessity of making the Grey Cup a truly national game. Looking back many years later, he commented that "one of the big contributing factors in building the great football structure we enjoy in Canada today were those early East-West games for the Grey Cup, despite the fact that we absorbed some bad beatings. It kept the principle of declaring a national champion alive… It developed an East-West friendship which has obtained through the years – something which is of immeasurable value."

Once Ritchie had become manager of the Regina Rugby Club, it did not take him long to get his team to the Grey Cup game. Finishing the 1923 Saskatchewan season with a 3-1 record, the club defeated the Edmonton Eskimos 9-6 and the Winnipeg Victorias 11-1 to earn the right to play Queen's University for the Grey Cup in Toronto. As they boarded the train for the two-day trip east, a Winnipeg reporter stated optimistically that "the Regina team is not flashy and will not score many points as their attack is not very brilliant. But they will be hard to score upon if they maintain the same kind of game which characterized their play in the [western] championship series."

Clearly the students from Queen's ignored this report because on December 3, in front of 8,528 spectators, they routed the western champions 54-0. Possessing a stronger line, skillfully using fakes and extension plays, and employing "interference" (what would now be called blocking) which was uncommon in western play, the Queen's squad completely dominated the game. As the *Leader-Post* put it, "touchdown followed touchdown with monotonous and heart-rending regularity," and the resulting score was the most lopsided Grey Cup result since Montreal beat Peterborough 71-9 in 1907. Ironically, when the dejected team arrived home three days later, it brought the game ball, a player having retrieved it when it was thrown in the air at the end of play. The local paper captured the public sentiment: "While Regina will scarcely be inclined to do honor to the sphere, it will nevertheless command a great deal of reverence, much like that accorded a captured Hun bomb." For those who played in that debacle, the humiliation was forever seared in their memories, and for many years after it was defensively referred to as the "five-four-oh" game.

To have failed in its first attempt to win the Grey Cup was no surprise to the Regina Rugby Club, but the magnitude of the defeat left it shell-shocked. This may have been the intention of the Queen's team, since the Toronto *Globe* reported that the eastern champions had run up such a high score to so humiliate the West that it would be discouraged from offering future challenges. Rather than being discouraged, however, the Regina Rugby Club was only more determined, and for the 1924 season it brought in Ed "Pete" Dolan, the substitute quarterback from Queen's, to teach its players the eastern training methods and style of play.

The more likely explanation is that "Roughriders" originated in the history of western Canada, where the term "rough riders" referred to horsemen.

1924 saw another – and ultimately more enduring – borrowing from the East. The Ottawa rugby club had since its beginnings in the 1880s used the name "Rough Riders," a term used to describe the lumberjacks who rode the logs down the turbulent rapids of the Ottawa River. As the 1924 season began, however, Ottawa dropped the name in favour of the "Senators," and the Regina Rugby Club soon began calling its team the "Roughriders," a name that the *Leader* had casually – and only once – used before, in 1915.

The term took on a different and more glamorous meaning in the United States during the Spanish-American War of 1898 when an American cavalry regiment under the command of Teddy Roosevelt, the future President of the country, became known as "Roosevelt's Rough Riders." It has been argued that the American ex-patriots in the Regina Rugby Club wanted to adopt the name in tribute to the ebullient Roosevelt.

The more likely explanation is that "Roughriders" originated in the history of western Canada, where the term "rough riders" referred to horsemen, specifically those who broke horses – as early as 1893 Buffalo Bill Cody called his travelling wild west show "Buffalo Bill's Wild West and Congress of Rough Riders of the World." According to Edith Patterson's *Tales of the Early West*, a contingent of North West Mounted Police officers who played two rugby matches in Winnipeg in 1890 were referred to as "Roughriders" because of their occupation of breaking the broncos used by the Force.

Whatever its origins the name "Roughriders" began to appear, without any fanfare or announcement, in the *Leader* reports in November, 1924, and the club has never relinquished it since, even when Ottawa reclaimed the name "Rough Riders" only a few years later. For many decades until the Ottawa franchise folded and re-emerged as the "Renegades," the situation of two teams with similar names in an eight- and nine-team league was a source of amusement to American observers.

Even with its new name, the Regina Roughrider Football Club did not have another opportunity to play for the Grey Cup until 1928. In 1924, the Roughriders lost the western final to the Winnipeg Victorias 22-1 and the following year they were beaten by the Winnipeg Tammany Tigers 11-1. In 1926, the Roughriders won the western title on an icy field in Edmonton by beating the University of Alberta 13-1, but when they looked east they found no enthusiasm for an East-West Grey Cup game. The eastern final was being played on December 4, and the eastern football officials argued that any game played after that would face prohibitive weather. Toronto sportswriter Lou Marsh was more candid when he wrote: "Take it from me, there is no demand for a playoff between the East and the West and there hardly will be until the West produces a team that stands out." In Regina they wondered how the East would ever know whether a team stood out unless they played it.

Eastern officials were no more receptive to an East-West Grey Cup game in 1927. After defeating the Winnipeg Tammany Tigers in Winnipeg, the Roughriders for the first time in history played a western final against a team from the west coast: the University of British Columbia. Eight hours after stepping off the train in Vancouver, the Regina team beat its hosts 13-1 and three days later won the two-game total-point final 19-0. When the Roughriders once again looked east, however, the East once again looked away, its position being that western teams did not belong on the same playing field as those of the East.

Photo courtesy of SSHFM

Angie Mitchell

Many western football officials shared the attitude of the East, believing that more humiliating Grey Cup losses would set back the progress of football in the West. Reginans, however, argued that exposure to the eastern game would bring increased football sophistication, and, as the *Leader-Post* suggested, only by being measured annually against the best in the country could western teams determine their progress:

"How in the name of Pete will the West ever find out how she stacks up against the East unless there is competition … How then are we going to determine the real strength of the Western team? It may be determined at a loss, at a heavy loss, too, but there's only one way to really answer the question. Get out there and play them, and find out how bad, or good we really are."

Looking back 40 years later, Al Ritchie was more succinct: "I knew that the Roughriders didn't stand much of a chance but I envisioned the day when the West would win the Cup. I felt we just had to keep challenging to win the trophy."

Driven by this sense of mission, Ritchie led the Regina Roughriders to six Grey Cup appearances in the next seven years. In 1928, with a perfect 6-0 season and a 12-1 western final victory over Winnipeg St. John's, the Roughriders sported a record that eastern officials could not ignore. They had not lost a game for three years, winning 17 in a row, and in the process outscoring the opposition 302-35. While their opponents had crossed their goal line only three times, the Roughriders had scored 47 touchdowns. They appeared to be a much stronger team than any previously sent east, and so it was arranged that the national championship be played on December 1.

Photo courtesy of SSHFM

Eddie "Dynamite" James

The Roughriders' opponents in the Grey Cup game were the Hamilton Tigers, considered to be the most formidable team fielded in the East since the war. To bolster their chances, the Regina club brought up five members of the junior Pats, who for the previous four years had won the western championship: Eddie "Dynamite" James, Saul Bloomfield, Andy "Red" Currie, Angie Mitchell, and Jim Doctor. The national junior final was to be played a week after the Grey Cup game, and several players – notably Eddie James – played in both.

James, described as a "human locomotive," was a fearless "plunger" (what would now be called a "rusher") and prolific scorer but also an excellent defensive player. After helping the Roughriders to western titles in 1929 and 1931, he moved to Winnipeg, where he played on the first western team to win the Grey Cup, in 1935. Inducted into the Canadian Football Hall of Fame in 1963, his superb talent as a running back led to the naming of the Eddie James Memorial Trophy, awarded annually to the leading rusher in the West.

Unlike James, the diminutive Angie Mitchell remained in Regina and performed brilliantly at quarterback for the Roughriders for a number of years. His career is remarkable in part because he weighed only 130 pounds, though his short stature would have been less noticeable in 1929, when the Regina players weighed an average of a mere 160 pounds.

The Roughriders were also helped in the 1928 Grey Cup game by the presence of Fritz Sandstrom, known in Regina as "the Crazy Swede." Off the field in civilian clothes, recalled teammate Al Urness, "he appeared the most unlikely athletic type: a mild milksop type with light gold-rimmed glasses and mousey blond hair." On the field, he was renowned for his ability to play any position, offence or defence, superbly, and to play them with reckless abandon. Helmetless in the 1928 Grey Cup game, he got kicked in the head and played most of the contest with blood streaming down his face. Despite this heroic effort and that of James – and the improved play of the team as a whole – the Roughriders lost to the Tigers 30-0.

Photo courtesy of SSHFM

Al Urness

The Roughriders were back in the Grey Cup final in 1929, having beaten Winnipeg St. John's 19-3 and the Calgary Tigers 15-8. The latter game, the western final played in Regina, was notable for several innovations: the first scoreboard, erected by the *Leader-Post*, and the first radio broadcast – by Regina's CKCK and a Calgary station – of a western game. The arrival of radio coverage immediately brought fears of reduced attendance, but it was soon obvious that the interest generated by radio broadcasts actually brought in spectators.

A more interesting innovation was the interception of a Calgary pass by the Roughriders' Fred Brown, his 55-yard return for a touchdown being the first ever scored from an interception in Canadian football. That there was even a pass to be intercepted was a new development in 1929, and the arrival of the forward pass in the West is an interesting example of the fluidity of early football rules and of the kind of borrowing that went on in the early days of the Canadian game.

A newcomer to the Calgary Tigers in 1929 was the American Jerry Seiberling, a star halfback from Drake University, where he had learned how to throw the ball accurately and at a great distance. Carrying the ball during one of Calgary's early games, Seiberling spotted a man downfield and instinctively passed it to him for a touchdown – a play permitted in the American college game. The Canadian officials, however, were dumbfounded and somewhat confused. In the moments that followed they hesitated to call the play back, and as a result the touchdown counted. With this historic precedent, Calgary continued to use the forward pass and gradually the other western teams followed suit.

Photo courtesy of SSHFM

Fritz Sandstrom

The Roughriders had used the forward pass only occasionally during the 1929 season, but sportswriters warned that the westerners had paid special attention to it in practice and might use it to devastating effect: "Tried out in the West this fall with only indifferent success, the aerial threat is nevertheless more or less familiar to the Roughriders ... they know how to use it, and they know its deadly potentialities." In fact, in the Grey Cup game, played against the Hamilton Tigers on a brutally cold day, the Reginans completed eight of 11 passes, a better aerial attack than most American teams were able to mount at the time. Much of the damage was done by Jersey Campbell, who was actually a "snapback" or centre as he would be known today. With few rules as to who could advance the ball from scrimmage, Campbell, with a strong arm, became the first player to throw a forward pass in Grey Cup competition. He actually threw nine of them, while quarterback Angie Mitchell threw two more.

Photo courtesy of SSHFM

Jersey Campbell

The Tigers were confused by this aerial attack, and the Roughriders themselves were surprised by their success, having always intended to beat Hamilton with a ground game. Trailing only 2-1 at halftime, they were optimistic that they could win with Campbell's passing, but a fumbled punt led to a Tigers touchdown and a final score of 14-3 for the Easterners. It was another disappointing loss, but one that earned the Reginans a new-found respect in Lou Marsh. "Western experts," he wrote, "said this was the best senior team the West had produced, but they did not tell the half of it. This team is a real team."

The 1930 season began with new team colours for the Roughriders – all black with red shoulder pads – and the grim prediction by the Hamilton coach that no western club would win the Grey Cup for twenty years. Al Ritchie, never one to remain silent in the face of a challenge, replied, "Gone is that inferiority complex and when the Roughriders walk into a game in Hamilton from now on, they are not a bit afraid of the Tigers – we both play twelve men a side, and the Westerners are not one bit less intelligent than the Easterners."

Photo courtesy of SSHFM

Stonewall Jackson

The 1930 season saw another first for the Roughriders, one signalled by the following *Leader-Post* headline: "DUSKY ATHLETE JOINS RIDERS." Using similar euphemisms of the time, the paper described this new player's debut: "The performance of 'Stonewall' Jackson was a revelation. Only twice did the dusky athlete touch the pigskin – but how he made those occasions count. Players, water boys and coaches alike looked on dumbfounded when the ebony-hued boy sped through the Moose Jaw line for 45 yards in the last quarter but the ball carrier did not seem the least excited and took everything in a matter-of-fact way." Thus did Robert Ellis 'Stonewall' Jackson, the Roughriders' first black player, make his appearance.

Working out of Regina as a porter on the Canadian National Railway, this natural athlete soon became a favourite of the Regina fans. When the Riders crushed the Winnipeg St. Johns' 23-0 in the western quarter-final before 2,000 fans in Regina, the cry of "we want Jackson" went up from the stands in the second half. Every move that he made brought a roar from the crowd, and, when he brought down Eddie James, then playing for Winnipeg, on an end run, the place exploded.

The Roughriders qualified for their third consecutive Grey Cup appearance in 1930 by beating the Calgary Tigers 9-6 in Calgary and then taking a two-game, total-point final against the Vancouver Meralomas by scores of 17-0 and 4-0. While en route to the East to play Toronto Balmy Beach, however, they once again came face to face with the determination of the eastern officials not to see the western teams win the Cup. The Roughriders had caught the easterners off guard with their passing the year before, and the Canadian Rugby Union ruled that the forward pass could not be used in the Grey Cup game unless both participating teams had employed it during the season. Toronto had not thrown the ball, so passing was banned, and 1930 became the last year that the national final was played without the forward pass.

Even without a passing attack, the Roughriders came closer to winning the Grey Cup than any western club ever had, and with a few breaks they might have triumphed. Down 10-0 at halftime, they narrowed the score to 10-6 on Fred Brown's touchdown, the first major score ever tallied by a western team in a Grey Cup game. Then, having the ball inside the Balmy Beach 10-yard line, the Roughriders attempted an on-side kick – a tactic with a high rate of success in that era – but in a play which has become part of Grey Cup lore, Toronto's Ted Reeve, playing with a dislocated shoulder, blocked the kick and killed the threat.

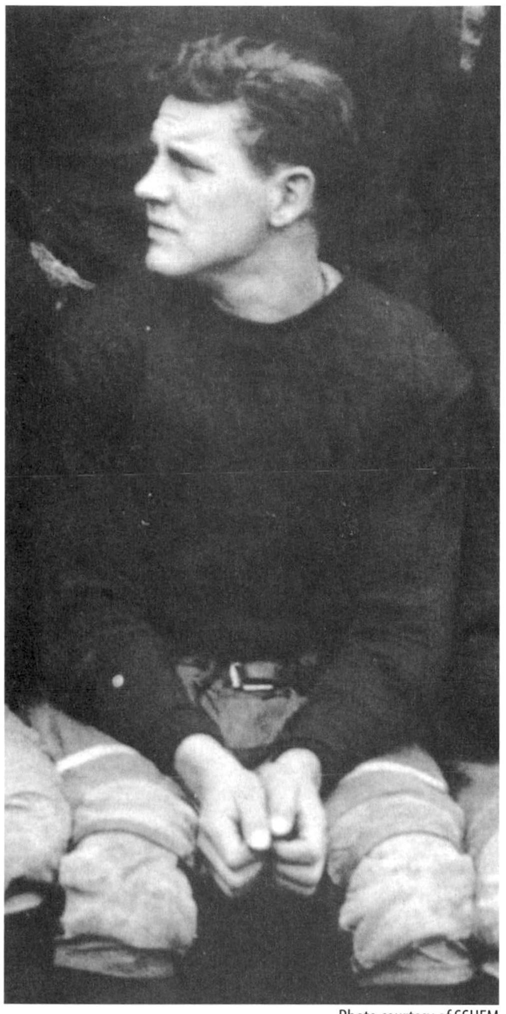

Photo courtesy of SSHFM

Fred Brown

Once again the Roughriders had improved the performance of the West in the national final, and western fans listening to Foster Hewitt give the first national broadcast of the Grey Cup game had a right to think that their day could not be far off. As the *Leader-Post* said, "The Roughriders' showing is accepted as almost guarantee that Western Canada will send their champions east from now on in the hope that eventually the title will go to the prairies."

This optimism was carried over into the 1931 season, a bright spot in a part of the country beginning to feel the devastating effects of the Great Depression. Eddie James rejoined the team from Winnipeg, and the Roughriders recruited Curt Schave, a halfback from the University of North Dakota who could run, kick, and pass with equal skill. Unlike the other Americans, who had played because they found themselves working in Regina, Schave was recruited to play football for about $200 a month and an apartment, thus becoming the Roughriders' first professional import.

Schave's triple threat, together with the return of such stalwarts as Gordon Barber, Tiny Thompson, Johnny Garuik, Jack Patrick, Albert Urness, and Tubby Renwick made the Roughriders a powerhouse again. They easily won the Saskatchewan title with four consecutive victories, and in the final game on October 24 saw the first touchdown

Photo courtesy of SSHFM

Curt Schave

Photo courtesy of SSHFM

John Garuik

pass ever thrown on a Regina field when Fred Goodman connected with Angie Mitchell. After demolishing Winnipeg St. John's 47-5 before 3,000 stunned Winnipeg fans, the Roughriders won the western final with a 26-2 victory over the Calgary Altomahs. In doing so, they completed a season record of 162 points for and 17 against, scoring 23 touchdowns while holding the opposition to one.

Before travelling east for the 1931 Grey Cup game, the Roughriders had to contend with the perennial problem of maintaining their game condition in the four weeks between their last western contest and the national final. When the scientifically trained and carefully conditioned players today argue that they lose their sharpness in a two-week layoff, it is easy to imagine the effect of a month of relative inactivity in a group of amateur athletes. In Regina's case this was compounded by the frigid and snowy training conditions nearly always gripping the prairies in November. Meanwhile, the eastern opponents were keeping sharp in rigorous interprovincial playdowns.

Little has been said about the effect of travel on western teams, which always played in the home parks of the eastern champions. The 1931 Roughrider excursion is typical of the way in which the travelers spent the days leading up to the Grey Cup game. On the Tuesday evening before the final, a thousand fans and the Regina Rifles band saw the team off on the CPR train for its two-and-a-half-day trip to Montreal. Local businessmen had donated enough apples and cigarettes for the trip, as well as a substantial number of magazines to combat the boredom. Greg Grassick brought along his portable gramophone, though the 100th playing of "Carolina Moon" somewhere in northern Ontario nearly led to fisticuffs among the players. Training during these final days before the championship game was confined to whatever limbering up could be done on the station platform in Winnipeg or Sudbury. When contemporary teams, travelling by air and enjoying the comforts of modern hotels, consider home field worth a touchdown, one can only imagine the effect that road trips must have had on the performance of western teams in the early days of Grey Cup competition.

Photo courtesy of SSHFM

Eddie 'Dynamite' James

In 1931 western officials did manage to win one concession from the CRU: for the first time one of the three officials doing the Grey Cup game would be from the West. This was a refreshing change from the previous year, when all three officials had been Ontario men, the head linesman being the former coach of Balmy Beach, the eastern team in the Cup final. In another move toward enlightenment, the CRU ruled that the forward pass would be permitted – a decision made easier because the eastern champions, the Montreal AAA Winged Wheelers, had brought in Warren Stevens, a brilliant American college quarterback, to teach them how to use the pass.

On December 5 Stevens threw the first touchdown pass in Grey Cup history, a 40-yard completion to Kenny Grant, in leading Montreal to a 22-0 victory over the Roughriders. The Reginans contributed to the loss through three fumbles by the usually reliable Eddie James, one behind the Roughrider goal line for a touchdown and another on the Winged Wheeler 10-yard-line following a brilliant Regina march. The Riders also contributed to their downfall through a miscalculation about footwear. Thinking that their ground attack would be strengthened by the use of leather cleats, the team paid a bootmaker $67 to change the team's cleats the night before the game. When the temperature on Grey Cup day plunged to 10 degrees above zero and the field was covered ice, the leather cleats became the worst possible footwear. The Wheelers, on the other hand, wearing running shoes in the first half and regular boots in the second, moved with ease on the gridiron.

Gordon Barber, who played on four Roughrider Grey Cup teams from 1929 to 1932, said the story of the footwear was more even galling because the Regina club had unwittingly assisted Montreal in its choice of running shoes. During the previous evening, Barber, Desmond Grubb, and Greg Grassick were at their hotel and while the others went to bed, Barber wandered into a dance in the ballroom, looking for excitement. Before going to bed, he stepped outside and found himself in a freezing snowstorm. He woke up Freddie Wilson, who made some phone calls and arranged to have a set of canvas lacrosse shoes sent to the Roughrider dressing room. They never arrived, however, and the players were forced to wear the ill-suited leather cleats. When the Winged Wheelers took to the field, the Regina officials were stunned to see each player outfitted in the lacrosse shoes. An errant delivery boy had taken them to the wrong quarters, and the delighted Wheelers, granted a 10-minute delay of the game by the referee, happily accepted and donned the gift.

Photo courtesy of SSHFM

Gordon Barber

However it happened, the loss in 1931 was a bitter defeat for many Reginans – perhaps even more painful than the shellacking by Queen's in 1923 – best summed up in the words of veteran player Bill Kerr: "Teams have gone down east before and we never expected them to win, but this year's lineup was what I have been dreaming about for years – the West's one big threat for the Dominion title."

1932 was the year that the Depression began to have a serious impact on the Roughriders, forcing many of their players – notably Eddie James, Johnny Patrick, Albert Urness, and Johnny Auld – to move to cities such as Winnipeg and Vancouver to find work. The effect of these losses was immediately felt when the Regina club lost its two exhibition games, marking the end of a truly remarkable domination of prairie football. It had been nearly *seven years* since the Roughriders had lost to a western team. During that time they had won 37 consecutive matches, outscoring the opposition 662 to 75, averaging 18 points a game and holding their opponents to a mere *two points* a game. In the process they had regularly trounced teams from Winnipeg, Edmonton, Calgary, and Vancouver.

Despite the exhibition losses, the Roughriders were not yet done with challenging for the Grey Cup. Playing under floodlights for the first time in Regina, the Roughriders retained the provincial title with a 6-1 record, and then repeated as western champions by beating Winnipeg 9-1 and Calgary 30-2. When they turned their sights to the east once more, they were met by the same disdain they had encountered years earlier. In 1931 the eastern football organizations had suggested that Regina play an elimination game against an eastern opponent in order to qualify to play for the Grey Cup, and in 1932 the Hamilton *Spectator* argued that there should be no East-West final at all: "Should the Tigers win the eastern title, the westerners could reasonably expect a trouncing, and it certainly would be no hardship for them to pass up the chance for the title and save the large expenditure entailed by the trip by staying at home."

The Roughriders, pushed by Al Ritchie's conviction that the West must continue to challenge the East, did travel to Hamilton, and on December 5 they lost their fifth consecutive Grey Cup game, this time to Hamilton 25-6. Though the team was considered the most tactically sophisticated ever assembled in the West, nothing went right on the day, and the troubles began on the opening kickoff. The Riders won the coin toss and, since their strength lay in their rock-hard defence, Ritchie decided to kick off and keep the Tigers in their own end of the field. However, as he later told sportswriter Trent Frayne, he was persuaded to change tactics by the fleet-footed kick returner Curt Schave:

Photo courtesy of SSHFM

Al Ritchie

> "He implored me to receive the kickoff. He pointed out that the field was in fine condition and he said he felt like running and, oh my, how that boy could run. So I said okay, we'll receive.
>
> Schave catches the ball and he starts up the field – he was a great runner, that boy. Five, ten, fifteen twenty yards, he comes and then he's at midfield. Bang! Somebody hits him. Pop! Goes the ball from his arms. Thud! A Tiger grabs it and goes all the way for a touchdown. Well, I know now we should have kicked off, but Schave comes over to the bench and says, 'Coach, make 'em kick off again. I'll get that one back for you.' He said he felt great, that he felt like running – and, my goodness, that boy could run! So the Tigers kick off to us again and Schave grabs the ball and starts up the field. Five, ten, fifteen, twenty yards he flies and then he's passing midfield, going like the wind. Bang! Somebody hits him. Pop! Goes the ball from his arm. Thud! a Tiger grabs it and goes all the way. We're behind 12-0 and the game has just nicely started.'
>
> 'One of the subs, I forget who now, slides along the bench beside me. 'Coach,' he says. 'I'm sure as hell glad that I'm not sitting in your spot.' I ask him why. 'Well,' he says, 'there's a lot of people back home hearing about this game right now. Most of 'em know that you've got the strongest defensive team in the west. I imagine most of 'ems gonna be wondering who was the genius who decided we shouldn't kick off.'
>
> But, oh my, how that Schave boy could run."

In addition to Schave's fumbles, the usually reliable quarterback, Austin DeFrate, threw three interceptions, one of which gave the Tigers yet another touchdown. In all, the Regina club played a better game than the score would indicate, its 13 first downs exceeding anything that any eastern team had been able to get against Hamilton, but once again it made the long trip home without the Cup.

The Roughriders had won the western title in 1932, but in 1933 there were clear signs that their 23-year domination of the West was coming to an end. Their opposition in the western semi-final was the new Winnipeg Football Club, an amalgamation of the St. John's team and the Winnipeg Rugby Club. Later to be known as the Blue Bombers, this team began to seriously import American players: Carl Cronin, a graduate of Knute Rockne's Notre Dame team, and University of Wisconsin alumni Russ Rebholz and Greg Kabat. Behind this recruiting lay a new determination to end the Regina reign, as voiced by Cronin in an address to the Winnipeg Knights of Columbus. "It is inconceivable to me," he said, "that a city of 300,000 should be satisfied to have Regina come down here year after year, belt them on the whiskers and make them like it. Al Ritchie is a great coach and he is able to put a good team on the field, but without the moral and financial support of the entire city behind him Ritchie would not go far." Cronin's urgings paid off and Winnipeg beat the Roughriders 11-1, though they then went on to lose 13-0 to the Toronto Argonauts.

Photo courtesy of SSHFM

Greg Grassick as a coach

The rebirth of Winnipeg football and its triumph in the western final created a rivalry between the Manitoba city and Regina which surpassed anything that had gone before. It began a period of fierce competition and this tradition has continued unabated – through the Labour Day Classic, the Banjo Bowl, and the periodic playoff battle – to the present.

In 1934 Al Ritchie stepped down as coach and was replaced by Greg Grassick, a tireless worker, popular with the players, who had coached the junior Regina Dales the year before. For the first time in its history the club named two assistant coaches, and it formally adopted the policy of recruiting imports. Steve Adkins, Oke Olson, and Bob Walker were brought up from the University of North Dakota, and Paul Kirk came from Minnesota. The most impressive American, however, was South Dakota's Ralph Pierce, called by Ritchie one of the greatest imports ever to play in Canada. The strength of the Regina club had always been its local players, but, in the face of the growing practice of Canadian clubs using imports, the Roughriders were forced to look south of the border or fall behind their opponents.

The Roughrider imports did not take long to show their skills in the 1934 season. In an early game against Moose Jaw Olson and Pierce combined to produce a passing attack on a scale never seen before in the West. The Riders completed 12 of 17 attempts for 210 yards, and in the last nine minutes Olson threw three touchdown passes. Against the Saskatoon Hilltops on Thanksgiving weekend, they did even better, completing 17 of 24 passes for 460 yards – the greatest aerial display ever seen in Canada. In this game Adkins caught 11 passes for an astonishing 231 yards, a club record which would stand for 49 years until Chris DeFrance gained 260 yards against Edmonton in 1983. Adkins' total is much more impressive when one remembers that it was gained in an era not dominated by the pass.

Photo courtesy of SSHFM

Steve Adkins

The Roughriders ended the 1934 season with a 6-0 record against Saskatchewan opposition and then, before 5,000 fans, defeated the powerful Winnipeg Football Club 8-0 in what Ritchie and Freddie Wilson called the greatest game ever played in Saskatchewan. After beating the Vancouver Meralomas 22-2 and 7-2, the Riders yet again lost the Grey Cup game, this time to the Sarnia Imperials by a score of 20-12. In defeat, though, the Roughriders had reasons to be proud. They scored more touchdowns than any western team had since the East-West finals had begun, and their 12 points were the most ever inflicted on an eastern team by western opposition. Moreover, this was accomplished against a Sarnia team that had allowed only a single touchdown for each of the previous two seasons.

Photo courtesy of SSHFM

Clair Warner

Following the game, reported the *Leader-Post*, "every player on the squad sat in the dressing room at Varsity Stadium and openly cried," and these tears were more fitting than anyone could have guessed. In the previous 12 seasons, the Riders had played in seven Grey Cup games and lost each one; 17 years would pass before they would be in another one, and it would take 32 years for a Saskatchewan team to bring home the Grey Cup. The dream of Ritchie, Grassick, Wilson, Clair Warner, and so many others would be deferred and many would never live to see it realized.

The Grey Cup would be brought west within a year, but that historic honour would not go to the Regina Roughriders. Stung by its loss to Regina in 1934, the Winnipeg Football Club brought in a further seven American players, among whom was Fritz Hanson, who would go on to play on four Grey Cup champion teams and become a legend in Canadian football. Behind Hanson's over 300 yards in punt returns, including a 78-yard return for a touchdown, the Winnipeg club beat Hamilton 18-12 to win the Grey Cup.

All across western Canada people basked in the glory of Winnipeg's victory, and few were happier than the Roughrider organization that had fought for so long for such a moment. No club had travelled so extensively in the country, taking football to the west coast and relentlessly taking the western challenge to the powerhouses of Ontario and Quebec. Enduring long periods of inactivity while the East named its champions, travelling always to their opponents' park, performing in front of the opposition's supporters before eastern officials enforcing eastern rules, the Roughriders had persevered in the belief that Canada's national football championship indeed had to be a championship for all the country. A catalyst and a pioneer, the Regina club had done much more than any other organization to move western football to the day when one of its clubs would bring home the Grey Cup.

The Winnipeg victory acted as a catalyst for two important developments in the 1936 season. First was the creation of a prairie league, the Western Interprovincial Football Union, comprising teams from Regina, Winnipeg and Calgary (the Edmonton Eskimos had folded in the mid-1920s and, except for two seasons in the late 1930s, would not return to competition until 1949). Second, the Canadian Rugby Union ruled that, in order to play in the Grey Cup game, players had to have lived in Canada for at least one year.

Photo courtesy of SSHFM

Dean Griffing (centering the football)

As the 1936 season wore on this rule would have a devastating impact on the Regina Roughriders and damage the development of football in Canada as a whole.

With the formation of the WIFU, football in Regina moved significantly into the modern era, and the Roughriders recruited heavily in the United States, bringing in Bill Cawley (Utah), Fred Ray (South Dakota), Louis Chumich (North Dakota), Fritz Falgren (North Dakota State), and Jim Lander (Kansas State). The most important addition, though, was Dean Griffing, a centre from Kansas who would share coaching duties with Ralph Pierce.

Photo courtesy of SSHFM

Ralph Pierce

Griffing was only 22 years old and had never coached before, but his intensity and forceful leadership were viewed as a needed change for a club that had perhaps become too comfortable with Ritchie and Grassick. As the Winnipeg-Regina rivalry grew heated in the 1936 season, Griffing's ferocious play soon earned him the hearty dislike of Winnipeg fans. The enmity, though tinged with admiration, was fuelled in part by Griffing's love of playing the antagonist and by sportswriters who loved to pen stories about "the big, bad man from Kansas." Ralph Allen, the witty reporter for the Winnipeg *Tribune*, for example, once spread the story that Griffing had taken advantage of pile-ups to take three bites from Greg Kabat's leg, and, for good measure, one from that of another player. Manitobans knew that the Roughriders were a hungry ball club, wrote Allen in mock indignation, but surely Griffing was going too far.

Allen's story became part of Canadian football folklore, but not before Griffing himself played along with it during a game several weeks later. Lining up opposite Winnipeg's giant Jewish lineman, Lou Mogul, before hostilities began, Griffing let a few moments go by and then said. "It's okay Lou. I don't think I'll have any kosher meat today." Mogul, it was said, laughed so hard that he could barely make a tackle all day.

Together with Chumich, Griffing made the 1936 Roughrider line, in Mogul's opinion, the toughest ever assembled in the pre-Second World War era, and it was intimidating. Winnipeg's Bob Fritz recalled attempting to block Chumich, who was always followed through the line by Griffing: "First thing I'd see would be Chumich's ham-like fist coming straight for me, so naturally I ducked. Then Griffing would be gone to give the kicker the business. Chumich never hit me but I've often looked back on those days and wished I hadn't ducked once just to see if he was trying to scare me or meant business. Darned if I know."

Until the late 1920s there were so few seats around the playing field at Park Hughes that it was difficult to ask a woman to a game.

With a new prairie conference and a strengthened team, the Roughrider Club decided that it was time for changes to make the game more comfortable for spectators. Until the late 1920s there were so few seats around the playing field at Park Hughes that it was difficult to ask a woman to a game. In 1928, however, a new gridiron had been laid out to take advantage of space adjoining Park Hughes and Park de Young, a tract of land donated to the city by John Marshall Young, a prominent Regina realtor. This arrangement offered far more seats around the field and, judging from one report, comforts previously unknown to the hardened football fan: "It was even possible to park one's car close to the touchline and enjoy the game with one's girl friend in the depths of comfortable upholstery."

Now in 1936 more new seating was provided at Park de Young, a crew of ushers were employed to keep crowds moving smoothly, numbers were put on players' uniforms, a press box was built, facilities provided for radio broadcasting, and a pep band entertained at half time. Gone forever were the days of crowds along the sidelines, standing throughout the game and fighting for a view of the action over the heads of others.

And there was plenty of action to be seen in 1936. In the regular season and playoffs, Regina played Winnipeg six times, and this still counts as one of the most competitive and exciting series played between two Canadian clubs. Except for the final game, none were decided by more than five points, and any one of them could have been won by either team. In the final game, trailing by 10 points in the second of a two-game total-point semi-final series, the Roughriders scored 20 points in the second half, achieving a comeback of the sort never seen before in western playoffs. It would not be until the Little Miracle of Taylor Field in 1963 that this comeback victory would be bettered. The Roughriders' 3-1 victory over the Calgary Bronks in the western final was almost anticlimactic though the win was never a sure thing: earlier in the year the Bronks had become the first Calgary team to beat Regina in 26 years of competition. It also set the stage for one of the sorriest episodes in Canadian football history.

Eastern football officials ruled that the five first-year Roughrider imports violated the CRU's residence regulation and were thus ineligible to play in the national final, providing, in the words of the CRU's past president, John de Gruchy, a preposterously exaggerated justification: "The Roughriders are a purely American team. We might just as well bring any team from the United States into the Dominion final. If we allow football to get down to this stage it would spoil the Canadian championship and discourage young Canadians from playing the game."

The Roughrider president, Piffles Taylor, was equally emphatic that his team would use all its players or not go east at all, and when the CRU upheld its ban, the Regina players packed away their uniforms for the year. The result was that, for the only time – except during the Second World War – between 1921 and the present, no western team contested the Grey Cup game. The Grey Cup was awarded to the Sarnia Imperials on the dubious grounds of its eastern playoff victory over Ottawa, the Canadian football season thus ending, not with a bang but with a whimper. The fans were denied a first-rate national final, and the Regina Roughriders were denied their greatest chance to win a Grey Cup. After watching the Regina team play a late-season game, Frederick Palmer, Canadian Trade Commissioner in England, aptly commented: "It's just as well if the east does not play Regina. I saw all the eastern teams in action and there is not a team in the same class as the Regina Roughriders. I never saw a line like Regina boasts. The east is not playing the same class of football."

Photo courtesy of the Canadian Football Hall of Fame

Piffles Taylor

The CRU and the WCRU had combined to prevent the Roughriders from playing for the Grey Cup in 1936, but the next year the WCRU adopted a limit of eight Americans dressing for any team. Other teams immediately began to accelerate their recruiting of imports, and with greater resources were able to attract many more highly talented Americans than was Regina, and this really spelled the end of Regina's 26-year domination of western football.

In 1937 the Roughriders had a far more serious problem than import players: sheer survival. By shrewd and cautious management, the club had made it through seven Depression years, but in 1937, a year in which the net farm income of Saskatchewan was an incredible *minus* $36,336,000, the province was facing the worst of its ordeal. In the previous year the Roughriders had gone all out to compete with the growing power of other centres, but now they realized that they did not have the financial resources to keep up to them. On August, 25, there was a very real possibility that the club might cease operations entirely.

In a three-hour meeting the 35-member executive discussed the Roughriders' financial future and examined a number of plans to keep the club alive. Rejecting the suggestion to ask Calgary and Winnipeg for a subsidy, the executive decided on a massive fundraising campaign, placing an advertisement in the *Leader-Post* under the heading "THE RIDERS NEED HELP!" It would hardly be the last time that the Roughriders would have to appeal to its supporters and citizens in general, and sportswriter Dave Dryburgh spoke for many generations of fans when he wrote:

> "The Roughriders aren't a mere football team. They're an institution that must be kept going even if we have to sell the city hall. Keeping up with the Joneses

> in Calgary and Winnipeg takes an oversized wad of the long green. Sooner or later the overhead will have to be spared and right now we don't have much more than grasshoppers to keep things moving, but the solution does not lie in the Riders folding up. Even the grasshoppers would leave us then, figuring that the country had definitely gone bad."

The Regina public responded generously to this call and the Regina Roughrider Football Club survived. On the field, however, the team was much less successful, ending up in third place with a 3-5 record and missing the playoffs. In a late-season game against Winnipeg, the Riders played so poorly that they gained only 78 yards rushing to their opponents' 282, and Griffing was so disgusted that he pulled himself out the game. As Dave Dryburgh pointed out, this fall from dominance hit Depression Regina particularly hard:

> "For 25 years Regina has ruled rugby on the prairies, the end had to come sooner or later. But it has arrived an inopportune time. For behind the Roughriders of 1937 is the story of a hard-up community that plunged on a football team, made a bold effort to keep up with the Jones. Regina staked all on the Riders. It has fallen hard."

Regina fans – and the growing numbers of supporters from the rest of Saskatchewan – would have to become accustomed to a hard struggle to assemble a competitive team or even to field a team at all. As the game became more professional and more reliant on American players, the first priority of the Roughrider organization would be to survive with its limited resources; if it could produce a championship team within that context, so much the better. In the years to come the Riders would produce their share of thrilling moments, but they would have to fight very much harder for each of them.

The 1938 season began against the backdrop of increasingly dark news from Europe as Hitler took the world closer to another war with his demand that the Sudetenland

Photo courtesy of SSHFM

Howard Cleveland

Photo courtesy of SSHFM

Leo Danaher

be returned to Germany. In Regina, nevertheless, the Roughriders continued to create new ways to generate interest in football. Backed by the Rider Booster Club, the first radio broadcast about the team was aired on CJRM on August 22. In this forerunner of the modern football talk show, a group of club officials, players, and fans – and, inevitably, the loquacious Al Ritchie – gathered to analyse the team and its opponents. The games themselves were enhanced by the addition of a loudspeaker system which carried a description and explanation of the action as seen by an announcer patrolling the sidelines. At a banquet in 1938 players and fans were fascinated by a movie film of a game and to hear Dean Griffing's rapid-fire commentary.

The games themselves were enhanced by the addition of a loudspeaker system which carried a description and explanation of the action as seen by an announcer patrolling the sidelines.

On the field the Roughriders began the season without the great Ralph Pierce, who had retired, but he was replaced by Howard "Highpockets" Cleveland, who had earned All-American mention at Kansas. Over the next two seasons he played brilliantly at halfback – passing superbly, kicking well, and making dazzling end runs; and in 1939 he was named to the Western All-Star team and chosen as the first winner of the McKinney Trophy as the most valuable player in the WIFU. Joining Cleveland was another Kansas recruit, Leo Danaher, who had a sensational rookie season, running brilliantly on offence and intercepting passes on defence. With these additions, the Roughriders won their first three games without giving up a point and looked as if they would run away with the league title. Griffing, however, tore a cartilage in the third game, robbing the Regina team of much of its intensity and drive, and it lost five of its six remaining games, including a 13-0 loss to Winnipeg in the western semi-final.

In 1939 the WIFU took a step forward by expanding its schedule to 12 games, but the entire season was undermined by the outbreak of war. Normally rabid football fans were soon sitting by their radios listening or scanning their newspapers for war reports from Europe. At least 200 worried Roughrider supporters returned their season tickets, and players began to leave the team for the armed services. By the end of the season the club had lost its president, Dr. E.A. McCusker, when he was appointed Deputy Assistant Director of Medical Services in Canada's first overseas division. Inevitably some of the men who had donned the Roughrider colours over the years lost their lives in the war, came back with wounds, or were interned in enemy prisoner-of-war camps.

Photo courtesy of SSHFM

Toar Springstein

On the football field the Roughriders' 2-6 record led to the first mid-season firings in the club's history. The public, which had grown more vocal with the increased media coverage of the team, demanded a shakeup, and the Rider executive axed Leo Danaher, whose play had fallen off badly, and two rookie imports. President McCusker explained that "the executive wants to make it known to all other players that any time they do not feel like co-operating and playing heads-up football, their resignations will be promptly accepted." It was a purge that left the team with only four imports and, with the addition of former Regina Dales players Lindsay Holt, Toar Springstein, and Harry Guest, it was the closest to a homebrew squad that the West had seen in years. Despite losing 24-17 to Calgary in the western semi-final, this young team went 4-2 in its remaining games in 1939.

Organized football survived the first year of the war, but by the summer of 1940 there were doubts that it could, or should, continue

Photo courtesy of SSHFM

Bob Walker

Photo courtesy of SSHFM

Ken Preston

during wartime. The Ministry of National Defence ruled that, apart from loss of players to the services, there should be no curtailment of competitive sports, but Canadian football clubs faced serious problems of manpower and resources. In 1939 the Vancouver Meralomas had folded when they lost most of their players, and in 1940 the Edmonton Eskimos once again disbanded, as did the Sarnia Imperials. In 1941 even the Hamilton Tigers would cease to play.

In Regina there were equally good reasons to suspend operations – except that the men and women in the street wanted to see football kept alive. While the Roughrider executive was debating the issue, the players found their own solution: if Dean Griffing would coach the team, they would continue on a co-operative basis. They would play on the understanding that, if there was any money left at the end of the season, it would be divided among the players; if the club lost money, the players would receive nothing.

The players' determination appealed to Griffing, and with the support of the president, Piffles Taylor, and Clair Warner, the first co-operative football team in Canada was born. Twenty-four players turned out to practice, among whom were former all-star lineman Bob Walker (who came out of retirement) and a newcomer from Queen's University who was to have a major role in the Roughrider fortunes for the next 36 years: backfielder Ken Preston. These "Co-operative Kids," as they were called, proceeded to play the season on a shoestring – but little more. On road trips they travelled without a manager or trainer, going overnight by ordinary coach, each player taking a blanket and trying to sleep without a berth. Once at their destination, they put their bags and blankets under their arms and walked to their hotel – and, as Griffing put it, "the boys didn't clamour for steaks; they made $2 last all day and liked it."

Griffing called the 1940 season his most enjoyable year, with the enthusiasm and determination of his young squad giving football fans some badly needed diversion from the grim news coming from overseas. The "Kids" won only two games, but one was a victory over the Grey Cup Champion Winnipeg Blue Bombers, and three of them – Griffing, Springstein, and Maurice Williams – earned places on the WIFU all-star squad.

Griffing was hailed as the "saviour of western football" for putting a team on the field in 1940, and in 1941 he had to work more magic. In eastern Canada all league play was discontinued, and in the WIFU the Calgary club disbanded on the grounds that there was no reason to keep the league alive just to send the Blue Bombers into the Grey Cup game again. Griffing was nonetheless adamant that a western conference was possible, and a new Vancouver team, the Grizzlies, took Calgary's place.

Among the 20 players that Griffing had for the 1941 season were some interesting newcomers. Steve Molnar joined the team, and from

Winnipeg came Bert Iannone. Up from Campion College was Bill Orban, who would go on to become Dean of the College of Physical Education at the University of Saskatchewan and the developer of the famous 5BX fitness program. Ken Charlton, who came out of Central Collegiate, the Westends, and the Dales, would go on to carve out an illustrious career in Regina and Ottawa over the next decade. A superb athlete who could pass and run, Charlton gave an early indication of his skills in his first season when he punted for a 54-yard average in one game.

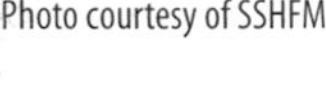
Photo courtesy of SSHFM

Maurice Williams

The Roughriders finished the 1941 season with a respectable 5-3 record, but lost a best-of-three western final to Winnipeg, the eventual Grey Cup champions. In 1942 all civilian football ceased in Canada, but armed forces teams in various centres kept competition alive. In Regina Al Ritchie and Ted Lydiard coached a Royal Canadian Navy team which had one game in the province, a 13-0 victory over the University of Saskatchewan Huskies, and then, strengthened by Dean Griffing, back from his job with an aeronautical firm in Prince Albert, lost a close 13-6 western final to the Winnipeg RCAF Bombers.

In 1943 Griffing and Piffles Taylor formed a team known as the "All-Services Riders" – an amalgam of players from the navy, army, air force, and the RCMP. In a three-team league with two Winnipeg clubs, the powerful RCAF Bombers and the United Services, the Regina team compiled a 2-4 record and qualified to meet the Bombers in a two-game total-point western final. After losing the first game 1-0, the All-Services Riders were trailing by only two points with 10 minutes remaining in the second game, but their hopes were dashed when a fumble on their 17-yard line gave the Bombers a clinching touchdown.

The year of D-Day and of the liberation of France, 1944, was the only year of the war without senior football being played in Regina. But the Roughrider organization, driven by individuals such as Dean Griffing, Piffles Taylor, and so many local players, many of them servicemen, had kept football and football enthusiasm alive in Regina and across southern Saskatchewan. It had taken ingenuity and perseverance, but they succeeded where other organizations in larger, more affluent centres had failed. Indeed, except for 1944 and two years during the First World War, when all organized football was suspended in western Canada, the Regina Rugby Club had mounted a team in every season since 1909.

While the Regina Rugby Club was maintaining this remarkable presence in western Canadian football, teams in other cities – notably Winnipeg, Calgary, Edmonton , and Vancouver – came and went. Thus the Roughriders are by far the longest continuous functioning football club east of Hamilton. The Winnipeg Blue Bombers were constituted in 1936, and the three other western clubs were formed after the Second World War: the Calgary Stampeders in 1948, the Edmonton Eskimos in 1949, and the British Columbia Lions in 1954. In historical terms, these clubs can genuinely be called Johnny-come-latelies.

Photo courtesy of SSHFM

Ted Lydiard

That there was a strong football tradition in the West on which to build a league in which Calgary, Edmonton, and British Columbia could play after

Photo courtesy of SSHFM

Paul Kirk

the Second World War is in no small way the result of the achievements of the Regina Rugby Club. No other organization was more catalytic in creating leagues, playoff systems, and common rules; and no other organization was as determined to achieve parity on the playing field with the eastern Canadian football powerhouses. Though the odds were always stacked against them, the Regina teams travelled to the East seven times to challenge for the Grey Cup, on each occasion chipping away another bit of eastern superiority. It is not stretching things to say that the road to Winnipeg's Grey Cup victory in 1935 was paved by the Roughrider teams.

Though the Roughriders did not win even one of those seven Grey Cup games, the years from 1910 to 1945 were a period of remarkable success, one in which they dominated western football in a way unmatched in any era by any other organization – even the Edmonton Eskimos dynasty of the 1970s and 1980s. Including regular season games, playoff matches, and Grey Cup contests, the Roughrider record during those 35 years was 145 wins, 60 losses, and two draws. This means that over three decades they maintained a winning record of a remarkable 75 per cent. Moreover, during that time they had once gone eight years without a defeat by anyone, and in the 1920s they went eight seasons without losing to a western team.

It was a golden age for the Regina Rugby Club, one which produced superb and exciting players who captured the imagination of its growing multitude of fans. Stars such as Freddie Wilson, Piffles Taylor, Brian Timmis, Eddie James, Dean Griffing, Greg Grassick, Ralph Pierce, Bob Walker, Paul Kirk, Louis Chumich, and many others were every bit as revered for their outstanding play, toughness, and character as later players such as Ken Carpenter, Ron Lancaster, George Reed, Kent Austin, Ray Elgaard, Ed McQuarters, Bobby Jurasin, and Eddie Davis would be worshipped by their fans. Sadly, because statistics were not kept by the Club or by the leagues until the late 1930s, there is not a detailed historical record of the magnitude of the achievements of the early players. As a result, it takes an effort of imagination for the modern fan to realize that these players were stars in their eras, that they brought acclaim to their club, their city and province, and to their followers. With each new generation of Roughrider fans, the achievements of the early players recede further into history, but they deserve to be as revered and celebrated as those of today's stars.

Photo courtesy of SSHFM

Bob Walker

The source of the Regina Rugby Club domination of western Canadian football in the early decades was twofold: terrific local talent and a strong community organization. In the beginning years players from elsewhere brought their football skills when they came to work and make a life in Regina. Before long, locally raised young men learned to play the game, and a well-organized system of junior and intermediate teams began to provide a steady stream of talented players who were as skilled as any in the country. This began Saskatchewan's long tradition of developing young players, and today the success of the University of Regina Rams, the Saskatoon Hilltops, the Regina Thunder and the University of Saskatchewan Huskies in Canadian junior and college football is proof of the province's outstanding community and school football programs and their coaching.

1940s action

Photo courtesy of SSHFM

The Roughrider Football Club was always a strongly committed community organization which, even in the toughest of economic times, found the resources to field a team. Community ownership – which means deeply committed community involvement and dedicated volunteers – has always been the backbone and the strength of the Saskatchewan Roughrider Football Club, and it remains that way. While most other Canadian clubs have gone into private ownership, the Roughriders have remained community owned, and thus – as they have for a century – they truly belong to the people of Saskatchewan.

Such a combination – strong local talent and strong community commitment – carried the Regina Rugby Club to great success in its first 25 years, but in the mid-1930s conditions were changing. Led by Winnipeg's seven imports in 1935, which gave them the West's first Grey Cup, western football clubs began to become professional and to import players from the United States. For the first time, teams were able to build outstanding teams, not by drawing on local players, but by luring highly skilled Americans north with high salaries. This immediately gave a huge advantage to football clubs in Winnipeg, Calgary, Edmonton, and Vancouver, large cities with much greater resources than Regina could muster. Until a truly enforced salary cap came into effect in 2007, the Saskatchewan Roughriders were always the "poor cousins" of the Canadian Football League, having to mount competitive teams against much richer, and therefore more powerful, clubs.

For the first time, teams were able to build outstanding teams, not by drawing on local players, but by luring highly skilled Americans north with high salaries. This immediately gave a huge advantage to football clubs in Winnipeg, Calgary, Edmonton, and Vancouver, large cities with much greater resources than Regina could muster.

When football began to be played again in western Canada in 1945, the Roughrider organization was undaunted by the odds against it. Elsewhere, however, there were doubts that the Saskatchewan club would ever again be competitive, especially in Winnipeg, where the *Tribune*'s Tony Allen argued that the Blue Bombers were "much too strong financially as well as in playing material for other prairie clubs." The Bombers, said Allen, should forget about the WIFU, leave Regina and Calgary behind, and join the eastern conference.

The football gods, if there are such deities, apparently do not take kindly to arrogant pronouncements, because, only two seasons following Allen's remarks, the Blue Bombers finished in last place in the reconstituted WIFU, ignominiously behind both the Roughriders and the Calgary Stampeders. Football was back in business in the West, the Roughriders, soon to become the Saskatchewan Roughriders with new green-and-white colours, were on the field again, and a new era had begun.

Outstanding Players
1910–1945

Because football in the early decades was a much different game from that played today, with players playing both ways in positions not comparable to those on a contemporary team, and in the absence of statistics (which did not start to be kept until the late 1930s), it is impossible to select a traditional all-star team. Below, however, are the names of 25 of the greatest stars of the Roughriders' first 35 years:

Freddie Wilson	Though he was only five feet, seven inches and weighed 140 pounds, he was a dynamic runner famous for launching booming kicks with either foot on the run. He once kicked 10 single points in a game in 1913.
N.J. "Piffles" Taylor	Both before and after the First World War, he was a strong and quick quarterback with a shrewd ability to analyse opposing teams' defences.
Brian Timmis	A superb fullback and defensive lineman for the Riders in the 1920s, he went on to play in eastern Canada and be named to the Canadian Football Hall of Fame.
Tare Rennebohm	A fierce player in the 1920s, he went on to have a nearly 40-year association with the Roughriders as player, manager, and equipment manager.
Dean Griffing	An all-star lineman and co-coach (at the age of 22) of the Roughriders in the late 1930s and during the Second World War, he became general manager in the 1950s.
Eddie "Dynamite" James	An outstanding two-way player for the Roughriders in the 1930s, he went on to play for the Winnipeg Blue Bombers and be named to the Canadian Football Hall of Fame and the Canadian Sports Hall of Fame.
Angie Mitchell	A 130-pound quarterback who came up from the junior Pats Football Club to play brilliantly for the Roughriders for a number of years in the 1930s.
Fritz Sandstrom	Known as "the crazy Swede," he was respected for his superb play at any position on offence (particularly quarterback) or defence in the 1920s.
Curt Schave	An outstanding Roughrider halfback in the 1930s from the University of North Dakota, he could run, kick, and pass brilliantly.
Harold Urness	An outstanding Roughrider right end in the late 1920s and early 1930s.

Al Urness	A stalwart of the Roughrider line in the late 1920s and early 1930s.
Gordon Barber	An extremely tough Roughrider lineman in the early 1930s.
Greg Grassick	A brilliant halfback for the Roughriders, he played in five Grey Cup games and later became coach of the team.
Ralph Pierce	An outstanding running back and defensive player for the Roughriders in the late 1930s, he was called by Al Ritchie one of the greatest import players ever to come to Canada.
Louis Chumich	A massive lineman from North Dakota who played for the Roughriders in the late 1930s.
Howard "Highpockets" Cleveland	A brilliant halfback, he was named to the Western All-Star team in 1939 and was awarded the McKinney Trophy as the most valuable player in the WIFU.
Rollo "Swede" Edberg	A superb receiver who was named to the 1939 Western All-Star Team.
Cliff Roseborough	A Saskatoon Hilltops player who joined the Roughriders in 1932, later won three Grey Cups with the Winnipeg Blue Bombers, and refereed 12 Grey Cup games.
Steve Adkins	An outstanding end in the 1930s who once caught 11 passes in a game for 231 yards, a club yardage record that would stand for 49 years.
Bob Walker	An outstanding lineman from North Dakota, he was named to the Western All-Star team in 1938 and 1939.
Howie Milne	A key player on the great Roughrider teams of the 1920s and later their coach.
Johnny Garuik	A tough and capable lineman for the Roughriders from the late 1920s to the Second World War.
Maurice Williams	An outstanding player who was named to the Western All-Star Team in 1940 and 1941.
Paul Kirk	An import halfback from Minnesota who could play offence and defence and could kick, he played for the Roughriders in the mid-1930s and he won the first recorded Western scoring title in 1937.
George Chiga	An outstanding player with the Roughriders in the 1930s, he was named a second-team Western All-Star in 1936; and off the field, as the Canadian heavyweight wrestling champion, he went to the 1936 Berlin Olympics.

1946-1962

BY JULIE FOLK/GORDON STASESON

CHAPTER 2

Photo courtesy of SSHFM

By 1939, the deepening of the Great Depression and the fear of war had caused many sports organizations to discontinue operations. The Regina Pats were no longer operational and only the Winnipeg Blue Bombers and the Regina Roughriders competed in western football. As for NHL teams, the Montreal Maroons folded and the fledgling New York Americans lasted only a couple of years. Many Roughriders like Ken Charlton, Jimmy Kinney and Lindsay Holt joined the service to fight for their country in the Second World War, and by the 1940 football season, the Roughrider club was operating on a tight budget with only 24 players on the roster. By 1942, competition ceased with the exception of service teams. The Royal Canadian Navy team (later the All Services Team) was coached by Al Ritchie and Ted Lydiard in Regina, and the RCAF Bombers operated in Winnipeg. Only in 1944 was competitive football obsolete in Saskatchewan.

Instead, Canadians were hunched around the radio listening to the CBC broadcasts; the Happy Gang singing, "There'll Always Be An England," and Lorne Greene, or, "The Voice of Doom," who later became TV star Ben Cartwright on the western weekly TV show *Bonanza*. With men gone to war, women worked in factories and munitions plants supporting the war effort. The void on the sports scene was filled by the creation of the All-American Girls Professional Baseball League in the midwestern United States that included Regina players Mary Baker, Daisy Junor and Millie Warwick. Hopes were kept alive through Frank Sinatra's hit on Broadway, "Oh What a Beautiful Morning," and Saskatchewan voted in Tommy Douglas and his CCF Party, the first socialist government in Canadian history.

As the war ended, football was kept alive in Regina by a band of dedicated volunteers led by Clair Warner and Greg Grassick. Grassick was the son of famous pioneer James

As the war ended, football was kept alive in Regina by a band of dedicated volunteers led by Clair Warner and Greg Grassick.

Sully Glasser (far right) heads for the end zone in the 1951 Grey Cup game with Martin Ruby (36) providing the blocking. (Top Photo)

Grassick. James settled in Regina with his father in 1882. James did a man's work at an early age and had little time for formal education. He drove a horse-driven army transport with arms and supplies for the RCMP from Fort Qu'Appelle to Battleford during the Northwest Rebellion. James later became a successful entrepreneur in many local companies and organizations. He was also deeply involved as a volunteer in the community, and was Mayor of Regina for five years on two separate occasions, from 1920-22 and 1940-41.

As football players began returning from the service in 1945, Warner recruited the assistance of former player Jack Rowand, Stacey 'Stack' Tibbits and Don MacDonald to head a group to again field a team to compete with the Winnipeg Blue Bombers and a new franchise in Calgary, headed by former Rider player Dean Griffing.

Photo courtesy of SSHFM

Johnny Bell

To many football seemed like a luxury at the time, but to others it was a necessity. Al Ritchie explained to Dave Dryburgh in a *Leader-Post* column:

> "Sport is the stamping ground for democracy. We mustn't forget this in the post-war years. Give me a man who has been an athlete and I'll have a clear thinker who is very fair in every decision he makes. Sport has far-reaching effects in this world … The Regina-Winnipeg gridiron rivalry is incomparable. It is something we cannot afford to let die. Down through the years it has created good fellowship between citizens. And in these coming years it will shut out much of the unrest that always follows a war … Regina needs the Roughriders. The 'Riders need the Blue Bombers, too, because those fellows have the finest football setup in Canada … Say, once the boys start coming back from Europe we can field three teams. We have so many football players in the services that if only 20 per cent are back this fall the 'Riders will have a helluva team."

Ritchie may have been slightly more optimistic than most, but at the time the talk wasn't the usual "how good will the Roughrider team be this season?" but "will there be a Roughrider team this season?"

Warner and his group attracted new players to Regina with the offer of employment with their respective construction companies. Former player Al Urness also assisted by offering employment at the Ford Motor Company Parts Department, where he was manager. Johnny Bell and Johnny Pope are just two players who came to Regina in search of work, with football an added incentive. Ken Charlton eventually came back, as did Toar Springstein, returning from stints in Winnipeg and Ottawa during the war years.

Throughout the 1930s, Park de Young was located next to Park Hughes, which was used mainly for soccer. There was no grass on Park de Young during those years and the forward pass was a restricted offensive tool. Play was somewhat limited to "two bucks and a kick" and the odd end run. On each buck through the line fans had to wait for the dust to clear to determine the position of the ball.

Shortly after the revival of the Roughriders, Park de Young, owned by the city, was revamped and consolidated with Park Hughes to become one recreational field accommodating football and baseball. The old main entrance, which also contained the players' dressing rooms, was removed to make way for field consolidation. Thereafter the team dressing rooms were located on the second floor of the grandstand at the nearby exhibition grounds and the team travelled by bus to the games until the major expansion of the west side grandstand in 1978, which included Rider offices and dressing room facilities.

As old stars returned and young players from the successful Regina Junior Dales filled the lineup, the first year of post-war competition followed through in 1945. Regina recruited many of its players from the successful Regina Junior Dales, while Winnipeg relied heavily on graduates from the Young Men's Hebrew Association.

When war ended, many hockey and football players who had been in the service returned to Canada, hopeful to resume their athletic careers.

The Edmonton Eskimos had discontinued operation in 1940, and would not re-enter the league until 1949, leaving only three clubs in the Western Football Conference: the Winnipeg Blue Bombers, Regina Roughriders and Calgary Broncs; all of whom struggled to field teams at first but quickly returned to form.

When the servicemen returned, there was a major senior hockey club in almost every community vying for the Allan Cup. Senior hockey in Canada, at that time, was second in calibre only to the NHL, and the Stanley Cup was emblematic of hockey supremacy. The old Western Hockey League consisted of five semi-professional hockey clubs: the Calgary Stampeders, Edmonton Flyers, Saskatoon Quakers, Lethbridge Maple Leafs and the Regina Capitals.

In Regina, the Capitals were a powerhouse, with former NHLers Sweeney Schreiner, 'Sudden Death' Mel Hill and Joe Fisher. Other players included Bev Bentley, Chuck McCullough, Gus and Bill Kyle, Vic Myles and the 'Buzz Saw' line of William 'Red' Tilson, Toby Brown and Gordie Staseson. Hockey was outdrawing football on the prairies; however that would change in 1948 when Les Lear took Toronto by storm and won the Grey Cup with his Cinderella Calgary Stampeders.

The spectacle of the trainloads of fans travelling by rail to Toronto, complete with parades, chuckwagons, street corner pancake breakfasts and cowboys on their horses in the lobby of the Royal York Hotel, changed the image of the Grey Cup game which thereafter became Canada's most important annual sports event. But football frenzy as we know it today really started after the war years, as football was welcomed back.

The return to football in 1945 was a new beginning for the Canadian Rugby Union. In the upcoming years positions would change, stadiums would be upgraded, and players would diversify. Tare Rennebohm, who was with the Riders from 1919 to 1949 as both a player and, later, equipment manager, put it this way in the *Leader-Post* in 1946:

> "Trouble with this modern football is that they haven't got the fight.... Just before every game, each lineman used to put a dollar in a hat. The money went to the guy who drew the first blood. The opening scrimmage was always a ritual. When we lined up for the second one we looked across at our man. If we saw blood we pointed to him and claimed the hatful of dollars. Those were the days! On the last play in every game, winning or losing, we went in

with fists swinging. We always ended the show fightin.' The Roughrider line was feared by man and beast clear across western Canada."

Lindsay Holt, an ex-Roughrider discharged from the services, returned to the Riders as coach for one last season, with Don King at his side. Sully Glasser, a hometown player, returned to Regina after his war years, beginning a long and successful career with the Roughriders. The team came together for the love of the game, playing in 10-year-old uniforms they had to exchange as they subbed into the game. Afterwards the families of the team would wash those same uniforms and towels for the players. Lights for night practices were provided by onlookers driving vehicles onto the field and turning on the headlights.

As the teams had formed so late in the season, there wasn't any league play in 1945; exhibition games and playoffs took place instead. Dean Griffing, a one-time Regina fan favourite as player and coach of the Riders, returned to football with the Calgary Stampeders. As the Roughriders prepared to play Calgary on Oct 22, the first game of the season, they made special plans for Griffing.

Before the first exhibition game between the Riders and the Stamps, Griffing was presented with a hunk of beefsteak and warned not to bite any Rider players, as Griffing was accused of biting Greg Kabat, a Winnipeg Blue Bomber, during a pile-up years before. A few weeks after the incident he lined up against another Winnipeg Jewish player, Lou Mogul, and said, "It's okay, Lou. I don't think I'll have any kosher meat today."

Despite the success of their practical joke, the Riders' performance on the field wasn't the same calibre. The young Regina Roughrider group lost 12-0 to the veteran Stampeders, as Griffing and Lindsay Holt stood toe-to-toe in argument. The crowd was into it, as it was for the start of the semi-finals between the two rival teams. Before the first semi-final game, Griffing was presented with a yellow rocking chair to remind him of his advancing age. A Model T, in the same Stampeder colours, carried Griffing from the station to the hotel. But despite the off-field show, the Riders didn't show much on the field, as they lost 3-1 and 12-0 to Calgary in the semi-finals, enough to send the Stampeders on to Winnipeg for the western championship, and for the Roughriders to end their own short-lived football season.

Photo courtesy of SSHFM

Sully Glasser

Yet the season was successful in the fact that football lived again in Saskatchewan. Competitively and financially the team didn't fare well, but players, coaches, and management alike were happy with the result. They weren't playing for money or for fame; they played because they loved football and they knew their fans did too. As Don King said in the November 6 edition of the *Leader-Post* that year, "We've made enough to buy the gang sports jackets and perhaps we'll have a windup dinner. It's been a good season for a starter and we'll be back again next fall."

Back they were in 1946, with a new, yet familiar, face at the helm. Ken Preston is now best remembered as 'The Dean' of general managers, a role he took on in later years, but his history with the Riders stretches far beyond that. Preston first played running back for Regina in 1940 before playing with the Winnipeg Blue Bombers for two seasons. He returned to the Riders in 1943, before the '44 break. When Canadian football resumed,

Photo courtesy of SSHFM

(Left to right): unknown, Mike Cassidy, Dean Bandiera, Matt Anthony, Roy Wright, Sully Glasser, Johnny Bell

Preston was playing with the Ottawa Rough Riders. When he returned to Regina in 1946, it was as player-coach, a position he would hold until Fred Grant arrived in 1948.

Preston's return to Regina came with high hopes for a new Roughrider beginning. But the season started slowly, with headlines such as "Rugby premier flat as a pancake" and "Rider collapse has all guessing" topping the *Leader-Post* after games.

Even Dean Griffing was said to be sympathetic to the Roughriders – but not for long, as he felt the Roughrider organization didn't properly respect and remember his past with the club.

"I hope the Roughriders never win a game," Griffing told Dave Dryburgh in September of 1946. "They have a lot of nerve using my old No. 26 on that guy Nagy. That's gratitude for you. I think it's a rotten deal."

Andy Nagy, a middle lineman, had been given the Dean's old number, and Griffing wasn't happy about seeing another player on the field in his old jersey. But Nagy just made things worse when he announced he was taking the jersey home with him to Ohio.

The rivalry with Calgary may have been exciting, but fans weren't happy the Riders most often came out on the losing side of each game. However, the Roughrider spirit was just as alive in 1946 as it is today, and fans stayed with the team that continued to disappoint.

"The easy way out would be to write off the 'Riders as a foul ball and start talking hockey," wrote *Leader-Post* columnist Dave Dryburgh, "but there's something about the Regina gridders that intrigues. They're like a race horse that shows a flash of speed, gets into trouble and winds up as also-ran every time out."

The Roughriders, however, would soon give fans a reason to celebrate. Despite Griffing's prediction that the Roughriders wouldn't win a game all season, the Riders won their first post-war game October 5, 1946, 10-9 against none other than their western rivals, the Calgary Stampeders. Griffing had been enjoying the beginning of the game, bantering with the crowd in addition to Clair Warner and Stack Tibbits. At one point Warner asked Griffing if he was afraid to get into the game himself. Soon after, Griffing was on the field and the Riders began to rack up points.

With a high came a low, and the next game Saskatchewan found out it would have to play the Winnipeg Blue Bombers outside of the city because rain had turned Park de Young unplayable. The loss of gate fares was huge for an organization that relied on the $3,000 the gate would bring in. It was one more factor leading toward the necessary changes needed to Park de Young, which, covered just in topsoil, caused dust and fumbles when dry and an unplayable mudbowl when wet. During one game, water had to be pumped off the field, which resembled a "giant custard pudding" according to Dryburgh.

The 1946 season was a short one for the Roughriders, who finished in third place among the three teams that comprised the Western conference, and out of playoffs. Andy Nagy, Sully Glasser and Johnny Bell were named western conference all-stars, but for the most part the season was not a memorable one. The city's attention soon moved onto the Regina Pats hockey club, which commenced post-war play that year with a star-packed team coached by ex-Pat Moose Stinson.

Regina had to deal with the death of 'Piffles' Taylor in May of 1947. Taylor, the backbone of the Roughriders, was associated with the club for three decades as both an athlete and a builder. To honour the man who led the team to a Western title in 1919, took on the role of club president from 1934-36 and in 1940, and was president of the Western Interprovincial Football Union in 1936, 1941-42 and 1946, the city council decided to rename Park de Young as Taylor Field.

The site of the field was originally purchased in 1913 by John Marshall Young. Known as JM, he founded Sun Electric, a company that still exists. He was active in real estate, and his wife was the sister of Premier Walter Scott. When Young purchased the land, he was hopeful that with his wife's connection to the first premier of Saskatchewan, he could convince the government to build the Legislative Building at his location.

But meanwhile, another pioneer entrepreneur, realtor Walter Hill, convinced the Saskatchewan government to construct the Legislative Building on land he controlled at the existing site in Wascana Park – Young's connections didn't pay off for him. Young was unable to develop his land closer to downtown Regina for other purposes and eventually he lost the land for taxes. Finally, Young agreed to relinquish ownership of the site to the City and did so with the understanding that it would be used as a recreational park with the name Park de Young. He chose the family name of Young and added 'de' in front to make it sound more exotic.

Later the City of Regina subdivided the land and created two separate adjoining parks. One was named Park Hughes for soccer and the other Park de Young for football and baseball.

The name change to Taylor Field didn't mean much more money or effort, as groundskeeper Howard Pink received only a rake, a hoe, and a wheelbarrow to care for the stadium. But the field had grass (in addition to huge dandelions), and through a borrowed lawn mower and a fire hose, Pink got the job done.

Photo courtesy of SSHFM

Jack Rowand

Fielding a team seemed to be as much of a struggle as the field itself. President Jack Rowand, general manager Clair Warner, Don MacDonald and Stack Tibbits worked tirelessly at bringing players together for what Dave Dryburgh described as "the biggest gamble of all sports," due to a large overhead, short season and unpredictable weather. But if Winnipeg and Calgary had teams, Regina would not allow itself to be left out.

Warner, Rowand, MacDonald and Tibbits were Regina businessman who contributed countless hours and money to keep football alive. The group became known as the 'Big Five' when Don McPherson joined the group in later years.

Warner and Rowand played for the Regina Rugby Club and later for the Riders in the 1930s. Warner was manager of Northern Electric and Jack Rowand owned Waterman-Waterbury Manufacturing Company in the plumbing and heating business. Tibbits ran Tibbits Electric, and Don MacDonald was the president of Bird Construction Co.

As a group they provided employment for many players who had been attracted to Regina to play football. Ken Charlton and Roy Wright became estimators at Bird Construction and import Del Wardien was employed as a carpenter. Paul Anderson was a staff member of Bird Building Supplies. Toar Springstein became a key project estimator at Waterman-Waterbury and Johnny Bell supervised the sheet metal department. The 'Big Five' arranged for former Rider all-star Al Urness to hire many players, such as Chuck Radley, Art McEwan, George Giokas and Ace Parker, to work at the Ford Motor Parts depot on Dewdney Avenue. Bob Pelling, Len Ortman and several players recruited by Riders from year to year worked for Tibbits Electric.

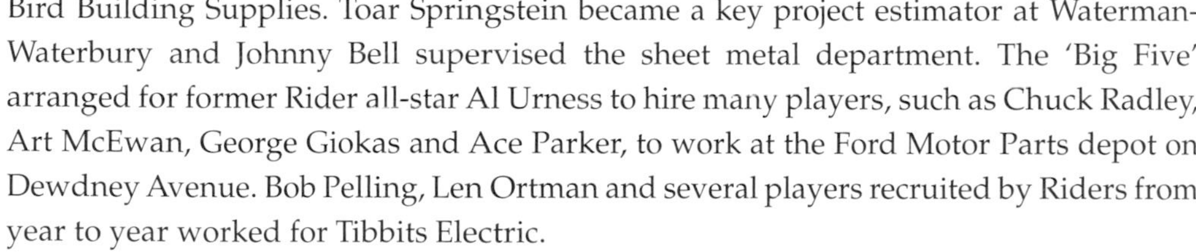

If the 'Big Five' didn't have employment for a player in one of its firms, they were able to contact other business owners in the community who were strong team supporters. Lindsay Holt and Taylor Paterson worked in the flooring department of T. Eaton Co. Ltd for the manager, former Rider great Larry Hegan; Bob Walker, another import, worked in the menswear department at the Robert Simpson department store. Rider supporter road contractor Beattie Ramsay gave players work with his road construction crew in the off-season. Players did not receive much money for playing football at that time and were attracted to Regina by the opportunity of obtaining year-round employment.

If the 'Big Five' didn't have employment for a player in one of its firms, they were able to contact other business owners in the community who were strong team supporters.

The management group kept the Roughriders going in 1947 after the death of 'Piffles' Taylor. Coach Ken Preston tested out his players with a pre-season road trip out east. Some questioned the decision of putting the Riders up against strong eastern teams, but Preston was hoping to toughen up his players, making them wiser and smarter as a whole.

The Riders did set a milestone, becoming the first western team to do an eastern exhibition tour. The Riders lost to the Hamilton Tiger-Cats 12-6 and 28-6; to the Montreal Alouettes 22-7, and to Ottawa 54-0. Tare Rennebohm, equipment manager, lamented the fact that both he and his son, Tare Rennebohm Jr., played on Roughrider teams on the losing end of such a score. Rennebohm Sr. played on the Roughriders in 1923 when they suffered a 54-0 loss to Queen's University.

Three games against strong teams took a toll on the Riders, but they were back and ready for the regular season.

On September 6, 1947, a pre-game ceremony dedicated Taylor Field. The Lions Band marched over the new turf as Rowand and Mayor Hugh McGillivray paid tribute to 'Piffles' Taylor, the driving force to build the new park.

That same day the Riders acquired backfielder 'Galloping' Gabe Patterson, the first black Roughrider since 'Stonewall' Jackson. The largest fan turnout to ever watch a practice came to watch Patterson. Dean Griffing, coach of the Stampeders, objected to the addition of Patterson, a late import signing, in addition to Stan Stasica. But the Riders were backed by the league and the Winnipeg Blue Bombers, and Patterson played against Calgary in his first game with the team. The Stamps won 16-11, but Regina had found a new star in Patterson, who ran for a 73-yard touchdown.

The Riders set another first for the Western Interprovincial Football Union in 1947. The Calgary Stampeders missed a road trip early in the season because of weather conditions. The tightened schedule meant the Riders had to play two games in three days, and wouldn't make it by train. Instead, they got on board a TCA plane and became the first team to fly to a football game. Some players were excited, others terrified; but they took to the air just as they did on the field.

Photo courtesy of SSHFM

Fred Grant

The Riders had quite a few skilled players that season, but following continued losses it was apparent they were definitely lacking something – but what? Scotty Melville referred to this in his column on October 6:

> "The time has come for Regina Roughriders to take stock. It doesn't need an efficiency expert to know something is wrong. Everybody knows it – the executive, the coach, the players and the Regina fans. They know it in Winnipeg and they know it in Calgary.... Gabe Patterson, Stan Stasica and Roy Wright are standout footballers in any league. Sully Glasser, although he has been hampered by injuries, is also top drawer. To that you can add hard-working, eager backs like Johnny Pope, Dave Gilbert, Stan Rose and Mike Yakymyk. Johnny Bell and Red Noel have no peers at end... Doug Cook has the reputation of being one of the finest centres in Canada... that's talent aplenty for any team, yet 'Riders lack the cohesion needed to weave victory."

But perhaps that cohesion was on his way – he just didn't know it yet.

Soon Calgary would file another objection, this time to import Fred Grant, even though Winnipeg was willing to let him play.

Grant came to the Riders from the Chicago Cardinals as a running back. He started his football career in high school in Virginia, leading his team to two undefeated seasons. In his last year he led the Southwestern District in scoring and was voted one of the most outstanding high school football players in Virginia.

In 1943 he entered Wake Forest College, North Carolina and as a freshman made the All-Southern Conference team as the Conference's leading scorer. He transferred to the University of Alabama and played in the Sugar Bowl and the Rose Bowl as an outstanding player on one of the most powerful undefeated teams Alabama ever turned out. In 1945 he led the Southwestern Conference in scoring and became the only college player to be the scoring leader of two major conferences.

In 1947 he joined the NFL's Chicago Cardinals but early in the season came to Regina. Don MacDonald got in touch with a coach of the Cardinals through Chicago Blackhawk Johnny Gottselig, who came from Regina. MacDonald found out the Cardinals had a running back – a great carrier with the potential of becoming an even better coach – but the team was letting him go. Grant arrived in Regina on September 4, three days after the date imports were to arrive in Canada to be eligible to play.

Grant did play one game with Winnipeg's permission but his eligibility was later challenged by Dean Griffing of Calgary.

The Riders were not doing well and so for the good of the game, Ken Preston stepped down to play regularly and Freddie Grant, 'The General,' took over as the youngest Roughrider coach ever at the age of 24. He chose not to continue playing after learning he had a heart condition.

Fred Grant introduced the Model T formation to the team, specializing in quick-breaking plays, as his line was a little light compared to others in the league. Stan Stasica, familiar with the Model T, became an important part of the system, and the Riders beat the Blue Bombers twice.

But the Model T – the system and the car Grant drove to the field – weren't enough, as the Stampeders broke it down, beating the Riders 6-5, leaving them in last place and out of playoff contention. Football fans were shocked and hearts were broken as badly as was the engine of the Model T, but more was to come from Fred Grant.

The season of 1948 was a new beginning for the team, who were now referred to as the Saskatchewan Roughriders. Moose Jaw and Saskatoon teams were officially defunct, and the team truly belonged to the province, although the name was not officially adopted until April of 1950. It was also the beginning of the green and white – a huge step in creating the identity of the football club.

Roughrider executive Jack Fyffe was in Chicago when he found two sets of green and white jerseys on sale. Not one to argue with the price, the team went with the new uniforms and Kelly green was adopted as the Roughrider colour.

"Roughrider executive Jack Fyffe was in Chicago when he found two sets of green and white jerseys on sale. Not one to argue with the price, the team went with the new uniforms and Kelly green was adopted as the Roughrider colour.

This was the start of big signings in the Canadian Rugby Union. Canadian teams were beginning to sign big-name passing quarterbacks. 'Indian' Jack Jacobs was picked up by Winnipeg; the Alouettes signed Frank Filchock, and the Edmonton Eskimos got Lindy Barry. The Roughriders signed Jack Hartman, who came with great credentials, but his output wasn't up to the high expectations of him.

Teams at that time had a budget of about $40,000 – less than what a single player is paid today. The largest percentage of the budget went to travel expenses, which were about $3,000 a trip – the reason for doubleheaders. Teams were most focused on recruiting imports, and would pay them anywhere from $2,000 to $4,000 a season, while homegrown players would make less than $500. Johnny Cook was paid $3,000 a season, while a player like Sully Glasser – a talented back who was with the club for 14 years – made only about $300 a year. Canadians didn't have any other football options, so money was spent drawing import players. The club executives felt they made up for it by offering players quality off-field employment.

A new concrete grandstand was revealed in the 1948 season, an optimistic outlook, as always, on the minds of players and coaches alike. Ken Preston returned for another go as a player. Despite the fact he announced he was retiring from football the year before, he came to watch practice in early August and next thing anyone knew, Preston was in a uniform and on the field.

Grant didn't have his best start to the season. In an exhibition game against the Toronto Beaches-Indians, Grant miscounted the downs and called for a pass instead of a punt. When Charlton fumbled, Toronto moved in for the rouge. After the game Grant said he "plumb forgot," but looked on the bright side – at least his players followed orders.

Others thought Grant's system wasn't working. Sportswriter Ted Reeve, former football and lacrosse star and Canadian Football Hall of Famer, thought the T formation was too much for Canadian footballers: "You've got to grow up with that kind of stuff. You can't learn it overnight," he was quoted as saying in the *Leader-Post*.

Photo courtesy of SSHFM

Left to right: Del Wardien, Ken Preston, Bob Early and Ken Charlton

But Grant's Model T merely needed a bit of repair. On August 21, the engine was revved, and with Ken Charlton and Bob Early in the backfield and Johnny Cook at quarterback, Grant took advantage of a new rule allowing unlimited substitutions. Of 29 players on the roster, Grant used 25, sending them in and out of the game constantly to wear down the Winnipeg Blue Bombers for a 17-6 victory.

Grant and the Riders were known for their sportsmanship, but their fans didn't follow suit in early September that year. Playing at Taylor Field, the Stamps fought back from a 7-0 deficit to tie the game 8-8. The Riders looked ready for the win, as Cook passed to Gabe Patterson, who was tackled. The ball slipped out of his hands, and the Riders, thinking the play was incomplete, stopped play while the Stampeders ran for a touchdown. With 12 seconds left, the Riders had the ball, but Grant had to take his team off the field as fans streamed onto the playing surface, protesting the call and throwing rocks and programs at officials Les Ferguson and Paul Dojack.

Grant scrapped the Model T in favour of the double-winged formation, but the Riders lost again to the Blue Bombers. After the game Grant looked at his gloomy players and said, "All right, this is no morgue. We've got to shake this off."

The Roughriders were a great team until the last five minutes of each game. On September 29, Scotty Melville wrote a new song for the Roughrider band: "Give Me Five Minutes More," dedicated to the "greatest 55-minute team in Canadian football:"

> "Give us five minutes more, only five minutes more! Hold that line, watch that pass and the Stamps cannot score. Big Les Lear's wet with tears and the count's 14-4. Keep that ball, hold it tight, give us five minutes more!"

The Roughriders didn't disappoint that season, as they went to Winnipeg to end the Bombers' season. A 10-car special train filled with 225 Roughrider enthusiasts left the Queen City to watch the game. The Riders satisfied fans with a 16-7 win. Del Wardien played almost all 60 minutes, making 27 tackles and numerous gains, catching four balls.

The team emerged victorious from the muddy playing field, everyone happy with one exception: Tare Rennebohm Sr. Scotty Melville explained: "The saddest man around was equipment manager Tare Rennebohm when Grant sent in the remainder of the subs during the last minutes of the game. It took one play for the bright uniforms to become as mud-plastered as the others."

After the semi-final win against the Bombers, the Riders went on to play their western rivals, the Calgary Stampeders. The first game of the final ended in a 4-4 tie at Taylor Field. The Riders put in a great effort in Calgary, but it wasn't enough as they lost 17-6. The Riders' season was over, but Calgary went on to beat the Ottawa Roughriders 12-7 in the Grey Cup final.

When the Calgary Stampeders took Toronto by storm in 1948 and the Grey Cup game became a national sports classic, the Grey Cup Parade and the Miss Grey Cup Pageant became important off-field events.

For a number of years in the late 1980s and early 1990s, the Grey Cup game was held indoors in Toronto's SkyDome. Poor organization and promotion by Eastern Division team hosts during that period ended the parade, and the Miss Grey Cup Pageant was discontinued because of lack of support and changing attitudes regarding the exploitation of female beauty.

The Miss Grey Cup Pageant was always strongly supported by the Roughriders and Miss Grey Cup was won by Miss Roughrider on five occasions. Myrtle Bainbridge was the first Miss Saskatchewan Roughrider and Miss Grey Cup winner of the pageant that would run until 1991. Candidates had to be residents of Canada between the ages of 17 and 22, single, not have taken a modelling course, attended a charm school, or practised modelling professionally. They were judged on charm, personality, deportment, makeup, figure, ability to speak in public, general intelligence, special ability and suitability of cheerleader costume, according to the 1966 Grey Cup program.

Miss Roughrider winners were:

Photo courtesy of *Leader-Post*

Miss Grey Cup 1951
Myrtle Bainbridge

1951 Myrtle Bainbridge* (Regina)
1952 Cleone Fleming (Weyburn)
1953 Joanne Baird* (Regina)
1954 Lynda Fleming (Swift Current)
1955 Frances Stewart (Swift Current)
1956 Colleen Todd (Regina)
1957 Rhonda Baker (Regina)
1958 Jane Wentz (Saskatoon)
1959 Anne Schnell (Regina)
1960 Lee Okenfold (Kinistino)
1961 Marilyn Craig (Regina)
1962 Anne Trenaman (Regina)
1963 Carol Erb (Regina)
1964 Deanna Bryden (Saskatoon)
1965 Lorayne Stevenson (Regina)
1966 Jo-Ann Martin (Regina)
1967 Anne Kennedy (North Battleford)
1968 Donna Hardy (Weyburn)
1969 Laura Medland* (Regina)
1970 Susan Pugsley (Weyburn)
1971 Janice Hogg (Moose Jaw)
1972 Pat Thompson (Saskatoon)
1973 Wendy Mills* (Saskatoon)
1974 Heather Anderson (Regina)
1975 Zelda Luchenski (Fillmore)
1976 Debbie Gamble (Moose Jaw)
1977 Kit Johnston (Regina)
1978 Terrene Whitney (Regina)
1979 Marlene Flaman* (Southey)
1980 Linda Minor (Regina)
1981 Michelle Frank (Southey)
1982 Leslie MacNaughton* (Regina)
1983 Cori Geisler (Moose Jaw)
1984 Carla Vermeulen (Regina)
1985 Lisa Hamernick (Regina)
1986 Olana Drebot (Regina)
1987 Sonia Girard (Regina)
1988 Pheona Wright (Wawota)
1989 Debra Jones (Regina)
1990 Kerry Beutler* (Moose Jaw)
1991 Lisa Stremick (Regina)
1992 Wanda Ferraton (Regina)
1993 Teresa Kivell (Regina)

* Denotes Miss Grey Cup winners.

Back on the home turf, Gabe Patterson, the second black player in Roughrider history, had been a fan favourite in 1948. Early on in the season he subbed in at quarterback for an injured Johnny Cook, and fans screamed every time Patterson set foot on the field. But there were stories about factions on the team around Patterson. Winnipeg broadcaster Doug Smith told a story of Fred Grant leaving the Roughrider windup when Patterson walked in. Scotty Melville defended Grant, calling the story a "malicious rumor that had absolutely no foundation." But rumours cropped up in Regina now and then about southern U.S. players objecting to Patterson's place on the team.

Patterson left the next season for personal reasons and was not invited back to play.

Other stars would pick up the slack the next year; a year of reorder in the league. Annis Stukus, a former Toronto Argonaut quarterback from the 1930s, reorganized the

Edmonton Eskimos, who began playing in the Western Conference in 1949; it was a team that would enjoy much success in the coming years. The Eskimos would go on to ruin Roughrider dreams with players such as 'Spaghetti Legs' Jackie Parker, Normie Kwong and Eagle Keys.

With the arrival of the Eskimos, the 1949 schedule was redone, adding doubleheader road trips for a 14-game season rather than the former 12 games. Instead of staying at hotels – most likely to cut costs – the Riders travelled in a caravan of three rail cars, two of which were sleeping cars, where the Riders would live throughout their stays. Warner said there was never a better way for a football team to travel, as the players could eat, sleep, listen to pregame chalk talks, and have their injuries treated all in one place.

Photo courtesy of SSHFM

Clair Warner

The late 1940s were tough financially for football and hockey clubs in a city of 65,000. As Scotty Melville wrote: "(It's) too much of a drag on wealthier citizens who now play the role of sugar daddies." He said "the little guy" had a hard enough time finding money for food and fuel, let alone sporting events. But the Saskatchewan Roughriders have always survived, and so they did in 1949.

The season started with an exhibition game against the Winnipeg Blue Bombers. The Bombers unexpectedly won 13-8, which general manager Clair Warner declared a good thing: "I'm tickled to death it finished that way… If the Riders had won we would have needed larger helmets."

Grant brought back the Model T, which purred to a 20-0 victory over the Blue Bombers in the first regular season game, played at Taylor Field in front of its largest crowd ever — 7,500. Fans came from all over Saskatchewan to take in the game, proving enthusiasm for the team really was province-wide.

But the Stampeders would again prove to be a formidable opponent. The Riders lost to the team 22-19 after leading 19-0. They followed this with another loss, this time 13-1.

Despite losses against Calgary, the Riders continued to be successful against Winnipeg, beating them 47-0 on October 15, the Bombers' worst defeat in their history.

Finally near the end of October the Roughriders "tamed the Calgary herd," beating the Stamps 9-6, their first win over the team in two years. Only 17 players saw the field for the Riders, but what they saw was questionable as a "near-blinding snowstorm" resulted in a low-scoring game. The Stampeders scored just once, when Roughrider receiver Johnny Bell accidentally deflected his own quarterback's pass, thrown by Doug Belden, into the arms of Stampeder Keith Spaith. The Riders didn't even score a touchdown, winning with rouges and field goals.

When the Riders returned to Regina, over 200 supporters greeted them.

The benchwarmers, clad in jackets sponsored by various Saskatchewan communities, had no regrets: "With a great whoop and a holler, the parka-clad alternates on the bench swooped out on the field at the final gun to hail their conquering teammates and touch off some wild victory celebrations in far-off Regina," according to the *Leader-Post*.

When the Riders returned to Regina, over 200 supporters greeted them. Wives and girlfriends had surprised players by hopping on the train in Moose Jaw to celebrate the long-awaited victory over the Stampeders for the last part of the ride home.

When playoffs rolled around, it was the Roughriders against the Stamps once again in the western final. In the first of the two-game total-point playoff, Calgary launched a terrific aerial show to win 18-12 in Regina as Roughrider fans looked on. One particular onlooker was Ruffie, the Rider mascot. He stood on the bench, disinterested in the game, slowly eating a roll of adhesive tape. Ruffie was a goat.

The Riders worked on their passing attack in days between games, as it was their ground game that had brought them this far. The Riders went to Calgary and spent the first three quarters trying to give the Stampeders the series. The Riders decided to come alive in the fourth, and had the chance to win the series with a field goal in the last seconds of the game. Kicker Buck Rogers just missed the field goal, leaving it low. Les Lear, player and coach of the Stampeders, was called for an offside, and the ball was moved five yards closer. Grant sent in Del Wardien, who heartbreakingly repeated Rogers' mistake. Johnny Bell rouged Pete Thodos, a future Roughrider, for a single, and Calgary just got by with a 22-21 series win.

But the season wasn't a write-off for the Saskatchewan Roughriders, at least not according to Scotty Melville:

> "Saskatchewan triumphs in Calgary, even though they failed to take the Western Football Conference title from the Stampeders, should have a two-fold effect on gridiron game in the West. First and most important is that Roughriders should be right in the thick of things again next year. Operating a club in a city the size of Regina is no easy chore. There is more money needed than the dollars taken at the gate and it's usually a long, hard pull for many centres to get incoming and outgoing reasonably closer to each other on the ledger. Friday's terrific comeback which won the game and just missed taking the series by a whistle has everybody in Regina and the outlaying precincts keener than mustard to take another crack at winning that title. Roughriders have something to sell and the long, hard pull will not be quite as tough when the Stack Tibbits and Company start off the collection campaign in the spring."

Photo courtesy of SSHFM

Bert Iannone

Spring came, and in 1950 the Saskatchewan Roughriders set another first, making the first player trade in Canadian Rugby Union history. Bob Early and Wilf Godfrey were traded to the Calgary Stampeders for Bert Iannone. Iannone, who ran a shoe store outside of his football life, would prove to be a terrific addition to the Roughriders.

The Riders tried for another player, and the result left the team the laughingstock of the league – for a few days at least. Leon 'Bull' Cochrane was a young fullback from Alabama who agreed to come to the Riders. His flight schedule included a transfer in Winnipeg. When Warner went to meet Cochrane at the Regina airport, Cochrane was nowhere to be seen. The Roughriders management committee decided the Blue Bombers must have drawn him to their team when he touched down in Winnipeg. Stack Tibbits and Jack Rowand agreed to go to Winnipeg to retrieve Cochrane. They loaded up Tibbits' truck and left Regina at 10 p.m. They showed up at Winnipeg's office the next morning, accusing the team of underhanded methods. When the

Blue Bombers denied any wrongdoing, the Rider management went in search of Cochrane. When they stopped at the airport, the customs official told them 'Bull' had signed his papers, looked at the strong wind and blowing snow out the window, turned around and bought a ticket back home.

Such situations began to be discussed at the newly formed Quarterback Club, hosted every Sunday by Johnny Esaw of CJRM at the Grand Theatre. Round Table discussions were held by managers, officials, players, sportswriters and the public. Over 700 people attended the first sessions, which would later move to the Rex Theatre. Sunday nights were a full night of football for fans, as Lloyd Saunders of CK Radio would compete against the Quarterback Club with Sunday Night Crossley's Sportslight.

They discussed players such as Del Wardien and Toar Springstein, captain and co-captain of the team in 1950. Wardien, in his fourth season, was from Montana; the halfback showed grit and determination in every battle. Springstein was a homegrown lineman from Manitoba Varsity.

Photo courtesy of SSHFM

Toar Springstein

They also discussed stories such as Bill Svoboda, who was to leave the Chicago Cardinals (also home at that time to a quarterback named Frank Tripucka) to come to Saskatchewan to play fullback with the Riders. When he went to say goodbye to his line coach, the coach talked him out of it, telling him, "they're just a bunch of bush leaguers up there… they'll promise you a lot of money but you'll never see it."

The Roughriders, however, were fine without Svoboda. They started off the season with a 35-12 win over the Calgary Stampeders. The largest crowd in the history of Saskatchewan football, 8,467, left the game with smiles on their faces.

The Riders looked sharp at the beginning of 1950, beating the Stampeders again 16-11. With a 6-5 lead at the beginning of the fourth, "the graying Charlton, who like wine seems to improve with age, uncorked his whirring feverish effort" and returned a punt from his own 10-yard line for the touchdown, according to the *Leader-Post*.

The middle of September was also the one-third mark of the season. Harvey Dryden of the *Leader-Post*, named the moments and players of the season that stood out in his mind, with a few Roughrider notables:

"Best all-around halfback in games witnessed: Del Wardien.

Longest runback – Ken Charlton's 65-yard hike in Calgary.

Happiest crowd: August 26th throng at Taylor Field gleefully watching the Riders beat the Stamps for the first time in Regina during Lear's reign.

Farthest runner: Bob Pelling.

Funniest guys: Buddy Tinsley of Winnipeg and 'Pistol' Pete Martin of the Riders in a dead heat.

Poorest dressing room facilities: Taylor Field, Regina (are there any?).

Best grandstand: Regina's concrete stand.

Photo courtesy of SSHFM

Ken Charlton

Most powerful tackler in the secondary: Al Bodine of Riders.
Most dangerous passer: Jack Hartman of Riders.
Laugh of the season: Bull Cochrane yarn.
Story of the season: The cutting down to size of the Stampeders.
Steal of the season: Riders trading Early and Godfrey for Bert Iannone.
Most eligible bachelor: 1) Royal Copeland of Calgary 2) Mike Cassidy of Riders (he's got a car now).
Most under-rated group: The Roughrider line.
Biggest man in the conference: Toar Springstein.
Sliver king of the conference: Doug Kelly of Riders.

A few new rules were introduced to the Canadian Rugby Union that season. The first was that a team could replace up to two of its American players before the third scheduled game; the second was that every player who was banished from a game for rough play would have to pay an automatic $25 fee to the league headquarters. Any subsequent banishment that season would be $50.

But the Riders were a sportsmanlike bunch. In fact, in late September they lost to the Bombers 26-13 and not a single penalty was called.

'Indian' Jack Jacobs, the backbone of the Bombers, didn't play one particular game in late October as the second-string Winnipeggers met Saskatchewan's second-string, each team resting starters because of injuries or to prepare for playoffs. The Riders won 36-1; they continued to prepare for the upcoming playoff games against the Eskimos. Annis Stukus, coach of the Esks, challenged the Rider nation, saying "we can beat them anytime" or anywhere.

Stukus followed through on his words, as the third-place team beat the Riders 24-1 in the two-game total-points semi-final.

Fans created a "Get Rid of Grant" club, and Fred Grant eventually announced his resignation in a sarcastic letter to the media. Broadcasters Esaw and Saunders were publicly critical of the management committee, and on November 11, Don MacDonald and Jack Rowand stepped down from the executive over the criticism of the Grant situation.

Photo courtesy of SSHFM

Bob Kramer

When the general meeting convened in December, the four- or five-man executive was converted through a new constitution into a 14-man executive. Bob Kramer returned to the club as president, Dr. Beattie Martin served as vice-president, and five directors-at-large were named, including Sam Taylor, son of 'Piffles.' Seven chairmen were responsible to a body of active members, each of whom paid $10 to the club. Members of the Booster or Quarterback clubs were associate members, who could attend meetings and discussions but could not vote. MacDonald, Warner, Rowand and Tibbits were named honorary vice-presidents due to their experience on the team.

It had been an interesting season, with many stories to tell, including the Calgary Stampeders' drop from first to last, Bob Pelling's first touchdown in four years with the Riders, and the dismissal of Fred Grant. But 1950 is forgettable to many considering what – or who – was to come next year.

Fans had greeted Fred Grant with great expectations for his new "Model T" offence, and the new green and white uniforms. Unfortunately the Model T sputtered and the team ended the 1950 season dismally.

The Riders had always rivalled the Stampeders, and they were not to be outdone by the Stamps' 1948 Grey Cup win. In 1951, Bob Kramer became president of the Saskatchewan Roughriders. The All-America Football Conference had just ceased operation in the U.S., talent was available from pro ranks and college football, and the price was right. CFL teams were offering better contracts than those in the U.S. and the surge of top talent to Canada began.

Glenn Dobbs was a first-round draft pick of the NFL's Chicago Cardinals. Previously, he was a Heisman Trophy candidate and All-American star at Tulsa University. He played four years in the All-America Football Conference, excelling until 1950, when he became a radio commentator at Oklahoma A & M college games.

That year Don MacDonald and Charlie Hay, Regina businessmen and Roughrider supporters, were in Tulsa on a business trip. MacDonald heard Dobbs was no longer playing football, and asked Hay to talk to the former player on another trip down south. Dobbs showed interest in playing in Saskatchewan, and so Jack Rowand headed down to chat with him. But there were a couple of issues to get over before Dobbs could make his way to Regina. The first was that he was under contract as a radio commentator until 1951. The second was that the NFL's Chicago Bears were just as interested in Dobbs. In the end, the Riders had a better offer, and Dobbs set out on a northern journey after he finished his radio contract.

It didn't take long for fans to rally around the friendly, likable and talented Glenn Dobbs. He met his fans in late February in 1951 at the Grand Theatre at a meeting of the Quarterback Club. The place was packed and fans lined the streets for a look at Dobbs. In minus-30 weather, Dobbs greeted his waiting fans.

New head coach Harry Smith was also introduced at the February gathering. Harry 'Blackjack' Smith had played on the offensive line with the University of Southern California's Rose Bowl teams in 1938 and 1939, earning All-American honours. His playing career extended to the 1940 season with the Detroit Lions. Afterward he was an assistant coach with the University of Missouri and the University of Tennessee before moving north to Saskatchewan.

Regina was most interested in Glenn Dobbs. The local store sold Dobber jeans and T-shirts, as people drove around with "Dobberville" license plates. Canada Post even received letters to "Dobberville, Saskatchewan."

Photo courtesy of SSHFM

Glenn Dobbs and Harry Smith

Photo courtesy of SSHFM

Glenn Dobbs

Photo courtesy of SSHFM

Red Ettinger

Photo courtesy of SSHFM

Jack Russell

Photo courtesy of SSHFM

Martin Ruby

Despite his big name, the tall quarterback was easy-going, down-to-earth, and just enjoyed living in Regina. He was the type of man who donated his fee for a half-hour radio program to the Roughrider club, or gave $1,000 to the reserve fund along with the Roughrider executive. One day he helped paint the fence of Taylor Field; so many people came to paint with him, the job was done in one day.

"In Regina, you knew these people," he told Rob Vanstone of the *Leader-Post* in 1998. "You knew everybody. You'd call everybody by their first name. It was wonderful. It was a blessing. It was the greatest part of my career."

Dobbs was a leader on and off the field, a triple threat as an excellent passer, deceptive runner and strong kicker. His calls were imaginative, and at 6-foot-4 and 215 pounds, he was hard to tackle. With his charismatic charm, people loved him for both his football and character.

In 1951, Dobbs was joined by Jack Russell, Martin Ruby, Donald 'Red' Ettinger, Jack Nix and Bob Sandberg. The regular season opener was set for August 25, and the green and white nation was anticipating big things from the Saskatchewan Roughriders.

Scotty Melville echoed fans' thoughts: "Today is August 25 when the greatest season of all gets under way and deeds on the gridirons take the place of prophecies. It will be the greatest season of all because never before in the history of the game in Canada has there been such emphasis on the gathering together of topflight United States talent and the very best that the Dominion can produce in the way of football heroes."

Martin Ruby's introduction to the Riders may have been slightly eclipsed by Glenn Dobbs, but he is certainly not to be forgotten. He was described by teammate Bill Clarke as one of the toughest men to ever play Canadian football. Sully Glasser also praised him, calling him the best lineman he ever saw play football. Glasser said Ruby would clear the way for him quickly as he was so powerful with his initial hit.

One player the Roughrider executive would later regret not signing was Rollie Miles. He played baseball for the Regina Caps in the summer of 1951. He was also known as an All-American football player, but for whatever reason – some say because he was black – he went unnoticed by the Roughriders, and ended up in Edmonton with Annis Stukus. He'd later rack up many points against the team from his former home. The Roughriders claimed they had invited him to play but he didn't show up; other accounts say the Riders wouldn't give him the tryout he wanted. Years later Miles would be inducted into the Canadian Football Hall of Fame.

There was another player in the league whose heroics often hurt the Roughriders; yet he helped create an important part of the team's history. 'Indian' Jack Jacobs, as he was known by all, was a quarterback with the Winnipeg Blue Bombers. After coming off a 33-1 victory against Winnipeg, the Riders were ready to take on the Bombers on the Labour Day weekend of 1951. The two teams were set to face off in front of 12,028 fans at Taylor Field. The Riders seemed to have the game after three quarters against a team whose star quarterback was sitting on the bench. Then Jacobs came in the game, and things changed. With three touchdown passes in 14 plays, he led his team to a 24-22 victory. It was the first of many Rider-Bomber Labour Day weekend games ingrained in fans' memories.

The Riders would go on to lose the next three games, after Glenn Dobbs injured his leg. He kept playing over the season, though perhaps not at full form as he lost 16 pounds along the way.

Nevertheless, by October the Riders had jumped into first place with two wins on an Alberta road trip. Dobbs was back in form and leading his team to victory. Jim Coleman, a syndicated sports columnist, claimed Dobbs just might bring the Grey Cup back to the West because he could run, pass, kick and breakout.

Dobbs wasn't the only star. The Saskatchewan Roughriders had six players on the first all-star squad that year: Glenn Dobbs of course, Jack Russell, Red Ettinger, Martin Ruby, Bert Iannone and Ken Charlton.

The best-of-three Western final was to be held against the Edmonton Eskimos, with the first game in Edmonton and the final two in Regina. The Roughriders lost the first game in Edmonton, and faced a problem with the second game in Regina – the possibility the field might freeze before game time. Saskatchewan fans, ever-resourceful and hard-working farmers, covered the field with straw and a layer of canvas to keep the field from freezing. Eight tonnes (325 truck carts) of straw was donated and laid on the field; then, of course, removed before game time. The Riders ended up winning 12-5 as they held the Eskimos to 25 yards rushing and Glasser, Charlton and Sandberg gained, a combined 190 yards. The series was capturing the public's attention like no sport in Regina ever had before.

On the Saturday of Game 3, held in Regina, the *Leader-Post* postponed delivery of the newspaper so that the carriers could watch the game, and on Monday the final edition was delayed to run an account of the game, which would end up reading: "This afternoon was dull and cloudy but in the hearts of Saskatchewan football fans everywhere, the sun was shining brighter than it ever had before."

> **Fans tore out the goal posts and paraded through the city as police officers smiled on them.**

Everyone in the city who could be was there – 12,463 people crammed into a stadium designed for 8,700 – to watch what the *Globe and Mail* called "60 minutes of the most wild and wonderful playoff football ever witnessed outside a Hollywood movie lot." The last 15 minutes was possibly the best football ever played in Regina. Rollie Miles – playing for the Eskimos – made a great one-handed catch, but Dobbs threw a touchdown pass to Sandberg. The teams traded touchdowns, and Edmonton scored again, but the Riders were able to hold them off for the 19-18 win.

Fans tore out the goal posts and paraded through the city as police officers smiled on them. Traffic stopped as fans marched to the Hotel Saskatchewan to deride Annis Stukus, head coach of the Edmonton Eskimos, but the makeshift parade instead decided to go to Dobbs' house and wait for him to get home.

The fans followed the Roughriders to Toronto for the Grey Cup game against the Ottawa Rough Riders. Dressed in blue jeans, plaid shirts and white Stetsons, 700 fans on 28 coaches on two special trains – labelled the 'Green' and the 'White' — headed to Toronto. On two cleared baggage cars filled with music, the fans danced all the way to Toronto. Al Ritchie was also on to Toronto, on his 11th trip east for a national sport final.

Photo courtesy of SSHFM

Sully Glasser

The team, however, wasn't quite as fit and cheerful as the fans. 'Pistol' Pete Martin had a broken leg, Jack Russell had injured a knee in the Western final, Al Bodine and Del Wardien had ankle injuries, Red Ettinger had bruised ribs injected with Novocain, and Martin Ruby had the same shot in his shoulder. Glenn Dobbs had a severe charley horse, three broken ribs, and a plastic protector from his waist to his armpits, was not noticeably visible to the public. Bob Sandberg was ruled an ineligible player as it was decided he would be classified as an import, which would put the Riders over their quota.

The Roughriders started on top, with a 2-0 lead, scoring on punt singles kicked by Dobbs. Ottawa answered with 20 straight points until Jack Nix and Sully Glasser scored touchdowns for Saskatchewan. It was too little, too late for the underdogs.

One major play that went Ottawa's way came at the mistake of Mickey Maguire, who fumbled two punts leading to an Ottawa touchdown and single. One fumble came late in the game when Saskatchewan needed the ball. As Maguire sat, inconsolable, in the Rider locker room after the game, none other than Glenn Dobbs came to give him a pep talk about the mistakes made by every player on the field – not just Maguire.

There was one Saskatchewan victory in Ottawa. Miss Saskatchewan Roughrider, 18-year-old Myrtle Bainbridge, was named Miss Grey Cup in the 1951 pageant.

Players were disappointed in themselves, but the fans still loved their football team. They danced all the way home, just as they had on the trip to Toronto. They made their own 'Grey Cup,' and once the fan trains made it back to Regina, they paraded around the goal posts they took from Varsity Stadium and had checked as baggage.

When the team returned, it was welcomed by fans as if they had won the Grey Cup. Players, in particular Dobbs, apologized for the loss, stressing the toll the Western final had taken on their bodies.

The love affair between Dobberville and the team wasn't over; Dobbs wasn't finished with the Roughriders – but Harry 'Blackjack' Smith was.

As it turned out, Sandberg could have played in the Grey Cup. Bob Kramer had protested to officials, telling them it wouldn't be much of a game without Sandberg due to the many injuries. He was told "rules were rules," and he stormed out, telling them he would play Sandberg anyway. Jerry McCaffrey, president of the Ottawa Rough Riders, caught up to him at the elevator, telling him he could play Sandberg as long as he kept the matter quiet. But Smith didn't play Sandberg, as he wanted to show up the executive in front of the media. When Kramer confronted him about it, Smith said "I'm sorry." Kramer replied, "You should be. You can pack up your suitcases and head for home as fast as you can."

It was said Smith and Dobbs were often at odds over how they treated other players on the team. To Dobbs, a player was a player, whether he was a Canadian or an import. Smith, on the other hand, did not have much love for Canadian players, and showed it to the team. Players lost confidence in him, and they shared this with the Rider executive. "Harry Smith was very hard on Canadian talent; very easy on American talent," said Sully Glasser, one who would know. After Sam Taylor asked the players what they thought of Smith, the coach didn't return.

But Glenn Dobbs did, and in a new role – player-coach. It was definitely a rebuilding year as many players from the successful 1951 team did not return, including Red Ettinger and Bob Sandberg. Jack Nix went to the U.S. Marines, and Jack Russell's season ended early due to injury.

Dobbs was on the field, but not in full form. He injured his right leg in training camp, and couldn't play a full game until the fourth outing of the season. Even then, he couldn't kick or run and wasn't the dominant presence of previous years. As the new imports that year were unproductive, the only plus was the new Canadian talent which included Harry Lampman and Reg Whitehouse. Dobbs secured the latter player, which took a lot of convincing – of Whitehouse's mother. Eventually Whitehouse, from Montreal, came to Regina, as he decided if he didn't make the team, he would join the RCMP. Not only did he make the Saskatchewan Roughriders, but he would stay for the next 15 years.

Photo courtesy of SSHFM

Reg Whitehouse

Photo courtesy of SSHFM

Ron Atchison

Ron Atchison was another new face to the team, but not to the province. Atchison was a farm kid who had played for the Saskatoon Hilltops until 1949. He sat out the 1950 and 1951 seasons, as he had never seen a professional football game and figured he wouldn't be good enough to make it. Cliff McClocklin, a Hilltops official, finally convinced Atchison to try out for the Riders. He walked into training camp, told them he was from the Hilltops, tried out, made the team, and played for the Riders for the next 17 years. Atchison injured his arm the next season, and the cast stayed on for 16 years, as he found it made a great weapon.

The Roughriders also welcomed a new mascot that season – another 'Roughie,' this time from Preeceville, a white goat who arrived on Train 88. Unfortunately due to foot and mouth disease in the province, the goat had to be put down – symbolic of the Saskatchewan Roughriders' 1952 season.

The Riders lost many games at the beginning of the regular season, and by the end of September, they were settled into the basement with little hope of a playoff berth. The season was full of fumbles, interceptions, loose balls, and calls against the Roughriders.

By the Thanksgiving Day game against the Winnipeg Blue Bombers, Glenn Dobbs announced he'd pull out a few tricks, as the team began a "Stop Jacobs" campaign against the Winnipeg quarterback. They lost that battle 37-1 in the last home game of the season, giving the Bombers a bye during playoffs.

Despite the dismal season with only three regular-season wins and no all-stars, the Roughriders set a new average attendance record of 10,789. Bob Kramer told the *Leader-Post*: "It can be truly said that Saskatchewan people are the best football fans in Canada. We didn't win many games for them, but they came to the park anyway."

Photo courtesy of SSHFM

Paul Anderson

This wouldn't be the last time in history Rider fans huddled around Taylor Field despite the awful performance in front of them.

When the Roughriders won against the Edmonton Eskimos 31-28 in the final game of the season, they did it for their fans, their pride and their reputation. The quarterback looked like the Glenn Dobbs of old as the back-and-forth battle ended with a bang. It was a positive way to close off the football season, as the club's new goals were focused on selling season tickets for the next year. Dobbs was expected to return in 1953, but as a player and most likely not a coach.

Halfback Bob Pelling felt that's where Dobbs' talent lay. "Dobbs was a heck of an athlete," Pelling told Rob Vanstone of the *Leader-Post*. "He came back in '52 and was a bad coach. Most guys who are good athletes are perfectionists and they expect everyone else to be that way. Everybody had to be that good… I really thought it was a bad year for Dobbs. He didn't bring in the ballplayers we needed to have."

Roy Wright, backup quarterback, told Vanstone the same thing about Dobbs, who threw only 14 touchdown passes that season: "They had Dobbs coach and play. That's a tall order. You can't do that. It's tough to play and organize who's on offence and defence. You lose the outside-looking-in on the various aspects of the game."

Obtaining quality players was a key issue at the end of that year. One thing was for certain – fewer hometown players were on the field each year. Teams were looking to Americans, and next eastern Canadians. In 1952, only nine players were actually from Regina – Roy Wright, Sully Glasser, Toar Springstein, Bob Pelling, Ken Charlton, Tony Hungle, Bill Clarke, Wayne Pyne and Len Ortman. Bill Ciz also came on as a rookie. Dobbs guessed at the explanation of fewer homegrown players, thinking perhaps Regina players were too busy with jobs after graduation. Most non-imports had to work in addition to playing football while Americans were paid enough to make a living. The quality of the American player was likely due to the exposure and coaching young players received in the States, with three years of football in junior high in addition to four in high school.

The Saskatchewan Roughriders did welcome a few players from the province. Up to the time of the draft system, there was automatic protection, which kept local players at home. In that year, Paul Anderson and Ray Syrnyk came from the Hilltops, Doug Killoh came from the Regina Junior Bombers, and Gordon Sturtridge, originally from Regina, returned from Winnipeg, where he didn't make the Blue Bombers. Joe 'The Toe' Aguirre arrived as line coach and kicker. Mario DeMarco came from the Edmonton Eskimos, and Mac Speedie, an American end, came from the U.S. Speedie was 33 years old and slightly past his prime, running slowly and slightly blind. Somehow, he still managed to catch the ball whenever it came his way, and when not on the field could often be found in the front row of cowboy movies.

John 'Heavy Hands' Wozniak came north from Alabama. His nickname stemmed from his tendency to welcome people be slapping them on the back so hard they just about fell over. Herb Johnson arrived, a great open field runner who set the Roughrider record for longest punt return at that time. Offensive end Stan Williams, halfback Bobby Marlow, and centre Mel Becket also made their way to Regina.

Bobby Marlow played seven years for the Riders. A legend in his own time, many fans consider him the best two-way running back/linebacker to ever wear the green and white. A fierce tackler on defence and a powerful running back on offence, Marlow was one of those rare players who comes along just every so often. He loved to play the game.

From Tuscaloosa, Alabama, Marlow had an outstanding football college career with the University of Alabama Crimson Tide and joined the Riders in 1953. In college he was referred to as 'Bama's Blazin Bobby.' He was a unanimous All-American in

Photo courtesy of SSHFM

John Wozniak

Photo courtesy of SSHFM

Bobby Marlow

Photo courtesy of SSHFM

Doug Killoh

1952 and he and Oklahoman Billy Vessels, who came to Edmonton in 1953, were considered the two best running backs in American college football in 1952. Marlow was a first-round draft choice of the New York Giants in 1953 and the Roughriders made North American sports headlines when they stole him away from the Giants, owned by the millionaire Mara family. Marlow played seven seasons and was an all-star halfback from 1953 to 1955 and an all-star linebacker in 1956 and 1957. His 4,291 rushing yards is third on the all-time Rider list behind George Reed and Mike Saunders; Marlow scored 10 touchdowns in 1957.

In describing Marlow's ability, Doug Killoh said that if you told him to go through a brick wall, he could do it. To illustrate Marlow's power and strength, Killoh tells how Al Pollard, celebrated running back of the B.C. Lions, attempted to go through an opening on the Rider line only to be stopped dead in his tracks with his head up by Marlow. The tackle was so devastating that Pollard never played football again.

Stan Williams began playing with the Roughriders in 1953 and would play until 1957. After a spectacular college career with Baylor University, he joined the Riders as an offensive end and defensive back. Coached by Frank Filchock, he was a WFC all-star defensive back in 1954 and offensive end in 1955. He was a coach's type of player, able to play both the offensive and defensive positions.

Another arrival who would make some waves, not just in 1953 but in years beyond, was Frank Tripucka.

Most importantly that season, Frank Filchock was named head coach. Filchock was a star in the United States for years, and ended up in the CFL in an unusual way. He was first drafted by the NFL's Pittsburgh Pirates in 1938 after an outstanding career at Indiana University. He played six games before being sold to the Washington Redskins, where he played until 1941, sharing the quarterback position with Sammy Baugh. The two were known as Slingin' Sam and Flingin' Frank. Filchock made NFL history in 1959, throwing a 99-yard touchdown pass, the longest play possible from the line of scrimmage. Filchock was out of professional football in 1942 and 1943 while in the U.S. Navy, but played for the Georgia Pre-Flight. After the 1945 season with the Redskins, Steve Owen (who would coach the Riders later in his career), wanted Filchock for the New York Giants. The trade created the first multi-year contract in Giants history.

Photo courtesy of SSHFM

Stan Williams

Filchock led his team to the NFL title game in 1946 against the Chicago Bears. The day of the game, a story broke that gamblers were trying to fix the game, and both Filchock and Merle Hapes, a Giant back, were involved. Later developments told the full story. Filchock and Hapes had been offered $2,500 each, profit sharing, and a $15,000 offseason job if Chicago won by more than 10 points. It was investigated by the New York City mayor, the police commissioner, the Giants owner, and NFL commissioner Bert Bell the day before the game. Hapes admitted he was approached, while Filchock denied it.

Hapes had to sit out of the game, while Filchock played almost all 60 minutes, and was responsible for all of the Giants scoring, throwing two touchdown passes. Chicago won 24-14 – the gamblers didn't win or lose their bets. But Filchock lost his reputation. He was booed at the beginning of the game, and suspended from the team when the gambling head was charged in January of 1947. At the trial, Filchock denied ever receiving or betting any money, as he and Hapes were accused of betting $500 on the Giants to beat the Redskins in the final game of the season. Both players were banned from the NFL, which included the NFL's minor teams. The All-America Football Conference wouldn't pick him up, and so Filchock came to Canada. He would be reinstated into the NFL in 1950, but wouldn't return.

Photo courtesy of SSHFM

Frank Filchock

Filchock was offered contracts by both the Ottawa Rough Riders and the Hamilton Tigers. He chose to play with the latter as a player-coach in 1947. He played with them for two years, with the Montreal Alouettes in 1949 and 1950, and with the Edmonton Eskimos as a player in 1951 and a player-coach in 1952, leading them to the Grey Cup game, which they lost.

In 1953, Filchock arrived in Saskatchewan. His first challenge as coach was to decide on a quarterback – Glenn Dobbs or Frank Tripucka.

Frank 'The Tripper' Tripucka had had a successful career with the Notre Dame Fighting Irish. In 1948, he went 9-0-1 and was named All-American. He was drafted number one overall by the Philadelphia Eagles in 1949, but was traded to the Detroit Lions before the season began. By the end of his fifth season, he wasn't producing the results the Lions required. He was then with the Chicago Cardinals, but when he got a call from the Roughriders to play for double the salary, up to Saskatchewan he went.

Winnipeg gossip reported rumours of a rift between Filchock and Dobbs, but obviously it wasn't so as Filchock decided to keep Dobbs at quarterback, cutting Tripucka before the October 1 roster deadline, but including him in plans for the future.

Not long after the import cutoff date, Dobbs' injuries began to catch up to him. Perhaps it was due to some of the doubleheader football games, or perhaps it just came down to his age. It was around that time that the league began reviewing import rules, with the possibility of upping the number allowed, or allowing replacements due to injuries. Unfortunately for the Riders, this wasn't allowed in 1953.

When Dobbs was injured, his replacement quarterback was none other than Frank Filchock. Near the end of October, the Riders had secured a playoff spot and headlines read "Filchock Sparkles for Riders." Scotty Melville declared Filchock proved wrong the theories that said coaching and playing don't mix. On October 23, Melville's column read: "There are some who feel the Old Man pilots his club from the seat of his pants after the fashion of the pioneer bush pilots. He improvises as he goes along. At Edmonton on Monday, some of his plays looked as if they were swiped right out of Darrell Royal's notebook. And certainly the Riders looked smarter than even the blonde queen some of the boys were ogling on Jasper Avenue in the afternoon."

Then things started to go slightly downhill for the Riders. "Frankie had his magic wand snatched away from him," read the *Leader-Post* October 29, after the Winnipeg Blue Bombers beat the Riders 43-5 in the first game of the two-game total-point semi-final. The Riders won the next game 18-17.

Filchock brought about another change in the rulebook that year. He played one game in Taylor Field, and was up 10 points into a big wind. Instead of punting, Filchock conceded four safeties, which at the time would allow the team to retain possession on its own 10-yard line. From then on, if a team conceded a safety with less than five minutes remaining on the clock, the team had to kick off. Today, the rule applies throughout the game.

It was the end of the season for the Riders, but not the end to Filchock's involvement in Roughrider football.

He had the same big decision to make as he had the season before, but changed his mind this time around. He cut Dobbs and brought on Tripucka as quarterback. Another familiar face returned to the Riders at the beginning of 1954; Dean Griffing became the general manager.

Television was introduced in 1954. Canadian Football games were now available in black and white to fans across Canada. *Hockey Night in Canada* expanded and Danny Gallivan, Frank Selke Jr. and Regina's own Dick Irvin broadcast the success of the Canadiens' dynasty from the Forum. The next year was the year of the Richard Riot, which occurred on March 17, 1955. Maurice Richard was suspended for a violent attack on a linesman. Hal Laycoe of the Boston Bruins had highsticked Richard in the head. The Canadiens retained possession of the puck as the referee signalled the penalty. Richard skated to Laycoe and hit him in the face with his stick. When the linesman tried to restrain Richard, he punched him twice in the face, later saying that he thought he was a Bruin. Richard was given a match penalty, provoking a riot – fans poured into the streets. It captured the attention of the entire country and possibly sparked Quebec nationalism.

As television programming developed, the *I Love Lucy Show* with Lucille Ball and Desi Arnaz, and *The Honeymooners* with Jackie Gleason and Audrey Meadows soon became popular sitcoms. Dinah Shore aired weekly with the Chevy show and everybody watched Ed Sullivan Sunday nights.

Fans who missed their great hero, Glenn Dobbs, didn't have to wait long before they saw him again. Dobbs had been picked up by the Hamilton Tiger-Cats, who played an exhibition game at Taylor Field in August. "It will seem strange seeing the tall Oklahoman cavorting about Taylor Field in the garb of a hostile club," wrote the *Leader-Post*.

The Ti-Cats beat the Riders, but Dobbs wasn't with the team much longer. Coach Carl Voyles said Dobbs "does not fit into my plans," as the 34-year-old Dobbs' knee was again acting up. It was the end to Dobbs' playing career, but not the end to his football days. Dobbs went on to become a successful coach at Tulsa University, from where he frequently sent players to the Saskatchewan Roughriders.

The Riders signed a player that year who would figure into their future in more ways than one: Ken Carpenter, a halfback from the Cleveland Browns. He would join Bobby Marlow, Stan Williams and Sully Glasser in enhancing the Riders' ground attack. Larry Isbell, a rookie import, also joined the Roughriders that year.

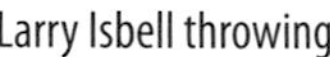
Larry Isbell throwing
Photo courtesy of SSHFM

Larry Isbell running
Photo courtesy of SSHFM

Larry Isbell kicking
Photo courtesy of SSHFM

Isbell was an immensely versatile football player who came to the Riders from Baylor University. He could play quarterback, end, halfback or defensive back. At Baylor, he was an All-American quarterback and an All-American baseball catcher drafted in the first round by both the NFL's Washington Redskins and the major league baseball team, the Boston Red Sox. He was also a great punter, whose unorthodox left-footed kicks confused punt returners who were used to the normal right-footed spiral on the ball. Isbell led the Riders in punting in all five seasons he was with the team. In 1954, he set a record with a punting average of 46.3 yards. His 539 career punts for 23,062 yards is fifth best in Rider history. He excelled offensively as a receiver, and was an All-Star in 1956, 1957 and 1958 as a defensive back. He is a member of the Texas Sports Hall of Fame and was inducted into the Plaza of Honor in 1999.

How fans came to watch their players changed as well that year. In the early 1950s, downtown merchants complained that when there was a Saturday afternoon football game at Taylor Field, the downtown was deserted as all the customers were at the game. City Council organized floodlights for Taylor Field through a fundraising committee headed by co-chairmen, local businessman David Isman and MP John Probe of the Elks Club. Service clubs and businesses united and raised the necessary funds. The Elks Club donated $10,000 and floodlights were installed in 1954 for night games.

Fans could now watch Filchock in action on the sidelines. Filchock had an easy-going policy that seemed to work, as fewer injuries resulted from practice. He was remembered as having a great football mind, but would coach without a lot of preparation. That is how Scotty Melville described him: "Filchock, as coaches go, is a modest type. If you ask him what he intends to do before a game in things like the imports he's going to use, strategy, or what have you, his answer is: 'I don't know.' For a guy who doesn't know he manages to come up with some pretty fair stuff on the gridiron and we believe that none of the others can equal his way of sizing up a situation and its possibilities within a matter of seconds."

Filchock was smarter than he let on. Many people underestimated him, but he really just let people think what they wanted to, keeping them guessing. What he could pick up during a game was phenomenal.

In *Rider Pride*, Bob Calder relates Bill Clarke's thoughts on Filchock: "He would improvise like crazy. He was really able to analyse on the field as things were going on but he didn't really prepare you for the football game. With Filchock we'd go to the park to start the game and in our pre-game chalk talk we'd diagram the defences on the board that we were going to use because we'd never practised them."

One of the first games the Riders played that season was against the newly formed B.C. Lions. Annis Stukus, Canadian Football Hall of Famer of the Argos who assisted the Edmonton Eskimos' entry into the Western Conference in 1949, was enlisted by the B.C. Lions to organize their entry into an expanded conference in 1954. Many players who were cut by the Riders ended up in B.C., where the slogan ran: "The Lions will roar in Fifty-Four." However their first game resulted in a 17-0 loss against the Roughriders on a rain-soaked field at Empire Stadium.

Photo courtesy of Heenan Studios

Frank Tripucka

Filchock brought in the new spread formation with Tripucka and Isbell working in at quarterback. It was one of the first times the spread formation – which is now played on almost every second down – was used in the league.

The rule that resulted in Filchock's safety plays in 1953 was enforced for the first time that season, against the Riders. The Riders, playing the Winnipeg Blue Bombers, conceded a safety touch in the last five minutes, and had to kick off from the 25-yard line. Kicking in western football played a large role. It wasn't used as often in the Big Four – the four teams of the Eastern conference – and so every year the leading kicker was a western player.

Tripucka wasn't the best all-around quarterback in the league, but he was certainly an excellent passer and the league's most consistent signal-caller. The Roughriders played Winnipeg in the semi-final that season. After a 14-14 tie in Winnipeg, the Riders lost 13-11 at Taylor Field; their first home loss of the season. Tripucka had been sidelined with a hip injury and without him the Riders couldn't get it done, as Gerry James, who had also played with the Riders and would later play for the Toronto Maple Leafs, scored an 87-yard touchdown on a kickoff return for the Blue Bombers.

It was the second year in a row – and not the last – the third-place Bombers would beat the Riders in a playoff series.

"The pin that dropped in the Saskatchewan Roughriders' dressing room made a noise like a clanging bell," wrote Scotty Melville after the game. "That's the way it is when a group of athletes come to the end of a trail in any sport. They changed into street clothes slowly Monday night, hardly believing that football was over for the season and that they had been beaten out by Winnipeg Blue Bombers. The silence was overpowering and when someone broke it he talked in a whisper, hoping someone else would take the cue and get the old after-game chatter going."

It was back to "next season" talk for the Roughriders once again, and Filchock returned to lead the troops into battle. Filchock's coaching philosophy was to keep things fun and light. He could always be spotted in practice in his red toque with Suds, his Weimaraner dog, who was with him everywhere – on the field, in the dressing room, or on a hunting trip. The only time the Riders ever watched films with Filchock was on rainy days, and then usually they would just watch for plays to laugh at. Regular practices usually ended with a game of some sort. Sometimes they'd play keep-away touch football; other times they would line up in teams and kick the ball back and forth to develop foot agility and hand-eye co-ordination. Some of the players still played for the fun of it at this time, practising at night after working all day.

Photo courtesy of SSHFM

Frank Filchock

There was a bit of a turnover for the Riders that season. Ken Charlton, who began his football career with the Regina Dales, finished his playing career with the Roughriders due to a previous injury. Del Wardien returned to Montana, and guard Art McEwan, from Montreal, didn't return to training camp. "Time marches on, even in football," wrote Scotty Melville. New Canadians took their place. The Riders had better Canadians than anyone else in the league with Reg Whitehouse, Ron Atchison, Sully Glasser, Bill Clarke, Pete Thodos, Rod Pantages, Doug Killoh, Gord Sturtridge, Paul Anderson, Ron Adam, Harry Lunn, Pete Martin, Harry Lampman, Ron Dundas and Fred Hamilton.

Doug Killoh was a tough hockey player, and brought that to the football field. Clarke, a defensive tackle, began playing with the Riders at 18 years old in 1951 and would play with the club for 15 years. He was also a deputy minister in the Saskatchewan government; a tall, distinguished, intelligent, and well-respected man. Reggie Whitehouse also played 15 years with the club, although he never quite made it to the All-Star team. Bill Clarke, who began playing with the Roughriders in 1951, was dominant in another sport as well – he won the Canadian Junior Curling Championship in 1950. Ron Adam was a Canadian backup

Photo courtesy of Heenan Studios

Bill Clarke

Photo courtesy of Heenan Studios

Ken Carpenter

quarterback and defensive halfback from the Hilltops, although he didn't see much playing time behind Tripucka at QB.

On Thanksgiving Day against the Calgary Stampeders, Filchock started an all-Canadian backfield, with the exception of Frank Tripucka, as a capacity crowd watched the Roughriders win a close game 18-16.

Tripucka always said the reason he didn't run the football was because they had running backs to do that for him. One time he did run and it took a second for anyone to react as they were so shocked. His passing game, helped by wearing child's shoulder pads, was what took him far, and he's still ranked third behind Ron Lancaster and Kent Austin as the best of Roughrider passers.

The Riders had a successful season, finishing league play in second place with a 10-6 record. A huge factor in their success was Ken Carpenter, who many thought was a contender for league MVP. He was awarded the Dave Dryburgh Memorial Trophy as the league-leading scorer before the first game of the western semi-final against the Winnipeg Blue Bombers, but couldn't play the game due to a knee injury. The Riders lost the playoff opener at Taylor Field 16-7, and went on to Winnipeg where they lost 9-8, upset by the third-place Bombers for the third year in a row.

The 1956 Saskatchewan Roughriders were possibly one of the greatest Canadian football teams in history. The only problem is they happened to play against an even greater Edmonton Eskimos, with players like Johnny Bright, Jackie Parker, Rollie Miles, and Norm Kwong, who would later become Lieutenant Governor of Alberta.

The Canadian Rugby Union became the Canadian Football Union that year, which would later become the Canadian Football League in 1958. Another rule change came about that year; a touchdown became worth six points instead of five so two field goals weren't worth more than a major.

An important part of the Roughriders that season was Bobby Marlow, a fullback, a linebacker, and a chain-smoker. Marlow was one of the toughest players to ever be on the Roughriders' roster. Filchock once said, "You know what? If a coach had four backfielders like Bobby Marlow, we wouldn't have any worries."

Filchock always hated the beginning of the season. He told Scotty Melville: "This cutting time is all right for the farmers but it gives me the heeby-jeebies. I can't even cut the roast on Sundays and when the grass gets long I stay away from the house for a week. It breaks my heart to cut a football player."

Quite the speech from a coach who rarely gave anything to the media. *Leader-Post* sportswriter Hank Johnson said he could never get Filchock to reveal his plans: "A major distinction between Frank Filchock and his faithful hunting hound, Suds, is that the latter will at least bark and wag his tail when spoken to. Suds is the extrovert in the Filchock family. His master, if pressed, will occasionally mutter, 'I dunno,' although he's apt to go off on a tangent if he should discover that Suds has been referred to as a hound dog."

The Riders played the season with fewer than 12 imports, and voted against a new import regulation which would allow clubs to replace two injured imports, and bring back the original players to the lineup when healthy.

It wasn't a rule that would help the Riders, who had so much great Canadian talent. Ken Carpenter continued to impress onlookers. His biggest critic was himself. After scoring two touchdowns in a winning game at home, Carpenter told reporters: "I wish that I could play one good game at Taylor Field... I made too many mistakes out there... Golly darn." He was unassuming and soft-spoken, but a great football player and well-respected.

He was one of eight Roughriders named to the 1956 all-star team, which also included Mel Becket, Martin Ruby, Larry Isbell, Bobby Marlow, John Wozniak, Ron Atchison and Gordon Sturtridge.

The Riders finally got past Winnipeg that season, winning the two-game total-point semi-final 50-26 overall. Perhaps the best help came from the water boy.

Allie Sherman, coach of the Winnipeg Blue Bombers, often introduced an entire new offence before a game. The night before the first game of the semi-final series at Taylor Field, the Bombers practised after the Riders. Later on that night, the Riders' water boy went to pick up a football, and found Allie Sherman's playbook next to the bench. On his way to return it, Filchock stopped him and said he was going Sherman's way and would give it back to him. The next day, the Riders were ready for everything that came their way; they held the Bombers to minus nine yards, and won 42-7.

They were then facing Edmonton for a best-of-three western final. The Riders were down 22-9 with nine minutes to go in the first game, and came back to score two touchdowns for the win. In the second game, Jackie Parker was unstoppable, and the Eskimos won 20-12. In the third game, Parker really let loose, and scored three touchdowns to win 51-7.

The Riders' season was done, but there was more to come that year in their history.

The all-stars went to Vancouver for the all-star game in December. Ray Syrnyk and Mario DeMarco went along to watch. DeMarco was Mel Becket's business partner and close friend. DeMarco was the comedian of the pair, while Becket was the straight man. They owned a gas station in Regina, and could always be found together. DeMarco, one of the biggest blocking guards in the league, hopped on a plane to watch Becket in the all-star game. It meant a lot to him, as DeMarco was a white-knuckled flier, and was often made fun of by his teammates for it.

The Western all-stars beat the Eastern all-stars 35-0. The Roughrider players took different routes home. Tripucka decided not to return to Regina, and instead took a flight from Vancouver to Toronto, and then home to New York to be with his family. Reg Whitehouse took an early flight home. He had asked his wife not to come because he had a bad feeling about the trip. Ron Atchison, who was named an all-star, didn't end up going to the game because of a foot injury.

Photos courtesy of Heenan Studios

Mel Becket

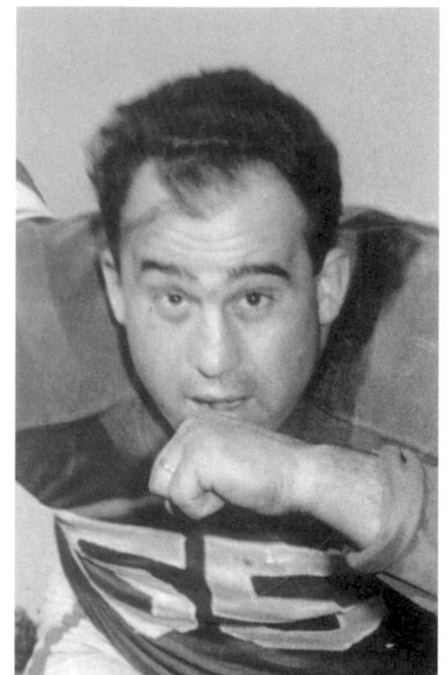

Photos courtesy of Heenan Studios

Mario DeMarco

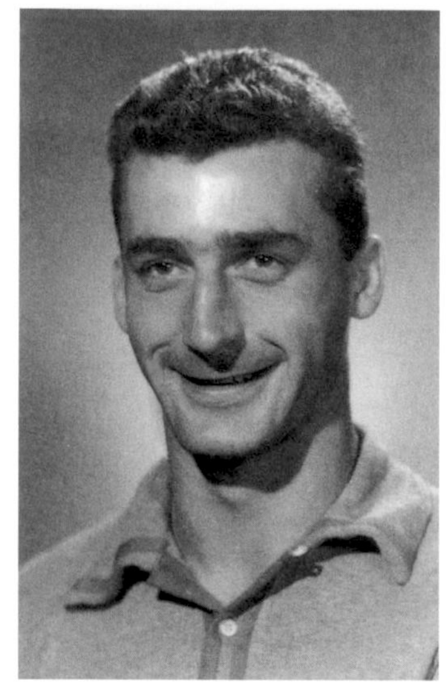
Photos courtesy of SSHFM

Gordon Sturtridge

Photos courtesy of SSHFM

Ray Syrnyk

> The crash sent shockwaves through Saskatchewan, affecting many people throughout the province and the country.

Mel Becket, Mario DeMarco, Gordon Sturtridge and Ray Syrnyk boarded Flight 810, a North Star aircraft. Engine troubles sent the plane into the 8,200-foot Mount Slesse in the Rocky Mountains near Chilliwack, B.C. on December 9, 1956. The crash sent shockwaves through Saskatchewan, affecting many people throughout the province and the country. In addition to the four Roughrider players, 58 other people were killed, including Roughriders director Harold McElroy, Calvin Jones of the Winnipeg Blue Bombers who had slept in and missed his flight that morning, and Mildred Sturtridge, Gordon's wife.

Sturtridge had come from the Winnipeg Blue Bombers in 1953, when he won Rookie of the Year in the Western Conference. Two years later he won the Tibbits Award for Outstanding Canadian. He and his wife left behind three children, who Ron Atchison had to inform that their parents were missing.

Ray Syrnyk, a guard from Redwater, Alberta, was a steady, quiet player, who had gone to Vancouver to have some fun.

The plane was lost for many months. Family, friends and fans at first waited for it to be found, but had to accept the fact that they had lost their loved ones. The papers discussed the loss and how much the team had needed the four players.

"It was only a few yesterdays back and you were talking to all of them," wrote Scotty Melville. "Gordon Sturtridge, sitting at coffee, reminiscing about the first Shrine All-Star football game in Toronto ..."

Sandy Archer was with the Saskatchewan Roughriders through many ups and downs in his time as trainer from 1951 to 1980. But this was something different. "It was a hell of a shock, because you're not going to see those guys again," he told Rob Vanstone. "We had four starting ballplayers who were suddenly gone. That's a fair part of a team. Losing those four guys made a big difference and it hurt a lot."

The uniform numbers of the four players – Becket (40), DeMarco (55), Syrnyk (56), and Sturtridge (73) — were retired, and the annual Becket-DeMarco Memorial Trophy was established to go to the top lineman in the Western Conference.

Citizens around the province were deeply affected. It was the same year John Diefenbaker of Prince Albert became the first western Prime Minister of Canada when his Conservative Party was elected. The next year he would win a landslide victory after his government fell.

But that year of 1957, the Saskatchewan Roughrider football team wasn't the same because of the accident. The locker room didn't have the same atmosphere, and many other players ended up leaving the team. John Wozniak retired, and Martin Ruby finished playing.

Ruby had been a force on the Roughriders. He made the All-Star team five times; three of those years as both an offensive and defensive player, as he was one of the last two-way linemen in the league. In 1956 he didn't even play defence but was still named to the defensive all-star team. He began playing with the Riders in 1951, and started the 1957 spring camp, but was last in sprints due to a knee injury and retired before the season. He ended up taking over the service station once owned by Becket and DeMarco.

Ruby had been a force on the Roughriders. He made the All-Star team five times; three of those years as both an offensive and defensive player, as he was one of the last two-way linemen in the league.

Jon McWilliams was drafted to the U.S. Army, Alex Bravo went back to Los Angeles, and Harry Lampman was traded. Bobby Marlow broke a hand and Ken Carpenter broke an arm. Atchison dislocated a thumb, while Vic Marks also broke a hand. Bill Clarke played the season with a bad knee. The season ended up being the worst year for injuries until 2008, when nine players broke legs and there were 21 on the injured list.

In October of 1957, team doctor T.J. Roulston told the *Leader-Post*: "It's just one of those years. The injuries haven't been caused because the players aren't in condition. They've just had a lot of tough luck."

The darkest period in Roughrider history stretched on until 1961. The 1957 season was dismal, as the Roughriders won only three games. Their first win came in early September, when Jack Hill ran 76 yards for a major. Tripucka and Carpenter were the stars that day but injuries continued to strike and performances got worse.

Jack Hill came to the Roughriders that year, in 1957. He played halfback and offensive end after a great college football career at Utah State University.

Hill was a complete player on offence and defence and also played on special teams. His greatest year as a Rider was in 1958 when he scored 16 touchdowns, including 14 on receptions. He was the first Rider to achieve over 1,000 receiving yards (1,065) and led the Western Division in scoring with 145 points in 1958. He was a Western All-Star running back in 1958 and established a club scoring record that lasted until broken by Dave Ridgway in 1988.

Tripucka, Stan Williams and Larry Isbell all had off years by their standards.

The one to take all of the blame on his shoulders was head coach Frank Filchock. He was driving home from a hunting trip with Suds when he heard on the radio that he had been fired. The Rider executive thought perhaps it was Filchock's coaching

Photo courtesy of SSHFM

Jack Hill

Photo courtesy of SSHFM
George Terlep

style that wasn't working, as his fun and relaxing practices were beginning to produce poor tackling, blocking, and playing in general.

In January, the coaching job was offered to Sammy Baugh, Filchock's old quarterback counterpart. But at the last minute Baugh decided to stay in his coaching position at Hardin-Simmons University in Texas.

A week later, George Terlep was named head coach. Terlep's playing career began with the Notre Dame Fighting Irish in 1943, but was cut short due to a leave from 1944 to 1946 for military service. Upon discharge, he signed with the Buffalo Bisons of the All-America football conference. He was fairly ineffective and in 1948 was sold to the Cleveland Browns as a backup quarterback. His coaching career was more successful. In 1949 he was with the University of South Carolina, and then was an assistant coach with Vanderbilt University from 1951 to 1952, with Marquette University in 1953, the University of Pennsylvania in 1954 and 1955, and Indiana University in 1956. He made the move to the CFL in 1959, coaching the backfield for the Hamilton Tiger-Cats. Then he moved up to head coach of the Saskatchewan Roughriders. He would later go on to be head coach and general manager for the Ottawa Rough Riders.

Photo courtesy of SSHFM
Ken Preston

Terlep wasn't the only new face on the Riders that year. Dean Griffing left his post of Roughrider GM to move to Tucson, Arizona to become general manager of a new team. A familiar face replaced him. Ken Preston was back with the Saskatchewan Roughriders, a team he had played for and coached in the 1940s. Since that time he had been running a company that manufactured paper boxes while coaching the Regina Junior Bombers, becoming a WIFU official, and helping manage the Riders. When Sam Taylor asked Preston to become general manager, Preston thought he could work half-days while working the other half at the paper-box plant. He soon realized that wouldn't suffice, and to do the job to the best of his ability he'd have to begin working full time with the Roughriders. One of Preston's greatest skills was recruiting quality players on a tight budget. The Riders would end up playing in five Grey Cup games under Preston, winning one, the Riders' first-ever Grey Cup, in 1966.

"He was a good general manager," said Al Benecick, who came to the Riders later that season and played with the team until 1969. "He used his money wisely. Each year he added two or three good ball players. You can see he worked his way up so eventually when we got to the pinnacle of 1966, we had a pretty good team."

Sam Taylor, son of decorated war veteran 'Piffles' Taylor, became president of the Roughriders in 1958. He wasn't the first son to follow in his father's footsteps as a member of the Roughrider organization. Howard (Tare Jr.) Rennebohm succeeded his father Tare in 1947; Al Urness' son Ted became a Rider in 1961 and was an all-star centre on six occasions; Paul Anderson's son Mike was an all-star centre in 1994.

Receiver Jack Hill, back Mike Hagler, and centre and linebacker Neil Habig also joined the Roughriders that season. The Riders have always been strong at the centre position with players like Dean Griffing, Toar Springstein, John Wozniak, Red Ettinger, Galen Wahlmeier, Mike Anderson, Larry Bird, Bob Poley and Jeremy O'Day. Neil Habig was no exception. He hailed from Indianapolis, Indiana. After a brilliant college career with Purdue in the Big Ten, Neil was drafted by the Green Bay Packers and ended up with the Riders in 1958. A colourful player and team leader, he played six years until 1964 and was an all-star every year. He also played linebacker in several critical short yardage situations.

Photo courtesy of SSHFM

Neil Habig

Another notable addition was Chester (Cookie) Gilchrist, a standout import running back who had been released by the Tiger-Cats due to a personality conflict.

One player had to leave the Roughriders that year, leaving a hole on the field and in the hearts of Roughrider fans. Sully Glasser was the oldest man in continual service with the Saskatchewan Roughriders, at 35. He played with six head coaches, and just began playing with a seventh. Glasser started playing football in Regina with the Eastend Bombers in the 1930s at age 15. He played with the Campion-Dales from 1940 to 1941, and during the war played with the Regina Navy. After three years of service, Glasser joined the re-formed Saskatchewan Roughriders in 1945. He didn't score many touchdowns, but played a big role in getting the ball down the field. He was actually told to forget football when he broke his leg in 1948, but he was back on the field – and the baseball diamond with the Caps – in 1949. He decided 1958 would be his last season, but it was cut short. After the annual intra-squad exhibition game, Glasser began complaining of stomach cramps. He was rushed to the hospital, and found out he had had a heart attack due to a coronary disorder and would have to spend a month in the hospital. It was the end of a memorable 13-year career.

"Glasser will be missed by the other players and fans alike," wrote Scotty Melville. "He was a great 'team man,' and always in high spirits and it was good to have him around. The fans always admired the redhead who played so long and so faithfully for the Riders."

Glasser was still involved in the community, and later that year was named the Wascana Kiwanis high school football "dad-of-the-year." The father of four was given the award for his work as a sportsman, citizen and businessman – the type of man the Wascana Kiwanis Club thought should be the perfect example of a father.

> **"The fans always admired the redhead who played so long and so faithfully for the Riders."**

Terlep noted the growing problem of Canadian football teams becoming short of home-grown players. This was true; as the imports coming to Canada improved each year, there was less space for local talent. The United States had more leagues to develop players, while Canada didn't have the players or money to do so.

Terlep changed the Roughriders' formation that year. He got rid of the double-fullback system and decided to go with a straight T and one or two flankers, as Gilchrist was bigger than most linemen but could run faster than most halfbacks.

Another area Terlep soon altered was the training regimen. Compared to Filchock's easy-going coaching style, it would have been a shock to many players. Some found it tough; others enjoyed it.

"This is the same kind of camp that the Cleveland Browns had when I was with them," said Ken Carpenter at the time. "The practices actually are more important than the games. That's where mistakes are corrected. I'm enjoying it all."

Ron Atchison said this was different than anything he'd seen before: "I guess I've played a lot of football but this is like going back to school. I'm learning things every day. I honestly didn't realize there was so much to football. I can appreciate what the coaches are trying to do and I'm doing my best to help them. I've never felt better. I've enjoyed the training although it's far tougher than anything I've had before."

> **"I can appreciate what the coaches are trying to do and I'm doing my best to help them. I've never felt better. I've enjoyed the training although it's far tougher than anything I've had before."**

Terlep treated football as a business. He didn't give out a lot of praise unless it was called for. Players soon realized that they couldn't get by without giving 100 per cent.

After Frank Tripucka separated his shoulder, the Riders started looking for a quarterback. The Blue Bombers offered quarterback Eagle Day in a trade, but the Riders said no. Ron Adam, the backup from the Hilltops, was to take over as QB. In August, the Riders played three league games in six days, impacting all of the players. George Terlep told the *Leader-Post*, "My forces are so depleted I think I'll ask the commissioner for permission to use the Shriners' drum and bugle corps for an attacking unit. At least they've got a formation that might fool the Bombers."

Terlep was mild-mannered, religious, and told the truth no matter how it sounded. In mid-October, Terlep was discussed as a possible coach-of-the-year, in his first job as head coach. The Riders, when they played like they could, were a strong football team. Four players were named to the all-star team: Cookie Gilchrist, Jack Hill, Ken Carpenter, and Larry Isbell. The Riders finished the season in third place with a 7-7-2 record; an improvement to the 1957 season. The Roughriders faced the Edmonton Eskimos in the two-game total-point semi-final.

Photo courtesy of SSHFM

Jack Gotta

The first game was at Taylor Field, which was becoming too small for the growing city of Regina with a 12,000 seating capacity. Jackie Parker, Normie Kwong and Johnny Bright once again proved too much for the Riders. Frank Tripucka had little time with the ball and didn't throw a single long pass. The Riders went into Game 2 down 27-11. The best moment of the game was when Ron Atchison was awarded the Stack Tibbits trophy for most valuable Canadian player.

It was on to Edmonton. The Riders were helpless against Parker, and lost 31-1 for a total point loss of 58-12. Terlep called it "junk" and said if it wasn't for Jackie Parker, the Riders would have won.

The post-season review left fans feeling it wasn't a bad season. They had seen worse but still needed some rebuilding. Scotty Melville wrote he'd never seen anyone work harder than Terlep, and he felt he would get his contract renewed.

Terlep did come back for the beginning of 1959, but Gilchrist and Tripucka were gone; Gilchrist traded to the Toronto Argonauts and Tripucka to the Ottawa Rough Riders.

Jack Gotta, the 'General of Scarth Street,' had been a star in 1958, but was injured in 1959. He was a two-way player, but also made a great assistant coach and the best practical joker around.

He got his nickname from standing on the corner of Scarth Street watching the good-looking girls go by. He'd have to rush to be on time for practice.

Gene Wlasiuk, who was acquired from the Blue Bombers in 1959, was a fan favourite because of his aggressive, competitive style. He played defensive back and was a punt returner for the Riders until 1967. He achieved a number of records throughout his career. 'Geno' was a member of the 1966 Grey Cup team and was considered the best punt returner in the league. He also played in the Grey Cup in 1967 and is still the Rider record holder in punt returns and second in total yards.

One key returnee was Danny Banda, who just missed being named rookie-of-the-year. The previous year, he was the only one who would take on Gilchrist at practice in tackling drills, despite weighing just 165 pounds.

Two new quarterbacks were added to the team: Don Allard and Bob Brodhead. Neither was exceptional, and both were better at throwing interceptions than touchdowns. Roughrider fans missed Frank Tripucka.

Terlep continued with his intense practice regimen. As one lineman was quoted in the *Leader-Post* after six days of Rider camp: "Maybe I should have listened to my old man when he told me to take up accordion playing ... I don't know where the coaches get the idea that a football player should look like Mr. America from the neck down. I'm 50 around the waist and I have to keep it at 50 because that's the size of my trousers."

The west side grandstand went up, adding 3,000 seats to the stadium, where fans continued to take in Rider wins and, more often, losses. The fans were the lifeline of the team in a centre like Regina, which didn't have a high population, but did have a high percentage of football fans.

The 1959 season was far from spectacular as the Roughriders continued to lose. Jack Wells, the voice of the Blue Bombers, put it this way: "During each financial crisis the Roughies came bouncing back and likely will again. This has been the saddest start for the Roughriders in many years. George Terlep is plagued with injuries. At last count he had 14 once-able bodies either hobbling or in the infirmary…. The fatal plane crash three years ago hurt the Roughriders more than any other club… they have yet to recover from the loss."

The Roughriders started looking for rescue, and added Ferdy Burkett and Al Benecick, both NFL players, in early September.

Benecick, born in Bristol, Connecticut, had success at Syracuse University, where he blocked for the legendary Jim Brown, one of the best running backs to ever play in the NFL. After college, Benecick became a second lieutenant in the U.S. Army

Photo courtesy of SSHFM

Gene Wlasiuk

Photo courtesy of SSHFM

Al Benecick

with the ROTC (Reserved Officer Training) program. "At that time, we had a military commitment," said Benecick. "It was either go into the army directly from high school, or to go college on an ROTC program. I did that and upon graduation I had to put in a commitment as an officer and six and half years reserve and six months active duty."

Benecick served his active duty in the U.S. with the Strategic Air Command outfit in Massachusetts. Benecick instructed officers on surface-to-air missiles, guided missiles which today are obsolete. In between his military duty, Benecick would play football. He'd put in his military duty for six months after the football season, and would be released two weeks early for training camp.

"I was drafted by the Philadelphia Eagles," explained Benecick. "I went to Philadelphia, tried out for that team. They put me all over: guard, tackle, defensive end. I stayed there for the entire training camp – six games – and I wasn't sure where I was going to be playing. So I approached them and said, 'I'm a player, I want to play." They said, 'Well, you've got to take time, you're too young really. You're young yet, just sit back.' I knew I had an offer from Saskatchewan because they also drafted me out of college. So I called Saskatchewan and said, 'I don't like it here.' They offered me more money than Philly. I wanted to get out of there, and they told me I couldn't because (Philadelphia) had my rights. But they had my American rights, not my Canadian rights. (Philadelphia) said if you really want to go, then go. And so I went."

Benecick returned to his family in Long Island for the off-season until eventually moving to Regina, where he got a job in a physical education department as an instructor and a wrestling coach for four years. He would teach in the morning and part of the afternoon, and then make it to the football field by 3 p.m. Wrestling started after the football season. Later on, Benecick worked as a distributor for a chemical company. When he finished playing with the Roughriders, he became a player-coach and later a coach with the Edmonton Eskimos. He would also be named to the Canadian Football Hall of Fame.

"I played tackle and guard, offence and defence," said Benecick. "I played the two-platoon system and special teams. I was on the field all the time – the Riders were getting their money's worth."

"I played tackle and guard, offence and defence," said Benecick. "I played the two-platoon system and special teams. I was on the field all the time."

The Riders also took over the Regina Rams that year to help develop junior players into professionals. It was a good idea for the future, but not enough to save the Roughriders that particular season. On September 30, George Terlep's 0-9 record sent him out the door. Terlep felt it wasn't his coaching ability that led to the downfall of the team, but the lack of Canadian talent. He said he did what he could with what he had.

> "It's hard to believe that my ability can disappear in a year," Terlep told Scotty Melville. "I feel sorry that nearly two years of work which I honestly believe was made has to be lost and that the club has to start all over again. I say this not for myself, but for football in Saskatchewan. It was been said that I tried to teach the players too much, that my plays were too complicated and the players were confused by it all. It has been said I worked too hard. Well, I think the other clubs use more plays than the Riders do and have to study just as much if not more. If working hard is a crime, then I'll plead guilty. I dedicated myself to the task of creating a football team in Saskatchewan. I like Regina and the football fans. I feel that most of the fans were understanding people and I should have liked to have stayed."

The Riders offered the head coaching job to assistant coaches Bob Maddock and Carl Schuette, but both declined. On October 1, it was unofficially learned the job would be offered to either Ken Carpenter or Frank Tripucka. The next day Tripucka was announced as Rider coach, as he was acquainted with the player personnel, the system, and Saskatchewan's setup. Al Ritchie said about him, "Tripucka has one of the best football minds of any man I ever talked to." The Riders had made a cash deal with Ottawa to get 'The Tripper' back to coach, not play. Before agreeing, Tripucka said he had to check with George Terlep, a friend of his. Terlep gave him the go-ahead, and Tripucka found himself back in Saskatchewan as the green and white province debated Terlep's firing.

"Who should take the blame? The coach or the quarterback? It just goes to show you. Nobody can coach and play at the same time."

Tripucka lost in his Roughrider coaching debut, 44-15 against Edmonton. The next game the Roughrider nation finally had a reason to celebrate. Don Allard played a good game with great passing, and the Riders beat the B.C. Lions 15-14 for their first win of the season. Tripucka proved to be just as good a coach as he was a leader on the field. The next weekend, Allard was injured and backups Ron Adam and Jack Urness were also most likely out. With Bob Brodhead gone by then, Tripucka tried to think about what to do: "About all we can do is go into a spread with Hill and Carpenter back there to throw," he said a couple of days before the game. "It probably won't make much of a game for the fans. But what can we do? Unless…"

Tripucka had been hired on October 1, the day after all imports had to be added to the roster, making Tripucka ineligible to play. With nothing left to lose, they went to both the commissioner of the league, Sydney Halter, and the Western Conference clubs, who gave permission for Frank Tripucka to play quarterback for the Roughriders. The game meant nothing in the standings, and at least with a quarterback the Roughriders could make the game entertaining. Tripucka replaced Ron Adam in the second quarter. The Riders had looked like they were going to win, but then Bill Smith picked off Tripucka's pass with 43 seconds left. On the final play of the game against the Edmonton Eskimos, Jackie Parker kicked a 33-yard field goal to give Edmonton the 20-19 win. Tripucka realized he should have run the ball instead of throwing but asked, "Who should take the blame? The coach or the quarterback? It just goes to show you. Nobody can coach and play at the same time."

The Riders did set a team record that year, for the most points allowed against in a season, as 567 points were racked up against them. Only one player, Neil Habig, was named to the western all-star team.

Tripucka had brought spirit back to the Saskatchewan Roughriders. He would be the last great quarterback to play for the Roughriders until Ron Lancaster joined the team.

The Riders had one more game left that season, on the road – against the Winnipeg Blue Bombers. It was both a win and a loss for each team. The Riders won on the scoreboard, but had to forfeit because Tripucka played. While the game didn't change the standings, Ferdy Burket set a single-game franchise record, scoring five touchdowns, and Bomber Ernie Pitts caught his 16th touchdown pass, breaking the record for a single season set by Jack Hill the previous year. For the Riders, this was the start of the 1960 football season; a moral victory. Tripucka had brought spirit back to the Saskatchewan Roughriders. He would be the last great quarterback to play for the Roughriders until Ron Lancaster joined the team.

Tripucka decided to stay in the United States with his businesses rather than coach another season. He then joined the Denver Broncos and his old coach Frank Filchock. The Denver Broncos were a charter member of the new American Football League that later merged with the NFL in 1970. Tripucka's number 18 is one of only three retired

Denver Broncos numbers. In 1986 he was inducted into the Ring of Fame on display at Invesco Field at Mile High Stadium.

The Roughriders in 1960 turned to Ken Carpenter, who had been named to the western all-star team multiple times, had been playing with the team since 1954 and was popular with the other players. It would be an interesting transition, as Carpenter knew all of the players but would now be looking at them on another level. Carpenter had always wanted to coach, was personable, commanded respect, and got along well with the other players. He once said, however: "There's a difference between playing and coaching. You can get cut as a player. As a coach, you can get fired!"

Photo courtesy of SSHFM

Bob Ptacek

Carpenter had faith, saying the Riders would get worse before they got better. They did get better – they won two games that season instead of just one. However, Carpenter was respected. He used two platoons and got as many players as he could out on the field. Still, the Riders had the same problems in the red zone, not able to score nor keep their opponents from scoring. Carpenter never gave up hope, and was proud of his team and the province of Saskatchewan. Bob Ptacek returned from injury near the end of September. In his first game back he passed for four touchdowns and ran for another to beat the Calgary Stampeders 45-35. Ptacek came to the Roughriders in 1960 for Jim Marshall in a trade with the Cleveland Browns. Ptacek played five seasons with the Riders as both a quarterback and linebacker; it was a toss-up which he excelled at more. He was the passing leader in 1960 when he held the best passing percentage in the Western Conference (60.6), and in 1962 when he set the longest completion in team history with a 104-yard touchdown pass to Ray Purdin. As of 2009, this remains as the third longest in team history. Ptacek didn't throw many interceptions, but caught 10 during his career when playing defence. Ptacek was one year short of playing with the 1966 Grey Cup winning team. In 1965 he snapped his Achilles tendon. After rehabilitating throughout the winter, he began training camp only to snap the other Achilles tendon in a game of racquetball. It caused his retirement.

Perhaps the highlight of the 1960 season – other than the 10-point win – was the Roughrider band debut. The 20-piece Roughrider band and 13 baton-twirling majorettes, led by Carol Gay Bell, were introduced to Saskatchewan football fans. It was a hit with the public and added colour to the games.

The budget for the Roughriders was raised to $600,000 to cover expenses. It cost $300 to outfit each player, $3,000 in tape a season, $15,000 went to medical bills, and phone calls to players in the States cost between $5,000 and $8,000. Prices had to go up at the gate to keep the team going. Roughrider fans weren't getting what they paid for. As Scotty Melville said, "The fans are not clamoring for a Grey Cup; they never have. But they want a team that is reasonably sure of scoring more than at the rate of one touchdown per game and at least has a 50-50 chance of winning at home."

The Roughriders finished in fifth place and once again failed to make the playoffs. The Roughriders executives met to discuss what was to happen to the team. Carpenter had taken over a weak team and didn't turn it around as fast as he had to. Carpenter resigned his coaching position to look at heading down to the Denver Broncos of the American Football League to coach with Frank Filchock. The Roughriders were $78,000 in debt, the team couldn't win, and fans were starting to give up on them. With the B.C. Lions in the league, the CFL didn't need the Roughriders anymore to make up their numbers in the west. Then in stepped Bob Kramer.

He decided to return as club president, and took complete control of club operations. He selected a management committee including Don McPherson, Clair Warner, Jack Rowand and Don MacDonald. Kramer formed a directorate of over 100 members with a strong committee, and made a goal to sell 10,000 season tickets, which the club just about met. Kramer knew business, and he knew when to take risks. His risks paid off and he started to bring around the team.

Another debate was raging at the time. It has oft been said that the three most important matters to the people of Saskatchewan are football, politics and four inches of good rain. As the Riders prepared for the 1961 season, the people of the province were locked in deep controversy as the Tommy Douglas CCF government introduced universal Medicare in the Legislature. Neighbours were divided against each other and the province's doctors went on strike. Medicare was eventually approved and implemented in 1962. Later, the Lester Pearson federal government approved Medicare nationally.

On the football field, optimism returned to Saskatchewan as Kramer named Steve Owen head coach. Owen, born before the start of the century, was 63 years old when he was named Roughriders head coach. He had an interesting, active and varied life, doing everything from trying to become a jockey to wrestling professionally under the name 'Jack O'Brien.' Owen served in the U.S. Army training corps, coached for a year at his alma mater Phillips University, and then in 1924 began playing professional football with the NFL's Kansas City Cowboys. The next year he played with both the Cowboys and the Cleveland Bulldogs, until he was sold to the New York Giants in 1926, where he played with his brother Bill. The Giants would become home for Steve. He was captain in 1927, when the team went 11-1-1. By 1930 he was a player-coach, and the next year he became the head coach. His last game on the field was in 1933. Under Owen, the Giants played in the NFL championship game eight times. Owen retired from the Giants in 1953 after 23 years with the team. He took a year off, and then helped coach the University of South Carolina and Baylor University. Owen then was an assistant coach with the Philadelphia Eagles for two seasons, and then moved north. He coached the Toronto Argonauts in 1959 and the Calgary Stampeders in 1960, and was dismissed after each season.

Photo courtesy of SSHFM

Steve Owen

He was what the Saskatchewan Roughriders needed – a coach with experience, who could get them back on track. Owen decided to use the same system he did with the New York Giants. The legendary coach told his team: "You can have your fancy frills – your split-T formation, your reserves, your option plays. It doesn't mean a bloody thing if you can't get down there on the dirt and beat the gizzard out of the guy across from you."

Owen was Al Benecick's second coach since joining the Riders. "He is renowned for coaching and playing with the New York Giants. He instituted what we call the umbrella defence. He solidified our defence. It's known, in a way, as the Steve Owen defence as he created it. We had a historical coach." said Benecick.

Stout Steve, so named by other jockeys during his early years for his body type, looked like a grandfather, but was tough. He wore thick glasses and a baseball cap, and was the unlikely leader of the Riders out of their "football wilderness."

Despite his age, he was tougher than many of the players. In one game between the Roughriders and the Edmonton Eskimos, Bobby Walden ran over Owen, who lay on the ground for a moment or two. But then Owen got up and asked Walden if he was OK. The team was beginning to follow his optimism, as Owen said, "Any time the ball is put on the field, we have a chance."

On August 21 of 1961, the Roughriders beat the Calgary Stampeders 23-16, and when the players returned to Regina they were greeted as if they had just won the Grey Cup. It was the start of a season that wouldn't bring the team all the way back, but would give the Roughriders back their pride.

The 1961 season was the first time the CFL had an interlocking schedule. One particular game that August would give Roughrider fans a glimpse of their future, although they had no idea of it at the time. The Ottawa Rough Riders came to play Saskatchewan with two quarterbacks: Russ Jackson and Ron Lancaster. The 1960 Grey Cup champions were no match for Saskatchewan, as Ottawa won 29-10 on Taylor Field.

The Riders were improving, if not yet at the top of their game. About 12,000 fans attended each game, even though a Winnipeg reporter felt the Riders should leave the league. But Kramer said the club's fund-raising campaigns were working well. "I do not like to leave a project unfinished," he said. "We started from scratch last November and made marked improvements on both the field and in our fund drives. As a team, the Riders are not far off a winning combination."

Photo courtesy of *Leader-Post*

Wayne Shaw

It was also Wayne Shaw's first year as a Saskatchewan Roughrider. Shaw played linebacker with the Riders until 1972. Under Steve Owen, the former Saskatoon Hilltop quickly developed into a star linebacker and was a Western Division All-Star six times and named All-Canadian in 1967. A graduate of Notre Dame College in Wilcox, Shaw was a member of the 1966 Grey Cup team and along with his teammates appeared in the 1967, 1969 and 1972 Grey Cup games. He was voted to the Roughriders' 75th Anniversary All-Star team. Known for his great attitude and unique tackling ability, his nickname was 'Ghost.'

The Saskatchewan Roughriders finished the season with a 19-13 win against the Winnipeg Blue Bombers. It wouldn't change the standings, but was a matter of pride for the Riders, who finished the season in fourth place with a 5-10-1 record.

The next season was an even greater improvement for the Roughriders. A few players left; quarterback Dennis Spurlock had personal problems, and Bill Johnson had to undergo operations. The previous year, Roughrider Vernon Vaughn passed away from leukemia, and the team had held a Vernon Vaughn Day to raise money for his family. A Roughrider jersey had also been sent to the U.S. for Vaughn to be buried in.

When Dean Griffing was general manager of the Roughriders, he always showed considerable interest in juniors playing for the Saskatoon Hilltops and Regina Rams. After he moved to Tuscon, he continued to show interest in Saskatchewan junior players. Through his American connections, he arranged for several Saskatchewan players to obtain football scholarships at the University of Arizona. Three of those players – Ted Urness, Larry Dumelie and Dale West – ended up as Roughriders and were members of the team during the 1966 Grey Cup win. All three players were later inducted into the Plaza of Honor.

A Scott Collegiate and Regina Rams graduate, Ted Urness joined the Riders as a guard in 1961 and later replaced centre Neil Habig. Urness became a perennial western all-star until he retired in 1970. In his 10-year career, Urness was selected to the western and CFL all-star teams six straight times. He was elected to the Canadian Football Hall of Fame in 1989.

Larry Dumelie was a farm boy from Fir Mountain, Saskatchewan, and never played the game of football until he attended Campion High School in Regina. Fred Wagman, who later became a Rider president, liked what he saw in Dumelie's talent and urged him to try out for the Regina Rams.

After two seasons with the Rams, Dumelie joined Ted Urness as a teammate at the University of Arizona. Upon graduation, he also joined the Riders.

Dumelie earned a reputation throughout the CFL as a hard hitter and tenacious tackler. In his eight years as a Rider, Dumelie made the playoffs six times, reaching the Western final three times and winning twice.

Dale West first played football at Bedford Road Collegiate in Saskatoon. He spent two years as a running back and in his final year, he rushed for 1,434 yards and scored 134 points. The following season he was offered a football scholarship at the University of Arizona, where he joined Saskatchewanians and future Roughrider teammates Urness and Dumelie.

West later played at the University of Saskatchewan as a receiver. He was also a track star, and ran the 100-yard dash in 9.8 seconds to break his own provincial senior men's record.

He came to the Riders, as they owned his territorial rights – where a player spent his minor football days would be the team he belonged to.

In his first year under coach Steve Owen in 1962, West would sometimes play defence, where later in his career he excelled, as a Western all-star from 1963 to 1965.

Photo courtesy of Heenan Studios

Ted Urness

Photo courtesy of Heenan Studios

Larry Dumelie

Photo courtesy of SSHFM

Dale West

"I started out as a wide receiver my first year," said West. "I was a flanker, basically because Steve Owen didn't know what to do with the 12th man. I played a little bit of defence in my first year, but not very much. I hadn't played defence before, except maybe a bit in high school… It's the most enjoyable thing to be paid to do something that's basically a game. It's kind of a unique time. I thoroughly enjoyed every minute of it except training camp, and I have not met a player yet who enjoyed training camp. In the old days, we did two-a-days for at least two weeks, we played four exhibition games, and then you're into the season. We would go down east and do doubleheaders. I can remember the time we got beat so badly by Hamilton 67-21. That was my first year. We went down and played Ottawa Saturday afternoon and Hamilton Monday night. We had small rosters too – 32-man rosters instead of 42. We had 17 Canadians and 15 imports, and everybody played. If you weren't starting, you were on special teams for sure. And when I played, I played defence and I played almost all special teams – punt return, kickoff return, kickoff … I didn't play on extra points or field goals, but you really earned your keep."

West stayed with the Riders until the end of the 1968 season.

Photo courtesy of SSHFM

Garner Ekstran

Garner Ekstran is the son of a dairy farmer from Bow, Washington. He attended Burlington-Madison High School in neighbouring Burlington where he learned to play football. Scouts noticed his talent and he was offered a football scholarship to Washington State, where he received several team and league player awards.

On graduation, pro scouts did not offer him the opportunity of a NFL tryout. He was uncertain of his future, but made contact with Rider coach Steve Owen through a college teammate, who had already signed a contract to come to Regina.

Although Ekstran had no idea where Regina was and who the Roughriders were, he accepted an invitation from Steve Owen to attend training camp.

Ekstran came to the Riders in 1961 as an unheralded tackle from Washington State. He soon became a four-time WFC all-star and a CFL All-Canadian, one of the most punishing tacklers in the CFL. Ekstran was a member of the 1966 Grey Cup team and his teammates and many fans say that it was the best game he played in his career.

In 1968 Ekstran was traded to the B.C. Lions so he could be closer to his dairy farm in Washington.

The 1962 season started well, although there was one game in particular most Roughrider players from 1962 would probably like erased. After beating the Ottawa Rough Riders 29-21 in

Ottawa, the team headed to Hamilton. The Tiger-Cats threw 10 touchdown passes, beating the Roughriders 67-21.

Danny Banda tells a story about Steve Owen during that game. At halftime Owen looked around and said, "Well you blew another one." When his players told him it was just halftime he said, "Well, you're going to do it again anyway."

The Roughriders played to an 8-7-1 record that year for third place, and took on Calgary in the two-game total-point semi-final. The Roughriders lost the first game 25-0 and the second 18-7. The Roughriders lacked an offensive attack and Ptacek had trouble at quarterback. Owen felt one of the problems was his players hadn't played in a playoff game in many years – some of them never at all. While their season ended early, making playoffs was a great achievement for the Saskatchewan Roughriders. Steve Owen was named coach-of-the-year for bringing the Riders back from their depths. He suffered a heart attack that year, and decided to resign. He did return to football as head coach of the United Football League's Syracuse Stormers in 1963 and scouted for the New York Giants, but he suffered a cerebral hemorrhage and died on May 17, 1964 at 66 years old.

Photo courtesy of SSHFM

Danny Banda

He may be remembered as coach of the New York Giants, but he was remembered for something different here in Saskatchewan.

From 1945 to 1962 there were many changes in Riderville. Sweater colors changed from red and black to green and white and 'the Jolly Green Giants' were fast beginning to be recognized as 'Canada's Team.' Park de Young expanded several times and was renamed Taylor Field in memory of 'Piffles' Taylor. Rule changes were many and the value of a touchdown increased from five to six points. The number of imports and roster size grew and the platoon system eliminated players playing both offence and defence. There were also firsts, as the Riders were the first team to make an eastern road trip and were also the first team to fly. The Saskatchewan Roughrider spirit was sparked to life upon the re-creation of the team after the war years. Fans followed the team as they sped to the top in 1951 and then hit a few bumps along the way in years following. The Rider Pride that would guide the team through coming years, riding the highs with the club and pulling them out of the lows, was founded in these post-war years. Fans never gave up on their team despite disappointments, and waited for key players to fill in the weak spots and guide the team to greatness. Like the farmers of Saskatchewan, the Roughriders lived in next-year country.

All-Era Team
1946-1962

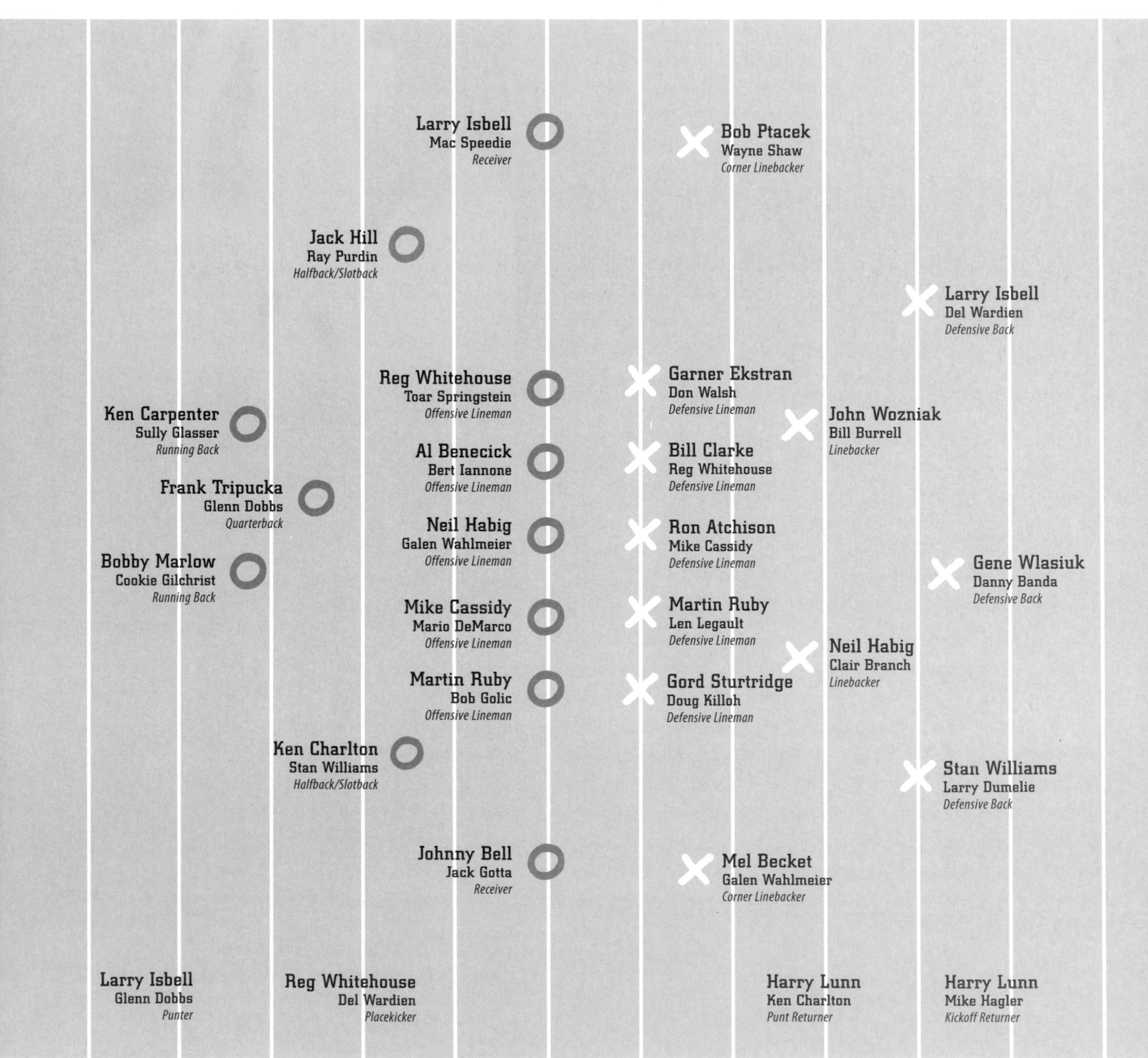

OFFENCE

Large print – 1st Team All-Star
Small print – 2nd Team All-Star
Position

DEFENCE

1963-1978

CHAPTER 3

BY BOB HUGHES

Photo courtesy of Solilo Studios

There was this time in the history of the Saskatchewan Roughriders when a sheer emotional love for the team, one that could be related to the relationship of a parent with a child, was formed. That came in 1951 when the remarkable Glenn Dobbs turned football in Saskatchewan on its ear, shook the daylights out of the province, gave birth to what would become the everlasting belief that, in Saskatchewan football, anything was possible. With Dobbs playing quarterback and also punting, the Roughriders mesmerized Saskatchewan fans by going to the Grey Cup game. So taken were the fans with The Dobber that a movement was underway to change the name of Regina to Dobberville. The Riders lost that Grey Cup appearance and head coach Harry (Blackjack) Smith was fired during a secret late-night meeting at a home on Leopold Crescent in Regina. But, the effects of Glenn Dobbs on Riderville were everlasting.

The effects of Glenn Dobbs on Riderville were everlasting. The best, though, was yet to come. The real relationship between fans and the team would be cemented more than a decade later.

The best, though, was yet to come. The real relationship between fans and the team would be cemented more than a decade later.

In 1963, Regina was so unlike what it would become. The city was small, yet growing at the rate of 4,500 people a year, and it seemed that weekday life revolved around what happened in the 1800 block of Hamilton. That block was an oasis of relaxation where fact and fiction danced together. The centerpiece of the 1800 block of Hamilton was The Leader Building, an imposing structure in the middle of the street. The Leader Building remains as the lone survivor of that time in Regina's history on the 1800 block of Hamilton. When the newspaper left downtown Regina in 1964 for the east side of Regina, it left part of its soul behind. It was downtown that the real *Leader-Post* was housed. Every day, business leaders, politicians, ordinary citizens and sports figures would drop in to chat, get the pulse of the city, and unload their gossip. Down the street, at the corner of Hamilton and

Ron Lancaster (23) is in the throwing motion while George Reed (34) and Gary Brandt (54) provide protection. (Top Photo)

11th, was Simpsons, and if you dropped into the men's clothing section you would find Big Bob Walker running the show. Walker came to the Riders in the 1930s from North Dakota, one of the the first Americans to play for the team, and he was outstanding along the line. When his career ended, he stayed, working for Simpsons for years, while he and his wife Helen raised their two children, Bob and Chrystal, in their comfortable home at 1256 Pasqua Street. Bobby Junior would go on to play for Regina Rams. Big Bob was among the early entries into the Plaza of Honor.

Across the street from The Leader Building was the LaSalle Hotel and a few doors north of that was the Balmoral Café. The LaSalle was operated by Jimmy and Harry Kangles, and they had the best cheeseburgers in town. The Balmoral was run by by Nick and Sam Pappas, and they were one of the few restaurants in town open on Sunday. For this I was eternally grateful. I was boarding in a house at 2341 McIntyre Street, but on Sundays you were on your own for meals. So, I worked a deal with Sam and Nick. I would type out their menu for the coming week if they fed me. They did, and usually it was a hot roast beef sandwich.

No matter what day it was, you could wander into the LaSalle or the Balmoral and run into the elite of Regina's sports fraternity. From legendary CKCK broadcaster Ken Milton to the remarkable coach Al Ritchie to the fiery Notre Dame priest Pere Murray to *Leader-Post* Sports Editor Tom (Scotty) Melville, to the political fund-raiser Staff Barootes,

Photo courtesy of SSHFM

Sports talk at the Balmoral Cafe – (seated left): Angie Mitchell, Ken Preston, Rider fan Charlie Stewart, sportscaster Lloyd Saunders, Al Ritchie. Standing behind Preston is cafe owner Nick Pappas and behind Saunders is Sam Pappas.

they could all be found there, trading their stories and starting rumours. Every once in a while Big Bert Neil, the owner of Neil Motors, would cruise by in his magnificent burgundy Imperial convertible, with its white leather seats, and the people would watch in absolute awe. Often, you would see Jack Gotta, the Riders' receiver, standing outside the LaSalle, handing out a card with his name and phone number on it, to every pretty girl that passed by. The old City Hall, an imposing structure, stood tall on 11th Avenue before ultimately giving way to the Galleria, and across the street could be found Kresge's.

"They say that Preston got Lancaster for a bottle of Scotch. "I'm not sure that is true," Preston once told me, "but it wasn't for much more."

The Roughriders had not been to the Grey Cup since 1951, so the fans still talked a lot about Glenn Dobbs. And in 1963, they were in for yet another new coach. They had gone through the Steve Owen era. He had been a remarkable coach with the New York Giants, but by the time he got to the Riders, the best was not yet to come. Stout Steve coached the Riders through a pair of not bad seasons and even was named the CFL's coach-of-the-year in 1962.

With Steve gone, the Riders turned to Bob Shaw, a tall former NFLer with a booming voice, an imposing personality and a domineering presence. Shaw had played in the National Football League, then served as an NFL assistant coach, and then as a head coach at New Mexico Military Institute. Shaw was a no-nonsense sort, and he could easily intimidate. So when Rider general manager Ken Preston made a trade with the Ottawa Rough Riders for quarterback-defensive back Ron Lancaster, Shaw was not impressed. They say that Preston got Lancaster for a bottle of Scotch. "I'm not sure that is true," Preston once told me, "but it wasn't for much more." Lancaster had played in Ottawa since 1960, much of the time at defensive back, but some of it at quarterback where he shared the duties with Russ Jackson. They won a Grey Cup in 1960. But in 1963, Ottawa coach Frank Clair knew he had to make decision. Jackson or Lancaster? He went with Jackson. And Lancaster was on his way to Saskatchewan.

"I didn't know a lot about the place," Ronnie would tell me years later. "But, what the heck, I wanted to play. So I flew out to Regina. There was nobody there to meet me. I got a ride to the Rider offices on Hill Avenue above that hardware store. I went up to the offices and they took me into to meet Shaw." Shaw sat back in his chair, staring out through those black eyes, looked down at his desk, and muttered, "You're a quarterback?"

Lancaster hardly looked like a quarterback. He was short, 5-foot-10 on a good day, he had this tight brushcut, and he was almost as wide as he was tall. This was not a good start to his first year in Saskatchewan. But if there was ever a defining moment in the Roughriders' history, one that has stood the test of time, then this was it. It was the beginning of the Ron Lancaster era in Saskatchewan, and by the end of it, nothing would ever be the same. Lancaster had played his college football at tiny Wittenberg College in Ohio after being born and raised near Pittsburgh. He was an excellent athlete and many felt he could have had a pro career in baseball.

Shortly before Lancaster arrived, another rookie to the Riders showed up. George Reed was his name.

Shortly before Lancaster arrived, another rookie to the Riders showed up. George Reed was his name. He had played college ball in Washington, and opted for the Riders over NFL offers. He was a running back and linebacker. "I drove up there, not having any idea where this place was," George remembered. "I drove right by Regina and was headed for Brandon when I finally figured out I had better turn around and go back."

George did. And his reception by Shaw was close to what Lancaster had experienced. "You're kind of small," Shaw said, and the words, like those he delivered to Lancaster, stung. Shaw never figured Reed would last long as a fullback. George was around six-feet tall and weighed just over 200 pounds. George only lasted 13 years and would become the greatest running back in the history of pro football in North America, surpassing the immortal Cleveland Brown fullback Jim Brown in a story that attracted the attention of *Sports Illustrated*.

> **George only lasted 13 years and would become the greatest running back in the history of pro football in North America.**

With Lancaster and Reed playing together, the Riders never once missed the playoffs, a remarkable achievement. The 1963 season was not easy on either Lancaster or Reed. Shaw never really seemed to have confidence in either one of them. And it probably didn't help Reed's cause when he fumbled the ball at the Riders' six-yard-line to set up a B.C. Lions' touchdown in a 40-0 loss in Vancouver in a pre-season game.

Shaw was fortunate in that he inherited a team that had plenty of talent. Names such as Dale West, Gene Wlasiuk, Clair Branch, Ray Purdin, Bob Ptacek, Neil Habig, Ted Urness, Bill Burrell, Al Benecick, Bill Clarke, Len Legault, Reggie Whitehouse, Dick Cohee, Jack Gotta, Ron Atchison and Garner Ekstran were among some of the solid players returning. The majority of those guys found their way into the Plaza of Honor. But, what the Riders didn't have was a proven starting quarterback and Shaw made it clear that he had his doubts Lancaster would be that guy.

At best, the 1963 season was a topsy-turvy one for the Riders. The Riders got off to a good start in their opening game in Edmonton, where they hadn't won since 1957. Shaw elected to go with Ptacek at quarterback, a move he didn't want to make. Because Bob Ptacek was a far better defensive back than he was a quarterback. Still, the move

Photo courtesy of SSHFM

Trainer Sandy Archer (left), Jim Copeland (30), Neil Habig (behind Copeland), Bob Ptacek (14), Hinckley Archer behind Ptacek, Bill Clarke (60), Dale West (12), Larry Dumelie (26), Bob Shaw standing

paid off. And, the Canadian Football League caught a glimpse of what would become a regular picture of George Reed. Reed displayed early flashes of what would be a career statement – slashing, punishing running. With Ray Purdin and Martin Fabi, who also punted, making sensational catches, the Riders won their opener 19-16, sending starting Edmonton quarterback Don Getty to the bench in the fourth quarter.

As the season unfolded, so too unfolded what Ron Lancaster would become during his storied career with the Riders. There is always a love-hate relationship with the starting quarterback. In a driving rainstorm, Lancaster got his first start at quarterback in a game against the Hamilton Tiger-Cats in Taylor Field. Lancaster completed only nine of 20 passes, but he had four drops. It was his scrambling that roused the crowd. Lancaster got several standing ovations from the drenched crowd. Hamilton quarterback Joe Zuger had more trouble throwing the ball than Ronnie did, but Zuger was also playing in the defensive backfield.

The season rolled along and the Riders sputtered, losing here, winning there. And the situation at quarterback became a controversial one. Shaw was often incensed at the lack of offence, saying that he could only do so much as a coach. It reached near rock bottom when the Riders lost 8-2 to the B.C. Lions in their eighth game of the season. The Riders went to Calgary next, and Shaw left Lancaster at home in Regina. With Lee Grosscup playing quarterback, the game ended in a 4-4 tie, and Shaw was spitting nails.

The following week, Lancaster was back at quarterback at home against the Eskimos. But Shaw benched him in the second quarter and sent in Frank Tripucka, who was 35 years old. Nothing happened, so he put Lancaster back in. Lancaster either had to produce or Shaw would likely have cut him. And, as he would his whole career, Ronnie pulled one out of the bag. He marched the Roughriders 109yards in 16 plays, sealing the victory when he hit Dale West on an eight-yard pass for the winning touchdown in an 8-7 victory. It was a play that highlighted Lancaster's ability to scramble away from imminent danger.

Photo courtesy of *Leader-Post*

Ron Lancaster

"I could see West in the end zone," said Lancaster, "but guys kept grabbing me. I could hear coach Shaw yelling from the bench to throw the darn thing, but every time I raised my arm, somebody would bump into me. When I finally got it away, I was sure it was going to hit the goalpost. It missed by a foot." And West caught it.

The game also was Hugh Campbell's first as a Rider receiver. They brought him in after he was cut in the NFL. Few could have guessed the impact Gluey Hughie would have on Lancaster, the Riders and, indeed, the whole CFL.

In their second-last game of the 1963 season, Lancaster played the whole 60 minutes and Reed had his best game as the Riders clinched a playoff spot. They went into Montreal and beat the Alouettes 32-20 with Lancaster throwing three touchdown passes in a row for the second straight game since Shaw benched him. And Reed rumbled for 123 yards on 21 carries.

The Riders lost their last game, 44-28, to the Argonauts in Toronto. They finished with a 7-7-2 record, which gave them third place in the West. It meant they would have to play the Stampeders in the two-game total-points Western semi-final.

The danger of a total-points series is that if you get wiped out in the first game, the second game takes on an empty meaning. And, that's exactly what happened. The Riders lost the first game in Calgary by a 35-9 score with Lancaster giving up three interceptions, all to Stampeder Art Johnson. "I made a lot of guys all-stars," Lancaster would say years later.

> **... Lancaster giving up three interceptions, all to Stampeder Art Johnson. "I made a lot of guys all-stars," Lancaster would say years later.**

Three days later, they came back to Taylor Field for the second game, and the Riders trailed by 26 points. They were somewhere between hopeless and no chance. Even the players had their doubts they could overcome that kind of a deficit. "It was over, we were done," said Lancaster.

A day before the game, Shaw was sitting at the kitchen table with his wife Mary. "Bob picked up a pencil and a napkin," she said "and he began designing plays." Whatever Shaw was in terms of his personality, he was a solid football man. One of the plays he drew up was called a "Sleeper Play."

The fans who came to Taylor Field on that chilly November night came expecting to see their beloved Riders play their last game of the season. Little did they know. Little did anybody know.

Photo courtesy of Heenan Studios

Ray Purdin

On the second play of the game, The Riders were at their own 34 yard-line. They called the Sleeper Play. With the team in the huddle, Purdin wandered over to the sideline, in front of the Calgary bench. Nobody paid attention to him. By the time the Stampeder defenders spotted him, it was too late. The ball was snapped, and Lancaster threw it to Purdin who was streaking down the sideline. The crowd went wild as Purdin ran untouched for 76 yards, and the Stamps had been hit by a bolt of lightning. Lancaster had a game for the ages. He completed 26 of 45 passes for 492 yards and five touchdowns. Of course, there was the usual batch of interceptions, four in fact, but it didn't matter on this storied night. Lancaster broke two CFL playoff records – for most passes thrown and most passing yardage. And, fittingly, Reed scored the winning touchdown on a 10-yard run. The Riders won the game 39-12, and the series by a single point. Thus was born, "The Little Miracle of Taylor Field." A crowd of 12,902 fans went home dazed and amazed.

Years later, Lancaster would look back at that game everybody called one of the greatest comebacks ever, and say, "You know what, that was a total fluke. There is no way we should have won by that big of a score. It was just a fluke. It wasn't really that great of a comeback on our part. But we won it, and that's all that mattered."

The city was beside itself. I remember the night as if it was yesterday. I was in the *Leader-Post* newsroom, and we were all listening on the radio. As the Riders mounted their comeback, I turned to the night sports editor, Hank Johnson, and said, "I've got to go to Taylor Field. I have to see this." I ran over to Taylor Field and watched the last half of one of the most amazing games in Rider history. Years later, I told Lancaster, "I don't care if you say it was a fluke. It was one of the most exciting things I have ever seen." He said, "Yeah, it was that."

It sent the Riders into the best-of-three Western final against Joe Kapp and the B.C. Lions. The Riders lost the first game 19-7, won the second 13-8 and were wiped out 36-1 in the decider. The Lions were 16-point favourites. They beat the spread.

It didn't seem to matter in Riderville. The fans spent the whole winter basking in the glory of the Little Miracle of Taylor Field. And for the organization itself, the season was a success. They made the playoffs. They saw glimpses of the future with Lancaster and Reed, even if nobody could gauge the magnitude of the impact those two would have on the Riders and the CFL. They set an attendance record of 111,526 fans and turned a profit of nearly $40,000.

The fans spent the whole winter basking in the glory of the Little Miracle of Taylor Field. And for the organization itself, the season was a success. They made the playoffs.

Seven Riders made the all-star team – Ron Atchison, Al Benecick, Bill Clarke, Garner Ekstran, Neil Habig, Wayne Shaw and Dale West. Lancaster led the team in passing and Reed in rushing. Optimism had wrapped its comforting arms around the Roughriders, for sure.

Bob Shaw's first season as head coach of the Riders had its moments, but in the end, it was a good season. And Lancaster and Reed had established themselves as forces that would have to be reckoned with. It was, no question, the dawning of a new era, one that would ultimately be unmatched in the history of pro football anywhere. The thing was, could the three of them work in concert? The 1964 season would be critical to that scenario, one that would reach a boiling point. Somebody would have to leave. This was not a marriage made in heaven.

Saskatchewan Roughrider fans always seemed to be tested by the gods of football. They always are asked to endure long waits between Grey Cup championships. Come the start to the 1964 season, they had yet to win a single Grey Cup, and the last time they were in one was 1951, which, of course, they lost to Ottawa. The wait would continue. And, thus, was born the time-honoured and occasionally tiresome phrase, "We're next-year country here." Farmers used it. The fans used it. The Riders used it.

There are all sorts of reasons why this was a time in the history of the Roughriders that they seemed as close to setting up a dynasty as they had ever been. And, it wasn't simply a matter of Bob Shaw's coaching, or the arrival of Ron Lancaster and George Reed. The building of the foundation to a team that would soon win the province's first Grey Cup came when Frank Filchock's days as Rider general manager ended after the 1957 season.

And, thus, was born the time-honoured and occasionally tiresome phrase, "We're next-year country here." Farmers used it. The fans used it. The Riders used it.

He was replaced by Ken Preston as GM. It would turn out to be one of the smartest moves, if not the smartest move, the Riders' executive ever made. Preston was not really a high-profile kind of football man. He was soft spoken and quiet, almost shy. His background was in football. He played at Queen's University from 1936-39, was with the Regina Roughriders in 1940, leaving to play with the Winnipeg Blue Bombers in 1941 and 1942, then onto the Ottawa Rough Riders in 1945, and finishing his playing career as a player-coach with Saskatchewan from 1946-48. He won one Grey Cup, as a player, in 1941 with Winnipeg.

Preston spent a few years in the private business world before agreeing to become Rider GM in 1958. It would be a career that lasted 20 years and saw the Riders play in five Grey Cup games and finally score a Grey Cup victory.

That Preston was able to accomplish such a feat given all the restraints and challenges itself is testimony enough to the football brilliance of the man. Very few things he did were done for the short term. He was a genius at developing home-grown talent. He organized a minor football program in Saskatchewan that to this day continues to grow from one end of the province to the other. He arranged for Canadian players to attend U.S. colleges on football scholarships. He was not only skilled at signing good football players on a tight budget, but he also was superb at ensuring they would stay with the team for long, fruitful periods of time.

George Reed

From Ron Lancaster to George Reed, from Ted Urness to Hugh Campbell, Preston was a whiz at finding sensational talent. How he got George Reed was in itself a great story. Reed played college football at Washington State, but broke his ankle in his second season. He came back to lead the Cougars in rushing in 1961 and 1962. But by then, the NFL had lost interest and made him only insignificant offers. The B.C. Lions put Reed on their negotiation list, then dropped him without telling him. He didn't find out about it until Preston, who had put Reed on the Riders' negotiation list, dropped by to see him. Within an hour Reed had signed with Saskatchewan.

Finding good coaches capable of milking the most out of that talent wasn't as easy. Preston went through George Terlep, Frank Tripucka, Ken Carpenter and Steve Owen before he finally found Bob Shaw. Whatever Shaw was, and there was always the suspected conflict between him and Reed and Lancaster, Shaw brought a form of discipline and excitement to the Riders. But it was another Preston move that turned out to be the final missing piece of the puzzle that had plagued Riders fans for the team's whole history. He brought in former Edmonton Eskimo player and coach Eagle Keys to serve as Shaw's assistant coach. That would last one season, Shaw would leave for Toronto, and Keys would take over as head coach. The man with the southern drawl, the piercing blue eyes and the big heart used to say he came from Turkey Neck Bend, Kentucky. But he would be the guy who was the glue in the coming Saskatchewan Roughrider dynasty.

"You know," Lancaster once told me, "Ken Preston took a lot of heat because everybody always thought he was cheap and wouldn't pay the players what they were worth. But he had only so much money to work with, and you kinda came to understand that. I mean, contract negotiations with Ken were ridiculous. You would go into his office, tell him you wanted a raise. He'd hand you a contract and the figure would never be what you wanted. He'd tell you, 'We don't have any more money. You know that, Ron.' So, you just shrugged your shoulders, signed the contract, and left. Every year, same thing. You'd walk into the hardware store vowing to be tough with him, drive home, and wonder just what the heck you had done. How'd he do that? I don't know."

"Ken Preston took a lot of heat because everybody always thought he was cheap and wouldn't pay the players what they were worth. But he had only so much money to work with, and you kinda came to understand that."

Ken and his wife Dorothy, or Dot as she was known, were always a part of the Regina scene. They were very social people, and Ken liked nothing more than golfing with his buddies at the Wascana Country Club, the cigar always close by. They raised their family in Regina, and their youngest son, Rich, who was a water boy with the 1966 Riders, went on to a successful career in the National Hockey League, first as a player, then as a coach.

The Ken Preston era in Saskatchewan was unrivalled, regardless of what measuring stick you used.

The Saskatchewan Roughriders had a lot to think about when they reported to training camp in 1964. There was little doubt they had the nucleus of a team that possessed unlimited potential. "There were times," said Shaw, "when I was so proud of them because no matter how much adversity they were facing, they didn't quit. And that is a big part of winning. Last year, they showed me they could play anybody in this league and win."

The Western Conference was anything but weak, and its strength could be found in the number of bona fide quarterbacks. Outside of the Edmonton Eskimos, who would again finish last, the West was indeed the best, as far as quarterbacking went. The B.C. Lions had the swashbuckling Joe Kapp, the Stampeders had the combination of Eagle Day and Jerry Keeling, the Blue Bombers had the efficient Ken Ploen, and the Riders had the scrambling Ron Lancaster.

And, football fever here was at its highest point in years. The Little Miracle of Taylor Field in the playoff comeback against the Stampeders the year before had captivated the province's football fans like never before, or at least since the days of Dobbs. Fans were buying season tickets, there was growing talk that Taylor Field had to be expanded, and optimism had embraced the Riders. Heading into training camp, Shaw said, "I think we'll be 25 per cent better this season."

Around the league, other coaches also were developing a fear of the Riders. Saskatchewan football was suddenly being taken very seriously by every other team.

It was kind of neat. And, you could see it happening everywhere.

There were two social events that fans could attend held every year where players and coaches could be found. There was the noon-hour luncheon in curling clubs put on by legendary curler Sam Richardson. "The Riders were always great about getting players or coaches to come out, have lunch, talk to the fans and take questions," recalled Sam. "But the best of them all was Ronnie Lancaster. He told me once, 'Sam don't schedule me for any of these. But the minute you need me to come over, just call Bev (Ron's wife) and let her know. I'll be there, no matter how short the notice is.' " The biggest draws for these luncheons were, of course, when Lancaster and Reed showed up. "The people couldn't get enough of them," said Sam.

Around the league, other coaches also were developing a fear of the Riders. Saskatchewan football was suddenly being taken very seriously by every other team.

Then there was Emmett Mooney's Smokers. Father Emmett Mooney was a Roman Catholic priest who was a huge Roughrider fan. He would often topic his Sunday morning sermons on game days with long prayers for a Roughrider victory. He would hold these Smokers at Christ the King Church in Regina where coaches and players and hundreds of fans would attend. They were huge successes, and a lot of fun too.

Those were signs that the Roughriders and the community were in this thing together, an important facet in selling season tickets.

But it helped, too, that the team itself was developing into an exciting and winning bunch, a Reign of Terror that would continue long into the 1970s.

When camp opened, the Riders had 33 holdover players mixed in with 32 rookies. There really weren't a lot of open spots. After all, they had Lancaster, Reed, Hugh Campbell, Ed Buchanan to move the ball, Al Benecick, Ted Urness and Reg Whitehouse on the line. The defence was anchored by Bill Clarke, Ron Atchison, Garner Ekstran, Dale West and so on.

But, there was a trio of rookies who would make a lasting mark. One was Jim Worden, a 235-pound tight end out of Wittenburg, the same school Lancaster came from. The other was Bobby Kosid, a Canadian defensive back who had played his college ball at Kentucky. And a third was running back/linebacker Henry Dorsch, a Saskatchewan kid who had played college ball at Tulsa. Those three would not only make the roster, but they would make it in big ways. And, ultimately, Dorsch would replace Preston as GM when Ken retired in 1978.

Shaw also had a new assistant coach in Eagle Keys, who had played and coached in Edmonton. He became an instant legend when he played in a Grey Cup game with a broken leg. Eagle and Lancaster hit it off almost immediately, which would play out into even greater things down the road.

Hugh Campbell

Photo courtesy of *SSHFM*

The 1964 season was pivotal for the Roughriders in so many ways. They continued to strengthen an already strong roster. Lancaster showed he was a quarterback capable of brilliance. Reed brought the whole package at fullback. Buchanan was the kind of halfback who could break open games. Campbell might not have been fast at wide receiver, but he could catch a hiccup in a hurricane. And, the defence was as mean as a junkyard dog. You never wanted to get on Ron Atchison's bad side.

It didn't faze anybody, or dampen the enthusiasm and optimism, when the Riders lost both of their exhibition games. "They don't mean a thing," Shaw said.

But they opened the regular season with a bang, with a lightning bolt. They went into Calgary and laid a 15-4 loss on the Stampeders. Bill Clarke played what many said was the best game of his career, chasing Eagle Day to the bench in the fourth quarter.

"We have to stop Lancaster," said Calgary coach Bobby Dobbs before the game. And, they did, sort of. They held The Little General to just five completions. But the ground game turned into a force Calgary couldn't reckon with. Buchanan ran for 187 yards as the Riders racked up 328 yards along the ground. Dobbs wasn't surprised. "They just ran the heck out of us physically," he said. "They wore us down. They didn't surprise us. They always give us trouble. There's no tougher team to play against in the nation."

What transpired after that was so much about what the Riders would become. One week, they would raise the spirits of your heart, the next week they might break it. They won their home opener against Winnipeg, 37-29, with Lancaster throwing for 326 yards and Campbell making three touchdown catches. The Riders had shown an early tendency to struggle in the opening halves of their first two games. In fact, two games into the season, they had scored but a single point in the first half, but exploded for 52 in the second half. "I've been saying all along that the Riders have a great club," said Bomber coach Bud Grant.

Then, the Riders went into a tailspin of sorts. They lost three games in a row, twice to B.C. and once Calgary, to drop their record to 2-3. Still, there was no panic.

They got it back together when they went into Edmonton to play the cellar-dwelling Eskimos. Lancaster gunned four touchdown passes, three to Campbell, and the Riders had 542 yards in offence with Buchanan getting 199 yards running all over Clarke Stadium. The Riders won 56-8.

During the game, Preston announced that he had signed an offensive tackle named Clyde Brock, who had been cut by the NFL. Brock was 6-foot-5 and 295 pounds and Preston had tried to sign him two years earlier when he graduated from Utah. But, Clyde went to the NFL where he played with the Dallas Cowboys and San Francisco 49ers. Brock would soon be a starter in Saskatchewan and would become an anchor for the offensive line.

The Riders were 3-3 after six games, and nobody was unhappy. In fact, Shaw was pleased. They had played six games in just 24 days and with a few breaks here and there, could easily have been 4-2 or 5-1. They were the real deal.

Then came a five-game winning streak in which Lancaster, Buchanan, Reed and Campbell got it all together and the defence, with West, Shaw, Ptacek, Atch, Ekstran and Clarke all excelling, dominated.

But in the 10th game in Ottawa, it all came apart. This was to be Lancaster's first game in Ottawa, the team that had traded him. It was his chance to show them they made a mistake, although keeping Russ Jackson was no mistake. But, in the first quarter, Lancaster took a shot, and broke a rib. He didn't play again until the last game of the season, a 26-20 win over Edmonton. The Riders finished third with a 9-7 record, their second-best record since 1956. They would once again meet the Stampeders in the two-game, total-points semi-final.

Would there be another miracle? The Riders opened the playoff in Calgary. The brilliance of Shaw showed itself. The Stampeders operated their offence out of the shotgun because Day was such a strong passer. "Why can't we do the same thing?" wondered Shaw.

So, the Riders put Lancaster in the shotgun and sent six receivers at the Stampeders' defence. They couldn't handle it. Lancaster completed 28 of 35 passes for 376 yards. Reed piled up 171 yards in rushing and receiving yardage. Saskatchewan's offence totalled 503 yards. And the Riders won, 34-25, giving Saskatchewan a nine-point lead in the second game. The joy was short-lived. The Stamps marched into McMahon Stadium and left with a 51-6 victory. Saskatchewan's season ended, once again, in the semi-final.

But, there was plenty to be happy about. Attendance was so good there were serious talks going on that would lead to the expansion of Taylor Field. The Regina Red Sox baseball team played out of Taylor Field, occupying space in the northeast corner. But their best days were behind them and the stadium was too big for them. It was felt that if they could find another more intimate venue to play out of, they would be content and the Riders could move ahead with plans to build a grandstand on the east side. Eventually, it would happen.

There was one unpleasant moment to the 1964 season, and it came early in the season. John Robertson, a gifted and colourful writer, covered the Riders for the *Leader-Post*. Robbie was the Riders' biggest fan and he worshipped Bob Shaw. Robbie was also a character. On road games, he would board the team bus for the ride to the airport. He and Reg Whitehouse would sit at the

Photo courtesy of SSHFM

Bob Kosid

back of the bus. Upon arriving at their seats, Robbie would pull out a jar of martinis, and he and Reg would enjoy the trip to the airport.

If riled, Robertson could turn that happy pen of his into a poison pen. I only remember him getting angry about the Riders on two occasions. One was when Shaw did something Robertson didn't like. He savaged Shaw in his column, the one and only time he did it. The other time was right after the opening game of the 1964 season, the victory in Calgary, where Buchanan had his 187-yard game.

This is what Robertson wrote the day after the game and it rocked the city:

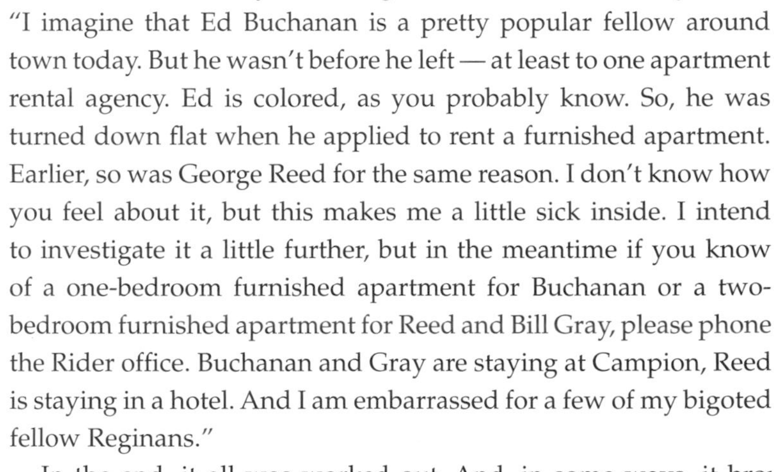

"I imagine that Ed Buchanan is a pretty popular fellow around town today. But he wasn't before he left — at least to one apartment rental agency. Ed is colored, as you probably know. So, he was turned down flat when he applied to rent a furnished apartment. Earlier, so was George Reed for the same reason. I don't know how you feel about it, but this makes me a little sick inside. I intend to investigate it a little further, but in the meantime if you know of a one-bedroom furnished apartment for Buchanan or a two-bedroom furnished apartment for Reed and Bill Gray, please phone the Rider office. Buchanan and Gray are staying at Campion, Reed is staying in a hotel. And I am embarrassed for a few of my bigoted fellow Reginans."

Ed Buchanan

In the end, it all was worked out. And, in some ways, it brought what would ultimately become a close team even closer.

And, so, in the offseason that arrived after the 1964 playoff loss, it came to pass that Bob Shaw left the Roughriders to become head coach of the Toronto Argonauts. And it was deemed as a good thing for everybody involved.

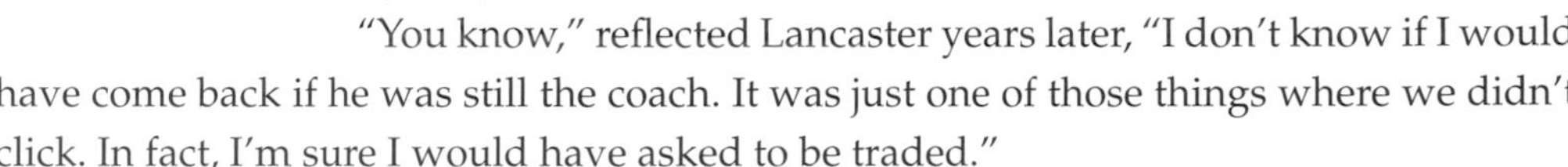

"You know," reflected Lancaster years later, "I don't know if I would have come back if he was still the coach. It was just one of those things where we didn't click. In fact, I'm sure I would have asked to be traded."

George Reed was of much the same mood. "Yeah, I probably would have left too. It was just not that good for me."

Imagine if Shaw had stayed, and Lancaster and Reed followed their hearts and left Saskatchewan? Would their careers have been as truly legendary as they became? Would the Roughriders have continued to build what Preston and Shaw had taken close to the mountaintop? Scary thought, that.

There was one interesting twist to Shaw's departure. *Leader-Post* sports columnist John Robertson ended his two-year reign atop the paper's sports pages by accepting a job offer from a Toronto newspaper. Most believed that Shaw had something to do with the move. Shaw and Robertson had become good friends and there was no stronger supporter among the Saskatchewan media of Shaw than John Robertson.

It did not take Preston, nor the Rider executive headed up by club president Bob Kramer, long to name Shaw's replacement. It was Eagle Keys, who had come to Saskatchewan in 1964 as an assistant coach. If Ken Preston had made two brilliant moves in his career by getting Lancaster and Reed, then this was his third brilliant move, one that would have a lasting impact on the franchise and take it to the greatest heights in its history.

Lancaster and Reed had established themselves as talented players in their first two seasons, despite the uneasiness they felt playing for Shaw. What Eagle gave them was his unabashed support. He set them free, let them play their game, and they soared. "I knew that Ronnie had everything you wanted in a quarterback," Eagle told me long after he had left the Riders. "He was tough, he was smart, he was a leader, and he was a winner. He would always find a way to beat you. There were times when I might be ready to give him hell, when he drove me nuts. Short yardage plays were an example. We'd be second and half a yard away from a first down. I'd send in a running play to George. The next thing I know, I look up, Ronnie fakes the handoff and throws a pass. The defence never expected it. I never expected it. But, he was a gambler. He'd come off the field and I'd tell him, 'It's a damn good thing you made that work.' "

"He was tough, he was smart, he was a leader, and he was a winner. He would always find a way to beat you. There were times when I might be ready to give him hell, when he drove me nuts."

Eagle would coach the Roughriders from 1965 through 1970 before joining his old buddy and Eskimo teammate Jackie Parker in B.C. where Parker was general manager of the Lions. But in the six years he coached in Saskatchewan, the Riders made the playoffs every year, made it to three Grey Cup games, winning one of them. Keys became the winningest coach in Rider history, a record that still stands. His 68 victories stacked against just 25 losses and three ties elevated him into the Plaza of Honor and the Canadian Football Hall of Fame. He was one of a kind, and you won't get much of an argument if you say he could rightfully claim the mantle of the best coach the Riders ever had.

By the time the Eagle landed in Saskatchewan, his background in Canadian football had been well established. He claimed to be from Turkey Neck Bend, which was always a source of fun moments with Eagle. He did play his college football at Western Kentucky University, playing centre and linebacker. He also lettered in baseball as pitcher or outfielder. And during the Second World War, he joined the Marines.

Eagle came to the CFL in 1949, playing for three years with Montreal Alouettes where he was an all-star every year. Then, he went to Edmonton and played three more seasons, again making the all-star team as a centre every season. He retired as a player and became an assistant coach for the Eskimos before being named head coach in 1959. He got the Eskimos into the 1960 Grey Cup game where they lost to Ottawa. Lancaster and Russ Jackson shared quarterbacking duties that season with the Rough Riders, although Lancaster saw a lot of time as a defensive back.

By the time Keys got to Saskatchewan in 1964, he already had proven his worth.

"Eagle knew football, there was never any doubt about that," Ken Preston said. "But I always thought his biggest asset was he knew how to handle a team and the players. He got them to play for him and for each other. He created a great bond among the players, and that's what made us good."

"Eagle knew football, there was never any doubt about that," Ken Preston said. "But I always thought his biggest asset was he knew how to handle a team and the players. He got them to play for him and for each other. He created a great bond among the players, and that's what made us good."

Keys could be tough when he had to be. "Old Eagle would just look at you through those blue eyes of his, and you knew you had better pick it up," laughed defensive lineman Ron Atchison. "He was a great coach, but you didn't want him to get mad at you."

One time in training camp, Eagle was growing steadily disenchanted with one of his running backs. "If you screw that play up again," Eagle drawled at him, "you might as well just keep on runnin' until y'all have left town." Sure enough, the running back screwed it up next time the play was called. He ran across the practice field, under the stands, up the dressing room, into the shower, and, presumably, out of town. He was never seen again in these parts.

> "The thing about Eagle," Lancaster said, "was that he let the players play. Everybody knew what was expected of them. He used to come into the dressing room and tell us, 'You guys are not that good individually, but as a team you can be damn good.' "

"The thing about Eagle," Lancaster said, "was that he let the players play. Everybody knew what was expected of them. He used to come into the dressing room and tell us, 'You guys are not that good individually, but as a team you can be damn good.'"

The Roughriders developed a rare closeness among each other during the Eagle Keys era. Many of them lived here year-round and held jobs away from football. They would spend time together in the off-season, at hockey rinks where their kids were playing, or at school gatherings. "We used to go out for dinner, a whole bunch of us, with our wives or girlfriends," Lancaster said. "If somebody didn't come, George or one of the other veterans would call the guy and ask him what was going on. We became pretty close off the field and it paid off on the field. And we had a lot of fun."

In many ways, Eagle came across as a quiet sort of guy and gave the impression he liked his own space and didn't want it to be intruded on. He was, in reality, not anything like that. He had a great sense of humour and developed some lasting friendships in Regina. He enjoyed going to Father Mooney's Smokers, or Sam Richardson's lunches at the curling club. He became great friends with broadcaster Ken Newans.

And Eagle knew how to enjoy himself. He spent a fair amount of time socializing with Gord Currie, who became head coach of the junior Regina Rams the same year Eagle became head coach of the Riders. In many ways, they were alike. They would get together in Eagle's house on Montague Street in south Regina to talk about everything under the sun. Usually, there'd be a bottle of gin and a bottle of rum nearby. Both men could handle the demon booze. And, often their gab sessions would last the night, ending when Eagle's devoted wife Joyce would come downstairs and make them breakfast.

Currie and Keys had much in common, their love of football and strategy part of that bond. But there was a certain irony attached to their relationship. In 1966, when the two of them were only in their second seasons as head coaches in Saskatchewan, they each won national championships. The irony could be found in the numbers. The Rams won the Canadian junior title by a 29-14 score. Fifteen days later, the Riders won the Grey Cup by an identical 29-14 score. The margin of victory in each case was 15 points. And, the Riders' victory came 15 years after their last Grey Cup appearance. I once asked each of them if 15 was their lucky number. It drew only blank stares.

Like Currie, Keys was a master of handling players, of knowing which players need a kick and which ones needed a pat to get them going. I remember one year when I was sent out to cover training camp. The Riders had a rookie fullback in camp and he was impressing a lot of people. So, I wrote a story about him.

The next day, I went back out to camp. And, Eagle came walking over to me.

"Hughes," he drawled, "we need to talk."

I had no idea what I had done, but we moved off the field and sat down.

"That story you wrote about the rookie running back was okay," Eagle said. "But I need you to do me a favour. George (Reed) read the story and he's all upset. He thinks he's going to get cut. Hell, that rookie's okay, but George is our guy. Could you write something nice about George so he settles down."

I did and Reed settled down.

You know, when the Riders went to training camp in 1965, there was a whole new atmosphere around them. It had everything to do with Eagle Keys.

George Reed remembers that time well.

"When I left after the 1964 season and went home (to Washington), I was very unhappy. I'd been home a couple of weeks when Angie finally said to me, 'George, what's wrong? You haven't been the same since you came back. What's the matter?' "

Reed paused and shook his head. We had this conversation one April night in 2009 when the two of us appeared at a Casino Regina event. We sat in a booth and talked. "I decided there was no way I was going back if Bob Shaw was still the coach," George said. "I just couldn't handle it. I had made up my mind I was getting out of football, going home, and getting a teaching job or something. But I wasn't going back up there." As things turned out, Shaw did leave and Reed did come back, to be greeted warmly by his new head coach, Eagle Keys.

"Eagle came to us in 1964 as an assistant to Shaw," Reed said. "He treated us a lot differently. While Shaw would go into his office, Eagle would come and sit with the boys. We talked a lot and we all grew very close to him. With Eagle, you always knew where you stood. There was never any bullshit with that man. If he had something to say to you, he said it. If you screwed up, you knew it. If he wanted more out of you, he told you to your face. That man, you wanted to play for him."

Reed laughed, a laugh that starts deeply somewhere inside of him and rolls out in claps of thunder. "I remember we had a rookie running back, and he said he didn't know how he was doing," Reed said. "I told him, go see coach Keys. He said his door was always open. So, the kid went into see Eagle, and he said, 'Coach, I'm just wondering how I'm doing.' Eagle looked at him and said, 'Not worth a damn. In fact I'm just getting ready to cut you.' "

There are always holes to fill in any roster on an annual basis. One of the team's outstanding players couldn't go another year so hometown boy Bill Clarke packed it in at the end of the 1964 season after 14 seasons as an offensive and defensive lineman with the Riders. He won all-star honours as a defensive tackle on two occasions and was twice named the most valuable Canadian on the team. He would be inducted into the Plaza of Honor and the Canadian Football, Saskatchewan and Regina sports hall of fames. But perhaps his biggest contribution in his life was to fight a disease that ultimately took his life. Clarke endured years of suffering from Parkinson's Disease. He headed up a golf tournament that raised tens of

Photo courtesy of SSHFM

Eagle Keys (left) and Bob Shaw

Photo courtesy of Heenan Studios

Bill Clarke

thousands for dollars for Parkinson's Disease research, a tournament held at Long Creek Golf Course in Avonlea which annually drew over 200 entrants.

Photo courtesy of *Leader-Post*

Al Ford

In many ways, the 1965 season was somewhat typical for the Roughriders. They'd win here, lose there. They'd make the playoffs. They'd lose in the playoffs. But much more emerged from the 1965 season than that. Three players who would ultimately have a huge impact on the Riders of the future arrived. The first was Al Ford, a Regina kid who had played college football in California. Ford would develop into one of the most versatile players the Riders ever had. He would play running back, receiver, defensive back and he could punt. Ford became an essential part of the Roughriders' roster because he could so many things well. And, he was a "team" guy. Before Ford's association with the Riders would end, he would have won a Grey Cup as a player (1966) and as a general manager (1989). He also was an assistant coach with the Riders when Lancaster became head coach. The other new face belonged to Jack Abendschan, who came to Saskatchewan from New Mexico. Not only would Abendschan develop into a great guard, he also became a reliable placekicker. And, then, there was defensive back Ted Dushinski, who came from the Saskatoon Hilltops and would develop into one of the toughest defensive backs the Riders ever had.

Keys also brought in his own assistant coaches. Remember now, these were the days when teams had only two assistant coaches, not the seven or more teams now have. Eagle hired Jack Gotta, whose days as a receiver with the Riders were over. And he brought in Jim Duncan, who had coached at Appalachian State in North Carolina. They were both gifted coaches who quickly earned the respect of the players. And both those guys would go on to head coaching careers in the Canadian Football League, Gotta winning a Grey Cup with Ottawa and Duncan winning one with the Stampeders. This was a quality group.

It would take a little while before Eagle blended the team into the kind of team he wanted. And, the blending began in 1965.

Eagle had total faith in Lancaster as a quarterback and he felt that Reed could become a great fullback. He knew he had an offensive line that was strong. And, the defence was one few offences in the CFL wanted to go up against.

The season started on a downer, of course, this being Saskatchewan. The Riders went into Calgary to take on the Stampeders, and it was no contest. They were bombed 37-8. The game was over early with Stampeder receiver Frank Budd turning on the jets on a 91-yard touchdown throw from Eagle Day. Budd was an Olympian as a sprinter so when he got behind Bob Kosid, there was no catching him. Budd was like a lot of world-class sprinters who tried their hand at football. There were times he would drop passes. But this time, he hung on. A touchdown by running back Paul Dudley put Saskatchewan behind 14-0 after the first quarter.

Lancaster completed only nine of 22 passes and gave up three interceptions. He could do that, and would throughout his career.

The season started with back-to-back games against the Stampeders. So, when they came back to Regina for the home opener, more was expected of the Riders. Keys had growled through practice sessions before the game and the players knew they had better produce. From the stands at Taylor Field, it appeared the Riders were headed for another disastrous outing. They trailed 18-0 at halftime. But neither Keys nor the players were worried. "Despite the score in the first half, I didn't think we played that badly," said Keys.

Photo courtesy of SSHFM

Jack Gotta makes the transition from player to assistant coach

The second half was a whole different story. Lancaster got the offence moving, mostly in the air. Calgary's great middle linebacker Wayne Harris virtually shut down the Riders' ground game. Harris and Reed would have many more battles as the years rolled along. Ford and Canadian receiver Gord Barwell, who came to the Riders in 1964 from the junior Saskatoon Hilltops, made big plays. And the Riders stormed back to win 20-18 on a late touchdown by Hugh Campbell. In all, Campbell caught 11 passes. Eagle felt the Riders needed to strengthen themselves at quarterback, to find somebody other than Ptacek to back Lancaster up. They found one in veteran Hal Ledyard, who they made a deal for with Winnipeg. Ledyard and Lancaster actually had played together in Ottawa.

"You know," Lancaster told me, "this was the first year I actually felt comfortable since coming to the Canadian Football League."

The Riders went on a tear in their third game, going into Edmonton and dismantling the Eskimos 34-15 on a night when everything clicked. Lancaster threw two touchdowns to Campbell as the Riders passed for 199 yards and ran for 241 yards. Reed and Bill Gray and Ford all had big games with Reed bulling and slashing for 71 yards.

Back in Taylor Field, it was a different story. The Riders ran into injury problems against the B.C. Lions, but were still able to squeeze out a 10-10 tie. The ground game was strong, but the passing game was limp. Reed hammered the Lions' defence for 106 yards on 17 carries. Eagle dressed Dushinski for the game on a whim, and it was a good move. Ted was thrown into the fray when Hank Dorsch broke a bone in his hand, and Dushinski came through in a large way. "How about that Dushinski?" Eagle said. "We throw him into the game and he plays like a veteran against a quarterback like Joe Kapp."

Photo courtesy of SSHFM

Ted Dushinski

The Riders began to rev up their engines. They went into Winnipeg and dazzled the Blue Bombers in a 25-6 victory. With

Al Benecick opening huge holes, Reed rolled for 99 yards on 21 carries. Lancaster and Campbell put on a dazzling show, Hughie catching eight of the Ronnie's passes. The Riders were in second place in the West, just a point back of Winnipeg.

There was once again joy in Riderville. But it was short-lived. The Riders lost their next game to the Hamilton Tiger-Cats, 30-6, with Hamilton setting a single-game CFL record with seven interceptions. Keys took the loss in stride, saying his players had played a lot of games in a short period of time and just didn't have any gas left. But, things got a little testier when the Riders dropped 24-22 thriller to Edmonton in Taylor Field. They just couldn't finish off their drives. Maybe, they were distracted. Maybe, they were distracted by what was coming next.

What was coming next was a trip to Toronto and their first game against their old coach, Bob Shaw. "Yeah, we were looking forward to that," Lancaster said.

The headline in the *Leader-Post* told the story. "Riders maul Argos for easy 28-9 win. Score settled with Shaw."

Shaw didn't take the loss easily. He left the field as soon as the game ended, not stopping to talk to any Rider players or shake Keys' hands.

"Well," said Shaw, "I didn't notice Eagle Keys coming to see me yesterday. I was in my office all day and he was here practising." Ouch!

Two days after playing in Toronto, the Riders went into McGill Stadium in Montreal. In those days, the eastern swing was brutal. "You'd play two games in three days, but we did it," said Reed. "It wasn't easy because you had no time to rest. But we did OK."

The Riders swept their eastern swing, knocking off the Alouettes 11-9. A late field goal by Abendschan after a Lancaster-engineered drive put the Roughriders into sole possession of first place in the West, a slim one point ahead of Calgary and B.C. It was vintage Lancaster who had to put together not one, but two, amazing comebacks in the last five minutes of the game to snatch victory from the jaws of defeat.

The ride back to the hotel was typical of all Rider victory rides on the bus. There would be the sounds of the players' fight song.

"

The ride back to the hotel was typical of all Rider victory rides on the bus. There would be the sounds of the players' fight song.

It went something like this, every time they won.

Somebody would start off by voicing words that sounded like …

"Mie, Mie, Mie…."

Then, the rest of the team would join in …
"We're the Raunchy Riders,
Raunchy are we.
We'd rather (bleep) than fight,
For victory!
We're the Raunchy Riders,
Raunchy are we!
We're from Regina,
The (bleep) of the world and all the universe!
Yes, we're the Raunchy Riders,
Raunchy are we!
We'd rather (bleep) than fight
For victoryyyyyyyyyyy!"

I guess you had to hear it.

The Riders came home from Montreal on Cloud Nine, and promptly found themselves at Ground Zero. The Roughriders came home to Taylor Field where the Stampeders were waiting, licking their chops.

It would be the beginning of a two-game skid for the team that just couldn't get it all together at the right time.

And a furious debate over whether Lancaster was indeed the quarterback they needed was born and it raged every time the Riders lost, or he had one of those games in which he served up a handful of interceptions. "Sometimes I would get stubborn," Lancaster would years later say. "If I got intercepted, I'd come back and call the same play. If the guy intercepted it again, I'd call it again until we finally beat him. A little dumb, eh?"

Nobody in the league could understand why the fans would occasionally turn on Lancaster. He was in his fifth season in the league, his third in Saskatchewan. Rogers Lehew, the general manager of the Stampeders, just shook his head. "Ronnie should be the Schenley Award winner as the league's outstanding player," Lehew said. Hamilton Tiger-Cat receiver and defensive back Garney Henley said that if Lancaster was playing in the Eastern Conference, he'd be the best quarterback, hands down.

The debate would go on for all of Lancaster's career. His stats, his victories, his Grey Cup appearances, his all-star awards … all of that … would be his response. And, it never really bothered him. He would take it in stride.

The Riders went into the second-last game of the 1965 season needing to beat the Lions in Vancouver to make the playoffs. The Lions were a formidable group. They had Joe Kapp at quarterback, Willie Fleming at running back and a handful of receivers that were as good as anybody.

But, the Riders had Lancaster and Reed. With a record crowd of nearly 40,000 fans packing every nook and cranny in Empire Stadium, the Riders put together their most devastating offensive attack of the season. Lancaster only threw 12 passes and completed eight of them. But as time went on, the old saying, "Let George do it!" took over. Reed had his greatest rushing game ever, He hit the holes opened by that great offensive line at full speed, the legs driving high, Lion defenders bouncing off his thick thighs. Reed set a Western Conference rushing record by pile-driving his way to 268 yards off 30 carries and the Riders won the game running away, 30-14.

Lions' defensive coach Jim Champion said, "If George Reed doesn't win the Schenley Award, there's no justice."

Eagle Keys wore a rare grin. "Ronnie called a great game, George ran a great game, and the rest played a great game."

The Riders flew home from Vancouver, arriving at 10.30 at night to be greeted by 2,500 fans who jammed into the airport.

The Riders closed out the season with a meaningless 15-12 win in Edmonton, and got ready for the playoffs.

Reed finished the season with over 1,700 yards rushing. And, the Riders ended up in third place.

Once again, they just weren't able to put it all together in the playoffs, losing to the Blue Bombers in Winnipeg.

The season ended in some disappointment. But when you remembered this was Eagle Keys' first year as head coach, the table had been set for something bigger and something better.

Photo courtesy of *Leader-Post*

Sandy Archer, the "Dean" of trainers

The Roughriders ended the 1965 season with a fourth straight third-place finish off an 8-7-1 record and a first-round playoff exit.

When the 1966 season arrived, nobody was really sure what to expect. But the usual umbrella of sheer optimism hovered over Saskatchewan and its football fans. Would this finally be the year "Next Year" arrived? Would Keys and Lancaster and Reed dare to venture where no other coach or player in Roughrider history had gone, to the promised land that would be the first Grey Cup win ever?

The additions to the roster in 1966 basically represented the final pieces in the puzzle. In came defensive tackle Ed McQuarters, cut by the St. Louis Cardinals. A large man, McQuarters' biggest attribute was his tenacity and his speed. There has likely never been a defensive lineman in the CFL who was as fast as Big Ed. Bruce Bennett arrived, a Florida grad, who would occupy a commanding presence at safety and also back up Lancaster at quarterback. Lanky Don Gerhardt, a defensive end, made the team and Paul Dudley came to provide relief at running back, his days in Calgary over.

In so many ways, the 1966 season was just another ordinary year for the Roughriders. It was the ending that was extraordinary.

The Roughriders launched the 1966 season with back-to-back wipeouts. They hammered the Eskimos 40-13 in the season opener, and followed that up with a 38-14 whuppin' of the Winnipeg Blue Bombers before a huge crowd in Taylor Field.

Lancaster passed for 192 yards and Reed ran for 118 and the Rider defence hounded Bomber quarterback Ken Ploen into throwing three interceptions. "I don't think I've ever been hit that hard that many times in a game," said Ploen.

Lancaster threw for three touchdowns, Reed ran for one, Campbell caught one, and offensive lineman Al Benecick scored on a fumble recovery. "Man," Keys said after the game, "that was a big one. The guys have never played better." Bomber coach Bud Grant agreed: "The Riders were simply superb. I can't say enough good things about the Riders."

The Riders ran their streak to three straight wins before getting bounced 26-1 by the Calgary Stampeders. Then, it was back-to-back losses, the Calgary loss followed by an 18-17 loss to Edmonton.

They got back on the winning track in one of the most exciting games ever played in the hallowed confines of Taylor Field. They beat the Lions 30-29 in a game in which the fans rarely sat down. It took a fourth-quarter field goal by Abendschan set up by a Lancaster to Worden pass to seal the victory. Lancaster passed for 361 yards and Reed ran for 80 as the Riders were able to answer everything that Joe Kapp and Willie Fleming threw at them.

Photo courtesy of *Leader-Post*

Ed McQuarters

"You know," said Keys, "I must have been involved in 400 games coaching and playing since I came to Canada 18 years ago. I can't honestly recall a more exciting game." The two teams combined for over 1,000 yards in total offence.

The victory launched the Riders on their biggest winning streak in years. They went on a four-game tear, starting with the win over B.C., followed by 44-0 shutout over the Montreal Alouettes, a 27-24 win over Winnipeg and a 23-7 win over Bob Shaw and the Argonauts.

The shutout win over Montreal was the Riders at their best. Gerhardt and linebacker Wayne Shaw had their best games of the season, shutting down Montreal's running game and smothering quarterback Bernie Faloney. Lancaster completed 13 of 14 passes for 219 yards, Campbell caught 11 passes, and Reed ran for 114 yards.

Against the Argos, Reed rose to the occasion against his old coach, Bob Shaw, rushing for 172 yards. Once again, Shaw had nothing to say. He kept the dressing room doors locked after the game and when they were opened, Shaw had slipped on to the Argo team bus.

It was almost too good to believe.

Actually, it was.

After they rang up four straight wins and sent the province into a state of delirious, unbridled joy, they hit a wall of sorts. The dreaded Eastern swing was up next on the schedule, two games on the road in three days. It turned into a nightmare of sorts.

They opened with a 29-7 loss to the defending Grey Cup champion Hamilton Tiger-Cats. With Joe Zuger enjoying a big night, the Ti-Cats jumped ahead early and never looked back. The game was costly to the Riders. Reed, Wayne Shaw and Benecick all were injured.

Two days later, they were in Ottawa to take on Russ Jackson and the Rough Riders. Saskatchewan limped to an 18-8 loss in a game that Keys labelled as a "courageous" one for his wounded warriors.

The Riders came back home to tie Winnipeg 11-11 and then lost 35-18 to Calgary in Taylor Field.

But there was no great concern. Injuries played a part in the Riders' skid, and if anybody was worried they were in a tailspin, it wasn't Eagle Keys.

With three games to go in the schedule, the Riders did what they had to do. They won two of them, a critical 22-21 win in B.C. that virtually nailed down first place in the Western Conference for them. They finished the season with a 28-26 road win over the Stampeders, and first place was theirs for the first time since 1951,

Photo courtesy of SSHFM

Al Benecick

Photo courtesy of *Leader-Post* archives

Wayne Shaw

Clyde Brock

Photo courtesy of *Leader-Post* archives

their last Grey Cup appearance. They finished with a 9-6-1 record in the tough Western Conference.

The season was highlighted by Hugh Campbell's 17 touchdown catches, a league record, Reed's 1,400-yard rushing season, and Lancaster's best passing year ever. He threw for almost 3,000 yards and 28 touchdowns.

There was little doubt that Keys and Preston had put together an extraordinary team. Lancaster and Reed escalated their games in 1966 and Campbell became the toughest receiver in Canadian football to stop. The offensive line of Ted Urness, Reggie Whitehouse, Jack Abendschan, Al Benecick and Clyde Brock was a force. Eddie Buchanan gave them breakaway speed at halfback. Gord Barwell was a game-breaker. The defence was tough with Ed McQuarters the anchor at tackle and Wally Dempsey everywhere at middle linebacker.

"I think one of the biggest things about that team was that we really believed in each other," remembered Lancaster years later. "We had good talent, and Eagle kept us focused. He told us that we weren't that good individually, but we were good when we played as a team. We were a close bunch, and we had a great belief in ourselves. And it was fun. If you're not having fun, why bother doing it?"

The Riders received a bye into the Western final in 1966 with the first game of the best-of-three Western final scheduled for Taylor Field. They were up against the Winnipeg Blue Bombers, who had beaten Edmonton 16-8 in the semi-final. The Riders knew they would have their hands full and they knew that had to get to quarterback Ken Ploen and control running back Dave Raimey.

Before a hometown crowd in a stadium that had not hosted a Western final since 1951, the Riders leaned heavily on their defence against the Bombers. McQuarters played his best game of the season since joining the Riders halfway through the schedule. He hounded Ploen mercilessly, even though he was double-teamed. Dempsey singlehandedly shut down the running game of Raimey, making incredible tackle after incredible tackle. And defensive back Bob Kosid intercepted two Ploen passes with his usual hell-bent-for-leather style of play. The Riders won the opener, 14-7, and now were just one win away from the Grey Cup game.

The buzz in Regina, indeed the whole province, was unlike anything ever witnessed here.

In a ferocious battle back in Winnipeg, two huge plays by the Riders made the difference. Ed Buchanan exploded for a 73-yard touchdown run. Then, Ed McQuarters scooped up a Ken Ploen fumble after Ploen was hit simultaneously by both Don Gerhardt and Ken Reed and McQuarters ran 50 yards for the touchdown.

The Riders went on to win, 21-19, and Saskatchewan was Grey Cup-bound.

Regina had never seen what transpired for the next week. The town was painted green from signs being put on front lawns to green and white streamers hanging off buildings. Christmas lights were turned on. There were Rider displays in the show windows of downtown stores. Fans were scrambling to get tickets to the Grey Cup game in Vancouver's Empire Stadium. Buses, trains and planes were booked as soon as tickets went on sale. Some drove to Vancouver. The fans had waited all their lives for this moment, and they wanted to be there.

Saskatchewan was up against Ottawa, and what a classic match-up this would be. Reed against Ottawa's Ron Stewart. Campbell against Whit Tucker. And, the marquee matchup? Lancaster vs. Jackson.

"You know, I never felt I had anything to prove to Russ or Frank Clair (Ottawa coach) in that game," said Lancaster years later. "It was just the way things worked out. I was the one who had to leave Ottawa and in the end it worked out for everybody. Russ had a great career and so did I and neither one of us had any regrets at all. As for the Grey Cup game, I wasn't worried about Russ. I was worried about us playing well and winning the game. That's all that mattered."

The game was played Saturday afternoon in Empire Stadium with 36,553 fans on hand. It was a cool, grey day. Ottawa was heavily favoured, so much so that CBC had set up its cameras in the Ottawa dressing room and that's where the cases of champagne were being chilled.

Photo courtesy of *Leader-Post* archives

Ed Buchanan

The streets in Regina went silent when the game came on television. House parties were everywhere. People had booked rooms in the city's hotels. I can remember Gord Currie, who 15 days earlier had coached the junior Regina Rams to a Canadian championship, joined myself, Ram players Bill Locke, Al Johnston, Richie Seitz, Mel Fiissel, Ken Newman and a few others. We had booked a room in the Holiday Inn, which is now the Seven Oaks.

The Riders had waited 56 years for this first Grey Cup victory. And, they weren't going to be denied. They'd played in eight previous Grey Cup games and were denied each time.

The eastern Riders were truly something special and the way the game started you thought maybe the fact they were eight-point favourites was justified. On Ottawa's fifth play of the game, Whit Tucker got behind Dale West and Jackson hit him for a 61-yard scoring play. But the Riders quickly rebounded when West intercepted Jackson at the Saskatchewan 50-yard line and returned the ball 51 yards. From six yards out, Lancaster found Jim Worden for the touchdown.

Saskatchewan took a 14-6 lead in the second quarter on an Al Ford touchdown, but Ottawa struck back, Tucker again getting behind West, this time for an explosive 85-yard touchdown. The teams were tied at halftime.

Two nights before the game, Winnipeg coach Bud Grant had predicted a Saskatchewan victory. "Eagle Keys' game preparation and ability to adjust will be the difference," Grant declared.

Photo courtesy of *Vancouver Sun*

George Reed's 31 yard touchdown run

Photo courtesy of *Vancouver Sun*

Eagle Keys

The Rider defence took over in the second half. They held Ottawa to just three first downs in the second half. The teams were still tied at 14-14 when they hit the fourth quarter. And, the game quickly became an all-Saskatchewan show.

From the Ottawa five, Lancaster threw a dart to Hugh Campbell for a touchdown. "If there was a turning point," said Rider defensive back Ted Dushinski, "that was it. It came when we were tied and Campbell caught that one in the end zone. We knew then we were on the way."

The game was wrapped up when Reed ran 31 yards up the middle for a touchdown. George finished the game with 133 yards rushing.

An explosion of emotion erupted in Empire Stadium as thousands of fans ran onto the field and back in Regina where fans poured from hotels and houses and headed downtown to celebrate in a four-hour-long horn-honking party that filled the Saturday night air.

The Riders themselves were stunned. Veteran punt returner Gene Wlasiuk broke down and sobbed in the dressing room. Geno was an outstanding punt returner, and, remember, he did it in the days when there was no blocking on punt returns. Dushinski wept. Reggie Whitehouse would end his career raising the Grey Cup. Reed sat in his stall, slouched forward. Once again, the pile-driving fullback had left nothing on the field.

"We never should have been eight-point underdogs," said Keys, who when the game ended said "I can't talk right now, I'm speechless."

"All week long, we heard about how good Ottawa was, how they were a super star team," said Reed. "We felt we were just as good and maybe a little bit better."

The victory celebrations didn't stop in Vancouver. When the Riders returned home Sunday night with the Grey Cup, they were met by thousands of fans in the Armoury on Elphinstone Street. There were speeches from Premier Ross Thatcher and Mayor Henry Baker.

The partying would go on all week. And why not? It was, after all, a party 56 years in the making.

And the long, cold Saskatchewan winter would not seem as long or as cold.

The winter went by swiftly. By the end of it, even after spring had turned into summer, and the Saskatchewan Roughriders had headed out to training camp, there was still this sense of elation in the air. After all, the Roughriders had never gone into a season defending a Grey Cup championship.

This would be Keys' third year as head coach and the nucleus of the club that had won the Grey Cup the year previous was basically intact. A little older, a little more experienced, a little stronger, and, hopefully, a little better.

A number of the players had settled into the community, choosing to buy homes, move their families here and get jobs. Lancaster was teaching and coaching at Central Collegiate and he and Bev had bought a home on

Emerald Park Road. It would be there that they would raise their three children, Lana, Ronnie David and Bob. Reed was selling beer for Molson's and living in Whitmore Park and it would be there that he and Angie would raise Keith, Georgette and Vicki. The players who stayed here spent a lot of time together in the off-season, and it brought them even closer.

"I always felt that the closeness of the players, which happened because they lived here, was a big part of our success in Saskatchewan," Keys would say. "They became a part of the community and because Regina was so small, the players couldn't help but get to understand how important the Roughriders were to the people of the province."

If the 1967 season was to serve as any sort of measuring stick to the success Keys and Ken Preston had in building this team, then they took big strides forward.

The Roughriders opened the season where they ended the last one, in Vancouver. With long-time CFLer Bernie Faloney quarterbacking the Lions, B.C. threw a scare into Saskatchewan by taking a 13-10 lead. But the Riders made some halftime adjustments that got their ground game going. They started to trap-block B.C.'s defensive line and it sprung Ed Buchanan loose for consecutive nine-yard gains on three plays. It seemed to turn the game around. The one thing about Lancaster, if he found something that worked, he would keep running it until the other team solved it.

Lancaster threw touchdown passes to Al Ford and Hugh Campbell and Saskatchewan opened with a 24-16 victory.

Less than a week later, the two teams were back in Taylor Field for the Riders' home opener. This time, the Rider defence gave Faloney no wiggle room while Lancaster got the Saskatchewan offence going. The Little General completed 13 of 16 passes for over 200 yards and Reed set the ground game alive with a 111-yard rushing show. The Riders won 36-13, but it was a costly win as tight end Jim Worden went down with a knee injury on the opening kickoff.

Two games. Two wins for the defending Grey Cup champs. An undefeated season, was that what was beckoning?

Not so fast. As they had the year before, the Calgary Stampeders snapped yet another Rider winning streak, welcoming Saskatchewan to Calgary with 36-10 spanking. It was the Pete Liske show. The Stampeder quarterback, who rewrote CFL passing records in his career, squashed a brief Rider comeback in the third quarter when Saskatchewan had pulled within six points of the lead. Liske promptly put together three touchdown drives and two of them were on long and sustained marches, including one that covered 102 yards.

McQuarters was the lone Rider to score a touchdown, this one coming on a 67-yard run after recovering a fumble.

Keys did not take this loss in stride. He was visibly upset after the game. "We had a few

Photo courtesy of SSHFM

Ed McQuarters

people that did nothing," he said. "You have to accept a loss sometimes, but not that way. We didn't make them work for that win."

The Riders obviously got the message.

They reacted to the loss and Eagle's spanking by going on a four-game winning streak. They began the streak with a shaky 24-18 victory at home over the Winnipeg Blue Bombers, a game that wasn't settled until the final seconds. It was vintage Lancaster. With time running out and on the short end of the scoreboard, Lancaster drove the Riders 82 yards in the final two minutes. The drive was launched with a 39-yard pass to Al Ford and ended when Lancaster dove into the end zone from a yard out with just 26 seconds left.

"We should have had this game won long before that, but we just didn't take advantage of all our chances," said Keys.

Next up were the Edmonton Eskimos, and the Riders came out firing rockets in a 20-10 victory.

"I'd like to say we lost because we made mistakes," said Eskimo coach Neill Armstrong. "But I can't because we were wiped out by the Roughrider defence." Dale West had a big night, laying on what were described as "vicious tackles." Ed Buchanan had a great night for the Riders, running for 132 yards. But, it was Saskatchewan's defence that was getting all the attention. They played their best game since the Grey Cup.

The Riders brought a record crowd of 21,673 to its feet at home to Edmonton, beating the Eskimos 18-6 for the first time in Taylor Field since 1964. Reed rushed for 101 yards and Lancaster became the Riders' all-time touchdown passer with two TD tosses to Campbell.

The dynasty had arrived, and was gaining steam.

Next up was a rematch of the 1966 Grey Cup combatants. Before another record crowd of 21,696, the Roughriders were way too much for Russ Jackson and the Ottawa Rough Riders, rolling to an exciting 32-23 victory, their fourth in a row. Buchanan had another big game, slashing for 132 yards and Reed added another 71. Lancaster hurt his ankle in the first quarter, which limited how much he could move around. But the ground game excelled.

And so did the fans. Ottawa coach Frank Clair was not amused by the Taylor Field crowd. The Professor remarked, "Yes, I guess that was a good game for the fans, but the fans don't deserve it. That's the most unsportsmanlike conduct I've seen and the CFL should have rules stopping the shouting when a team is calling signals. We never scored a point once those buzzards started screeching."

Taylor Field crowds were notorious for their, ah, rabid support of the Roughriders. When the fans were allowed to sit on the sidelines, opposing players who wandered out of bounds did so at their own peril.

Taylor Field crowds were notorious for their, ah, rabid support of the Roughriders. When the fans were allowed to sit on the sidelines, opposing players who wandered out of bounds did so at their own peril. And, the especially vocally gifted Rider fans always seemed to find their way to seats directly behind the visiting team's bench. There was a certain element of personality involved in being a Rider fan.

The Riders' win streak was stopped in Winnipeg by the Bombers, who won 17-16 when they stopped a third down Saskatchewan gamble and turned it into a short drive for the winning touchdown by quarterback Billy Van Burkleo, who was replacing the injured Ken Ploen.

"We've had some great moments on this club, but this wasn't one of them," said Keys.

In what turned into an aerial show with Liske and Lancaster trading bombs, the Riders' next game against Calgary was decided by a safety touch when Liske was tackled in the end zone by Wayne Shaw and Ron Atchison for the margin of victory in 28-27 Saskatchewan victory. Liske completed 21 of 31 for 351 yards while Lancaster was good on 13 of 21 for 248 yards. There was another Taylor Field record crowd of 22,038 on hand. The game ended on a bizarre note. Calgary's Larry Robinson was wide with what would have been the winning field. Al Ford tried to soccer kick the ball out, but whiffed. Gene Wlasiuk rushed over, picked it up and managed to kick it out of the end zone. The ball rolled 90 yards before Robinson got to it. There was nothing he could do with it.

Next up was the eastern swing. The Riders opened in Toronto with a 17-15 win in a game in which they never trailed. The Argos controlled Saskatchewan's running game, but they couldn't handle the Rider defence and that was the difference.

The Roughriders took over sole possession of first place in the West with a 22-12 win in Montreal, running their record to 9-2, the best in the CFL.

They came home to Taylor Field riding their second significant winning streak of the season and despite some nagging injuries were poised to keep it going when the Hamilton Tiger-Cats roared into town. Lancaster put together another fourth-quarter game-winning drive, this one covering 52 yards, and ending when Ford scored from a yard out for a 22-21 Saskatchewan victory. Reed had his best game of the season, rushing for 182 yards on 31 carries. Barwell had a big game with five catches for 97 yards and a touchdown. The Taylor Field crowd of 21,405 wiped its collective forehead, and went home to be left limp by yet another electrifying Roughrider comeback.

In Edmonton, the Roughriders again found themselves trailing on the scoreboard. And Lancaster responded, sort of. He did lead them on an 88-yard touchdown drive which cut Edmonton's lead 21-17. But there wasn't enough time left on the clock for another comeback as the Eskimos got the ball with a couple of minutes left and simply ran out the clock.

The Riders closed out their season by dropping their next game to Calgary, 19-11, before finishing with back to back victories, 24-14 over B.C. and 24-14 over Winnipeg.

They ended up finishing in second place in the West with a 12-4 record. But, even though first place eluded them, they went into the playoffs as the team to beat. The Stampeders finished first, Saskatchewan second, and Edmonton came in third.

The Riders opened the playoffs at home to the Eskimos in the semi-final. The Eskimos had won seven of their last nine games,

Photo courtesy of SSHFM

Gord Barwell

Photo courtesy of Wyatt Photography

Jack Abendschan

and represented a scary opponent for Saskatchewan. But, the Riders rode a 150-yard rushing game from Reed, a big defensive performance and a late Jack Abendschan field goal to a 21-5 victory. "We stopped the guy everybody said was on Edmonton's side," said Rider assistant coach Jack Gotta. "We stopped Mo Mentum."

It put the Riders into the Western final against Calgary, a best-of-three affair in which Calgary had the extra home game. It would come to that.

In a bruising battle, which saw players from both teams carted off the field, the Stampeders prevailed 15-11 in the opener to move within one game of a Grey Cup berth. Back in Saskatchewan on Wednesday night for the second game, the tide turned against Calgary.

One play seemed to settle the series. Calgary's great wide receiver, Canadian Terry Evanshen had already caught five passes when he cut across the middle searching out another Peter Liske pass. Evanshen snared the pass on a slippery field. He was hit by four Roughriders, one of whom had a hold of his leg. When he went down, he heard something snap. "I knew I had broken my leg," said Evanshen. He had. He was done for the season. And, so were the Stampeders. That injury took the life out of them. The Riders went on to win 11-9.

The game ended on a sour note, though. On the last play of the game, Lancaster took the snap from centre and knelt down. Reed had been knocked to the turf as he stepped up to block. From the side came Calgary defensive tackle Don Luzzi. Luzzi came in slowly, and then dove helmet first into Reed's exposed back. George would be helped off the field with injured ribs.

They headed back to Calgary for the third and deciding game. But Evanshen's loss seemed to take the sting out of the Stampeder offence and in a game that was likely closer than the final score indicated, the Roughriders won 17-13 and they were off to the Grey Cup for the second year in a row.

It was becoming old hat for them, these Grey Cup trips.

The dynasty rolled into Ottawa's Lansdowne Park to take on the Eastern champion, the Hamilton Tiger-Cats, who had labelled themselves The Beasts from The East. They were.

If Saskatchewan's Grey Cup win over Ottawa a year earlier was exhilarating, this game was equally as deflating. The Roughriders were never in it, for whatever reasons. The game seemed to hinge on one play. Lancaster called Buchanan's number on a pass play over the middle of the Ti-Cat secondary. The play unfolded as it was drawn up. Lancaster dropped back into the pocket. The protection was good. Buchanan streaked up the middle and broke into the clear. Lancaster put the ball in the air. It was a perfect pass, the ball spinning out of the sky and right into Buchanan's out-stretched hands. Lancaster couldn't have thrown a more perfect pass. Buchanan dropped it.

Lancaster put the ball in the air. It was a perfect pass, the ball spinning out of the sky and right into Buchanan's out-stretched hands. Lancaster couldn't have thrown a more perfect pass. Buchanan dropped it.

Whenever anybody talks about the 1967 Grey Cup game, that's the only play they talk about. The Riders were hammered 24-1.

They were back in "Next Year" country.

But they would have to do it without the incomparable Garner Ekstran on their defence. Ekstran had come to the Riders from Washington State in 1961 and played defensive end and linebacker through the 1967 season. He was a dominating figure every time he put on the green and white, capable of turning a game around with his quickness and his toughness. He wasn't a big man. In fact, his voice was bigger than he was. You could hear Garner talking across town and you hear his laugh from one end of the province to the other.

Garner finished off his CFL career in 1968 with the B.C. Lions. But, his heart never left the Roughriders. In fact, to this day, he often will drive from his home in Washington to visit old friends in Regina.

"Garner was probably one of the toughest guys I ever played with or against," Lancaster said.

Ekstran was a four-time Western Conference all-star and a three-time All-Canadian.

It would not be an easy chore replacing him as the Riders headed into the winter and got ready for the 1968 season.

Ed Buchanan was also gone from the 1968 team as was Geno Wlasiuk, who also had packed it in, ending a wonderful career as both a defensive back and outstanding punt returner.

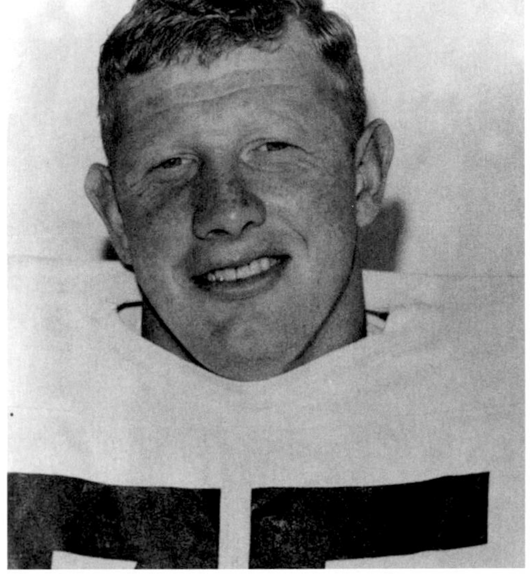
Garner Ekstran

And for Ron Atchison, this would be his final season of play. He had joined the Riders in 1952 from the junior Saskatoon Hilltops and his career lasted 18 years. He played for eight different coaches. He was an all-star. He was on a Grey Cup winner. And he was one of the most feared defensive linemen in the league, for a number of reasons, but mostly his tenacity. A gentle man off the field, Big Atch turned tiger when he hit the turf. And, he was tough. One year, he broke his arm, so they put a plaster cast on it, and he played with that. "It was kinda good," he said, "because I could club guys with it." There were a lot of complaints about how Atch used that cast as a sledgehammer, but there were no rules against it.

And, then there was the night Big Atch gained the stuff of legends. The Riders were playing the Calgary Stampeders in a game at Taylor Field. The field was covered in a sheet of ice. And, footing was treacherous. So, Atch took off his football cleats and put on his ordinary pair of Hush Puppies. It worked, this moment of genius. He was the only player on the field who wasn't sliding all over the place. "Yeah," recalled Atch, "that was quite a deal. I got a bunch of free Hush Puppies out of it."

"You never had to worry about Atch showing up for games," said Eagle Keys. "He was always there ready to play."

"He was one tough son of a gun," remembered Ron Lancaster. "I mean, he was tough."

Atch wanted 1968, his last year, to be a special year. He knew the Roughriders had a team capable of finishing in first place and he knew they had a team capable of going to the Grey Cup for the third straight year.

The Riders knew the only thing standing between them and the Grey Cup could be found across the vast prairie land of Saskatchewan and Alberta. Nestled in the foothills of Alberta, up against the Rocky Mountains, could be found the Calgary Stampeders. Head coach Jerry Williams had built a passing attack the likes of which the CFL had never before seen. It centred around quarterback Pete Liske and featured the sensational Terry Evanshen, a mighty mite of a receiver, and Herman Harrison, one of the greatest tight ends in the history of the game.

The Riders felt they had a more balanced attack. They had Reed, of course, who was coming off another all-Canadian season. And they replaced Buchanan with Silas McKinnie, who not only was a slippery kind of running back but could also catch the ball.

Wally Dempsey

Photo courtesy of *Leader-Post* archives

Both teams boasted strong defences. Calgary's defence was anchored by Wayne Harris, perhaps the greatest middle linebacker to play the game in Canada, while Saskatchewan had Wally Dempsey in the middle and Ed McQuarters running free at defensive tackle.

The table, then, was set. Let the football feast begin.

The Riders opened the season in Calgary against the Stampeders, the first of a couple of Titanic-like battles these two would wage against each other in 1968. The game came down to the final minutes, which was no surprise. And, when Larry Robinson missed a 31-yard field goal by three feet, the Riders slipped out of town with a 25-24 victory. Larry Robinson did not always miss game-winning field goal tries, as Rider fans would come to know.

The game stuck to the menu. The Stampeders only ran the ball 13 times while Liske threw 35 passes, completing 25 of them for 419 yards and three touchdowns. Lancaster only threw 17 passes, but their ground game was effective with Reed running for 67 yards and McKinnie for 63. And Evanshen had come back from his broken leg of last year's playoffs by catching 10 passes for 162 yards and a touchdown.

The game was on, and football fans in Saskatchewan were in for a treat of a season.

The Riders won their first two games, whacking Winnipeg 27-8 before getting tied 10-10 by Edmonton and then losing two straight, 37-23 to Ottawa and 9-3 to Hamilton. Then, as had become their habit, they settled into a five-game winning streak. In order, they beat Toronto and new coach Leo Cahill 32-17, hammered Edmonton 29-2, outlasted B.C. 14-8, whipped Winnipeg 31-3 and nipped B.C. 16-12.

Then came the second showdown of the season with the Stampeders, again in Calgary. In a game for the ages, the big guns on both teams let it all hang out, and the defences were essentially left helpless to defend against this offensive explosion.

Liske had a career day, firing 39 passes and completing 29 of them for 553 yards. Tight end Herm Harrison caught 11 for 237 yards and Terry Evanshen caught three touchdown passes.

The Riders answered. Lancaster completed 12 of 22 for 240 yards. Reed had a huge running day, gaining 149 yards.

In the end, it all came down to the fourth quarter and usually in those situations, he who has the ball last wins. The Stampeders stopped Reed and the Riders on a third-down gamble that set up a Pete Liske to Rick Shaw 66-yard touchdown pass that gave the Stampeders a 38-35 victory.

It was a game of cat and mouse between Wayne Harris and George Reed when the two collided. Earlier in the game, the Riders caught Harris blitzing and Reed exploded through the hole for a 68-yard run that set up a Lancaster touchdown. On the third-down gamble, it was Harris who made the play.

It was a game of cat and mouse between Wayne Harris and George Reed when the two collided. Earlier in the game, the Riders caught Harris blitzing and Reed exploded through the hole for a 68-yard run that set up a Lancaster touchdown. On the third-down gamble, it was Harris who made the play.

The victory gave the Stampeders a one-point cushion over the Riders in the race for first place, Calgary sitting at 8-3, the Riders at 7-3-1.

Then, the Roughriders went on a tear. They won their last five games, the second five-game winning streak of the season. They beat Montreal 11-7, Calgary 19-15, Winnipeg 24-7, Edmonton 34-20 and closed off the regular schedule with a 12-6 win over B.C.

The Roughriders actually clinched first place with their victory over Edmonton and it was George Reed Night all over again. Yes, they let George do it. There have been very few football players in North America who were as capable of responding to big moments as often as George did in his storied 13-year career, or for as long. On this night, George scored four touchdowns and rushed for 140 yards.

Photo courtesy of Solilo Studios

Jack Abendschan (53) leads the blocking for George Reed (34)

The 1968 season would another banner year for Reed. He picked up 78 yards in the last game of the schedule in Vancouver as the Riders dumped the Lions. It gave Reed 1,223 yards and the CFL's rushing title, three yards better than B.C.'s Jim Evenson. Reed made up a 19-yard deficit on the game's final three plays.

The Roughriders went into the playoffs on an absolute high. They were as good as they'd ever been, and figured they could get better. And they knew the Stampeders would be their likely opponents.

With winter showing signs of arriving, the Riders went back to practice, enjoying a two-week break, but itching to get back on the field of play. The practice field had turned hard, and much of the grass had been worn off. This was fall football conditions.

For years, the Riders dressing room was housed under the grandstand at the race track in the exhibition grounds. The practice field was on the infield of the racetrack, and players regularly had to dodge the horses who were working out. For rookies, this would result in a lot of close calls.

"Nothing ever came easy for this football team," Lancaster recalled. "Our dressing room was crappy, the practice field was dangerous with all those horses running around. But it was fun."

When the Stampeders hammered the Eskimos 29-13 in the semi-final, the mood changed within the Rider dressing room. Now, they knew that the only thing standing between them and the Grey Cup game was Pete Liske and Wayne Harris and the rest of the Stampeders.

Getting a two-week break may not have been the best thing to happen to the Riders. Some coaches like it because it gives the players a chance to heal. But when you are on a five-game winning streak and have clinched first place, you are anxious to play. You can

Photo courtesy of *Leader-Post* archives

Bobby Thompson

lose your edge, whether you know it or not. And, that's pretty well what happened to the Roughriders.

They were easy pickings for the Stampeders in the best-of-three Western final, never really regaining the momentum they had built up throughout the season. The Stamps won the opener 32-0 in Taylor Field, and closed the Riders out with a 25-12 win at home to go to the Grey Cup game.

Calgary would lose to Ottawa, 24-21, and Saskatchewan would go back to the drawing board and try to figure out a way to end the growing playoff jinx.

The winds of change were blowing across Western Canada as the 1969 Canadian Football League season approached.

And it would change for the better for the Saskatchewan Roughriders, who simply kept improving each year under the tandem of Ken Preston and Eagle Keys.

In Calgary, the Stampeders would undergo an off-season shakeup that rocked the team to its very foundation. Coach Jerry Williams left to become head coach of the Philadelphia Eagles of the National Football League. And, quarterback Pete Liske would sign with the Denver Broncos of the AFL. Just like that, Calgary's offence had gone from outstanding to mediocre. The Stampeders would ultimately pull defensive back Jerry Keeling to replace Liske at quarterback. And, they hired Jim Duncan from the Riders to take the place of Williams.

The Roughriders brought in another running back to go with George Reed and Silas McKinnie in Bobby Thompson, a speedster who would make a big impression. And, they started the season with a four-game winning streak that immediately set them apart from the rest of the Western Conference.

But, the season opened on a note of some controversy and much hilarity. In the aftermath of Saskatchewan's 22-20 win over the B.C. Lions in a rowdy Taylor Field, the Lions were still snarling days later. So much so that they issued a formal protest to CFL commissioner Jake Gaudaur.

> "That's the trouble with those football people down in Regina," wrote *Vancouver Sun* columnist Denny Boyd. "They don't just kill the visitors ... they loot the bodies."

The Lions' protest was based on officiating, a time clock that broke down, sideline telephones that wouldn't work and the fence that surrounded the end zones at Taylor Field.

B.C.'s Craig Murray crashed into the fence trying to cover Riders' Hugh Campbell and initially looked as if he was seriously injured. It turned out he was just shaken up, but everybody agree the fence had to be padded, or, better still, taken out before somebody did get seriously hurt.

"Great!" exclaimed Lions' coach Jim Champion when he heard the fence would be gone. "The Riders have figured out that a fence like that can kill people. That's probably the greatest discovery Saskatchewan has made since potash."

Champion also suggested the Riders have telephone repairmen on hand, with badges on, so coaches would know who to go to when sideline phones were not working.

"Preston should try using the phones even without the crowd noise and see if he can hear anything," snarled Champion.

"That's the trouble with those football people down in Regina," wrote *Vancouver Sun* columnist Denny Boyd. "They don't just kill the visitors ... they loot the bodies. They've got a six-bit clock that doesn't work and a fence that'll probably kill somebody before they move it. They've got howling whiskey-drinking fans that hover right over the sidelines and intimidate players and officials ...

"In fact, a referee named Taylor Paterson was shot in the face with a BB gun pellet while working a game in Barnyard Stadium."

Well, what did the B.C. people expect? Taylor Field has never been known as a hospitable place for visiting teams. You can look it up.

And the beat went on. After coming back from a 16-point deficit to beat the befuddled Lions, the Riders edged Edmonton 21-20, stomped the new-look Stampeders 24-8 and took out the Eskimos 21-20. The only Western team they hadn't played was Winnipeg and the Bombers responded to Saskatchewan's surge by nipping them 16-14 to end the Riders' win streak.

The Riders rebounded with another win over B.C., this time by a 32-14 count. Six games into the season, and the Riders had established that in Reed, McKinnie and Thompson, they had a running game that was second to none in the CFL. And Campbell, Barwell and Worden gave the Riders plenty of balance in their passing attack. Worden also had established himself as one of the great blocking tight ends.

"Nobody on defence ever wanted to have to line up across from Jim Worden," recalled Lancaster. "Not just because he was a great blocker, but because you never knew when he was going to throw up. Yeah, he would get down in his stance and the next thing you knew, he had thrown up all over the guy across from him."

After B.C., the Riders headed out on their eastern swing, two games in three days. They opened in Toronto where the Argos were the hottest team in the East, bringing a five-game winning streak with them against Saskatchewan. Leo Cahill, one of the true coaching characters in CFL history, had assembled a bunch of castoffs from other teams. He had Wally Gabler at quarterback, Dave Raimey at halfback, Mel Profit at tight end. In a game in which the officiating didn't endear itself to the Riders, the Argos rolled to a 34-15 victory, and the Riders headed for Montreal to face Sonny Wade and the Alouettes.

Photo courtesy of *Leader-Post* archives

Jim Worden

The Als were no match for Saskatchewan. Even though the Rider offence turned in a lacklustre performance, Saskatchewan still left town with 27-8 victory. They came back to play the Hamilton Tiger-Cats. The Ti-Cats beat them 31-29 when a Jack Abendschan kick was blocked. "The snap was high and Ronnie had to stand up to get it," said Abendschan. "It threw off my timing."

The Roughriders got back on the winning streak in their next game against the Stampeders in Calgary. Although Reed ran for over 100 yards, it was the defence that sealed the 31-12 win, recovering six Stampeder fumbles and intercepting two Jerry Keeling passes.

That game would launch the Roughriders on a seven-game season-ending winning streak as they knocked off first one then another pretender to their throne. The Roughriders finished the season in first place with a 13-3 record, their best record since Keys took over as head coach.

In his first season as head coach and having to rebuild the key components of the offence, Duncan got the Stampeders to a second place finish in the West. Keeling started to come on in the latter part of the season. But, it was the defence that made Calgary tough. They still had Wayne Harris anchoring the middle, Frank Andruski had developed into one the top cornerbacks in the league and John Helton would become one of the greatest defensive tackles in the history of the CFL.

So, when the Stampeders beat the B.C. Lions 35-21 in the semi-final, the Riders knew they would be challenged.

The best-of-three Western final opened in Taylor Field and it took a huge effort by the Roughriders to turn back the Stampeders 17-11. Jerry Keeling had his best passing game of the season, throwing 25 completions in 43 attempts for 408 yards. But he also coughed up three interceptions, which hurt.

The Roughriders needed a big goal-line stand, 11 points from Jack Abendschan and a fourth-quarter touchdown by Bobby Thompson to open the playoffs with a crucial win. Lancaster threw the ball 20 times, but he completed just eight. The goal-line stand saw Calgary back Rudy Linterman stopped by Ken Frith and Wayne Shaw and then Keeling stuffed by almost the whole Rider defensive line.

Photo courtesy of SSHFM

Cliff Shaw

Photo courtesy of SSHFM

Gary Brandt

The Riders headed to Calgary for Game 2. And, it didn't start off well. Right off the bat, the Roughriders lost all-Canadian centre Ted Urness when he took a blow to the head. Keys moved guard Gary Brandt to centre and Cliff Shaw went in as a guard. The two played tremendously well.

The Riders rolled over the Stampeders with relative ease, grounding Calgary with a 36-13 stomping. Keeling was intercepted three times as the Riders erupted for 24 points in the second half.

And once again, the Riders were off to the Grey Cup game for the third time since Keys became head coach.

And for the second time since Eagle took over, they were no match for their opposition. It was the Ottawa Rough Riders who would be prevail, 29-11 in Montreal's Autostade on a bitterly cold day in the first Sunday Grey Cup game ever.

The Roughriders got off to a good start, opening with a safety touch and then a 27-yard Lancaster to Ford touchdown pass for a 9-0 lead. Saskatchewan decided to blitz Ottawa quarterback Russ Jackson all day, but Jackson easily fended it off, either by running the ball himself or getting rid of it quickly. In all, Jackson threw four touchdown passes. It was his final game in the CFL and he left with a new car after being named the Grey Cup's most valuable player.

The season had ended for Saskatchewan, a season so full of promise, so full of hope, and so full of accomplishment.

The beginning of a new decade would mark the end of an era for the Saskatchewan Roughriders.

As the Saskatchewan Roughriders prepared for the start to the 1970 season, they were haunted by past playoff and Grey Cup failures. Those defeats all resounded through the province with a mean sting to them. But, for the team itself, their resolve grew even stronger. They still had the main core of the dynasty intact. Ron Lancaster was still there, so was George Reed and the offensive line that was the best in the league remained. The defence stood as Saskatchewan's version of the Great Wall of China.

Little did they know that the 1970 season would represent the best of times and the worst of times. Stuff happens, but it seemed to happen too many times to the greatest football dynasty the Saskatchewan Roughriders ever fielded.

The Roughriders opened the season by winning seven of their nine first games, and then they went on a tear that saw them run the table. They won their last seven games to finish in first place and establish the best won-lost record the franchise had ever known (14-2).

The Roughriders served notice in the first game that they were not to be messed with. They went into Empire Stadium in Vancouver and the first game ever in the West that was played on artificial turf. The Riders took to the new turf with great glee, enjoying the sure footing it gave them until rain began to fall and the field turned slick. But, it didn't really slow down the Riders as they won 42-9. Silas McKinnie scored three touchdowns for Saskatchewan and Lancaster, who had been bothered by a sore arm heading into the game, was as efficient as he could be.

Photo courtesy of *Leader-Post*

Silas McKinnie

The Riders played their home opener on a Friday night against the Edmonton Eskimos, whose defence had been rebuilt to the point where it was one of the stronger ones in the league. But, it was Saskatchewan's defence and Jack Abendschan's foot that made the difference. Abendschan tied a CFL record with five field goals in a 17-point night as the Riders turned back the Eskimos 23-11.

The Riders headed out on their eastern swing, a trip that wasn't always kind to them. But they survived it quite nicely, thank you. They opened with a 23-22 win in Hamilton over the Tiger-Cats when Silas McKinnie turned a swing pass from Lancaster into a thrilling 90-yard touchdown.

Three days later, they were in Ottawa, and they easily trumped the rebuilding Rough Riders 24-1.

The Roughriders came home to play Calgary. George Reed did not play because of a knee injury suffered in Ottawa, and it did hurt the Riders' ground game. But Calgary's Jerry Keeling and the Stampeder pass rush on Lancaster were likely the two major reasons the Riders suffered their first loss of the season, a 30-0 shutout. Keeling shredded the Rider defence with an on-the-money short passing game that Saskatchewan just couldn't handle. And the Calgary front four was all over Lancaster from start to finish.

The Roughriders went into Calgary just over a week later vowing that this time things would be different. And, they were. The Riders had the game well in hand when Calgary mounted a fourth-quarter comeback that produced 14 points. It took a late Henry Dorsch interception of a Keeling pass to seal a 21-17 Saskatchewan victory. The Riders would rack up victories over Toronto and Winnipeg before losing only their second game of the season, 10-6 to Edmonton.

The Riders were definitely banged up. Lancaster had been nursing a sore arm since the season began and wasn't even throwing in practice. Both Reed and McKinnie were playing on sore knees. "You never know for sure how injuries will affect a player," Keys said. "Ronnie was underthrowing guys, and maybe it's because his timing is off."

Still, to show the resolve of Saskatchewan's tenacity, the Riders never lost another game the rest of the way. Their fast finish gave them a bye into the best-of-three Western final. And they would end up going against the Stampeders.

The Riders had the extra home game if it went the distance, and, indeed it would.

The Stampeders of Jim Duncan were a solid bunch and Jerry Keeling had established himself at quarterback. He had an excellent receiving corps in Gerry Shaw, Rudy Linterman, Dave Cranmer and Herman Harrison and a great running back in Hugh McKinnis. The defence was as nasty as ever.

The Stampeders stunned the Riders and the Taylor Field crowd in the opening game of the Western final by romping to a 28-11 victory. Keeling passed for over 230 yards while Lancaster didn't even get 100 yards in the air.

"We had a great regular season," said Keys, "but when the playoffs come around, it's an entirely new season. The Stampeders were just a better team today."

The Stampeders weren't sure how they would fare going into Saskatchewan for the opening game. When they won, their confidence soared and they couldn't wait for the second game, a Wednesday night in McMahon Stadium.

It turned into one of the hardest-hitting, most viciously fought games either Duncan or Keys had even seen, and the game turned on a brilliant 87-yard fumble recovery for a touchdown by McQuarters as the Riders won 11-3.

It turned into one of the hardest-hitting, most viciously fought games either Duncan or Keys had even seen, and the game turned on a brilliant 87-yard fumble recovery for a touchdown by McQuarters as the Riders won 11-3.

But the price the Riders paid for the victory was steep. They lost tight end Nolan Bailey with a knee injury. Worse, Ron Lancaster was nailed by Calgary defensive end Dick Suderman. "I saw him coming," Lancaster said. "But I was twisted around and couldn't protect myself. When he hit me, I couldn't breathe and I had trouble standing up. I don't know how it is."

Lancaster had suffered cracked ribs. His status for the deciding game back in Regina on Saturday was up in the air.

At the time, I was covering the Stampeders for the Calgary *Albertan*. On the plane ride to Regina for the third game, I was sitting with Calgary's tough defensive end Craig Koinzan. He knew that Lancaster and I were good friends from my days in Regina. Craig leaned over to me, and said, "Tell your little buddy that I'm going to take a shot at his ribs the first chance I get."

I got off the plane and Lancaster was waiting for me. As we were driving downtown, I told Ronnie what Koinzan had said. "Yeah, that won't surprise me," Lancaster said with that crooked grin of his. He knew what was coming.

I ran into Eagle Keys the day before the game. "Well, we're going to start Ronnie, that's the only way he'll have it," said Keys. "If he can walk, he wants to play. But I don't know how long he'll last."

Game day dawned wrapped in a Saskatchewan winter storm. The wind was howling and the wind chill temperature was well into the minus 30s. It was freezing, and there was no way to keep warm.

In the Rider dressing room, Dr. Jim Chatwin was inserting a needle filled with painkiller into Lancaster's side. You could have heard a pin drop in the Saskatchewan dressing room as Lancaster grimaced. Across the way, Craig Koinzan sat in his locker, in full uniform, and stared at the floor.

Tensions were high as the game started. Lancaster came onto the field for the first Rider series. He was moving as if he was in pain. The wind was whipping into every player down there. Lancaster came up over the ball. Koinzan dropped into a three-point stance. He drew back his right leg and planted the foot into the frozen Taylor Field turf. He was lined up at right defensive end. He would be coming at Lancaster from the back side. Lancaster took the snap, and dropped back. He brought his arm up and then through, and released the ball. My eyes never left Koinzan. He kept coming. As he neared Lancaster, his head dropped. Lancaster now saw him, but it was too late. Koinzan buried his helmet into Lancaster's side. Ronnie went down as if he had been shot. He was done for the day. And somebody named Gary Lane would quarterback the rest of the way. "You know, I didn't take any pleasure in doing that to Lancaster," said Koinzan. "But this was the playoffs and we knew what he was capable of." Koinzan was flagged for rough play.

The game ended on a bizarre note. Because of the weather, neither team really had much success moving the ball. But the Stampeders somehow found a way late in the fourth quarter. Keeling and McKinnis hooked up on a brilliant swing pass that set up Larry Robinson for a last-second field goal from 32 yards out. There seemed no way he could make it, not with that wind. Robinson hit the ball solidly, sending it about 20 yards wide of the north end goalposts. It seemed likely to be sailing wide. Then, the wind grabbed it and carried it through the goal posts, sending Calgary to the Grey Cup with a 15-14 victory.

There seemed no way he could make it, not with that wind. Robinson hit the ball solidly, sending it about 20 yards wide of the north end goalposts. It seemed likely to be sailing wide. Then, the wind grabbed it and carried it through the goal posts, sending Calgary to the Grey Cup with a 15-14 victory.

The Riders were stunned. They were angered because they thought Lane had scored a touchdown on a one-yard plunge, but the officials didn't see it that way. Keys alluded to how tough it was to win without Lancaster. And Duncan was virtually speechless. Robinson later would tell me, "I could try that kick in these conditions 100 times and never make one."

Indeed, the end to the season also marked the end of the Eagle Keys era in Saskatchewan. It wasn't really surprising. Eagle's long-time buddy Jackie Parker had been coaching in B.C. When Lions' general manager Denny Veitch left, Parker was named general manager. Everybody knew who he would go after for his head coach.

The phone rang in Ken Preston's office.

"Ken, it's Jackie Parker. I'd like permission from the Roughriders to talk to Eagle Keys."

Preston wanted no part of this. But what could he do? He gave the Lions permission, but he told them it would come with a cost. Although Keys was perfectly happy in Regina, he loved Vancouver, the mountains and the ocean and Jackie Parker. He took the job, for more money of course. But the B.C. Lions had to give the Roughriders $20,000 in compensation.

That was a lot of money in those days, but it did little to weaken the impact of Eagle Keys' departure from Saskatchewan.

The Stampeders, meanwhile, went to the Grey Cup a wounded bunch. The three-game series with Saskatchewan had taken everything out of them, especially the last game. Players such as defensive tackle John Helton had split open the skin on their fingers from frostbite. The Stampeders were easy prey for the Montreal Alouettes, losing 23-10 in the Grey Cup game in Toronto.

The Roughriders did not have to go far to find a successor for Keys. On December 29th of 1970, they announced that Dave Skrien would be the new head coach. Keys had hired Skrien as an assistant when Jim Duncan left to take over as head coach in Calgary.

Skrien had an impressive background. He had been a head coach with the B.C. Lions for six years, getting them to two Grey Cups and winning once. He had been named the CFL's coach-of-the-year. And because he had served as an assistant in Saskatchewan, he knew the players and they knew him. It was not an easy transition because the players loved Keys. But, it wasn't that tough of a transition, either, because they respected Skrien.

It wasn't that he was taking over a team in need of a major repair job. In fact, Skrien had landed at the centre of the dynasty when it seemed to be at its zenith. The year before, the Riders had gone 14-2. Lancaster had been named the outstanding player of the year and won his first Schenley Award. Lancaster and Reed were entering their ninth seasons with the Riders and Lancaster was in his t12th year in the CFL. How much better could it get for any new head coach?

Lancaster and Reed had formed perhaps the most powerful tandem in CFL history. Reed was well on his way to becoming the most productive running back in pro football history. And Lancaster was erasing passing records on his way to a career that would take a long time to be matched.

When he was out of football, Eagle once told me, "You know, when I had Ronnie and George, they said I was a great coach. It's not all that hard to be a great coach when you have those two. When I didn't have them, I'm not sure people thought I was such a great coach."

Photo courtesy of SSHFM

Ron Lancaster (23), George Reed (34) and Clyde Brock (67)

"When you have a fullback like George," Lancaster said, "it makes everything else work. Defences have to respect him, and that opens up the passing game. And when George was on, he could control a whole game all by himself. There were times, though, when I wondered if I was going to kill him out there. We would have drives where he would carry the ball almost every play, and he was as strong at the end of it as he was when we started out. I remember one game, we had about a 15- or 16-play drive. George carried the ball every time. I remember him coming back to the huddle near the end of the drive. There were tears coming out his eyes. Blood was coming out his nose and mouth. He had that glazed look. I didn't know if he could any further. 'George,' I said, 'are you OK?' He just looked at me as if to say, 'How the hell do you think I am?' So, I called his number again and he took it into the end zone. Man, I don't know how he did it."

Reed endured so much punishment in his career, it is absolutely amazing he lasted 13 years. He played with broken bones. He played with wounded knees. There were times after games when he passed blood. For 13 straight seasons, something always hurt.

"He was one of the toughest guys I ever saw," long-time Rider trainer Sandy Archer said. "You could never tell if George was hurt because it would take him forever to get off the ground and get back to the huddle. But once that ball was snapped, it was something to see."

Photo courtesy of SSHFM

George Reed

Photo courtesy of SSHFM

George Reed

It is legendary stuff that during his career Reed, whose thighs measured 29 inches around, broke the arms of two defensive players who made the mistake of trying to arm tackle him.

They said Reed's pain threshold was among the highest you would find anywhere. One year, George dislocated a big toe, which is one of the most painful injuries you could have, especially for a running back. Reed should have sat out for a couple of games to heal it. But he wouldn't. What happened was one of the most excruciating scenes you could imagine. Before every game, the team's medical staff would take a large needle and push it into the joint of the big toe.

"The pain from putting that needle into him was awful," recalled Sandy Archer. "There were times it brought tears to George's eyes. And, if you had trouble getting the needle in, and had to wiggle it around, it was even more painful."

The procedure was done before every game, and at halftime.

He played six games in 1970 with a broken bone in his leg.

George had a great sense of humour too. I can recall going out to training camp one year at the university in June. It was a cold, blustery day, and nobody really was enjoying themselves. George came running over to me, yelling "Hughes! Hughes! Come over here, you're not going to believe this."

I went over to him and said, "What do you want George?"

He held out his right arm, and exclaimed, "Look! Look! I'm turning white!" That deep laugh of his rolled out. I looked at his arm. It was covered in goose bumps, and, indeed they were white.

When you look back on his career, and his life, it is to marvel. He lasted 13 seasons, retiring at the end of the 1975 season. In his last season, he carried the ball 323 times, gained 1,454 yards and scored 11 touchdowns. He was named to the CFL's all-star team nine times. He won the Schenley Award as the outstanding player once. He's been inducted into every Hall of Fame he was eligible for. In 1973, the province declared October 9th as George Reed Day in Saskatchewan. His career stats show he gained 16,116 yards, scored 134 touchdowns rushing and three more on receptions.

Nobody was more involved in the community. George hooked up with Special Olympics for years, and it was a genuine thing with him. He started the George Reed Foundation, which raised millions of dollars for the disabled. In 1976, he was named the first winner of the CFL's Tom Pate Award for community service. He was named to the Order of Canada.

They often used the term, "He was one of a kind." But, in this case, George Reed was one of a kind.

Head coach Dave Skrien (left), George Reed (34) and Gord Barwell (71)

Photo courtesy of *Leader-Post* archives

George Reed was one of the reasons Dave Skrien didn't have to think long to accept Ken Preston's offer to be head coach of the Riders in 1971.

In a four-year span, from 1967-1970, the Saskatchewan Roughriders were clearly the most dominant franchise in the Canadian Football League. In that span of time, they won 41 games, tied two and lost only 12. They made it to the Grey Cup twice, but their only Cup win was their 29-14 victory over the Ottawa Rough Riders in 1966.

So, while Dave Skrien obviously took over a team that was pretty well set and really wasn't facing a whole lot of changes, his biggest challenge was in keeping that big winning record going and, in the process, getting back to the Grey Cup, and winning another one.

It was easier said than done. Not that the Roughriders didn't continue their streak of making the playoffs every year, a streak that began in 1962 when Steve Owen was the coach. But their days of dominating the West were soon to end.

The Western Conference overnight had become a tightly bunched one with no real obvious favourites. Everybody, it seemed, was getting stronger, except perhaps the Lions, where Eagle Keys was finding out that life was indeed different without the Ronnie and George Show.

When the 1971 regular schedule ended, a mere seven points separated first place from last. The Riders and Stampeders tied for first place, each with 9-6-1 records, and Calgary got the pennant, pushing Saskatchewan to second place. The Blue Bombers were third, the Lions fourth and the Eskimos last.

A year later, the Bombers, with Don Jonas at quarterback and Jim Spavital as coach, finished in a first-place tie with the Edmonton Eskimos, coached by Ray Jauch, each with 10-6 records. The Riders caught the last playoff spot with an 8-8 record, their worst record since 1961. The Stampeders slipped to fourth place and B.C. brought up the rear.

This was when the West became a conference where survival of the fittest was in vogue. There some huge battles between Western teams in 1971, and nobody was running away from the pack.

The season got off to a nostalgic beginning in more ways than one. The Riders opened in Vancouver against their old coach Eagle Keys and his rookie-laden Lions. Keys and Jackie Parker had taken the stance they would rebuild the Lions from almost scratch.

The Riders needed a huge effort from their defence and a dose of Lancaster to hand Eagle his first loss. And it was done in a way very familiar to Keys. One of the hallmarks of Keys' journey in Saskatchewan was the ability of the Riders to come from behind late in games. He tried it again with the Lions. Trailing 14-3 going into the fourth quarter, the Lions started to flex their muscles. With Keys calling the plays for quarterback Paul Brothers, the Lions began to move towards the Saskatchewan end zone. But, the defence held and Keys had no choice but to gamble on third down. Fullback Jim Evenson, a powerful runner, slammed into the Saskatchewan front four. But the wall of defenders didn't budge and Evenson was turned back. Saskatchewan got the ball back, and Lancaster simply ran out the clock, cementing a 14-10 win. As soon as the game ended, Lancaster sprinted towards his old coach and two spoke for quite some time. "I want Eagle to do well in B.C.," Lancaster said, "but not against us. It was kind of strange seeing him standing on the other sideline."

Photo courtesy of *Leader-Post*

Ron Lancaster

The Riders' second game, their home-opener against Calgary, was a downer. The Stampeder defence, led by linebacker Wayne Harris, tackle John Helton and linebacker Joe Forzani slammed the door shut on Lancaster and his offence. The Riders didn't cross midfield until the fourth quarter. Skrien didn't like what he was seeing, so he pulled Lancaster and sent in backup Bubba Wyche. But Wyche had to leave the game when he was hammered by Helton. Lancaster came back in, but by then the barn door was open and the horse was gone. The Stampeders galloped out of town on the wings of a 21-0 shutout of Saskatchewan.

It was only the start of a four-game losing streak for the Roughriders. And the boobirds were out in full force, squawking as one loss after another happened. The Riders were dumped 29-16 by the Montreal Alouettes as the Riders went on their eastern swing. Saskatchewan tried to mount a fourth-quarterback but Lancaster was intercepted by Larry Fairholm, who returned it 86 yards for the clinching touchdown.

The Riders took their sorry act in Toronto to take on Leo Cahill's Argos. Quarterback Joe Theismann and running back Leon McQuay were just too much for Saskatchewan's defence to handle as the Argos won 22-7. Four games into the season, and the Riders had already lost one more game than they did through 16 games the year before.

The Riders came home on Friday the 13th to play the Bombers. The Bombers had a high-powered offence that revolved around the passing of quarterback Don Jonas and the running of Mack Herron. The Riders defence, especially end Bill Baker and linebacker Wally Dempsey, pressured Jonas. But it wasn't enough. Offensively, Saskatchewan couldn't put it together. They didn't get a first down until the second quarter and Lancaster wasn't sharp until the fourth quarter. But, by the time he got the offence going, it was too late and the Bombers won 32-22. The Riders left the field serenaded by a chorus of boos as they lost their fourth straight game to drop their record to 1-4.

In what was turning into a topsy-turvy kind of season for the Roughriders, they suddenly turned it all around. It all began with 31-25 win over the Bombers in Winnipeg, then a 42-21 throttling of Jack Gotta and the Ottawa Rough Riders. The game marked the return to the lineup of defensive tackle Ed McQuarters, who had suffered a freak off-season eye injury.

They snared their third straight victory when Keys made his first visit to Taylor Field with the Lions. Lancaster threw for two touchdowns and the Riders' pass rush harassed three different B.C. quarterbacks into throwing seven interceptions as Saskatchewan ran away 35-14. McQuarters, Baker and Don Bahnuik beat up the B.C. offensive line as they beat a steady path

Photo courtesy of *Leader-Post*

Bill Baker

Photo courtesy of *Leader-Post*

Don Bahnuik

to whichever Lion quarterback Keys had in the game – Don Moorhead or Rusty Clark or Brothers.

"McQuarters makes a big difference for them," said Keys. "He certainly complements Baker and Bahnuik and it's pretty tough to stop all three of them. You know, I thought we should have won the first game we played them. But, there was no doubt who was the better team today."

The Riders ran their winning streak to four games when they went into Edmonton and beat the Eskimos 19-3, intercepting seven Eskimo passes. For the ball-hawking Rider defence, led by Ted Dushinski, this was the second game in a row they had racked up seven interceptions.

The Riders and Eskimos returned to Taylor Field for the rematch, and it was another romp in the park for Saskatchewan. They beat the Eskimos 28-14 in a game that produced two CFL record-breaking moments. Reed scored a touchdown on a 17-yard run that gave him a career high 92nd TD, a CFL record. And Lancaster became the all-time CFL passing leader with 25,585 yards, three better than former Alouette quarterback Sam Etcheverry.

Saskatchewan had posted its fifth straight win, and all was well in Riderville.

Well, for a few days it was, until the Riders went into Winnipeg and were embarrassed 35-2 by the Blue Bombers. It was just a disastrous night for the Riders. Reed fumbled three times. Lancaster served up two interceptions and was replaced by Wyche in the fourth quarter. As bad as it was for the Riders, it was as good for the Bombers. Jonas threw four touchdown passes, two each to Paul Williams and Jim Thorpe.

The loss didn't send the Riders into a tailspin, though. They came home to play Hamilton and with George Reed rushing 161 yards on 21 carries and Lancaster tossing a pair of touchdowns, the Riders romped back into the win column with a 28-20 victory over Joe Zuger and the Ti-Cats.

"I've never seen anything like it," said Skrien. "We don't get injuries that keep our players out for a game or two. We lose them for the full season. Heck, we even lost our equipment manager for a couple of games."

The Riders paid a price, though. Defensive back Bob Kosid tore his Achilles tendon and was gone for the season. The week before, Bob Pearce had suffered a leg injury that sent him to the sidelines. "I've never seen anything like it," said Skrien. "We don't get injuries that keep our players out for a game or two. We lose them for the full season. Heck, we even lost our equipment manager for a couple of games." Skrien was referring to an injury suffered by equipment manager Dale Laird, when he severed a tendon in his hand working on a drink machine in the Rider dressing room.

The Riders still had a shot at finishing in first place. And it would likely depend on what happened when they played the Stampeders in Taylor Field in their next game. You had to figure, it just wasn't meant to be. Abendschan made only one of six field goal tries and a late Calgary touchdown off a Jim Lindsey to Gerry Shaw pass gave Calgary a 7-7 tie, and virtual assurance they would finish in first place.

The Riders finished off the season by hammering B.C. 50-18 with Bobby Thompson scoring three touchdowns, and then losing 28-12 to Edmonton in a game that meant nothing.

The second-place finish gave the Riders home field in the semi-final against the Bombers and the Riders easily won, 34-23, to advance to the Western final for the sixth straight season.

The Roughriders opened the Western final in Calgary's McMahon Stadium, and it appeared as if they would win. They were ahead in the fourth quarter but a Reggie

Holmes' interception of a Lancaster pass and a fumble recovery that led to another Calgary major saw the Stamps come from behind and win 30-21.

"We had them right in the bag and we let them out," said Skrien.

"Now we have to do it the hard way," said assistant coach John Payne.

Calgary's great defensive coach Dick Monroe admitted he was worried coming into the game. "Saskatchewan does a lot more things on offence than they did last year," said Monroe. "It makes it tougher to defend against them."

The Stampeders' ground game was the difference in the second game. Fullback Hugh McKinnis and halfback Jesse Mims ran for over 200 yards as Calgary's offensive line beat up the Riders. And a 71-yard pass from quarterback Jerry Keeling to receiver Rudy Linterman carried the Stampeders to a 23-21 victory, a two-game sweep of the Western final and into the Grey Cup in Vancouver against the Toronto Argonauts.

That Grey Cup served up a crazy finish. The Argos were moving in for a score that would have given them the championship when running back Leon McQuay slipped at the Calgary 14-yard line on a soaking wet Empire Stadium turf, and fumbled the ball away. Calgary won the Cup 14-11.

The 1972 season began for the Saskatchewan Roughriders the way it would end. A loss in Hamilton to the Tiger-Cats on an Ian Sunter field goal.

A 33-yard field goal in the last minute of play gave the Tabbies a 20-17 victory and started the Roughriders off on a season that would have more turns in it than driving through downtown Regina, and the 19-year-old Sunter had launched a remarkable season.

Photo courtesy of SSHFM

Bob Pearce (12), Jack Abendschan (53), Ralph Galloway (59), Bill Manchuk (75), Larry Bird (42) and Bobby Thompson (26)

The Roughriders had little offence going for them for much of the game. Hamilton's front four of Angelo Mosca, Gary Innskeep, John Baker and Bruce Smith overpowered Saskatchewan's offensive line of centre Larry Bird, guards Gary Brandt and Jack Abendschan and tackles Ralph Galloway and Clyde Brock. Thus, no running game. But, Lancaster, who didn't have a good first-half throwing the ball, almost pulled this one out in the second half, hooking up with receiver Bob Pearce, a genuine speedster, on a handful of big plays. Nevertheless, the Riders fell short.

"Anybody who sets up a schedule like this – two games in 48 hours – doesn't know anything about football. You have no time to prepare. You're in the hole before you even start."

The second game of their eastern swing took them to Ottawa where the Rough Riders easily beat them 22-7. Saskatchewan coaches and players felt that playing two games in just 48 hours was unfair, and they were right. The Ottawa loss illustrated that.

Part of the problem was Ottawa was starting an almost all-rookie defensive backfield. Names such as Dick Adams and James Elder were playing their first games in the CFL, and the Riders knew nothing about them. There were times in the games when Lancaster took a long time getting the ball snapped. "I'd go up to the line, and call out numbers that meant nothing just to buy some time," he said. "I was trying to figure out if I could read them. But, I couldn't."

Head coach Dave Skrien was furious. "Anybody who sets up a schedule like this – two games in 48 hours – doesn't know anything about football. You have no time to prepare. You're in the hole before you even start."

Photo courtesy of *Leader-Post*

Tom Campana

The Roughriders came home with two straight losses weighing them down. But, although a little bruised, they were hardly beaten. They were taking on the defending Eastern champion Toronto Argonauts.

The Riders unleashed a fast and furious attack, on both sides of the ball. Rookie Tom Campana, from Ohio State, who was brought in as a defensive back, gave a few glimpses of why he should move to a receiving position on offence.

Years later, Lancaster would tell me, "Everybody is talking about the West Coast offence and the Run and Shoot offence and how receivers have to read the defensive backs before deciding where they're going. Well, Campana could do that and we were running that kind of offence long before anybody else was."

Despite a few new faces – the Roughriders went back to their old bread and butter to secure a 15-6 win. The Ronnie and George Show was again in fine form. Lancaster completed 12 of 16 for 166 yards and Reed rushed for 129 yards on 35 carries. Defensively, linebackers Charlie Collins and Wally Dempsey shut down Leon McQuay.

The Riders weren't out of the woods yet. The Edmonton Eskimos came to town on a two-game winning streak and after taking a 14-point lead, the Riders fell apart and the Eskimos raced to a heart-stopping 31-29 victory. With Tom Wilkinson and Bruce Lemmerman alternating at quarterback, the Eskimos hit for 22 points in the second quarter and hung on the rest of the way.

Lancaster had his second great game in a row, producing sizzling passing yardage of over 300 yards on 18 completions and three of those went for touchdowns. Reed rushed for 81 yards and Bobby Thompson ran for 58. Campana made yards both catching and running the ball.

"We had the game in our hands and we let it slip away," said Skrien.

The Riders next faced the Stampeders in a home and home series, opening in Calgary, and it took a late field goal by Jack Abendschan to win 12-10. Lancaster was at his absolute best. Just when it looked as if the Stampeders were on their way to victory, Lancaster went to a higher gear, journeyed to that never-neverland he had visited so many times in his storied career.

Calgary offensive line coach Ron Payne said, "He's a fantastic quarterback. He's probably the best in the country. He worked on our weaknesses. I've never seen the screen pass work so well that often."

Stampeder defensive coach Dick Monroe was equally impressed. "If anybody in this league can do it, it's him. I've seen it for so many years. You just can't stop him."

Photo courtesy of *Leader-Post* archives

Bruce Bennett

Nobody knew it, or perhaps even could foresee it, but that victory in Calgary was just the start to what would become a runaway train. They went on one of their winning streaks, this time winning five straight games.

On a sweltering hot Sunday afternoon in Taylor Field, the Riders and Stamps hooked up again. The Riders blew it wide open with 17 points in a wild second quarter that saw them intercept two Jerry Keeling passes and return them for touchdowns. Bruce Bennett ran his back 112 yards. "I was running as hard as I could, but I could keep hearing footsteps behind me and they seemed to be gaining on me," said Bennett. "But when I looked back, I couldn't see any Stampeders." It turned out to be one of the officials who was following, and almost passed, Bennett on his way to the end zone. And Lewis Cook, Rider defensive back, also got into the act when he intercepted a Keeling pass and returned it 98 yards for a touchdown.

Any hope the Stampeders had of overcoming the 24-3 halftime deficit evaporated when Reed roared through a gaping hole and ran 59 yards for a touchdown. "Our defensive backs were so shocked seeing him come through that hole, they just stood there and watched," said Monroe. The Riders won 35-3.

The Riders would continue on their merry way, beating Winnipeg 32-21, thumping the B.C. Lions 24-13 and edging Edmonton 14-12 before their win streak was stopped.

If you were a writer covering the Roughriders then, it was so much fun because every game they played offered up something different. I had started my career at the *Leader-Post* in 1962, then left to write a column for the Saskatoon *Star-Phoenix* for a year and then spent two and one-half years writing a column and covering the Stamps for the Calgary *Albertan*. When I was offered a job at the *Leader-Post* in June of 1972 with the promise I would be covering the Riders, I didn't have to think twice about it. It was something I had dreamed about. When I started at the *Leader* in 1962, I would spend many a Saturday night going into the office in the old Leader Building at 1853 Hamilton St. I was the only one there. Tom (Scotty) Melville was the Sports Editor at the time. I would

Photo courtesy of *Leader-Post* archives

Bill Baker

Photo courtesy of SSHFM

Jack Abendschan

sit at his typewriter pounding out imaginary columns, columns that saw only the bottom of his garbage can. I began covering high school sports in 1965 and quickly became close friends with Lancaster, who was coaching the Central Gophers basketball team. I always wanted to cover the Riders, especially while he was still playing. Can you imagine? Watching almost every game Ron Lancaster and George Reed played and then getting to write about them. How good was that!

And they gave me plenty to write about in 1972.

Because the Western Conference boasted four teams capable of winning at any time, the race to the playoffs burned with a white heat. Winnipeg, Calgary, Saskatchewan all took turns at securing a playoff spot, but in the end Calgary and, as expected, B.C. fell short.

The Riders five-game win streak ended when they lost 18-16 to Winnipeg. They won only two of their remaining six games to finish at 8-8. The Bombers and Eskimos tied for first with identical 10-6 record and Winnipeg was given first place and home advantage.

The Roughriders went into Edmonton to face the Eskimos in the semi-final, and Edmonton, which had become a strong team under Norm Kimball and Ray Jauch, was clearly the favourite. And there were hard feelings between the two teams. Kimball had all but put a bounty on the head of Rider defensive end Bill Baker earlier in the season when Baker put three Eskimo quarterbacks out of the game with shots to the head in a viciously played game in Taylor Field. It was around about that time that he got the nickname The Undertaker.

The Riders and Esks hooked up in another hard-hitting battle, but Saskatchewan was ready. "We were high," said Lancaster. "We were ready for this one. I know when I'm ready for a game and you could just tell before the game that all 32 guys were ready."

The Roughriders won it 8-6 on the strength of a fourth-quarter Abendschan field goal.

And, then, it was off to Winnipeg to tangle with the first place Blue Bombers, who had Don Jonas and Mack Herron and who were on a 12-game winning streak in Winnipeg Stadium. The Roughriders had no chance, everybody figured.

Well, everybody figured wrong.

The Riders and Bombers traded blows through another dramatic Western final, considered by observers to be the toughest game to win of the season. It came down to a final field goal attempt by Abendschan. He missed it, and in an unreal scene, the Bombers kicked the ball out of the end zone. Lancaster caught it and wanted to kick it back into the end zone. The only option he had was to kick it left-footed because the Bombers were fast closing on him from the right. He kicked it just as he was leveled. But wait! There was a penalty flag on the play and Abendschan got another chance. With the scored tied at 24-24, the Riders pulled off the upset of the year when Jack made the kick for a 27-24 win and a trip to Hamilton for the Grey Cup game.

It almost seemed that by getting to the Grey Cup was going to be too much for the Riders. They would be playing the hometown Hamilton Tiger-Cats in Ivor Wynne Stadium. Hamilton had a new wonderkid at quarterback, Chuck Ealey. They had the great Garney Henley. And Jerry Williams was coaching them. Lurking in the shadows was tight end Tony Gabriel, waiting to crush yet another Rider dream.

With over 33,000 fans packed into the stadium, the Ti-Cats opened quickly with a 10-0 first-quarter lead. But the Riders struck back and tied the game at 10-10 at halftime. There would be no more scoring until the final play of the game.

Ealey and Lancaster both had big games. Ealey completed 18 of 29 for 291 yards while Lancaster was 20 of 29 for 239 yards. There were only two touchdowns scored in the game. Ealey hit Dave Fleming on a 16-yard pass that the Riders claimed shouldn't have been allowed because they said Fleming was out of bounds when he caught the ball. Lancaster threw an eight-yard touchdown toss to Campana.

The game came down to the final series. Ealey masterminded a scintillating drive, throwing three passes to tight end Tony Gabriel that set up Ian Sunter's field goal from 34 yards. On the final play of the 1972 Grey Cup game, a 19-year-old kid kicked the winning field goal in the biggest game of the year to win 13-10.

Once again, the Saskatchewan Roughriders checked into the Heartbreak Hotel.

The loss was devastating to some of the Roughriders. Linebacker Wayne Shaw was so upset with one of the coaching decisions that he left Ivor Wynne Stadium after the game, drove to Toronto, and flew home to Regina by himself. He never played another game with the Riders. For much of the game, he had lined up opposite Gabriel. His job was simple. Hit Gabriel at the line of scrimmage and prevent him from getting off the line. It worked until the final drive of the game. Bill Manchuk, an inexperienced linebacker, replaced Shaw. The Riders felt Manchuk could run with Gabriel, keep up with him, cover him. It didn't happen the way the coaching staff thought it would. "The reason Gabriel didn't do anything in the game before the last drive was because it's hard to catch a pass when you're on your ass," Shaw said.

"The loss was devastating to some of the Roughriders. Linebacker Wayne Shaw was so upset with one of the coaching decisions that he left Ivor Wynne Stadium after the game, drove to Toronto, and flew home to Regina by himself.

There were further ramifications that spilled over from that loss that would shake the Rider world.

A few hours after the 1972 Grey Cup game, I had finished writing and went downstairs to the hotel coffee shop. We were staying at the Holiday Inn in Hamilton. The streets were fairly quiet, considering the hometown Tiger-Cats had just won the Grey Cup game. And, there wasn't a Saskatchewan Roughrider fan to be found. To lose the way the Riders did, on a last-play field goal, had gutted everyone of any enthusiasm.

The restaurant was virtually empty. I had ordered a hamburger and finished it. I was enjoying a cup of coffee when Roughrider assistant coach John Payne came in and sat down with me.

"That was a tough way to lose, John," I said.

Payne just shook his head.

"But you guys had a great season, and there's nothing to be ashamed of."

John Payne

"Well, we did pretty well but gosh-darn when you get that close to the Grey Cup, you don't want to lose. You never know how many chances you'll get."

We talked for about a half an hour, maybe longer. And, we talked a bit about the next season.

"You can't write anything about it now, but there's going to be some big changes, I think," Payne said. "There's going to be some big changes."

"What changes?"

"Well, I don't think that Dave (Skrien) will be back," Payne said. "I'm pretty sure he's going to resign."

"Why? Why would he resign? He's in his second year as head coach here and he got the team to the Grey Cup."

"Things aren't too good between him and some of the executive members," Payne said. "Some of them aren't happy with the job he did."

So, with a little nudge from some of the board members, Skrien did indeed resign, and Payne was ultimately named the Riders' head coach.

This wasn't the first time a head coach from the Riders had been pushed aside right after losing in a Grey Cup game. In 1951, shortly after the Roughriders lost the Grey Cup game, Harry (Blackjack) Smith was shown the door.

Go figure.

The 1973 season was the beginning of one of the most incredible rivalries ever in the Canadian Football League. For three straight years, the Roughriders and the Edmonton Eskimos would meet in the Western final in Edmonton. For three straight years, the Eskimos would finish first and the Riders second. For three straight years, the Western final was played on the frozen tundra of Clarke Stadium. For three straight years, the Riders would lose the Western final.

> **If ever there were two teams that didn't like each other, then it was these two. They hated each other and they respected each other. And, they feared each other. Every game they played was war. Every hit was delivered with a little extra power.**

If ever there were two teams that didn't like each other, then it was these two. They hated each other and they respected each other. And, they feared each other. Every game they played was war. Every hit was delivered with a little extra power. These were not games for the faint of heart. But they were games that underlined and put an exclamation mark behind the reason the Canadian Football League can be so filled with drama and excitement and sheer, raw entertainment.

The Eskimos' success was based entirely on how general manager Norm Kimball ran the organization. Norm was a tough, no-nonsense guy who not only had a vision, but he had the ability to make it happen. He wanted the Eskimos to become the marquee franchise in the Canadian Football League, and few could argue that he didn't succeed. The Eskimos' unprecedented string of successes really began in 1973 and didn't end until well into the 1980s. There was a time when they won an unprecedented five straight Grey Cup championships. Kimball put together an incredible scouting machine. No CFL team has ever recruited the number of Hall of Fame quarterbacks the Eskimos did. From Tom Wilkinson to Warren Moon to Matt Dunigan and Damon Allen, the Eskimos always had great quarterbacks. He hired solid head coaches. Hugh Campbell was likely the best one. But Ray Jauch also had a hand in turning around the Eskimos' fortunes on the field.

When the 1973 season opened, the Riders and the Eskimos were considered the top two contenders for the Western crown. And, did they go at it.

John Payne settled into the head coaching job with relative ease. He knew the players and they knew him from when he was Skrien's assistant. Payne was a low-key kind of guy who was consistent in how he operated and he was a thorough head coach. Ken Preston had made another good choice in who he selected to continue the Riders' incredible run.

The Roughriders opened the '73 season in Vancouver against the Lions. And it was another no-brainer. The Riders won 21-5. Then, they lost 23-15 to the Stampeders in Calgary in a nutty sort of a game that featured 12 turnovers. The Riders' first home game was against Eagle Keys and the Lions. For the 23rd time in the last 24 games between these two teams, the Roughriders won.

George Reed had a lot to do with the 38-19 victory. He only gained 60 yards on the night, but they were key yards, and he did score a record-setting 107th career touchdown. And, he was within less than 100 yards of surpassing Cleveland Browns fullback Jim Brown's all-time rushing record.

I wrote a column after that game which said, "If God designed a fullback, he would have made George Reed."

I asked Eagle Keys about Reed after the game. "George is something special," Eagle told me. "When he gets near the goal-line, his nose starts twitching and there is just no way you are going to stop him. All the great ones have it"

One game later, a headline in the *Leader-Post* said it all. "George makes football history" bellowed the large black type. Reed needed 80 yards going into the game to equal Brown's record. That he did it in front of Eagle Keys was special, because it was Keys who showed complete faith in Reed when he took over as head coach in Saskatchewan

Photo courtesy of *Leader-Post*

George Reed (34), recognized by then Lt. Gov., and former Rider Dinny Hanbidge while Premier Allan Blakeney looks on.

in 1965. The Riders would beat the Ottawa Rough Riders 18-12 that night, August 21, 1973 it was, but it was George Reed who stole the show. Oh, did he steal the show. There was a photograph in the next day's paper, taken by the great *Leader-Post* photographer Peter Blashill, spread across the top of the sports section, showing George lowering his shoulders as he ran for the record-breaker.

Here's how it happened, as I wrote in the paper.

"There were 40 seconds to go in the game and the Riders were second and eight at their own 17 with a bit of unfinished business still to go. It was a professional football record and Lancaster promptly dialed Reed's number. George hit into the line, off the left side, cracked into a lineman and rolled off to snap up his 81st rushing yard of the night. Jim Brown's record became history. It was 10.31 p.m. CST when George Reed made history."

Brown had rushed for 12,312 yards in a nine-year career. In his 11th year, George had rushed for 12,313 yards. A crowd of 21,032 had sat in some sort of a trance throughout the game, waiting for George to break the record. When it happened, they went crazy. You could have heard them cheering all the way to College Avenue in Regina. In fact, I think the roar of the crowd roared across the mighty Wascana.

"This record probably means more to me than the touchdown record," Reed said. "Because it was tougher to get. It took a long time to get it." But, he got it.

Reed's story caught the attention of media throughout North America. *Sports Illustrated* magazine assigned a writer named Joe Marshall to come to Regina to do a story on this amazing athlete. Marshall followed the Riders for a week or two, and his story did appear in *Sports Illustrated*. George had made the big time. All of North America knew about George Reed.

"Reed's story caught the attention of media throughout North America. *Sports Illustrated* magazine assigned a writer named Joe Marshall to come to Regina to do a story on this amazing athlete. Marshall followed the Riders for a week or two, and his story did appear in *Sports Illustrated*. George had made the big time. All of North America knew about George Reed.

The night seemed to inspire the Roughriders, who promptly went on a three-game winning streak, including a 28-27 victory over the Eskimos. That one, it was special.

The Riders put together a 100-yard drive, highlighted by a 55-yard burst from Bobby Thompson, and sealed by George Reed's touchdown run to nail the victory. The game ended with Dave Cutler missing a 39-yard field goal.

The win gave the Riders a four-point cushion atop first place over the Eskimos and Lions, who were tied for second. The Riders intercepted Bruce Lemmerman three times. Ted Provost got one, Ted Dushinski got one and Charlie Collins got one.

Eskimo head coach Ray Jauch, never a good loser, laid down the gauntlet for the Riders. He said the game showed him that his team was capable of going the distance. "And," he vowed, "we'll win before it's over."

The Roughriders would play the Eskimos two more times before the regular-season schedule ended, and they lost both those games.

It cost them. Edmonton ended up in first place in the West and the Riders were second and had to play the B.C. Lions in the semi-final.

The Lions, of course, were no match for the Riders, who smashed them to smithereens, 33-13. The real story of that game was, nobody in town seemed to care. Less than 10,000 fans showed up in Taylor Field to watch the game. Rider general manager Ken Preston said it was the lowest crowd in 20 years. Why? Three reasons. The Lions were not a big draw in Saskatchewan. The cost for a single ticket to the game was $10, which was a big price in 1973. And, the game was played on a Saturday afternoon, when a lot of people were working. Preston phoned me a few days before the game. "We're not selling any tickets, can't you write something?" I tried. But this was a no-sale from the beginning.

That game mattered little anyway. The real matchup people wanted to see would come a week later at Clarke Stadium in Edmonton when the Riders and Eskimos would clash in the Western final.

"It was one of the greatest playoff games people almost didn't get to see," is what I wrote the day after the Western final. One thing about the Western final, you could always be assured something wild, weird and unpredictable would happen. In 1973, it was a blanket of fog that enveloped Clarke Stadium. Anybody 10 rows up and beyond couldn't really see a thing. There were reporters who had to leave the press box and go down to the sidelines if they wanted to see what was going on.

What was going on was an incredible game by both the Riders and the Eskimos. And it came down to the final moments. Tom Wilkinson had started at quarterback for the Eskimos, but he pulled himself from the game. "I hurt my shoulder and I hurt my hip," he said. "I couldn't get anything on the ball. There was no point in me staying in there when Bruce was ready to do the job."

Both offences had their moments. Reed rushed for 168 yards, the highlight for Saskatchewan. But the game came down to the final moments.

With 2.32 to go, Lemmerman put together the game's most important drive. The biggest play was a second-and-nine pass to Larry Highbaugh streaking down the sidelines. He beat Lorne Richardson for 39 yards to the Saskatchewan five and two plays later Lemmerman hit George McGowan for the winning touchdown in a 25-23 Edmonton victory.

"I turned around," said Richardson, "and I couldn't find the ball. If it hadn't been under-thrown, I would have had a chance at it."

Lancaster tried to bring the Riders back, but his pass was intercepted by John Beaton, and that was all she wrote folks.

The game was one that would impact the Riders greatly. Assistant coach Bud Riley, a defensive genius, would soon be on his way to take over the Blue Bombers. And defensive end Bill Baker, upset with what he considered a lack of monetary interest by the Riders, would leave and go play for the B.C. Lions.

All good things must come to an end. And, in 1974, the Saskatchewan Roughriders went through a tumultuous season that created strong cries for change from the vocal minority out there in Riderville. By the time the season was approaching the final stages, the stinging criticism from open mouth radio shows, letters to the editor and the boos from the Taylor Field crowd had reached a crescendo that even the players couldn't ignore.

By then, even quarterback Ron Lancaster and fullback George Reed, two of most remarkably successful and honoured players in CFL history, were wondering if, perhaps, they had reached the end of the line. That old adage of "It's not what you did yesterday that matters, it's what you do today that counts" had come into play. Rider head coach John Payne and his two outstanding assistants, Jim Eddy and Don (Pops) Powell, were equally as befuddled about what

Photo courtesy of SSHFM

Lorne Richardson

was going on with the team they thought was going to take a run at first place and the Grey Cup.

"That season was not a whole lot of fun," Lancaster would say when his playing days had ended. "We had a lot of injuries so it was tough to get any consistency going. We had some great players. Lorne Richardson was a hell of a defensive back, Rhett Dawson was a receiver who kind of reminded me of Hugh Campbell. Ted Provost was the best safety in the league. George was still the greatest fullback anybody ever saw. But, for whatever reasons, we just couldn't put it all together. It really got frustrating and, yeah, I was wondering if enough was enough and maybe I should retire."

There was a lot of talk that the Toronto Argonauts were interested in hiring Lancaster as their head coach. As well, it was round about this time that Lancaster was this ( ) close to asking to be traded. He had heard that Montreal's Sonny Wade had become the highest paid quarterback in the CFL, and it ate away at him. Because he felt he should be the highest paid. And he was right. He should have been. Ronnie finally took his case to general manager Ken Preston, and Preston wisely increased Lancaster's salary.

Preston had been around long enough to know that was happening to the Riders in their hit and miss 1974 season was no reason to hit the panic buttons. Payne had made 21 roster changes since becoming head coach in 1973, and it takes time for all those pieces to fit themselves in. Preston still possessed great confidence in Payne and his coaching staff and he was certain the Riders did have talent. He practised patience, and it paid off.

But, oh, was it tested. The Riders opened in Edmonton against the Eskimos, and a big crowd turned out wondering if Saskatchewan was about to lay down the law to Edmonton right off the bat.

The headline in the next day's paper pretty well summed it up.

"OUCH! ... the embarrassment of it all. Eskimos 31, Riders 7."

I began my story with:

"EDMONTON - John Payne was bewitched. Ron Lancaster was bothered. And anybody who wears a green and white sticker over their heart was bewildered."

Eskimo quarterback Tom Wilkinson pounced on the Riders early and had an astounding game in a downpour of rain. He completed an amazing 13 of 14 passes and threw four touchdown passes. Eskimo defensive ends Ron Estay and Leroy Jones manhandled the Saskatchewan offensive line all night and hounded Lancaster into submission. They chased Lancaster to the bench in the fourth quarter, Ronnie being replaced by Randy Mattingly, who was being groomed as Lancaster's successor. Mattingly engineered the Riders' only touchdown of the game when he passed to wide receiver Steve Mazurak. Other than that, there wasn't much else good about the Riders on this soggy late July night.

"They just intimidated us," was the way one Rider put it. "They just wound up and came at us and we couldn't stop them."

"I just couldn't believe we played that bad," said Payne. Well, believe it John, because they did.

Photo courtesy of SSHFM

Steve Mazurak

The Riders went into Calgary the following week, got a big performance running and catching the ball out of halfback Pete Watson, and beat the Stamps 24-18. Lancaster had a great game, completing 22 of 30 passes, and guiding a ground game that saw Reed gain over 100 yards.

"I don't know how the hell they got beaten so badly in Edmonton," Calgary defensive tackle John Helton told me.

The Riders came back to Taylor Field for their home opener against the Eskimos, and they were chomping at the bit to get at them. The Roughriders dominated the Eskimos throughout the first half. Reed would rush for well over 100 yards and Lancaster passed for over 200 yards. But, it still came down to the final two minutes before it was decided, and the Riders needed a miracle of sorts.

Dave Cutler was lined up to kick a 41-yard field goal for what would be the winning points with only a minute and 41 seconds left. Lorne Richardson provided the miracle. He roared in from the left side and blocked the kick, saving a 24-23 Saskatchewan victory. "Pete Wysocki and I were lined up on the left side and they had one guy to block us," said Richardson. "Wysocki took him out of the play and I had a free shot."

One Rider told me after the game, "I've never seen the veterans so keyed up about a game. It was like if we lost the whole season would have gone down the drain."

"I have never seen George Reed like that," Rider offensive lineman Jim Hopson said.

The Riders had to do some adjusting on the fly in the game. Offensive tackle Elbert Walker broke his ankle and Tim Roth had to switch from defensive end to offensive tackle. He did the job.

And Rider guard Ralph Galloway did a number on Edmonton's great John LaGrone. "I don't like LaGrone and he doesn't like me," said Galloway. "It makes it interesting."

The Riders won two more games – 24-13 over Winnipeg and 10-8 over Calgary before their season started going off the rails. They went into a deep tailspin, losing five of their next six games, and reached a point where making the playoffs was even in question.

Photo courtesy of SSHFM

Tim Roth

Their only win in that six-game span was in Vancouver against the Lions. They hammered the Lions 38-16 and it could have been more. Reed rushed for 142 yards despite a couple of leg injuries. Lancaster passed for over 200 yards and threw touchdowns passes to Campana, Mazurak and Thompson.

The Riders' joy was short-lived as they came home and were spanked 24-18 by the Eskimos, and once again the debate over whether Mattingly should be given the start at quarterback caught fire. Payne was clearly irritated by the same question being asked over and over again. Finally, he snapped. He looked at the surrounding media, and said, "You guys just let me coach the club and you write your articles, and we'll be fine." Then, he turned and walked away. It was the only time I ever saw him that mad.

But the cry for Mattingly was causing everybody to be a little irritated, and it had its comical moments.

Mattingly definitely did have talent, perhaps more than anybody the Riders had brought in to back up Lancaster. But Payne was a Lancaster man and unless Ronnie was having a miserable night, or the game was out of hand, he wasn't going to pull him.

I can remember the Riders played a Sunday afternoon game in Winnipeg, one they lost 24-21. Lancaster completed only eight of 22 passes and gave up two interceptions. But Payne left him in for the whole game because the score was close, and with Lancaster, you never knew. He was capable of playing lousy for 58 minutes and great for two minutes. Often, that would be the difference between winning and losing.

The Riders had chartered a plane home, but it wasn't going to leave until five or six hours after the game. They went back to the International Inn near the Winnipeg Airport, had a meal, and then retired to their rooms to drink beer, or watch television.

When the bus arrived, I got on and sat down. Payne got on and sat down at the front of the bus, which he always did. Mattingly came on and sat down beside me. I figured he had had a few beers. We talked for a while, and then he looked around, and turned back to me.

"I know you are a good friend of Ronnie's, but I have to ask you something."

"What's that?" I said.

"Am I ever going to get to play more than just a few minutes?"

"Nope," I said. "Not as long as the game is close, or he doesn't want to come out."

Tears came to Mattingly's eyes.

"Oh, for God's sake," I muttered to myself. I got up and went to Payne.

"John, you better go back and talk to Mattingly. He's really upset that he's not getting to play more."

"This is all I need now," said Payne, who went back and rode the rest of the way to the airport calming Mattingly down.

He still didn't get to play much more, unless Lancaster got hurt.

The Riders reached rock bottom when they went on their eastern swing and lost back-to-back games in Hamilton and Ottawa. The Ottawa game was perhaps their sorriest show of the season. They turned over the ball nine times on seven interceptions – four by Mattingly and three by Lancaster – and fumbled it away two more times. The Riders lost Lancaster with hip and shoulder injuries in the first quarter, but Mattingly didn't do much better when he came in.

The Riders' record had dropped to five wins and six losses, and they were dangerously close to missing the playoffs.

While around them it was chaotic, the Riders withdrew to their inner sanctum, grew closer together during the storm of criticism.

As they had done so many times in so many years, they gathered themselves the week before their next game. The practices were shortened. The players held team meetings.

"I told coach Payne that we were at rock bottom, that we couldn't go down any further, that we had to come back," Lancaster said.

And come back, they did. They hammered the Stampeders 34-10, lost their next game 24-21 in Winnipeg, then finished off the schedule with two victories over B.C. and one over Montreal. It gave them second place in the west, ahead of B.C. and behind Edmonton.

Here we go again.

The Lions came to town for the semi-final. They beat the Lions 24-14 for the second straight year in the semi-finals.

"Lancaster did a great job of throwing the ball in the second quarter," said B.C. coach Eagle Keys. "Once they got ahead of us, they did a good job of running the ball. But you know, it still comes down to Lancaster. He's the difference. You get him going, it's tough."

Rider defensive end George Wells also had a huge game for the Riders, knocking down anybody who got in his way, and manhandling B.C. quarterbacks Pete Liske and Don Moorhead.

The victory sent the Riders to Edmonton for the second straight year to face the Eskimos in the Western final.

Yes, here we go again.

In another stunningly wild Western final, the Eskimos prevailed 31-27 in a game that will forever be remembered as a classic. It was open season on quarterbacks Ron Lancaster and Tom Wilkinson. Lancaster was harassed all day long, and gave up four interceptions. Wilkinson was chased all over Clarke Stadium by Wells, and he was hurting when the game ended. "Who said you can't hurt fat?" the rotund Wilkie smiled after the game. He gave up a pair of interceptions.

The Eskimos seemed to have the game won after the third quarter. They were leading 27-17. But Lancaster mounted another one of his patented comebacks, and the Riders inched closer and closer, and Clarke Stadium was going wild. The Riders moved within four points after Lancaster carried them on a daring 85-yard march that included three third-down gambles. It ended when Ronnie found Al Ford alone in the end zone on a third down pass that narrowed the score to 31-27. The TD came at the 13:58 mark of the last quarter. It was the last time the Riders saw the ball.

"Turn back the clock a year," said Lancaster.

Ray Jauch perhaps summed it up best.

"You know, there is something you cannot buy in football," he said. "It's something that Saskatchewan has got. They've got pride and tradition. When they pull on that sweater, something happens, and you know you've got one hell of a team on your hands."

There they went again.

They had, without a doubt, become one of the most resilient teams in the Canadian Football League. For two straight seasons, the Saskatchewan Roughriders had battled tooth and nail with the Edmonton Eskimos and for two straight seasons they had ended up second. For two straight seasons, they had travelled to Edmonton for the Western final. And for two straight seasons, they had lost heartbreakers.

They were like the little kid with his face pressed against the candy store window. They had become the most successful losers in the CFL. Because, you had to understand, anything short of a Grey Cup victory was a losing season as far as they were concerned. They were Saskatchewan Roughriders of a golden era in the CFL, the winningest team over a span of magical years that began in 1962. There were filled with pride, possessed by a never-say-die attitude and they played the game with a "take no prisoners" fire raging in their bellies.

"We just never believed we would lose," quarterback Ron Lancaster said after he had retired. "Every game we played, we figured we would win it. We didn't, of course, but it didn't matter. It didn't matter how many games in a row we lost. We always felt we'd win the next one. I think that probably started when Eagle Keys was coaching us. He was the same way, and it rubbed off on us. Nobody hated losing more than he did, and if he really had a bad game, the next week of practice was no fun."

"Lancaster did a great job of throwing the ball in the second quarter," said B.C. coach Eagle Keys. "Once they got ahead of us, they did a good job of running the ball. But you know, it still comes down to Lancaster. He's the difference. You get him going, it's tough."

Ray Jauch perhaps summed it up best.

"You know, there is something you cannot buy in football," he said. "It's something that Saskatchewan has got. They've got pride and tradition. When they pull on that sweater, something happens, and you know you've got one hell of a team on your hands."

"We just never believed we would lose," quarterback Ron Lancaster said after he had retired. "Every game we played, we figured we would win it. We didn't, of course, but it didn't matter. It didn't matter how many games in a row we lost. We always felt we'd win the next one."

When the Riders went to training camp in 1975 at the University of Regina, the ghosts of two straight years of Western final losses hovered above them. Not until they won a Western final would they be exorcised.

They went into 1975 with a strong team. Lancaster and George Reed were back, Rhett Dawson and Tom Campana had merged into a potent receiving team, the offensive and defensive lines were strong. In fact, there really weren't any weaknesses.

John Payne and his assistants Lee Snider and Jim Eddy oozed confidence as they herded the team through camp and the exhibition season. In those days, teams played four exhibition games so by the time regular season arrived everybody had a pretty good idea of how things would be. Trouble was, with the Roughriders you could never be sure. They always seemed to get caught in these mini-losing streaks. That, of course, would drive the whole province nuts, send the media into a tizzy and leave Payne and his staff going in dizzying circles. General manager Ken Preston, of course, would simply chomp down on his cigar and go golfing with his buddies at the Wascana Country Club. Preston had seen this act enough times before to know it wouldn't last all that long.

The Riders got off to a rapid start, thanks in some part to a fairly easy schedule. They opened with a 20-2 win over the Stampeders, a 24-20 win in Montreal and 14-12 victory in Toronto. Then, they were beaten by the Lions 28-27, the first time the Lions had won in Taylor Field in 10 years.

Then, the Riders found themselves on one of those roller-coaster rides. They would win one, lose one, win one, lose one and so on. Not until the final five games of the season did they catch fire, winning four in a row before closing out with 12-8 loss in Vancouver. One more time, they ended up in second place, this time with a 10-5-1 record. They were three points back of the … you guessed it … Edmonton Eskimos.

One of the real highlights of the early moments of the season came in Toronto. George Reed rushed for 109 yards. It was the 59th time in his career George had gone over 100 yards rushing, eclipsing by one the pro football record that had been held by Jim Brown.

Photo courtesy of SSHFM

George Wells

The 36-year-old Reed went into the game incensed. A Toronto newspaper had printed a story the day of the game labelling Reed as "aging and slowing down." George answered them.

"I don't know why people say that," Reed said. "A lot of people say we're too old to play the game. Well, we've got a few players over 30 but the rest are young. Yeah, it bothered me."

Said Lancaster, "One thing you never want to do is get George mad."

The game also had its angry moments. Defensive end George Wells had to leave the game after Argo tackle Wayne Cuncic kicked him in the … well, you know. As Wells was leaving the field, he went over to the Argo huddle and said something to Cuncic.

"What did you say to him?" I asked George after the game.

"I told him 'Don't you go away because I'm coming back to get you.' "

Wells was back in one play. He blew past Cuncic and hammered quarterback Bill Bynum so hard the bells didn't stop ringing for the rest of the game. "Of all the hits I took, that one hurt the most," said the dazed Argo quarterback.

The Riders had their usual batch of comeback victories. The most stirring might have been in Winnipeg in late August when Lancaster took them on an 81-yard drive that started and ended with the ball in running back Steve Molnar's hands, the last time for a touchdown. Molnar bolted for a 14-yard TD run, the Riders made a two-point convert and they beat Dieter (call me Ralph) Brock and the Bombers 20-13. And Reed had another 100-yard plus game.

If there were promising moments in the season, and there were many, then it was how the Riders did in three games against the Eskimos. They lost the first meeting in Edmonton when Tom Wilkinson caught fire. In just over a quarter of play, Wilkinson completed 13 of 17 passes for over 200 yards and two touchdowns and the Eskimos won 28-24. But the next two meetings went the Riders' way. They beat Edmonton 28-18 in Edmonton and hammered the Eskimos 36-27 in Taylor Field.

The season was not always kind to the Riders. Over the course of the year, they lost guard Jack Abendshan and tackle Clyde Brock to injuries. Defensive back Ken McEachern went down with knee problems. Safety Ted Provost injured his arm. And both Lancaster and Reed didn't have a day when something wasn't hurting on their bodies.

In a 20-14 mid-October victory over the Blue Bombers in Winnipeg, Reed and Lancaster continued their assault on the all-time record books. Reed carried the ball 34 times for 150 yards to become the first player in football anywhere to rush for nine miles in a career. And Lancaster surpassed the pro football all-time passing record held by his hero, legendary Baltimore colts quarterback Johnny Unitas. Lancaster had 40,510 career yards passing, Unitas had 40,239. Earlier that year, Ronnie got to meet and spend time with Unitas when he came to Regina to speak to a sports dinner.

Photo courtesy of *Leader-Post*

George Reed, Johnny Unitas, Ron Lancaster . . . three legends talking football

The playoffs had arrived. And throughout Saskatchewan there was a buzz quite unlike any seen before. Because the fans were sure the Riders were finally going to beat Edmonton. So, too, were the Riders.

Saskatchewan played host to the Bombers in the semi-final in Taylor Field, and most saw this game as a mere formality. It was. Lancaster passed for 328 yards, Reed ran for 101 yards, Campana and Dawson each caught five passes and George Wells sacked Brock five times as the Riders roared 42-24.

They were ready for Edmonton!

Lancaster hated playing in Edmonton. For him, it was the toughest park in the country to play in. The Eskimos had a fire truck that would sound the sirens after an Edmonton touchdown. At halftime in one game, Lancaster had not played well. When the Riders were on the way to their dressing room, the guys in the truck taunted him by turning on the sirens. Lancaster exploded. It was hilarious. He jumped up on the truck and was scrambling to get at the guy sounding the sirens. If big Clyde Brock hadn't reached up, and hauled him into the dressing room, kicking and screaming, heaven knows what would have happened.

The last two Western finals had been head-knocking, bruising, tightly contested affairs. They were both survival of the fittest games. It was the Western Conference at its very best with neither team willing to give an inch.

This one?

It was a titanic battle. If you remember the Titanic sunk. It was a rumble in the jungle, if you remember Custer at Little Big Horn.

What it was, was a massacre. The Riders got caught walking down a back alley, and they were mugged. They played as if they didn't have a worry in the world. They played as if they figured all they had to do was show up because it was their turn.

"If you don't play well, you won't win," said a totally dejected Lancaster in the haunting quiet of the Saskatchewan dressing room after the Eskimos had won 30-18. Lancaster had a cold hand for most of the day, and he served up three interceptions. Reed was held to just 46 yards rushing on 18 carries. The game turned in the second half when Ray Jauch pulled starter Tom Wilkinson and put in Bruce Lemmerman, and Lemmerman shredded the Rider defence, scoring 22 points in the fourth quarter. It was all she wrote.

"We didn't get any breaks," said Payne.

"You make your own breaks," said Jauch.

After the game, Lancaster said he wasn't sure he would be back, that he might retire. Reed would retire, ending the kind of career that words simply are inadequate to describe. Suffice to say he was the greatest of them all.

And the Riders flew home, late on that dark, cold Sunday night, wondering if they would get another shot at the Eskimos in 1976.

It was the strangest of times. It was surreal, in a way. The Saskatchewan Roughriders went to training camp in 1976. And George Reed was not there. He had retired. And, now there was this massive hole to be filled right behind Ron Lancaster. The Little General had thought about retiring after the third straight loss in the Western final. But, he still loved the game and he still believed the Riders had a shot at the Grey Cup. And he could still play. Still, it was strange to wander out to training camp, and there would be no George Reed. If the season started out as being the strangest of times, eerie almost, then that would be how it ended. The dynasty was crawling towards its conclusion, and everybody seemed to realize that this could be the last kick at the cat.

Steve Molnar, a Canadian kid out of Saskatoon who had played college ball in Utah, was Reed's replacement going into the season. He had joined the Riders in 1969 and played a fair amount in the years following. He was a good size, over 200 pounds, could catch, and was a strong runner. But as long as Reed was around, Steve would mostly stay in the shadows. He earned the label, "The best starter not starting in the CFL." Nobody expected Molnar to be Reed's equal. But, in 1976 he did get the job done, especially in the playoffs.

Photo courtesy of *Leader-Post*

Tim Roth (66), Gary Brandt (54) and Alan Ford (21) present George Reed with a grandfather clock upon his retirement.

In some ways, the 1976 season was not unlike the seasons that had gone before it. The Riders got off to a quick start, winning five of the first six games. And, then for the rest of the season, they fell back into that win one, lose one pattern.

Still, Lancaster was having one of his best years ever. He had a great balance in his receiving corps with Leif Pettersen, Rhett Dawson, Tom Campana, Steve Mazurak, Al Ford and tight end Bob Richardson. As with every other season, the Riders were always in the playoff hunt, reaching for that elusive first-place finish that would give them home field in the final. That was so important because they had yet to find a way to win in Edmonton. And, the Eskimos were still a veteran-laden team led by the quarterbacking duo of Bruce Lemmerman and Tom Wilkinson.

The Riders opened the season with a bang, going into Vancouver and hammering the Lions 35-8. Campana returned a punt 80 yards for a touchdown. Cornerback Paul Williams ran back an interception for a touchdown.

Molnar rushed for 87 yards and scored a touchdown. Halfback Pete Van Valkenburg picked up another 45 yards. The Riders held a 35-0 lead going into the fourth quarter and Lancaster gave way to backup Dave Syme.

The Riders went home and lost to Montreal, then headed out on their eastern swing. They opened in Ottawa and the defence came up big, especially middle linebacker Cleveland Vann. His late interception of a Condredge Holloway pass sealed a 29-16 victory for Saskatchewan. Then, they went into Hamilton and bombed the Tiger-Cats 24-8. Lancaster used seven different receivers in the game.

Next up were the Edmonton Eskimos in Taylor Field. The Riders played one of the greatest games in their history as they shut out the Eskimos 40-0. Lancaster was on fire, completing 23 of 27 passes for 290 yards and three touchdowns in barely one half of play. Dawson caught six passes and scored a touchdown, Richardson caught five. The defence bottled up Lemmerman and forced him into throwing four interceptions.

Photo courtesy of SSHFM

Roger Aldag's career begins

"Look," said Ray Jauch after the game, "we get to play these guys again."

"You know," said Lancaster, "when I look back at all the years we've been playing those guys, I can never remember beating them that bad."

The Riders would play the Eskimos again, back in Edmonton. And, this was beginning to look as if Saskatchewan finally had crossed that bridge and figured out how to beat Edmonton. It was indeed a long time coming. The Roughrider defence owned Clarke Stadium on this mid-September afternoon. They intercepted Wilkinson and Lemmerman six times and got a seventh turnover on a fumble. The final score? Saskatchewan 34, Edmonton 7.

Rider defensive coach Jim Eddy was giddy over the play of his defence. "They are," he said, "the toughest defence that's ever been assembled in the CFL."

Both Wilkinson and Lemmerman were shaken up in the game. Wilkinson left after George Wells ripped his helmet off. Lemmerman went out after getting hammered by Roger Goree.

And Lancaster continued his dominating play, passing for 185 yards and guiding a ground game that produced over 100 yards.

"I guess you could say I'm a little surprised we beat them that badly again," said Payne. "But, remember, this is the team that's kept us out of the Grey Cup the last three years. We get a little fired up when we play them."

Game 11 saw the arrival of a true Saskatchewan Roughrider legend. When centre Larry Bird tore a ligament in his knee, Payne had no choice but to turn to his Canadian taxi squad for a replacement. The kid's name was Roger Aldag. He had come to Regina from Gull Lake to play for the junior Rams and head coach Gord Currie. He was taught by line coach Doug Killoh, a star when he played for the Riders in the 1950s.

Roger Aldag started his first game as a centre. And he did an outstanding job.

There has never been a quieter offensive lineman than Roger Aldag. To him, a sentence is a speech.

"I heard him yell huddle once today," laughed Lancaster.

"I heard him yell second and six once," said Al Ford.

In his very first game as a starter, Aldag was solid and the Roughriders hammered Calgary 35-10 as Lancaster threw for 351 yards. The game gave the Riders sole possession of first place in the West.

The Riders built a three-point cushion on the Eskimos with two games to go after they beat the Lions 28-15 in Vancouver. The two biggest plays of the game came from defensive back Lorne Richardson. They called him LR Superstar, and this game he lived up to his billing. He intercepted a Rick Cassata pass and returned it for a touchdown. And in the fourth quarter on a third and three gamble by the Lions, Richardson knifed in from the outside like he'd been shot out of a cannon and cut down Mike Strickland for a three-yard loss.

The Roughriders needed a victory in the last game of the regular schedule in the CFL in 1976 to clinch first place. They went into Calgary to play the Stampeders. The Eskimos were already assured of finishing third, and a Saskatchewan loss would mean Winnipeg would get first place.

For the longest of times, it looked as if the Roughriders were about to cough up another loss. The Stampeders burst into a 24-0 lead. But then Lancaster got things rolling in the second half. He gunned them to 25 points. In the final four minutes and 14 seconds of the game, he threw touchdown passes to Leif Pettersen and Rhett Dawson, Dawson's coming on the final play of a game won 33-31 by Saskatchewan.

That play to Dawson was one for the ages. The Riders were at the Calgary four. Everybody expected a running play. "I told Rhett in the huddle to line up on the right side, start out left into the end zone and then come back to the sideline," Lancaster said. "The ball will be there when you come back."

Dawson ran the pattern, and then stopped and turned back. Lancaster had already thrown the ball. "I let it go and looked and nobody was there. Not Rhett. Not anybody. And, then out of the closing darkness came Dawson, arms stretched out, and he brought the ball in for the biggest Saskatchewan victory since 1972.

"Everybody always talked about that 1963 playoff against Calgary as the greatest comeback we ever had," Lancaster said years later. "But that one was a fluke. We never should have won that game. This one, this one was for real. This is the best one we ever had." Over the course of his career, Lancaster would engineer 50 comeback victories, but this was the keeper.

Calgary centre Basil Bark, who had played against Lancaster for years, first in Montreal and then in Calgary, just shook his head. "I know that little guy," said Bark. "I know what he can do. If you get him down, you better keep your foot on his throat. I've seen him do this to teams too many times."

The Eskimos went to Winnipeg for the semi-final, while the Riders rested at home, and Edmonton upset the Bombers 14-12 in a yawner.

Photo courtesy of *Leader-Post*

Rhett Dawson

Photo courtesy of SSHFM

Steve Molnar

Then came the much-anticipated fourth straight Western final meeting between the Eskimos and the Roughriders. Only this time the game was in Regina's Taylor Field. Only this time the Roughriders had all the momentum.

The record Taylor Field crowd of 21,896 fans jammed the place for Saskatchewan's first Western final in Regina since 1970, and from the very beginning to the end they were a wild bunch. "I've never seen our fans like that," Lancaster said.

The Riders pulled a fast one on the Eskimos. "I don't think Edmonton expected us to run the ball," said Lancaster. The Riders' running game had been OK all season long, but it essentially revolved around Molnar, who did gain over 800 yards on the season. But they needed another back to open things up and they got one late in the season when they claimed Molly McGee on waivers from Ottawa.

In the Western final, the running game they had needed all season long exploded.

On the frozen tundra of Taylor Field, on a cold but dry November afternoon, the Saskatchewan Roughriders rocked and rolled their way to a 23-13 victory over the Eskimos. It was something to see, and the voice of the crowd grew louder with each play. There was no grass on the middle of Taylor Field, just dirt. And it looked like old time football. When Molnar ran clouds of dust swirled beneath his cleats. And did he ever run! Steve had the best game of his career, bulling up the middle for 144 yards on 27 carries. And McGee gave the Riders the outside running game, carrying the ball 20 times for an even 100 yards. "I never even thought of passing," said Lancaster. "I didn't even know what coverage their defensive backs were in because I never looked at them."

The Riders only scored two touchdowns in the game, one by Molnar on a one-yard run, the other by tight end Bob Richardson on a sensational-one-handed catch while he was running backwards. "That wasn't a pass," said Lancaster. "It was a catch." The rest of Saskatchewan's points came from kicker Bob Macoritti.

"Our guys did everything they could," said Ray Jauch. "We just lost to a great team and there's no shame in that."

The Taylor Field crowd poured onto the field as soon as the game ended, surrounding the players, and going absolutely nuts with joy. Yes, there was joy in Riderville. The mighty Riders, the greatest dynasty in Saskatchewan's history, was going to the Grey Cup game.

Lancaster had his best passing season since 1966, completing over 60 per cent of his throws for 3,869 yards and 25 touchdowns.

The Roughriders flew into Toronto on Wednesday for the Grey Cup game against the Ottawa Rough Riders. Ottawa quarterback Tom Clements and the reliable tight end Tony Gabriel, an old thorn in Saskatchewan's side.

But Saskatchewan had momentum, and the Riders were quickly established as seven-point favourites to win the Grey Cup.

The week prior to the Grey Cup, everything seemed to point to a Saskatchewan victory. On Thursday, Lancaster was named the most outstanding player in the league.

He was also named to the all-CFL team, as were guard Ralph Galloway, receiver Rhett Dawson, linebacker Roger Goree, and defensive backs Lorne Richardson and Paul Williams.

It seemed like a season and a week made in heaven. And, it ended in hell.

Tom Campana, who didn't play in the Western final because of an ankle injury, was ready to come back. But to get him on the roster, coach John Payne cut Robert Holmes, the only back-up running back the Riders had. Molly McGee broke his ribs halfway through the Grey Cup game, and that killed Saskatchewan's ground game. And, it was eerie watching the retired George Reed standing on the sidelines at the Rider bench. If only …

But Saskatchewan made some critical mistakes. They gave up an easy touchdown to Bill Hatanaka on an 79-yard punt return. Lancaster had trouble with the wind, and the Riders had trouble connecting on key second-down passes.

Photo courtesy of *Leader-Post*

Roger Goree

It didn't matter. The 1976 Grey Cup game came down to one play. The last one, with only 20 seconds left on the clock. Ottawa was at Saskatchewan's 24 yard line. Everybody in the park knew who Clements would try to get the ball to.

"We knew he would go to Gabriel and we had the perfect defence called," said defensive coach Jim Eddy. That defence was supposed to see end Jesse O'Neal step across the line of scrimmage and prevent Clements from rolling out to his right. Goree was to hit Gabriel and make it tough for him to get off the line of scrimmage. Cornerback Ray Odums and safety Ted Provost were to drop back and not let Gabriel get behind them. The ball was snapped. O'Neal didn't get across the line of scrimmage and Clements easily rolled to his right. Goree never touched Gabriel and he came off the line at full speed. He threw an inside move on Provost, and both Provost and Odums bit on it and hesitated long enough for Gabriel to get well behind them. Clements let the ball go and Gabriel caught it with Odums and Provost trying to catch up. Ottawa had won the Grey Cup 23-20.

Things would never be the same again in Saskatchewan. An era had ended. A dynasty was about to crumble. And the photo of Tony Gabriel catching that pass has haunted Saskatchewan football fans to this very day.

If only …

Regina was not the same place when 1977 arrived. The downtown had changed dramatically. The SaskPower Building on Victoria had been hailed around the world as a wonder of architecture. The old City Hall on 11th Avenue would soon be torn down in one of this city's biggest heritage mistakes. And a new City Hall would spring up on Victoria Avenue. The new city hall was designed by Regina architect Joe Pettick. He also would design the Bank of Montreal Building and the Civic Centre in Moose Jaw. A lot had been going on as the city grew and expanded.

And change was sweeping through the Saskatchewan Roughriders. Head coach John Payne left to become an assistant coach with the Detroit Lions of the National Football League. Rogers Lehew, former general manager of the Calgary Stampeders, had taken

Photo courtesy of the *Globe and Mail*

Not the end of the world . . . just the end of an era!

on a similar position with the Lions. And, he hired Tommy Hudspeth as head coach. Hudspeth and Payne were good friends.

Ken Preston replaced Payne with defensive coach Jim Eddy, and nobody questioned that move. Eddy had developed into one of the best defensive coaches the Riders ever had. The Riders lost receiver Rhett Dawson when they wouldn't pay him the $38,000 he wanted. He retired. So did Al Ford. Lorne Richardson wanted more money too and he found it in Toronto, signing with the Argos.

Change was coming to the Roughriders, on and off the field.

The Roughriders had made the playoffs for 16 straight seasons. They appeared in 12 Western finals. They made five Grey Cup appearances and won one of them, in 1966. But that was yesterday and yesterday was certainly gone.

Something happened to the Roughriders in 1977 that nobody really saw coming. For whatever reasons, they lost that killer instinct, that desire to do everything possible to win. And, they replaced it too many times with a team that had too many players willing to run up the white flag.

Right off the bat, the fans saw what the Roughriders would become. They went into Winnipeg, and were hammered 33-11. Then, they came home and were splattered 34-14 by the B.C. Lions. The Riders put together their best game so far when they went to Vancouver and broke a two-game losing streak with a 24-5 win. They got their running game going and everything else seemed to fall into place.

"We've got to remember what we did here," said Lancaster. "Everybody played well. If we don't all play well, we lose. If we do, we have a chance."

The Riders then went on a bit of a tear which saw them win four of five games, but once the season moved into the last half, they couldn't keep up with the rest of the pack. They finished with an 8-8 record and missed the playoffs by four points.

Any chances the Riders might have had of making the playoffs ended with three games to go when Lancaster banged up a knee that ended his season. Backups Eric Guthrie and Mike Nott couldn't replace the Little General. The season ended in humiliation in the last game in Edmonton. It was 38-0 Eskimos.

Somebody asked Steve Molnar how it felt to miss the playoffs. "It hurts, it really hurts," he said. "It's embarrassing."

Guard Ralph Galloway was the only Roughrider to make the all-CFL team. That tells you something.

And it would be Ken Preston's last season as general manager. He retired and Henry Dorsch replaced him.

Throughout the off-season, all anybody talked about was how important it would be for the Roughriders to get off to a winning start in 1978. Everybody circled Wednesday, July 19 on their calendar. That was the date of their opening game in Hamilton against the Tiger-Cats.

The game started out as if it would be a Rider romp. It turned into one of the most incredible coaching decisions I'd ever seen. Lancaster came out on fire and the Ti-Cats were no match for him. By halftime, he had taken the Riders into 20-3 lead, and for all purposes the game seemed over.

At halftime, Lorne Richardson, who had driven over from Toronto to watch his old teammates, came up to the press box and asked me to come out and sit with him in the stands for the second half. "This one's over," said Richardson, "you don't need to take notes anymore."

When the Riders came out for the second half, Larry Dick, a rookie, was at quarterback. I looked down at the Rider bench. Lancaster had his helmet off and was on one knee at the end of the bench, all by himself.

Photo courtesy of SSHFM

Ralph Galloway

"He must be hurt," I said to Richardson.

The Ti-Cats thought the same thing. And, they came after the inexperienced Dick. The whole game quickly turned. The Ti-Cats took over. Hamilton scored eight unanswered points in the third quarter. More importantly, they had stolen the momentum from the Riders.

I left Richardson and went back to the press box. I went into the Riders' coaching box and asked Walt Posadowski if Lancaster was hurt. "Nope," said Walt, "the coach just decided to put Larry in."

In the fourth quarter, Eddy put Lancaster back into the game. But by this time it was over. You don't just flick a switch and everything good happens.

Lancaster had a great night throwing the ball, completing 21 of 29 passes, but the Riders lost 27-23.

Jim Eddy and Ron Lancaster

Photo courtesy of *Leader-Post*

When I went into the Rider dressing room after the game, I knew the season was over. The players were seething. And Lancaster was one of them. They had all lost confidence in Jim Eddy as head coach. So much emphasis had been put on winning that first game, and then Eddy didn't leave Lancaster in to finish off the Ti-Cats.

Over the next couple of days, things reached a boiling point. I heard that Lancaster was either going to retire or ask to be traded. I phoned his house one morning and Bev answered. "Tell him to call me," I said. "I will," she said, "but I don't know ... it's not good around here right now."

I left the newspaper office and drove over to Lancaster's house in Whitmore Park. As I was walking up to the front door, Bev came charging out. "What the hell are you doing here?" she said. "Oh, alright, come in, he'll probably want to talk to you."

We went into the kitchen, and Bev put a finger over her mouth. She pointed to the backyard. I looked out the window and there was Lancaster sitting with Hank Dorsch by the swimming pool. Ronnie was going to quit and Hank was trying to talk him out of it. Lancaster came in to get some more coffee. When he saw me sitting at the kitchen table, he shook his head and, said, "What the hell are you doing here?" "Your wife already said that to me," I told him. "Just stay here, Hank's going pretty soon."

When Dorsch left, I went outside and sat with him by the pool. He said he was ready to quit, but that he had never been a quitter in his life and he couldn't let his teammates down. So, he was going to play out the season and then retire.

The Riders just kept losing after that. When they went into B.C. to play the Lions, they were 0-5, and going nowhere. I talked to Rider president Bruce Cowie before the game.

"When are you guys going to do something?" I said.

"If we lose this game, Jim is gone," Cowie said.

The Riders lost 24-23. Lancaster didn't even make the whole game. He was knocked dizzy when Lions' receiver Jim Young ran over him on a Grady Cavness interception.

The next day, Jim Eddy was fired. And Walt Posadowski was named head coach.

The rest of the season was a virtual write-off. But it did have its comical moments. The Riders were in Toronto in late August to play the Argos. The usual routine was the players would board a chartered bus a couple of hours before kickoff and go to the stadium. A little less than two hours before the game, I went down to the lobby of the Hotel Toronto and saw that the whole team was standing outside.

I asked Lancaster what was going on. "Nobody thought to order the bus," he said, giggling.

"Well, Walt," I said as Posadowski came over.

"The five Ps, Bob, the five Ps," Posadowski said.

"What is that?" I said.

"Prior preparation prevents a piss-pot full of problems."

The season ended on a strange note. In his last game as a Rider in Taylor Field, Lancaster was badly booed by the crowd. It shocked people from around Canada, who called the *Leader-Post*'s sports department and the open line shows to voice their disgust and wonder how fans could treat so poorly someone who had done so much for the franchise.

Ron Lancaster's playing career ended a week later in Edmonton against the Eskimos, who had already clinched first place. Posadowski started Larry Dick at quarterback. The Eskimos were ahead 26-20 when one of the strangest things I'd ever seen in sports happened.

As Ronnie trotted onto the field, the crowd's roar grew and grew to a deafening crescendo. They rose to their feet, one after the other, until all 46,673 of them were screaming to the sky.

The crowd began to chant, "We want Ronnie! We want Ronnie!" Signs started to pop up. "Thanks for the memories, Ronnie." The fire truck that used to circle Commonwealth Stadium when the Eskimos scored now circled it calling for Lancaster.

Posadowski turned to Lancaster and told him to go in at quarterback.

As Ronnie trotted onto the field, the crowd's roar grew and grew to a deafening crescendo. They rose to their feet, one after the other, until all 46,673 of them were screaming to the sky. Dick shook Lancaster's hand as he passed him. Edmonton cornerback Larry Highbaugh came over and shook Ronnie's hand. Players on the Edmonton bench were applauding.

It didn't take the 40-year-old Lancaster long before he put together a touchdown drive, hitting Joey Walters on a nine-yard pass. Again, the crowd roared its approval. The big scoreboard clock in Commonwealth Stadium lit up and flashed the word, "Wow!"

"Wow!" was right. Before the game was over, Lancaster had engineered the last touchdown drive of his career. He carried it in himself from the one-yard-line. The Riders won, 36-26, and the crowd went wild.

Lancaster said he felt the emotion of the moment. But all he really wanted to talk about was how the team played and that they won their last game of the season. "You always want to win that last game."

The greatest player in the history of the Roughriders was retiring. It was a moment of some sadness. But, for all of those who had had the pleasure of playing with him, coaching him, or just watching him, it was a moment of thanks and joy for having had that golden opportunity.

There would never be another like him. There would never again be a number 23 at quarterback.

Photo courtesy of the Willie Jacobs family

Ron Lancaster

All-Era Team
1963-1978

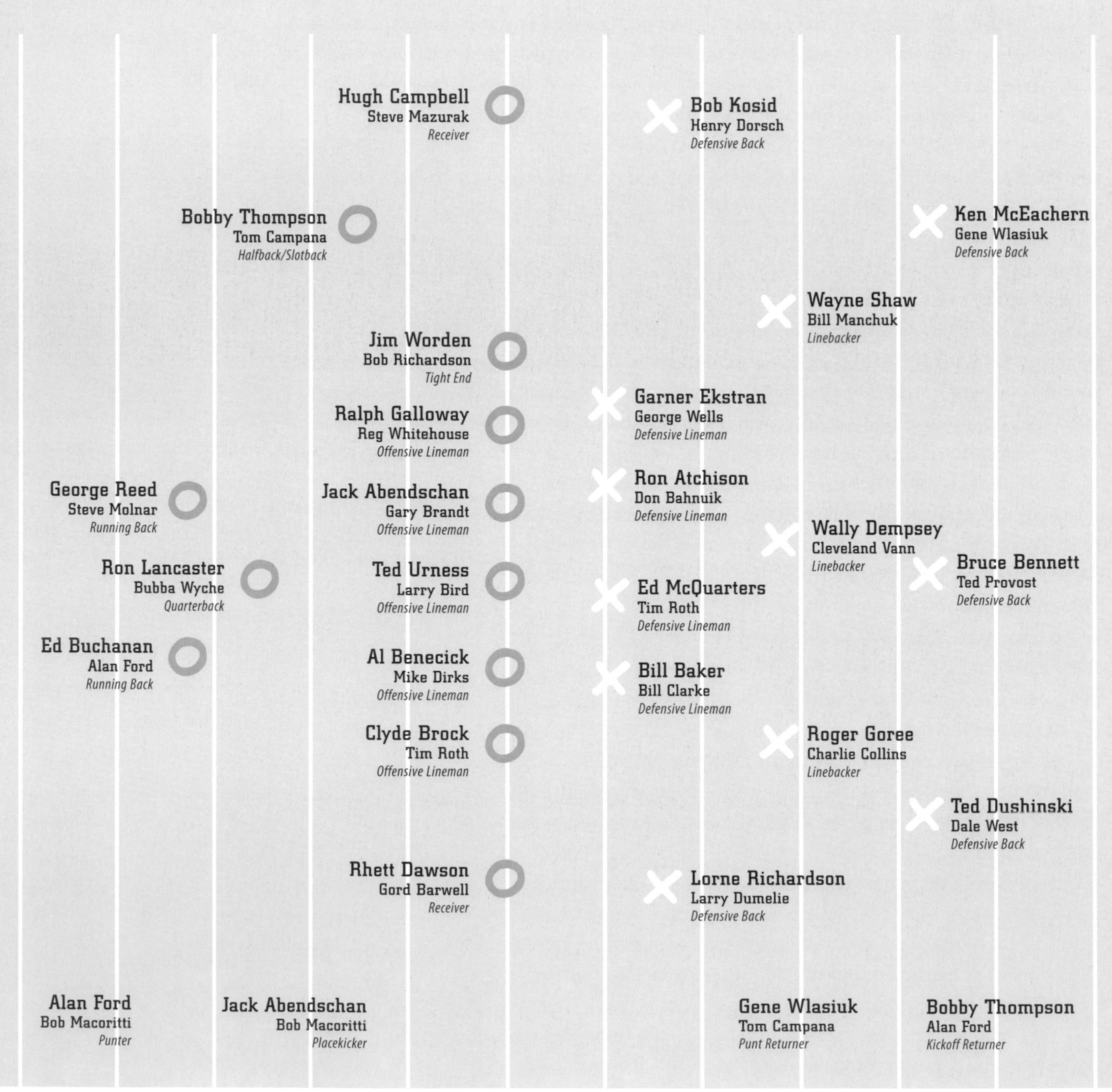

OFFENCE

Large print – 1st Team All-Star
Small print – 2nd Team All-Star
Position

DEFENCE

1979-1989

BY ROB VANSTONE

CHAPTER 4

Photo courtesy of Royal Studios

As the Saskatchewan Roughriders' head coach, Ron Lancaster's initial challenge was to replace Ron Lancaster. The Little General's retirement following the 1978 Canadian Football League season left the Roughriders without a bona fide quarterback. Larry Dick, who had received some playing time in 1978, was viewed by the team's braintrust as a passer of some promise. But there were doubts as to whether Dick was prepared to fill the cleats of the legendary Lancaster.

With that in mind, Lancaster and Roughriders general manager Hank Dorsch went hunting. Phil Simms, who had starred at Morehead State University in Morehead, Ky., was in their sights. "What a nice guy," Lancaster recalled. "Morehead State is not exactly a great football power. He was told he was going to be drafted in the second round. He said, 'If I don't get drafted in the second round, I might just sign and come up there.' "

> "He was told he was going to be drafted in the second round. He said, 'If I don't get drafted in the second round, I might just sign and come up there.' "

Sure enough, Simms was *not* drafted in the second round. The New York Giants selected Simms seventh overall in 1979. "When he went in the first round, I remember calling him and wishing him well, because there's no way in hell he's coming to Regina after being drafted Number 1 by the Giants," Lancaster continued. "He was concerned about who was going to play quarterback for us. I said, 'Don't you worry about that. You just have a good career.' " And he did, becoming one of the elite quarterbacks in the history of the Giants, with whom he enjoyed a near-flawless performance in a 1987 Super Bowl victory over the Denver Broncos.

Even if the Roughriders had successfully landed Simms, they would have faced a dearth of experience at football's most crucial position. To address that deficiency, they began negotiating with the Ottawa Rough Riders. The Eastern Riders knew that 1979 would almost certainly be Tom Clements' last season with the team, given his desire to try the NFL after playing out his option.

Perhaps the most recognizable photo in the club's history is that of Dave Ridgway's last-second field goal which gave the Riders their second Grey Cup victory, a 43-40 triumph over Hamilton in 1989.
(Top Photo)

Clements' contractual situation, along with the presence of future Hall of Fame quarterback Condredge Holloway in the nation's capital, made the Ottawa brass amenable to a trade. Despite the prospect of losing Clements in a year, Saskatchewan was not in a position to quibble. A deal was consummated shortly before training camp. Suddenly, quarterbacking was an area of strength, given Clements' glittering résumé.

Clements would soon be introduced to his Roughriders teammates, along with the new artificial turf at Taylor Field. The SuperTurf was part of an extensive renovation to the stadium. The upgrade had been approved during a future-spending vote held by the City of Regina on December 7, 1977, when 12,859 burgesses favoured the City's expenditure on the football facility, compared to 9,005 against. Voters gave the City authorization to borrow $4 million of its $4.5-million share of the expansion plan. The provincial government was also on board, providing $2.5 million and agreeing to match, dollar for dollar, all funds raised by the Roughriders – who targeted $1 million. The renovation plan extended to the dressing-room facilities at Taylor Field, a plan that would end the long-standing tradition of the Roughriders holding workouts on the infield at Regina Exhibition Track.

Photo courtesy of *Leader-Post*

Gordon Staseson (left) and Ron Lancaster check out the newly renovated Taylor Field and artificial SuperTurf playing surface in 1979.

The $9-million project was to be completed in time for the 1978 season. There was a snag, however, in the form of a construction strike/lockout. The dispute continued well into 1978, meaning that renovations to Taylor Field – including 8,000 new sideline seats on the west side – were incomplete throughout the football season. The upgrades were finally finished in 1979, and not a moment too soon. The last strip of SuperTurf was not installed until a few minutes before the Roughriders' home pre-season opener on June 20, 1979.

"Because of the humidity and daily heat, the turf continued to bubble after being laid, and the turf rolls had to be stripped and relaid several times," said Gordon Staseson, who was the Roughriders' president at the time. "This caused a serious delay in the completion schedule and great concern as to whether the field would be ready for the first pre-season game and the grand opening of the newly renovated Taylor Field."

Complicating matters, SuperTurf was having difficulty recruiting enough rug layers in Regina to complete the installation. Therefore, the turf company decided to import experienced installers from the United States. "The day before the first pre-season game, I visited the new Rider office at Taylor Field and faced a long-faced Hank Dorsch, who informed me that we had big trouble," Staseson recalled. "The rug layers that SuperTurf brought in were arrested by immigration officials for working in Canada illegally. Completion of laying the turf now loomed as an impossibility."

The rug layers that SuperTurf brought in were arrested by immigration officials for working in Canada illegally. Completion of laying the turf now loomed as an impossibility.

Staseson made a bee-line to the courthouse to obtain the rug layers' releases while Dorsch negotiated with immigration officials. A judge heard the case and fined each rug layer $350. The rug layers were to be released upon payment of the fine but, to Staseson's chagrin, the courthouse would not accept a cheque. He then rushed to the Bank of Nova Scotia's branch at the nearby Plains Hotel, cashed the cheque, and paid the fines. The crew worked frantically and completed the installation, just in time for kickoff.

The stadium was ready but, for the Roughriders, the building process was just beginning during what the team billed as "The New Era." A club that had been one of the CFL's finest well into the 1970s was in need of a full-scale overhaul. Saskatchewan had reached the Grey Cup in 1976, losing 23-20 to Ottawa when Tom Clements hit Tony Gabriel on a last-minute touchdown pass. "[The 1976 season] was our last hurrah," Lancaster said. "That was a bunch of guys who had been together for a while and you could see it falling apart." The Roughriders, who had made the playoffs from 1962 to 1976 inclusive, missed the post-season in 1977 and 1978. After going 8-8 in 1977, the Roughriders went 4-11-1 the following year – the team's first losing season since 1961.

Signs of age were especially apparent along the offensive line. Lancaster was quick to take action, initiating an infusion of youth. The onus was on the likes of Roger Aldag, Bob Poley, Neil Quilter, Gerry Hornett and Bryan Illerbrun (who was converted from defensive tackle during the 1979 season) to provide protection for Clements.

"When Ronnie made the transition from player-coach to head coach, he understood that change had to be made with the old guard," Poley said. "They were right at the tail end. They might have had another year, maybe two. He made changes and it gave guys like me a chance to play. I'm forever in his debt about that. He put his neck on the line for guys like me. Roger Aldag had been there for a couple of years, but he was like a raw rookie, too. He started that [mostly] Canadian offensive line." The growing pains were intolerable, and Clements was often running for his life. After seven games – all defeats – Clements had two touchdown passes, 11 interceptions and an untold number of bruises. In a merciful move, he was traded to the Hamilton Tiger-Cats for tight end Lawrie Skolrood, who was converted to an offensive lineman the following season. "When you're zero-and-seven, you've got to do something," Lancaster said at the time.

Photo courtesy of SSHFM

Bob Poley

The Roughriders' record eventually worsened to 0-and-11. At one point during that swoon, Saskatchewan had gone four-plus games without a touchdown. The protracted drought – spanning 266 minutes 48 seconds of playing time – ended September 15 against the visiting Calgary Stampeders, when Willie Wilder caught a short pass from Craig Juntunen, turned up the left sideline and sped 96 yards to paydirt. The nickname of Willie (Touchdown) Wilder was born. For the Roughriders, the highlight reel began and ended there. Calgary won 52-10.

The threat of a winless season was very real as the Green and White prepared for an October 14, 1979 date with the Edmonton Eskimos, who would soon win their second of five consecutive Grey Cups. Against all odds, the Roughriders won 26-25 at Taylor Field on Lancaster's 41st birthday. The contest ended in dramatic fashion, when Edmonton's Dave Cutler lined up to attempt a 32-yard, game-winning field goal on the final play. Cutler's kick went wide and was retrieved by Emil Nielsen, who booted the ball out of the end zone to prevent Edmonton from registering a game-tying single. Tom Wilkinson, who was holding for Cutler, caught the ball and booted it back into the Saskatchewan end zone. Roughriders kicker Bob Macoritti retrieved Wilkinson's punt and again hoofed it out of danger. Wilkinson caught the ball once more, but did so while out of bounds. Macoritti, meanwhile, was writhing on the turf with a serious knee injury. For everyone else, the victory had alleviated the pain.

Photo courtesy of *Leader-Post*

Joey Walters

"As much as we were able to celebrate the win and get the monkey off our back for a minute, I was still thinking, 'Let's just keep this in perspective. It's just one win. We've lost 11 of them. Let's not get too carried away here,' " said Joey Walters, who had nine receptions for 212 yards in that game, including a 52-yard touchdown pass from Danny Sanders. "We could breathe for a minute, but we were still at the bottom of the pole."

That improbable victory served as a catalyst for Rider Pride. After upsetting Edmonton, the Roughriders had one regular-season home game remaining – an October 28 clash with the British Columbia Lions. With Winnipeg-based sports writer and broadcaster John Robertson (formerly of the *Leader-Post*) leading the charge, the occasion of the B.C. game would be known as "Rider Pride Day." The objective was to pack an expanded Taylor Field – capacity: 27,606 – for the first time.

In the 10 days leading up to the game, Robertson made five trips to Regina while paying his own travel and accommodations expenses. "There is a magnet here," he told the crowd at the Roughriders' $200-a-plate dinner. "It's like an old lover I keep coming back to." Robertson was offered a $500 speaker's fee, but declined any compensation. He was also a guest on open-line radio shows that were used to sell tickets for the game.

"But if you're like me, sometimes you're so busy telling them what they are doing wrong, you forget to tell them that you still love them as much as ever."

If that wasn't enough, Robertson penned a column which appeared in a full-page advertisement that was published in the October 23, 1979 *Leader-Post*. "I know that many thousands of you have grown to love the Roughriders over the years, as if they were your own sons," Robertson wrote. "And I know that you don't quit being proud of your sons just because they lose a few football games. But if you're like me, sometimes you're so busy telling them what they are doing wrong, you forget to tell them that you still love them as much as ever. Sometimes you forget to tell them how proud you are of them, even when they make mistakes – and recent Rider teams and their executives have made more than their share of mistakes. Sometimes you let them grow away from you – perhaps because they stopped reminding you how much they needed your support – until one day when you decided to put on your coat and go and see them, you discovered to your horror that they were gone … forever."

The impassioned blitz was successful, as 28,012 eyewitnesses watched Saskatchewan win 26-12. The overflow crowd raised an estimated $80,000 in additional funds for the Roughriders, who would lose more than $400,000 on their 1979 operations. "When you have 28,000 fans in there, that's all they talked about leading up to the game, and after the game," Lancaster said. "For the next X number of years, that was the slogan – Rider Pride. To be part of that and to be on that field when there were 28,000 in there, that was quite a place to play. On that particular day, it was very noisy and it was a fun place to be."

"To be part of that and to be on that field when there were 28,000 in there, that was quite a place to play."

The atmosphere was funereal more often than it was fun in 1979. Saskatchewan posted a 2-14 record – the second-worst in franchise history – while being outscored 437-194. Saskatchewan had a meagre 17 touchdowns to show for 16 games. Perhaps the ugliest statistic pertained to the quarterbacks. Clements, Dick, Sanders, Lloyd Patterson and Craig Juntunen combined for nine touchdown passes and (get this) 38 interceptions.

Entering the 1980 season, a quarterback was once again atop the Roughriders' wish list. Dick had suffered a career-ending knee injury on Labour Day weekend against the Winnipeg Blue Bombers. Patterson and Juntunen were not invited back. Sanders' late-season heroics were not enough to convince Lancaster and general manager Jim Spavital – who had succeeded Hank Dorsch after the 1979 season – that the quarterbacking situation was stable.

For the second straight off-season, the Roughriders went shopping for a veteran, signing John Hufnagel (previously of Calgary) as a free agent. The hope was that Hufnagel, operating behind an offensive line that had steadily improved in 1979, would enliven the Roughriders' offence.

With Hufnagel at the controls, Saskatchewan was able to register its first victory much more quickly than in 1979. The 1980 Roughriders won in Week 4, edging the host Tiger-Cats 19-18. That was the first game in which Hufnagel had gone the distance for Saskatchewan. He had missed most of the first three games after tearing ligaments in a thumb in the regular-season opener.

Saskatchewan waited until its 13th game for its other victory of 1980 – an 18-14 conquest of the visiting Stampeders. Joe Barnes, a mid-season acquisition from the Montreal Alouettes, was the quarterback of record for the Roughriders in the second win.

Photo courtesy of *Leader-Post*

John Hufnagel

Photo courtesy of *Leader-Post*

Ken McEachern returns one of his 38 interceptions for big yardage in 1980, when his 10 pickoffs led the league

> "I remember walking though the locker room and Bob Poley goes, 'Coach! Come here!' " Lancaster remembered. "I said, 'What's up?' He said, 'You've got to tell Doug MacIver to quit using these big words. He's using the word empathy.' "

The 1980 Roughriders were often competitive, scoring 90 more points than the 1979 edition while boasting an all-Canadian safety – Ken McEachern, whose 10 interceptions led the CFL. The fans took notice, as overall attendance increased from 169,484 in 1979 to 196,456 in 1980. The atmosphere at Taylor Field was enhanced by a fight song, "Green Is The Colour," which is played at Roughriders games to this day.

The record, however, was the same, old, unsightly 2-14. "It was excruciating," Joey Walters said. "I would show [the frustration] more when I was alone as opposed to in front of my teammates, because I wanted to keep everybody positive. Ronnie wanted to keep everybody as positive as possible, saying, 'OK, this is going to be the week. Let's put what we got into it. Everybody concentrate.' There were a number of us on the team who were the cheerleaders, per se, and tried to keep the morale up because obviously it's tremendously tough when you're going through a season like that to keep from saying, 'Here we go again, another loss.' "

Despite the almost-weekly defeats, the Roughriders were somehow able to maintain a sense of humour. "I remember walking though the locker room and Bob Poley goes, 'Coach! Come here!' " Lancaster remembered. "I said, 'What's up?' He said, 'You've got to tell Doug MacIver to quit using these big words. He's using the word empathy. I told him before that we don't understand anything bigger than handkerchief and marmalade. That's all you can use in here.' I'll never forget that."

"Bobby bends down over the ball, turns around before he snaps, and says, 'Now, Bob, do you want the ball in the air or do you want it to bounce like you get it in the game?' I thought that was funny as hell."

Nor would he forget an anecdote involving punter/placekicker Bob Macoritti and the head coach's son, Bobby Lancaster. "We were at practice one day," the elder Lancaster said. "I looked down at the other end of the field and Macoritti's down there kicking, and Bobby's down there. We go into the locker room and Macoritti says, 'Coach, come here.' Macoritti said that Bobby had asked if he wanted him to snap the ball and he said, 'Sure.' Bobby bends down over the ball, turns around before he snaps, and says, 'Now, Bob, do you want the ball in the air or do you want it to bounce like you get it in the game?' I thought that was funny as hell."

The events that soon followed the 1980 season were no laughing matter for Lancaster. Everything began agreeably enough, as Lancaster signed a contract extension in November. But within hours of the announcement, he experienced second thoughts, saying he "just didn't feel like going through it anymore." "I knew that it was over when the press conference ended," Lancaster told the *Leader-Post* at the time. "Before I made the decision, I had a weight on my shoulders. When I left the press conference, it was still there. I knew things weren't right. After I had decided to stay, I should have felt pretty good about it. I didn't. When I left the office to meet my wife Bev for lunch, I didn't feel that good about it.

"It was the hardest decision I ever had to make. I just never really had the time I needed to think it all out. I wanted to wait until after the Grey Cup. I needed to get out of here, to get away from everything so I could think about it, but they wanted a decision this week and I can understand that. They treated me fairly."

After 18 years – 16 as a quarterback and two as the head coach – Ron Lancaster was an ex-Roughrider. "I think I had kind of been around there long enough," he reflected. "I was part of that scene for a long time."

Joe Faragalli's association with the Edmonton Eskimos' scene was one reason why the Roughriders coveted him as a head coach. Six days before Christmas in 1980, general manager Jim Spavital unveiled Faragalli as the field boss. "He really impressed me," Spavital said. "He had a lot of knowledge about our team. And Hughie [Campbell, the Eskimos' head coach] told me that Joe was the guy who designed Edmonton's offensive strategy."

That is why the Roughriders had designs on Faragalli. "The worst is over," the affable Faragalli said at his introductory media conference. "I can smell it. I can feel it. I want to be a part of it." Faragalli then examined his diamond-studded Grey Cup ring, earned while he was a part of the Eskimos' dynasty, and said: "I won't be wearing this anymore, I guess."

In Faragalli and Spavital, the Roughriders had two football-operations people who quickly endeared themselves to the community and the team. Faragalli, nicknamed Papa Joe, had an appropriately paternal relationship with the players. The players were not quite as enamoured of Spavital, who was a tight-fisted contract negotiator, but the fans adored him. Spavital rarely, if ever,

Photo courtesy of *Leader-Post*

Joe Faragalli (left) and Jim Spavital

Photo courtesy of *Leader-Post*

Joe Barnes warms up in 1980

declined an invitation to appear at social function, regardless of where it was in Saskatchewan. The folksy general manager was especially conspicuous at Roughriders pep rallies and pancake breakfasts, which preceded home games.

The bond with the fans was strengthened when the Roughriders, having missed the playoffs for four consecutive seasons, reversed their fortunes in 1981. The defence was led by rush end Vince Goldsmith, who registered 18½ sacks en route to being named the CFL's rookie-of-the-year. Faragalli was, as advertised, a tonic for the offence. The 1981 Roughriders scored 431 points – 147 more than in 1980, and 237 more than in 1979 – while relying on a high-powered aerial attack.

Veteran quarterbacks John Hufnagel and Joe Barnes formed an effective tandem – which was dubbed J.J. Barnagel. Oftentimes, Barnes would start the game before giving way to Hufnagel. In one complete-game effort, Barnes threw five touchdown passes in a blowout victory over his former team, the host Alouettes. When the Roughriders next opposed Montreal, at Taylor Field, Hufnagel led a stirring second-half rally from a 26-8 deficit by helping his team amass 27 unanswered points. That was the nature of the

Joe Barnes, Joe Faragalli and John Hufnagel ... Barnes and Hufnagel were dubbed "J.J. Barnagel"

Photo courtesy of *Leader-Post*

1981 Roughriders, who were nicknamed the Cardiac Cowboys for their heart-stopping finishes. By season's end, Barnagel had produced 33 touchdown passes (including 21 by Hufnagel) and 4,873 aerial yards. One out of every 14 attempts by Hufnagel went for a TD.

Hufnagel and Barnes worked effectively with a talented quartet of receivers – Walters, Chris DeFrance, Emanuel Tolbert and Dwight Edwards. Walters and DeFrance were especially dangerous at the slotback positions, both eclipsing the 1,000-yard mark. Walters was named the Roughriders' most outstanding player after catching 91 passes for 1,715 yards and 14 touchdowns. The yardage figure remains a Roughriders single-season record, having rarely been approached.

The acrobatic slotback, who was noted for leaping and diving catches, thrived under Faragalli. Walters had been primarily a wide receiver until late in the 1980 season, when head coach Ron Lancaster utilized No. 17 at slotback. Walters become entrenched at that position when Faragalli took over. "Joe told me, 'Joey, I want to move you inside,' " Walters recalled. "Joe probably got that from being with Edmonton and having Tommy Scott. He felt that he could use me in the middle like they used Tommy Scott. To be honest with you, I said, 'Joe, I don't know whether I want to move inside. I like where I'm at.' He said, 'Joey, I need you inside. This is where you're going to best help the team and that's where I need you to be. Believe me, you'll enjoy it there.' It worked out great."

So did the 1981 season, for the most part. By the eight-game mark, the Roughriders had a 4-4 record – matching their victory total for the previous two seasons combined. Rider Pride reached a state of hysteria when Saskatchewan's slate improved to 7-4. Suddenly, a Rider ticket was a prized possession. Unlike 1979, when John Robertson was the energy behind "Rider Pride Day," a ticket blitz was not required. The team's performance was enough to pack the park. In 1981, five of the eight regular-season home games – including the final four – were sold out. The 1981 Roughriders ended up entertaining 222,626 spectators, an average of 27,828 per game (or 222 more than Taylor Field's seating capacity). The extras spilled over into the south end zone, known as Hemorrhoid Hill.

Having completed the regular-season home schedule, the Roughriders travelled to Vancouver for the finale against the B.C. Lions. The winner was to earn the Western Conference's third and final playoff berth. The game proved to be as ugly as the weather. Relentless rain, which was

Photo courtesy of *Leader-Post*

Dick Rendek (left) and Jim Spavital preview promotional flashcards washing out roads and bridges and causing mudslides, pelted Empire Stadium. "It was horrible," athletic therapist Ivan Gutfriend said. "You're standing on the sideline and there's water going over your ankles. That's how hard it was raining."

The Roughriders' high-octane passing attack was grounded by the inclement conditions. Even so, Saskatchewan was in the game until 2:45 remained in the fourth quarter. Faragalli, who had a magic touch for most of the 1981 season, sent in a trick play to quarterback Joe Barnes. The Riders' field boss called for a reverse to wide receiver Dwight Edwards. However, Barnes collided with running back Greg Fieger while preparing to flip the ball to Edwards. The ball popped loose and the Lions' Nick Hebeler recovered. The Roughriders never did. Larry Key ran for a touchdown on first-and-goal from the two-yard line. The Lions won 13-5. "I wish there was a dome then," centre Bob Poley said.

Saskatchewan emerged from the downpour with a 9-7 record – its first winning season since 1976. Had a crossover playoff format been in effect at the time, the Roughriders would have easily made the playoffs. The Roughriders were fourth in the West, but their record would have placed them second in the East, well ahead of Ottawa (5-11), Montreal (3-13) and Toronto (2-14). Montreal and Ottawa were second and third, respectively, in the East and advanced to the post-season. "We were better than the weak sisters who got into the playoffs in the East," Poley said. "That was our fate and we accepted it, but it was tough to watch those guys play."

Photo courtesy of *Leader-Post*

Marshall Hamilton (24) and Joe Faragalli celebrate

The tough times were on hold in Riderville. A $704,600 profit from the 1981 operations easily eliminated the accumulated deficit of $47,400. Some of the profits were used to sign Faragalli to a contract extension. Faragalli also found himself $5,000 richer, courtesy of Molson's, when he was named the CFL's coach-of-the-year. "We had no superstars on our team … no Vince Ferragamos … no big-salaried players," Faragalli told Bob Hughes after receiving the award. "But the players were all-stars in my eyes. On game days, it was up to them. I pray and they play. We have the best fans in the whole world. They are everywhere. They sing their little songs and wave those pompoms and people think they're weird, but it affects the whole team." There was only one downside to moving to Regina, according to Faragalli. "Leaving Edmonton to go to Saskatchewan cost me a fourth Grey Cup ring," he quipped.

Under Faragalli, the Roughriders never recaptured the magic of 1981 – except at the gate. In 1982, Saskatchewan established a franchise single-season attendance mark of 224, 824, averaging 28,103 customers per game, en route to finishing last in the Western Conference. The Roughriders' success at the turnstiles was largely attributable to a record season-ticket count – 21,686.

However, the fans had much less to cheer about in 1982. The sour notes began even before the season. In early May, the Roughriders dealt quarterback Joe Barnes to Toronto for cornerback Marcellus Greene, whom Faragalli labelled the best defensive back in the Eastern Conference. "What happens to J.J. Barnagel?" John Hufnagel, one-half of the Roughriders' quarterbacking hybrid, wondered after being informed that Barnes had been dealt. Faragalli defended the deal by pointing out that Hufnagel had a greater comprehension of the offence. The head coach also noted that "by the end of the year, John was ahead" in terms of performance, suggesting that it was "60-40, 65-35 in John's favour."

> Faragalli defended the deal by pointing out that Hufnagel had a greater comprehension of the offence.

"Another reason we traded Joe," Faragalli continued, "was because I did not want the Saskatchewan Roughriders to end up in the same position they were in when Ron Lancaster retired – and they had no quarterback to replace him. Joe and John are about the same age and we would be in that same situation if they retired at the same time … This didn't take place overnight. I must have looked at it 20 different ways and there is no doubt that Joe played a great part in our turnaround, but I felt this was the only way to go." With Barnes suddenly out of the equation, Faragalli looked toward rocket-armed Joe (747) Adams as the quarterback of the future.

With Hufnagel as the starter, the 1982 Roughriders staggered out of the gate – losing their first two games. The only bright spot during that span was provided by Walters, who made one of the most spectacular receptions in franchise history – a diving, one-handed touchdown catch – during a 26-24 home-field loss to B.C.

Photo courtesy of *Star-Phoenix*

Joey Walters makes a typical circus catch

Fearing a nosedive, Faragalli opted to start Adams at quarterback after the offence continued to falter under Hufnagel. He regained the No. 1 job near mid-season, but Papa Joe again turned to 747 shortly thereafter. Adams was at the controls for the Roughriders' most-inspired showing of the 1982 campaign – a 53-8 victory over the visiting Stampeders. The Sunday afternoon slaughter was televised on NBC as the American network sought to satisfy fans' football fixes during an NFL strike.

The Roughriders were operating without a full-time general manager. Jim Spavital had resigned in late August to become the GM of Detroit's franchise in the fledgling United States Football League, which was to begin play early in 1983.

By that time, the Roughriders were operating without a full-time general manager. Jim Spavital had resigned in late August to become the GM of Detroit's franchise in the fledgling United States Football League, which was to begin play early in 1983. "Detroit gave me a hell of a deal," Spavital told the *Leader-Post*. "Money was the big thing, but the benefits also had a lot to do with it … I really enjoyed Regina and working for the Roughriders. I enjoyed the fans and I enjoyed working for the people that I worked for. It was fun. They treated me fairly, and I feel we accomplished a lot. In a way, I am sorry that I am leaving before the job is finished, but this is the kind of business where you have to make the best of opportunities when they're presented to you. This was something I just couldn't afford to turn down."

Minus Spavital, the Roughriders had to improvise for the remainder of the 1982 season. "I made an arrangement with Joe Faragalli," said Dick Rendek, who was the Roughriders' president at the time. "I told him, 'I will take care of the business end, but you take care of the football side because I don't pretend to be a football [person].' I did this because it's not an easy task trying to find a GM midway through the year. It resulted in me being at the Rider office from seven o'clock in the morning to noon, going to the law office for the rest of the afternoon, going home for supper, and then going back to the Rider office. It was interesting times."

Photo courtesy of *Leader-Post*

Joey Walters makes a touchdown catch on Rider Pride Day in 1979

There was only one interesting aspect of the Roughriders' 1982 season finale: Would Walters set a CFL single-season receptions record? He entered the game with 92 catches, eight shy of a standard the Blue Bombers' Eugene Goodlow had established the previous season. As the Eskimos assumed an insurmountable lead, the Roughriders turned their attention to ensuring that Walters would at least threaten the record. He ended up with 10 receptions on the day, finishing the season with 102 grabs for 1,692 yards. A Taylor Field crowd of 27,830 gave an emotional Walters a standing ovation. For Roughriders fans, it was a rare opportunity to cheer. A 46-22 loss to Edmonton left Saskatchewan with a 6-9-1 record. On a positive note, the Roughriders had a $788,600 profit to show for 1982, fattening their Heritage Stabilization Fund to $1,456,200. It helped that the Roughriders had 28,103 spectators per game, or 497 more than capacity.

A Taylor Field crowd of 27,830 gave an emotional Walters a standing ovation. For Roughriders fans, it was a rare opportunity to cheer.

Having closed the books on a disappointing season, the Roughriders brass turned its attention to finding a general manager to replace Jim Spavital. The short list was eventually whittled down to two candidates – Paul Robson and John Herrera. The Roughriders thought they were close to a deal with Robson, who was the Blue Bombers' assistant general manager. Those plans were scuttled when Earl Lunsford resigned as the Bombers' GM, creating a vacancy that Robson quickly filled. The Roughriders then intensified their courtship of the 36-year-old Herrera, who had spent two seasons as the B.C. Lions' director of player personnel.

A disciple of Oakland Raiders boss Al Davis, Herrera wore a diamond-studded Super Bowl ring when he was introduced at a media conference on December 8, 1982. Herrera had scouted for the Raiders when they won the 1981 Super Bowl.

He also had player-personnel experience with the Washington Redskins and Tampa Bay Buccaneers before joining the Lions. In addition, Herrera had a background in public relations and marketing, which were two other prerequisites for the Roughriders' new GM. "I can't describe how happy I am," Herrera said when the announcement was made. "This is something I have worked towards. It's what I wanted to be."

Herrera's involvement with professional football dated back to 1963 when his father, Andrew, mentioned to Davis that he had a teenaged son who loved sports. The owner of Herrera Buick knew the Raiders' boss as a business acquaintance. "Al said, 'Well, send him down and I'll talk to him and see if I can find a spot for him at training camp when he's not in school during the summer,' " Herrera recalled, flashing back to the fourth year of the American Football League. "So I went down and talked to him and we hit it right off and he hired me immediately to work summer camp. The first thing he told me was, 'I'm not bringing you up so that you can run around the field and chase balls and pick up jockstraps. I'm hiring you because you told me you can type. You can answer a phone. You can talk. You can drive, so you can run errands for me. I expect you to work 24 hours a day while you're in camp and be an asset for us.' So I gladly accepted those terms, for $25 a week."

Photo courtesy of *Leader-Post*

John Herrera

After agreeing to terms with the Roughriders, Herrera's first priority was to meet with head coach Joe Faragalli. A general manager typically appoints his own head coach, but Herrera ended up inheriting Faragalli. "I knew when Spav left, I became in a very precarious position," Faragalli told the *Leader-Post*. "In my heart, I knew I could be in trouble. It's nothing surprising. Football is my business and I know my business as well as anybody knows their business." Herrera soon met with Faragalli and endorsed him as the head coach for 1983.

That being done, Herrera shifted gears and dove into negotiations with Joey Walters, who was about to become a free agent. The spectacular slotback had earned all-Canadian status in 1981 and 1982, receiving the Roughriders' most-popular-player award in both of those seasons.

In the early stages of contract talks, Herrera expressed optimism that a deal would be reached. No such luck. Walters ended up signing with the Washington Federals of the USFL. "It was like leaving a part of your family, especially from a fan perspective," he said. "It wasn't anything that I wanted to do. I felt that the team could have definitely kept me there, because it wasn't a big demand. All that they would have had to have done was pay me in American money. They were offering Canadian money, and I wanted them to pay my changeover rate so that I wouldn't lose so much money.

"I'll bet you it wasn't any more than $20,000 or $30,000. I didn't think that was an out-of-the-world request – I really didn't. The changeover was killing me. They didn't want to do that." Herrera felt it went beyond being a matter of choice. "There were two things," he recalled. "One, it probably wouldn't have mattered how much money we

Photo courtesy of SSHFM

Eddie Lowe tracks down Winnipeg quarterback Tom Clements (2)

would have offered him. He wanted to go back and play in the States. He wanted that opportunity. And, two, they did pay him a lot more money than we could. In the end, they were just going to pay him whatever it took. We really didn't have a real great chance there with Joey."

With Walters off to the USFL, the Roughriders signed another former Clemson University standout. Homer Jordan, who had quarterbacked Clemson to the NCAA title in 1981, was one of Herrera's first major recruits. The rookie GM also made it a priority to upgrade the defensive line, signing three graduating collegians – J.C. Pelusi (from the University of Pittsburgh), Karl Morgan (UCLA) and Ron Mackey (Central Oklahoma). With less fanfare, Herrera also recruited linebacker Eddie Lowe, who had sparkled for iconic head coach Paul (Bear) Bryant with the Alabama Crimson Tide. Herrera also engineered a steal in the second round of the 1983 CFL draft, selecting Utah receiver Ray Elgaard.

The Roughriders' Canadian talent was depleted by a March deal that sent non-import safety Ken McEachern – a fixture with the Green and White since 1974 – to Toronto for American slotback Dave Newman. Newman, it was reasoned, would help the Roughriders weather the departure of Joey Walters. As it turned out, Newman never played a regular-season game with Saskatchewan. After an unimpressive pre-season, he was shipped to Ottawa for future considerations.

Nonetheless, Herrera was exuding optimism about the future. "We have all the parts to be a solid contender," he told Nick Miliokas of the *Leader-Post* as the 1983 season approached. "I would be very disappointed if we're not a solid contender." Herrera ended up being very disappointed. After winning their regular-season opener, the Roughriders lost the next five games. Faragalli lost his job as a consequence. The *Leader-Post*'s Bob Hughes referred to the purge, which also included the firing of assistant coach Mike Murphy, as The Night of The Long Knives.

"The firing of Faragalli was the messiest [of any Roughriders coaching change]," Hughes wrote in the Saturday, August 20 edition, taking dead aim at Herrera and the Roughriders' management committee. "It lacked class, showed no sense of decency and, in fact, was cruelly done. They have no conscience. They stuck him on a spit last Sunday night, following a 36-28 loss to the Calgary Stampeders, the fifth straight defeat, and left him spinning on

Photo courtesy of *Leader-Post*

Joe Faragalli (left) and John Herrera

it until yesterday when they finally got around to telling him he was fired. It made you want to puke.

"Not until this morning did they officially announce it, even though everybody in town knew about it last night. The publicly owned team, operated like a highly secretive private corporation, concerned more at times with making money than the playoffs, continues to wander aimlessly through its make-believe world, the Reign of Error guaranteed to run another year, the Relapse Roughriders assured of another year out of the playoffs, the Grim Machine just that."

> **"That's the first time I can remember going to a staff function where people were crying. It was almost like we lost a family member."**

The atmosphere was equally grim at the Faragalli residence. "It was very sad when he was fired," equipment manager Norm Fong remembered. "When he got fired, Joe and his wife had kind of a going-away party for everybody. That's the first time I can remember going to a staff function where people were crying. It was almost like we lost a family member. It was sad, because he didn't have to do that. I don't know if he ever had a bad day. Getting fired didn't bother him. He was more worried about his assistant coaches and what was going to happen to them. He was really special."

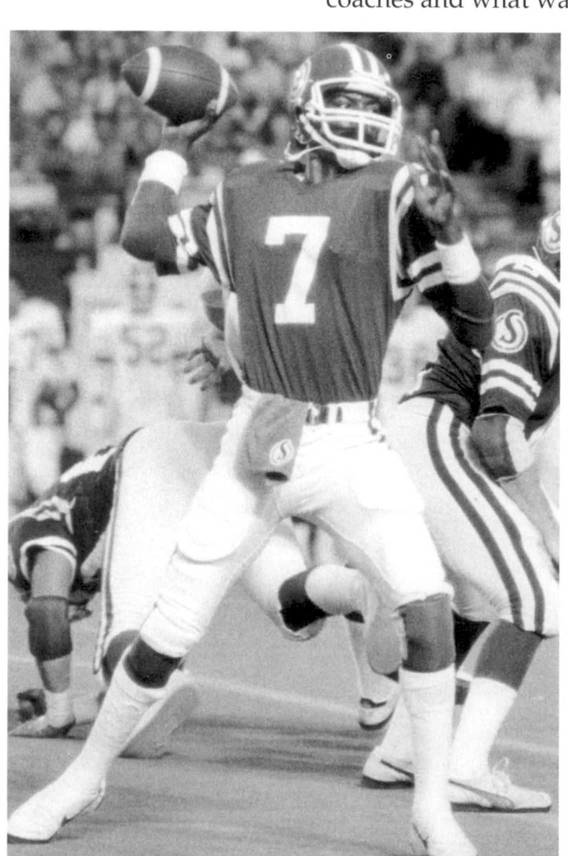

Photo courtesy of *Leader-Post*

Joe (747) Adams

Faragalli was initially reticent about his firing, but he opened up late in 1983 when interviewed by Nick Miliokas. "As a head coach, I wanted the right to make my own decisions, and to live and die with those decisions," Faragalli said. "The ground rules were laid down between Spav and me. Anytime we had our differences, I'd say to him, 'You promised me I could do it my way,' and that always ended the argument. When they hired the new man, I could see right away that I might have a problem. I'm no dummy. I knew I didn't have the same agreement anymore. Spav's gone. The agreement's gone. The ground rules changed … I have only myself to blame. Thinking back, the smartest thing I could have done was say, 'Forget it.' I could have saved myself a lot of aggravation, a lot of disappointment. The thing was, I didn't want to let it go. You let loyalty affect your decisions."

Faragalli's loyalty to his players ultimately worked to his detriment, at least in the case of Joe (747) Adams. Papa Joe was in awe of Adams' physical attributes and gave him every opportunity to become the quarterback Saskatchewan had coveted since the retirement of Ron Lancaster. But once Faragalli was gone, so was 747. "Adams could throw a mile," centre Bob Poley said. "Roger Aldag had a great line for him. He said, 'He's got all the tools, but he has no toolbox to put 'em all in.' Joe Faragalli was comparing him to a young Warren Moon. Joe got fired over that." Aldag also weighed in on 747, noting: "You knew there was a pretty good chance the pass was going to be completed, but it wasn't always to our guys."

Adams did figure in a classic play with the Roughriders. When the Roughriders faced Edmonton on August 5, 1983, Chris DeFrance had 260 receiving yards – a single-game franchise record – on nine catches. Included was an 88-yard touchdown hookup with Adams. On that play, DeFrance lost his helmet after absorbing a punishing hit over the

Photo courtesy of *Leader-Post*

Chris DeFrance makes a catch between two B.C. Lions defenders

middle, but maintained his balance and sprinted untouched into the end zone. More than a helmet was lost on that evening. The Roughriders fell, 36-21.

The departures of Faragalli and Adams left the Roughriders in need of a head coach and a starting quarterback. The latter position was filled by John Hufnagel, who was reinstated as the No. 1 signal-caller. The choice of field boss was less obvious, except to Herrera. Reuben Berry, who was a colleague of Herrera's with B.C., was chosen to head the Roughriders' on-field operation. Berry had been a head coach in the American college ranks (most notably at Northeastern, where he spent five years), but his professional experience was limited to four seasons as an assistant with B.C. – first as the offensive backfield coach, then as linebackers coach. When Herrera called about the Saskatchewan job, Berry was a junior partner with an oil company in his native Oklahoma.

Herrera touted Berry as a "motivator of men and a sound fundamentalist." The sounds of Berry resonated long after his departure, due to the slogans and sayings for which he was noted. Berry quickly coined the term "Saskatchewan Tough" and wanted his players to adhere to that template. Berry's own toughness was on display with the United States military. He was stationed in New York at the time of the Korean War. "I defended the East Coast," the ever-quotable Berry said. "I kept the Koreans from invading. If you check the record, you'll find that they never did advance inland." Berry

Photo courtesy of *Leader-Post*

John Herrera (left) and Reuben Berry announcing a coaching change in 1983.

was most concerned with contributing to the advancement of the Roughriders and their generally inexperienced players. "We have some young pups over there," he observed. "I'm hoping to make howling hounds out of them."

Berry's head-coaching debut was inauspicious. With less than a week to become acclimatized, Berry watched Saskatchewan lose 36-15 to Toronto, which would go on to win the 1983 Grey Cup (with Joe Barnes playing a key role). Next on the agenda was the annual Labour Day weekend clash with Winnipeg. At 1-6, the Roughriders were expected to be easy prey, but unusual things have been known to occur at Taylor Field on the final long weekend of the summer. The Blue Bombers were ahead 30-29 with 1:31 remaining in the fourth quarter, at which point Saskatchewan assumed possession on its 37-yard line. Hufnagel crisply moved the Roughriders into field-goal range, thanks largely to a 37-yard connection with DeFrance. There was only one snag: Saskatchewan was without its placekicker. Dave Ridgway had sustained a mild concussion after tackling Nate Johnson on a kickoff return early in the third quarter and was taken to hospital as a precautionary measure. That left the placement duties in the hands – or feet, as it were – of punter Ken Clark, who had last handled field goals on a regular basis seven years earlier with Hamilton.

Nonetheless, Clark was Berry's best/only bet. The veteran kicker nailed a 41-yard field goal into the wind with 43 seconds remaining. That proved to be the winning kick as Saskatchewan prevailed 32-30. Adding to the drama, Clark had just returned to Regina from Toronto and the bedside of his dying mother, who had suffered an aneurysm. "I had to come back and play," Clark, who also unloaded a team-record 101-yard punt during that memorable game, told the *Leader-Post*. "My mom, she was such a good fan. She wouldn't have had it any other way. This was a special day. I had dedicated it to her."

Veronica Clark died hours after the game. "I knew that kick was going through," Ken Clark said. "I didn't have any doubt … During the game, I felt that my mother was there for that amount of time – and gone as soon as the ball went through the uprights."

Photo courtesy of *Leader-Post*

Ken Clark kicking a game-winning field goal

Hufnagel led another come-from-behind victory the following week, celebrating a 29-28 conquest of the host Ottawa Rough Riders. The progress ended there. Five successive losses ensued. During a 40-23 loss to the visiting Montreal Concordes, an effigy of Herrera was hung over the top railing of the upper deck by some frustrated fans. "[Criticism] does hurt a little bit when people can't see the overall picture," Herrera told the *Leader-Post*. "The bottom line is that I came here to do a job. I charted a course and I'm sticking to it. I'm not going to let a fringe element deter me from that task."

By then, Herrera had become known as Trader John. Ron Robinson, another unsuccessful candidate to replace Joey Walters at slotback, was dealt to Montreal. Hufnagel, meanwhile, was sent to Winnipeg along with defensive lineman J.C. Pelusi – one of the Roughriders' most-ballyhooed off-season signings – for wide receiver Nate Johnson, quarterback Nickie Hall, offensive lineman Jason Riley and a draft pick.

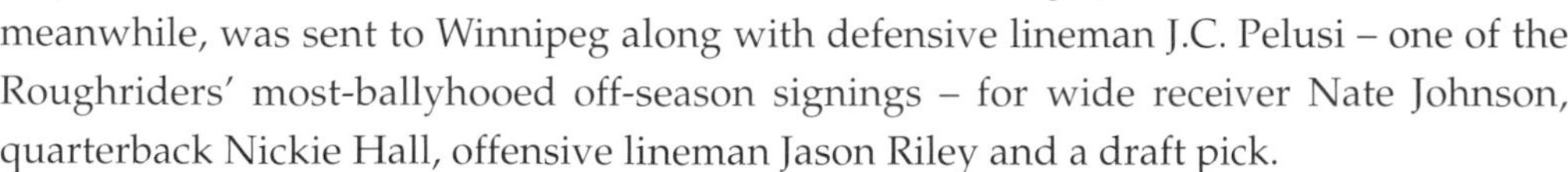

In another deal of note, Herrera sent punter Ken Clark – the hero of the Labour Day weekend game – to Ottawa for non-import fullback John Park and future considerations (import receiver Carl Powell, as it turned out). Clark was unloaded shortly after voicing frustration over the Hufnagel trade. "He asked to be traded, and we accommodated him," Herrera told the *Leader-Post*. "This isn't the first time. He's been a clubhouse guy all along, a guy who's got a lot to say about everything, a bit of a lawyer. He demonstrated to the club that he wasn't a team player. When you've got some enthusiastic young guys who want to play football, and one or two guys who drag it down, you've got to get rid of them."

Clark was quick to retort. "To the people that really count, and that includes the fans, I don't think asking to be traded puts me in a bad light," he said. "Everyone here knows what the problem is, but nobody wants to believe it. It's a big decision for me to say adios and to move my family out of Regina, but the majority of the fans know what's going on here."

Certainly not a playoff game. In 1983, Saskatchewan would finish out of the post-season for the seventh consecutive year. Back-to-back victories to conclude the regular season were of little solace as the Roughriders finished last in the five-team Western Conference, posting a 5-11 record while surrendering nearly 33 points per game. In the final analysis, the 1983 Roughriders set an ignominious record – auditioning or dressing 164 players, the most in franchise history.

> **Five seasons after Ron Lancaster's retirement as a player, the Roughriders were still looking to replace him at quarterback. Over that time span, 12 quarterbacks had thrown passes for Saskatchewan.**

Five seasons after Ron Lancaster's retirement as a player, the Roughriders were still looking to replace him at quarterback. Over that time span, 12 quarterbacks had thrown passes for Saskatchewan – Tom Clements, Danny Sanders, Lloyd Patterson, Larry Dick, Craig Juntunen, John Hufnagel, Joe Barnes, Tom Rozantz, Joe (747) Adams, Homer Jordan, Nickie Hall and Steve Clarkson. The Roughriders' hierarchy was so impressed that it resolved to add to that list. Hello there, Joe Paopao.

"He's one of the premier quarterbacks in the Canadian Football League," GM John Herrera said in March of 1984 after signing Paopao, a free agent, to a four-year contract. "He's a proven leader, and a proven winner. He's also one of the hardest-working players I've ever been associated with." Herrera and head coach Reuben Berry both knew Paopao from their days with the B.C. Lions.

Also imported from the Lions was Sammy Greene, who had been released by B.C. late in the 1983 season despite having amassed 75 receptions. He was immensely talented but equally troubled. A problem with drugs and alcohol largely explained why, at 25, Greene had already been with 11 professional football teams – seven in the NFL, one in the USFL, and three in the CFL.

Greene was released by Saskatcheawn in late August, and he did not depart quietly. "I can tell you one thing," he told the *Leader-Post*. "None of the receivers they have are better than me … We've only scored four touchdowns through the air, and I've caught three of them." Greene also reportedly said: "If they drop a bomb on Regina, there would only be 67 cents damage." And that was part of the problem – Roughriders receivers were known for dropping bombs … on the field.

While referencing the not-so-grand total of four aerial touchdowns, Greene underlined one of the myriad reasons why the Roughriders were struggling. An inability to finish drives with touchdowns was a major contributor to the chronic losses. One beneficiary of the stalled drives was third-year placekicker Dave Ridgway, who set a CFL single-game record on July 29, 1984 by kicking eight field goals. The man who would eventually be dubbed Robokicker connected from 41, 30, 21, 27, 20, 40, 50 and 46 yards.

The timing was ideal for Ridgway, who had been on thin ice as the Ottawa game approached. Reuben Berry had held a kicking contest in practice, pitting Ridgway against Paul Watson. The latter had been erratic as Saskatchewan's placekicker in 1981, although he did boast a 59-yard field goal that season. Ridgway staved off the challenge from Watson, who soon disappeared after the 46-24 trouncing of Ottawa.

> **"The offence is in a shambles, coming apart, like loose shingles in a Saskatchewan wind."**

"His job was on the line," Berry said of Ridgway, "but so was everybody's. Mine. His. Everybody's. You've got to perform or you'll wake up the next morning unemployed." The convincing victory in Ottawa did not signal a trend. The Roughriders lost their next four games, to the chagrin of the increasingly frustrated fan base. At one game in August, ticket-holders demonstrated their dissatisfaction by wearing bags over their heads. "The offence is in a shambles, coming apart, like loose shingles in a Saskatchewan wind," Bob Hughes wrote in the *Leader-Post*. Hughes also quipped that quarterback Joe Paopao "is close to considering having his sweater number unlisted."

By midseason, the 1984 Roughriders had a 1-6-1 record, prompting Hughes to opine that the Roughriders "may be the only team in the Canadian Football League which could be called for objectionable conduct just by the way they play." The repeated losses were objectionable to Berry, who lamented: "Losing is worse than dying because you've got to live with losing." The cause seemed lost. A *Leader-Post* headline read: "Hope has been drained from Taylor Field." The ink had barely dried when, unexpectedly, the Roughriders altered their course. Beginning on Labour Day weekend, Saskatchewan won five times in a six-game span – thanks in part to sophomore slotback Ray Elgaard, who had become a major weapon in the Roughriders' arsenal. The second-half surge created the possibility of Saskatchewan making the playoffs for the first time since 1976.

Saskatchewan won five times in a six-game span – thanks in part to sophomore slotback Ray Elgaard, who had become a major weapon in the Roughriders' arsenal.

Fans salivated at the notion of a post-season berth, packing Taylor Field for the only time in 1984 when the Hamilton Tiger-Cats paid a visit on October 14. It was a must-win game for the Roughriders, who succumbed 31-8 before 28,414 dissatisfied customers. Saskatchewan proceeded to lose its regular-season finale in humiliating fashion, with the host Edmonton Eskimos emerging victorious, 52-7. The optimism had dissipated in barely a fortnight as Saskatchewan finished fourth in the five-team West with a 6-9-1 record.

Those two lopsided losses weighed heavily into management's decision to dump Herrera, Berry and administrative assistant Tim Ruskell one week into November. "They were the two worst games of the season for us," president Dick Rendek said. "It gravely concerned us that we ended the season on that note." Rendek went on to say that "we felt the team had to improve and the only way to do that was to make a change. We were 6-9-1 two years ago [the season before Herrera was hired] and we were 6-9-1 this year. It's the bottom line that leads to these decisions."

Herrera's reaction? "Disappointment," he said at the time. "Not anger or frustration – just disappointment." Given the passage of time, however, Herrera was able to look back more fondly on his time with the Roughriders. "It was a really interesting two years in Saskatchewan," he said in 2006, having returned to the Oakland Raiders as a senior executive. "If things had gone a little bit differently, I would have stayed there a lot longer than two years. I was very happy there, actually. I really enjoyed the community. I love the Canadian Football League. I probably had more fun in the four-plus years I was up there in Canada than I have had anywhere. I really loved it."

"The only thing that bothered me – and I let it bother me probably a little more than it should have – was the constant criticism in the paper."

Well, most of it, anyway. "The only thing that bothered me – and I let it bother me probably a little more than it should have – was the constant criticism in the paper," Herrera reflected. "Maybe if I'd had a few more years under my belt when I came there, I would have handled it a little bit better. But the people there always treated me great in general. There was an uprising or two when we weren't going too well. The people were publicly not real nice but, personally, nobody was ever mean-spirited to me. In the two years I was there, nobody personally ever came up to me and said, 'You're really horse(bleep), Herrera! Why don't you pack up and go back where you came from?' "

Although Herrera had his detractors, he did make some inspired personnel moves during his two-year tenure. Draft picks were astutely spent on slotback Ray Elgaard (1983) and safety Glen Suitor (1984). A fellow Canadian, Mike Anderson, was a territorial protection who became a mainstay on the offensive line. Veteran cornerback Terry Irvin, whom Herrera brought to Saskatchewan after Calgary deemed him expendable, registered a franchise-record 11 interceptions in 1984. Billy Jackson, whom Herrera signed in 1984, would go on to become an all-star. Fellow linebacker Eddie Lowe, who joined the team in 1983, became a mainstay. "[Herrera] got Dan Rambo and Tim Ruskell

Ray Elgaard Photo courtesy of SSHFM

Glen Suitor Photo courtesy of SSHFM

Mike Anderson Photo courtesy of SSHFM

to do the scouting," athletic therapist Ivan Gutfriend recalled. "Look at Tim Ruskell now. He's the president of the Seattle Seahawks. I think John started to get some of the things on the right track by having permanent scouts working out of here."

Despite the string of disappointing seasons, the Roughriders still had a seven-figure savings account. The team incurred a $269,600 deficit in 1984, reducing the Heritage Stabilization Fund to $1,191,700. "Financially, what kept us afloat was our vigorous marketing program," said Rendek, whose three-year term as the Roughriders' president concluded in 1984. "Everyone in the league would tell you, whether it was green and white pompoms or fight songs or game day sponsors or whatever, that we had the best marketing team in the CFL. [Former Roughriders president] Bruce Cowie used to say, 'If you don't have the steak, sell the sizzle,' and that is what we did."

"Everyone in the league would tell you, whether it was green and white pompoms or fight songs or game day sponsors or whatever, that we had the best marketing team in the CFL."

Ultimately, the objective was to sell winning football. Upon being hired as general manager, Bill Quinter suggested that the best public-relations scheme is a successful football team. "That's the bottom line," Quinter said after being appointed John Herrera's successor. Like Herrera, Quinter came to Saskatchewan after spending two seasons in a player-personnel capacity with B.C.

What we were looking for was long-term leadership and stability in the general manager's position," outgoing president Dick Rendek said. "Bill has met the criteria. His experience and knowledge of Canadian football is excellent. He has played in the league on both sides of the football, he has coached in the league on both sides of the football, and he has been heavily involved in the player-personnel department everywhere he's been. He has experience in all facets of the organization, from playing to coaching, and from coaching to management."

Quinter was not the Roughriders' first choice for GM, but that was hardly novel. Before hiring Jim Spavital late in 1979, Saskatchewan had attempted to pry Joe Tiller away from Calgary. Herrera was chosen following the 1982 season after efforts to lure Paul Robson away from Winnipeg were unsuccessful. Two years later, the Roughriders' brass once again attempted to raid the Blue Bombers – wooing Cal Murphy. Kindly Cal declined a lucrative offer, but still had an impact on the Roughriders' hiring. He suggested to Rendek that Quinter should be the GM. "That is exactly what Cal said," Rendek said. "It meant a lot."

"I am absolutely delighted," Quinter said. "Twenty-five years in the CFL – you can't beat that. I've known him a long time. I played against him. I coached against him. And now we're working together. He has a lot of talent. He knows what it takes to put a winning football team on the field."

Shortly thereafter, Quinter completed negotiations with Jack Gotta, who was named the head coach. "I am absolutely delighted," Quinter said. "Twenty-five years in the CFL – you can't beat that. I've known him a long time. I played against him. I coached against him. And now we're working together. He has a lot of talent. He knows what it takes to put a winning football team on the field."

Gotta was well-acquainted with the concept of a winning Saskatchewan football team. He was an assistant to head coach Eagle Keys from 1965 to 1967, and played a role in the Roughriders' first-ever championship season in 1966. Previously, Gotta had been a receiver with the Roughriders. It was in Regina that he met his wife, Joan.

"Jocko," as he was widely known, was named the CFL's coach-of-the-year with Ottawa in 1972 and 1973, and with Calgary in 1978. "I'd like to commend the general manager," Rendek said at a media conference. "He hired the best coach available in the country, as far as we're concerned. This is a tremendous accomplishment in his first act as GM. I think this gives us a solid one-two punch. We now have the two things we need: The stability of a quiet, behind-the-scenes general manager, and an all-star, high-profile head coach."

Before hiring Gotta, Quinter wondered if his initial hiring would be content to be solely the head coach, as opposed to controlling the entire football operation. As Quinter put it: "My concern with Jocko was, I didn't think he could accept the role as just head coach." Those apprehensions vanished, at least for the time being, after Quinter spoke with Gotta. "There's no problem there," said Gotta who, like Quinter, signed a three-year contract. "He understands the coaching environment and I understand his environment."

Gotta acquired that understanding by spending six seasons as a CFL general manager – six more than Quinter at the time – before joining the Roughriders. "I don't have any problem with Jack Gotta's background," Quinter said. "In fact, I welcome it. I always learn from people and I always listen to what they have to say. And he certainly has some good experience and some talent that I can rely on. I have no problem with anything concerning a power struggle. Jack is the head coach. He knows that that is his title. But … it's very encouraging for me to have someone like that whom I can rely on."

Photo courtesy of *Leader-Post*

Jack Gotta (left) and Bill Quinter … a marriage not made in heaven

Three not-so-old reliables were dispatched to Calgary in Quinter's first major trade as the Roughriders' GM. In May of 1985, he sent centre Bob Poley, offensive tackle Gerry Hornett and fullback Greg Fieger westward for three offensive linemen – Willie Thomas, Kevin Molle and Ken Moore. The departures of Poley and Fieger were particularly notable, being that they had joined the Roughriders after starring for the junior Regina Rams. "You kind of hear it, and there were rumours and stuff," Poley recalled. "Jocko sort of grabbed me by the neck and said, 'Oh, you're going to love Calgary. It's a good place. I loved it before I got fired out of there.' OK, Jocko …"

Ray Elgaard, a starter at slotback from Day 1, was squelching overmatched defensive halfbacks with his bruising runs after the catch en route to his first of eight 1,000-yard seasons.

Early in the 1985 season, it was reasonable to wonder whether Gotta would receive his fourth coach-of-the-year award. A 42-34 victory in Edmonton gave Saskatchewan a 4-3 record and enlivened talk of a long-awaited playoff berth. Joe Paopao and Homer Jordan were providing solid quarterbacking. Craig Ellis was contributing as a ball-carrier and a receiver out of the backfield. Ray Elgaard, a starter at slotback from Day 1, was squelching overmatched defensive halfbacks with his bruising runs after the catch en route to his first of eight 1,000-yard seasons.

The Roughriders' encouraging start energized ticket sales for the annual Labour Day Classic against Winnipeg. The night before the game, the Roughriders held their annual fundraising dinner – at which the 75th-anniversary dream team was unveiled. The select squad consisted of quarterback Ron Lancaster, running backs George Reed and Bobby Marlow, receivers Hugh Campbell, Joey Walters, Rhett Dawson and Chris DeFrance, centre Ted Urness, guards Al Benecick and Jack Abendschan, offensive tackles Martin Ruby and Clyde Brock, defensive linemen Bill Baker, Ed McQuarters, Ron Atchison and Garner Ekstran, linebackers Wally Dempsey, Roger Goree and Wayne Shaw, and defensive backs Bruce Bennett, Lorne Richardson, Ken McEachern, Ted Dushinski and Steve Dennis. Abendschan was chosen as the placekicker. Glenn Dobbs was the punter. Eagle Keys and Ken Preston were selected as the head coach and general manager, respectively.

At the time, little did anyone imagine that, for the Roughriders, the 1985 season would peak in late August. On September 1, the Roughriders lost 18-10 to Winnipeg and were promptly sent reeling. Saskatchewan lost all five of its games in September, being outscored 160-49. After a 27-15 home-field loss to Edmonton on September. 15, Gotta described his team's sloppy tackling in this fashion: "They weren't exactly a bunch of hungry bulldogs going after a meatball, were they?"

Through it all, Gotta maintained his sense of humour, along with his penchant for one-liners – the most memorable being: "When lightning hits the outhouse, the whole joint stinks."

The Roughriders arrested the losing streak by beating Calgary 21-10 at home, only to lose their last three games by a combined score of 123-58. Attendance was below 20,000 for each of the Roughriders' final three home games as the team missed the playoffs for the ninth consecutive season. The optimism buoyed by a 4-3 start evaporated as Saskatchewan finished 5-11 – a regression from the 6-9-1 slate in the final season under John Herrera and Reuben Berry. Through it all, Gotta maintained his sense of humour, along with his penchant for one-liners – the most memorable being: "When lightning hits the outhouse, the whole joint stinks."

The Roughriders also incurred devastating losses off the field in 1985, losing $947,500 on operations for that woeful season. The Roughriders watched their Heritage Stabilization Fund dip to $233,400. "This fund has often been referred to as our Rainy Day Fund and never was it more needed than in 1985 when, not only did it rain, but it poured," read a portion of the financial report, delivered at the annual general meeting.

"Thankfully, the fund was in place to absorb our 1985 loss but in doing so the fund has been severely depleted and cannot absorb continued losses of this magnitude."

Complicating matters, treasurer Tom Shepherd announced the team was anticipating a budget of $6 million in 1986, meaning that it needed to generate $1 million more in revenue than was the case in 1985. However, the revenue was slow in arriving during a long winter. By March, just over 10,000 season tickets had been renewed – an ominous figure, considering that the team had 17,983 subscribers in 1985. Club president Keith Critchley referred to "a very desperate and fragile time in the life of the Saskatchewan Roughrider Football Club." Critchley also told the *Leader-Post* that "if the same thing which happened in 1985 happens in 1986, it means two years in a row of that and we will have dropped $2 million. I don't know what would happen then. I don't even want to think about it."

"What happens if we lose the Roughriders? You can tear down 53 grain elevators and people will be upset, but there are lots of other grain elevators. But there is only one Saskatchewan Roughrider football team. And if we lose that, what have we got?"

Neither did Tom Shepherd, who had ascended to the role of vice-president. "We want everybody to understand what the situation is," he said. "We have $200,000 left from last year and the money from the season-ticket sales this year. And it isn't enough. In terms of today's dollars, that can go fast. But it goes beyond all of that, beyond dollars and cents. What it comes down to is that the Roughriders are an institution in Saskatchewan. They mean something to Saskatchewan, to all of us. What happens if we lose the Roughriders? You can tear down 53 grain elevators and people will be upset, but there are lots of other grain elevators. But there is only one Saskatchewan Roughrider football team. And if we lose that, what have we got?"

A power struggle, that's what. General manager Bill Quinter and head coach Jack Gotta had barely stopped short of singing "Kumbaya" when the latter was hired in mid-December of 1984. Late in the 1985 season, Gotta intimated that he wanted more power, citing a desire to be in full control of the football operations – as he was in Calgary. The head coach also indicated that he was not thrilled with the recruiting done by Quinter or director of player personnel Dan Rambo.

Entering the 1986 season, a running back was high on the list of priorities – even though Craig Ellis had scored 17 touchdowns (14 along the ground and three through the air) the previous year. Ellis's rushing average was a substandard 3.8 yards per carry, although he did tie Joey Walters' single-season franchise record by catching 102 passes.

With the intent of bolstering the running game, the Roughriders made a debatable choice in the first round of the 1986 CFL draft. On the surface, the selection of Washington State star Rueben Mayes was a no-brainer, given that he was born in North Battleford. But at the time of the choice, Mayes was widely expected to try the NFL. He did just that after the New Orleans Saints claimed him in the third round of the 1986 NFL draft. That proved to be an astute pick, as Mayes rushed for 1,353 yards in 1986 en route to being named the NFL's offensive rookie-of-the-year.

"Saskatchewan began the season with Bobby Johnson as the featured tailback. The San Jose State product did not disappoint, rushing for 869 yards and 12 touchdowns in 13 games. He added another major on one of his 43 receptions.

Despite swinging and missing on Mayes, the Roughriders decided against retaining Ellis, who was dealt to the Toronto Argonauts. In his place, Saskatchewan began the season with Bobby Johnson as the featured tailback. The San Jose State product did not disappoint, rushing for 869 yards and 12 touchdowns in 13 games. He added another major on one of his 43 receptions. But even the success story of 1986 would have an unhappy ending. Johnson damaged a vertebra in his neck during a 29-11 victory over the visiting Montreal Alouettes and never played again.

The first defeat of the season was the worst – in franchise history! After doubling the visiting Calgary Stampeders 28-14 in the opener, the Roughriders travelled to Winnipeg and absorbed a 56-0 defeat. Jack Gotta referred to the loss as a "devastating damn thing." Never one to mince words, he also offered: "I'm glad we didn't leave town tonight. There would probably be an air crash."

Photo courtesy of *Leader-Post*

Joe Paopao in the pocket against Montreal

When the Roughriders and Blue Bombers next collided, the story would be drastically different. Saskatchewan won 34-30 on Labour Day weekend, courtesy of a 56-yard scoring bomb from Joe Paopao to Ray Elgaard with 22 seconds left. "It was ironic, because we talked about that coverage during the week," Paopao reflected. "Ray said, 'If I see that coverage, I'm just going to go right between [the defensive backs].' I said OK. It just so happened that, on that particular play, it worked out. It happened so quick and fast. Ray just caught it, slid away from Scott Flagel at safety, and the rest is history. Ray's a great Hall of Famer and was a great player with the Riders and that's one of my fondest memories as a quarterback."

Paopao and Elgaard had also made news three days before the game, when they had a heated disagreement at a local nightspot. "It's ironic," Paopao said. "During those days, when anybody got released, it was customary for the players to go and have a drink – coffee, beer or a soda – and say your goodbyes. That year, it seemed like there was a guy going home every week."

That week, the players had gathered to bid farewell to quarterback Harold Smith. "There was a disagreement between Ray and I," Paopao said. "Those things can happen. You're looking at two competitive people. Words were said. We made our peace. I think people made a bigger deal of it than it was. I disagree with my wife. That doesn't mean I don't like her anymore. It's just one of those things where it happened that week of Labour Day. [After the game-winning touchdown], we looked at each other and said, 'Hey, we should fight more often.' "

Asked for his recollections of a classic touchdown, Elgaard said: "I guess it was a good play and it was a win that we needed, although it didn't save the season or anything." In retrospect, Elgaard perceived that game – and that play – as a sign that the situation in Riderville was gradually improving. "In '83, it was a mess. In '86, it was getting better," Elgaard said. "We had a veteran quarterback like Joe. We were fighting to win some games and some good things started to happen. Maybe that game was one of them. We couldn't keep it going long enough to get into the playoffs, but we were starting to do some of those kind of things more often than we had in the past – win the game at the end with a big play, and that kind of thing. That's kind of when it started to change a little bit. Joe was a big factor in that. He was a pro quarterback and he had that sort of way about him. He wasn't going to put up with anything less. That was part of the positive changes."

Photo courtesy of *Leader-Post*

Ray Elgaard

Assuredly, there would be changes. Shortly after the 1986 season, in which the Roughriders finished 6-11-1 and missed the playoffs for the 10th consecutive year, it appeared Quinter would be retained and Gotta would be dumped. As expected, the Roughriders' brass pulled the trigger on Gotta – as Quinter had recommended following the 1986 campaign. "The areas where we broke down most were leadership and head coach," Quinter told the *Leader-Post*. "I don't think he had a strong coaching staff, in terms of teaching." The management committee acted on Quinter's recommendation, but went one step further – relieving the GM of his duties.

The news shocked Quinter. "I don't feel betrayed, but I do feel disappointed," he said. "I think the administrative end of the operation is in good hands. What the team needs is a good, solid head coach who could show some leadership, and a quarterback. There are some good football players here who are capable of winning."

Quinter-Gotta did not prove to be a winning formula. Upon being dismissed, Quinter revealed that the decision to hire Gotta was not autonomous. "It was strongly recommended that I interview Jack," Quinter said. "I would've liked to interview several candidates that I had on the list, and I didn't do that. It was impressed on me that I do [the hiring] quickly." Quinter was not as quick to fire, and he resisted any temptation to depose the head coach. "The mandate I had from the president [Keith Critchley] was for continuity," Quinter said.

Although Quinter made it clear that he was unimpressed with the coaching, he downplayed reports that there was friction between the head coach and GM. "It's been a very professional relationship," said Quinter, he of the trademark stetson. "I don't think a general manager and head coach have to have any relationship other than the Number 1 goal of putting a winning team on the field. They don't have to be buddies, but Jack and I are friends."

Nonetheless, the arrangement did not produce the desired results. "It never worked because it never had a chance," Bob Hughes wrote in the *Leader-Post*. "They were opposites. Quinter wanted a teacher as coach. Gotta was an excitable motivator, given to changes of the mind at any moment. Quinter was happy just to be given the chance to be a GM. Gotta wanted to run the whole show. Mostly, Jack drew from the lips. And Bill wore THAT hat. Even after Gotta lashed out at Quinter at the end of the 1985 season and, in fact, much of the Rider operation, the upper management was never able to bring

> "The brass could not see the trees for the forest. So badly did they want this combination to work that they wore blinders and ear muffs (hear no evil, see no evil, and maybe catch a playoff spot)."

itself to admitting its mistake. There were some who felt Gotta should have been fired for taking his beefs to the public, if only because it showed a certain disloyalty. But Quinter did not push hard enough for it, intimidated (he now suggests) by the wish of the upper management to salvage continuity.

"And management suffered a serious delusion in feeling that Quinter and Gotta had ironed out their differences. The brass could not see the trees for the forest. So badly did they want this combination to work that they wore blinders and ear muffs (hear no evil, see no evil, and maybe catch a playoff spot)."

Gotta was headed west on a ski trip when the change was made. Once he could be contacted, he expressed his sentiments on his two years as the Roughriders' head coach. "I signed a three-year contract when I came here and to me that meant a three-year mandate," he said. "I understand that you have to win, but I really thought that we were progressing, that good things were happening. I thought we were on track, but it has become an aborted mission. I knew coming in here that it was going to be a more difficult job than anything I had done before. The Riders had been out of the playoffs for so many years ... I had to change the attitudes of everybody – the fans, the players, the management, the executive. All my predecessors and people in football I know had told me before I came here that it was a no-win situation. I was told by a lot of people not to take the job because I wouldn't have a chance."

> Tom Shepherd's first decision as president was to sack Gotta and Quinter. "They didn't work together," he said. "It was always one against the other and their actions were doing nothing when it came to the betterment of the club."

Tom Shepherd's first decision as president was to sack Gotta and Quinter. "They didn't work together," he said. "It was always one against the other and their actions were doing nothing when it came to the betterment of the club." Shepherd expressed the view that "Bill Quinter could have been a good GM" but "in retrospect, he probably never got a fair chance."

At the same time the dismissals of Gotta and Quinter were announced, Shepherd revealed that former Roughriders defensive lineman Bill (The Undertaker) Baker would be the new GM. Days earlier, Baker – then a vice-president at IPSCO – had been appointed to the team's executive. A fellow executive member, former Roughriders centre Ted Urness, spoke up in favour of Baker. "Ted just turned and pointed to Bill and said, 'We have the man right here,' " Shepherd said. "We knew instinctively that he was right. I assure you that Bill Baker was not on anybody's list. He was as surprised as any of us."

Baker then approached IPSCO president Roger Phillips, who granted a two-year leave of absence. "I'm a sucker for a challenge," Baker said. "I had been with IPSCO for 15 years but I've always said I will take substantial risk because I truly believe in the challenge of life and I have a great passion for learning new things ... I had a great job with IPSCO and spent too much time working but I still had a great passion for the team. I sat in the stands and watched some awful, awful games."

> "So instead of having him piss all over us from outside for what was going on, like Bill is apt to, I decided to make him part of the solution."

That factored into Shepherd's conclusion that Baker was the perfect candidate to succeed Quinter. "Bill Baker was a real bull-in-the-china-shop type of guy," Shepherd said. "His desire to see the Riders succeed was similar to mine. He had been upset and disappointed and vocal, as only Bill can be, with what he was seeing. In my business career, I always felt if someone is a constant problem to you, make him part of the solution. So instead of having him piss all over us from outside for what was going on, like Bill is apt to, I decided to make him part of the solution. You know it's not as easy as you think when you are on the outside looking in being critical, so I will make him part of the solution."

Photo courtesy of *Leader-Post*

Bill Baker (left) and Tom Shepherd

Baker believed he had a solution, despite the on- and off-field adversity the Roughriders were encountering. "I had a passion to see the Riders become successful and, quite frankly, I thought I knew what to do to make that happen," he said. "One thing about sports that's so interesting is you have to perform on certain days and get graded by fans and media every day, especially on game day. That creates a very challenging environment and it's one I was ready to embrace."

The challenge facing Baker, and the entire organization, was daunting. A $723,000 loss on 1986 operations exhausted the Heritage Stabilization Fund and put the team nearly $600,000 in the hole. "I wouldn't describe it as the greatest challenge I've ever faced," Baker said at the time. "I think it is the most worthwhile. I feel so strongly about it, I felt I had no choice but to accept the challenge. Saskatchewan and the Roughriders have been such a big part of my life. I can only hope the people of this province realize, as I do, how important it is to have this team here."

"I felt I had no choice but to accept the challenge. Saskatchewan and the Roughriders have been such a big part of my life. I can only hope the people of this province realize, as I do, how important it is to have this team here."

As well as slaying a financial monster, Baker had some personnel issues to address and a no-nonsense philosophy to instill. "I came in and immediately made it clear – and long-term, I realized it was a mistake – that I wanted a lot more control than the board was used to giving," Baker recalled. "I thought I needed the freedom to take some pretty strong actions and it wasn't going to be very pretty. One of the troubles you have with any organization like the Riders when you go through a dramatic change is that it's hard. People want change, but they want it done in a certain way and sometimes it's not a pretty process. I came in and very quickly established the rules. Any bad players we had – any players that were going to be a distraction – would not be invited back."

Photo courtesy of *Leader-Post*

Dan Rambo at training camp

Baker also decided that "rightly or wrongly, we were going to terminate all football staff, or consider it, which we basically did." That included veteran player-personnel man Dan Rambo, whom then-GM John Herrera had brought to Saskatchewan in 1983. "One of the best things I did do was I went in to Dan – not knowing him – and explained very bluntly that tough actions were going to be taken," Baker said. "I explained to him he didn't have a job and, if he had another one on the horizon, that he should take that job. Dan came back to me and said, 'I'm still interested in being here,' so I said, 'Let's you and I work together with Al [Ford] over the next few weeks to see if we can get along and agree on the same principles.' That was a very fortunate thing because Dan and I became very good partners. Having Dan around gave us the knowledge I didn't have on the player-personnel side. Talking to Dan and retaining Dan turned out to be one of the most fortunate things I did."

Photo courtesy of *Leader-Post*

John Gregory on the day he was hired

The next priority, in terms of staffing, was to appoint a head coach. Baker decided on John Gregory, who had spent the previous four seasons as Winnipeg's offensive line coach. Baker hired Gregory on the recommendation of then-Bombers boss Cal Murphy. "Clearly, he is the right man for the job," Baker said when introducing Gregory. "I feel very confident about that. I'm very pleased with John Gregory. His experience is excellent, but the thing I'm most pleased about is the kind of man he is – a very mature individual with tremendous integrity. Those are qualities you can win with." Gregory was actually Quinter's first choice two years earlier, but he said the Riders' executive steered him in the direction of Gotta.

Baker was hired, in part, because of his ability as a crisis manager. As it turned out, Gregory had the same pedigree. "In my life, I've been the guy who went in and fixed things for people in the football world, not only when I coached in high school but when I coached in college and junior college," he said. "I like those kind of challenges. We had Bill Baker and he was a very strong asset at that point in time. He was certainly the man to have at the head of the organization because he was real strong and he was able to fight through a lot of the B.S."

At times, it *was* a fight. "We had a lot of people locally who didn't like the direction we were taking," Baker said. "I remember at our meetings, the board was not happy because of what we were doing. They would say, 'We don't think this is going to work,' or they would voice concerns they had. I kept telling them, and everyone else who would listen, that it will work. I did ruffle a lot of feathers with my approach, but in the end it did work and we survived."

The cash-strapped Roughriders were in survival mode for much of 1987. While Baker attempted to make ends meet, he was also hit between the eyes with a player-personnel folly that was not of his making. During the 1986 season, the Roughriders gave a first-round draft choice to Edmonton for offensive lineman Bryan Illerbrun. As part of the deal, the Eskimos were given the option of choosing between a future third-round draft pick or veteran kicker Dave Ridgway. Then-head coach Jack Gotta, who had an icy reception with Ridgway, gave Edmonton that option – to be exercised after the 1986 campaign. Edmonton took Ridgway and soon dealt him to Montreal. Baker labelled the Ridgway trade "one of the dumbest deals I've ever heard of."

Baker responded by engineering another deal – one that worked in the Roughriders' favour. Joe Paopao, who had been Saskatchewan's starting quarterback for most of the previous three seasons, was shipped to Ottawa for Tom Burgess, who was 23 at the time.

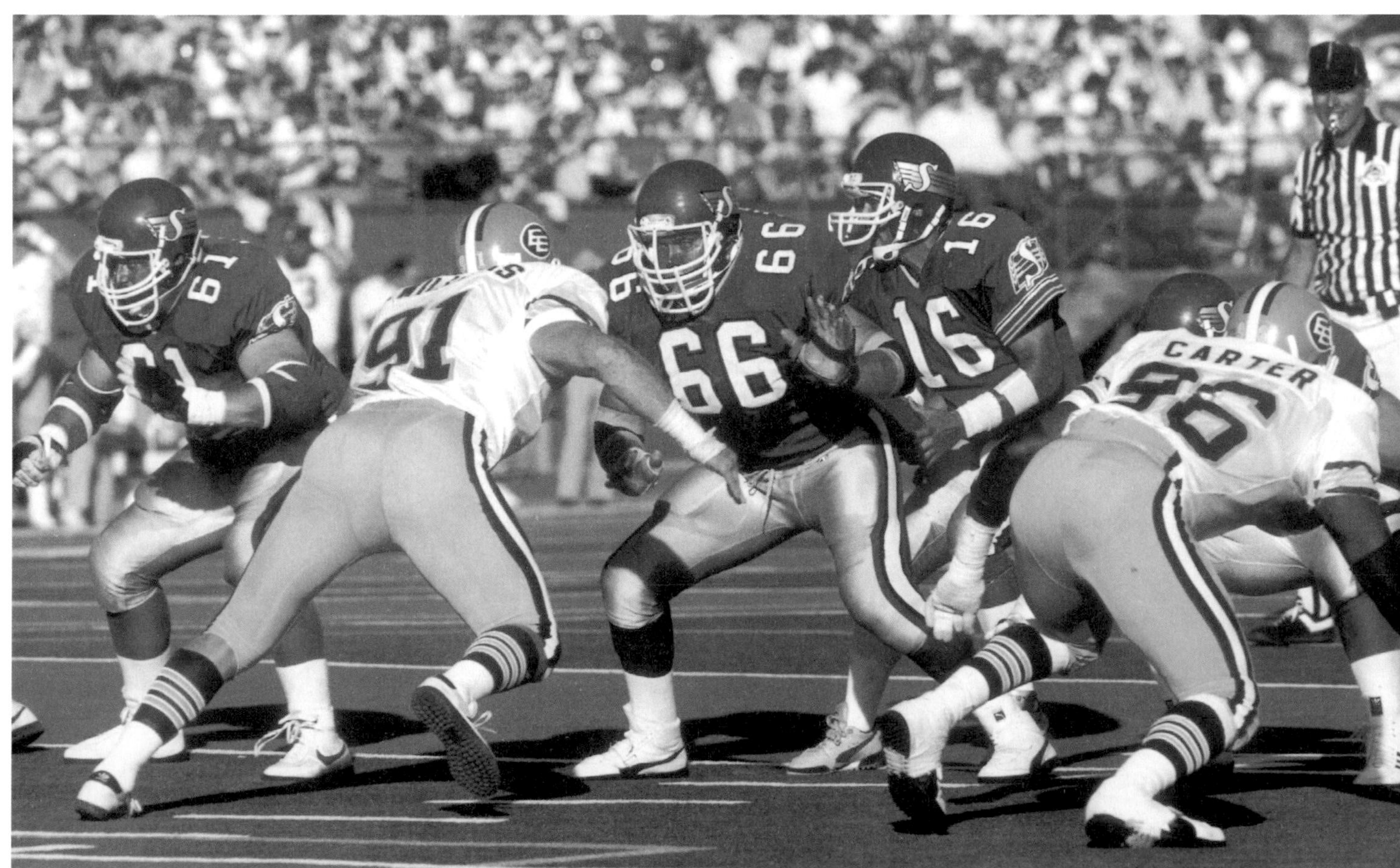

Photo courtesy of SSHFM

Bryan Illerbrun (61) and Mike Anderson (66) block for Tom Burgess (16) as he prepares to throw a pass

Paopao exhibited typical class when discussing the deal. "[Saskatchewan management] feels there might have been some negative feelings toward me for not being able to get the job done and I was disheartened because we fell short of our goals – making the playoffs and becoming respectable," he said. "I'll take my share of the blame, but there's a lot of stress there. When you mess up, everybody lets you know it. And when it doesn't go well, it hurts."

The pain was especially acute on the financial side. In late April of 1987, Baker assembled the media and declared that the franchise's future was tenuous. He stated that the Roughriders could be broke by late August or early September if matters did not improve on the field and at the box office. "Nobody quite believes it," Baker said, "but I tell you, it can really happen." The message was emphasized in a *Leader-Post* headline which read: "Roughriders' franchise in its darkest moments." At the time, the Roughriders had sold a meagre 11,500 season tickets. Baker said the team needed to average at least 22,000 fans per home game in 1987 to remain solvent. While looking to increase revenues, Baker and his associates also strived to pare expenses by $1 million. They did so by asking players to take pay cuts, with a ceiling of $70,000 established for most players. Slotback Ray Elgaard and guard Roger Aldag took two of the biggest hits, salary-wise. "It was handled as well as it possibly could have been," Aldag said. "My first reaction was, 'Why me?' After looking things over, the guys who want to play football in Saskatchewan took the cut. I know myself I want to see this thing through."

Photo courtesy of *Leader-Post*

Roger Aldag

Most of Aldag's teammates felt similarly. "There's still a few of our top-performing players who haven't joined in, but most of them have," Baker said in late April. "They're one of the only groups in North America to take a salary cut and some of them took a 20- or 30-per-cent cut. The players have given us a chance. We became one of the highest-paying clubs in the league when we should have been one of the lowest. Traditionally, we're one of the bottom one or two. We're a small unit."

One month later, the grim message regarding the Roughriders' balance sheet was disseminated more emphatically. Baker appeared at a media conference, to which sports and news reporters were invited. The Riders' GM said the team could fold by July unless it: (a) Sold 100,000 more tickets for its 10 home games; (b) Received a $407,000 park-rental and amusement-tax abatement from the City of Regina; and, (c) Generated another $700,000 in the third "Friends of the Riders" lottery, founded by Tom Shepherd. "I don't think people realize how fragile it is," Baker said of the club's status. "I don't think people really believe it will happen – that the club might not be here."

The club had sold 12,750 season tickets as of May 19, but that was far from satisfactory. Baker said the team faced a $1.8-million deficit in 1987 unless a survival strategy was successful. "We have to, first of all, find someone who will allow us to be $1.8 million in debt," said Baker, who was poised to negotiate with the banks. "If you have any advice, we'd appreciate it." The gravity of the situation was outlined in an interview the *Leader-Post*'s Bruce Johnstone did with Bill Watt, the Royal Bank's vice-president of retail banking. "There's little justification for a bank to be lending the Roughriders money in 1987, based on their own figures," Watt said.

In order to avert a monstrous deficit and allay fears that the team would fold, an ambitious ticket blitz was launched. The Roughriders set a goal of selling an additional 100,000 game tickets for 1987 and announced that a 16-hour telethon would be held June 13 and 14. Game tickets and active memberships were to be sold during the "Tickethon," to be held in co-operation with the Saskatchewan media. "Whether we win or lose on the field, while important, is no longer the paramount issue," said *Leader-Post* executive vice-president Jim Struthers, who headed the media committee. "It is whether the Roughriders will survive beyond this year."

"Whether we win or lose on the field, while important, is no longer the paramount issue ... It is whether the Roughriders will survive beyond this year."

The Roughriders' plight attracted nationwide media attention. "How bad is the situation?" Jim Taylor wrote in the *Vancouver Province*. "Last season, the Riders held two lotteries that brought in $700,000, took their $1.3-million share of TV money – and still lost $723,000. This year, that TV money will be cut in half. What happened? What felled the Jolly Green Giants? Losing, of course, but let's not forget stupidity. Last year, the Riders' salaries totalled $3.5 million, which put them among the top three in the league. About $1 million of that was in bonus clauses. When the Riders signed quarterback Joe Paopao, who was not exactly in high demand, they gave him a $91,000 signing bonus. When the Ottawa Rough Riders traded to get running back Robert Reid from Regina, they saw his contract and almost threw up. It had 106 bonus clauses."

Taylor's column was picked up by the *Leader-Post* and headlined: "Fans ignoring pleas to save the Roughriders." In the words beneath, Taylor had a chilling message. "Among the once-rabid fans, the bad news is being greeted with a yawn. The theory is that the fans don't believe it, that they've heard the same song for three years and refuse to be fooled again. That's incorrect. They know it's true. They just don't care."

The Roughriders were left to hope that their fans did, in fact, care. The Tickethon was to begin on a Saturday evening at 8 o'clock. The volunteer-run effort included entertainment by local acts, along with contributions from football and media figures such as Ron Lancaster, George Reed, Eagle Keys, Ron Atchison, Angelo Mosca, John

Photo courtesy of *Leader-Post*

Sportscaster Johnny Esaw, George Reed and Ron Lancaster support Tickethon while former player Gene Wlasiuk and Regina Pats hero Fran Huck man the phones

Wells, Dick Irvin and, once again, John Robertson. Then a columnist for the *Toronto Star*, Robertson – the principal figure behind the landmark "Rider Pride Day" in 1979 – flew in from Toronto for the Tickethon. Robertson said during the Tickethon that "if the lights go out in the CFL, the last light will go out in Saskatchewan's stadium."

By Sunday at 10 a.m., the Roughriders had sold 51,000 tickets during the Tickethon. That figure jumped to 58,000 at 11 a.m., before settling at 77,138 at noon. It was not the 100,000 they had targeted, but it was enough.

That infusion of revenue, along with the aforementioned concession from city hall, provided optimism that the Green and White would be able to endure the 1987 season. "Financially, we don't have to sweat July," Baker said, relievedly. "We're now into August and that gives the team a chance to do their job. If they can come through, we'll sell the place out."

But would the team come through? Entering the 1987 regular season, Ray Elgaard was optimistic that a long-awaited turnaround was imminent, thanks largely to John Gregory and his coaching staff. "I do have a good feeling about what they're teaching," the star slotback said. "It's good stuff – great stuff, actually." Elgaard was impressed with what he had seen of the offensive package. "It's definitely more challenging," he noted. "It's a good challenge, though – a challenge we need here. It's an offence that demands that the players be smart. You don't go to the line of scrimmage with one play in mind, because two yards up the field it may change, and five yards up the field it may change again. In the past, once the play was called, that was it. If your opponent was in the right defence, hell, there was nothing you could do. This offence gives us some options. It's definitely more complicated and, sure, it's tougher to grasp. But we should be able to handle that. We're professionals."

Photo courtesy of *Leader-Post*

Glen Suitor (27) holds for a Dave Ridgway field goal attempt

The regular season began auspiciously enough. Elgaard caught a touchdown pass from rookie quarterback Jeff Bentrim to help the Roughriders assume a 16-0 first-quarter lead against the visiting Stampeders. However, the Roughriders wilted in the latter stages and lost 29-28. Rick Worman hit Larry Willis for a game-winning touchdown pass with 31 seconds remaining. The following week, the Roughriders suffered a 44-1 loss in Vancouver. That game was most noteworthy because it marked the return to the Roughriders of kicker Dave Ridgway, whom Saskatchewan had claimed in a dispersal draft when the Montreal Alouettes folded with the regular season looming.

Next on the agenda was a July 4 home date with the Toronto Argonauts – featuring a pre-game show unlike any other. Arrangements were made for a World Wrestling Federation card to be held at Taylor Field on the afternoon of the game. "People thought we were nuts," Baker recalled. "The good news was we had a lot of media attention, not just from Saskatchewan but across Canada, and it translated into people wanting to

Photo courtesy of Dan Marce

Plaza of Honor cairn in front of Mosaic Stadium

be there. That event and the Tickethon certainly turned out to be milestone events. We gained tremendous momentum from these events and by July we could see some light at the end of the tunnel on the financial side." A crowd of 23,927 watched the Roughriders tie Toronto 33-33, having earlier witnessed victories by Bret (The Hitman) Hart, Jim (The Anvil) Neidhart, Brutus (The Barber) Beefcake, and friends.

In 1987, the Roughriders attracted no fewer than 21,340 spectators to each of their nine regular-season home games. That was a pronounced contrast to 1986, when Saskatchewan had only two crowds exceeding 20,000.

Also of note in 1987 was the establishment of the Roughriders' Hall of Fame – the Plaza of Honor. Ron Lancaster, George Reed, Ron Atchison, Ken Preston, Eagle Keys, Bob Kramer, Dean Griffing, Fred Wilson and Al Ritchie were enshrined at the $250-a-plate dinner. The following month, Kramer entered another shrine, joining the Canadian Football Hall of Fame as a builder.

The Roughriders did not perform at a Hall of Fame level in 1987. They finished 5-12-1 in after going 6-11-1 the season before. But there were signs of advancement.

Photo courtesy of *Leader-Post*

Kent Austin

When healthy, Tom Burgess demonstrated that he was a capable quarterback. So did mid-season addition Kent Austin, who joined the Roughriders after being released by the St. Louis Cardinals. Austin won his first start as a Roughrider, piloting the team to a 23-20 victory in Hamilton on October 11 while throwing for 292 yards – 98 more than Saskatchewan had gained through the air in its previous two games, combined.

"The guy with the toughest job in all of Canada on Sunday was named Kent Austin," Bob Hughes wrote in the *Leader-Post*. "What made his Sunday so tough was, he was playing quarterback for the Saskatchewan Roughriders, and lately you would not wish this on your worst enemy. Recent history nudged you and suggested one of two things would happen to him in Hamilton. He would throw six interceptions, or get to leave the field on a stretcher." Austin was one of five quarterbacks to play for Saskatchewan in 1987, the others being Burgess, Bentrim, Jeff Tedford and 35-year-old John Hufnagel. The latter, an assistant coach with the '87 Roughriders, was pressed into duty for one game, in which he suffered an Achilles tendon injury.

"What Kent Austin proved on Sunday in Hamilton was, if you give the Roughriders of 1987 a thread of hope, they will rise to the occasion, and give themselves a chance to win," Hughes continued. "That thread of hope, that incentive, was there when Tom Burgess was the quarterback and when John Hufnagel made his cameo appearance. It wasn't there, lately, for Jeff Bentrim and you could see it in the offence, which played like it knew something was wrong behind the centre. Now, Kent Austin didn't break any CFL passing records on Sunday. But he didn't break any bones, either, and so from the wishing well of eternal hope has sprung the thought that the Roughriders have come upon something good here."

Austin also won his second start with the Roughriders, guiding them to a 34-25 victory over the visiting Eskimos. Along with Austin's play, there were other positive signs in 1987. Wide receiver Don Narcisse – like Austin, a cut of the St. Louis Cardinals – arrived in Regina in time to play the final eight games. Tailback Tim McCray, who was obtained from Ottawa during the previous season, rushed for 457 yards and averaged 5.3 yards per carry in six games with Saskatchewan. Dave Ridgway hit 49 of 57 field-goal attempts, including a league-record 60-yarder on Labour Day weekend. The defence was taking shape, with five Roughriders (Harry Skipper, Glen Suitor, Dave Sidoo, Joe Fuller and Mike McGruder) making at least five interceptions, and middle linebacker Dave Albright recording 118 defensive tackles.

Photo courtesy of *Leader-Post*

Don Narcisse

And then there was rush end Bobby Jurasin, who exploded into prominence as a sophomore CFLer, racking up 22 quarterback sacks.

Photo courtesy of *Leader-Post*

Bobby Jurasin

Jurasin had seen spot duty in 1986 as a rookie out of Northern Michigan. He registered three sacks while being used primarily on special teams. "Jack Gotta gave me a lot of chances," Jurasin reflected. "I owe a lot to him. He opened the door and I made sure I shoved my foot in that door and wouldn't let it get closed on me. Nothing was given to me. I had to earn it. But at least he put me in that spot with a chance to make or break." When Jurasin enjoyed a breakthrough season in 1987, his patented bandana also skyrocketed in popularity. "I didn't start wearing it until I earned it," said Jurasin, who had worn the bandana in college. "I started wearing it in 1987. I wore a smaller version of it in '86. It was just like a headband with a red dot." The fans snapped up the bandanas when the Roughriders began selling them at The Store. "It was unreal how they took to me," Jurasin said.

Jurasin contributed to a resurgence of Rider Pride, creating some optimism that the team would be better in 1988. The bottom line: There would be a team in 1988, despite fears to the contrary leading up to the 1987 season. The Roughriders were far from out of the woods, registering a $284,000 deficit in 1987, but the amount was manageable. Under general manager Bill Baker, the Roughriders had weathered a crisis. "I've never believed that we would be forced to call it quits or that the league would have to call it quits," Baker reflected 20-plus years later. "I've always thought the CFL had great venues for the size of the country and that there was always a great amount of talent available because the U.S. football factory is enormous. I thought we might have to fold the team and start over again just to get rid of the debt. In fact, I think we were closer to extinction as a league in '89 than we were as a team in '87 because of some of the things that went on. Yes, the Riders could have passed on, but I truly believe they would have been reborn the next day."

Photo courtesy of *Leader-Post*

Vince Goldsmith sacks Tracy Ham

The Roughriders faced a different off-season issue in 1988. Financial issues were newsworthy, but primarily because it cost $843,000 to install Omniturf at Taylor Field. After playing on SuperTurf for the first nine seasons at an expanded stadium, the Roughriders – along with the junior Regina Rams and high school football – required new carpet. The Omniturf, which was $300,000 cheaper than the more conventional

Astroturf, appealed to the user groups because of a sand-infill system which was designed to create a softer landing.

> In addition to the speedy Fairholm, there was an infusion of veterans. Defensive halfback Richie Hall and defensive end Vince Goldsmith were obtained from Calgary.

There were also new players to go with a new playing surface. Slotback Jeff Fairholm was claimed second overall in the 1988 CFL draft. In addition to the speedy Fairholm, there was an infusion of veterans. Defensive halfback Richie Hall and defensive end Vince Goldsmith were obtained from Calgary. Goldsmith had been dealt to Toronto after a 20-sack season in 1983, spending one season with the Argos before joining Calgary. Rick Klassen, previously of B.C., was also added to improve the defensive line. The running game received a boost when non-import fullback Milson Jones, who was cut by the Eskimos, was quickly snapped up by Saskatchewan.

From the outset, the 1988 Roughriders had a winning formula. Saskatchewan posted victories in each of its first three games, defeating the host Ottawa Rough Riders 48-21 before posting home-field wins over Edmonton (26-15) and Winnipeg (46-18). Against Edmonton, Dave Ridgway tied his own CFL single-game record by making eight field goals.

The Roughriders' first 3-0 start since 1975 sent the fans into a frenzy. Even in July, the Rider Nation was buzzing about the prospect of snapping a drought of 11 years out of the playoffs – the longest such dry spell in league history. As the victories continued to mount, many of the players appeared in a music video, entitled "11 Years, That's Enough."

Bob Poley, meanwhile, had enough of the situation in Calgary. The veteran offensive lineman, a Roughrider from 1978 to 1984, had a dispute with then-Stampeders head coach Lary Kuharich during the 1988 campaign. Poley felt kicker J.T. Hay had absorbed

Photo courtesy of Royal Studios

Mike Anderson (66) and Roger Aldag (44) protect Kent Austin (5) in the 1989 Grey Cup too much criticism for the Stampeders' struggles and made those sentiments known to Kuharich. "I guess he didn't like hearing that," said Poley, who was soon dumped, along with Hay. "[The Roughriders] were in second place in '88 when I got released out of Calgary," recalled Poley, whose cause was advanced by long-time teammate and close friend Roger Aldag. "There was no room for an old offensive lineman, and things were turning there in Saskatchewan. Rog went to bat for me, saying, 'We need him. He can help us.' " Soon enough, Poley was once again resplendent in green.

"Rog went to bat for me, saying, 'We need him. He can help us.'" Soon enough, Poley was once again resplendent in green.

The stretch run was especially meaningful for warhorses like Aldag and Poley, who had endured the Roughriders' lean years. Aldag had seen it all, having made his debut with Saskatchewan in 1976. After a taste of success as a rookie, Aldag would face disappointment as a playoff berth was perennially unattainable. "We had a lot of teammates in those years," he said. "There were years when we had well in excess of 100 people at training camp. It just seemed like we really stuck together. I mean, nobody else really wanted to be with us, so we stuck together as teammates as much as we could. The guys who stuck it out and hung around became really close. I think that's the thing that made it the easiest. We had great teammates. We just went out there and tried to do the best we could."

The efforts eventually paid off for veteran players such as Aldag, Poley, Eddie Lowe, Dave Ridgway, Mike Anderson, Ray Elgaard, Vic Stevenson, Glen Suitor and Ken Moore. For them, a 28-25 victory over the B.C. Lions on October 15 was especially sweet. The win secured a playoff berth. "We couldn't miss the playoffs forever," said Elgaard, who caught a 75-yard touchdown pass from Tom Burgess in the clinching game.

Following the game, Aldag's teammates presented him with the game ball. "There should have been a bunch of game balls today," he said. "They just felt sorry for me, I guess." The Roughriders were sorry no more. The victory over B.C. gave Saskatchewan a 10-5 record, good for a first-place tie with Edmonton.

"By the time 1988 rolled around, I felt we could be a force because we learned some lessons in losing some close games in '87," Bill Baker said. "We had a hell of a defence and we had two quarterbacks who on any given day were the best in the league. We could compete with Edmonton, B.C. or Toronto and we created a winning atmosphere."

With Tom Burgess and Kent Austin sharing the quarterbacking, the 1988 Roughriders scored 525 points – the second-highest total in the league. Ridgway led the way, scoring-wise, by setting CFL single-season records

Photo courtesy of *Leader-Post*

Tom Burgess (16) throws as Roger Aldag (44) and Vic Stevenson give him time for points (215) and field goals (55). Robokicker was one of the Roughriders' four all-Canadians, along with Aldag, Elgaard and Bobby Jurasin. Goldsmith and Hall were West Division all-stars – along with Anderson and defensive tackle Gary Lewis – after coming over from Calgary.

Their contributions helped Saskatchewan finish 11-7, tying Edmonton for the best record in the West. The Eskimos were awarded first place based on a better points differential in their season series with the Roughriders. By virtue of finishing second, Saskatchewan would play host to B.C. in the West semifinal.

Even though the Roughriders were staging a home playoff game for the first time since the 1976 West final, Taylor Field was not sold out when the Lions visited. A total of 26,229 fans braved a minus-25 wind chill to watch B.C. pulverize Saskatchewan 42-18. B.C. led 18-17 at halftime before dominating the final two quarters. The Lions' Tony Cherry led the way with 184 yards on 17 carries.

"It was disappointing because we got our heads too high during the season," Roughriders president Tom Shepherd said. "We got so hyped about having a playoff game. We had a big pep rally. We did everything we could. It was a new experience for everyone involved and while we partied, we forgot B.C. had a good team and they kicked the shit out of us. It was disappointing, but not end-of-the-world disappointing, because we knew we could compete and we were looking forward to '89. We thought we were there when, in reality and in hindsight, we were a year away."

Photo courtesy of *Leader-Post*

Jeff Fairholm – speed kills . . . the opposition

There was one more road trip in 1988 for Aldag, Fairholm and Elgaard – all of whom were West Division finalists for CFL player awards. Aldag was named the league's outstanding offensive lineman for the second time, having previously won in 1986. Elgaard was also called to the podium, earning outstanding-Canadian honours after a 69-catch, 1,290-yard season. Fairholm, with 10 touchdown receptions, was the runner-up to Ottawa's Orville Lee for rookie-of-the-year.

Shortly after the season, there was more big news in Riderville. Rampant speculation that Bill Baker was headed for the CFL office provided to be correct. In mid-December, he stepped down as the general manager to become the league's president and chief operating officer. In that capacity, he was to work closely with newly appointed chairman and chief executive officer Roy McMurtry. The CFL had decided to hire two people to replace outgoing commissioner Doug Mitchell. The search committee was chaired by Shepherd. "A classic example of good news, bad news," Shepherd said after the announcement was made in Toronto. "For me, it's a classic case of mixed emotions, too. It's a great move for the league, but I don't know about going back to Saskatchewan and facing the people. We're losing our Number 1 asset, no question about that, but I think the abilities he'll give to the league are more important at this time, and I think the people back home will understand that."

Baker had become the third consecutive Saskatchewan GM to serve for only two years, following John Herrera (1983 and

1984) and Bill Quinter (1985 and 1986). "I wouldn't say the challenge is no longer there, but it isn't what it was two years ago," Baker said following his appointment. "Still, I would have liked to spend one more year [with the Roughriders]. I would've liked this to happen next year. And if it didn't happen at all, I would've stayed one or two more years and then I would have gone back into the private sector."

In two short but eventful years, Baker had done a remarkable job. He played an instrumental role in rescuing the Roughriders from the precipice of insolvency. A year and a half after holding a Tickethon to remain afloat, the Roughriders were able to announce a modest profit – in the neighbourhood of $30,000 – on their 1988 operations. The accumulated deficit was still a shade over $1 million, however, and it would have to be tackled by whomever succeeded Baker in 1989.

"Whatever happens, I'm undoubtedly going to be compared to Bill Baker," Alan Ford said after being named the Roughriders' general manager on January 5, 1989. "If it's good, it's because Bill Baker left a good foundation. If it's bad, it's because somebody left town … I don't have Bill's personality. I demand the same excellence. I just do it in a different way." Ford, who had spent the previous four seasons as a member of the Roughriders' office staff, was promoted from assistant GM. He was accustomed to changing job descriptions, having earned the nickname Mr. Versatility during a CFL playing career that lasted from 1965 to 1976. While wearing green and white, the Regina-born Ford played offensive and defensive halfback, tight end and linebacker. He also punted and returned kickoffs.

"Whatever happens, I'm undoubtedly going to be compared to Bill Baker … If it's good, it's because Bill Baker left a good foundation. If it's bad, it's because somebody left town."

Upon taking over from Baker, Ford appointed two assistant GMs. Head scout Dan Rambo was promoted to assistant GM in charge of player personnel. Larry Mueller was hired as assistant GM for sales and administration.

Photo courtesy of *Leader-Post*

Tom Shepherd and Alan Ford

Photo courtesy of Royal Studios

Don Narcisse

At long last, the Roughriders had a winning team to sell. The marketing extended to The Store – the team's sales outlet, based at Taylor Field. But after finally making the playoffs following 11 years of futility, fans were most anxious to see what was in store for 1989.

Unlike the first two years under head coach John Gregory, the Roughriders would not be making major player-personnel alterations. The 36-man roster with which Saskatchewan began the 1989 season bore a distinct resemblance to the 1988 squad. Why mess with success after a breakthrough year?

There was one notable change involving a returning player. After an injury-plagued 1988 season, wide receiver Don Narcisse was 100 per cent to begin the 1989 campaign. Narcisse had but one touchdown reception to show for his first 18 games as a Roughrider, spread over 1987 and 1988, but doubled that total in the 1989 regular-season opener against Calgary.

Narcisse caught two touchdown passes late in the fourth quarter as Saskatchewan rallied from a 26-6 deficit and defeated Calgary 32-29 at Taylor Field. The rally began when Tom Burgess, in relief of Kent Austin, found Ray Elgaard for a 35-yard score early in the fourth quarter. Burgess then hit Narcisse from 11 yards away with 1:51 left. Dave Ridgway promptly attempted an onside kickoff, which Narcisse tipped to teammate Albert Brown.

Photo courtesy of Royal Studios

Tom Burgess hands off to Tim McCray

Four plays later, facing a third-and-10 on Calgary's 42-yard line, Burgess spotted Narcisse in the end zone. Ridgway's convert tied the game. The Roughriders regained possession in time for Ridgway to hit a 42-yard, game-winning field goal with no time remaining. "That was amazing," Bobby Jurasin said. "If you wanted to have a beer and take a pee, you would have missed us putting 17 points on the board, because it went quick." With Burgess at the controls of a quick-strike offence, the Roughriders roared out of the gate, winning four of their first five games while amassing 178 points. In the fourth victory, a 58-22 conquest of visiting Ottawa, Saskatchewan established a single-game franchise record for points.

The next week, Saskatchewan's offence could hardly be blamed for the team's second defeat of the season, as the Roughriders fell 46-40 in Hamilton. It would not be the only time the losing team scored 40 points in a Roughriders/Tiger-Cats meeting in 1989.

Burgess had five touchdown passes against Hamilton, giving him a staggering 19 after six games. He soon cooled off, leading some fans and media types to lobby for the deployment of Austin. Gregory bristled at any mention of a quarterback controversy and stuck with Burgess until he was unable to move the offence September 9 in Toronto. As was the case in the season opener, a quarterbacking change sparked the team. Austin led the

Roughriders to 19 unanswered fourth-quarter points and a 29-24 victory. Eight days later, Austin threw for three touchdowns in a 48-35 home-field victory over Edmonton, handing the Eskimos one of only two losses they would absorb during the 1989 regular season.

The momentum was arrested, though, as Saskatchewan lost its next two games – falling 36-27 in Ottawa before donating a 32-30 victory to the visiting Lions on September 30. The Roughriders were apparently poised for victory, as the Lions were on Saskatchewan's 53-yard line with five seconds remaining.

For B.C., the only option was to attempt a Hail Mary pass and hope, against incalculable odds, for a miracle.

The miracle happened. Dunigan fired a pass toward three Lions receivers at the Roughriders' 18-yard line. Before the ball arrived, Saskatchewan safety Glen Suitor crashed into B.C. wideout David Williams. It was a flagrant pass-interference penalty, and flags flew. "All he had to do was wait for me to catch it, then tackle me, and the game was over," Williams said.

No time remained on the clock, but the Lions were given one more play because a game cannot end on a penalty. From the 18, Dunigan again looked to Williams. The Lions' receiver was hit by cornerback Albert Brown in the end zone and, once again, Saskatchewan was called for pass interference. The ball was moved to the one-yard line and B.C. was given yet another play. The snap bounced off Dunigan's chest and facemask before hitting Lions offensive linemen Leo Groenewegen and Jim Mills. Dunigan, playing with a sprained right thumb, grabbed the ball and fell into the end zone for the winning touchdown before 25,013 stunned spectators.

"That's the toughest loss ever, no question," John Gregory said. "I don't know what else can happen to this football team, but I don't think one play by one person determines a football game. The easiest thing to do is to point fingers after a loss and to start shuffling players." But people did point fingers – directly at Suitor, who was inconsolable.

Despite the devastation, the veteran safety sat in his locker-room stall and answered questions from all members of the media. "I knew time was running down, but I didn't know it had expired," he explained. "I just tried to time my jump." Fans were jumping all over Suitor, who was vilified on the post-game phone-in show.

In the sombre aftermath of that game, Suitor pondered his football future, even though he had not yet turned 27. "I sort of went through a complete re-evaluation of why I was playing and the investment of time and effort that I had put in to that point," he recalled. "It was the first time in my entire life that I ever thought about quitting and not playing, after that B.C. game. That was the first time ever in my career that I had thought, "I don't need football. I'll go do something else.' That didn't last very long, though, because of my desire to compete. Within the next 12 hours, with it going over and over in my mind and not sleeping and people calling me and saying this and that, my feelings changed." But his basic philosophy did not. True to form, Suitor faced the music. Much like he submitted to pointed questions from the media horde after the Saturday night collapse against the Lions, Suitor was a guest on CKRM's Monday night phone-in show and took calls from fans. In so doing, he defused the firestorm.

Meanwhile, Suitor's teammates rallied around him. "I told him we're all in this together and one play doesn't win or lose a football game," defensive backfield cohort Richie Hall said. "He was very hard on himself. He took sole responsibility for the loss, but we didn't lose that game because of Glen. To me, that was a defining moment because

"That's the toughest loss ever, no question," John Gregory said. "I don't know what else can happen to this football team, but I don't think one play by one person determines a football game. The easiest thing to do is to point fingers after a loss and to start shuffling players."

Suitor was a guest on CKRM's Monday night phone-in show and took calls from fans. In so doing, he defused the firestorm.

> Gregor impressed upon the Roughriders' coaches and players that a new season was to begin after the B.C. game. That team would be referred to, internally, as the 89'ers. From that point, players wore tape on their fingers to simulate a Grey Cup ring and to provide a constant reminder of the objective.

the worst possible thing that could happen did happen. We let something slip away but, because we had an experienced group of guys, we weren't going to let that play stop us from our goal. Believe it or not, it brought us closer together. It made us refocus, not take things for granted." The change in focus was aided by Gary Gregor, a psychologist and motivational speaker from Moose Jaw. Gregor impressed upon the Roughriders' coaches and players that a new season was to begin after the B.C. game. That team would be referred to, internally, as the 89'ers. From that point, players wore tape on their fingers to simulate a Grey Cup ring and to provide a constant reminder of the objective.

"We were a team in turmoil," said Ray Elgaard, whose team's record had slipped to 6-7 after a 4-1 start. "That was the real turning point in that season. After we lost that game, John Gregory did some things that were pretty creative in that dressing room." For the remainder of the season, Gregory and Gregor were never far apart on the sideline. "He had more impact on Coach Gregory than he had on me," Hall said. "He brought a sense of levelness to John, who was a very emotional guy. It calmed him down. For the players, how much of an influence he had is something that was very small to some guys to very large for others." Gregory felt Gregor's impact extended far beyond the head coach. "He did some really nice things with the players," the head coach said. "He had a real positive air about him. He was one of those guys who was sort of a psychologist who tried to make everybody believe they could win, and I think that was good. Those guys never have a place in their souls for what happens if you lose." At the time Gregor was enlisted, the Roughriders were losing games and players. Elgaard suffered torn left knee ligaments during the third quarter against B.C. He underwent arthroscopic surgery the following day and was to miss the remainder of the regular season. For the B.C. game, the injury-riddled Roughriders had already been without their other accomplished Canadian slotback – Jeff Fairholm. The absence of the Slot Machines did not bode well for the Roughriders, who were preparing for an October 8 road game in Calgary.

Photo courtesy of *Leader-Post*

Kent Austin

Somehow, the Roughriders were able to erupt offensively without Elgaard and Fairholm. Austin passed for 492 yards and three touchdowns in a 39-26 victory over the Stampeders. Two of the touchdown passes were caught by Narcisse, who had four receptions for 122 yards. Regina-born slotback Rob Bresciani, starting for the first time in the CFL, enjoyed a career day – catching six passes for 194 yards, including a 59-yard TD, plus a spectacular one-handed catch along the sideline. James Ellingson, another homebrew inside receiver, added five receptions for 72 yards.

One week later, the Roughriders went above .500 (8-7) by beating Toronto 24-18 at Taylor Field. Saskatchewan then split a home-and-home set with Calgary before concluding the regular season with a 49-17 loss in Edmonton.

At 9-9, the Roughriders finished third in the West, and appeared to be staggering into the playoffs – literally. Elgaard was still out of the lineup. Fairholm was hobbling. The torrent of injuries was such that third-string quarterback Jeff Bentrim was required to play slotback and return kickoffs. The athletic Bentrim was to fill those roles when the post-season began.

The Roughriders were in the playoffs for the second consecutive season, but without the giddiness of 1988. Having concluded the regular season in inglorious fashion, the Roughriders were off to Calgary for the West Division semifinal. The Stampeders, who finished second in the conference at 10-8, seemed to be a good bet to advance to the division final after Terrence Jones (who was inserted after the starting quarterback, Danny Barrett, suffered an ankle injury) lobbed a 36-yard touchdown pass to 6-foot-3 Marc Zeno, who outjumped 5-foot-6 Roughriders defensive halfback Richie Hall in the end zone. That major put Calgary up 26-23 with 2:24 remaining.

Photo courtesy of Royal Studios

Tim McCray in the 1989 Grey Cup

Tim McCray returned the ensuing kickoff to Saskatchewan's 20-yard line. Two completions from Austin to Bentrim helped the Roughriders advance 40 yards, to the Calgary 50-yard line. John Gregory then sent Brian Walling, who had been claimed off Edmonton's practice roster three weeks earlier, into the game with a play. Walling, who spelled Milson Jones alongside McCray in the offensive backfield, relayed the information to Austin.

"What I basically wanted to do was get really good field position," Gregory said. "They'd been playing a lot of zone and double-covering the receivers, so we just ran a draw play." Austin was all for it. "The ironic thing was, I was going to call the same play," the third-year Roughriders pivot said.

"I was on the same page. I was playing for the win. We weren't thinking field goal to tie." Austin handed off to Walling, who followed the blocking of Roger Aldag. Meanwhile, fellow guard Bob Poley had eliminated Stampeders middle linebacker Doug (Tank) Landry. As Walling burst through a gaping hole, Ellingson KO'd two Stampeders – defensive backs Junior Thurman and Chris Major – with one devastating block. Walling sprinted to the end zone and scored untouched from 50 yards away with 1:38 left before a mere 16,286 spectators at McMahon Stadium. Ridgway's convert gave Saskatchewan a 30-26 lead.

Shortly thereafter, linebacker Eddie Lowe stripped the football from Calgary fullback Andy McVey. Defensive tackle Chuck Klingbeil, a late-season addition who made an immediate impact, pounced on the loose ball – setting up a Ridgway field goal, his fourth of the day, that completed the scoring.

On the game's final play, Jones' desperation pass was intercepted by Hall, who made amends for the Zeno touchdown.

"I felt like I had let my teammates down when they scored that touchdown to go ahead," Hall recalled. "I was very disappointed but, knowing the character we had on this team, others were quick to let me know I shouldn't worry about it because we'll get it back. That's the kind of team we had. We were a team. We weren't a bunch of individuals." One individual was especially verbose as the West Division final loomed.

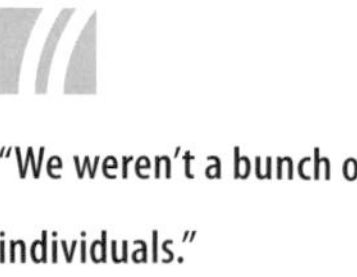

"We weren't a bunch of individuals."

Eskimos defensive tackle John Mandarich told everyone who would listen that the game against the Roughriders would be a cakewalk. "People are expecting us to blow them out of the water," Mandarich said. "The bottom line is I expect to blow them out of the water. It's not being arrogant. It's not being cocky. It's being determined. There's no reason why we shouldn't blow them out of the water." The Eskimos had been established as 12-point favourites after registering a CFL-record 16 victories, with only two losses, during the regular season.

Edmonton, which won all nine of its home games, amassed 644 points over 18 contests while being quarterbacked by Tracy Ham – who would soon be decorated as the league's most outstanding player for 1989.

Photo courtesy of Royal Studios

Eddie Lowe

With Ham at the controls, Edmonton briskly marched 69 yards in seven plays en route to scoring a touchdown on its opening drive. The Eskimos were ahead 10-0 midway through the first quarter. But, in a sense, Edmonton's robust start benefited Saskatchewan. "It couldn't have worked out any better for us," Ray Elgaard said. "They came out and in two minutes marched for a touchdown. It made them think they're gods. We said, 'OK, let's do the same thing.' It showed our offence that if we're going to win, we've got to shove it down their throats." The Roughriders answered with a Dave Ridgway field goal to reduce Edmonton's lead to 10-3, but things still looked promising for the Eskimos, who had scored on their first two possessions. Edmonton was making it look easy.

"Maybe too easy," Eskimos centre Rod Connop told Cam Cole, then of the *Edmonton Journal*. "Not that we got overconfident, but they scrapped their whole defensive game plan after that first drive. They just threw caution to the wind and came after Tracy with everything they had." That was especially true barely two minutes into the second quarter. The Eskimos were second-and-15 at Saskatchewan's 30-yard line when Ham was hammered by a Lowe blow. A blitzing Eddie Lowe jarred the ball loose. Middle linebacker Dave Albright scooped up the football and lumbered 62 yards to paydirt. One Ridgway convert later, the game was tied.

"Eddie just smashed Ham," offensive tackle Vic Stevenson recalled. "I'll always remember the sound of it. I remember a woman screaming when he hit him. You hear the crowd noise, and all of a sudden I hear this woman just shriek." The Roughriders were screaming for different reasons. "I think every player on that sideline was running with Dave Albright when he picked up that ball," tailback Tim McCray said. "Myself, I was running, and I think the coaching staff was even running. After that play, we were all jacked up. It just electrified everyone." Lowe struck again shortly thereafter, intercepting Ham to give Saskatchewan possession on Edmonton's 42-yard line. Five plays later, Kent Austin found Elgaard – playing for the first time since September 30 after recovering from a knee injury – for a touchdown. The convert, Saskatchewan's 17th consecutive point, put the visitors ahead 17-10. Austin, however, would soon be out of the game after injuring his right knee. But the Roughriders had also inflicted some damage on the Eskimos, who unexpectedly trailed 17-13 at halftime.

"I think every player on that sideline was running with Dave Albright when he picked up that ball," tailback Tim McCray said. "Myself, I was running, and I think the coaching staff was even running. After that play, we were all jacked up. It just electrified everyone."

As was the case in the first half, Edmonton emerged from its dressing room and quickly scored. Ham's 10-yard touchdown run, converted by Jerry Kauric, gave the Eskimos a 20-17 advantage after their first possession of the third quarter. Little did anyone suspect that the high-powered Eskimos would score only one more point that afternoon.

Saskatchewan's offence, by contrast, was poised for an eruption. At 9:52 of the third quarter, Tom Burgess – quarterbacking in place of Austin – shrugged off pressure and looked deep for Jeff Fairholm, who was open down the left sideline. Fairholm hauled in the bomb for a 47-yard touchdown, helping Saskatchewan regain the lead, 24-20.

The ensuing kickoff was fumbled by Edmonton's Keith Wright. Don Narcisse recovered the ball at the Eskimos' 39-yard line. Four plays later, Burgess looked to Elgaard with six points in mind. The veteran slotback made a spectacular leaping catch in the right corner of the end zone while keeping both feet in bounds, recording a 14-yard major that put Saskatchewan ahead 31-20. "I said to Ray, 'Dude, that's the best [bleeping] catch I've ever seen you make,' " Bob Poley said.

Photo courtesy of *Leader-Post*

Ray Elgaard in the open field

Eighteen minutes remained, but the Eskimos were hardly a threat to score. Ham was bothered by the Roughriders' blitzing tactics. Glen Suitor, in particular, was conspicuous in the Eskimos' offensive backfield throughout the game. By the time the final gun sounded, signalling a 32-21 Saskatchewan win, the sixth-year safety had registered five defensive tackles, an interception and a quarterback sack. "Suitor played the way a

Photo courtesy of Royal Studios

Glen Suitor (27) and Bobby Jurasin sandwich Edmonton runner Reggie Taylor

"If anything positive could have come out of that B.C. game, this was it," Suitor said as 35,112 spectators filed out of Commonwealth Stadium. While the Eskimos' supporters moped, the Roughriders contingent was going bonkers.

safety is supposed to play," Nick Miliokas wrote in the *Leader-Post*. "He was all over the field." Frustrated fans had been all over Suitor after the collapse against the visiting B.C. Lions, but he made amends many times over in the West final.

"If anything positive could have come out of that B.C. game, this was it," Suitor said as 35,112 spectators filed out of Commonwealth Stadium. While the Eskimos' supporters moped, the Roughriders contingent was going bonkers.

"No one gave us a chance in the world to beat the Eskimos," then-president Tom Shepherd said. "Even as passionate as I am about the Riders, I didn't think we could beat the best team perhaps in the history of the CFL. They were 16-and-2 and we were 9-and-9. There's not one chance in a million we will win at Commonwealth because they were so good. It was so unexpected."

Except, perhaps, within the Roughriders' dressing room. 'I don't think any pro athlete goes into a game thinking they're going to lose," Fairholm said. "If you don't totally believe and prepare like you're going to win a game, don't go on the field. You're going to get hurt. No, that never crossed my mind. I can safely say that nobody would say that [they expected to lose to Edmonton]. I think we all expected to win." Afterwards, the media was magnetically attracted to Mandarich – with some imploring from Austin, who wondered: "What's he saying now?" The Eskimos' defensive tackle, full of bravado before the game, sat quietly in his cubicle and faced all inquiries. "You've got to learn from this experience," he told reporters. "We all make mistakes. I wasn't trying to be malicious when I said those things. It's just my personality. I guess I've got to get a big spoon and eat some words. It was tongue-in-cheek. I was just trying to get the fans going and sell a few tickets. I guess I've got a long time to think about it." The Roughriders, meanwhile, were packing their bags with two trips in mind – a return flight to Regina, where they would be mobbed at the airport by more than 1,000 fans at 2 a.m., followed by an excursion to Toronto for a Grey Cup date with the Hamilton Tiger-Cats.

"I decided that because Hamilton was going to play so much zone, and they were going to play a lot of crazy-type zones, Kent was the guy."

THE question as the Roughriders prepared for the Grey Cup pertained to who would start at quarterback – Austin or Burgess? Head coach John Gregory chose the former. "That was really an interesting deal because of the way that Tommy played up in Edmonton," Gregory said. "We had used both quarterbacks during the year. We used Tommy when we were playing against man-to-man coverage. We used Kent when we were playing against zone coverage. They both were very effective in their own right based upon the kind of coverage they were going against. I decided that because Hamilton was going to play so much zone, and they were going to play a lot of crazy-type zones, Kent was the guy." Burgess felt he was worthy of a start after completing nine of 12 passes for 120 yards and two touchdowns after Austin injured his right knee late in the first half of the West final. Burgess had led the Roughriders in touchdown passes, with 22, during the regular season. Austin, who had 16 TD tosses, threw for 2,650 yards – 110 more than Burgess. Austin had taken over the quarterbacking September 9, after Burgess cooled off. The Grey Cup game was to be Austin's 11th consecutive start.

"I've quarterbacked this team to where we're at – I deserve to start," Austin told Grant Kerr of The Canadian Press on the Wednesday of Grey Cup week. "I helped turn this team around when we had a four-game losing streak." During that dry spell, a debate had raged as to whom Gregory should start. "There was a big quarterback controversy in my mind," Burgess told Kerr. "Anytime you get to the point where you don't know

Photo courtesy of Royal Studios

Kent Austin throws over the outstretched arms of former Rider Frank Robinson (43)

who to play, there's controversy. There was a lot of public pressure ... to see the other guy. I got very frustrated, but the best thing to do is not to dwell on it." Burgess put personal interests aside and concentrated on his team's first Grey Cup appearance since 1976. Meanwhile, back in Saskatchewan, fans were making last-minute plans to head to Toronto for the game. Arrangements were made for additional airline space. Some fans took the bus, or even drove.

The night before the game, two long-time Roughriders offensive linemen – Roger Aldag and Bob Poley – realized they had no choice but to win the Grey Cup. "We were watching the tube in our hotel room," Poley said. "Rog rolled over and said, 'We can't go back without it.' And I go, 'No, we've got to take it back with us.' " By game day – November 26, 1989 – the Roughriders' ardent fan base was well-represented in Toronto. Green-clad supporters were heard loud and clear on Sunday during a pre-game pep rally at Maple Leaf Gardens. "The week before no one had a ticket for the game, and a week later the place is full of Saskatchewan fans," Tom Shepherd marvelled. "Al [Ford, general manager] and I are leading the cheers on the stage. It was fantastic." Then it was off to the SkyDome – now the Rogers Centre – which had opened earlier in 1989. "We walked on the field for our pre-game warmup and it seemed like the whole SkyDome was green and white," Austin said. "It was awesome. We definitely had the majority there, at least from a vocal standpoint." The circumstances left a few Roughriders players somewhat star-struck. "The biggest memory I have is running on the field for introductions because they introduced the defence," defensive halfback Richie Hall

"We walked on the field for our pre-game warmup and it seemed like the whole SkyDome was green and white," Austin said. "It was awesome."

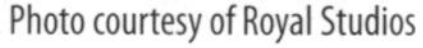

Photo courtesy of Royal Studios

Richie Hall celebrates

Photo courtesy of Sun Media Corp.

Jeff Fairholm scores on a bomb from Kent Austin

recalled. "Right at the end, I looked at the big screen to see my face and thought, 'Gosh, for these two or three seconds, everything is focused on myself.' To see myself up there and knowing my parents were in the building somewhere was just a dream come true." The first quarter did not meet that description, from the Roughriders' perspective. Hamilton led 13-1 after the opening 15 minutes. Adding to the discomfort, many Saskatchewan players could not escape reminders of plays that went awry. "At Taylor Field, we never had a replay screen," Bob Poley said. "We go to the SkyDome and it had a big screen. You'd finish a play and there it is again. So we got going in the game and it wasn't going great early. It was a struggle. Guys are kind of feeling each other out. We ran a play, it didn't work, and the way the field was, we were huddled up and looking at the screen. We're all looking up. Elgaard comes into the huddle and he's cussing us out. He said, 'Are you going to [bleeping] watch yourself play or are you going to play? Let's play.' Nobody was watching the screen anymore." There was every reason to watch the game during a scintillating second quarter. The Roughriders and Tiger-Cats combined for 35 points – the most ever in one quarter during a Grey Cup. Austin, in particular, was lethal. He fired touchdown passes to Elgaard (from six yards away), Jeff Fairholm (on a 75-yard bomb) and Don Narcisse (a five-yarder) to help Saskatchewan narrow the deficit to 27-22 by halftime.

Fairholm caught the long pass from Austin even though Hamilton defensive back Stephen Jordan was flagged for pass interference on the play. "I remember sitting on the bench before that series," said Fairholm, who was the runner-up to Tiger-Cats slotback Rocky DiPietro for most-outstanding-Canadian honours in 1989. Burgess came over to me and said, 'Can you beat Jordan deep?' I said, 'I can do anything you want. Yes, I can beat him deep.' And I never said that. I would never say anything like that. That was not like me. And I said, 'I'll beat him. I know I can.' Tommy went over to Kent and said, 'Jeff just told me this.' The first play, Kent called it. He said, 'Run,' and I ran. How intricate. Kent just threw it up there and I was able to catch it." Saskatchewan was playing catch-up until 12:09 of the third quarter, when Tim McCray's one-yard touchdown run, converted by Ridgway, gave the Roughriders a 34-30 lead. The West Division champions remained in front until 44 seconds remained in the game when, on third-and-goal from the nine, Hamilton's Tony Champion made a spectacular catch of a Mike Kerrigan aerial in the end zone.

Champion, who was playing with injured ribs, twisted in midair and made the catch by falling backwards. Paul Osbaldiston's convert knotted the game at 40-40. "[Austin] put the game on his shoulders after Tony Champion made that catch," said McCray,

Photo courtesy of Royal Studios

Kent Austin (5) audibles near the Hamilton goal line

who returned the ensuing kickoff 23 yards to the 36-yard line. "He came into the huddle and told us, 'Look, we're going to take this ball down and we are either going to score a touchdown or we are going to get into position for a field goal so that Dave [Ridgway] can win it for us.' Everyone believed in Kent that day. I think that game took his career to a new level because he proved to everyone what a leader he was." On first down, Austin looked deep for Narcisse, but overthrew everyone. As much as anything, the pass was intended to loosen up the Hamilton defence.

"Everyone believed in Kent that day. I think that game took his career to a new level because he proved to everyone what a leader he was."

The Roughriders' quarterback then found Elgaard near the right sideline for a 20-yard advance. On the next play, Austin looked over the middle for first-year wide receiver Mark Guy, who caught the ball for a 18-yard gain while absorbing a wicked hit. Guy was also the target on the next play, connecting with Austin for a 10-yard gain.

"I didn't say anything to Kent in the huddle," said Guy, who had four receptions for a team-high 100 yards. "I was the same guy I had always been. I was very happy to know the ball was coming my way. I remember that first catch. I was coming into some traffic. When he threw it, I knew we needed that first down so I just jumped up and made sure I had it before I went down. That was the most important thing – to just catch the ball. On the second catch, it was just a simple out pattern. I don't know if Kent's confidence grew in me after the first catch, but I was impressed that he went back to me, knowing

Photo courtesy of Royal Studios

The Kick

Photo courtesy of Royal Studios

The Joy

that I had to do what I was getting paid for – catch the ball and then get out of bounds – so Ridgway could make his kick." Before Ridgway stepped on the field, the Roughriders called one more offensive play. Austin grounded the ball between the hash marks to give Robokicker a straight-on attempt from 35 yards away. "Hamilton called a timeout to make Ridgway think about the kick, but [holder Glen] Suitor took care of that," remembered Poley, who snapped the ball on placements.

"Suitor had him so deflected that he wasn't even thinking about the kick." Ridgway chuckled at the recollection. "He was just trying to get my mind off the game," Robokicker said. "The true story is that we were talking about camping. He wanted to go to the Rockies and camp – and I was worrying about bears. He then talked about a blond who was sitting behind the bench and we started laughing. He did exactly what he had to do for me. He was like my coach at the time." With the timeout out of the way, Ridgway lined up for the kick. He nodded. Suitor called for the ball. The snap was flawless. "All I said to Suitor was, 'Do what you want. Once the ball hits your hands, it's not my problem anymore,' " Poley said. "Glen said, 'Once I pin the ball, it's not my problem anymore.' " Ridgway made The Kick – no problem. "I remember looking up and seeing the ball on its way," he said. "It was close to being right down the middle. I remember my eyes shooting wide open. I remember thinking, 'Oh my God, we did it!' " Two seconds remained. There was time for one more play. Ridgway's kickoff was a squibber. Hamilton's Steve Jackson retrieved the ball and punted it downfield. The ball ended up in the hands of Suitor, who ran out of bounds – hands in the air – as the clock read 0:00. "The feeling was just exhilaration," Suitor said. "You don't know what to do or what to say. You're running around. You're screaming. You're celebrating with your teammates." It was a long-awaited celebration for the franchise, which won its second Grey Cup 23 years to the day after the first. "I was going around hugging people and shaking hands," said Aldag, a 14th-year Roughrider at the time. "I don't really know what I did. I think I just kind of wandered around the field. One of our main jobs was we were supposed to go get the Grey Cup presented to us, but that didn't seem to enter our mind. We missed it. It was no big deal. It seemed like it was a Fantasyland type of thing. It was quite a feeling." And quite a game for Austin, who was named the Grey Cup's outstanding offensive player after completing 26 of 41 passes for 474 yards and three TDs. "Hamilton was playing zone coverages and he just was great at breaking down zone coverages, reading them, and laying the ball into a hole and letting the receiver go get it," John Gregory said. "He had a great game – one of the best games

Photo courtesy of Royal Studios

We are the champions!

ever played by a Grey Cup as far as I was concerned." The game itself was also touted as the greatest ever. "I defy anybody in any city in Canada to show me an NFL game that could touch this one for exciting football," fullback Milson Jones said. That appraisal was shared by legendary Roughriders quarterback Ron Lancaster, who was the analyst on CBC's telecast of the 1989 Grey Cup. "It was great to do it, because of the fact that it was such a great game – one of the best games ever played. It may be the best Grey Cup ever played. Who knows? But it was an outstanding football game, back and forth," Lancaster said in 2008. "I can still remember Tony Champion's great catch in the end zone. Naturally, you remember the field goal. You were there for the first Grey Cup, and being there for the second one was kind of unique." Bill Baker had just missed being part of the organization in both Grey Cups the Roughriders had won to that point. He joined the team as a defensive lineman in 1968, two years after the ice-breaking Cup conquest. In 1989, Baker was completing his first (and only) year as the CFL's president and chief operating officer. He had spent the previous two seasons as Saskatchewan's general manager. As a significant consolation prize, Baker had the honour of presenting the trophy to his former team.

The game itself was also touted as the greatest ever. "I defy anybody in any city in Canada to show me an NFL game that could touch this one for exciting football."

Photo courtesy of *Leader-Post*

Coach Gregory leads the team on to the field to celebrate

"What was so great was the players we had brought in had made a contribution – guys like Kent Austin and Dave Ridgway. They were a bunch of high-quality people and you're very proud for the people like the volunteers whose efforts are often ignored."

"I was very, very proud of the team," Baker said. "Al Ford and all of the guys had a hell of a team, even though they only won nine games in the regular season. I was pleased for Saskatchewan. What was so great was the players we had brought in had made a contribution – guys like Kent Austin and Dave Ridgway. They were a bunch of high-quality people and you're very proud for the people like the volunteers whose efforts are often ignored. When you look at the day and the amount of people we had in Toronto that day, it was a celebration of what Saskatchewan had become to the CFL." Amid the revelry in the dressing room, Suitor was subdued. "I kind of went in the back," said the veteran safety, who had experienced such a variance of emotions in 1989. "A lot of my buddies were wondering why I wasn't on any of the post-game interviews in the locker room. I had heard that they were searching for me, but I went into the back with just one can of beer and was kind of like a baby, emotionally by myself, for a good 20 minutes."

Meanwhile, back in Saskatchewan, fans spilled out on to the streets. Traffic was bumper-to-bumper on Albert Street in Regina. The intersection of Albert and Victoria Avenue was the central gathering point. Motorists honked their horns. Passengers hung out of windows and sunroofs. Revellers climbed lightposts and lit fireworks. And, yes, beer was spilled.

The partying continued the next day, when the Roughriders flew back to Regina with the Grey Cup. "I was really looking forward to all the people at the airport when we landed," Jeff Fairholm said. "We landed and there were, like, 100 people. I was expecting 100,000. Nobody had told us what was going on when they took us over to the stadium." At Taylor Field, the Roughriders had a welcoming committee of 17,000 people. "That was special when we walked out on to the field," Fairholm said. "The whole west stands was packed with people, and it was cold. I remember that my neighbourhood had changed the street signs from Rae Street to Fairholm Street within a three-block radius. I remember not buying a drink for two straight weeks. There were tons of fun things. The whole place was up in arms." The Grey Cup was supported by the arms of Bob Poley and Roger Aldag, who carried the trophy on to the field on the evening of November 27, 1989. "They came up to us and said, 'You guys are carrying it,' " Poley remembered. "I said, 'OK, I can handle it. Grab on, Rog! I'll just go along for the ride.' It was a wonderful thing." The merriment endured long past that Monday night. "It was pretty special, bringing it back to Taylor Field," Aldag said. "After that, we took it to all the small towns in Saskatchewan. Just to see those people drive for miles to come to some little community hall to be with the Grey Cup was amazing." It was especially rewarding for the players who had experienced the other end of the spectrum during an 11-year playoff drought, known as the Reign of Error. Veteran members of the 1989 Roughriders had every reason to reflect on a journey that began when success was sporadic or simply non-existent.

Photo courtesy of *Leader-Post*

Bob Poley (left) and Roger Aldag – two good 'ol Saskatchewan farm boys – lead the team to the cheers of 17,000 fans at frigid Taylor Field

"It was a contrast in every sense of the word – everything from hopelessness to exhilaration," reflected Ray Elgaard, who joined the Roughriders in 1983. "It was total satisfaction – total joy and glee, as opposed to glum. It couldn't have been any more of a reverse situation.

"In its totality, it was a very cool thing to be a part of. It was really a cool chunk of time because it ended up good. If you look at '83 to '88 and that was the end of the story, it would have been a mess. When you factor all those different scenarios into it and the fact that in '89, we ended up on top, it's a pretty cool story."

All-Era Team
1979-1989

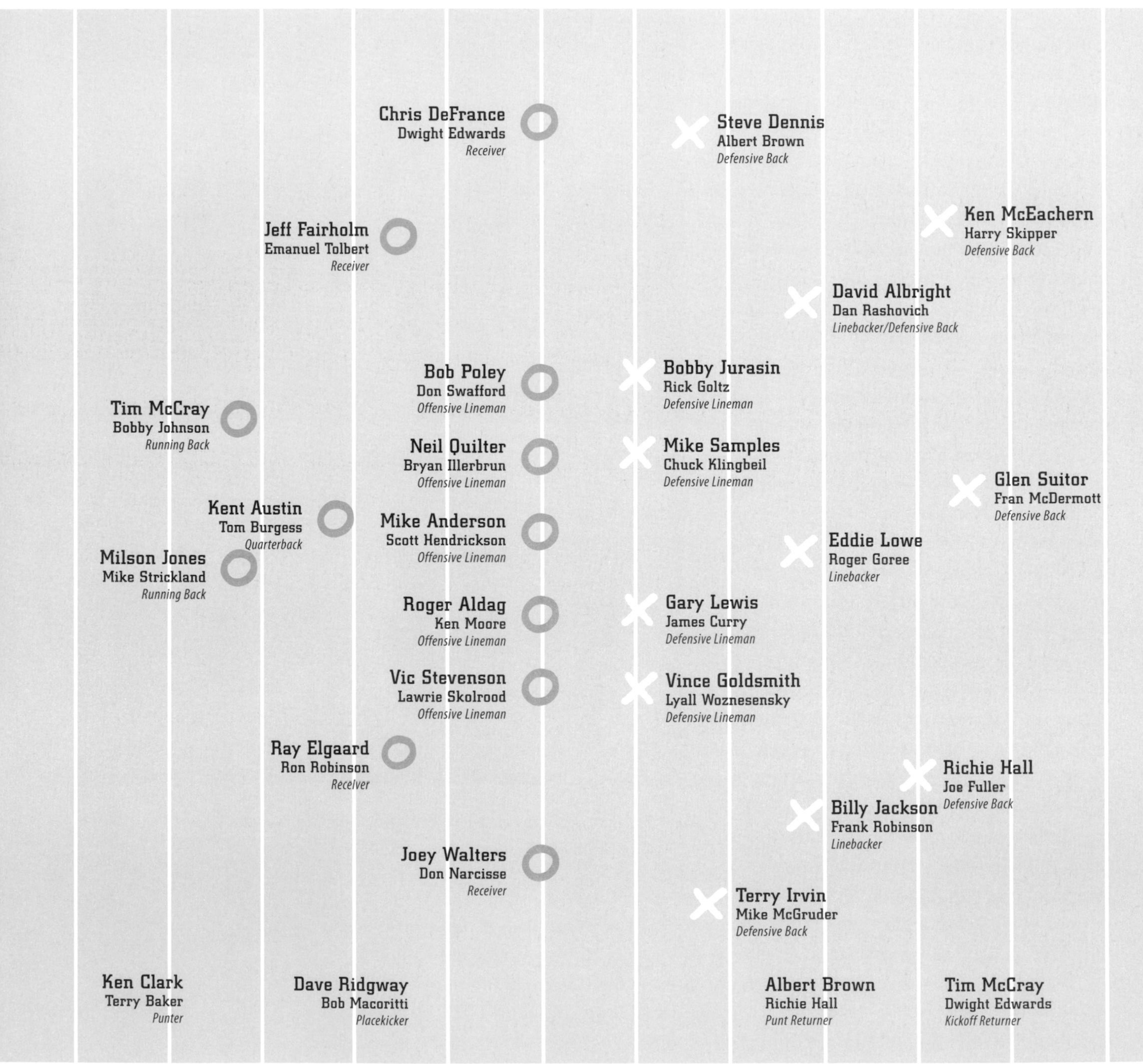

OFFENCE

Large print – 1st Team All-Star
Small print – 2nd Team All-Star
Position

DEFENCE

1990-2009

CHAPTER 5

BY DARRELL DAVIS

Photo courtesy of Royal Studios

Funny what winning a Grey Cup will do. Following the team's victory in the 1989 Grey Cup, general manager Al Ford and John Gregory, Saskatchewan's first CFL coach-of-the-year since Joe Faragalli in 1981, had their contracts extended through 1991. "This had been a long process," Gregory said after receiving the Annis Stukus Trophy. "It's taken three years to teach our players how to win." Roughriders president Phil Kershaw told CFL governors that Saskatchewan wanted to play host to the 1995 Grey Cup, "contingent on Taylor Field expansion" that would add 4,000 permanent seats and allow temporary seating capacity to almost double to 50,000. The Roughriders commissioned an economic impact study that showed Regina would benefit from $25 million in economic activity because of the Grey Cup. The franchise also saw that hosting the Grey Cup was a means to eradicate its $1.5-million debt. Despite selling $150,000 in souvenirs during January – and $1.7 million in merchandise during the past 13 months – the Grey Cup-winning team made only $220,000 on its 1989 operations. It was fiercely protective of the province-wide blackout for televised home games and, knowing that gate receipts were its major source of income, waged numerous battles to prevent people in Saskatchewan from seeing games – unless they bought tickets at Taylor Field. But the community-owned Roughriders remained one of the league's most stable franchises and wanted to be involved in setting policies that would guarantee the CFL's existence. "I believe the Saskatchewan Roughriders will exist as long as the Canadian Football League exists," said Kershaw. "So we can't sit and watch the league take a wrong turn. We won't be intimidated by anyone else during league meetings." Saskatchewan's history was honoured by the Canadian Football Hall of Fame, which announced that Ken Preston and Eagle Keys, the team's general manager and head coach of the 1966 Grey Cup champions, were being inducted. Later in the year,

"I believe the Saskatchewan Roughriders will exist as long as the Canadian Football League exists," said Kershaw. "So we can't sit and watch the league take a wrong turn."

Jeremy O'Day and Gene Makowsky, celebrate the Riders third Grey Cup victory in 2007. (Top Photo)

Photo courtesy of *Leader-Post*

Jeff Fairholm

Photo courtesy of Royal Studios

Milson Jones

the team's Plaza of Honor welcomed Jack Rowand, Stack Tibbitts, Don MacDonald, Toar Springstein, Peter Martin, Garner Ekstran, Bill Baker and Joey Walters.

The biggest issue throughout Saskatchewan's march to the Grey Cup was its quarterbacks. A quarterback controversy continually bubbled because Gregory had two solid pivots in Kent Austin, who had been named the Grey Cup's outstanding offensive player, and Tom Burgess, who had replaced an injured Austin and led the team to its victory over Edmonton in the West final. Knowing their roles as they entered the option years of their contracts, Burgess had publicly demanded a trade and Austin had balked at signing a four-year, million-dollar contract. When rookie camp opened, Austin, veteran third-stringer Jeff Bentrim and rookie Tony Rice, a Notre Dame product, were in attendance. "I don't have any formal letter asking me to go to rookie camp," said Burgess, when asked about his absence. Second-year slotback Jeff Fairholm was also upset about his contract and announced his retirement at a hastily called media conference in front of the Legislative Building. It turns out the Roughriders weren't allowing him to cash in on an all-star bonus stipulated in his contract because he had made the West team, not the CFL squad. "You can read into it what you want," said Fairholm, who worked out a deal a few days later and appeared at training camp in Saskatoon, on the grass fields across the street from the University of Saskatchewan campus. Burgess also attended training camp, where one rainy day he was being closely watched by Ford and Cal Murphy, the long-time Winnipeg Blue Bombers head coach/general manager, who was wearing green Riders rain-gear while huddled under a nearby tree. Murphy wouldn't admit to anything, but days later he sent quarterback Lee Saltz, receiver Allan Boyko and first-round draft picks in 1991 and 1992 to the Roughriders for Burgess. Burgess instantly became Winnipeg's starting quarterback and ultimately led the Blue Bombers to victory in the 1990 Grey Cup. Burgess had celebrated quietly after the '89 game, but he was downright giddy after winning the 1990 championship as Winnipeg's starting quarterback.

Gregory made very few changes to his roster. He added a new assistant, Larry Donovan, a Grey Cup-winning coach with B.C. in 1988, to handle linebackers and special teams. Assistant general manager Dan Rambo also hired Tom Dimitroff Jr. Although Dimitroff was hoping to become a coach, Rambo made him a personnel assistant and started the youngster on a career that ultimately led him to become general manager of the NFL's Atlanta Falcons.

The Roughriders opened their season with a 38-35 victory over the visiting Tiger-Cats, with fullback Milson Jones running for the game-winning, 33-yard touchdown in the final minute. Despite tallying 506 yards in offence, the Riders scored only one touchdown in their next game and lost 30-25 in Calgary, followed by a 54-16 loss that completed the home-and-home set. Austin began calling his own offensive plays and completed 27 of 52 passes for 389 yards with one interception and one touchdown in a 36-25 victory in B.C. A 10-sack performance by the Eskimos gave them a 57-31 victory over the visiting Riders, which dropped Saskatchewan's record to 2-3. They fell to 2-4 after losing 32-30 to the Lions.

Austin began calling his own offensive plays and completed 27 of 52 passes for 389 yards with one interception and one touchdown in a 36-25 victory in B.C.

Days after making a trade for the Roughriders – fullback Shawn Daniels and a draft pick to Ottawa for tailback Orville Lee – Dan Rambo announced he was leaving the organization after 7½ years to become pro personnel co-ordinator for Canada and Mexico with the upstart World League of American Football. Fred Glick, a former Ottawa Rough Riders head coach, would be hired as the U.S. scouting director.

More news came off the field when Sandy Monteith, AKA "The Flame," was charged and found guilty of keeping explosives in an unsuitable, unmarked container. A 15-year-old helper had suffered burns to 25 per cent of his body after a carrying case exploded following a game on July 12. Monteith, who gained nation-wide notoriety for igniting a canister of gunpowder atop his football helmet to celebrate Riders touchdowns, was banned from Taylor Field until his act was "safe," according to Ford. Monteith would make regular appearances at Grey Cup festivities, plus he made one, closely monitored appearance at Mosaic Stadium in 2006 as a 65th birthday celebration for then-GM Roy Shivers.

Three straight victories – 49-24 against the Eskimos, 46-33 in Hamilton and 55-11 against the Blue Bombers in a Labour Day Classic that drew a Taylor Field-record crowd of 31,121 – got the Riders back to 5-4. Then they split a home-and-home set with Ottawa, losing 30-21 in the capital and winning 45-19 at home, as Don Narcisse caught 13 passes for 145 yards and one touchdown. Tailback Tim McCray, who had set a team record with 2,684 all-purpose yards in 1989, was injured and had to be replaced by Lucius Floyd. Burgess, playing for the Blue Bombers against his old teammates, conducted a game-opening touchdown drive that helped Winnipeg sink the Riders 36-7. A 37-34 victory against the Lions cost Saskatchewan the services of safety Glen Suitor, slotbacks Ray Elgaard and Jeff Fairholm and quarterback Kent Austin, whose injured knee required arthroscopic surgery. Jeff Bentrim replaced Austin, losing 23-16 in Calgary and winning 29-24 against the Eskimos. Austin returned for a 59-15 loss in Toronto, during which he tossed three interceptions. Dave Ridgway's 47-yard field goal on the last play of a 33-31 victory against the Argonauts clinched a third straight playoff berth for the Riders, who finished third in the West at 9-9 after losing 35-28 in B.C.

Dave Ridgway's 47-yard field goal on the last play of a 33-31 victory against the Argonauts clinched a third straight playoff berth for the Riders.

They lost a sixth straight road game, 43-27 in snowy Edmonton, as Eskimos quarterback Tracy Ham threw three touchdown passes in the West semifinal. Ray Elgaard was later named the CFL's outstanding Canadian, but he didn't make the CFL all-star squad, unlike teammates Kent Austin, Roger Aldag, Don Narcisse and Dave Ridgway, whose 233 points tied the CFL single-season record.

The feel-good atmosphere that followed the 1989 Grey Cup victory showed explicitly when the team revealed its financial statement: With help from $650,000 in league-generated revenues, the Roughriders made $378,000 in 1990 and reduced their deficit to $917,000. All the CFL teams expected to generate more funds by signing a one-year television deal with TSN and CBC, which would televise 53 of the 72 regular-season contests, and disbanding the CFL-run TV network known as CFN, which sometimes cost $3 million annually to operate. Naturally the CFL's governors were unhappy with commissioner Donald Crump, who was halfway through his three-year deal. "I'm a dedicated employee," said Crump, who would resign at the end of the year amid complaints about paying the Hamilton Tiger-Cats to lift TV blackouts, the delay in getting (reduced) television revenues and the $2.3 million the rest of the teams paid to operate the floundering Ottawa Rough Riders for three months. "If these guys have lost confidence in me I don't know who else they're going to get." CFL meetings were held in Regina in early June. John Candy, a well-known comedic actor, was the star of the show when he agreed to chair the expansion committee. Candy and hockey superstar Wayne Gretzky were minority owners, along with majority owner Bruce McNall, of the Toronto Argonauts.

Friends of the Riders Inc. had contributed $330,000 through its annual lottery and Tom Shepherd, president of the organization, was attempting to raise another $300,000 annually through a liquor distribution franchise that initially earned $325,000 in federal tax rebates. Selling liquor put the Roughriders in competition with government-run corporations, which upset some of the province's unions and ultimately led to the end of that idea.

Photo courtesy of Royal Studios

Dan Farthing

With offensive backs coach Pal Sartori joining the Winnipeg Blue Bombers, John Gregory added veteran CFL head coach Ray Jauch to his staff as offensive co-ordinator. Although most assistant coaches worked on one-year contracts, Jauch signed a two-year deal. In player moves the team drafted University of Saskatchewan slotback Dan Farthing second overall, signed journeyman quarterback Rick Worman, cut Jeff Bentrim and tailback Tim McCray, and traded linebacker Tuineau Alipate and defensive end Vince Goldsmith to Hamilton for defensive back Sonny Gordon. The Roughriders also tried to get Doug (Tank) Landry. On the day they traded defensive lineman Tony Simmons to B.C. for the troubled linebacker, Landry was charged in a Regina court with assaulting his common-law wife. Landry would receive a two-month jail sentence and never played for the Riders, although there were sometimes indications he might appear on the 37-man roster (20 non-imports, 14 imports, three quarterbacks and two players on the reserve list).

The 1991 season began for the Roughriders with very few roster changes to their aging lineup but with a few new rules to deal with, including a 10-yard penalty being assessed to anyone found with an illegal substance on their jersey. No longer could players coat their hands in Stickum to help them hold onto the football! Because drug testing had never been officially conducted on CFL players, that led some observers to note that "Stickum is the only illegal substance in the CFL." A seventh on-field official was added to game crews. And the Roughriders stopped wearing the silver pants they had been sporting, changing to green pants. "Now we all look like jolly green giants," said kicker Dave Ridgway. "Except for (diminutive defensive back) Richie Hall.

He's the little sprout." Later in the season the Plaza of Honor would induct Al Benecick, Del Wardien, Bruce Bennett, Mike Samples, Tare Rennebohm, Johnny Garuik, Sully Glasser and W.E. Clarke.

Disaster struck the Roughriders in their 1991 season opener, which was delayed by a 20-minute blackout while the 1966 Grey Cup-winning team was feted on its 25th anniversary. A hit by Eskimos linebacker Larry Wruck dislocated the right (throwing) shoulder of quarterback Austin during a 34-25 Edmonton victory. Austin was placed on the 30-day injury list. But they had acquired Worman for a reason, primarily because of the success he had in playing against the Roughriders. Worman was sacked eight times in his Riders debut, a 48-28 loss in Calgary, in a game that was offered on a pay-per-view basis by Cable Regina. About 3,000 subscribers paid $19.95 for the telecast. In a battle of winless teams, the Roughriders dumped the Tiger-Cats 52-16, but the Roughriders followed with a 54-24 loss against the visiting Eskimos.

Co-owner John Candy escorted his Argonauts onto Taylor Field for an August 9 game. The game was nearly sold out – 27,093 of 27,637 seats – and the province-wide TV blackout had been lifted, with prompting from the Argos owners. They wanted everyone throughout Saskatchewan, indeed the whole country, to see Raghib (Rocket) Ismail, the speedy receiver/returner they had wooed away from possibly being the NFL's first overall draft choice with a personal-services contract worth $3.5 million per year. The league would eventually decide that each team could have a marquee player whose contract was exempt from the salary cap. Although Argonauts quarterback Matt Dunigan was hurt, backup Rickey Foggie led the visitors to a 37-35 victory. Saskatchewan's next game was a debacle, with the home-town Argonauts beating them 62-10. "Everybody in the organization needs to be be evaluated," said Ford. "We sit down and see what we have to do to be successful." After the game Gregory was quizzed about his job security by members of the media, who were sitting high in SkyDome's press box filing their stories a short while later as Gregory made a lonely walk to one of the stadium's elevators. Roughriders president Phil Kershaw was, indeed, interested in replacing Gregory with Don Matthews, a successful CFL coach who was working in the World League of American Football. They couldn't work out a deal right away, so Gregory remained in place for one more game, a 50-47 heartbreaker against the visiting Lions – quarterback Doug Flutie engineered two touchdowns in the final 2½ minutes – that dropped Saskatchewan's record to 1-6. Austin had returned from the injury list and the team looked respectable, but at 2:30 a.m. the following morning the Roughriders issued a press release stating that Ford had just visited with Gregory and terminated his coach. They were both crying when they were contacted minutes later by the *Leader-Post*. Gregory was the longest-tenured CFL coach at that time; he had a regular-season record of 38-45-1 and was 3-2 in the postseason. "I sold my soul to the team," said Gregory, who attended a media conference the next day. "I did it all for the Saskatchewan Roughriders. I appreciate the players' efforts and I appreciate their class through the five years I've known them.

Photo courtesy of Leader-Post

John Gregory

Photo courtesy of *Leader-Post*

Don Matthews

Photo courtesy of *Leader-Post*

Roger Aldag

They've worked very hard." Within two weeks, Gregory was hired to coach the Hamilton Tiger-Cats.

Matthews, 54, arrived the day of Gregory's departure with numerous suitcases; a vagabond coach, joking that he should have brought along ice skates. A two-time coach-of-the-year in the CFL (1983 and '87) who won the Grey Cup with B.C. in 1985, Matthews also coached the Toronto Argonauts and would eventually become the winningest coach in CFL history with future stops in Toronto (again), Baltimore, Edmonton and Montreal. "This is a bold stroke and it proves we are ready to do things," said Kershaw. Brash and confident, Matthews insisted it was players who won football games. He didn't set many rules for his charges, but he demanded they play their hardest during games or he would replace them. During his first night at a Regina hotel he got a call from the front desk. "Someone better have died," he growled, before being told that one of his players was crawling on the hotel's balconies. When he arrived at the office the next day, Matthews asked executive assistant Jill McDougall about the player: "Do we have a John Bankhead on our team?" When told that Bankhead, indeed, was on the Riders' practice roster, Matthews replied, "Not anymore he isn't." Matthews signed a multi-year contract to be the head coach and director of football operations. Ford was relegated to looking after the financial and administrative sides of the organization, specifically dealing with the $3-million cap for coaches' and players' salaries, recruiting and training camp costs. "There are a couple of things that really excite me," said Matthews. "It's a challenge to build a football team with the tools I've been given."

Matthews' new team won his first game, 44-41 in Edmonton, when Dave Ridgway kicked a 35-yard field goal with nine seconds remaining. "I feel happy for Don Matthews," said Ridgway. "At the same time I feel sad for John Gregory." Kent Austin, after signing a five-year deal worth a reported $1 million – "I wish," he said in response to questions about the deal's net worth – passed for 461 yards and Glen Suitor intercepted two passes in a 56-23 win against the Blue Bombers in the Labour Day Classic. They lost the rematch 49-41, despite Austin's four passing touchdowns and a team record of 507 yards, and followed with a 41-36 loss to the visiting Eskimos. Jeff Fairholm caught three of Austin's six touchdown passes during a 49-47 victory in B.C., which they followed with a 41-40 victory over the league-leading Stampeders. "That's the living-on-the-edge philosophy we're trying to instill here," said Matthews, who had called two fake punts in the contest. Two losses followed – 42-25 in Ottawa and 42-21 in Hamilton – which dropped the Riders to 5-10 and out of playoff contention. "The playoffs are not our immediate goal," said Matthews. "Our goal is to play hard every game." In the next contest, veteran guard Roger Aldag was presented with a hunting rifle for playing 250 straight games, the fourth-longest streak in history, but he didn't finish the match because he suffered torn left knee ligaments. The Roughriders finished the season at 6-12 with a 36-5 loss to the Lions and a 39-27 defeat in Calgary. The 710 points allowed by the Roughriders during the season were a CFL record, signaling the departure of defensive coaches Dick Adams, Ted Heath and Larry Donovan. Scouts Fred Glick and Tom Dimitroff Jr. were dumped, while offensive coaches Gary Hoffman and Ray Jauch were retained. Feisty linebacker Tyrone Jones was acquired from Winnipeg for receiver Allan Boyko and a first-round draft choice. "I'm not a bad guy, but I will be a bad guy on the football field," said Jones. Aldag and Vic Stevenson made the West's all-star team as offensive linemen, with safety Glen Suitor, defensive tackle Gary Lewis and kicker Dave Ridgway joining them.

Photo courtesy of Royal Studios

Vic Stevenson

Austerity was the name of the game in 1992 when the team announced it had lost $939,700 from the previous year's operations and was $1.87 million in debt. "We can't afford another loss like this," said Riders treasurer Tom Shepherd, whose devotion to his volunteer job would get him feted at the end of the season with the Commissioner's Award. It was easy to see why CFL teams were struggling – they weren't adhering to the $3-million salary cap because they weren't being punished, although there were announced plans to penalize teams by taking away draft choices and negotiation-list players. Calgary Stampeders owner Larry Ryckman and B.C. Lions owner Murray Pezim spent most of the season bickering because of a trade involving devalued stocks that were part of a ridiculous trade that sent quarterback Danny Barrett to B.C. Hamilton Tiger-Cats owner David Braley was trying to sell his franchise, which had lost $5 million since he bought it from Harold Ballard in 1989. Hamilton's status was so uncertain the league drew up a tentative schedule with only seven teams (instead of eight) before ownership of the franchise was transferred to a community group. The league was eyeing its future when it scheduled a preseason game in Portland, Oregon, the first time a CFL game had been played in the United States in 34 years. With high-profile quarterback Doug Flutie leading the Calgary Stampeders, they beat the Toronto Argonauts 20-1 before 15,362 fans in Portland's Rose Bowl. Interim commissioner Phil Kershaw, the Riders' volunteer president, served on the committee to hire Larry Smith, a Montreal businessman and former CFL player, as the full-time replacement for departed commissioner Donald Crump. Smith's big plan was to have the

Photo courtesy of *Leader-Post*

Phil Kershaw

CFL expand into American markets, particularly after crowds across the CFL dropped by an average of 2,000 per game.

> There was money coming in through various methods, such as $250,000 from the Friends of the Riders lottery, $300,000 from its short-lived liquor distributorship and an undisclosed amount from CKRM radio.

There was money coming in through various methods, such as $250,000 from the Friends of the Riders lottery, $300,000 from its short-lived liquor distributorship and an undisclosed amount from CKRM radio, which won a bidding war against rival CKCK to get a three-year deal for broadcast rights, keeping Geoff Currier as the play-by-play announcer and Carm Carteri as the analyst. The City of Regina helped out by giving the Roughriders a rent-free lease at Taylor Field, but if the community-owned franchise made money, 25 per cent of the profit (to a maximum of $200,000) would be paid to the city. The city also forgave $560,000 in past taxes and rent, allowed the Roughriders to take over concession rights and began allowing beer sales in the stands. Still, general manager Al Ford needed to cut his players' salaries. "We can't have the same guys earning the same amount as last year," said Ford. "It's the only option I have." While Ford was chopping salaries, head coach Don Matthews was assembling a new staff of defensive assistants. Darryl Edralin was hired to handle linebackers and special teams, Bob Price joined as defensive co-ordinator/secondary coach and James Parker, a legendary pass rusher during his playing days, became the defensive line coach. When the proposed Professional Spring Football League failed to materialize – a common occurrence in the 1990s as idealistic football leagues would be proposed almost annually – Jim Popp, who was going to be in charge of scouting, didn't have a job, so he was hired as the Roughriders' player personnel director.

Photo courtesy of Royal *Studios*

Ray Elgaard

Backup Rick Worman was released when the Roughriders acquired quarterback Warren Jones from Edmonton for third- and fourth-round draft picks. The team drafted Virginia Tech linebacker Mark Scott second overall – his career would be short and inconsequential. They got better contributions from Bishop's linebacker Ray Bernard, drafted 10th, and 15th pick Scott Hendrickson, an offensive lineman from the University of Minnesota, whose brother Craig was already with the Roughriders. The team re-signed slotback Ray Elgaard and also enticed free agent Jearld Baylis to leave B.C. as a free agent. Elgaard would, at the end of the year, win his third award as the CFL's outstanding Canadian, while teammate Vic Stevenson was runner-up as the league's top offensive lineman. Training camp was held in Saskatoon; Matthews arrived there after riding his Harley-Davidson motorcycle north from Regina.

Saskatchewan lost its opener 44-26 to the Stampeders, as Flutie threw for 429 yards and four touchdowns. The Riders were wearing their old silver pants because Matthews had ordered the change – he didn't like the all-green, cucumber look. The Riders lost 34-31 in Winnipeg, beat the Rough Riders 23-14 in Regina and lost 38-24 in Hamilton before knocking off the undefeated Stampeders 30-21 at Taylor Field. Pezim's Lions lost their sixth straight game, 46-43 in overtime to the visiting Roughriders, who got 536 passing yards from quarterback Kent Austin. Within two weeks Pezim was pushed aside and the CFL took over his franchise until it began sharing ownership with Bill Comrie, owner of The Brick furniture stores, and the B.C. Pavilion Corporation. Comrie would eventually hire a former Montreal Concordes scout, Eric Tillman, as B.C.'s general manager.

With 14 players suffering from the flu, the Roughriders lost 20-9 in Ottawa. Austin threw five interceptions against the Rough Riders. He suffered a neck injury during a subsequent 47-36 victory over the Lions, who were hurt by two interceptions each from Riders defensive backs Stacey Hairston and Glen Suitor. The Roughriders were 4-4 and averaging only 20,230 fans per game, below the budgeted break-even mark of 23,000. That would translate into a $300,000 loss at the gate. But 29,298 fans attended the Labour Day Classic, which the Roughriders won 32-20 over the Blue Bombers in a feisty contest that featured an on-field brawl. That game and the second part of the home-and-home set weren't on television, so Riders' stay-at-home fans couldn't see the Roughriders get two punts and a field goal blocked in a 37-16 loss. Matthews was tinkering with his roster, getting Warren Jones some playing time when Austin was hobbled, replacing punter Mike Lazecki with Brent Matich and dumping tailback Lucius Floyd for an unknown, Curtis Delgado, before giving the job to Mike Saunders, a former receiver whose pass-catching prowess fit into Saskatchewan's offensive plans. The Roughriders won their fifth straight home game, 22-10 against the Eskimos, but they fell to 1-5 on the road when the lost 39-32 in Toronto to a team that had just replaced head coach Adam Rita with offensive co-ordinator Dennis Meyer. Saskatchewan won the rematch 43-18. Toronto didn't care much about the struggling Argos, not while the Toronto Blue Jays were winning the American League pennant and World Series.

Photo courtesy of *Leader-Post*

Mike Saunders

Former Riders head coach John Gregory brought his Tiger-Cats to Regina, where the visitors lost 44-6. The next game, in Calgary, was turned into a pay-per-view telecast on Cable Regina, which got about 2,000 subscribers to pay $14.19 for the telecast; Saskatchewan lost 34-30. Mike Saunders had 280 all-purpose yards in a 41-22 victory against the Lions, which was followed by a 30-24 victory in Edmonton.

The season-ending game featured a Flutie-Austin showdown – it was the first time two CFL quarterbacks had exceeded 5,000 passing yards in a season. Riders linebacker Tyrone Jones stole the show, drawing four penalties and getting ejected at halftime for a run-in with the officials that would earn him a $1,000 fine. Saskatchewan lost 40-17 and finished at 9-9 for the third time in four years. The Roughriders placed third in the West and qualified for the division semifinal in Edmonton. Playing on Commonwealth Stadium's tricky, grass field on a wintry day, the home-town Eskimos escaped with a 22-20 victory because Riders kicker Dave Ridgway – who insisted he was wearing the right cleats for the conditions – slipped while attempting a game-winning, 40-yard field goal. Kent Austin's great year left him serving as a TV commentator for CBC during the postseason while teammates Ray Elgaard, Vic Stevenson, Jearld Baylis, Bobby Jurasin and Glen Suitor were named to the West's all-star team.

Expanding the CFL into the United States was a mandate of new commissioner Larry Smith, who realized any expansion fees paid by American owners could prop up the financially ailing league.

Expanding the CFL into the United States was a mandate of new commissioner Larry Smith, who realized any expansion fees paid by American owners could prop up the financially ailing league. Six of eight CFL teams would have to approve any expansion plans. While the Winnipeg Blue Bombers opposed any venture into the U.S., outgoing Roughriders president Phil Kershaw, who was about to be replaced by Regina businessman and former city councilor John Lipp, said his team would have to consider all financial implications with the realization that it would cost more to travel. The Roughriders were adamant that Canadian players, the non-imports, would not be eliminated from rosters. "I don't want to say this is our last-gasp plan to support the franchise," said Lipp. "It's not going to be disastrous because I really believe the league is more stable as we head into 1993, especially with expansion teams in Sacramento and San Antonio." Lipp's team was $2.2 million in debt after losing $887,000 on 1992's operations. The provincial government upped its support, increasing its guarantee on the Riders' loan to $2.1 million from $1.5 million. Treasurer Tom Shepherd concocted an idea for the Riders to obtain a Watkins dealership, selling health and beauty products in a pyramid scheme that could earn the Roughriders six figures annually. The plan petered out over the next few years. More money came from Great Western Brewery, the Saskatoon-based brewer that was awarded the right to sell beer at Taylor Field. But money was outgoing, too, when the CFL used at least $300,000 to prop up the Hamilton Tiger-Cats, who had already arranged a $700,000 line of credit from their regional government. David Macdonald, an investment banker, would eventually lead a $3-million limited partnership that assumed ownership of the Tiger-Cats. It was a difficult situation in southern Ontario, which was going gaga over the Blue Jays – CBC proved that by dropping from its late-season schedule a B.C.-Hamilton game to show the World Series victory party.

Fred Anderson and Larry Benson accepted the terms of U.S. ownership and got tentative approval from CFL governors in January. Anderson wanted a team in Sacramento, California, while Benson wanted a franchise in San Antonio, Texas. They were willing to pay $3 million apiece in installments on a six-year payment plan. When the next CFL meetings convened one month later in Edmonton, a 16-player trade that sent Eskimos quarterback Tracy Ham to Toronto nearly overshadowed the fact that Anderson was there, but Benson wasn't. "I guess I'm going to be the Lone Ranger," said Anderson, who followed through on his plans to establish the Sacramento Gold Miners, a ninth CFL franchise and the first based in the U.S. Convinced that American laws could not force the team to employ Canadians, the Gold Miners did not have to dress any non-import players. Another potential franchise would soon appear in Las Vegas. Nick Mileti, who had ties with the American Hockey League, World Hockey Association and Major League Baseball's Cleveland Indians, presented the CFL commissioner with

Anderson wanted a team in Sacramento, California, while Benson wanted a franchise in San Antonio, Texas. They were willing to pay $3 million apiece in installments on a six-year payment plan.

two cheques, one a non-refundable deposit of $50,000 and another for $1 million as an installment on the franchise fee. Smith was never asked if the cheques cleared. Baltimore also became a potential site when Jim Speros submitted a $50,000 cheque.

In 1993, teams were supposed to abide by a $2.5 million salary cap – average salaries had slipped to $60,521 – but the rules had changed to make the cap include basically only players' salaries. Although marquee players were exempt from the cap, Argonauts owner Bruce McNall released Rocket Ismail from his four-year, $14-million personal-services contract so the latter could play in the NFL.

The Riders had been $120,000 under the cap during the 1992 season, so they were awarded a draft choice in the bonus round. They used it to take Queen's running back Brad Elberg, a Regina product who wouldn't make the squad but had a short CFL career as a special-teams player. They also drafted Portland State linebacker Brooks Findlay. Offensive line coach Gary Hoffman departed (and was hired by the B.C. Lions) after feuding with head coach Don Matthews, who recruited long-time friend Steve Buratto as a replacement. It was Buratto's third stint as a Riders assistant coach. In Ottawa, confusion reigned when general manager Dan Rambo, a former Riders assistant GM, was dumped five days before training camp opened.

Offensive lineman Roger Aldag retired after a 17-year career at the age of 39. He had played 271 regular-season games, all with his home-province team, been named a CFL all-star five times and the league's outstanding offensive lineman twice. Aldag would be honoured with a special night on July 15, which was temporarily renamed July 44 to honour his uniform number. Offensive lineman Bob Poley also retired, while linemates Vic Stevenson and Mike Anderson were waived after refusing paycuts and Chris Gioskos departed as a free agent. Stevenson benefited when he became part of B.C.'s spending spree, signing with the Lions as a free agent. "No chance we'll be under the cap," said Lions general manager Eric Tillman. Defensive end Stew Hill left B.C. for Saskatchewan. Troublesome linebacker Tyrone Jones was dealt to B.C., leaving the Roughriders to deploy two non-import linebackers in their starting group – Ray Bernard in the middle and Dan Rashovich on the short side of the field.

Photo courtesy of Royal Studios

Offensive line Stalwarts – Bob Poley (57), Mike Anderson (66), Roger Aldag (seated with jacket) and Vic Stevenson (62) together for one of the last times

Dave Ridgway

Photo courtesy of *Leader-Post*

The Roughriders lost their season-opener in B.C., 33-26 in overtime. Kent Austin was sacked six times. They beat the visiting Eskimos 23-22 on a 50-yard field goal by Dave Ridgway with 1:41 remaining, then committed six turnovers while losing the rematch 35-3 one week later in Edmonton. The Riders had to leave Alberta via charter flight immediately following the game because they had only two days before they made their American debut, on July 24 in Sacramento. It was a tough, six-hour trip with a late-night stop at U.S. Customs in Seattle. Temperatures hit 35 degrees Celsius during their pregame walk-through at Hornet Field in the California capital, so afterwards several of the players cooled off by jumping into plastic garbage cans that were filled with ice cubes and water. The next night was marginally cooler as the Gold Miners won their first game, a 37-26 decision that dropped Saskatchewan's record to 1-3. The league was still deciding upon its playoff format – should three or four West teams make the playoffs? – when the Roughriders' defence, sparked by the on-field arrogance and excellence of former NFL cornerback Barry Wilburn, helped turn around the team's fortunes. Nose tackle Jearld Baylis became so dominant he was later named the West's outstanding defensive player. Defensive end Bobby Jurasin posted his 90th sack, surpassing Vince Goldsmith for the team record, in a 36-17 victory over the Argonauts. They won 37-10 in Hamilton, as Ray Elgaard caught 12 passes for 212 yards and two touchdowns, and forced eight turnovers during a 45-28 victory against their Ottawa namesakes, the Rough Riders. Saskatchewan won the rematch 27-26 in Ottawa.

> Into Regina came the Gold Miners, on their own Boeing 737 replete with team logo, for a regular-season game that was being touted as Keep the Pride Alive Friday.

Home attendance was dismally low at 18,269 per game. The Riders needed 24,000 fans per game to break even; a 25 per cent decrease would cost them $900,000, a drastic loss that could kill the franchise. "I'm saying that if we don't have better attendance for the rest of the year, we have some real question marks about 1994," said Riders treasurer Tom Shepherd. Into Regina came the Gold Miners, on their own Boeing 737 replete with team logo, for a regular-season game that was being touted as Keep the Pride Alive Friday. With a record-setting 33,032 fans inside Taylor Field, the Roughriders avenged their earlier loss by beating Sacramento 26-23. It was Saskatchewan's fifth straight victory, its longest winning streak since 1972. The streak ended in the Labour Day Classic, when the Blue Bombers got 10 points in 70 seconds, finishing with a 37-yard field goal by Troy Westwood with four seconds remaining in a 25-24 victory. Winnipeg won again at home, intercepting four passes and injuring one of Austin's shoulders and fingers in a 41-23 victory. The Roughriders improved to 7-5 and knocked the visiting Gold Miners to 3-9, out of playoff contention, with a 27-20 win at Taylor Field. Following a 31-6 victory in B.C., Lions general manager Eric Tillman and Riders head coach Don Matthews had a minor set-to when the latter wouldn't shake the former's hand. Tillman believed Matthews, who wouldn't discuss the matter, was upset he didn't get the B.C. job, that the Lions had signed Vic Stevenson and also given a job to assistant coach Gary Hoffman. Tillman didn't return to Regina with his team to witness B.C.'s 50-28 victory, in which Austin strained knee ligaments. Austin watched the next game from McMahon Stadium's spotter's booth, helping to call plays because offensive co-ordinator Ray Jauch was on the sidelines for the first time since 1982. Jauch had been pressed into duty as Saskatchewan's head coach when Don Matthews checked into a Calgary hospital for an emergency appendectomy. Calgary won 34-18. Matthews got phone reports in his Calgary hospital room during the next game, a 33-10 victory over the visiting Tiger-Cats.

Austin passed for 546 yards and Doug Flutie for 542 in a 48-45 win over the Stampeders, followed by a season-ending, 30-24 victory in Toronto that gave the Roughriders an 11-7 record. The Riders were on a three-game winning steak when they travelled to Edmonton for a West semifinal. Matthews spent his pre-game evening in hospital because of a bowel blockage, but he was on the sidelines for the Eskimos' 51-13 victory. Former Riders tailback Lucius Floyd had 294 all-purpose yards. Despite the deflating finish to Saskatchewan's season, Al Ford tried to keep his coach. "I want Don back because I think he's the best guy for the job." It looked like Matthews was coming back to a team that had five CFL all-stars – Jearld Baylis, Glen Suitor, Barry Wilburn, Dave Ridgway and Ray Elgaard. "My contract's not up," said Matthews. "I say I have a lifetime deal. As long as we win, that's a lifetime." The new franchises in Las Vegas and Baltimore wanted to hire Matthews, who was away golfing on December 31 when he resigned from the Roughriders "to pursue other opportunities."

> Orlando? New England? Worcester? Where would the CFL look next in its expansion plans? A televised media conference was scheduled one morning in Orlando, Florida, apparently to announce the formation of another CFL franchise for the 1994 season.

Orlando? New England? Worcester? Where would the CFL look next in its expansion plans? A televised media conference was scheduled one morning in Orlando, Florida, apparently to announce the formation of another CFL franchise for the 1994 season. TV cameras were in attendance from TSN and CBC Newsworld. They showed a microphone on its stand. Nobody showed up for 45 minutes. Already reeling from cash-flow problems and being laughed at for its attempts to implement a $2.5-million salary cap that was ignored by five of its nine teams – Hamilton, Saskatchewan, Calgary and Winnipeg were rewarded with extra draft picks for abiding by the spending regulations — the CFL took another blow to its image. There was no financing in place for the Orlando franchise, so there was no deal, but somebody neglected to cancel the televised media conference. The Ottawa Rough Riders were in a similar situation – they were being operated by CFL commissioner Larry Smith after the owners, Bernie and Lonie Glieberman, disappeared to pursue an expansion franchise in Shreveport, Louisiana.

> There the Roughriders were awarded hosting privileges to the 1995 Grey Cup. Saskatchewan won the game away from Winnipeg.

Although the CFL wanted $3 million in fees for a new franchise, the Gliebermans got theirs for $1.7 million. Bruce Firestone took over ownership of Ottawa's franchise and hired Phil Kershaw, on leave from Saskatchewan's board, to run the Eastern Riders. With backing from Calgary Stampeders owner Larry Ryckman, a committee that included past Riders presidents Dick Rendek, Gord Staseson and Bruce Cowie, plus a host of dignitaries including Saskatchewan Premier Roy Romanow and Regina Mayor Doug Archer, attended a March 3 league meeting in Sacramento. There the Roughriders were awarded hosting privileges to the 1995 Grey Cup. Saskatchewan won the game away from Winnipeg because Romanow tossed another $500,000 into the kitty and assured CFL governors that the Saskatchewan government would guarantee the league a $1.8 million profit from the game. There were drawbacks because Regina had only 2,683 hotel/motel rooms, about half what the league demanded. But the organizing committee – led by chair Bob Ellard – would establish a home-stay program that encouraged Regina

The Roughriders were about to be the last established CFL franchise to play host to the championship game and it created a ticket-buying frenzy for the 50,000 or so tickets that would be available.

residents to have relatives or paying guests stay at their homes as part of a homecoming for Saskatchewan's 90th birthday. The Roughriders were about to be the last established CFL franchise to play host to the championship game and it created a ticket-buying frenzy for the 50,000 or so tickets that would be available. The Riders capitalized on that point by giving their season-ticket holders first crack at Grey Cup tickets. Although the Riders had made $109,000 on their 1993 operations, the on-field product was losing its luster and didn't appear to be a candidate for appearing in the 1995 championship.

With the departure of his head coach, Don Matthews, Riders GM Al Ford began looking for a replacement. Ford spent two hours interviewing Mike Riley, an assistant at the University of Southern California, who had been the Winnipeg Blue Bombers head coach for their 1988 Grey Cup victory. Riley said, "No, thanks." Riders assistants Steve Buratto and Ray Jauch were also on Ford's list. He hired 55-year-old Jauch, who had been a Grey Cup-winning head coach with the Edmonton Eskimos between 1970-76 and been named 1980 coach-of-the-year with the Blue Bombers before joining the United States Football League in 1983. Meanwhile, Matthews was formally introduced as head coach and director of football operations for the CFL's expansion franchise in Baltimore, which owner Jim Speros tried calling the "Colts" until the National Football League obtained an injunction forbidding use of the departed NFL franchise's nickname. The U.S. franchises were appealing destinations, partly because they weren't required to have non-imports on their rosters. Matthews began poaching Jauch's staff, luring away Darryl Edralin, Bob Price, Steve Buratto and Jim Popp. Jauch replaced them with defensive co-ordinator Jim Daley, defensive line coach Greg Marshall, defensive backs coach (and former Rider) Richie Hall and offensive line coach Pat Perles. Matthews also signed free-agent nose tackle Jearld Baylis away from Saskatchewan, while free-agent slotback Jeff Fairholm joined the Toronto Argonauts. Roughriders quarterback Kent Austin was also interested in leaving. Although Austin initially denied it, he had apparently written a note to Ford requesting a trade during the offseason. Ford granted Austin's wish, sending the quarterback to B.C. in a three-way trade that sent Danny Barrett to Ottawa and Tom Burgess to Saskatchewan. Also going to Ottawa were defensive back Cory Dowden and offensive lineman Andrew Greene. Also heading to Saskatchewan were defensive back Anthony Drawhorn, linebacker Ron Goetz and defensive lineman Paul Yatkowski. Austin's arrival in B.C. was rocky as he tried to get a new contract from Lions general manager Eric Tillman. Austin retired for a while, declaring, "I don't want to deal with the B.C. Lions anymore." It was also revealed that Austin owed the Roughriders $125,000 from his old contract. Some of the numbers never seemed right. While the CFL Players' Association was revealing salaries to show how little its members were being paid, it stated that Calgary quarterback Doug Flutie was making $170,000 annually. Obviously the side deals and personal-services contracts he had with Ryckman weren't included.

Austin's trade request wasn't well-received by Rider fans, who felt betrayed by the departure of the seven-year, Grey Cup-winning veteran; they would welcome him rudely during subsequent trips back when he was with the Lions, Argonauts or Blue Bombers.

Austin's trade request wasn't well-received by Rider fans, who felt betrayed by the departure of the seven-year, Grey Cup-winning veteran; they would welcome him rudely during subsequent trips back when he was with the Lions, Argonauts or Blue Bombers. Coinciding with Austin's first return, disgruntled fans were paying to whack an Austin mini car with a sledgehammer.

Bill Baker, Riders GM from 1987-88, a former defensive end who spent eight of his 11 CFL seasons (1968-78) with Saskatchewan and for two years the president of the CFL, was named to the Canadian Football Hall of Fame.

CFL governors put a playoff format in place before the season that would allow four teams from each conference to make the playoffs. There were six teams in the East: Winnipeg, Baltimore, Toronto, Ottawa, Hamilton and Shreveport. There were six teams in the West: Calgary, Edmonton, B.C., Saskatchewan, Sacramento and Las Vegas. (The teams are listed in the order they would ultimately finish in the regular season – Baltimore was the only American team to make the playoffs.) The Roughriders drafted Portland State offensive lineman Chris Burns second overall as they began assembling their 37-man active roster and two-man reserve list, plus dispatching players to the practice roster, 30-day injury list or waived/injured list, which was where slightly injured players were supposed to be placed. The waived/injured list would soon become a haven for hiding healthy players – they were paid full salaries while stashed there and weren't going to be claimed by rival teams who thought the players might actually be injured. The highlight of the preseason was a power outage during the third quarter of a 19-4 victory over the visiting Gold Miners.

Tom Burgess made an immediate impact when the season began at home against the Stampeders. The reacquired quarterback rallied the Roughriders from a 21-3, fourth-quarter deficit with a 15-yard touchdown pass to Don Narcisse at 14:57 of the fourth quarter, giving the home team a 22-21 victory. The Roughriders' next game was much more memorable because it marked the CFL's debut in Las Vegas, where the Posse played home games at the Sam Boyd Silver Bowl. On game day the temperature was 106 degrees Fahrenheit, although it cooled somewhat by kickoff to 37 degrees Celsius. Just before recording artist Dionne Warwick – who had berated Regina during a recent concert stop there – sang the U.S. national anthem, a lounge singer named Dennis K.C. Park was recruited to sing "O Canada". Park, an American, remembered most of the words to the Canadian anthem, but he forgot the tune and made it sound like a rendition of "Oh, Christmas Tree!" Most of the 12,213 fans in attendance didn't know better, but irate Canadians watching on television or listening on the radio began calling the CFL office to complain. The Posse apologized for the gaffe. They should have apologized for the whole season, during which they averaged only 8,000 spectators and had to play their final home game in Edmonton. Nick Mileti, the supposed owner of the Posse, was removed by the team's directors after $5 million of the $6 million in public shares had disappeared. Hamilton, Shreveport and Sacramento, whose owner was rumoured to be moving the franchise to San Antonio, were also suffering at the gate.

Photo courtesy of *Leader-Post*

Tom Burgess

Park was invited to Hamilton later in the season, where he sang a better rendition of "O Canada" before a Rough Riders/Tiger-Cats game that attracted a slightly larger crowd of 12,399 fans. Crowded onto their bench along the sideline inside Sam Boyd Stadium, the Roughriders were sometimes surrounded by the pooping horses, scantily-clad cheerleaders and odd sideshows that were contracted to provide entertainment during the game. The Posse, whose impressive roster included such talented players as Curtis Mayfield, Greg Battle, Tamarick Vanover and Anthony Calvillo, won 32-22 in overtime. Riders slotback Ray Elgaard tied Rocky DiPietro for the CFL all-time lead with 706 catches, a mark he broke – before fumbling the reception – during a 35-24 victory at home against the Argonauts.

The Roughriders remained winless on U.S. soil after losing 30-27 in Sacramento. They lost 42-23 in Edmonton as Burgess was sacked five times and threw three interceptions. During a 20-7 victory that completed the home-and-home set with the Eskimos, Jauch was bowled over on the sidelines and suffered torn knee ligaments. The Roughriders lost 54-15 in Calgary, giving them an 0-4 mark in road games. They improved to 4-0 at home with a 35-19 victory over Ottawa, with Warren Jones earning the win after relieving Tom Burgess 11 minutes into the first quarter. Jones started the next game, a 42-31 victory over the Blue Bombers in the Labour Day Classic. It drew 28,738 fans, who watched the Roughriders score their first two first-quarter touchdowns of the season. Jones hurt his ribs and was replaced by Burgess during a 49-18 victory in Winnipeg.

> **"Don Matthews brought his new team to Regina for Saskatchewan's next game. "I was a little nervous before this game and I didn't think I would be," said the Riders' former coach, whose no-name squad won 35-18. "Once the game started I was more focused, so I forgot about coming back here."**

Don Matthews brought his new team to Regina for Saskatchewan's next game. "I was a little nervous before this game and I didn't think I would be," said the Riders' former coach, whose no-name squad won 35-18. "Once the game started I was more focused, so I forgot about coming back here." A trip to Louisiana netted the Riders their first U.S. victory when they beat the Pirates 29-11. Fullback Shawn Daniels was pressed into duty as a tailback; he scored two touchdowns even though he had been traded before the game to Calgary for a second-round pick in the 1995 CFL draft. The Gold Miners made their last visit to Regina a profitable one, knocking off their hosts 19-16 and injuring Riders receiver Larry Thompson, linebacker Dan Rashovich and quarterback Warren Jones. Next came the home-and-home series that had been circled on lots of calendars: Two games against B.C., starting in Vancouver. Austin, evidently upset about his treatment by the Regina newspaper, refused to be interviewed by the *Leader-Post*. His team won 23-22 inside B.C. Place Stadium, where the fans were incited to disrupt Saskatchewan's offensive play-calling by a Fan-Meter that measured the noise they created. The noise couldn't hide the sideline yelling match between Riders quarterback Tom Burgess and offensive line coach Pat Perles; it was evidently about the team's play-calling. The Riders brought back a loaner from Vancouver – promising kicker Paul McCallum joined them from B.C.'s practice roster while veteran Dave Ridgway recovered from a thigh injury. McCallum played four games, making 11 of 13 field goals, but his biggest impact would come one year later when he became a full-fledged member of the team. McCallum's arrival was overshadowed by the return of Austin, whose appearance at Taylor Field was greeted by heckling, derogatory signs and four security guards around the Lions' bench. Lions cornerback James Jefferson became so enraged he slapped a fan in the stands. Saskatchewan won 38-27, improving its record to 9-7 while B.C. dropped to 10-4-1. The Las Vegas Posse, on life support through loans that would supposedly be repaid upon the sale of the team, lost 37-18 at Taylor Field as the Roughriders were compiling a four-game, season-ending winning streak that would help them finish with an 11-7 record. A 41-29 win in Ottawa clinched fourth place in the West and a semifinal visit with first-place Calgary. McCallum kicked a 49-yard field goal as time expired to win the regular-season finale, 16-14 in Hamilton. In their West semifinal, McCallum tallied Saskatchewan's only postseason points with a field goal in its 36-3 loss against the home-town Stampeders. "That stuff about defences winning championships is B.S.," said Riders linebacker Ron Goetz, a West all-star with teammates Albert Brown, Mike Saunders, Mike Anderson and Bobby Jurasin. "We can't beat Shreveport with three points." The Roughriders obviously were not destined to be Grey Cup contenders, something Austin and Matthews apparently realized when they escaped. Matthews and Austin met again in the Grey Cup game

> **"That stuff about defences winning championships is B.S.," said Riders linebacker Ron Goetz, a West all-star with teammates Albert Brown, Mike Saunders, Mike Anderson and Bobby Jurasin. "We can't beat Shreveport with three points."**

in Vancouver, where the Lions (with 20 Canadians on their 37-man roster) beat Canadian-less Baltimore 26-23. Austin was replaced by backup Danny McManus, who would become the starter the next year when Austin was dealt to Toronto.

Photo courtesy of Royal Studios

Albert Brown excels as a return specialist

Fred Smith, the CEO of courier company FedEx, was granted a franchise for 1995 in Memphis by a league in which 11 of 12 teams (excluding Baltimore, which made $500,000) lost money. Insurance magnate Art Williams got a franchise in Birmingham. The CFL took over Ottawa and attempted to sell the Las Vegas franchise for 20 cents on the dollar. Meanwhile, the Roughriders increased their ticket prices for the first time in six years. "We still have the lowest, or one of the lowest, prices in the CFL," Riders president John Lipp said after season tickets in the highest-priced Green zone increased to $260 from $250.

When Mike Saunders hired agent Gil Scott to represent him, there was little doubt the all-star tailback was leaving the Roughriders. Scott had shepherded two other clients, Kent Austin and Don Matthews, out of Saskatchewan. Saunders had great stats – 1,205 rushing yards, 613 receiving yards, 15 touchdowns – so he got an opportunity to join the NFL's Green Bay Packers. After being cut by Green Bay, Saunders was signed by the San Antonio Texans, formerly the Sacramento Gold Miners, who had moved to the Lone Star State. Though the league had been re-aligned into the North Division, comprising the eight Canadian teams, and five-team South Division (Baltimore Stallions, San Antonio Texans, Birmingham Barracudas, Memphis Mad Dogs and Shreveport Pirates), there was going to be more travelling costs for the Roughriders. They had just spent $5.4 million to operate in 1994, the most ever, and incurred a loss of $139,000. The team was $2.066 million in debt, which was nearly equal to what the Sacramento Gold Miners had lost in 1994. The Riders had abided by the league's $2.5-million salary cap, but the CFL had spent $2 million to carry cash-strapped clubs in Las Vegas, Hamilton and Ottawa. It wasn't only the CFL that was looking southward – the National Hockey League's Winnipeg Jets moved to Phoenix, Arizona. Why? The CFLPA salary survey may have shown the reason: 504 players on Canadian teams made an average of $53,882 Cdn apiece, while 262 players on American teams averaged $32,083 US each. Even with an exchange rate of 30 per cent, American labour was markedly cheaper.

Saskatchewan's hopes for a profitable year depended upon making money by playing host to the Grey Cup on November 19. If the Roughriders made it to the championship, it would be even better because Taylor Field was being expanded with temporary bleachers to accommodate more than 50,000 fans. Ticket prices would be $90, $120 and $135, plus seven per cent GST (general sales tax). Information was available on-line to computer users because the Roughriders had joined the booming Internet and started their own website. Luxury boxes were being built in the west-side press box while the east-side grandstand was being topped with a new press box; it would seat 300 media members

Photo courtesy of *Leader-Post*

All-Time Attendance Record – 55,438 . . . Oct. 14, 1995

and afterwards be converted into mainly club seating, except for a tiny portion above the east end zone that was turned into an uninhabitable, sweltering, sun-splattered press box.

Losing Saunders was a bad sign. The Riders had nine potential free agents. One of them, defensive back Anthony Drawhorn, balked at a 20-per-cent pay cut and instead signed with Birmingham. Defensive stalwarts Glen Suitor and Gary Lewis retired in April; Suitor joined the broadcast team at TSN and Lewis returned home to Oklahoma City, where two weeks later a domestic terrorist bombed a federal government building, killing 168 people and injuring more than 800.

Linebacker Ray Bernard signed with Ottawa. The Riders re-signed all-star linebacker Ron Goetz, lured defensive tackle Glenn Kulka away from Ottawa and, after free-agent QB Warren Jones was dumped by Winnipeg, re-signed Jones as a backup to Tom Burgess. Burgess was Saskatchewan's marquee player, with his salary ($175,000 plus $85,000 in potential bonuses, according to a survey released by the CFLPA) being exempt from the salary cap. They drafted Eastern Washington defensive lineman Troy Alexander fourth overall, St. Mary's defensive back Dwayne Provo 10th, Western Illinois offensive lineman Rob Lazeo 12th and Saskatchewan offensive lineman Gene Makowsky 23rd. Makowsky surrendered his final year of college eligibility to remain with the team, which had promised that he would receive full salary on the active roster or two-man reserve list. "I'm going to sign a contract with the Roughriders and I'm going to trust their word," said Makowsky, who was about to embark on a Hall of Fame-worthy career. "I believe they're not going to screw me. With me being from Saskatchewan, that would be a bad p.r. move." Head coach Ray Jauch was true to his word and Makowsky

Makowsky surrendered his final year of college eligibility to remain with the team, which had promised that he would receive full salary on the active roster or two-man reserve list. "I'm going to sign a contract with the Roughriders and I'm going to trust their word."

would soon be a starting lineman, while getting blocking help from all-star slotback Ray Elgaard, who was inexplicably being converted into a fullback to let him run shorter routes and exploit his blocking ability. Elgaard had been tested at fullback when he joined the Roughriders in 1983. "Yeah," the future Hall of Famer said after a training-camp workout in Saskatoon. "Two carries for six yards." Jauch also tried convincing one of his predecessors, John Gregory, to join his staff. Gregory, Saskatchewan's head coach from 1988-91, instead signed a three-year deal with the Arena Football League's Iowa Barnstormers. Ron Lancaster Jr., son of the Hall of Fame quarterback, was also a potential assistant, but he stayed at the University of Manitoba. Jauch's assistants were Jim Daley, Greg Marshall, Richie Hall, Pat Perles and long-time University of British Columbia coach Frank Smith, who replaced Tom Cudney. Daley stayed after turning down an offer to coach the Ottawa Rough Riders, who had been purchased by elusive Chicago businessman Horn Chen.

There had been plans for a sixth U.S. franchise in Jackson, Mississippi, where the Las Vegas Posse was looking to relocate. But commissioner Larry Smith scuttled those plans two months before the season opened. A dispersal draft was held of the Posse's players – the Riders selected slotback Prince Wimbley, linebackers Tim Broady, Zock Allen and defensive end Lance Cook. None made significant contributions. Neither did ex-Hamilton players John Hood, a tailback, quarterback Bob Torrance or receiver Joey Jauch, the head coach's son. When tailback Wolf Barber, another short-lived, ineffective candidate to replace Saunders, was dispatched, he complained about Jauch's decision. "No way I'd come back here," said Barber. "I'm not one of Jauch's best friends."

Barber played the first game of the season, rushing nine times for 44 yards and catching five passes for 31 yards in a 37-16 loss to the visiting Tiger-Cats. During the loss, Riders defensive tackle Sean Brantley had arranged for the public address announcer to relay a marriage proposal – Brantley's fiancée accepted by nodding her head. "It would have been perfect if we had won the game," said Brantley, who played only one more game for the Roughriders before being waived. That game was a 26-19, overtime loss against the Eskimos which included a 36-minute, third-quarter power outage at Taylor Field. Saskatchewan led 16-3 at halftime. With their 0-2 record the Roughriders faced an unfamiliar road trip to Memphis, but after getting Glenn Kulka through U.S. Customs (he was routinely detained because of an old narcotics charge) they weren't going to check out Graceland or Beale Street. The Roughriders were meeting the 0-2 Mad Dogs, quarterbacked by Damon Allen, who played on a CFL field crammed into the Liberty Bowl. End zones were 12 yards deep, rather than 20, with concrete grandstand supports jutting into the field and making the end zone only six yards at the shallowest points. The grass playing surface was bordered by artificial turf, but because 11-man U.S. football was played on fields 53 yards wide and 12-a-side Canadian football on 65-yard fields, about 12 yards of artificial sidelines were used. The field was supposedly 110 yards long, but CFL officials admitted years later that they had actually shortened the yard markers to 33 inches apart, rather than 36. Any rushing totals or passing totals weren't entirely accurate. During a pre-game media conference, held in an air-conditioned room, away from the stifling daytime heat that reached 113 degrees Fahrenheit on the humidex, Pepper Rodgers held court. "We should play 11-man football with the same (Canadian) rules," said Rodgers, who was the Mad Dogs' managing general partner, head coach and general manager. "I'm not sure what the 12th guy does . . . We also need 100-yard

The Roughriders were meeting the 0-2 Mad Dogs, quarterbacked by Damon Allen, who played on a CFL field crammed into the Liberty Bowl. End zones were 12 yards deep, rather than 20, with concrete grandstand supports jutting into the field and making the end zone only six yards at the shallowest points.

> The Riders had plenty of time to tour the facility because they were thrown out of their hotel rooms at noon on game day to make room for the NASCAR fans flocking there for the nearby race in Talladega.

fields. The extra 10 yards screws up the American fans. And for the Canadian teams to be successful, the American teams have to be successful." There were 11,748 fans watching the Mad Dogs and Roughriders play one of the most boring games of all time, won 11-5 by Memphis. The Riders were 0-3 for the first time since 1980 and they had another American date eight days later in Birmingham, Alabama, roughly 250 miles away. So the Roughriders flew home on a charter and flew back to the Southern States a week later. Legion Field was a beautiful facility that could almost accommodate a CFL field, except the end zones were shortened by six yards. The Riders had plenty of time to tour the facility because they were thrown out of their hotel rooms at noon on game day to make room for the NASCAR fans flocking there for the nearby race in Talladega. The Barracudas, quarterbacked by Matt Dunigan, coached by Jack Pardee and assembled by general manager Roy Shivers, the first black GM in CFL history, beat the Roughriders 24-14 before 25,321 fans. Saskatchewan was 0-4 for the first time since going 0-12 in 1979. Warren Jones, Saskatchewan's starting quarterback, was sacked five times. The American teams, with their all-American rosters, were dominating the Canadian squads. "I'm not saying anything about that," said Jauch. "All I'm saying is the league has changed and the game is changing and we have to change with it."

With the San Antonio Texans coming to Regina, the Roughriders offered their fans a deal – a home-team victory would earn every fan in attendance a free ticket to one of the two home games in August. Only 22,215 fans appeared at Taylor Field to see former Riders tailback Mike Saunders rush 24 times for 170 yards and one touchdown in the Texans' 36-15 victory. No free tickets. The Roughriders needed six games to get their first win, a 31-20 victory in Ottawa, the home-town of Saskatchewan tailback Darren Joseph. Joseph gained 185 all-purpose yards in the victory, but he was about to be replaced by Robert Mimbs, a former CFLer who assistant general manager Dan Rambo had recruited to participate in the offseason filming of a football video game. Wideout Larry Thompson was on his way out; having requested a trade he was dealt to Hamilton for a third-round draft choice. "I wanted this since the offseason because things weren't happening here," said Thompson. "I'm happy now because I can't go anywhere worse." The B.C. Lions scored four rushing touchdowns in a 43-25 victory over the home-town Roughriders, who dropped further into the North basement at 1-7 after losing 32-13 in Edmonton. The Eskmos were playing their third game in 10 days. Riders cornerback Albert Brown lost his starting spot after getting beaten for two touchdowns. "I'm not happy with a lot of guys' play," said Jauch. "We have to pick it up." They did, winning 31-16 against the Rough Riders and 54-4 against the Blue Bombers during a Labour Day Classic that featured five fans running onto the playing surface and getting viciously tackled by security guards. How bad were the Riders? They lost their next game 25-24 in Winnipeg, even though Blue Bombers quarterback Kevin McDougal was making his first start. The Riders were undone by a third-and-two gamble that was stopped early in the fourth quarter, when they were leading 24-15. Jauch defended his decision by saying he thought it was closer to a one-yard gamble. And quarterback Tom Burgess, appearing in relief of Warren Jones in pre-video replay days, twice sneaked into the end zone (according to various camera angles) but neither touchdown was acknowledged by the on-field officials. Under pressure for his team's 3-8 record, Jauch was getting more outspoken about the disparity between the Canadian and U.S. teams. "It's ridiculous, absolutely ridiculous, that we have two sets of rules in the same league," said Jauch. "Something

> Under pressure for his team's 3-8 record, Jauch was getting more outspoken about the disparity between the Canadian and U.S. teams. "It's ridiculous, absolutely ridiculous, that we have two sets of rules in the same league," said Jauch. "Something has got to be done about that."

has got to be done about that." The Roughriders responded by beating the visiting Mad Dogs 34-32 before 27,787 fans. Mimbs scored two touchdowns and wideout Don Narcisse – who would be the team's lone CFL all-star – caught a pass for a record-setting 138th straight game.

The Roughriders were evidently out of playoff contention, except that the collective bargaining agreement had not been ratified because the CFLPA had never agreed to the north/south divisional alignment. When the CBA was ratified, it allowed fourth-place Winnipeg to become a wild-card entry into the South playoffs and it also withdrew coaches' salaries from the cap in future years. Also off the field, the Riders inducted into their Plaza of Honor: Eddie Lowe, Clyde Brock, Geno Wlasiuk, Tom Shepherd and Wally Dempsey.

The Roughriders won 23-20 in Toronto, lost 28-24 against the Stallions and again 29-27 in Baltimore. With the temporary seats installed for the Grey Cup game, a record crowd of 55,438 came to watch the Calgary Stampeders, even though starting, superstar quarterback Doug Flutie was injured and replaced by Jeff Garcia. They had to come to the stadium because the province-wide television blackout was not lifted. Saskatchewan won 25-20, but an 18-15 loss in Calgary and a 30-25 defeat in B.C. eliminated the 6-12 Riders from playoff contention. Saskatchewan had lost four of its last five games and Jauch had stirred up a hornet's nest by replacing veteran kicker Dave Ridgway, a fan favourite, with Paul McCallum, who had been reacquired permanently from B.C. Ridgway and Jauch had feuded during the season. While the kicker made 74 per cent of his field goals and grumbled about the holding by Joey Jauch, Ray's son, the head coach was irate about Ridgway's feeble tackling abilities. Ridgway vowed that he wouldn't participate in a kicking derby to decide who was going to be the kicker. "If one guy won't compete," said Jauch, "it's like me telling a wide receiver to run a route and he won't. What's your decision then?" Because McCallum had signed a three-year contract, the issue was evidently decided beforehand. "The closing of the door on my career in Saskatchewan is being handled with little or no class," said Ridgway. Jauch insisted the change would benefit the club "in the long run."McCallum kicked in the last two games and made eight of nine field goals. "It's a tough spot," McCallum said. "But whether I came in now or next training camp, there's still going to be a situation like this."

The Roughriders could only wait uncomfortably during Grey Cup Week while the Calgary Stampeders and Baltimore Stallions took over their stadium and lobbied for support from the Rider Priders. Baltimore won the Grey Cup game 37-20 with 52,564 fans at Taylor Field, about 1,000 shy of a sellout. It marked the end

Photo courtesy of *Leader-Post*

Don Narcisse

Photo courtesy of Royal Studios

Paul McCallum

of U.S. expansion because Baltimore, the only successful franchise south of the border, was about to be dislodged as the only professional football team in Maryland by the Cleveland Browns, who were moving there.

Shortly after the Grey Cup festivities had worn down, general manager Al Ford had his contract extended for one year. But Ray Jauch – with two years remaining on his contract – resigned as Saskatchewan's head coach. He would resurface for the next Arena Football League season as head coach of the 4-10 Minnesota Fighting Pike. Irate about his treatment during the latter stages of the season, he refused to be interviewed by the *Leader-Post*, but he told CBC-TV, "I didn't appreciate getting tagged personally by certain parties. Certainly (the Ridgway issue) was a traumatic time, but I didn't do anything that wasn't for the betterment of the team."

Photo courtesy of *Leader-Post*

Jim Daley

After failing to field a winning team with two of the CFL's legendary head coaches, Don Matthews and Ray Jauch, Roughriders general manager Al Ford began looking at replacements who had never been a CFL head coach. John Hufnagel, a former CFL quarterback who was Calgary's offensive co-ordinator, led the pack. Riders defensive co-ordinator Jim Daley was next; he had been a head coach with the University of Ottawa. Ford's third serious candidate was believed to be Bob Price, a former Riders assistant who had been defensive co-ordinator with the Baltimore Stallions. Ford selected Daley, a meticulous 41-year-old from Ottawa, and signed him to a two-year deal. "Do you want to know how prepared Daley is?" said Riders linebacker Ron Goetz, a veteran of Daley's defence. "He went over the kick-back before every game! In detail! How many times do you see a kick-back? Once a season?" Daley admitted he paid attention to the intricacies of the game. "I know I'm a hard-working, detail guy," said Daley, who would get married before the season opened. "But through the last decade I've become flexible. I know that the players can help you determine what's best. This is a people game, so the people playing it need access to you."

Daley's salary was now exempt from the league-mandated, $2.3-million salary cap, as were the salaries of his assistant coaches. Some players took pay cuts, including wideout Don Narcisse. "You've got to make sacrifices," Narcisse said about his 20-percent reduction. Daley kept some of the previous staff, promoting defensive line coach Greg Marshall to defensive co-ordinator, plus he added Paul Chryst as offensive co-ordinator, Bill Dole as offensive line coach and Jerry Friesen as special teams/linebackers coach. The Riders had exceeded the old, $2.5-million cap by $25,000 in 1995 while spending $5.753 million on operating costs. The Grey Cup committee gave its $1.525-million profit to the Riders, who lost $272,000 on last season's operations. New president Fred Wagman, the CEO of Cable Regina, took over a team that was $948,000 in debt. Other franchises were in worse shape: Calgary and Winnipeg were teetering on bankruptcy, but they committed to play in the 1996 season. Ottawa also committed to the season, but asked the CFL for a loan of $750,000, a ridiculous gesture from a team that was paying an exorbitant salary of $650,000 to quarterback David Archer. All except one of the U.S. franchises – Birmingham, Memphis, San Antonio and Shreveport – folded, leaving the reigning Grey Cup champions from Baltimore to take up residence in Montreal as the reborn Alouettes. The ensuing dispersal draft of defunct franchises netted the Roughriders 16 players – their first three selections were receivers Curtis Mayfield and Rod Harris and linebacker Shont'e Peoples, who was dealt away and played for two other teams before joining Saskatchewan in 2001. In the equalization draft of non-imports, designed to help Montreal stock its team, the Riders lost slotback Bruce Boyko. But they quickly reacquired him and offensive lineman Dan Payne in exchange for the rights to kicker Dave Ridgway and fullback David Pitcher. Ridgway would retire soon after from a career that landed him in the Canadian Football Hall of Fame, along with former Riders Al Benecick and Bill Clarke, two offensive linemen who were feted in 1996. In August, on Dave Ridgway Day, he would become the eighth player to have his Riders jersey retired (Number 36). Ridgway would also earn enshrinement into the Plaza of Honor, whose '96 inductees were John Gregory, Bob Poley, Ralph Galloway, Jim Worden and Stan Williams.

In the Canadian college draft the Riders selected Northern Illinois offensive lineman Mike Sutherland third overall. The Riders were also looking for a free-agent quarterback, hopefully eyeing Danny McManus from B.C., Danny Barrett from Ottawa and Damon Allen from Memphis. They got Mike Johnson from Shreveport, who had had a short tryout with the Riders in 1994. They signed him to a three-year contract and cut him before the regular season opened. When quarterback Tom Burgess and centre Mike Anderson refused pay cuts, they were dumped. Saskatchewan's quarterbacks were Warren Jones, Heath Rylance and Kevin Mason. There were 12 new players on the 36-man roster when they opened the season with a 33-13 loss against the Stampeders. Veteran slotback Ray Elgaard was platooning with Dan Farthing. "We're definitely not spelling each other because I can't physically play a full game," said Elgaard. "There's no doubt I can play a full game. This is a transition, I guess. Dan's got lots of good years left." The Roughriders won 29-14 in Ottawa, before a crowd of 10,125, and 27-24 in Edmonton. The deciding points were scored on Aaron Ruffin's 99-yard punt return with 1:01 remaining. Tailback Robert Mimbs was averaging 25 carries for 147 yards per game. When Hamilton beat the visiting Roughriders 27-24, starter Warren Jones was replaced during the fourth quarter by unproven quarterback Heath Rylance. Kicker Paul McCallum had been suffering injury problems and been replaced by Darcy Dahlem. When McCallum tore knee ligaments on the opening kickoff of a 40-16 loss to the visiting Argonauts, punter Brent Matich took over. While the Riders were adding kicker Frank Jagas from Edmonton's practice roster, Montreal was plucking Mike Sutherland from their practice roster. Stampeders kicker Mark McLoughlin tied a CFL record with eight field goals in Calgary's 38-11 victory over the visiting Riders, who gave Heath Rylance his first start in their next game, a 32-20 loss to the Alouettes. Saskatchewan led 17-6 at halftime. Rylance suffered a concussion in the fourth quarter, which convinced Ford to contact Tom Burgess. The veteran quarterback almost returned before deciding to stay and look after his nursery and greenhouse in New Jersey. After losing

Photo courtesy of Royal Studios

Ray Elgaard

25-8 in Edmonton, the Riders waived Warren Jones and obtained quarterback Jimmy Kemp from Montreal. In his first Riders game, played in Montreal, Kemp relieved starter Kevin Mason in a 23-16 overtime loss that was memorable for an injury to defensive lineman Glenn Kulka, who walked off the field despite suffering a broken back! That was the last CFL game played by slotback Ray Elgaard. A 14-year veteran, Elgaard retired after playing 220 games and catching a CFL-record 830 passes for 13,198 yards (with 78 touchdowns). These weren't good times for the league – the B.C. Lions had missed a payroll, the Montreal Alouettes needed a $500,000 loan, the Ottawa Rough Riders were seeking $1.6 million and to cut costs, the entire CFL staff took a 7.5 per cent pay cut. Financial problems among its franchises would ultimately cost the CFL $5 million in support payments and convinced the league to demand that each team sell at least 10,000 season tickets before mid-January, which would give the CFL some certainty moving into 1997.

The Roughriders were struggling, too, but their concern was about finding a quarterback. Kevin Mason was the starter on Labour Day when a crowd of 25,876 saw Riders receiver Curtis Mayfield catch touchdown passes of 95 and 87 yards in a 41-23 victory over Winnipeg. Meanwhile, pass-rushing linebacker Gary Rogers rejoined the team after being cut by the Alouettes, who had signed him as a free agent. A 31-13 loss in Toronto preceded an 18-16 defeat against Ottawa, which the home team lost by allowing two touchdowns in the final 90 seconds. The Riders were six points out of a playoff berth, but so were their next opponents, the B.C. Lions. B.C. sacked Heath Rylance four times and improved to 4-9, dropping the Riders to 3-10. They were 3-11 after losing 37-15 in the Labour Day Classic; Winnipeg's quarterback was Kent Austin while the Riders started Jimmy Kemp because Rylance had a concussion and Mason had torn knee ligaments. Quarterback Marvin Graves, who had played for three other CFL teams, was recruited. But Ford and Daley were facing mounting criticism. President Fred Wagman said an assessment on both men would be conducted after the season. On the first offensive play of Saskatchewan's next game, Rylance got sacked and suffered torn knee ligaments. In relief, Kemp threw three TD passes in a 37-26 victory over the Tiger-Cats. The Riders, in turn, hurt Blue Bomber pivots Kent Austin and Reggie Slack during a 20-14 loss in Winnipeg. B.C. was missing quarterback Damon Allen and Chris Vargas when it lost 27-19 in Regina. The Roughriders finished fifth in the West, out of the playoffs, with a 5-13 record after losing 46-23 in Calgary. The lone bright spot: Tailback Robert Mimbs (292 carries for 1,403 yards and eight touchdowns), was the West's outstanding-player nominee. He lost to Toronto quarterback Doug Flutie in balloting to determine the CFL's outstanding player.

The league rescinded its marquee-player rule for everybody except Flutie, who was making $1 million annually while the top salary was supposed to be $200,000. "Quarterbacks deserve more, but not $600,000 more," said Riders defensive end Bobby Jurasin. Horn Chen had his debt-ridden Ottawa franchise revoked, allowing the remaining teams to hold another dispersal draft. Quarterback David Archer was the "first choice," according to Ford, who had just signed another one-year contract. The over-spending by their rivals meant the Roughriders were $422,000 short in their expected league revenues, and with average crowds down by 3,000 per game they were on track to lose $1.7 million, pushing the debt to a near-fatal $2.6 million. Riders president Fred Wagman tried conveying the seriousness of the issue during a media conference that was televised on provincial cable networks. "The crisis is real," Wagman said. Pressed on the issue, Wagman tersely replied, "Read my lips." That didn't exactly rally the fans, who were told they had to purchase 200,000 game tickets by March 15 or the franchise would fold. Commissioner Larry Smith resigned after a five-year term and there was real concern that the CFL could not afford to even pay the bonuses due the Toronto Argonauts and Edmonton Eskimos, who staged a memorable Grey Cup in Hamilton on a snowy evening. Toronto won.

Selling tickets and signing a quarterback. Those were the primary tasks facing the Roughriders in 1997. To stay afloat financially, the Riders, according to their volunteer executive, had to sell 200,000 game tickets by March 15. To stay competitive, they needed a quarterback. Riders director Bob Ellard had been commissioned by team president Fred Wagman to meet with the team's long-time volunteer support system, known as the Rider Reps, whose efforts had sustained the franchise for most of its 87 years. The media and public were kept out of the meetings, but Ellard discovered the supporters' deep-down optimism was wearing thin because of the team's on-field ineptitude. It showed at the ticket counter in 1996, when the team's gate receipts fell $575,000 from the 1995 total of $2.875 million. With another $500,000 drop in souvenir sales, $200,000 in extra injury costs and a $425,000 loss in CFL revenues, the Roughriders were $2.6 million in debt. Pre-selling 200,000 tickets would supposedly help the Roughriders surpass $4 million in gate receipts. A profitable year could lie ahead.

Fred Wagman

Photo courtesy of *Leader-Post*

When only 40,368 tickets had been sold by mid-February, fans were reminded they needed only to put down a $30 deposit to show they were going to buy season tickets – each season-ticket package would add 10 tickets to the total. One week before the deadline, with only 68,428 tickets sold, CFL chairman John Tory added some urgency by stating, "We have contingency plans in place in the event that things don't work out for Saskatchewan." Players and coaches joined the volunteers answering phones at the ticket-thon on March 11, as the number cracked 85,000. Bill Baker, a former CFL president, player and Riders general manager, scoffed at the tactics, and at the notion that the executive of a non-profit, community-owned franchise could simply terminate the team. "How can you say that?" Baker wondered. 'If you don't support us by March 15, we're going to take our ball and go home?' It's not your ball! I would hope that people realized that whoever is saying these things doesn't have the authority to say them." Baker said he would lead a group that would "pick up the traces" if required. Although the executive was trying to convey the proper sense of urgency regarding the team's plight, it seemed like the taxpayers and ticket buyers had grown tired of hearing about the problems. There really wasn't a sense of foreboding. Few people believed the Roughriders would fold.

Tom Shepherd

Photo courtesy of *Leader-Post*

Doug Archer, Regina's mayor, and Dwain Lingenfelter, the provincial government's economic development minister, supported the Riders' ticket-selling campaign by answering phones alongside Edmonton Eskimos head coach Ron Lancaster and return specialist Henry (Gizmo) Williams and current Riders Bobby Jurasin and Don Narcisse, along with many others. The governments couldn't provide financial support (the province was already guaranteeing $2.1 million of the team's loans) as the clock ticked down. Only 113,879 tickets had been sold by March 14 and 134,223 by midnight of March 15. It wasn't enough. Into the picture waded Riders treasurer Tom Shepherd, who announced that "a consortium of private companies" had donated $500,000, which equalled 29,412 tickets. Through creative mathematics, the Roughriders declared they had sold 215,222 tickets for the upcoming season and were guaranteed $3.4 million in gate receipts. That was apparently enough, as Shepherd rushed off to meet with the banks.

Shepherd's anonymous "consortium" turned out to be the National Football League. The NFL and CFL had reached an agreement in principle for the U.S. league to loan the Canadian loop $4 million in support money. There were strings attached, so no details were supposed to be revealed beforehand. Shepherd had obtained approval from Edmonton Eskimos president Hugh Campbell, who was negotiating the deal with the NFL, to say that the Riders were getting $500,000 from anonymous donors. One month later the details emerged: The NFL was going to help the CFL promote its sport and advance a loan provided NFL teams could have the ability to sign players who were either about to become free agents or were entering the option years of their CFL contracts. The player-signing deal would become a major issue of contention in the ensuing years, but the Roughriders and their cohorts sorely needed the money. The NFL's loan would be paid back on a five-year plan. "The Saskatchewan Roughriders will not be repaying one cent," said Shepherd, even though the team would not be receiving as many league revenues while the CFL was repaying its loan.

Meanwhile, head coach Jim Daley was trying to land a quarterback. He met with David Archer in Ottawa and reported that the Rough Riders' QB would be willing to join Saskatchewan if he were selected in the upcoming dispersal draft of the defunct franchise. That was before Archer discovered his $650,000 salary would be reduced to the league maximum of $150,000 (for everyone except Toronto quarterback Doug Flutie). Because the league realized they really needed help, the Roughriders were awarded the first two picks in Ottawa's dispersal draft. Archer was the first pick, linebacker Lamar McGriggs was second, fullback Shawn Daniels was 10th, running back Dave Dinnall was 18th and return specialist Profail Grier was 26th. McGriggs signed a three-year deal and became, as did Grier and Daniels, for a short team, a contributor to the squad. Archer didn't. His agent, who had already attempted to have the quarterback declared a free agent, pleaded for his client to get marketing deals and endorsements that could increase Archer's income. "They've grandfathered only one player (Flutie) and that's ludicrous," noted Archer. "I've also got a contract." When Archer announced he was retiring to become an analyst on CBC and TSN telecasts, the Roughriders signed quarterback Reggie Slack, who had a history of knee problems and had been backing up Kent Austin in Winnipeg. Linebacker K.D. Williams also joined the Roughriders in a six-player deal from Winnipeg and, upon his arrival, asked for Number 44, a number that had been retired to honour Roger Aldag. "It's OK with me," said Aldag. Williams was given No. 43. Bruce Boyko, Paul Vajda and Dave Van Belleghem were released after refusing pay cuts, and the Riders drafted Calgary offensive lineman Ben Fairbrother second overall and Windsor offensive lineman Dan Comiskey 42nd. Punter Brent Matich and defensive back Aaron Ruffin were cut while free-agent defensive linemen Will Johnson (Calgary) and John Kropke (Ottawa) were added.

Assistant coaches Paul Chryst and Jerry Friesen left the staff, so did assistant personnel director Brendan Taman. While defensive backs coach Richie Hall was being wooed by the Winnipeg Blue Bombers and the University of Idaho, Daley replenished his support group with long-time Winnipeg GM/head coach Cal Murphy and convinced Gary Hoffman, an assistant from 1987-92, to return as offensive co-ordinator. Dick Rendek, Dale West, Lorne Richardson and Bob Kosid were inducted into the Plaza of Honor.

Despite getting a new owner for the Montreal franchise in Robert Wetenhall, who hired ex-commissioner Larry Smith as the team's president, the Quebec city withdrew as Grey Cup host. Baltimore had initially been awarded the game, so the rights went along when the Stallions became the Alouettes. Edmonton begrudgingly stepped in on short notice to replace Montreal. And the Alouettes re-signed their quarterback, Tracy Ham, to a deal worth $500,000 annually, salary cap be damned!

Slack separated his clavicle in the preseason, allowing Kevin Mason to open the campaign as the starting quarterback. The Riders won their opener 24-23 in B.C. with a 10-play drive capped by a 10-yard touchdown pass from Mason to Dan Farthing with four seconds remaining. They lost 24-18 in Edmonton. With a synthetic lubricant injected into his damaged left knee that allowed him to play, Slack won his first start, 27-23, in Toronto. Slack was ineffective in his next start and was replaced late by Kevin Mason as the home-town Stampeders got five field goals from Mark McLoughlin to win 22-13. Ex-Stampeder Will Johnson suffered torn knee ligaments. Although the fans were adamant that Mason should start, Daley anointed Slack as the starter. Slack had a great game before hurting his ribs and right knee during a 37-34 loss in Edmonton. Slack's penchant for injuries rubbed off, literally, on assistant coach Cal Murphy during a 30-20 victory in Hamilton; the quarterback got pushed out of bounds while running and he bowled over Murphy, who suffered a broken and dislocated right wrist while tumbling into the concrete dugouts the teams used for benches at Ivor Wynne Stadium.

Even though a crowd exceeding Taylor Field's capacity of 27,732 saw the Riders lose 39-26 to B.C., the province-wide television blackout wasn't lifted. During the game, linebacker K.D. Williams got into a sideline altercation with defensive co-ordinator Greg Marshall. After defensive lineman Lybrant Robinson was waived a few days later, Lamar McGriggs and K.D. Williams skipped a team meeting after missing their flight to Toronto. Evidently it was intentional. Saskatchewan lost 27-1 in Toronto, which didn't surprise recently released linebacker Henry Newby. "It's a team in turmoil," said Newby. Winnipeg got its first victory in nine starts by beating the 4-6 Roughriders

Photo courtesy of Royal Studios

Mike Saunders outruns a Baltimore defender

43-12. McGriggs and Williams, Saskatchewan's leading defensive tacklers, were afterwards quoted in a newspaper article claiming there were rifts in the locker room. The twosome held a media conference the next day and downplayed their comments, saying they were "misconscrewed," but a trade was already in the works that sent them to Hamilton for a second-round draft pick and future considerations. Said McGriggs, "Since I'm being treated as the virus, I guess they should remove the virus." After the players departed, their jerseys were thrown on the floor of the locker room and several players danced on them. Nobody would admit who it was. About then a stabilizing force rejoined the team – popular tailback Mike Saunders was reacquired from Toronto for two draft choices. Saunders rushed 24 times for 155 yards and scored two of Saskatchewan's six touchdowns in a 46-12 victory over B.C. The Roughriders lost for the 14th straight time in Calgary, 28-24, and afterwards wideout Don Narcisse said, "I guess we're waiting for the playoffs to get our two wins in a row."

With their 5-7 record the Roughriders weren't threatening to play host to a West playoff game, but because they were in fourth place there was a chance they could move into the East as a wild-card qualifier. Maybe that playoff game would be moved to Regina because Montreal, which sat second in the East, was being kicked out of Olympic Stadium for a rock concert by U2. It turned out to be a great move for the Alouettes, who found a new home at quainter Molson Stadium, on the campus of McGill University partway up Mount Royal, and began a lengthy string of sellouts. Slack was bothered by a numbness in an arm during the 24-22 loss in Montreal. The Alouettes intercepted four passes and quarterback Tracy Ham had a touchdown run and threw for two majors. Saskatchewan next intercepted four passes in a 29-15, windy (gusts to 100 km-h) victory over the Eskimos. There was still roster shuffling going on: Brigham Young quarterback Steve Sarkisian was activated, offensive guard Andrew Greene returned from three years in the NFL, fullback Shawn Daniels was sidelined 10 games with a sprained ankle, linebacker Ron Goetz missed most of the season with back spasms, wideout Curtis Mayfield was upset about being moved to slotback and tailback Robert Mimbs, suddenly ineffective, was cut. "It's not that I wasn't performing," said Mimbs, whose 10-game totals were 113 carries for 493 yards and two touchdowns. "It's that I wasn't getting the ball." The Roughriders won 26-19 in B.C. and 22-19 against Hamilton for their first two-game winning streak of the season, before being pulverized 55-9 in Winnipeg. The season-ending loss placed them third in the West at 8-10. They moved into Calgary for the West

Photo courtesy of Royal Studios

Andrew Greene returns from the NFL

semifinal, which turned on a first-quarter hit by Riders linebacker Gary Rogers on Stampeders quarterback Jeff Garcia. Using an option attack during their 33-30 victory, Slack ran for 102 yards and one touchdown, plus he passed for 278 yards and one touchdown. Four veteran players on the team recognized intimately the path the Roughriders were taking was the same that led to their 1989 Grey Cup appearance (and victory) – through Calgary and Edmonton. In Edmonton for the West final, Curtis Mayfield returned a punt 95 yards for a touchdown and caught a 37-yard touchdown pass that helped the Riders win 31-30. The Roughriders returned home to begin their preparations for the Grey Cup game, also at Edmonton's Commonwealth Stadium. They would meet the Toronto Argonauts, whose quarterback, Doug Flutie, won his sixth award as the CFL's outstanding player in 1997. "Toronto hasn't had the troubles we had," said Riders defensive end Bobby Jurasin, his team's only CFL all-star. "Toronto took the interstate to the Grey Cup. We took the grid roads." Another 10,000 Grey Cup tickets were sold to Saskatchewan fans in the wake of their team's victory. When Slack missed a mid-week practice, ostensibly because of the flu, it caused some concern. But the Roughriders were outmatched 47-23 by the 15-3 Argonauts. Flutie's team accumulated 540 offensive yards. For taking the team from league-worst to Grey Cup finalist, Daley and Ford got two-year contracts. Dan Rambo retired as player personnel director, a job he had been doing out of Ottawa, and became a regional scout for the NFL's Denver Broncos And, amid derogatory shots from Slack, Gary Hoffman resigned, leaving the team to find its sixth offensive co-ordinator in six seasons. "I didn't get coached this year," said Slack. Replied Hoffman: "I'm not going to be the goat."

Photo courtesy of SSHFM

Curtis Mayfield

Defensive end Bobby Jurasin was coming off an all-star season. He had been the Roughriders' outstanding defensive player and their inspirational leader, helping them make an unexpected Grey Cup appearance in his 12th season with the club. His 142 career sacks were second in CFL records to Grover Covington's 157 and Jurasin had his eye on that total. Until something happened on cutdown day of 1998, when Jurasin walked by a group of people standing sheltered from the rain beside the Roughriders' locker room at Taylor Field. "That's it," he said, before jumping in his car and driving away. "I'm out of here." One of the people in the group, a Roughriders employee who knew this was coming, summed up the surprising release of Jurasin this way: "(Head coach Jim) Daley just made a decision that might cost him his job." Daley believed newcomers R-Kal Truluck and DeWayne Patterson were good enough to replace Jurasin. "We have to make a decision, weigh it and live with it," said Daley. "We have to decide when the crossroads of our younger players pass the crossroads of our older players." The Riders also cut offensive lineman Vic Stevenson, defensive lineman Ernie Brown, defensive back Charles Anthony and,

Photo courtesy of *Leader-Post*

Bobby Jurasin

in roster shuffling moves, linebacker Dan Rashovich and quarterback Kevin Mason. None were as surprising as Jurasin, who had been offered a job as an assistant coach. He declined and, instead, got an invitation from former Riders coach Don Matthews to join him with the Toronto Argonauts. Jurasin's first of two games in Argo blue was at Taylor Field, where the Roughriders won 19-10 and Truluck had three sacks. Jurasin, who got a pregame ovation but was barely noticeable, didn't conduct interviews afterward. Jurasin's denouement wouldn't deprive him of future enshrinement in the Plaza of Honor, where he would ultimately join the 1998 inductees – Roger Goree, Johnny Bell and Glen Suitor.

The Roughriders had spent most of their offseason trying to get a quarterback, a need that intensified when Reggie Slack requested a raise from his $80,000 base salary (plus bonuses). They made a pass at Anthony Calvillo, who had been cut by the Hamilton Tiger-Cats before joining the Montreal Alouettes as a backup to Tracy Ham. Calvillo was one of the few people heading to Montreal – a storm replete with freezing ice ravaged the area in the late winter and left three million people without power; some of them needed a month before their power was restored.

Ham became the CFL's highest-paid player (estimated salary: $350,000) when Toronto quarterback Doug Flutie joined the NFL's Buffalo Bills. With the US dollar worth $1.50 Cdn, Flutie had extra reasons for leaving Canada. Danny McManus played out his option with the Edmonton Eskimos and, while he was a free agent, visited Regina. His exploratory trip included a stop at the Scott Tournament of Hearts, where he was warmly greeted by the crowd inside the Agridome watching the Canadian women's curling championship. McManus instead joined his former Eskimos coach, Ron Lancaster, in Hamilton and was replaced in Edmonton by David Archer, who ended his one-year retirement and tried explaining why he had not wanted to join Saskatchewan the previous season. "The team was 5-13 in '96 and had a new offensive co-ordinator," said Archer. "It had nothing to do with the fans or the city, it was the nuts and bolts of the football operations that I was scared of. Fortunately for them I didn't come. Reggie Slack had a heroic postseason and they made it to the Grey Cup." Archer's salary in Edmonton was announced as the league-maximum $150,000, but it's doubtful anyone in Canada believed that. The Roughriders couldn't have afforded Archer anyway, not after making only $540,000 in 1997. That figure included the team's $520,000 share of the $4 million US loan from the NFL, according to new president Bob Ellard, a local architect, who assumed his position when Fred Wagman resigned after only two years at the post for "personal reasons." After making $4.07 million in gate receipts and spending $4.5495 million to operate the previous year, the Roughriders were back to $2.1 million in debt. That was exactly even with the CFL's salary cap before it expanded by $28,000 to allow CFL teams to add a third, developmental quarterback to their rosters. Players' salaries had fallen by $4,100 and, according to the CFLPA survey, an average salary in 1997 was $43,119. Slack eventually re-signed with the Roughriders for a reported $110,000 plus bonuses, after insinuating he couldn't play his hardest if he wasn't among the league's top-paid quarterbacks. The Roughriders released linebackers Ron Goetz and Greg Clark and defensive lineman John Kropke, lost free agents Troy Alexander, Scott Hendrickson, Carl Coulter and Dale Joseph to other CFL teams and saw Andrew Greene become their first option-year player to leave for an NFL team when he signed with the Seattle Seahawks. Quarterback Steve Sarkisian, who had left the team prior to Grey Cup because he felt

Archer's salary in Edmonton was announced as the league-maximum $150,000, but it's doubtful anyone in Canada believed that.

Photo courtesy of Royal Studios

John Terry (51) and Scott Hendrickson block for Reggie Slack (17)

slighted by his treatment, rejoined the team. The Riders also drafted UBC defensive back Curtis Galick seventh overall and Ottawa receiver Ousmane Tounkara eighth. Defensive lineman Andrew Stewart (via trade) and linebacker Ken Benson (free agent) came from Toronto to join a team that now had Bob O'Billovich as its player personnel director. Training camp was in Saskatoon.

The aforementioned Toronto-Saskatchewan Grey Cup rematch kicked off the season, with Riderss winning 19-10. The Roughriders fell to 1-1 by losing 30-24 in Montreal. They won 28-14 against the visiting Eskimos before losing six straight games – 25-20 against B.C. by allowing Robert Drummond to rush for 187 yards; 26-8 in Hamilton as Slack threw four interceptions; 46-27 against Calgary; 47-24 in Calgary; 13-12 against Montreal; and 35-13 in Edmonton because Eskimos cornerback Kavis Reed intercepted Heath Rylance's first pass and returned it 56 yards for a touchdown. Rylance was playing because Slack had strained abdominal muscles.

Fans were furious. They didn't care that the Riders were missing 10 starters during their skid, including Slack, who was getting cortisone shots for a pulled groin. Because of a strike at Air Canada the Blue Bombers came to Regina by bus for the Labour Day Classic, which contained a celebration honouring Riders receiver Don Narcisse, who had just passed former teammate Ray Elgaard's record of 830 career receptions. Saskatchewan won 32-18, but the Blue Bombers won their first game in 11 starts in the rematch when their backup quarterback, Troy Kopp, rallied the home team from a 28-10 fourth-quarter deficit to a 36-35 victory. After losing 35-18 in Calgary, Slack returned from visiting his ailing mother in Florida, where Hurricane Georges had been swirling, to pass for one touchdown and run for another in a 27-22 victory over the Stampeders. The Roughriders didn't win on the road until they beat Toronto 18-15, giving them their only two-game winning streak of the season. They lost 34-31 to the Tiger-Cats on a last-play, 34-yard field goal by Paul Osbaldiston. The Roughriders were eliminated from postseason contention before losing 42-37 to the Lions and 46-24 in Edmonton. The season-ending fiasco dropped the Roughriders' record to 5-13 and embarrassed the team's longest-serving veteran, Dan Rashovich. "(Eskimos quarterback) David Archer said to me, 'I can't believe this is happening to you,' " said Rashovich, a 12-year veteran. "This is what happens to us!" The dropoff from Grey Cup finalist to playoff non-qualifier didn't go unpunished. General manager Al Ford decided the team needed a new head coach, so Jim Daley was dumped with one year remaining on his contract.

Daley held a media conference in the Riders' offices and answered all questions. He had never been one to duck an issue. "As a coach I want to go back and correct it," said Daley, who had a 20-37 mark during his three seasons as Saskatchewan's head coach. "The only regret I have is not winning more games."

Photo courtesy of *Leader-Post*

Cal Murphy – add his Super Bowl ring with the Indianapolis Colts to this pot of gold!

Offensive co-ordinator Cal Murphy was convinced to take over the job. Despite Saskatchewan's poor record, its offence had placed fifth in productivity; the defence had been last with 132 rushing yards against per game and league lows of 12 interceptions and 39 sacks. Murphy, 67, had spent 23 years in the CFL with five teams, was a part of nine Grey Cup championship teams, and had spent 14 years with the Winnipeg Blue Bombers as their head coach or general manager. He was six years removed from receiving a heart transplant. "I assure you I had no intentions of taking this job," Murphy said upon being hired as the Roughriders 24th head coach. "When I was approached about this job, the first person I spoke with was Jim. And he told me he was behind me all the way." Murphy offered Daley a job as an assistant coach. Daley declined.

Ford wanted an experienced coach because the upcoming year could be his last in charge if the team faltered. "I told the executive, 'Don't point the gun anywhere else after the '99 season,' " said Ford.

General manager Al Ford was adamant: The team's fortunes were his responsibility. If the team didn't improve markedly, he would no longer be in charge. "I've been associated with this team for 25 years," Ford said at the Roughriders' annual general meeting. "That will end after this season if we don't make the playoffs." The team did make money the previous year – a profit of $337,000 helped trim the debt to $1.78 million – and began looking at overhauling the managerial structure. "The purpose is to put to sleep any statements that this is an old boys' network," said former president Fred Wagman, who had been appointed to review the team's structure and constitution. The

Riders had sold 13,000 season tickets and made $3.6 million in gate receipts, but they also got $1.05 million from its share of CFL revenues, which, for a change, didn't have to be used to help support troubled franchises. The Roughriders tried bolstering their own roster with free agents. They got offensive lineman Jeremy O'Day from Toronto and linebacker Willie Pless, an 11-time all-star and five-time winner of the CFL's outstanding defensive player award, who had been cut by Edmonton. They didn't get linebacker Mike O'Shea from Toronto, defensive end Joe Montford from Hamilton or receiver Terry Vaughn, who had been booked on a flight to Regina for a press conference announcing his signing with the Roughriders, before he decided he would instead leave Calgary for Edmonton. Offensive lineman Andrew Greene returned from his NFL sojourn and they scooped up free-agent defensive back Douglass Craft. They drafted Indianapolis defensive back Stephane Fortin 10th overall and Idaho State running back Kennedy Nkeyasen, a Regina product, 18th overall. Because of the NFL/CFL agreement, they also lost six players to NFL tryouts – defensive linemen Ernie Brown, Herb Coleman and Paul Spicer, linebacker Aaron Collins and defensive backs Eric Sutton and Curtis Galick. Defensive lineman Andrew Stewart didn't return after being indicted for mail fraud in the U.S. Head coach Cal Murphy added Mickey Mays as an assistant coach in charge of linebackers, moving Alex Smith to running backs/special teams on a staff that still included Sam Garza, Richie Hall, Greg Marshall and Bill Dole. Murphy was featured prominently on billboards throughout the province, peering out stern-faced beside the slogan, "Excuses? Not in our house!"

Photo courtesy of Royal Studios

Andrew Greene dominates defensive linemen around the league

The Roughriders hadn't had a winning season since 1994, but things started poorly at training camp when veteran defensive back Terryl Ulmer was a no-show. Ford didn't know what happened and was unable to reach him. Ulmer's teammates claimed they had no idea why Ulmer was AWOL. Ulmer had been issued a plane ticket, but he missed the flight and didn't call. It turned out that the New Orleans branch of the Drug Enforcement Agency, after a lengthy investigation in Ulmer's home town of Laurel, Mississippi, conducted a raid that resulted in 37 individuals receiving 17 indictments for distributing crack cocaine. Ulmer was one of the indicted. He pleaded guilty and was sentenced in September to 37 months in a federal penitentiary, followed by five years of supervised relief. He was given a one-month respite before beginning his sentence so he could be with his pregnant wife. When the Roughriders broke camp, their 39-man roster (19 non-imports, 17 imports and three quarterbacks) included explosive returner/slotback Eric Guliford, who had served an NFL suspension after testing positive for marijuana, and linebacker Trevis Smith, who had taken over the team's impromptu barber duties from Ulmer. There were nine newcomers on the roster, five players who had shifted positions and four rookie backups. Among the cuts were quarterback Heath Rylance and defensive end DeWayne Patterson. Because punter/kicker Paul McCallum was hurt to begin the season, Wayne Lammle returned as a short-term kicker and Cory Stevens was punting. The Riders had tried to get punter/kicker Matt Kellett, a Regina product, from B.C.; he played a pre-season game with the Riders before the CFL ruled that he had actually been traded to Edmonton.

There was a new Voice of the Riders on CKRM. Geoff Currier had left the radio station before the 1998 season and been replaced by Steve Brown, another Ottawa product, who lasted only one campaign. Rod Pedersen, from nearby Milestone, took over as CKRM's sports director and, in addition to handling the junior Regina Pats hockey broadcasts, became the Riders' play-by-play announcer (alongside analyst Carm Carteri) for the station's province-wide network. It took a few years before Pedersen was invited to host the annual Plaza of Honor induction dinner, which in 1999 was going to fete Kent Austin, Ray Elgaard and Larry Isbell.

The Roughriders began their season with two straight road games while the City of Regina had $1.8 million in repairs being done to the concrete, structure and old seats in the west grandstand of Taylor Field. The reigning Grey Cup champions began defending their crown by beating the Roughriders 28-18 in Calgary; Stampeders quarterback Dave Dickenson was sacked six times, but he engineered four touchdown drives. Edmonton quarterback Nealon Greene carried 14 times for 180 yards and threw four touchdown passes, including three to Rider-shunner Terry Vaughn, to beat Saskatchewan 39-6. The Riders dropped – literally because they committed six turnovers – to 0-3 with a home-opening, 32-21 loss to the undefeated Lions. "I was cussed at and booed," said Riders quarterback Reggie Slack, who suffered a strained calf muscle and was replaced as the starter by Steve Sarkisian for a 20-15 victory against the Argonauts. Things got worse for Slack. Although he wasn't expected to play in Hamilton, he missed the team's flight out of Regina. While the Roughriders were trying to contact Slack, a fan reported seeing him in Regina. Slack was suspended, but apparently earning 60 per cent of his salary while he was on the disabled list. That left Steve Sarkisian and John Rayborn as the quarterbacks for a 63-17 loss in Hamilton. Slack met his teammates shortly after they returned to Regina, confessing to them and the media that he had a "medical addictions problem." That insinuated that Slack was addicted to painkillers, but it was a more serious addiction that he was battling. Slack admitted he had been in a rehabilitation facility during the offseason and was heading back to the same place in Toronto, on the Riders' tab. "I feel confident that I can get through this thing with my teammates' help," Slack said. Slack – inconceivably to anyone familiar with addictions treatment – missed only one game, a 37-22 loss to the Stampeders,

Photo courtesy of Royal Studios

Nealon Greene

who scored 21 points in the fourth quarter. He was at Taylor Field, watching from the sideline, as Paul McCallum kicked a 52-yard field goal to give the Roughriders a 29-27 victory over the Eskimos. Only 16,544 fans were watching that game, the third-smallest crowd since Taylor Field's expansion in 1979. The Roughriders, with a season-ticket base that had shrunk in one year from 13,000 to 10,500, were averaging only 18,304 fans per home game and were on track to lose $700,000. Slack went with the Roughriders to Vancouver, relieving Sarkisian during a 28-21 loss to the Lions. "Recovery is a life-long process," said Slack. "I want to put things in place to help deal with my recovery." With Saskatchewan in the midst of a provincial election campaign that would see Premier Roy Romanow's NDP keep power away from the Saskatchewan Party's Elwin Hermanson and Liberal Jim Melenchuk, the 1999 Roughriders won their last game in the Labour Day Classic. They improved to 3-6 by handing the hapless Blue Bombers their fifth straight loss, 42-17, on the strength of tailback Mike Saunders rushing 27 times for 162 yards and one touchdown. The victory was the 99th of Murphy's career as a CFL head coach, prompting Riders communications director Tony Playter to inform the media that Murphy was poised to become the ninth CFL coach to record 100 victories. The media chuckled, realizing that the pitiful Riders likely weren't going to help Murphy reach that milestone. Indeed, they didn't. They surrendered 549 offensive yards while losing 28-3 in Toronto, watched former Riders quarterback Kevin Mason run for 116 yards while leading the Eskimos to 28 straight points in a 41-36 victory over the hometown Roughriders, and fell 24-18 in Winnipeg. The Riders also lost guard Andrew Greene with a torn Achilles tendon, Slack to arthroscopic knee surgery and linebacker Trevis Smith with one of the sport's most painful and rare injuries, a dislocated hip. The Montreal Alouettes scored 27 straight points to beat the Roughriders 41-26, then beat them again 43-7 in Montreal as Sarkisian threw two interceptions, Rayborn threw two and third-stringer Mike Cawley threw two. The Riders were 3-11 and president Bob Ellard realized any mid-season changes to the team's hierarchy would be futile. "At this point in the season there are no people available," said Ellard. "If we were to fire Al or Cal it would turn us upside down." A miniscule crowd of 16,448 saw the Roughriders lose 34-31 to the visiting Stampeders. Ron Lancaster, head coach and football operations director of the Hamilton Tiger-Cats, was bringing his team to Regina for the last home game of the regular season and the city was abuzz about the Riders legend perhaps rejoining the franchise as the replacement for Ford and Murphy. Said Lancaster: "It's not really the time to talk about this, but they should get a younger guy." The Riders lost 42-12 to the Tiger-Cats. True to his word, with a fifth straight losing season looming

Photo courtesy of Royal Studios

Steve Sarkisian (12) and Paul McCallum watch the ball sail through the uprights

> "As the losses kept building I was afraid to listen to the radio or look in the newspaper," said Ford, who wiped away tears at his farewell media conference. "I knew this was going to be the toughest day of my life."

and a second straight without a playoff appearance, Ford submitted his resignation as general manager and chief operating officer. Although the Riders won the 1989 Grey Cup during his first season in charge, they never had a home playoff game while Ford was general manager, an 11-year tenure during which the team had an 82-116 record. "As the losses kept building I was afraid to listen to the radio or look in the newspaper," said Ford, who wiped away tears at his farewell media conference. "I knew this was going to be the toughest day of my life." The Riders lost 34-21 in Edmonton and 19-18 in B.C. Their season-ending, nine-game losing streak – their longest skid since 1980 – left them with a 3-15 record. They had three all-stars: Linebacker Willie Pless, defensive end Neal Smith and offensive tackle John Terry. On November 11, Cal Murphy resigned as head coach and director of football operations. Murphy and Ford represented the Roughriders during the Grey Cup festivities in Vancouver, where Bob Ellard began compiling a list of candidates to replace them. Ron Lancaster was quickly scratched from that list because after Hamilton won the Grey Cup, the Tiger-Cats owners signed him to a four-year contract.

Looking back from, the general manager's perspective:

ALAN FORD:

"I never thought I'd be GM. Who would want that job? Everybody hates you. Why would you want it? Not everybody, I guess, but all the players hate you. The fans, hatred grows about five per cent a year, it keeps mounting. Once you get past the 51 per cent mark you've got problems. I think Ken Preston gave me a vision of what it was like to be a general manager. Times have changed so much. Obviously when I took the job and I was thinking back about it, I was thinking that, 'Gosh, I sure hope I can be even close to as successful as Preston was.' That didn't happen. That was kind of how I saw myself: As a Canadian here in the community. I don't know how much actual scouting Preston did. Who knows his contacts? I didn't do much scouting. It was different times. We were just worried about keeping the franchise alive. The worse the club and league got in terms of the finances, the bigger the job got for the, in quotes, general manager. I think it was Edmonton who split the jobs and gave one job to the player personnel guy, put him in charge of football operations, and gave somebody else the business side. There's only a handful of really good personnel guys. I think it was Hughie (Campbell, Edmonton's general manager), who knew you couldn't just take the personnel guy away from one club and hire him. The smart guys made him the general manager and would have the club president overseeing the business stuff; if he didn't have a football background, he at least had a feel for professional sport or for running an operation. He was smart enough to not put his nose where it didn't belong.

> "I think Ken Preston gave me a vision of what it was like to be a general manager. Times have changed so much. Obviously when I took the job and I was thinking back about it, I was thinking that, 'Gosh, I sure hope I can be even close to as successful as Preston was.'"

"I didn't have a lot of player personnel experience in the States. (Assistant general manager Dan) Rambo was already in that position in the States. Leaving him in that position made sense while I was working on whether the team would survive. The closest the team came to folding was if we didn't get the NFL money, we probably were toast. There were some things Shepherd did, like the liquor distributorship and the lottery, things only Tom could have done, that were very important in keeping this thing alive. We kind of hope people don't forget that. Everything is kind of rosy throughout the whole league, but it can change pretty quickly if Toronto or Hamilton goes through a couple of bad years and we'll see if the guys who are supporting it are still hanging around. We

Photo courtesy of SSHFM

Dan Rambo

needed that U.S. expansion money, too. Larry Smith gets blamed for that, but that and the NFL money gave teams a chance to keep going. There were some real dollars in franchise fees. There were some real expenses and some stupid things people did, but the net effect was positive for the league. Sometimes you have to get into bed with people you don't want to. What bothered me the most is you're competing on the football field, the football guys are competing like hell, but the business guys have to understand that you can't be 'Poor Saskatchewan, you guys are always going to be there, drawing fans.' It doesn't work that way. I don't know how many times in my tenure I heard that: 'We need this quarterback.' Wait a minute, we do, too. All of a sudden the money doesn't equate for the quarterback coming here, he goes somewhere else and gets paid a lot, then the next year that club goes under.

"The league was so wild, with all these guys buying franchises who had no background in the league. From a league perspective, they didn't care. That was something I could never change. I cared about the league. It wasn't going to be me on the watch when this club went under. If the whole league went, we were going to go under. But it wasn't going to go under when I was the general manager.

"Sometimes you get guys who come together like they did in 2007. I don't think anybody would have predicted that team would have won the Grey Cup. Maybe nobody would have predicted 1989 either."

"It's harder to attract players here from all over, especially players who have been in big cities. The ones who come and stay, they get it. The ones who come here and go back home, they don't get it and are ready to leave when somebody comes after them as a free agent. You limit your chances a little bit of getting free agents and players when you're here. That's the way it is, the way it's been the whole time. Sometimes you get guys who come together like they did in 2007. I don't think anybody would have predicted that team would have won the Grey Cup. Maybe nobody would have predicted 1989 either.

"John (Gregory) was there in 1988, so I knew him when I was the assistant general manager. I had been around him for that year. I was doing the Canadian college scouting, so I had been around the personnel end a bit and was working a little in the business end. Every team has a lot of really good players, but it depends on how you do when things are going really well and how you do when you're going in the tank. There were a few small things that happened in '89 that made it look like we were going in the tank, but we didn't. All of a sudden people start believing we've got the talent to do it, guys start playing like they believe it.

"Of all the stuff I did, firing John was the toughest. After we got hammered 62-10 in Toronto and then again the next week when (Doug) Flutie came from way behind to beat us 50-47 at home, it seemed like we had to do something to turn this around. If we don't do it now and we keep going the way we're going, what are we going to do in the off-season? When's the best opportunity to make that change? We were fortunate that Don Matthews, a proven head coach with extensive CFL experience was available. So we decided to go in that direction.

"If I was looking for a guy who prepared during the week, John Gregory was one of the top coaches ... Don Matthews on the sidelines was the best I know."

"One of the downsides of expansion: American players and American coaches would rather be in the States because that's their home. Each of the coaches had their own styles. If I was looking for a guy who prepared during the week, John Gregory was one of the top coaches. Maybe he didn't have the talent that was necessary, or maybe injuries changed that. Don Matthews on the sidelines was the best I know. When Ray (Jauch) took the job, Kent (Austin) had left, Mike Saunders left, all of a sudden the coaching staff and personnel guy (Jim Popp) goes. U.S. expansion, in terms of our club, cost us a lot of talent, but not so much on-the-field talent, but coaching talent. We were starting to rebuild. Ray had to find new people and new players. I don't want to speak for Ray, but his days when he was really successful in Edmonton, if you needed somebody you would make a call and they would be there.

"In 1997, all of a sudden we got on a roll. We acquired Mike Saunders in late August or early September, he comes in, has a spectacular game and everybody thought we might have a chance. Reggie (Slack) started making the plays that were necessary as an athlete, rather than a quarterback. All of a sudden we were started on the same trail as 1989. Guys bought into it because they thought if those guys could do it in '89, we can, too. Who knows, if Reggie had been able to rise above his personal problems? He was a great talent. In 1998, if you look back at it, I don't know what our record was, 5-13 or something, but I bet we lost eight games by less than a touchdown. You go through that year and think, 'If Reggie can take that next step . . .' He's got the ability to do it. Mentally can he do it? Physically does he want to do it? Who else is out there? I'm trying to sign Damon Allen and a bunch of people who were free at the time. Anthony Calvillo was in Hamilton and wasn't doing very well. We came pretty close. Montreal offered him the chance, 'Come with us and learn.' After being in Montreal for a couple of training camps I've been able to see Anthony, with his demeanour, why he was able to do that. He would get hammered so he needed that. He didn't have the personality of Kent Austin – knock me down five times and I'll get up for a sixth time. He had some early success in Las Vegas, went downhill with Hamilton big time, so it didn't matter what we were going to offer him, he was going to go to Montreal and work behind Tracy Ham.

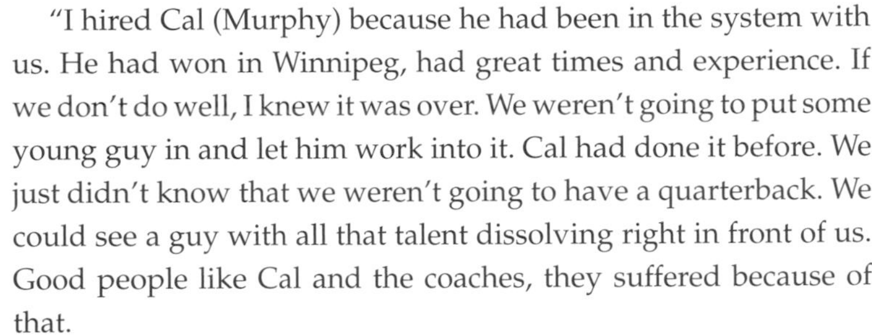

"I hired Cal (Murphy) because he had been in the system with us. He had won in Winnipeg, had great times and experience. If we don't do well, I knew it was over. We weren't going to put some young guy in and let him work into it. Cal had done it before. We just didn't know that we weren't going to have a quarterback. We could see a guy with all that talent dissolving right in front of us. Good people like Cal and the coaches, they suffered because of that.

Photo courtesy of Royal Studios

Dan Rashovich

"The guy who keeps popping back into mind is Dan Rashovich. He played above his level all the time. He was a pretty talented guy. If he was playing special teams he would go at an unbelievable rate. He didn't get along with Matthews. I remember at the Grey Cup in 1997, he yelled something at the bench to Matthews. He needed to be spoon-fed, but he played hurt, probably on some teams Razz could have been in a position to start. He was kind of in the wrong place for us. He did start some for us. He made a big play for us in '97 on our way to the Grey Cup. For a guy who played a fair amount and quite a bit on special teams, we had some run-ins with things that happened. I put them beside me now. I'm sure Preston had a few of those, so you put them aside. There's a bunch of guys like Roger (Aldag), who were going through all the pay cuts. He probably could have played hardball and didn't because he and Bob Poley and Bryan Illerbrun and Dan Farthing went though the system and understood the situation. In the 1990s if they were with another team they probably would have had more success.

"Getting to the Grey Cup and winning it was great. So was getting to it in 1997. I didn't have that much to do with the personnel, maybe people thought I had more to do with it, but working on the business side and just surviving was my legacy. I made a lot of calls to people we owed money to for, two to three years in the middle saying, 'Hang with us, we will pay you.' I'm most proud of that. There were a bunch of clubs that went under. And we didn't. But it wasn't just me."

The Saskatchewan Roughriders were a floundering CFL franchise when the 2000s approached. Coming off a 3-15 season in 1999 – their worst since back-to-back 2-14 campaigns in 1979-80 – the team parted ways with long-time general manager Al Ford and head coach Cal Murphy, whose previous successes coaching the Winnipeg Blue Bombers, Edmonton Eskimos and B.C. Lions couldn't be transferred to the debt-ridden, talent-starved Roughriders in his only season as Saskatchewan's bench boss.

Roughriders president Bob Ellard needed to reinvigorate the franchise and its ever-adoring public, who were becoming exasperated with the team's annual shortcomings. The Roughriders had persevered through league- and self-inflicted financial disasters, the CFL's short-lived U.S. expansion and the folding of rival franchises. It simply couldn't survive another prolonged streak of fielding bad football teams. The Roughriders had last posted a winning record (11-7) in 1994 and attendance, the lifeblood of CFL franchises, was waning at Taylor Field. The community-owned franchise lost $700,000 in 1999 and was $2.5 million in debt, with the provincial government guaranteeing a $2.1-million loan from four local financial institutions. Showing that public support remained for the Roughriders, a group of 17 private and corporate sponsors, led by former Riders president Bruce Cowie, raised $1.7 million to replace Taylor Field's worn-out OmniTurf. Although there were newer, innovative, "artificial-grass" products available, the City of Regina was reluctant to again try an unproven product and elected to cover the city-owned field with AstroTurf for the upcoming season. The artificial turf was installed just before the regular season began. Cowie, coincidentally, was among the team's inductees that year into its Plaza of Honor, along with former kicker Dave Ridgway and former linebacker Cleveland Vann.

Showing that public support remained for the Roughriders, a group of 17 private and corporate sponsors, led by former Riders president Bruce Cowie, raised $1.7 million to replace Taylor Field's worn-out OmniTurf.

Still, something had to be done about the on-field product. But who would take on such a task? Ron Lancaster, a former Riders head coach and Hall of Fame quarterback, was entrenched with the Hamilton Tiger-Cats after leading them to victory in the 1999 Grey Cup. The Tiger-Cats owners quickly re-signed Lancaster to keep him from considering Saskatchewan's offer. Tom Higgins, who had a short stint as a Riders player, didn't want to leave his job as the Edmonton Eskimos assistant general manager, a role that later allowed him to win a Grey Cup as that team's coach. Lancaster and Higgins were Ellard's first two choices. Eric Tillman was also offered the job and declined. Ellard was running out of prospects.

Calgary Stampeders assistant general manager Roy Shivers was interested. That's what he told the *Leader-Post* during the 1999 Grey Cup Week in Vancouver. Ellard read the newspaper story and it piqued his curiosity. Shivers, through his extensive contacts in U.S. colleges, had been responsible for accumulating talent in B.C., primarily for head

Shivers had been general manager of the Birmingham Barracudas in 1995, the one year of their existence in the CFL. Shivers was also black, a fact unknown to Ellard until they met to discuss the job.

coach Don Matthews, and Calgary, where his working relationship with Stampeders head coach/general manager Wally Buono had made the squad a perennial contender with such great players as Allen Pitts, Kelvin Anderson and Alondra Johnson. Shivers had been general manager of the Birmingham Barracudas in 1995, the one year of their existence in the CFL. Shivers was also black, a fact unknown to Ellard until they met to discuss the job. Unlike the NFL, the CFL had long given opportunities to black quarterbacks such as Warren Moon, Condredge Holloway and J.C. Watts, but it hadn't been as generous with its top administrative jobs. Shivers had been the CFL's first African-American general manager and, until then, only the Toronto Argonauts had once employed a black head coach – the unsuccessful Willie Wood in 1981-82.

Shivers apparently impressed Ellard and the board of directors with his plans to restock the Roughriders' roster. Shivers was 58 when he took the job and signed a three-year contract on December 24, 1999; he became the team's general manager and director of football operations. Ellard had put a time limit on his search and, after getting approval from his board to hire Shivers, told everyone he wanted to give "a Christmas present to the fans of the Saskatchewan Roughriders." Shivers didn't believe race played any role in his hiring. "I don't think so, but Thurgood Marshall said snakes come in many colours." Shivers' first hiring was an assistant general manager, Bob Vespaziani, a white man who had worked for 21 years as a coach in the CFL. They had built a friendship together in Calgary, so Shivers brought him in to handle the team's business affairs, a move that shocked the Roughriders' board of directors when it was announced at a media conference. Neither Shivers nor Vespaziani had any experience handling business affairs, so many of the GM's monetary tasks were ultimately handled by the directors and accountants. Shivers initially handled most of the contractual negotiations with players, while Vespaziani busied himself with the team's schedule-making process and later stepped back onto the field where he could fulfill his passion by coaching Saskatchewan's defensive linemen. The front-office shakeup created mayhem among the team's experienced staff, causing several resignations, but Shivers and Vespaziani were certain they were setting up a franchise model that would rival Calgary's, so they soldiered on.

Photo courtesy of *Leader-Post*

Roy Shivers

Shivers' next hiring also had no experience at being a CFL head coach, but Shivers had seen Danny Barrett when they were together in B.C. and Calgary. He believed Barrett was ready to don the headset. Shivers didn't really consider hiring anybody else, but he did speak with R.D. Lancaster, a CFL assistant coach and son of the Roughriders legend. Barrett, a Boynton Beach, Florida, product who attended the University of Cincinnati before spending 13 seasons as a CFL quarterback (although early in his career he also got pressed into duty as a slotback and defensive back) with four teams, had worked only as an assistant coach when he signed a three-year deal to be Saskatchewan's head coach on January 28, 2000. Barrett was 38. Black. Race played a role in Barrett's hiring. "I was always taught that when you go through a door you should pull someone with you," said Shivers. "My father would have turned over in his grave if I didn't hire a man of colour. The only thing Danny is lacking is opportunity. And if I don't give it to him, who will?" They became the first all-black management team in professional football, a newsworthy event by U.S. standards but largely ignored in Canada. Indeed, when Barrett and his friend, Mike (Pinball) Clemons, who became Toronto's head coach later in the season, coached against each other, it would be the first meeting of African-American head coaches in a major, professional football game. Clemons was a player-coach for that first meeting. Barrett and Clemons subsequently spoke about how much they would like to meet in a Grey Cup, so a black man could achieve another goal, winning a CFL championship as a head coach (which Clemons did in 2004). "Down the road a few years this may be an outstanding moment," Barrett said. "Pinball will be dressed out (in uniform), so it might take away a little of the impact that there are two black head coaches."

Photo courtesy of *Leader-Post*

Danny Barrett

Upon his hiring, Barrett retained two assistant coaches from the previous staff, Richie Hall (defensive backs) and Alex Smith (linebackers), plus he hired defensive co-ordinator Gary Etcheverry, offensive line coach Bill Dobson and quarterbacks coach Harold Smith. Barrett decided that he would be the team's offensive co-ordinator so he could make sure his philosophy was properly integrated. Barrett relished the idea of being a teacher, the fatherly veteran with quarterbacking experience who could impart his knowledge to the young players, particularly Henry Burris, a strong-armed, outgoing quarterback the Roughriders would woo away as a free agent from Calgary. Indeed, Burris was the team's first big acquisition after the arrivals of Barrett and Shivers. Shivers also enticed flamboyant linebacker Anthony McClanahan to leave the Stampeders, a move that backfired early in Saskatchewan's training camp when the linebacker's chronic neck problems forced him to retire (and get paid for the season).

Photo courtesy of *Leader-Post*

Roy Shivers

Opinionated, candid, articulate, intelligent, street-smart and flamboyant, Shivers was a Vietnam War veteran who had played NFL football as a running back/returner with the St. Louis Cardinals. In Regina he would often wear blue jeans, dreadlocks and sometimes have a toothpick in his mouth, a sharp contrast to the white-bread nature of the football team's supporters. Shivers had years ago wanted to be a football coach and worked at it for a while, but because of his ability to assess players he switched to personnel. An aficionado of jazz music and U.S. history who had gone to school in Oakland, California, with founders of the Black Panther Party, Shivers never shied away from meeting the Roughriders' supporters or from returning their calls. "If you don't want to hear the answer," he said, "don't ask me the question." So he was asked about his new team's potential. Replied Shivers: "I was feeling OK today, but then I looked at our team's depth chart and I got sick."

That was about to change. When tailback Mike Saunders, who led the team in all-purpose yardage the previous season, and receiver Curtis Mayfield, the team leader with 12 touchdown catches, announced their retirements early in 2000, they were the 13th and 14th departures from the previous year's squad. Their retirements were unexpected because, to the chagrin of Shivers and Vespaziani, both players cashed contract bonuses days before retiring. The anticipated signing of free-agent defensive lineman Steve Anderson fell apart – even though a press conference had been called – when there wasn't a Riders staffer available to get the ex-Stampeder a contract written up. Anderson instead bolted for B.C. Receiver Reggie Jones (San Diego) and defensive back Todd McMillon (Chicago) joined NFL teams as per the agreement that allowed CFL players to leave entering the option years of their contracts. The Roughriders dumped troubled quarterback Reggie Slack, who later claimed he was owed money, said he was moving to Winnipeg to work in the financial world, joined the Montreal Alouettes, retired without playing and would resurface two years later with the Argonauts. Linebacker Willie Pless, a one-season acquisition from Edmonton, was let go, as were veteran linebacker Dan Rashovich and receiver Don Narcisse, who had caught at least one pass in every one of the 216 games he played for Saskatchewan. "I can't say retire, I just can't," said Narcisse, who would end up retiring and being feted at an early season barbecue. Quarterback Steve Sarkisian, defensive back Glenn Rogers, defensive end Neal Smith, who unexpectedly left during camp, and linebacker Ken Benson were among the departees. So was newly signed quarterback Keith Smith, who fled after attending the first workout of training camp while his girlfriend huddled nearby in the freezing rain at the University of Saskatchewan's fields in Saskatoon. Smith and his new teammates were miserable during that first morning because the U of S cafeteria had failed to provide the players with breakfast – a foreboding start for the new squad. Or else Smith had found out that the average salary for a CFL player was $43,776 (Cdn) in 1999 and quarterback Damon Allen, then in the 16th of his 23 seasons, was getting paid $340,000, an amount that didn't break any of the league's unenforceable salary rules, according to CFL president/CEO Jeff Giles. By the end of the season Giles would be gone, having been replaced as commissioner with Michael Lysko by the finicky CFL governors.

Under their previous general manager, Alan Ford, the Roughriders had been forthright with their roster and happily showed how they were trying to abide by the salary cap, a rule that had been implemented to help the community-owned team compete with the richer owners of the privately owned teams in Toronto, Montreal and Vancouver. Shivers, Barrett and Vespaziani were more secretive, sometimes not announcing their roster moves, only revealing a new player's identity if pressed on the subject and trying to hold discreet workouts for their rookies.

There were 19 newcomers on Saskatchewan's roster for its 2000 season opener against the Toronto Argonauts, who were coached by CFL newcomer John Huard. Deploying a double tight-end offence and switching quarterbacks willy-nilly from Jimmy Kemp to Jay Barker, the Argonauts beat the Roughriders 36-28 before 20,995 fans at Taylor Field. The Roughriders lost their next two games, 30-28 in B.C. when Henry Burris threw four interceptions, and 40-34 in Hamilton, where they gained only 15 rushing yards and the five rookie DBs in Richie Hall's secondary were scorched for 479 passing yards.

Shivers publicly guaranteed his new team would beat his old team, Calgary, in their next meeting, but all they got was a 52-52 tie. The teams played overtime and the Stampeders had taken a 52-49 lead when Barrett, not realizing that his team had already earned a point in the standings because of the regulation-time tie, sent Paul McCallum to kick a game-tying, 37-yard field goal on the final possession of overtime. "I would have done nothing different," Barrett said when quizzed about the nonsensical move, which extended the Roughriders' winless skein to 13 games, their longest in 40 years.

"Barrett, not realizing that his team had already earned a point in the standings because of the regulation-time tie, sent Paul McCallum to kick a game-tying, 37-yard field goal. "I would have done nothing different," Barrett said when quizzed about the nonsensical move.

Losses followed against Montreal (62-7), Hamilton (29-23) and Edmonton (28-22), dropping the Roughriders to 0-6-1. When new receiver Darryl Hobbs had two passes taken away from him by defensive backs in the late stages of the last two losses, he was cut in a rare demonstration of retribution by Barrett. The Roughriders, dating back to the previous regime, were winless in 16 games, second-worst in CFL history to Hamilton's 20-game winless skid in the 1940s. The Roughriders had also lost 14 straight road games when they gave their new coach his first victory, a 30-28 decision in Edmonton. Typical of Barrett's tenure, the Roughriders followed with a hot streak, winning their Labour Day Classic 38-29 at home against the Blue Bombers and dropping the visiting Lions 28-20 in a game that B.C. quarterback Damon Allen convinced the officials to assess a penalty to the Roughriders' Pep Band for playing too loudly after his team broke its offensive huddle. Barrett's squad followed with a victory over Clemons' Argos, 44-17 in Toronto, before losing to Calgary (40-17), in Winnipeg (38-30) and in Calgary (28-19). On the day the Roughriders visited Calgary, SaskEnergy, a Crown corporation, announced there would be a 27 per cent increase in gas prices to its consumers inside Saskatchewan; hours later SaskEnergy president Ron Clark (a future Riders president) was entertaining TransGas clients in a $15,000 suite at Calgary's McMahon Stadium. Future Saskatchewan premier Brad Wall, then the opposition critic for Crown Corporations, said with his tongue firmly in his cheek, "This gives new meaning to (the promotional slogan) Huddle Up, Saskatchewan!"

Photo courtesy of Royal Studios

Omarr Morgan

The Roughriders were 4-9-1, with an outside chance at making the playoffs, as they prepared to meet the visiting Lions. Two days before that game, Riders receiver Curtis Marsh, who was leading the CFL in yardage, got into a scuffle during practice with defensive back Antoine Hunter and stomped off the field. Barrett told reporters his mercurial star had "personal issues," which turned out to be $70,000 (US) in unpaid child-support payments to a former partner in Florida. She had found him through legal channels and was trying to get the money she was owed. Marsh never spoke about the issue, but three days after the Riders lost 39-15 he publicly apologized for disrupting his teammates. Barrett promptly closed his team's locker room to the media, except for post-game interviews. A 39-22 loss to Montreal cost the Roughriders the services of Henry Burris and his wild touchdown-to-interception ratio (30-25) for the rest of the season. Journeyman Marvin Graves became the starting quarterback. Graves led the Roughriders to a 54-52 overtime victory in Edmonton and through a bizarre 27-26 loss in B.C., which featured a tribute to retiring Lions punter/kicker Lui Passaglia. A computer malfunction caused a 22-minute power outage inside domed B.C. Place Stadium and, later, Passaglia was put into the game as quarterback, from where he was awarded a rushing touchdown even though it appeared as if he hadn't crossed the goal line. The Roughriders' outrage couldn't change the fact they were 5-12-1 and out of the CFL playoffs for the third straight year. It didn't help that the team allowed a CFL-high 133 rushing yards per game and 626 points, most in the league. Guard Andrew Greene, part of an offensive line that helped tailback Darren Davis rush for 1,024 yards in 12 games, and linebacker George White (rookie) were West Division nominees for players-of-the-year, plus they were chosen as all-stars, along with Marsh and defensive tackle Demetrious Maxie.

Photo courtesy of Royal Studios

Curtis Marsh

There were hardly any blinks when quarterback Henry Burris, who was entering the option year of his Riders contract, started looking at NFL options before the 2001 season. Defensive tackle Demetrious Maxie had already left Saskatchewan for the NFL, signing with the Chicago Bears. Defensive tackle Scott Schultz, a Moose Jaw product who attended the University of North Dakota and became Saskatchewan's first overall draft choice, signed with the San Diego Chargers. The Roughriders' draft choices also included slotback Jason French and offensive lineman Jocelyn Frenette, both of whom would become important members of the team. Slotback Eric Guliford and kicker Paul McCallum would join teams in the Xtreme Football League, a made-for-TV league financed (for its lone season) by the World Wrestling Federation. XFL teams were paying salaries of $45,000, roughly the average salary of a CFL player. The notion of losing Burris was mentioned repeatedly at the team's annual meeting, whose attendees heard Barrett say, "We're going to get into the playoffs." The financial report revealed the team had earned $3.655 million in gate receipts but still lost $70,000 in 2000, increasing its deficit to $2.518 million. Mike Lysko, the CFL's new commissioner, revealed that five of the eight teams exceeded the $2.128-million salary cap, but no punishments would be meted out. And the future was brighter for the Roughriders, who were slated to play host to the 2003 Grey Cup game. Grey Cup president Marty Klyne vowed the festival would make at least $500,000 for the Roughriders.

After three seasons as a novice passer in Calgary, Burris had become a starter upon joining the Roughriders and completed 308 of 576 passes for 4,647 yards with 25 interceptions and 30 touchdowns in 2000. As a player entering the option year of his CFL contract, Burris drew interest from 15 NFL teams, but the Green Bay Packers recruited him as the latest potential replacement for legendary Brett Favre. Said Barrett: "You know my feelings towards Henry. It feels like one of my children just left." Having already replaced two coaches, defensive co-ordinator Gary Etcheverry and Bill Dobson, who joined the B.C. Lions, Barrett was ready to promote Marvin Graves into Burris' spot, based on the former's late-season performance. Of the five quarterbacks on Saskatchewan's roster, including the re-appearing Keith Smith, only Graves had played in the CFL. Graves got a new contract. The new coaches were defensive line coach Ron Estay, a former all-star defensive lineman in the CFL, receivers coach Tim Kearse, who had played for the team in the 1980s, and offensive line coach Marcel Bellefeuille, who had led the University of Ottawa to a Vanier Cup championship the year before.

Photo courtesy of Royal Studios

Henry Burris

Long-time assistant Richie Hall, a close friend of Barrett's, became the defensive co-ordinator while Barrett remained offensive co-ordinator. The biggest offseason acquisition was defensive back Eddie Davis, a solid citizen, outstanding performer and a free-agent from Calgary who was brought in to stabilize the inexperienced defensive backfield. The Roughriders were hoping defensive end Shont'e Peoples could also help with maturity. They were right about Eddie Davis, anyway.

The team assembled for its training camp at the University of Saskatchewan – minus all-star receiver Curtis Marsh, who missed an early workout to force a negotiated upgrade to his $55,000 salary – with a noticeable swagger, an attitude that was mentioned repeatedly during the upcoming season. "We do have a little swagger," said linebacker George White. "That's because we know what we're capable of." Slotback Dan Farthing tore a hamstring during workouts, leaving the Roughriders with only 13 players on their 39-man, opening-day roster who were with the team in 1999. The marketing slogan was "Loud and Proud!" It referred to the team's fans, but it could have referenced the players.

Playing before 23,421 fans in their season opener, Marsh, evidently a reinstated part of the team's family atmosphere, caught seven passes for 132 yards and two touchdowns as the Roughriders beat Hamilton 30-28. "What we have here is real," said Barrett. "We have a real camaraderie." The Roughriders lost their next game, 13-11 in Edmonton, won 12-7 in B.C., and lost their next four – 50-24 against Toronto (which featured a late-game punch-up between Saskatchewan's Demetris Bendross and Toronto's Adrion Smith); 32-14 in Winnipeg (because of five Riders turnovers); 35-4 against Calgary; and 37-13 in Calgary. The Roughriders coaches had expected Graves to show the prowess he had displayed as a late-season starter in 2000, but he was missing open receivers. After the Roughriders went seven quarters without scoring an offensive touchdown, Graves was replaced later during the hometown loss against the Stampeders by rookie Kevin Glenn. Graves started the loss in Calgary, completing only 14 of 30 passes for 169 yards with one interception. Sharing a taxi to the Calgary International Airport the following morning with two reporters, Graves spoke quietly about his poor play. "My neck is sore, too," said Graves, who would never play another CFL game and would finish the season on Saskatchewan's nine-game injury list after having a spot discovered on one of his lungs. "The Saskatchewan fans deserve better. I didn't play the way I should have and didn't give them the performance they deserved. I wish I could come back here and give the Riders what I should have. I've had injuries before, but never an injury that makes me miss the rest of the season. Or ends my career."

Glenn became the starter, although he would sometimes get hurt badly enough to let Keith Smith take over. The Roughriders won 14-11 in Toronto before losing 20-18 against Winnipeg and 31-3 to Montreal. Their 3-7 record was easy to explain: The Riders had scored just 13 offensive touchdowns in 10 games. Somewhere during that span the Roughriders posed for one of their regular team photographs, except the players

Photo courtesy of *Leader-Post*

Kevin Glenn

were wearing black jerseys! Sacrilege, apparently. An informal campaign to stop the Roughriders from wearing black emerged throughout the community, with former team president Tom Shepherd being one of the most outspoken critics. It dissuaded the Roughriders from wearing the black jerseys for their Labour Day Classic against Winnipeg. Formed in 1910, the Roughriders began wearing red and black sweaters in 1912, but switched to the more familiar green and white colours in 1948 after an executive member found a good deal on jerseys. Silver was added to the scheme in 1985. Black was never part of the equation, until Shivers spent $25,000 to purchase the set of third jerseys. It was only a matter of time until they were again taken out of their boxes, but a bigger concern was on the horizon.

On September 11, 2001, the entire world was shaken by terror attacks that resulted in four U.S. planes being hijacked and crashed – two were flown into New York's World Trade Center, one crashed into the Pentagon and another, thanks to the heroic efforts of its passengers, plunged into an empty field. Airports across the world were closed. Regina's airport was left virtually empty, but the Roughriders were supposed to leave two days later for a September 14 game in Calgary. They chartered buses while the world reacted to the events. Canadian Prime Minister Jean Chretien declared a day of mourning. Major League Baseball and the National Football League suspended their schedules through the weekend. CFL commissioner Mike Lysko waffled, initially believing his league's games should go as scheduled before being pressured into deciding they would be postponed. His decision came too late for the Roughriders. Although planes were again flying out of Regina on September 13, most of them eerily empty, the team took a nine-hour bus trip. "This is a relative inconvenience compared to everything else," said veteran offensive lineman Gene Makowsky, a bit of a non-flying fan anyway. But the team had to live in its downtown Calgary hotel for three extra days as the game was being rescheduled. The players, used to bringing only a T-shirt, jeans and a change of underwear to go with their dress-up-for-the-plane clothes, were seeking nearby laundromats and changing their per diems into quarters. "We're the only CFL team on the road right now and that's unfair," said Riders defensive back Omar Evans. "We shouldn't have left Regina until everything was settled." The game was postponed until Monday, September 17. Beforehand the U.S. national anthem was played and the American players were introduced. Calgary won 21-14. The Roughriders won a few concessions from the CFL, getting their expenses

"

On September 11, 2001, the entire world was shaken by terror attacks that resulted in four U.S. planes being hijacked and crashed – two were flown into New York's World Trade Center, one crashed into the Pentagon ...

covered and getting their next home game pushed back one day from Saturday to Sunday, September 23. They still lost 17-15 to the Lions; during the game Smith was sidelined with a concussion.

The black uniforms made their debut in Saskatchewan's next game, September 29 against the visiting Eskimos. Smith was OK to play, but Curtis Marsh's short CFL career was ending because of knee surgery. The Roughriders lost 35-19. With a 3-10 record the Roughriders travelled to Montreal, where they had lost 13 straight games. But they didn't allow a touchdown and won 13-7. A 29-26 loss against Calgary and a 30-24 defeat in Hamilton, during which Smith and offensive tackle John Terry suffered torn Achilles tendons, ended the team's playoff aspirations for a fourth straight season, even though they reeled off a 12-3 win in Edmonton and an astounding 42-10, regular season-capping victory in Vancouver. "Understand that our record is not indicative of our team," said linebacker Jackie Mitchell. "Teams don't like to play against us."

With their 6-12 record the Roughriders would have again earned the first overall draft choice in 2002, but they had dealt it away to select offensive lineman Andrew Moore in the 2001 supplemental draft. Moore spent two injury-plagued seasons with the Roughriders, who could have instead used that choice to draft University of Regina slotback Jason Clermont. That oversight became a contentious issue that would be thrown back at Shivers for years. In the off-season the Roughriders announced that ticket prices would increase $2 per game for 2002.

Photo courtesy of *Leader-Post*

Gene Makowsky stretches before practice

After a season in which his team led the CFL offensively in rushing yards and was last in passing yards, Riders head coach Danny Barrett was again hinting that he would give up the offensive co-ordinator's position. All six assistant coaches returned – Richie Hall, Alex Smith, Ron Estay, Marcel Bellefeuille, Harold Smith and Tim Kearse – with Hall, the defensive co-ordinator, getting a promotion to assistant head coach. But nobody was named o.c. The biggest shakeup still came on offence, when tailback Darren Davis re-signed with the team and was promptly dealt, along with offensive lineman Dan Comiskey, to the Edmonton Eskimos for quarterback Nealon Greene and fullback Simon Baffoe. "I guess that's what this business is all about," said Davis. "You get somewhere you like, you get traded. The Riders wanted Nealon Greene and Edmonton wasn't going to give him up for nothing."

On the defensive line, the Riders added free-agent Ray Jacobs from Calgary but lost two other tackles when Demetrious Maxie joined the Buffalo Bills and Scott Schultz had a short tryout with the Pittsburgh Steelers. They were the 10th and 11th players the Roughriders had lost because of the CFL/NFL agreement. They waived unpredictable receiver Curtis Marsh and subsequently dumped slotback/returner Eric Guliford, who was trying to become the top receiver in several ways. "I want Curtis Marsh's money," said Guliford, while negotiating his contract. Replied Shivers: "We're looking to replace Eric anyway. Why should we sign a 30-something-year-old receiver who hasn't played a full season in three years?" Another veteran receiver was on his way out, evidently, when

"I want Curtis Marsh's money," said Guliford, while negotiating his contract. Replied Shivers: "We're looking to replace Eric anyway. Why should we sign a 30-something-year-old receiver who hasn't played a full season in three years?"

Roger Aldag and Ray Elgaard were being inducted into the Canadian Football Hall of Fame. Aldag had played 253 games for the Roughriders, including 250 straight, from 1976-92 and was five times a CFL all-star and twice the league's outstanding offensive lineman. "It means a lot to me being inducted with Ray."

There were few changes to the 39-man roster after training camp ended in Saskatoon. That was a hallmark of Barrett's tenure – few surprises – and it was certainly going to be that way as he and Shivers approached the final seasons of their three-year contracts.

Shivers was asked at the team's annual general meeting about the status of slotback Dan Farthing, who had played the previous season with a pulled groin and a broken ankle (which hadn't been properly diagnosed). "It may be time (for Farthing) to try something else," said Shivers. That shocked Farthing, who said, "I was a little surprised to hear it, but at this point in my career I guess it is something I have to consider." Farthing retired soon after it was announced that two of his former teammates, Roger Aldag and Ray Elgaard, were being inducted into the Canadian Football Hall of Fame. Aldag had played 253 games for the Roughriders, including 250 straight, from 1976-92 and was five times a CFL all-star and twice the league's outstanding offensive lineman. "It means a lot to me being inducted with Ray," said Aldag. "We both played for one team for our whole careers and it would be nice to hoist a Grey Cup one day. We got to do that, but we were no more important than anyone else on that team." Elgaard, a member of Saskatchewan's 1989 Grey Cup champions, retired in 1996 after a 14-year career in which he became the CFL's all-time leading receiver (830 catches for 13,198 yards). "I always thought those were the most important things: To be respected internally, by the people you play with. But this is pretty special, too." The year's Plaza of Honor inductees were also announced: Bobby Jurasin, Gary Brandt and Larry Bird.

The Roughriders' annual meeting had a familiar timbre as a loss of $130,000 was announced from the previous campaign. That increased the team's debt to $2.741 million, dangerously close to the $3-million mark that had often been predicted as the fatal number by Tom Shepherd, a long-time treasurer whose 22-year tenure as a Riders director came to an end. Shepherd remained as president of Friends of the Riders, a non-profit organization established to help raise money for the community-owned team. The reason for the losses was a drop in attendance (to 22,100 per game from 24,300 in 2000), which caused gate receipts to fall to $3.54 million from $3.65 million. The Roughriders abided by the $2.28-million salary cap, plus they received $937,000 in league revenues, helped by an initial share of the franchise fee paid by the new owners of the expansion team in Ottawa. That was about the only good news from the CFL, where commissioner Mike Lysko was embroiled in a scrap with Toronto Argonauts owner Sherwood Schwarz, who was enraged about unflattering comments made by Lysko. Other owners were upset about the commissioner's handling of the September 11 weekend and a drop in league sponsorships. The Roughriders supported Lysko, but that was irrelevant when he got fired 15 months into his term and replaced on an interim basis by power-hungry B.C. Lions owner David Braley. "There is not one defining moment (for Lysko's ouster)," said Riders president Tom Robinson, who had another year remaining on his term until newly elected vice-president Ron Clark was scheduled to replace him. "We've just gone through a bad patch of highway and reached a point where it was irreconcilable."

The Roughriders tried to make a trade during the CFL draft, which perhaps would have given them an opportunity to select University of Regina product Jason Clermont, who went fourth overall to the B.C. Lions. Nothing materialized, leaving the Roughriders to select Laval offensive lineman Francois Bouliane 15th overall and later choose St. Mary's receiver Patrick Thibeault and Manitoba defensive back Darnell Edwards. Saskatchewan's other acquisition was slotback Quincy Jackson, a free agent whose contract with Edmonton had been voided because of a deal he had with the Arena Football League. There were few changes to the 39-man roster after training camp ended in Saskatoon. That was a hallmark of Barrett's tenure – few surprises – and it was certainly going to be that way as he and Shivers approached the final seasons of their three-year contracts.

The Roughriders opened their season with a 30-27 victory in Ottawa and followed with a 32-21 win over Calgary, sparked by two touchdowns apiece from receiver Derick Armstrong and multi-purpose back Corey Holmes. A 26-20 loss followed in Montreal, where the Riders rarely won. But with a 17-carry, 128-yard performance from tailback Sedrick Shaw they rebounded by shellacking the Eskimos 45-11. The Roughriders lost four of their next five games – 26-21 in Calgary; 34-31 in Hamilton followed by a 30-14 victory to complete the home-and-home set; 18-10 in Toronto and 23-9 against the Alouettes. The Roughriders had 149 offensive yards against Montreal. "Horrible, horrible offensively," said Barrett, the offensive co-ordinator. Quarterbacks Nealon Greene (hamstring) and Kevin Glenn (thumb) were sidelined with injuries for the Labour Day Classic, so Rocky Butler got his first start against the Blue Bombers. He ran for two touchdowns in Saskatchewan's 33-19 victory. Wearing their black jerseys, the Roughriders defeated the visiting Argonauts 40-11 – which caused Toronto head coach Gary Etcheverry to be replaced by Mike (Pinball) Clemons. In their road whites, the Riders lost 31-25 in Edmonton to drop their record to 6-6. Only 20,098 fans saw the home team defeat the expansion Ottawa Renegades 29-11. The team was facing some external upheaval as it dropped a 35-32 overtime decision in Winnipeg. Linebacker K.D. Williams, in his second stint with the team, played two games and left for Winnipeg. Defensive tackle Ray Jacobs was missing because of "personal problems," according to Barrett. And when the Blue Bombers tried claiming linebacker George White, who had returned uninjured from the NFL's Green Bay Packers, off Saskatchewan's waived/injured list, Barrett called the move "underhanded" and closed practices to the media. "We need to be able to do things that not everyone knows about," said the head coach. Saskatchewan lost 20-11 in Winnipeg, but followed with a monumental, 13-11 victory against B.C. That assured the Roughriders of their first playoff berth since 1997. They lost 27-21 in Edmonton and 38-3 in B.C. to complete their season. With an 8-10-2-0 record (includes two overtime losses), the Roughriders placed fourth in the West and were en route to what everyone considered the easier playoff path, as a wild-card qualifier in the East. They were visiting the 8-10-0-0 Toronto Argonauts, whose quarterback had been the pivot in Saskatchewan's last playoff game five years earlier – Reggie Slack. The Argonauts had won the last three games of their regular season. The Roughriders suffered their ninth straight road loss, blowing a 12-0 lead and falling 24-14 in the East semifinal. "That road stuff's a pile of shit," said Riders defensive tackle Nate Davis. "I don't think it's tough to win any game. It was just our lack of making plays. It's a disappointing season. We finished under .500, didn't get a home playoff game, then we lost in the playoffs to a team we had no business losing to." Corey Holmes, Derick Armstrong and cornerback Omarr Morgan were later named CFL all-stars,

Photo courtesy of Royal Studios

Corey Holmes

with Holmes getting the added distinction of being chosen as the league's outstanding special teams player.

Following the season, Shivers signed a new three-year contract and he hastily re-signed Barrett, who promptly announced that Marcel Bellefeuille would replace him as the offensive co-ordinator. "I want to be a part of something from Day One until we can look back in 10 years and see what we accomplished," said Barrett. "That there's a finality to it." There was optimism for the upcoming year because the 2003 Grey Cup was being played in Regina. Ticket sales were booming because of an arrangement that gave first dibs on Grey Cup tickets to season-ticket holders. The Roughriders desperately wanted to be the home team.

Money was again a pressing issue with the CFL and the Roughriders. The team actually made money in 2002 – sparked by record-high gate receipts of $4.2 million, a profit of $220,000 was announced at its annual meeting – and there was more financial optimism because the pending 2003 Grey Cup game at Taylor Field would likely reap a $1 million bonus. By April, 12, 5,000 season tickets had already been sold, an increase of 3,700 from the year before. And 70 per cent of the Grey Cup tickets were sold before the season began, at prices of $119, $159 and $189. The league also had a new television deal in place, a five-year pact with TSN and CBC that would bring the CFL about $9.5 million annually, an increase of $2 million. All of the Riders' away games would be televised within Saskatchewan, basically serving as three-hour commercials, plus the TV deal specified that the province-wide blackout had to be lifted for two of their televised home games. The influx of money evidently spurred some teams more than others, as B.C. signed quarterback Dave Dickenson for a reported annual salary of $400,000, a pretty big chunk of their (supposed) $2.5 million salary cap.

> The Riders lost 6-foot-2, 195-pound wideout Derick Armstrong, who had led the Roughriders and was fourth among CFL receivers in 2002 with 70 catches for 1,104 yards and five touchdowns. He signed with the NFL's Houston Texans.

The Riders lost 6-foot-2, 195-pound wideout Derick Armstrong, who had led the Roughriders and was fourth among CFL receivers in 2002 with 70 catches for 1,104 yards and five touchdowns. He signed with the NFL's Houston Texans. Roy Shivers sought replacement players at a variety of free-agent camps he slated throughout the U.S., plus he acquired receiver Travis Moore and linebacker Chris Hoople from Calgary for a draft choice. The Riders drafted St. Francis Xavier linebacker Mike McCullough 23rd overall; he made the team during training camp at the University of Regina.

While seven free agents departed, including Calgary-bound linebacker George White and defensive tackle Sheldon Napastuk, kicker Paul McCallum got into a contract tussle with Shivers, a scrap that ended only after Barrett smoothed out the details. The player McCallum had replaced on the Roughriders, Dave Ridgway, was among the inductees into the Canadian Football Hall of Fame, along with Riders defensive line coach Ron Estay, who had been a defensive end with the B.C. Lions and Edmonton Eskimos. From 1982-95, Ridgway played 238 games and was the league's most accurate kicker, making 78 per cent (574 of 736) of his field goals. He also held records for the longest field goal (60 yards), the most in a game (eight) and the most consecutive (28), plus he was best remembered for making a 35-yarder that lifted Saskatchewan to a 43-40 victory over the Hamilton Tiger-Cats in the 1989 Grey Cup game. "I was asked if I thought I was being inducted because of the kick," said Ridgway. "I said, 'I hope not.' I hope it's because of seven divisional all-star selections and some other things I might have accomplished." Cup-winning wideout Don Narcisse, former president John Lipp and defensive back Larry Dumelie, the 22nd member of the 1966 Grey Cup champions to be inducted, were enshrined in the Plaza of Honor.

Plagued by hamstring and hip injuries in 2002, quarterback Nealon Greene was expected to be Saskatchewan's key weapon when the Riders opened the season in Toronto. "We've got to start galloping and start getting to the front of the pack," said Greene. "The only way we can do that – especially me – is to stay healthy." Toronto was having its own problems; the city was under a SARS (severe acute respiratory syndrome) scare and travellers were being warned to stay away from Hogtown. The team doctors said the players had no cause for concern, unless they had to visit a hospital. There were rumblings that the game might be cancelled after Argonauts owner Sherwood Schwarz confessed his finances were tied up in family matters, probably because he didn't want to add to the $10 million in losses he had suffered since taking ownership of the team in 2001. The CFL assumed ownership of the Argonauts and later, again, of the Hamilton Tiger-Cats, with commissioner Tom Wright ultimately finding stable owners for both franchises – Howard Sokolowski and David Cynamon took over in Toronto, Bob Young in Hamilton. Former Riders GM Al Ford served as Hamilton's interim general manager after owners George Grant and David Macdonald were out of the equation.

Defensive tackle Ray Jacobs again went missing on the Roughriders. His absence was said to be caused by migraines. Marcus (Chunky) Adams was a last-minute replacement for Jacobs, who actually was appearing in court that day to explain why he hadn't made child support payments. Jacobs wouldn't rejoin the Roughriders after he confessed to having "binge-drinking" problems. A tribunal of teammates, appointed by Barrett, decided that Jacobs couldn't be trusted. He was dealt to the B.C. Lions, falling out of favour the next season when he was charged with drug possession near a house of ill repute. Defensive end Shont'e Peoples, who was on Barrett's tribunal, had an interesting resume: He had been charged with shooting at a police officer during his college days, was later charged with marijuana possession while visiting Saskatoon, and had to make amends for missing curfew on a road trip. When that news broke following Saskatchewan's regular-season trip to Montreal, guess what Barrett did – he convinced the players to vote against conducting media interviews.

The Roughriders pulled out an amazing, 20-18 victory in their opener, with Greene tossing last-minute touchdowns of six yards and 53 yards to little-used receiver Corey Grant. It was the only offensive flourish the team produced. Barrett believed his faith in Greene was being rewarded, but the decision to not pull Greene would be detrimental as the season progressed. "At some point we considered if we should make a move (and replace Greene with Kevin Glenn)," Barrett said. "We decided it wasn't the quarterback's fault. We believed in the young man and we wanted to give him his Opening Night." The Roughriders won their next game, 32-30 against the Lions, but lost their next two. They lost 32-31 against the Alouettes when Jeremaine Copeland caught a late-game touchdown pass, which was followed by a missed 35-yard field goal from Paul McCallum on the game's final play. Winnipeg's Troy Westwood kicked a 55-yard field goal to defeat the visiting Roughriders 29-27; Saskatchewan started Kevin Glenn because Greene had a sore shoulder and Roughriders linebacker Reggie Hunt set a CFL record in the game with 16 defensive tackles. Meanwhile, speculation was rampant that Henry Burris would

Photo courtesy of *Leader-Post*

Reggie Hunt

Photo courtesy of *Leader-Post*

Kenton Keith

be rejoining the Roughriders after being waived by the NFL's Chicago Bears.

Speedy tailback Kenton Keith debuted for the Riders in their next game, carrying 11 times for 88 yards and one touchdown in a 42-9 victory over Hamilton. The Roughriders followed with a 32-14 victory against Edmonton and a 27-11 win in Calgary, their first regular-season victory in Cowtown in 14 years. After losing 29-24 in Ottawa, there were many public debates about whether Greene or Burris, who had just rejoined the Roughriders, should be the starter. Barrett stayed with Greene and the Roughriders, who hadn't played in 11 days, beat the Renegades 51-41. Ottawa had lost 34-29 five days earlier in Winnipeg.

The CFL's schedule was disrupted by a huge, disastrous power outage that affected the Eastern seaboard and Eastern Canada. A Montreal-Hamilton game was delayed by one day while the Eskimos, who needed $30,000 in per diems to be hand-delivered by the commissioner during their extended stay in Toronto, had their game against the Argonauts delayed by two days. Edmonton rebounded nicely, beating the visiting Roughriders 49-31 in their next game while Greene struggled mightily, completing just seven of 15 passes for 68 yards with one interception. The Roughriders lost again, 36-18 to the Blue Bombers, with a crowd filling the temporary Grey Cup seats and helping 40,320 fans watch the Labour Day Classic. Greene struggled again. Saskatchewan beat B.C. 28-2 and headed to Hamilton, where the Ti-Cats were winless in 13 games. They beat Saskatchewan 27-24 in overtime; it was Hamilton's lone victory of 2003.

After losing 28-23 in Montreal and dealing with the aforementioned Peoples issue, the Roughriders charged from their locked practice field and blasted the visiting Argonauts 41-24. Glenn played quarterback, but Keith was the game star with 167 rushing yards and one touchdown. Corey Holmes added 264 all-purpose yards. "It was a week in which we had some situations, but we felt we dealt with them in the right manner, "said Barrett, whose team followed with back-to-back victories (24-22 and 34-6) against the Stampeders to improve its record to 10-7. "If anything came out of this, it's that the players realize they have to stick together." The Roughriders had a chance to place second in the West, provided they won their finale in B.C. Even though the game was garnering more attention than the upcoming provincial election – during which Premier Lorne Calvert's New Democratic Party was re-elected over Elwin Hermanson's Saskatchewan Party by winning 30 of the 58 seats available – the match wasn't on television. So Tom Shepherd, acting on behalf of Friends of the Riders Inc., brokered deals with Access Communications for broadcast time and TSN for technical people and announcers. The game was shown on a cable network throughout Saskatchewan. The Riders beat the Lions 26-23 and, with their 11-7 record, were tied for second with B.C. and Winnipeg, which had moved into the dominant position by beating the Edmonton Eskimos 34-30 in their final contest. Tie-breaking formats placed the Blue Bombers second, so they would play host to the West semifinal against third-place Saskatchewan. Any Saskatchewan-Winnipeg matchup is a good rivalry, but this one was stoked by Blue Bombers kicker Troy Westwood, who had described the Roughriders' fans as "banjo-pickin' inbreds." Westwood later explained himself and intentionally made the issue more explosive. "I was wrong to make such a statement and I apologize," said Westwood. "The vast majority of people in Saskatchewan have no idea how to play the banjo." Westwood stood alone on the sidelines of Canad Inns Stadium, listening to catcalls from Riders and Bombers fans, as the Roughriders got 14 carries for 130 yards and three touchdowns from Keith while winning the West semifinal 37-21. To be the home-town team for the Grey Cup, the Roughriders had to win the West final in Edmonton. Nealon Greene's former team had a 13-5 record, but the Roughriders were on a five-game winning streak and had legions of fans heading to the Alberta capital. Edmonton led 30-2 before Greene was replaced by Kevin Glenn, who helped the Roughriders score 21 points and narrow the gap to 30-23. Eskimos tailback Mike Pringle, the CFL's all-time rushing leader who had been cut by Montreal in the preseason, scored two touchdowns to put Edmonton into the championship game against the East-champion Alouettes. "I'd imagine in Saskatchewan it will be just like it is in this locker room," Riders fullback Chris Szarka said afterwards inside Commonwealth Stadium. "It's going to be a letdown."

Photo courtesy of *Leader-Post*

Kevin Glenn

Szarka was the West's top Canadian, but he would lose the CFL award during Grey Cup festivities to Montreal slotback Ben Cahoon. Andrew Greene, Saskatchewan's veteran guard, was chosen the league's outstanding offensive lineman over Montreal's Scott Flory, a Regina product who attended the University of Saskatchewan. Both teams were trying to win support from Saskatchewan's fans. Eskimos receiver Ed Hervey wore an "I Love Regina" T-shirt while Alouettes head coach Don Matthews, a former Riders coach, declared, "If I'm a Rider fan, I'm ticked at the Eskimos for knocking us out of the playoffs. We were cheering for the Riders. So their fans can come and cheer for us." The teams wanted to entice them away from Riderville 2003 at Exhibition Park, where the out-of-towners, who filled the city's 2,500 hotel rooms and any space available from a Home-Stay Hosts program, joined CFL commissioner Tom Wright and the locals while partying to music by Canadian bands Trooper, Harlequin, Streetheart and April Wine. Scores of tickets were available in the *Leader-Post*'s classified ad section. One of the biggest stories during the week was a *Calgary Herald* report claiming that new Stampeders president Ron Rooke was poised to hire Roy Shivers and Danny Barrett away from the Roughriders. Barrett pooh-poohed the idea when asked; Shivers demurred until after the Grey Cup, when it was revealed that the Riders brass discussed an offer from Rooke. "Either all of us went

Photo courtesy of *Leader-Post*

Chris Szarka

or none of us went," said Shivers. "The vote was very close." Barrett was also mentioned as a candidate to become the head coach at his alma mater, the University of Cincinnati.

A not-quite-sold-out crowd of 50,909 was inside Taylor Field for the Grey Cup game. The temperature was minus-4 Celsius and there was a 19 km-h wind. Eskimos quarterback Ricky Ray exploited Montreal's rookie-laden secondary and threw two touchdown passes to Jason Tucker, who was chosen the game's outstanding player. Playing host to the Grey Cup, which required 3,300 volunteers to organize the week's festivities, helped the Roughriders make $2.1 million. It was $600,000 more than estimated and $900,000 more than the team made from the 1995 Grey Cup. But the Riders needed the money because the league had drained $1 million to support the Toronto Argonauts and Hamilton Tiger-Cats. Another ticket increase was coming for Riders supporters: $1 per game for season tickets and $2 for individual tickets, increasing the top seat to $47 per contest.

Photo courtesy of Royal Studios

Matt Dominguez

After being spurned by Roy Shivers and Danny Barrett, who was nominated as a coach-of-the-year candidate along with Toronto's Mike Clemons and Edmonton's Grey Cup-winner Tom Higgins (the coach chosen to receive the Annis Stukus Trophy by the Football Reporters of Canada), the Calgary Stampeders made former CFL quarterback Matt Dunigan their head coach and general manager. Barrett retained his six assistant coaches in Saskatchewan, but early in the season he dispatched quarterbacks coach Harold Smith without any public explanation and replaced him with Sam Garza, a former CFL quarterback who earlier had a short stint as a Riders assistant. The Roughriders lost elsewhere, with receiver Matt Dominguez and tailback Kenton Keith joining the New York Jets, linebacker Terrence Melton signing with the Atlanta Falcons and offensive lineman Tango McCauley somehow getting a $100,000 signing bonus from the Dallas Cowboys. McCauley signed a five-year deal, but he didn't get to the Cowboys' training camp. Keith and Dominguez would return after being released. The Roughriders were one of the few teams who wanted out of the agreement that allowed NFL teams to sign players entering the option-years of their CFL contracts. Shivers noted that the Roughriders were not financially compensated for losing their players. The Roughriders were, however, like the other eight CFL teams in terms of following the league's $2.5-million salary cap. Nobody followed the cap and nobody was punished for violating it. "We look at it as a guideline," said Roughriders president Tom Robinson, who was in the midst of revamping the governance of the community-owned franchise. The top volunteer would no longer be the president. Instead, the chairman would be in charge of the board of directors and they would hire a full-time, paid president/chief executive officer. Ron Clark, formerly the vice-president, replaced Robinson and became the first chairman during the team's annual meeting. Clark was a volunteer.

The Roughriders were the last CFL team to have a full-time president, but they saw the wisdom in such a move after the community-owned Winnipeg Blue Bombers nearly eliminated their $5.4-million debt in the five years after hiring Lyle Bauer. The Roughriders also began selling shares for $250 apiece. Buyers were deemed as shareholders and were given a vote at the annual meeting. There was still virtually no way of overthrowing the volunteer board, something that was discussed whenever the Roughriders fell upon hard times, but the shares allowed for more participation from the fans and served as a fund-raising idea. Robinson hoped the shares would ultimately generate $5 million, but only 2,200 were sold in the first four months. Still, the Roughriders were making money. Helped by Grey Cup profits of $2.1 million, a payment of $637,000 from the CFL for television and marketing revenues and $5.2 million in gate receipts (generated by a team high, per-game average of 29,353 fans), the Roughriders made $27,000 in 2003. The team's directors boldly declared the Riders were "debt-free," but the franchise still had a $2.8-million loan that had to be repaid to the provincial government by 2014. Following a Grey Cup-induced sales frenzy that generated 17,000 season tickets being sold, the Roughriders still managed to sell 14,500 for 2004.

Before training camp opened at the University of Regina, the Roughriders drafted Villanova fullback Ducarmel Augustin sixth overall. They also signed undrafted tailback Neal Hughes from the University of Regina. Augustin lasted one season. Hughes developed into a solid CFLer. The team also traded quarterback Kevin Glenn to Toronto, which promptly shipped him to Winnipeg, a West rival. And offensive lineman Scott Flory, a Regina native, signed a free-agent pact with Saskatchewan before reconsidering and re-signing with Montreal. "Things came to light after I signed the contract," said Flory. "The relationship in Saskatchewan deteriorated." Flory never joined the Riders. Instead he was dealt back to Montreal for a first-round draft choice in 2005 and the Alouettes repaid his signing bonus, which was reported to be $25,000.

The team again opened its regular season on Toronto's bumpy artificial turf, but Nealon Greene's day was nothing like the year earlier. Two offensive series into the first quarter, Greene's left leg was broken in two places on a tackle by Argonauts linebacker Michael Fletcher. Rocky Butler replaced him because Henry Burris, the anointed backup, had a sprained ankle. Toronto won 21-10. Butler also played the home opener, throwing four interceptions in a 33-10 loss to the Stampeders. "It would be easy to . . . make excuses," said Barrett. "We're not going to do that. Some days you walk the dog, some days the dog walks you. Today the dog walked us. We just had the string in our hands."

Burris became the starter while Greene recuperated, leading Saskatchewan to a 42-29 victory over B.C. and a 32-15, turnover-filled loss in Winnipeg. Before improving to 2-4 with a 40-21 victory in Calgary, Barrett addressed the notion that he would be replaced as head coach. "If that's the direction they need to go, I'm OK with that," said Barrett, who still had the confidence of his general manager. Higher up there were changes, because chairman Ron Clark stepped aside. The CEO of SaskEnergy, a Crown corporation, Clark had been on

Photo courtesy of *Leader-Post*

Henry Burris

paid leave during a review of the company's creative compensation programs. Treasurer Garry Huntington, the Riders' vice-chair, replaced Clark and Tom Robinson re-assumed his role as governor. "There was no pressure, no votes," said Clark. "It was just from everybody's point of view a prudent thing to do. If somebody is harbouring any ill will toward me, I didn't want it in any way, shape or form to impair the football club."

The Riders beat the Tiger-Cats, jumping into a 23-0 lead before downing the visitors 33-24. They lost 24-20 in Montreal because Alouettes quarterback Anthony Calvillo passed for 410 yards, then rebounded with an ugly, 46-16 victory over the Stampeders in Regina. Dunigan accused Barrett of running up the score. "(Dunigan) needs to worry about his players," said Barrett. "They're poking guys in the eyes and stuff like that. If anything I'm frustrated because that's bush-league stuff. But that's not the story. The story is that we kicked their butt." A typical, mid-season swoon followed as the Roughriders lost 31-7 in Montreal, 17-4 in the Labour Day Classic against the Blue Bombers and 27-24 in the rematch. The game in Winnipeg was dubbed the "National Post Banjo Bowl." The Roughriders hated the idea, which was sparked by derogatory comments about Saskatchewan's fans by Winnipeg kicker Troy Westwood, but the winning team would take home $10,000 for its local United Way. Also true to form, the Roughriders compiled a winning streak, next beating the Tiger-Cats 32-30 in Hamilton's Ivor Wynne Stadium, which had been "Never Win Stadium" since 1997. They beat the Renegades back-to-back, dumping them 36-22 in Regina and 32-25 in Ottawa, to improve to 8-8. In the midst of a winning streak that would stretch to five games, Roughriders returner Emery Beckles and receiver Jamel Richardson were charged with assault from different incidents. It didn't slow the Riders, who got 146 rushing yards and two touchdowns from Kenton Keith in a 35-19 victory over the Alouettes. They clinched their third straight playoff berth by beating the Eskimos 40-16 before 30,087 fans at Taylor Field. One season-ending victory against the B.C. Lions would earn the Roughriders their first home playoff game since 1988 (and second since 1976). The Roughriders, would soon be under the direction of CEO/president Jim Hopson, were ready to purchase hosting rights to the playoff game from the CFL for about $1 million; the team could have conceivably made $300,000 by selling out its stadium. It would have been quite a splash for Hopson, an ex-Rider offensive lineman and Regina product who had been the director of education for the Qu'Appelle Valley School Division. The Lions didn't want it to happen. B.C. slotback Geroy Simon told reporters the Roughriders were a cocky bunch, boastful like Shivers and Barrett. "We want to shut them up," said Simon, whose team pulled out a 40-38 victory that kept the Roughriders marooned in third place and dashed their dreams of a home playoff game. B.C. won on an amazing last-play touchdown toss from backup quarterback Spergon Wynn to Simon,

Photo courtesy of Leader-Post

Jim Hopson

while Saskatchewan defensive backs Darnell Edwards and Santino Hall collided in the end zone.

The Riders' disappointment was tempered by what was happening outside the sports world, where the U.S. military was waging war in Iraq. U.S. President George W. Bush, who had just won re-election against Democratic challenger John Kerry, insisted Iraq president Saddam Hussein was stashing weapons of mass destruction inside the ravaged country. Such weapons were never found, but Hussein was captured and later executed for his actions.

Photo courtesy of *Leader-Post*

Nate Davis

The Roughriders were travelling to Edmonton for the West semifinal. Roughriders defensive tackle Nate Davis stoked the rivalry by claiming that some of the Eskimos couldn't play for his high school team and that the only good thing about the Alberta capital was a steak house across the street from the Roughriders' hotel. "I wasn't going to apologize for anything I said," said Davis, whose team upset the Eskimos 14-6 and earned a rematch in B.C. Barrett again clamped down on his players and prevented them from doing interviews with the B.C. media beforehand, so there were some happy reporters in the B.C. Place Stadium press box when the Lions defeated the visitors 27-25 in overtime. The Roughriders had again surrendered a late-game scoring drive that tied the contest 24-24. In overtime, the Roughriders marched to B.C.'s 11-yard line before setting up for an 18-yard field goal. A chip shot, right? Not exactly. McCallum missed the easy field goal, which went for a single point. On B.C.'s subsequent possession, Duncan O'Mahony made a 40-yard field goal that gave the Lions the victory. (B.C. would lose the Grey Cup to the Toronto Argonauts, but Lions slotback Jason Clermont was chosen the league's top Canadian and Riders tackle Gene Makowsky was the top offensive lineman.)

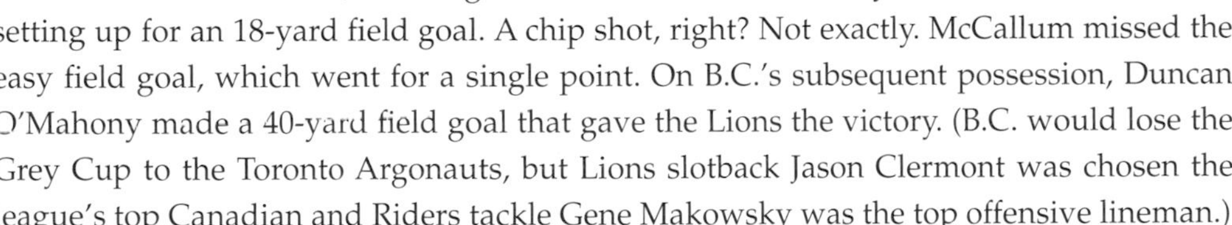

McCallum somberly conducted media interviews in an area beside the Roughriders' locker room. He didn't want to go in. "Shit, yeah," he said. "I don't want to face anybody. I let a lot of people down, especially the guys in this locker room." At McCallum's Regina home, misguided fans were driving past, scaring his wife and young daughters. Some people yelled nasty comments. Some threw objects. Somebody tried dumping manure on his driveway, but instead dumped it on a neighbour's driveway. "I can face the music," McCallum said. "I screwed up. I have to live with that forever, really. Who knows how long? For (my family) to have to deal with anything like this is ridiculous." Dozens of letters were written to the *Leader-Post*. Riders chairman Garry Huntington spoke on the matter: "Anyone convicted of these actions is no longer allowed in Taylor Field." Two people were charged with mischief under $5,000. Another was charged with uttering threats.

Riders quarterback Henry Burris was facing a different situation. He was coming off his best performance as a professional. Despite losing in Vancouver, Burris had completed 28 of 39 passes for 416 yards and three touchdowns. Stampeders president Ron Rooke stated publicly he wanted Burris, a free agent, to join his team. Barrett, who also did not have a contract for next season, knew Burris was pivotal for Saskatchewan's success. Shivers re-signed Barrett for two years (and an option year); the coach had a 39-50-1 record. Two of his assistants, Richie Hall and Marcel Bellefeuille, were candidates to become the Edmonton Eskimos' new head coach, a job that went to Edmonton assistant Danny Maciocia. Hall and Bellefeuille stayed with the Roughriders, who added a new coach for their offensive line, Carl Brennan. Riders wideout Matt Dominguez, who

Photo courtesy of *Leader-Post*

Henry Burris

had returned midseason from the New York Jets, signed a new contract and implored Burris to join him, to little avail.

Saskatchewan's psychotic football fans were making headlines in *Sports Illustrated*, the *New York Times*, *USA Today* and on CNN. Trying to dump manure on his driveway, threatening the family and egging the house of Roughriders kicker Paul McCallum – only because he had missed a crucial field goal in a CFL playoff game – evidently made Riders' fans worthy of ridicule across North America. Those fans were apparently more interested in the fate of the province's lone professional football team than they were in the disaster that had hit Asia in late December – a huge tsunami that resulted in 140,000 people dying or going missing.

Three of the Riders' misguided fans were charged with mischief or uttering threats, leading to them being found guilty when they appeared in court. Their actions may have played a small part in hurrying the departure of quarterback Henry Burris. Burris' contract was about to expire. As Burris and his agent began discussing contracts with Riders GM Roy Shivers, he mentioned the uneasiness of playing before such rabid fans. Trust was certainly becoming an issue. The negotiations boiled down to a distrust between Burris and Shivers. Shivers had trusted his kicker, McCallum, enough to allow him to attend a tryout with the NFL's Tennessee Titans. The flow of CFL players was slowing, but offensive tackle Charles Thomas still got a tryout with the New York Jets.

Burris was no longer interested in trying the NFL. He seemed intent on staying put. "You don't have to worry about me going anywhere else," Burris said. "We'll make sure we've won a Grey Cup here first." His intentions changed when Shivers signed Nealon Greene, ostensibly the backup quarterback, to a contract that carried through 2008. Suddenly there was doubt about which passer was the team's starter. Upset about the perceived betrayal, Burris waited past the February 15 deadline and became a free agent. Before February ended, Burris signed a three-year contract with the Calgary Stampeders, who had a 4-14 record in 2004 before being purchased by a 12-man consortium led by Doug Mitchell, Ted Hellard and John Forzani. Tom Higgins, Calgary's new on-field boss, assured Burris the new-look franchise would be constructed around him. Higgins proved it by dumping veteran quarterbacks Marcus Crandell and Khari Jones. Crandell would soon join the Roughriders. The Stampeders also offered more money than Saskatchewan. The Roughriders had money to spend: They were about to get $1 million from Harvard Broadcasting for continuing to hold their radio rights through 2014, meaning play-by-play commentator Rod Pedersen and analyst Carm Carteri could have long-term job security. The Roughriders' $2.8 million loan had been fully forgiven by the provincial government, provided the money was used for improving Taylor Field. It was part of a $9 million plan – the City of Regina was chipping in $1.65 million and the Roughriders vowed to raise another $5 million – that would upgrade the grandstands, sound and lighting and purchase a gigantic video board. SaskTel eventually stepped forward to sponsor the MaxTron, an $800,000 video board that is 21 feet high and 35 feet wide.

The scoreboard, which would occasionally remind patrons that smoking was no longer permitted in the city-owned stadium, was placed behind Taylor Field's southeast end zone. That meant grass-covered "Hemorrhoid Hill," which had served as overflow seating, had to be removed. A sellout was now 28,800 fans.

The goal of the spending was to make the team more attractive for players. It didn't work on Burris. According to Shivers, the three-year pact he offered Burris to stay in Saskatchewan was worth $301,000 the first year, $326,000 the second and $337,000 the third, plus bonuses. Long known as "Smilin' Hank" around Saskatchewan because of his effervescent personality and non-stop smile, the team's fans were now calling him "Bank" and much worse on Internet chat rooms. Said Burris: "They're saying I'm being selfish and taking the money. The thing is, a couple more bucks would have got the deal done with Saskatchewan. But one side was willing to meet my number and the other side wouldn't come close to it. I just wanted Saskatchewan to be competitive and try to get the deal done. But to ignore what these guys are trying to get done here (in Calgary) is hard to do." When the teams were scheduled to meet for the first time in the regular season, Shivers joked that his players would "try to break Burris' neck." The league didn't laugh and fined the GM $1,000.

Photo courtesy of Saskatchewan Roughriders

SaskTel MaxTron

Burris' contract – plus a $460,000 deal for Edmonton Eskimos quarterback Ricky Ray -- seemed extravagant in a league whose commissioner, Tom Wright, wanted teams to follow the $2.55-million salary cap. The cap was going to be increased to $2.66 million in 2005. All nine teams had ignored the cap in 2004 and admitted they each had spent more than $3 million on salaries, an act that made the future of the three-year-old Ottawa Renegades look uncertain. Ottawa's owners nearly filed a lawsuit agains the CFL for not abiding by the salary cap, as they had been promised; the league spent $10 million to stop the suit. "Ultimately what we're looking for is a level playing field where small markets can compete with the large markets, where there is transparency and enforceability," said Wright, whose methods had created a rift among the CFL's governors and convinced them to offer him only a one-year contract extension, which he ultimately accepted.

The blatant overspending left the Roughriders with a $268,000 shortfall, as announced by incoming treasurer Garry Huntington at the team's annual general meeting. It cost $6.3 million for the franchise to operate the previous year, up from $5.48 million in 2003. There was a dropoff of $1.1 million in sponsorships and merchandise sales, but the team did receive $1.1 million in league revenues, up from $600,000 the year before. The team's new governance was also on display for incoming chairman Graham Barker, as 157 shareholders attended the meeting and another 135 (of 2,441) had sent along their votes by proxy.

Right after an announcement that Jeff Fairholm, Tim Roth and John Wozniak would be inducted into the Roughriders' Plaza of Honor, training camp opened on a FieldTurf facsimile at the University of Regina. The roster featured three players who had previously been named the CFL's outstanding offensive lineman: Gene Makowsky (2004), Andrew Greene (2003) and Calgary castoff Fred Childress (1998). All eyes were on McCallum, to see how he would respond. Barrett was watching him, too. "He was frustrated and disappointed by what transpired," said Barrett, who was beginning his sixth season, making him the CFL's longest-tenured head coach following the Winnipeg Blue Bombers' offseason dismissal of Dave Ritchie. "You try to talk about it and say, 'Hey, it shouldn't have come down to one play.' He made the comment, 'I let down a whole bunch of guys in the locker room.' At the same time, we should have kept it off his shoulders." The first preseason game was in Calgary, where the Roughriders lost 18-14. It was Nealon Greene's first game since recovering from a broken leg suffered in the previous season-opener. Burris, naturally, was asked about Saskatchewan. "It would have been good to have Nealon and I playing together," Burris said. "But if they were telling me I'm their guy and saying, 'We haven't signed Nealon yet,' then I find out he had a three-year deal done already . . . I think that speaks volumes right there."

Corey Holmes started the 2005 regular season by returning the opening kickoff 81 yards for a touchdown in a 42-15 win over the visiting Blue Bombers in a game that featured a 30-minute storm delay. The Roughriders won 23-21 in Hamilton and, despite leading the Argonauts 26-14, lost 27-26 in Toronto. After beating the Tiger-Cats 32-13, the Roughriders lost four straight games – 44-18 in Calgary as Burris completed 21 of 30 passes for 302 yards and two touchdowns; 21-16 against Ottawa because they had only nine offensive yards in the third quarter and Nealon Greene had a shovel pass intercepted; a nine-turnover, 42-13 debacle in Montreal; and a 22-17 defeat in Ottawa during which Greene hurt his neck and was replaced by Marcus Crandell. The Roughriders had a 16-day break while Regina was playing host to the Canada Summer Games, an event that recruited 6,000 local volunteers. Saskatchewan's next game was at home against the B.C. Lions on Aug. 27, the same day City of Regina employees staged a one-day walkout to highlight their need for a new contract. Employees of CBC, who were scheduled to televise the game, had been locked out by the corporation because of a contract squabble, so the game was shown without commentators, relying almost exclusively on Taylor Field announcer Evan Bray to keep the audience updated on the proceedings. CBC tried several similar telecasts and was surprised to see an increase in its ratings; announcers were brought back after the lockout ended.

Saskatchewan stretched its losing streak to five straight games and its record dropped to 3-6 with a 19-15 loss to the Lions.

The next game was Barrett's 100th regular-season contest. He was tied with Eagle Keys for the longest tenure as Saskatchewan's head coach, with six seasons, but his 42-56-1 record was below Keys' winning record of 68-25-3. Barrett was also 2-3 in the playoffs; Keys was 9-8. The Roughriders responded with a 45-26 victory in the Labour Day Classic and completed the home-and-home set with a 19-17 victory over the Blue

Bombers, their first regular-season win in Winnipeg since 1994. While news filtered north about Hurricane Katrina flooding the dykes in New Orleans, the Roughriders went on one of their late-season winning streaks. They beat the visiting Eskimos 37-36 because Omarr Morgan returned an interception 46 yards for a touchdown, plus he blocked what would have been a game-winning, 31-yard field goal on the final play. A fourth straight victory came in Toronto, 24-13 against the reigning champions. A fifth came in B.C., when Elijah Thurmon caught two touchdown passes to hand the Lions their first loss of the season, 28-19. The Roughriders followed with a 38-34 loss against the Alouettes and a controversial 19-18 loss in Edmonton. Just before that game the Eskimos, needing an offensive lineman and a running back, sent little-known defensive back Tay Cody, slotback Brock Ralph and a first-round draft choice to Hamilton for guard Dan Comiskey and tailback Troy Davis. There were also rumours the trade contained future considerations, specifically highly regarded Eskimos quarterback Jason Maas. "They didn't break any rules or anything," said Riders defensive tackle Nate Davis. "Somebody just decided to help them out. But with all the underhanded stuff, I bet that Maas is in Hamilton next year." Davis was right, by the way. Barrett described Saskatchewan's next game as "a total collapse." His team led 21-3 before allowing the visiting Stampeders to rally for a 29-21 victory. Saskatchewan could make the playoffs as a wild-card entrant in the East Division by winning or tying its finale in B.C. The Riders did that by eking out a 13-12 victory to give them a 9-9 record, good enough for fourth place in the West and a postseason trip to Montreal. The victory in B.C. was gained after the Roughriders, again following a Barrett dictum, turned inward to shield themselves against another unwanted glare.

Photo courtesy of *Leader-Post*

Omarr Morgan

Veteran linebacker Trevis Smith, a seven-year veteran and the only American player on Saskatchewan's roster from before Barrett and Shivers arrived, had been charged with aggravated sexual assault. RCMP in Surrey, B.C. also announced that Smith was HIV positive. He was ultimately accused of having unprotected sex with a woman in Surrey and another in Regina, both of whom tested negative for the disease, which can cause AIDS. The Roughriders had gotten Smith tested, but because of privacy issues they insisted they were unable to keep him from playing. "Any information of a health-related issue relating to any employee at any organization is private," said Riders chairman Graham Barker, who vowed the team would establish a code of conduct to govern the behaviour of its personnel. "The employer has zero right and zero obligation to release that information." Medical experts declared the chances of transferring AIDS during

Photo courtesy of *Leader-Post*

Nate Davis

Corey Holmes

Photo courtesy of *Leader-Post*

a football game were miniscule, but there remained a public belief that more players would soon come forward with similar stories. It didn't happen.

The Roughriders' season ended in Montreal's Olympic Stadium, where the visitors – perhaps bothered by travel problems that kept them from arriving in Quebec until 22 hours before kickoff – fell behind 24-0 before losing 30-14 in the East semifinal. The CFL quickly decreed that all visiting teams would in the future have to arrive at their destination two days before any playoff game. Gene Makowsky (offensive lineman), who played on a unit that averaged 135 rushing yards per game and allowed a league-low 23 sacks, and Corey Holmes (special teams), who led the CFL with 3,455 all-purpose yards, were winners of two of the league's outstanding player awards. Holmes had won before, in 2002, as had Makowsky, in 2004. Another early playoff exit left the futures of Shivers and Barrett in doubt. Shivers told the 10-member board of directors about his future plans and stayed with the team.

CFL governors held their major offseason meeting in Phoenix, where they finally decided that if the league was going to survive, thrive and allow all its teams to be competitive in 2006, they needed to implement an enforceable salary cap. Voila! Out of the fax machines and over the Internet, the CFL revealed a 14-point plan called the Salary Management System (SMS). Although the governors decreed that video replay challenges would be allowed for specific on-field rulings during preseason and regular-season games, the most important point was this, according to Riders chairman Graham Baker: "Two words – cost certainty." A salary cap of $3.8 million would be enforced in 2007. Not in 2006! "We were over that amount last year," said Roughriders CEO/president Jim Hopson. "So we can't sit here and say, 'Poor Riders!' There's no more whining." Teams would be fined $1 for each dollar they over-spent up to $100,000, $2 for each dollar over-spent between $100,000 and $300,000 and $3 for each dollar over the cap above $300,000. Teams would also lose first- or second-round draft picks for exceeding the cap by more than $300,000. Those draft choices were supposed to be given to the law-abiding teams. All players and teams were supposed to sign compliance forms that listed every deal contained within a contract, plus the league was going to hire people, mainly auditors, to ensure the teams were complying by the rules. Teams that broke the rules could be fined between five and 20 per cent of their league revenues. The cap limit would be reset each January, allowing teams to know how much they could spend when the free-agent market opened in mid-February. Active rosters were increased to 46 from 40 players, but only 42 players could dress while the remaining four were paid full salaries. That allowed teams to make roster changes up to three hours before kickoff. A six-man practice roster was established, with room for a seventh player if he was a non-import. The practice roster expanded to 12 players after NFL cuts were announced in early September, allowing coaches and scouts to bring in prospects for late-season assessments. One final clause prevented teams from trading players back to their previous teams for one year. In other words, no more lending of players to needy franchises.

All of this came too late to save CFL Commissioner Tom Wright – who, despite increased sponsorships and attendance throughout the league, would resign when his non-renewed contract expired in December – or the Ottawa Renegades. After losing $4.6 million in 2005, the franchise was revoked from majority owner Bernie Glieberman, a former owner who had assumed some debts from the previous partnership, and minority owner Bill Smith. Soon after, the league held a dispersal draft to scavenge Ottawa's players. The Roughriders traded safety Scott Gordon and tailback/returner Corey Holmes to Hamilton to acquire the first overall pick, which they used to select Renegades quarterback Kerry Joseph. "It surprised me to see the players who were traded away," said Joseph, who would jump into community work and assume the role as a KidSport fundraiser previously held by Don Narcisse and Paul McCallum. "That showed I was really wanted." The Roughriders, who had been relatively quiet in the offseason, also selected receiver/returner Jason Armstead. "Fans have been waiting for a big splash," said head coach Danny Barrett. "They've been waiting for news, so have (the media). If today wasn't big enough, you need to get a bigger pool." The Riders subsequently traded Nealon Greene to Montreal, ending the four-year saga of an underachieving quarterback. "I have no regrets," said Greene. "Danny and Roy gave me an opportunity when I didn't have an opportunity. It just didn't work out the years I was here. It came close. We turned it around, we just didn't turn things all the way over."

Wideout Jamel Richardson was declared eligible for the NFL draft because he met the American league's college eligibility requirements – it was four years after he had begun his college career – but the Riders refused to let him out of his contract; he wasn't drafted. Receiver Elijah Thurmon, who led the Riders with 88 catches for 1,048 yards and seven touchdowns, and linebacker Walter Spencer-Robinson, the team's leader with 29 special-teams tackles, signed free-agent deals with Calgary. And kicker Paul McCallum, upset with Shivers' negotiating tactics after being offered, he said, a 30-per-cent cut following a season in which his field goal proficiency slipped to 73.8 per cent from his career average of 75.2 per cent, signed with B.C. "I only talked to Roy once," said McCallum, who had been with the Riders since 1994 and was their longest-serving veteran. "He said, 'Take it or leave it.' I told them I would look at what I was worth on the market. They told me to take it." The Roughriders replaced McCallum in the draft by selecting punter/kicker Luca Congi, a Simon Fraser product, 12th overall. They had opened the draft with the third pick, using it to select Western Ontario receiver Andy Fantuz, a Hec Crighton Trophy winner as the outstanding player in Canadian college football.

Photo courtesy of *Leader-Post*

Andy Fantuz

Defensive end Bobby Jurasin, who held the team record for sacks when he was released before the 1998 season, was inducted into the Canadian Football Hall of Fame. One of his long-time teammates, defensive tackle Gary Lewis, was placed in the Riders' Plaza of Honor with receiver Rhett Dawson and defensive end

Ken Reed. "I'm only as good as Gary Lewis, as James Curry, as Vince Goldsmith, as Chuck Klingbeil," said Jurasin, praising his former teammates. "They's no way one guy can go out there and dominate. I'm reaping the benefits of 11 other guys' hard work."

Long before training camp opened at the University of Regina, offensive co-ordinator Marcel Bellefeuille, who had been taking heat for his non-prolific offence, declared he wanted to move his family closer to its Ottawa home. The Roughriders were coming off a season in which they led the league with 135 rushing yards per game, but were last among CFL passing offences with 235 yards per game. After returning east, Bellefeuille was hired as an assistant by the Montreal Alouettes. Offensive line coach Carl Brennan joined the Edmonton Eskimos. Bellefeuille was replaced by Tommy Condell, who had been working with Ottawa's offence for two years, and long-time CFL assistant George Cortez returned from the U.S. college ranks to spend one year as Saskatchewan's offensive line coach. All of the coaches took turns attending workout camps that Shivers scheduled throughout the U.S., where they would recruit hopefuls and sometimes sign prospects for training camp. Those camp expenses were among the $7.05 million it cost to operate the Roughriders in 2005. Because they generated $5.87 million in gate receipts, the Riders announced a profit of $243,391, which turned out to be $182,544 after the City of Regina – according to the renewed rental agreement – received 25 per cent of the team's profits for renting Taylor Field. The city and the Roughriders also agreed to share the $1.2 million cost of replacing the stadium's six-year-old AstroTurf. This time they chose FieldTurf, an "artificial grass" product that was softer than previous products because of the rubber pellets used as in-fill. The stadium was also about to undergo another transformation. The name was changed from Taylor Field to Mosaic Stadium after the Saskatchewan-based Mosaic Company, one of the world's largest potash producers, paid $4 million for naming rights to the stadium for a period of 10 years. Even the family of Piffles Taylor, after whom the stadium had been named, gave its consent to the new name of the facility now located on Piffles Taylor Way.

The season began with fans and media wondering how Shivers and Barrett would handle being in the final years of their respective contracts. The *Leader-Post*, in its annual preseason preview, labelled the regime's performance in a huge headline: "Mediocre." The campaign started poorly against B.C. when Lions quarterback Dave Dickenson threw five touchdown passes in a 45-28 victory. Worse: Three of Saskatchewan's first four games were against the Lions. The Roughriders rebounded with a 32-24 victory at Mosaic Stadium, helped by a 34-yard interception return for a touchdown by Riders defensive back Eddie Davis. Henry Burris threw two touchdown passes to another ex-Rider, Elijah Thurmon, in Calgary's 53-36 victory over the home-town Roughriders. With the Roughriders at 1-2, star tailback Kenton Keith was charged with assaulting a bouncer at a local nightclub. The charges were eventually stayed, but it didn't help the team's image. Following a 29-28 victory in B.C., which was punctuated by a head-snapping hit inflicted on Dickenson by Riders linebacker Jackie Mitchell, the biggest news emanating from the newly named stadium was an announcement that the Rolling Stones, the world's best-known rock band, would be playing a concert at Mosaic Stadium on October 8. A second show was added for October 6 when 48,000-some tickets were sold on-line in 20 minutes. Prices ranged from $62.50 to $302.50, with 8,000 being reserved for Roughriders season-ticket holders, employees of Casinos Regina and Moose Jaw, and others.

A surprising, 26-23 loss ensued against the visiting Toronto Argonauts, who were left with third-string quarterback Eric Crouch at the controls. Saskatchewan beat the visiting Stampeders 19-9 in their next game, but lost 23-7 in Calgary and 24-18 in Edmonton. Shivers blasted his players following the loss in Edmonton, which dropped the Riders' record to 3-5. "If somebody's feelings were hurt, I really don't care," said the general manager. "I told them you better get your head out of your ass. Some of you aren't as good as you think you are." Even with strong-armed (if somewhat inaccurate) and strong-running Kerry Joseph at the controls, the Roughriders had scored only one touchdown in their last 10 quarters of football. The heat was on Barrett and Shivers. "I truly believe that this thing is going to work itself out to the utmost," said Barrett. "I continue to hold my faith. That's what keeps me going each and every day."

Photo courtesy of *Leader-Post*

Jackie Mitchell

The team was averaging 23,275 fans through four home games before beating the lowly Hamilton Tiger-Cats 46-15. With Joseph slightly injured and ineffective, Marcus Crandell became the starter until dislocating an elbow in the first quarter. It seemed like the impressive victory might have saved some jobs, except the board of directors was evidently eager to get a new coach to inspire the troops. Shivers had the final say. "When a move is made on Danny, it will be up to me," said Shivers, when asked if he had been instructed to dump his head coach. "I just don't want Danny to have a three- or four-game losing streak. I can't tolerate anything like that. If we're in a funk, I would have to do something. It would be a no-brainer. But the board hasn't told me anything."

Shivers was fired the next day. Immediately speculation began that he would be replaced by Eric Tillman, a former general manager in B.C., Toronto and Ottawa, who had turned down Saskatchewan's job before it was offered to Shivers. Indeed, Roughriders CEO/president Jim Hopson had already spoken to Tillman about the possibility of assuming the post.

Shivers' overall record as Saskatchewan's general manager was 52-64-1. The team had made the playoffs for four straight years and the reworked roster had only five players remaining from the group Shivers had taken over in 2000.

Upset about losing his mentor, and realizing the planned chain of command that would have seen him move into the GM's office wasn't going to materialize, Barrett didn't speak to the media for two days. Unaware that some players were happy about Shivers' departure, Barrett kept them from doing interviews, too. Barrett said he wanted to keep them focused. He also instructed long-

Photo courtesy of *Leader-Post*

Roy Shivers

time equipment manager Norm Fong to order decals bearing the initials RS, which Barrett wanted attached to the players' helmets in homage to Shivers.

When Tillman, who was hired as the Roughriders general manager and vice-president of football operations on August 21, heard about the decals he squelched the idea. Tillman also insisted that all future practices be open to fans and the media, an expected move from someone with a journalism degree who had been working as an analyst on CFL telecasts. Tillman was 49 and a product of the University of Mississippi. He had held numerous jobs with football teams, ranging from general manager with three CFL teams to a scout with the Montreal Concordes to being the man in charge of recruiting players for the Senior Bowl in Mobile, Alabama. He won Grey Cups with the Toronto Argonauts in 1997 and the B.C. Lions in 1994. He turned down the chance to succeed Al Ford as Saskatchewan's general manager in 1999, he said, because he was starting a new relationship in Ottawa and partly because of the cold weather that chilled him during his winter visit to Regina. "I liked everything about the situation here, but I made a decision based on a personal (choice)," said Tillman. "I don't apologize for doing that. I would say now, the fact that we're married and have two children that I made the right decision for the right reasons."

Kent Austin, a former Riders quarterback who had recently been fired as the Toronto Argonauts' offensive co-ordinator, was a good friend of Tillman's and quickly became the odds-on favourite to replace Barrett as Saskatchewan's head coach.

Kent Austin, a former Riders quarterback who had recently been fired as the Toronto Argonauts' offensive co-ordinator, was a good friend of Tillman's and quickly became the odds-on favourite to replace Barrett as Saskatchewan's head coach. But Tillman insisted he would evaluate Barrett on the remainder of the season. Barrett intended to get his players ready. "To a man they're ready to play hard, like we always do," said Barrett. "As a team we first play for ourselves, but Roy's still a part of that. Roy believed in me, gave me an opportunity and I'm eternally grateful for that. A lot of guys in the room feel the same way."

The Roughriders forced eight turnovers and third-string quarterback Rocky Butler constructed four touchdown drives in their first game after Shivers' firing, a 51-8 victory in Hamilton. With Joseph back in the lineup they won 39-12 against the Blue Bombers but lost the rematch 27-23 in Winnipeg, a game that cost veteran Mike McCullough his job as the starting middle linebacker because of a knee injury. A crowd of 27,592 watched the Roughriders beat the visiting Lions 23-20 in overtime, when Andy Fantuz pounced on Kerry Joseph's fumble in the end zone for the winning touchdown. A 30-25 loss to the Eskimos ended Saskatchewan's chances of earning a home playoff game. The Riders took to the road, leaving the Rolling Stones to fill Mosaic Stadium for two memorable concerts, and lost 35-8 in Montreal. The Alouettes had just lost their coach, Don Matthews, who retired with a CFL-leading 231 victories, because of health issues. When the Alouettes came to Regina, the home team won 27-26 on a last-play, 29-yard field goal by Luca Congi. It was the last home game of a season in which the team averaged 25,244 fans per game, down from 25,733 in 2005, even though season-ticket sales increased to 13,471 from 13,013. The Riders completed their schedule on the road by not allowing a touchdown in a 13-9 victory over the Toronto Argonauts and, with 14 starters left at home, losing 20-18 in Edmonton. For the third straight year the Riders had a 9-9 record. They were headed to the West semifinal in Calgary, where the biggest issue surrounded the Stampeders' refusal to allow Riders mascot Gainer the Gopher on the sidelines inside McMahon Stadium. Alberta premier Ralph Klein got involved, somewhat facetiously: "We've always made it clear that we welcome all visitors and animals from our great neighbour to the east, except those that are a nuisance to crops and fields, including football fields." The Riders would force seven turnovers and score 25 straight points in their 30-21 semifinal victory over Calgary, in which Henry Burris tossed four interceptions and fumbled once. Four Riders – Fred Perry, Jeremy O'Day, Gene Makowsky and Eddie Davis – were named to the CFL all-star team before the team ventured, again, to Vancouver for a West final against the Lions. Despite their supposed familiarity with the noise and humidity inside B.C. Place Stadium, the Riders committed four time-count infractions and Kerry Joseph was sacked five times. B.C. quarterback Dave Dickenson wasn't sacked once in the Lions' 45-18 victory, their second over Saskatchewan in two (of the last three) West finals. The team had never made it to the Grey Cup or played host to a home playoff game during Barrett's seven years as head coach. That was the primary reason why Tillman – after debating the limited merits and the win-or-else pressure of offering a one-year contract – decided against re-signing him. Barrett attended a media conference, at which he described his family's affection for and acceptance in Saskatchewan. He took no questions. "There's two ways you can look at this," Barrett said. "You can either be bitter or you can be better and I like to think that I am a better man for coming here. I know I am a better coach and I leave a better person." Barrett left as Saskatchewan's longest-serving coach; his seven seasons were one more than Eagle Keys amassed from 1965-70. Including playoffs, Keys' record was 88-43-3. Barrett's was 69-78-1.

Photo courtesy of Royal Studios

Jeremy O'Day

There was little doubt that Tillman would bring in Austin. Although Tillman vowed to conduct an extensive search, he really only sat down for one serious interview before hiring the man. They met for a sit-down in Toronto and spent hours discussing the team's roster, ways to upgrade and numerous what-if scenarios. The only problem, it seemed, would be ingratiating himself with Riders fans who had long memories, who recalled that he had asked to be traded away from Saskatchewan in 1994. Austin handled every question with aplomb once he returned to Regina, admitting he might have made a mistake leaving Saskatchewan and confessing how much he wanted to return. "I cherish the challenge," said Austin, who had been the Grey Cup-winning quarterback and game's outstanding offensive player when Saskatchewan won the CFL crown in 1989. "There are other reasons, too. There have only been two Grey Cups won in Saskatchewan – 1966 and 1989 – and the

Photo courtesy of *Leader-Post*

Eric Tillman (left) with Kent Austin at a press conference

thought of being a part of the third one was too good to pass up." Austin signed a three-year deal.

Looking back from the general manager's perspective:

ROY SHIVERS

"We heard from everybody that you couldn't win there and dah-dee-dah-dee-dah. I wanted to give it a try. I was extremely motivated by that, by the fact that everyone was telling us we couldn't win in Saskatchewan. I never want to turn away from a challenge, but it was worse than I thought. When I looked at the roster I went, 'Holy shit!' We had to do a lot of surgery. I talked to Don Matthews, to Ron Lancaster, to Wally Buono. Wally thought I was nuts. It was a challenge, but we knew it was all about finding football players. We had to find good football players.

Photo courtesy of *Leader-Post*

Eddie Davis

"Eddie Davis might have been the best of all the players we had, because of what he contributed through the years. He was the guy who held that defence together. We had some good football players. Curtis Marsh was a good player, but he was a knucklehead. We had some good running backs, like Kenton Keith, who was one of the best athletes of the time and one of the best running backs I've seen in quite a while. The three linebackers they won the Grey Cup with (Maurice Lloyd, Anton McKenzie and Sean Lucas) were good players. We revamped the team with two new cornerbacks, LaDouphyous McCalla and Omarr Morgan. Kerry Joseph, we drafted him, and he's a good athlete. But Eddie Davis might have been the best because of what he brings to the table. He kept all those guys together. Jackie Mitchell was one of my favourites. Jackie had limited ability and limited speed, but he made up for what he lacked in quickness and speed by knowing the game. We had one of the best offensive lines, too, with Gene Makowsky and Jeremy O'Day. It was a group that finally got together and played good football, when we added guys like Corey Holmes, who played good football and was one of our best because he played multiple positions. After we got it whittled down and turned it around, we had a good football team. We proved it. By 2004 on we could play with anybody.

"Yeah, I should have taken (the job offered to move the Roughriders' entire coaching staff to the Calgary Stampeders in 2003). Then I wouldn't have had all the aggravation I had. We all got together and made a family choice. We said we were all going or nobody was going. We had a meeting and voted. It was 5-3, or 4-3, or something like that. It was close. Hindsight is always perfect, but the big thing was we wanted to finish something. We got to the point where we thought we could beat everybody and we wanted to see it through, maybe win two or three. I used to tell those guys all the time – and I hate to say I was prophetic looking back at it – but I would say, "One of these days we're going to get fired, somebody's going to come in here and win the Grey Cup." I would tell Tony Playter that somebody could win the Grey Cup with this team. That's exactly what happened. It was a very good football team. We got jobbed one time in the West final with a phantom call, with Jason Clermont in B.C., they were second-and-19 and they got 36. We just made crucial mistakes at the wrong time. Everybody thinks it was the missed kick the one year, what was it – 18 yards? The turning point was at the end of the first half, when (Riders kicker Paul McCallum) missed a 37-yarder or something and we didn't even get a single point. That would have changed everything because (B.C.) would have needed to score a touchdown to force overtime. He missed it and they didn't kick it out, they ran it out. That one point changed everything. The other time I could have killed Paul McCallum was when he said afterwards he didn't know we had to win a game by 25 points to earn a home playoff game. I said, 'Why do you think all those people were sitting there at the end of the game?" We messed that up because we were playing a soft defence and let them score two touchdowns so they could get within 24 points. If we had kept playing hard they never would have scored. When he told me that I nearly went ballistic. Shee-e-e-t! It was in the paper all week. There were 30,000 people still sitting in the stands and we were leading by more than 30 points.

"That one year we played shitty against Montreal in the playoffs, another against Toronto. We played crappy games in the playoffs, except for the year we beat Edmonton. We could have won it that year. We had a chance to get home-field advantage that last game against B.C., too, except for that last touchdown. We got jobbed on that one. We're right there at the end, we just have to knock the ball down except Santino Hall and Darnell Edwards run into each other on the last play and (Geroy Simon) catches a touchdown to win.

"The year we go 11-7 with Nealon (Greene) as our quarterback was the best, because everybody's saying, 'Nealon's not a quarterback.' 'You can't win with Nealon.' We played a great playoff game in Winnipeg. That's one of the proudest moments. Overall I was proudest of what we accomplished, how we turned it around after totally gutting it. The most frustrating part was the first year. Things happened that I couldn't believe. We had players retiring who were supposed to come back. They got their bonuses and retired. Bob (Vespaziani) and I looked at each other and said, 'What the hell is going on here?' It sure was frustrating. We signed Steve Anderson, then he changed his mind after he went back to the hotel because the secretary couldn't get the contract written up. The (Scott) Flory thing didn't bother me. I let Marcel (Bellefeuille) and Danny (Barrett) handle most of that, until they told me he reneged. It was short and to the point from me: If he didn't report, if he wanted to go back to Montreal, they had to give us our money back and a first-round draft pick. We got the pick and our money back – $100,000. It didn't hurt us.

"The year we go 11-7 with Nealon (Greene) as our quarterback was the best, because everybody's saying, 'Nealon's not a quarterback.' 'You can't win with Nealon.' We played a great playoff game in Winnipeg. That's one of the proudest moments ..."

"We were going to pay him $315,000 and it went up to $350,000. He was going to have two cars. Henry, I think, didn't want to play in Saskatchewan. The board of directors knew that because I checked with them. We were going to give him a contract stating $250,000 and another $100,000 up-front. It was a three-year deal for more than $300,000 every year. I wasn't a math major, but I knew that was a million-dollar contract. I don't think he wanted to play in Regina. He's good at making himself look good: Smilin' Hank. I haven't spoken to him since. If I saw him I would probably slap him in the mouth. ... Sure, he won a Grey Cup with Calgary . . . finally. I think we should have won a Grey Cup when he was with us. Paul McCallum won a Grey Cup, too, with B.C. I had forgotten about him (joining B.C. as a free agent) when I went to training camp (as the new player personnel director) with the Lions. Clean forgot about it. Walking down the pathway one day and who's coming the other way? Paul McCallum. You've got to be kidding me! I haven't said a word to him. ... He said Danny and I had screwed him out of something. He said we were really squeezing him. I can't understand why I came out on the bad end in the public relations area. I told the truth the majority of the time. People don't like to hear the truth, but I'm not going to change it for anybody. I don't know how to sugar-coat things. ... When guys have you, think they've got you, they squeeze you. With Paul, we really gave him lots of things, letting him go to an NFL camp, he played in the XFL, anything he wanted. We gave him lots of money. ... But I didn't keep yapping about it. Henry is still yapping about it. ... When we offered him that money, he hadn't won anything, but I was going to give him $300,000.

"I thought Danny was ready to coach and he deserved a chance. I was with Calgary when he was with them. I saw him coach and play for two years. The only thing Danny was lacking was experience. You don't get experience until somebody gives you a job."

"I thought Danny was ready to coach and he deserved a chance. I was with Calgary when he was with them. I saw him coach and play for two years. The only thing Danny was lacking was experience. You don't get experience until somebody gives you a job. I see lots of teams hiring younger guys now, guys who are 30, 32, 35 years old. It goes back to the racial thing. I promised myself I was going to help somebody out. That's the only way we get a chance. Nobody else was going to make him a head coach. You need an opportunity. Bob Ellard gave me a shot. The guy down in Alabama gave me a shot – Art Williams. Danny deserved a shot. I'm glad to see (long-time Riders assistant coach) Richie Hall got a shot. Finally. It's like he was in a rut. You just need somebody to give you a shot instead of getting passed over. I was happy for him and I was happy for Marcel (Bellefeuille) too.

Photo courtesy of *Leader-Post*

Richie Hall

"I feel a lot of pride. I was happy to be at the vanguard of it. I made a vow to myself that if I ever got in a position I was going to hire some people of colour for positions that they wouldn't be getting. If I wasn't going to do it, who was? My father taught me that when I walk through a door I should take someone with me. My whole plan was to bring somebody with me. I thought I brought some people with me. Danny has a great football mind. They should have gone to the Grey Cup the year I left. They could never clear that last hurdle. That upset me more than anything in all our time there, we couldn't get past that last hurdle. He could have written his own ticket. I tried putting my finger on the reasons, but other than getting outplayed or screwing it up sometime during the game, what else can you say? I probably thought about firing Danny only once and it wasn't at the end because I knew he was going to get back in the race. I was mad at the players at the end because they were playing so shitty. I was ticked at the team. Guys who were getting paid all the money, they played crappy. When you confront them they get all pissed off and everything, guys like Reggie Hunt, Nate Davis, the offensive line played crappy, so I called them out after that game in Edmonton. Maybe, if we hadn't made the playoffs at the end of that year, I might have fired him. We got off to a bad start that year, but like I told the board, we had two games against Hamilton and beat them 51-8 – they fired me the next day. We had a game against Winnipeg, so we were going to get back in it. That's what they did. There was subtle pressure put on me because they were always asking me, 'What are you going to do? And yah-dee-da.'

I didn't get fired because I didn't fire Danny. I got fired because it was a power struggle. The team's governance was changing. (Riders chairman Rob) Pletch said it in a column in the newspaper that it was changing and I said I wouldn't work for (CEO/president Jim) Hopson. In the first part of the year they tried to get me to go along with everything, but I wouldn't do it. ... I said, 'I can work with you, but not for you.' "

General manager Eric Tillman and head coach Kent Austin began reworking the Roughriders in earnest, starting with the coaching staff, as they prepared for the 2007 season. Austin quickly re-hired defensive co-ordinator Richie Hall, an ex-Rider teammate whose defence had allowed a league-low 82 rushing yards per game, was second-best with only 302 total yards per game and second with 52 sacks. Linebackers coach Alex Smith and line coach Ron Estay were retained. The new offensive coaches were Ken Miller, who had worked with Austin in Toronto, Mike Gibson and Paul LaPolice. Miller became offensive co-ordinator while Gibson and LaPolice, who had each served as offensive co-ordinator for the Winnipeg Blue Bombers, were named assistant head coach/offensive line coach and receivers coach, respectively. With his three years of professional experience, all as an assistant, Austin was the least experienced member of the staff. Former Riders head coach Danny Barrett spoke with the Blue Bombers about joining their staff before joining Turner Gill, a former Montreal Concordes quarterback, as assistant head coach/quarterbacks coach at the University of Buffalo. Another former head coach, Jim Daley, joined the CFL as its senior adviser. The Roughriders also added Joe Womack as their player personnel director. A good friend of Tillman, Womack had begun his off-field career in football as a Roughriders scout in 1982.

Players were departing, as veteran linebacker Jackie Mitchell, defensive tackle Nate Davis, guard Andrew Greene and tackle Charles Thomas were released, free-agent DB Davin Bush signed with Winnipeg, tailback Kenton Keith joined the NFL's Indianapolis Colts, wideout Jamel Richardson inked a pact with the Dallas Cowboys and third-string quarterback Rocky Butler was traded to the Hamilton Tiger-Cats for Wayne Smith, one of the league's highest-ranked offensive linemen, and feisty slotback D.J. Flick. Veteran slotback Jason French was also traded to Hamilton. Many of the moves were made to clear space under the salary cap – Saskatchewan had exceeded the $3.8-million cap by $1.1 million and was committed to $4.9 million in salaries again for 2007. Somehow the Roughriders had posted a miniscule profit of $455, barely enough to buy a season ticket, helped by $6.1 million in gate receipts. It cost $15.379 million to operate the franchise in 2006, with about $600,000 earmarked for the team's share of the FieldTurf that was being installed inside Mosaic Stadium before training camp opened in early June. The team also slated one workout for Saskatoon, which would be used as a preseason intrasquad game. For the upcoming year the cap was going to be increased to $4.1 million. Incoming commissioner Mark Cohon was given the task of enforcing the cap implemented by his predecessor, Tom Wright, whose rehiring had been blocked by three negative votes from unhappy CFL governors. Cohon had been CEO of a software corporation, plus he worked with Major League Baseball and the National Basketball Association. He took over as the Canadian dollar surged against the U.S. dollar and, for awhile, the Canadian loonie was worth five cents more than the American greenback.

Veteran lineman Mike Abou-Mechrek was signed to bring some leadership into the locker room. The Riders drafted Guelph receiver David McKoy ninth overall and Wilfrid

Laurier linebacker Yannick Carter 20th. They also signed wide receiver Kahlil Hill and his younger brother, running back Hakim Hill, who had been plagued by off-field problems throughout his career. Austin and Tillman believed Hakim Hill had cleaned up his act, but when the brothers got into a booze-influenced fight in Arizona a few days after their signings, the younger brother was immediately dumped. Devastating news came from Virginia Tech, where 32 people were shot to death and others injured in the worst massacre by a single shooter in the gun-infested history of the United States. It served as quite a backdrop for the court case of linebacker Trevis Smith, whose playing career with the Riders ended 16 months earlier when he was charged with aggravated sexual assault. Smith was found guilty on charges that he did not tell two female sexual partners that he was HIV positive. Smith was sent to prison for 5½ years plus six months for a parole violation. "I apologize to this province, to the team that I represented for the last seven years," Smith said after his trial ended. "I also want to apologize to the women I was involved with during this time, and my wife, for my actions. I ask that she forgive me for committing adultery."

Photo courtesy of Saskatchewan Roughriders

Graham Barker

Graham Barker, an outspoken critic of bad off-field behaviour by the players, stepped aside as Riders chairman after two years and was replaced by Rob Pletch, the managing partner of a local law firm. Although Barker left one year early, insisting he didn't have time for the demands of the job, he had implemented a code of conduct for the franchise. Breaking the code of conduct could lead to "a reprimand or a suspension or a termination of employment." It stated that "club personnel . . . must make every reasonable effort to ensure that their conduct will measure up to that of good citizenship."

True to his nature, Austin supervised an organized, brisk training camp. He rarely wandered towards the defence, staying instead with the offensive players as he explained – in detail – the nuances of the read-and-react offence. His presence was captivating, on the field and off. His players paid close attention to every word and soaked up the advice he gave them, his first-hand knowledge of what it's like to win a Grey Cup in Saskatchewan. His team had eight new starters on its roster. Austin had insisted throughout training camp that Marcus Crandell and Kerry Joseph would battle for the starting quarterback's job. It surprised few that Joseph won the job. "It was very close," said Austin, "but we feel like this is the best way to go to start." It would be a good decision.

The Roughriders opened their season in Montreal, where lo and behold they won for only the second time since the Alouettes had rejoined the CFL in 1996. "I got sick and tired of answering that question," said Austin. "Every football field has the same dimensions. Wherever we play, we play to win. No matter where it is." Defensive backs James Johnson, Eddie Davis and Tristan Clovis intercepted passes inside Saskatchewan's 10-yard line and Montreal quarterback Anthony Calvillo was sacked eight times. A 49-8 victory followed against the visiting Stampeders, who were torched by Joseph's four touchdown passes and two rushing touchdowns from tailback Wes Cates, who had just been acquired from Calgary. Joseph followed with a "horrible" performance at home against B.C., getting replaced by Crandell with his team trailing 21-0 in a game it would lose 42-12. In their next game, in Edmonton, the Riders led 20-1 when Luca Congi hit an upright on a 19-yard field goal attempt. The Eskimos rallied to win 21-20. That game cost the Riders the services for nine games of defensive back Eddie Davis, their on-field leader who kept playing after the injury, because of torn shoulder ligaments. Andy Fantuz's drop-filled performance also cost him a starting job, but when replacement Mike Washington was sidelined because of heart murmurs, Fantuz regained the spot for Saskatchewan's 54-14 victory in a rematch with the Eskimos. The Roughriders improved to 4-2 by handing B.C. its first loss, 21-9 in Vancouver. Next came Austin's much-hyped return to Toronto, where he had been fired one year earlier as the Argonauts' offensive co-ordinator. Although Austin downplayed the importance of the game, Tillman and offensive co-ordinator Ken Miller were quite intent on showing the Argos had made a mistake. Saskatchewan won 24-13. "Saskatchewan is my team," said Austin. "I'm proud of how our guys played. It's not about me." One of the reasons the Riders were 5-2? They had forced 21 turnovers and committed only two.

Photo courtesy of *Leader-Post*

Wes Cates

A sold-out crowd of 28,800, enthralled by the enthusiasm Austin was instilling in his players, was at Mosaic Stadium to see the Roughriders rally for a 39-32 victory over the Eskimos on August 18. The home team was losing 32-27 when a 59-minute break was caused by a serious rainstorm. Although CBC didn't televise the final 13:20 of the fourth quarter, to the chagrin of the team's loyal fans across Canada, the teams wanted to play and most of the spectators waited to watch the conclusion. "We'll all remember that," said Riders CEO Jim Hopson. Fans retained the momentum from that memorable night and the Riders were starting to sell out the ballpark well in advance of the next home game. Customers were also going wild about the third retro jersey added to the team's wardrobe, a green-and-white version similar to what the Roughriders wore from 1948-85 complete with an old-style S adorning the helmets. When the team traded with Hamilton to bring back fan favourite Corey Holmes, a crowd met him at the airport. "It feels good to come home," said Holmes, who was dealt along with University of Regina product Chris Getzlaf for Jason Armstead, who hastened his departure by letting it be known he was unhappy with his role as a part-time receiver/returner. Labour Day actually provided a classic matchup for the sold-out crowd – with just over one minute remaining and trailing the Blue Bombers 26-24, the Riders began a seven-play, 91-yard drive that Kerry Joseph capped with a 27-yard touchdown run. Who called the play? Austin, apparently. After the game, linebacker Mike McCullough scurried into the stands to summon Chris Knox, a 24-year-old fan who was afflicted with a brain tumour. Knox came into the locker room, where the Riders prayed for him and handed him the game ball. Kerry Joseph would also about that time befriend a 20-year-old girl, Erin Lawrence, who died August 6 from stomach cancer. Joseph, touched by "her spirit," wore an "I Love Erin" bracelet during games to honour her memory. Away from the football field, the NFL was dealing with the public and legal uproar over Atlanta Falcons quarterback Michael Vick financing a

Photo courtesy of *Leader-Post*

Kerry Joseph scores the winning touchdown on Labour Day

kennel that staged dog fights; the charges ultimately sent him to prison.

The Riders then endured their longest losing streak of the season, dropping a 34-15 decision in Winnipeg, falling 44-22 in Calgary (Burris threw five TD passes) and a 37-34 loss to the Lions. Wide receiver Matt Dominguez suffered torn knee ligaments in Winnipeg, so he was replaced by 15-year pro Yo Murphy. Austin was irate after the Calgary loss and, in a rare yelling fit, told the players, "It's going to cost a lot more than they're giving." The first-place showdown against B.C. revealed the hatred the teams were developing for each other. With Lions quarterback Jarious Jackson on the bottom of a pileup, offensive lineman Sherko Haji-Rasouli tore off the helmet of Riders defensive lineman Scott Schultz and rolled it down the field while Lions tackle Rob Murphy grabbed Schultz, then defensive end John Chick, holding the latter down by the facemask and threatening him. Saskatchewan was leading 24-15 at the time, but faltered afterwards. Murphy and Lions receiver Cory Rodgers, the lone player ejected, each got fined while Haji-Rasouli was suspended for one game. The tactics worked during the game, but they infuriated Tillman, who had some strong words for Lions head coach/general manager Wally Buono. "Being Sir Wally doesn't mean the rules apply to you or your team," said Tillman, who drew a $1,000 fine from the CFL.

Joseph passed for 365 yards and three touchdowns as the Riders completed an unprecedented season sweep of the Alouettes with a 33-22 victory in Regina. Two road victories followed, 33-21 in Calgary and 40-23 in Hamilton, but the most amazing thing was that slotback D.J. Flick played in both games. While preparing for the game against Calgary, Flick was told his in-laws had been injured in a Pennsylvania traffic accident. He went to see them, found out that everyone was going to be OK, and headed to Calgary. Before the next game his wife gave birth to premature twins, so Flick flew home to Montgomery, Pennsylvania, and met the team in Hamilton. Between those two games the Roughriders put their playoff tickets on sale, even though their 9-5 record hadn't clinched a playoff berth. "We're not being presumptuous," said CEO/president Jim Hopson. "If we get a home playoff game we needed 20,000 fans and it would be impossible to sell all of those in one week." Although there were playoff vouchers contained in the 17,000 season tickets that had been sold, fans hadn't witnessed a home playoff game since 1988, so only one per cent of the season-ticket holders had purchased their playoff tickets in advance. On the first day tickets were available, 3,000 were sold. The victory over Hamilton, coupled with a subsequent Blue Bombers victory over Calgary, ensured the Roughriders would end their 19-year drought and place either first or second in the West, thus earning a home playoff game. Tailback Wes Cates, who had a "foot issue," and fullback Chris Szarka were destined to miss the game. Szarka suffered an injury at home: During an off day he was operating a table saw, which partially sliced the tops off his left thumb and forefinger. Offensive linemen Jermese Jones and Mike Abou-Mechrek also earned some notoriety. They had been ejected from the Hamilton game for their parts in a fracas. Tillman and Austin questioned why they had been ejected and, because they had done so publicly, got fined $2,500 apiece by the league office. The team also got dinged $5,000. The discipline prompted patrons at the Plaza of Honor Dinner to give a light-hearted chorus of "boos" to Commissioner Mark Cohon, who was there as a guest to honour inductees Vic Stevenson, Bobby Thompson and Steve Dennis. The dinner attracted 1,412 people to Queensbury Centre and raised $255,000 for the franchise. The year's Touchdown Lottery, conducted by Friends of the Riders Inc., added $650,000 to the team's coffers, bringing the total raised through the lottery to $10 million since it began in 1986.

A fifth straight sellout was on hand for the next home game, a 38-11 victory over Hamilton. During the telecast, receiver Matt Dominguez told a TSN interviewer he was unhappy about waiting for surgery and sparked a public debate. "I said my knee felt OK, but I hadn't had surgery yet, thanks to our great Canadian health care system." Canada's socialized health system got him in for surgery soon after.

Despite missing 10 starters, the Roughriders won their 12th game by beating the home-town Eskimos 36-29 in overtime. The Eskimos thought they had won the game with a 47-yard field goal on the final play of regulation, but they were assessed a questionable penalty that negated the game-winning points. The Riders finished their season with a 12-6 record because of a surprising, 41-13 loss to the visiting Argonauts. Kerry Joseph had a poor performance and was yanked, an unexpected showing considering he had just been nominated as the West's outstanding player. Joseph was one of eight Riders named to the conference all-star team, along with linebackers Maurice Lloyd and Reggie Hunt, slotback D.J. Flick, defensive end Fred Perry, centre Jeremy O'Day, tackle Gene Makowsky and cornerback James Johnson. It was the first time the CFL included ballots from fans who voted on-line; their votes were calculated along with the voting conducted by the Football Reporters of Canada.

The Roughriders placed second in the West with their 12-6 record – the first time they had won 12 games since going 14-2 in 1970 – and prepared to play host to the third-place Calgary Stampeders (7-10-1) in the West semifinal. Another sellout crowd greeted the teams. Saskatchewan had claimed a home playoff victory for the first time since 1976 – it had lost 42-18 to B.C. in the 1988 West semifinal – and the players celebrated on the field before their boisterous fans. "They got so loud late in the game that it hurt my ears," said Flick. Unbeknownst to the players and most fans, there were two good luck charms planted under the new turf at Mosaic Stadium – employees of Site Management

Photo courtesy of *Leader-Post*

D.J. Flick

Photo courtesy of *Leader-Post*

Maurice Lloyd

Services, a local company that installed the FieldTurf, had placed two "Lucky Loonies" about 1½ inches below the carpet.

Cates and Szarka played in the West final. It was the third time in four years the Riders were headed to B.C. for the contest, but this time they won 26-17. Kerry Joseph threw touchdown passes to Neal Hughes and Andy Fantuz. Luca Congi kicked four field goals and two converts as all of the Roughriders points came from Canadian players. "I know coach Austin doesn't like to hear about all that old stuff," said Makowsky, who had missed a month of action with mononucleosis. "But he hasn't been around for those losses. (B.C. Place Stadium) is an extremely tough place to play, so coming here and winning . . . Oh, boy!"

Saskatchewan's Grey Cup opponents were the Winnipeg Blue Bombers, usually their divisional rivals, who had become the CFL's swing team, moving between the East and West conferences depending on the existence of East franchises in Ottawa and/or Montreal. It was the first Winnipeg-Saskatchewan matchup in 95 Grey Cups and the Blue Bombers were hurting: Quarterback Kevin Glenn, who would be the runner-up to Kerry Joseph as the CFL's outstanding player, had broken his left arm in the East final, leaving Ryan Dinwiddie to make his first pro start. "We don't get a free pass to the Grey Cup," cautioned Riders DB Eddie Davis. Fate may have been on Saskatchewan's side. During the provincial election, it was pointed out the Riders had never won a Grey Cup with an NDP government controlling the legislature. As Grey Cup week began in Toronto, Brad Wall was being sworn in as Saskatchewan's new premier because his Saskatchewan Party had unseated the NDP – led by Premier Lorne Calvert – by winning 38 of the province's 58 seats. Wall attended the Grey Cup, taking along with him Chris Knox, the cancer patient who had touched the Riders earlier in the season. Because the premier's flight had been arranged for Knox, that allowed 10 kids, all of them battling cancer, to attend the Grey Cup. They met the Riders inside Toronto's Rogers Centre following the team's final workout.

Photo courtesy of Royal Studios

Eddie Davis

The Roughriders won the third Grey Cup in franchise history on November 25. Before 52,230 spectators and a national television audience they defeated the Blue Bombers 23-19. Cornerback James Johnson was named the game's most outstanding player after he set a Grey Cup record by intercepting Dinwiddie three times, including one that he returned 30 yards for a touchdown and the game-clincher in the final minute. Defensive co-ordinator Richie Hall, who had played with Austin on the 1989 championship team, was elated inside the victors' locker room. "Nothing ever replaces being a player," said Hall, who was finishing his 14th season as an assistant coach. "That's why I'm so happy for these guys. I had my moment in the sun 18 years ago. I know what it's like." Added Tillman: "If you don't dream big, you don't achieve big . . . We play to be the champion."

Fans had been well-behaved during Grey Cup celebrations throughout Saskatchewan, including Regina, where the Regina Police Service had added extra personnel to the post-game shifts, just in case. There were 8,000 fans at Mosaic Stadium to welcome back the champions, plus a parade was slated for November 27. In temperatures of minus-14

Celsius, 15 trucks carried players and coaches along The Green Mile, a section of Albert Street, to the Legislative Building, where they were feted by Premier Brad Wall. "This is crazy," said defensive tackle Marcus Adams. "I hope it's warmer when we do this next year. I've never been so cold in my life."

Austin's dream had come true. "One of the reasons why I wanted to come back is there is no greater place to win a championship in the CFL than with the Saskatchewan Roughriders," said the head coach. "To win it as a player and a coach, in whatever small part I played in it, it was just too enticing to pass up." There had been stories that Austin was a candidate to become head coach at his alma mater, the University of Mississippi, also known as Ole Miss. In truth, he was never considered to be the head coach before legendary Houston Nutt was signed to run the program. "Why would they be interested in me?" said Austin.

Photo courtesy of *Leader-Post*

James Johnson

Head coach Kent Austin was wanted in two places for 2008. As the reigning Grey Cup-winning coach – and soon to be named the Annis Stukus Trophy winner as the CFL's top coach in 2007 – he was certainly coveted by the Roughriders. General manager Eric Tillman, realizing he might lose his friend to a more lucrative career opportunity, offered Austin a contract extension. The offer might have made Austin the highest-paid coach in the CFL. Meanwhile, at the suggestion of David Lee, a long-time college assistant who had coached Austin and left Ole Miss to work for the NFL's Miami Dolphins, newly hired Mississippi coach Houston Nutt interviewed Austin for the job as the Rebels' offensive co-ordinator. Austin didn't think he had a chance. He had never coached college football and wasn't connected to the U.S. university ranks. He wasn't looking for another job. "Typically, coaches hire who they know," Austin said upon returning to Regina from visiting his old school. "I'm not anticipating an offer. I'm not. I went down there to listen. It's Ole Miss!" Austin still had two years remaining on his Riders contract when he got an offer from Nutt. He was torn between continuing what he had started in Saskatchewan and returning home. He went home, even though the Ole Miss offer – reported to be $300,000 annually – was less than Saskatchewan's offer. "What (Saskatchewan) presented to me was an unbelievable offer to stay," said Austin. "I was appreciative of that and I probably didn't deserve it. But it wasn't based on money. If it was all about the money I'd be staying here." Out of professional courtesy and friendship, Tillman let him leave, a move that infuriated some fans who believed Austin should honour the remaining two years of his contract. Tillman swayed most of the Riders faithful by reminding them Austin hadn't been looking to leave, he simply

Photo courtesy of *Leader-Post*

Kent Austin

received an offer to return home. And besides, Austin had accomplished what he had set out to do: Win another Grey Cup with the Roughriders.

"Ken is . . . thoughtful, bright, full of wisdom, has worked both sides of the ball and brings a scroll of attributes. And don't mistake his kindness for weakness – he'll bite a hole in your anatomy if it's warranted."

Assistant coaches Richie Hall and Ken Miller topped a list of potential replacements for Austin. Tillman considered numerous others, including veteran CFL coaches Dave Ritchie and George Cortez. Tillman interviewed Hall first, but soon after began believing Miller would be his best choice. Miller, 66, had spent five seasons with the Toronto Argonauts – including 2004 when, with Austin, the team won a Grey Cup – and 35 years coaching U.S. college and high school teams. He had been a head coach once, from 1984-88 at the University of Redlands in California. When Tillman announced he had hired Miller, he said, "Ken is . . . thoughtful, bright, full of wisdom, has worked both sides of the ball and brings a scroll of attributes. And don't mistake his kindness for weakness – he'll bite a hole in your anatomy if it's warranted." Miller's soft-spoken approach evidently hid a highly competitive nature. "We might not win (a Grey Cup) every year," Miller said. "But we are going to be in the hunt for it all the time, with a great opportunity to win."

Photo courtesy of *Leader-Post*

Ken Miller and Eric Tillman

Miller promoted Paul LaPolice to offensive co-ordinator, kept the rest of the assistant coaches – although defensive line coach Ron Estay would be sidelined most of the season with various ailments – and added Jamie Barresi to handle the running backs and former defensive co-ordinator Gary Etcheverry as a defensive consultant. Big changes were coming to the roster, however, as all-star defensive end Fred Perry was traded to the Edmonton Eskimos for quarterback Steven Jyles. Perry had led the team in sacks the previous two seasons, slipping from 14 to eight in 2007, and he had just signed a new contract. When Perry wanted to rework his new deal, Tillman dealt him. In on-line chats Tillman defended the move by claiming Perry had financial problems, which seemed to hold some merit because a car-restoration business he co-owned with teammate Marcus Crandell had recently closed. "I haven't heard all these stories," said Perry. "But I don't owe anybody anything." Linebacker Reggie Hunt, who had missed only one game because of injuries during his six years with Saskatchewan, turned down a reduced offer and signed as a free agent with the Montreal Alouettes. Then came the big deal: Quarterback Kerry Joseph, the reigning MVP who had stated publicly that he wanted to get a new contract that would give back some of the money he had lost upon agreeing to a pay cut one year earlier, was dealt to the Toronto Argonauts. Along with a draft choice, Joseph was exchanged for two draft choices, offensive tackle Glenn January (who played sparingly during his one season) and defensive lineman Ronald Flemons, who was sent back to Toronto early in the regular season. Joseph never received a formal offer from Tillman, so he was shocked about being traded. "I didn't want to be traded," Joseph said. "I wanted to come back and lead my team to back-to-back championships."

Tillman was intent on trimming salaries again. Although Tillman had tried to trim $800,000 from his payroll, he had overspent the $4.1-million salary cap by $54,330 and the team was fined that amount by the CFL. Still, the Roughriders recorded a record profit of $1.73 million during their Grey Cup-winning campaign, helped by all-time high gate receipts of $7.4 million, $5.08 million in merchandise sales and $1.5 million from playing host to a home playoff game. Rider Fever was in full flight as the team was poised to – for the first time in history – sell out every home game. Former treasurer Tom Shepherd would have been proud – he never recorded such a profit during his 22 years as the team's treasurer, but his volunteer work was rewarded when it was announced he was being inducted as a builder into the Canadian Football Hall of Fame. Shepherd was being honoured with a stellar group, along with quarterback Doug Flutie, tailback Mike Pringle, returner/tailback Mike (Pinball) Clemons and offensive lineman John Bonk.

Photo courtesy of Hamilton *Spectator*

Left to right: Tom Shepherd, John Bonk, Pinball Clemons, Doug Flutie, Mike Pringle – 2008 inductees in to the Canadian Football Hall of Fame

None of the team's top three draft picks were in attendance when training camp opened at the University of Regina on June 1. One night earlier, the Roughriders were presented with their Grey Cup rings during a Dinner of Champions at the Conexus Arts Centre. There were 100 rings made for distribution, varying in size and value depending on a person's contribution to the team. Of course the coaches and players got the most elaborate rings. Also on the eve of training camp, Ted Provost, Tom Campana and Lawrie Skolrood were named as the year's inductees into the Plaza of Honor. And the Grey Cup kept hovering around the province, making appearances at schools and shopping malls and one special stop at the home where Erin Lawrence – the young woman befriended by Kerry Joseph during her fight with cancer – had lived with her family. "When the Cup came in, I saw my sister," said Erin's 16-year-old brother, Jared. Two Roughriders alumni, Roger Aldag and Steve Mazurak, also escorted the Grey Cup to Afghanistan for a Canada Day visit with some of the 2,500 Canadian troops stationed there.

The team's top draft choice, Keith Shologan, a defensive end from Central Florida taken fourth overall, had a short-lived tryout with the NFL's San Diego Chargers before joining the Riders in September. Regina-born defensive end Michael Stadnyk, a University of Montana product taken 14th, and offensive lineman Jonathan St. Pierre, an Illinois State product taken 10th, had college eligibility remaining. Most of the attention was focused on quarterback Teale Orban from the University of Regina. The Riders had made a draft-day trade to pick him 41st – he saw little preseason action and was waived on cutdown day.

Photo courtesy of *Leader-Post*

Darian Durant

The Roughriders flew out of the starting gate. Marcus Crandell, a 10-year CFL veteran who had led the Calgary Stampeders to their 2001 Grey Cup victory, was Saskatchewan's starting quarterback. He tossed a 73-yard touchdown to rookie receiver Adarius Bowman, an NFL prospect from Oklahoma State who came to Canada after marijuana possession charges sidetracked his U.S. career, in a season-opening, 34-13 victory over the Eskimos. When Crandell got hurt early in the next game, Steven Jyles replaced him, but his ineffectiveness convinced Miller to insert third-stringer Darian Durant. Saskatchewan won 26-16, but lost slotback D.J. Flick and defensive back Leron Mitchell with broken legs. They would be the first of nine players who suffered broken legs during the campaign. Athletic therapist Ivan Gutfriend said during the season it was rare for a team to have two players break legs in one year, let alone during a single game. Durant, who had been recruited by Roy Shivers out of North Carolina, won his first start, 33-28 in Hamilton. Durant passed for 347 yards and two touchdowns, plus the Riders were helped by a video-replay challenge that let them keep the football on Hamilton's one-yard line despite a fumble by Weston Dressler.

With his team undefeated in three games, Tillman signed a contract extension that carried him through 2010 and could extend itself further based on his team's performance. "It's based upon the kind of things that you measure football success by," said Riders CEO/president Jim Hopson, "such as wins and home playoff games and playoff appearances. They're achievable. They're realistic." The wary Roughriders also made sure Tillman wouldn't be leaving, like Austin, without paying heavily before his contract expired. "There's a punitive part (for leaving early)," said Tillman.

The Roughriders won three more games – 41-33 over the Alouettes in a game delayed 50 minutes by a rainstorm; 28-22 against the Argonauts, who seemed to be in disarray while short-termed head coach Rich Stubler decided whether Kerry Joseph or Michael Bishop should be his quarterback; and 22-21 in Calgary, where the Roughriders lost three more players (Nos. 11, 12 and 13) to injuries, including torn knee ligaments by wideout Matt Dominguez and a fractured left fibula by fullback Neal Hughes. That prompted Tillman to criticize the injury lists described in the league's Salary Management System, saying there were better ways to control costs than by forcing an injured player to the sideline, receiving full salary, for a specific time frame. Tillman got fined $2,500. The Roughriders were 6-0 for the first time in 38 years, partly because they had outscored their opponents 68-32 in the fourth quarters of their contests. "In a dogfight, it's the pit bulls that always win," said middle linebacker Maurice Lloyd. Tackle Belton Johnson cracked his right fibula during a 30-25 loss to the Stampeders – Saskatchewan's first loss came after going ahead 4-0 and surrendering 30 straight points. The Roughriders led 10-0 in their next game, before losing 27-10 in Edmonton. Crandell completed seven of 24 passes for 135 yards and one touchdown before being replaced by Jyles. Durant had cracked ribs. It was Crandell's last game. He was unceremoniously waived, not coincidentally just before the deadline when contracts of players with six or more years of CFL experience had to be honoured for the rest of the season. "It's a shock," said Crandell. "But it's the kind of business that I chose and this is a part of it that I have to deal with."

Photo courtesy of *Leader-Post*

Maurice Lloyd

Crandell was replaced by Michael Bishop, the sometimes-good, sometimes-bad pivot who had been mired in a quarterback controversy in Toronto. Bishop, following a season in which he was 11-1 as a starter, had re-signed with the Argonauts just before they acquired Kerry Joseph from Saskatchewan. Bishop was dealt to Saskatchewan for a conditional draft choice. "I'm glad that chapter in my life is past," said Bishop. "I'm happy to be with an organization that is honest and up-front from the top." Bishop won his first two games in a home-and-home set with the Blue Bombers. With 30,945 fans filling Mosaic Stadium, which had been expanded by 2,065 temporary seats to help accommodate the demand for tickets, the Riders beat Winnipeg 19-9. Saskatchewan won the rematch 34-31 in Winnipeg, despite trailing 31-14 in the fourth quarter. Linebacker Brandon Lynch became the sixth victim of a broken fibula – receiver Adam Nicolson would be the seventh – on the opening kickoff of a 28-23 loss in B.C.

When the teams met to complete the home-and-home series, Taylor Field had "23" painted on the 23-yard lines. The numbers were placed there to honour Hall of Fame quarterback Ron Lancaster, who died Sept. 18 at the age of 69. Lancaster's image, wearing Riders jersey No. 23 in a huge mural along with Hall of Fame teammate George Reed, continued to adorn the exterior of Mosaic Stadium.

Saskatchewan lost 27-21. The Lions were pelted with beer cans thrown by fans and the game was temporarily halted while the players went to the middle of the field to escape danger. It was decreed afterwards that beer would be sold in the east grandstands only in plastic cups, which couldn't be used as projectiles. Bishop was replaced by Durant in the B.C. loss. He didn't manufacture any touchdowns in a 37-12 loss in Montreal that dropped Saskatchewan's record to 8-5. A 37-34 victory over the Stampeders clinched a seventh straight playoff berth before the Roughriders embarked on a season-ending trek that would see them play four games in 17 days. Michael Bishop started a 42-5 loss in Calgary and a 30-29 victory against the Tiger-Cats, although he was replaced by Jyles in that contest. Jyles got his first start against his former team, the Eskimos, which Saskatchewan won 55-9 in Regina. Bishop started the finale in Toronto and threw four interceptions, forcing the head coach to think about yanking his quarterback. Bishop begged for one more chance and rallied the Roughriders to a 45-38 victory with four touchdowns in the fourth quarter. Saskatchewan placed second in the West with a 12-6 record and, although he had used three different starters in his last three games, Miller decided Bishop's year-end rally had earned him the playoff start. He should have held an election – it was election year in the U.S., where Barack Obama, the Democratic candidate, became the country's first black president by defeating Republican challenger John McCain, whose ties to unpopular, outgoing president George W. Bush were too strong to overcome. Obama's first official visit was to Canada, where he met Prime Minister Stephen Harper, whose Conservative party earlier in 2008 had retained a minority government. The defeat cost Liberal leader Stephane Dion his position.

Saskatchewan's home playoff game sold out in 35 minutes. Some season-ticket holders hadn't been aware they missed the deadline to purchase playoff tickets and some fans were irate that tickets were being resold at inflated prices, even though that wasn't illegal. Playing before an 18th straight sellout, the Roughriders were dreadful while losing the West semfinal 33-12 to the B.C. Lions. Bishop threw three interceptions but wasn't pulled until Ryan Phillips returned the last one 54 yards for a touchdown. Miller's judgment was questioned publicly by the fans and media, quietly by Tillman and the Roughriders brass. "It's all on me," said Bishop. "I didn't play well." Two days later, Bishop was released to start a furious off-season. Four Riders were commended as CFL all-stars – linebackers Anton McKenzie and Maurice Lloyd, offensive lineman Gene Makowsky and tailback Wes Cates – while rookie receiver Weston Dressler, a speedster from the University of North Dakota, was the CFL's outstanding rookie. Defensive co-ordinator Richie Hall met with Marcel Bellefeuille, a former Riders assistant who had become Hamilton's head coach, and speculation began that Hall might be leaving. He did leave, but the discussions with Bellefeuille were informational. Hall was hired to become head coach of the Edmonton Eskimos by GM Danny Maciocia, who had stepped down from the position. "(Saskatchewan) is a place I've been for the last 20 years as a coach and player," said Hall, who had been interviewed for seven other jobs during his tenure. "At the same time, all good things must end." Gary Etcheverry was promoted to defensive co-ordinator while Mike Gibson, the assistant head coach and offensive line coach, joined Bellefeuille as his offensive co-ordinator. Saskatchewan's roster was bolstered by the signing of slotback Jason Clermont, a University of Regina product and native son, who had been released after seven seasons with the B.C. Lions.

Photo courtesy of *Leader-Post*

Wes Cates

There were a couple of uproars over ticket sales – the Riders limited the number of 10-game flex packs they would be selling – and about a planned, all-expenses-paid directors meeting in Palm Springs, California, which convinced the board members they should be paying their own expenses for such a trip. The biggest issue was the appearance of the NFL in Canada, sparking a debate about the CFL's continued existence. The Buffalo Bills played the NFL's first regular-season game in Toronto on December 7. A crowd of 52,134 saw the Miami Dolphins beat the Bills 16-3. Average ticket prices were $185, three times the top price of a Roughriders ticket.

Hall was hired to become head coach of the Edmonton Eskimos by GM Danny Maciocia, who had stepped down from the position. "(Saskatchewan) is a place I've been for the last 20 years as a coach and player," said Hall, who had been interviewed for seven other jobs during his tenure. "At the same time, all good things must end."

News broke on February 3, 2009 that Eric Tillman, the Roughriders' general manager, had been charged with sexual assault, an allegation that involved a 16-year-old girl. The alleged incident occurred August 9, 2008, and charges were laid January 29. While the legal process was unwinding, Tillman was placed on paid administrative leave, but he continued to be used as a "resource" and was constantly being consulted by head coach Ken Miller and the team's personnel department, comprising Tony Playter and Joe Womack. Tillman called a media conference after the Regina Police Service announced that charges had been laid. "I have told the truth and that won't change," said Tillman, who pleaded not guilty in April. "I have faith in the process and that will not change." When asked whether Tillman had broken the team's code of conduct, CEO/president Jim Hopson replied: "A charge did not automatically kick in any kind of sanctions or disciplinary action or anything like that." A normal series of legal moves was to delay the case until January 2010.

Player negotiations continued normally, with quarterback Darian Durant signing a new contract that made him "the lead rabbit," according to Tillman, in the derby to become the starter. The team evidently wasn't interested in Kevin Glenn, a former Rider, or Casey Printers, a former outstanding-player winner, quarterbacks who had been dumped by Winnipeg and Hamilton. All-star linebackers Maurice Lloyd and Anton McKenzie departed as free agents, signing respectively with the Edmonton Eskimos and B.C. Lions. Safety Scott Gordon also joined Edmonton, while defensive line coach Ron Estay – after completing cancer treatments – returned home to Louisiana. With defensive co-ordinator Gary Etcheverry slated to handle the linemen, Nelson Martin was hired to oversee the secondary, Bob Wylie became offensive line coach and Kavis Reed took over the special teams and running backs. Veteran coach Alex Smith was placed in charge of linebackers and returnee Jamie Barresi got the quarterbacks while Mike Scheper became defensive line coach. Wide receiver Matt Dominguez, who had suffered four knee injuries, was waived with a chance of returning if he could pass physical tests. Offensive lineman Mike Abou-Mechrek wasn't re-signed. Cornerback James Johnson, who had been relegated to backup duties after being named MVP of the 2007 Grey Cup, and second-year receiver Adarius Bowman were traded to Winnipeg in separate deals. The Roughriders got a 2011 draft choice for Johnson and offensive lineman Jordan Rempel, a Saskatchewan product, from Hamilton in a three-way trade. In addition to signing slotback Jason Clermont, the Riders landed another free agent in Joe McGrath, an offensive lineman from Moose Jaw who had been with the Edmonton Eskimos. McGrath was shipped back to Edmonton during training camp. The Eskimos also grabbed undersized defensive end Kitwana Jones. On draft day, because of earlier trades the Roughriders had only two selections and used them to select University of Regina teammates Tamon George, a defensive back, ninth overall and offensive lineman Nick Hutchins 17th overall.

The Roughriders again were charged with exceeding the salary cap. They were the only team that overspent the league-mandated $4.2-million limit and were fined an equal amount – $87,147 – which the Riders insisted was caused by their unbelievable rash of injuries. "The goal was to stay under," said Hopson. "Clearly as we got down to the end of the year and everyone wanted to stay competitive, we had to balance the cost of gong over the cap with achieving a second- or third-place finish." The cost was evidently worthwhile

In addition to signing slotback Jason Clermont, the Riders landed another free agent in Joe McGrath, an offensive lineman from Moose Jaw who had been with the Edmonton Eskimos.

– the team made $500,000 for playing host to a playoff game and recorded a profit of $1.6 million on its 2008-09 operations. As the football team's 100th season approached, there was the usual speculation about the upcoming year, with high hopes for everything from a home playoff game to another Grey Cup championship to a new, domed stadium. Because Mosaic Stadium at Taylor Field was 63 years old, different levels of government began looking at options for the facility. Should the taxpayers, with help from private contributions and the Roughriders, pay $100 million to properly upgrade the stadium? Or would it be better to build a new, domed stadium in downtown Regina for approximately $350 million?

Looking back from the general manager's perspective:

ERIC TILLMAN

"I had always been fascinated by the Saskatchewan Roughriders, in every sense of the word, the passion the fans had for the team. The warmth and friendliness of the province. It reminded me, other than the weather, so much of home. It, more than any other place in Canada, felt like home when I came here with the visiting team. I always had this image as a big-city guy because I was the GM in the capital, Vancouver and the Republic of Toronto. Every time I came to Regina I felt this incredible draw to everything the province represented.

"I remember when Jim (Hopson) called to invite me to fly out. I was talking to (my wife) Francine before I got on the plane. She was the factor, the only reason why I didn't take the job in December of 1999. She said, 'You want to do this, don't you?' We had a great home in Ottawa, great neighbours, I enjoyed the broadcasting thing. She looked at me and said, 'Do it!' I'll always be grateful for that support. She knew that in my mind, even though I never regretted the decision because of how it worked out on a personal level, that I played the what-if game with a wistful sense that I would love to be there. Every time I watched a game, even sitting in the TSN studio in Toronto, I would see the people there and think about it. I developed so many good friendships with people who love the place. Not only Glen Suitor, but Kent Austin and James Ellingson and Vic Stevenson, they told me what a great place it was if you won there. Everything they said resonated. You would get a sense of how important the game was to the people. And every time you went out there, there was such a connection. But it's way more than I thought. You think you know, coming in, that you have a good feel for it but you don't. There's no way to understand the passion or emotion, the DNA connection with the team, unless you're here. I joke that people in Saskatchewan aren't born with birthmarks, they're born with logos. It's a way of life. Family events are built around when the Rider games are scheduled. People compare an offensive line from 2007 to an offensive line from 1988 and speak in specifics of who the right and left guards were. You know they're devoted when they're spending hours a day before the game on Riderville.com debating about who the four people should be on the reserve list. People care at a level that's incomparable throughout the country.

"I had always been fascinated by the Saskatchewan Roughriders, in every sense of the word, the passion the fans had for the team. The warmth and friendliness of the province. It reminded me, other than the weather, so much of home."

"When we talk about what this team has accomplished over the past several years, you have to be fair to Al Ford on a comparative basis. Al Ford is a good man, a fine person, and he bleeds Green and White. The reality is he didn't have near the resources that we have now. The level of resources we have been afforded are at a completely different basis from what Al had. It's important to establish that on a comparative basis. There's no question that Roy Shivers built a solid foundation in many regards. When we came in there were some definite, significant positives to build around. The biggest challenge when I came in was – and how it got there you'll have to ask other people because I don't know how the relationships became fractured – how the distrust had reached such a high level. We wanted to try to become One again. We had to become One. There was distrust and disharmony; the factions were staggering at multiple levels. For example, it was in so many ways at so many levels, one of the first things when I came in was Danny (Barrett) asked Normie (Fong) to order 100 RS stickers to put on the helmets (to honour fired GM Roy Shivers). Even though they were never worn, they were ordered and there was a plan to wear them during the season. I had just been there a few weeks. Danny pulled three or four people together in football operations, where I work, and talked to them about me. I don't have to name names because everybody knows who they are. He pulled that little group in and told them, 'Don't share anything with him because he's going to get rid of us at the end of the year.' It was extreme distrust in football operations. It was splintered. When I came in it was made clear to me that there were three, maybe four groups, in there. I was an intruder in football ops. Then you had Jim Hopson's group that the football people did not trust, interact with or have anything to do with. Then there was the big, bad wolf, the board. It was incredibly dysfunctional because of distrust, total lack of communication, and as a result of that there were individual goals rather than team goals.

"I almost kept Danny because I saw so much good in Danny. I respect him and care for him as a person. So many times in my life I thought with my heart as opposed to my head. Danny and I progressed a million miles in those 2½ months in a personal sense. I did everything I could: Going to his kid's high school football games, trying to be inclusive and establish a rapport. I let him make every football decision. One of the first things I told him when I got in was, 'I understand that this is a very emotional time for you because of the relationship you have with Roy and the loyalty you have for him. And certainly there's the fear you and your family face now. As such, out of fairness for you because we'll be making an evaluation at the end of the year, I'm going to let you make every major football decision as we go forward, unless there's an economic component or something that would affect this team long-term, such as trading draft picks. Otherwise I'll let you make the decisions. If I implement A, C and D and it doesn't work, does that mean I impeded you? At the same time, if we go on, the dynamic will change and my role as general manager from 2007 and beyond will be very different. Because it's midseason and the relationships you have, I'm going to give you every opportunity to be successful. Anything you need from me to help in that regard, I'm going to try.' If you look back with a sense of humour, one of the funniest things looking back – and it's easy now because of the success he's having at the University of Buffalo, so I'm thrilled for Danny and Alison because he's well-positioned for a tremendous career in the business – because I told him I was going to offer advice, although he could make the final decision. The first advice I gave him was I thought the team was really suffering from poor field position because Luca (Congi) was struggling as a young kicker. Because he was dressing two or three American running backs, I suggested he bring in an American punter and kickoff guy. I understand some people might view that as unorthodox. In Ottawa we had done that with Lawrence Tynes, although he's a field goal kicker, but the kicking game is such an important element. Danny listened to me and elected to keep the status quo. Two or three times during the course of the year I suggested it again. We never went that route. But two to three times during the season and looking at the Western final, when we got thrashed by B.C., we got killed in field position. A couple

"I let him make every football decision. One of the first things I told him when I got in was, 'I understand that this is a very emotional time for you because of the relationship you have with Roy and the loyalty you have for him."

weeks after that I was in Saskatoon for the (University of Saskatchewan's) Dogs Breakfast. A guy walked up to me and said, 'Tillman, you need to do what you should have done months ago and get our kicking game fixed up.' Tony Playter was with me. He nearly fell down. I told the guy I appreciated the advice, but it was the first thing I had suggested.

"I always said that hiring somebody you don't know, or hiring somebody off a good interview, is like getting married after a blind date. How many of us had great blind dates, then within a month neither person wanted to be within 100 kilometres of the other? I knew Kent (Austin) at so many different levels. We have a special relationship. I negotiated a contract with him with B.C. (in 1994) and after we won the Grey Cup I traded him. I'm still amazed that after I traded Kerry Joseph (from Saskatchewan to Toronto), nobody wrote that I had also traded our starting quarterback after winning the Grey Cup in B.C. It wasn't personal, just like it wasn't personal trading Danny (Barrett away from B.C. in 1994). You have to do what you believe is best. The best relationships are often forged through a combination of highs and lows. Kent and I had tremendous respect for one another from a long and shared philosophy of how to build teams. It goes beyond athletes, to the kind of people and the environment you want. I've been pretty candid about how fractured it was when I got there, but it's critical for the general manager and the head coach to have a shared philosophy, good communication and the ability to disagree without it being personal. As much as in my heart, and I knew that Danny and Alison and their family loved Regina, how deeply rooted they were here and the strong bond they had, I thought so long and hard about giving Danny a one-year extension and trying to make it work. When I stepped back, I realized by extending just one year – and I wasn't willing to go beyond that – it would be a week-to-week thing. One week we win, he's OK. Then we lose, is he on the hot seat? That wasn't conducive to long-term success. When I made the decision it wasn't going to be Danny, that we weren't going to extend the relationship, in my mind there was no doubt Kent was the right guy. The shared philosophies we had, the communication, those were the strengths we had in bringing the organization together. Kent was intense and guarded, genetically gifted as a player. From an athletic standpoint everybody knows about his football prowess, plus he was an all-state basketball player who was recruited by Kentucky. Not offered, recruited. His dad finished fifth or sixth in Heisman Trophy balloting. Intellectually, I have never met anyone like him in any walk of life who is his superior. There are some who are his equal. He's scary. And he's so competitive. If he had an IQ of 75 he'd be successful because of his tenacity and his work ethic. Since it's double that or more, that combination is really something. I had seen the evolution, the natural maturity, when we hired him in Ottawa as a coach. The biggest misnomer when we hired him was people wondering if he would connect with the players. I heard whispered, and we hear all the whispers in Saskatchewan, 'Is he going to be too hard on the players? Is he going to be too critical?' I had seen first-hand in Ottawa one of his greatest assets, what a positive teacher he was, that he built players up and made them believe they were better. That dynamic was different from what the public had seen when he played quarterback. We sat at Novotel in Toronto and went from 30 minutes of conversation to pulling out our shirt-tails, rolling up our sleeves and drawing up our plans. I had the roster and salary cap with me. It was unspoken that we wanted to do this. Without the job even being offered, the dynamic was, 'We'll do this. We should do that. What about this guy?' There was no question those hours we spent together, eight to 10 hours that day, from noon until almost

"You have to do what you believe is best. The best relationships are often forged through a combination of highs and lows. Kent and I had tremendous respect for one another from a long and shared philosophy of how to build teams."

"The biggest misnomer when we hired him was people wondering if he would connect with the players. I heard whispered, and we hear all the whispers in Saskatchewan, 'Is he going to be too hard on the players? Is he going to be too critical?' I had seen first-hand in Ottawa one of his greatest assets, what a positive teacher he was, that he built players up and made them believe they were better."

midnight, I knew without question he was the right guy. If there was any question before, there wasn't now and I knew we were going to be successful.

"I thought he was going to be here a long time. He did, too. He was really enthused about coming back. We had a special relationship. He thought it was going to be really good for his family. He had a perspective different from that of a young player: It was safe, the people were good, the community, the sense of shared values. He asked me what I thought and I told him I was hoping to work into my 70s. He didn't seek the other job. I was at home in Mississippi when I got a phone call from Langston Rogers, the sports information director at Ole Miss. Langston wanted to know if it was OK for Houston (Nutt) to call me. I knew it was going to happen. My Adam's apple dropped. David Lee, who was like a father figure to Kent, had been Houston's offensive co-ordinator and was with him for a few days at Ole Miss before leaving to join the Miami Dolphins. Knowing that Kent was not only an alumnus but in the school's hall of fame, and that David was championing his cause, as soon as those two got together it was game, set, match.

"It was important to stay within when we hired a replacement. We had so much success. Even though there was George Cortez, Dave Ritchie, so many people I believe would have been successful coaches, I knew we didn't win because we had the most talented team. We were not the most talented team in the Canadian Football League in 2007. We were extremely well coached, but we had such unity within and a sense of oneness through the football team and the whole organization. It goes back to what I said about being fractured. All the divisions, all the walls separating us had been knocked down. We had a tremendous relationship with the board, Jim helped as much as he could. There was a sense of trust, such an environment that was conducive to success. It was such a huge difference from what I had walked into in late August of 2006. It was important to maintain that environment with our players and throughout the organization. Hiring Kenny (Miller) was easy. Not hiring Richie (Hall) was one of the hardest things I ever had to do in the business.

"Hiring Kenny (Miller) was easy. Not hiring Richie (Hall) was one of the hardest things I ever had to do in the business."

"I hope that our legacy will be that we understood that we were fortunate. When I talked to people about the job, like I did when Bob Ellard had been such a tremendous host in December 1999 – when I got on the plane to come out there I wanted to take the job, and after spending a couple days with him I really wanted to take the job because he was just phenomenal – there was always the questioning. Can you win in Saskatchewan? Will the players come here? Can it be done? I hope the thing we're able to do is completely negate that mindset and change it to knowing this is the best place to be in the Canadian Football League. The best fans. The most passionate support. It matters more, at a deeper level, than anyplace else in the country. If you're a player, a coach, the general manager, you're lucky to be there. Not vice versa. There had been an attitude of other people, and I'm not talking about Roy in this sense at all, that Saskatchewan was lucky to have them. There was a sense that nobody wanted to be there. Whether you're a player, a coach or an administrator you're lucky to have this job, this opportunity, rather than them being fortunate to have you. It's fortunate to be in a place where it matters so much. I hope that's part of our legacy. I also hope we return that with absolute, total dedication, in trying to give people the type of football team they can be proud of. Roy left a strong foundation. There's no way we would have won in 2007 without the foundation he and Danny built."

"The best fans. The most passionate support. It matters more, at a deeper level, than anyplace else in the country. If you're a player, a coach, the general manager, you're lucky to be there. Not vice versa."

All-Era Team
1990-2009

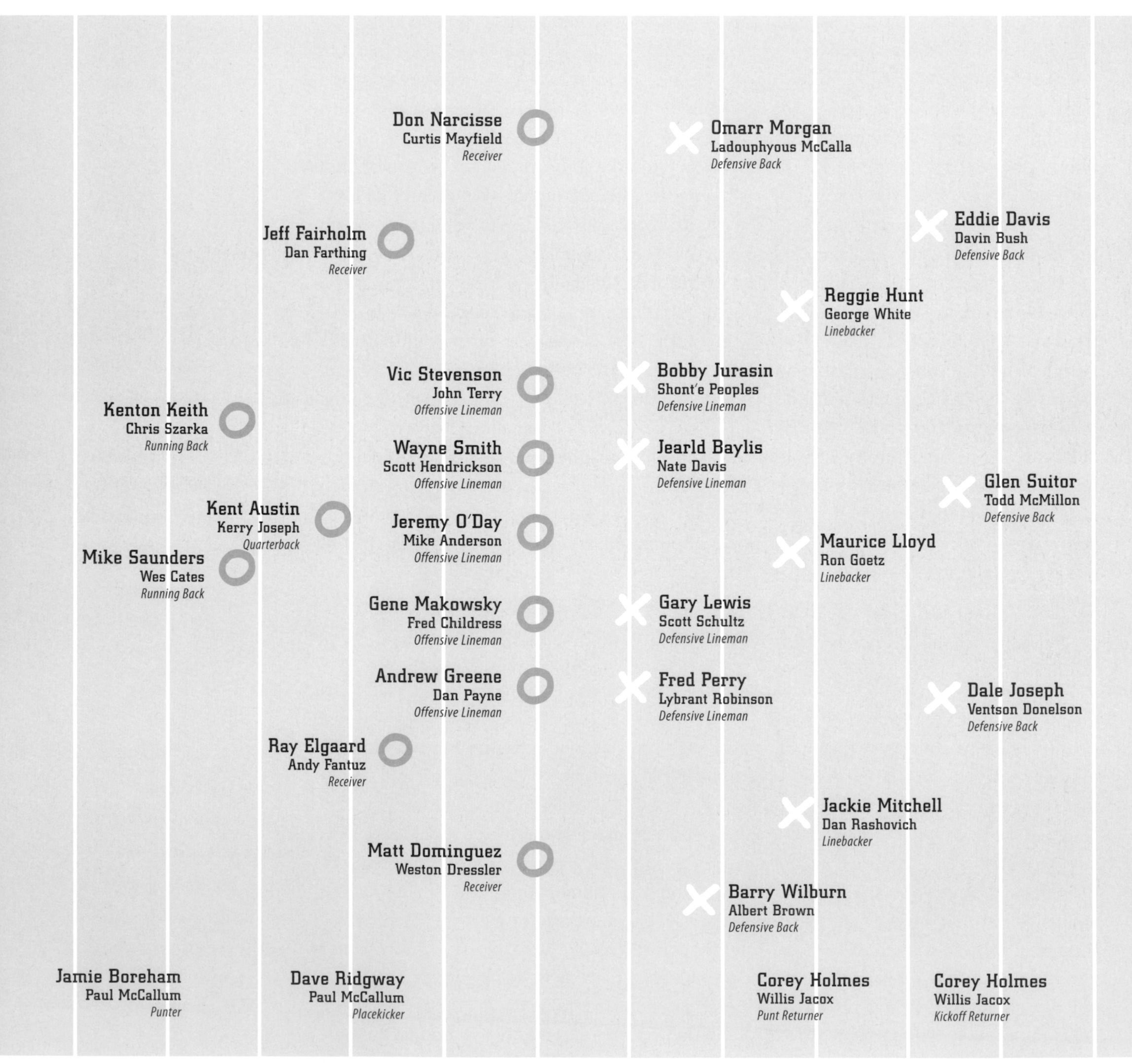

OFFENCE

Large print – 1st Team All-Star
Small print – 2nd Team All-Star
Position

DEFENCE

Photo courtesy of Dan Marce

CHAPTER 6

The Plaza of Honor

BY DAN MARCE

Located outside the main gates on the west side of Mosaic Stadium is a 10-sided cairn supporting solid granite tablets that symbolize the rich tradition, strength and history of the Saskatchewan Roughriders.

The cairn, which is formally known as the Plaza of Honor (the Roughrider equivalent of a hall of fame), includes the names of over 100 individuals who have been building blocks of this renowned franchise. The fact that the cairn stands outside the stadium allows for the accessibility of the shrine to Rider fans at any time.

In the fall of each football season the list of honorees grows as more heroes of the past are feted upon induction into the Plaza of Honor.

Historically the club, by virtue of its small provincial population base, has had to look off-field to raise much-needed revenue in order to compete with the larger CFL member partners.

The club's Board of Directors, which has long been comprised of prominent volunteer business people who have had a passion for football and "bled green", conjured up a fundraising Roughrider Sportsman's Dinner in 1953 charging the then-substantial sum of $50 per plate.

The inaugural fundraising format of having Rider players, coaches and management in attendance, often with a guest speaker unrelated to the Roughriders, continued until 1987 with the unveiling of the Plaza of Honor and the inaugural induction ceremonies, honoring nine Rider greats. After a few catch-up years of a similarly large slate of inductees, the annual honorees now generally numbers three, often representing the contribution of different eras.

Over time the cost of the fundraiser has gradually increased to the $350 ticket price of 2009. Since 1953 the previous dinner and current induction format has raised in excess of $7 million, and contributes over $200,000 annually towards the operation of the club.

Listed on this page are the names of the esteemed inductees and the year each was inducted.

1987
Ron Atchison
Dean Griffing
Al Ritchie
Ken Preston
Ron Lancaster
Bob Kramer
George Reed
Fred Wilson
Eagle Keys

1988
Sandy Archer
Ken Charlton
Martin Ruby
Glenn Dobbs
Hugh Campbell
Greg Grassick
Don McPherson
Gord Barber
Bill Clarke

1989
Ken Carpenter
Bob Walker
Ed McQuarters
Jack Hill
Frank Tripucka
Bob Marlow
Clair Warner
Al Urness
Ted Urness

1990
J.D. Rowand
D.S. MacDonald
Bill Baker
Garner Ekstran
S.D. Tibbits
Pete Martin
Joey Walters
Toar Springstein

1991
Bruce Bennett
Mike Samples
Al Benecick
Tare Rennebohm
Sully Glasser
Del Wardien
John Garuik
W.E. Bill Clarke

1992
Alan Ford
Howie Milne
Jack Abendschan
Neil Habig
Reg Whitehouse

1993
Gordon Staseson
Maurice Williams
Ken McEachern
Piffles Taylor
Ted Dushinski
Roger Aldag

1994
Wayne Shaw
Chris DeFrance
Vince Goldsmith
Mike Cassidy
Gordon Barwell

1995
Eddie Lowe
Geno Wlasiuk
Wally Dempsey
Clyde Brock
Tom Shepherd

1996
Bob Poley
John Gregory
Ralph Galloway
Jim Worden
Stan Williams

1997
Bob Kosid
Dick Rendek
Dale West
Lorne Richardson

1998
Roger Goree
Johnny (Red) Bell
Glen Suitor

1999
Kent Austin
Larry Isbell
Ray Elgaard

2000
Dave Ridgway
Bruce Cowie
Cleveland Vann

2001
John Payne
Doug Killoh
Bob Ptacek
Bill Manchuk

2002
Bobby Jurasin
Larry Bird
Gary Brandt

2003
John Lipp
Don Narcisse
Larry Dumelie

2004
Hank Dorsch
Mike Anderson
Steve Mazurak

2005
John Wozniak
Jeff Fairholm
Tim Roth

2006
Ken Reed
Gary Lewis
Rhett Dawson

2007
Vic Stevenson
Bobby Thompson
Steve Dennis

2008
Lawrie Skolrood
Tom Campana
Ted Provost

2009
Norm Fong
Dan Farthing
Tom Burgess

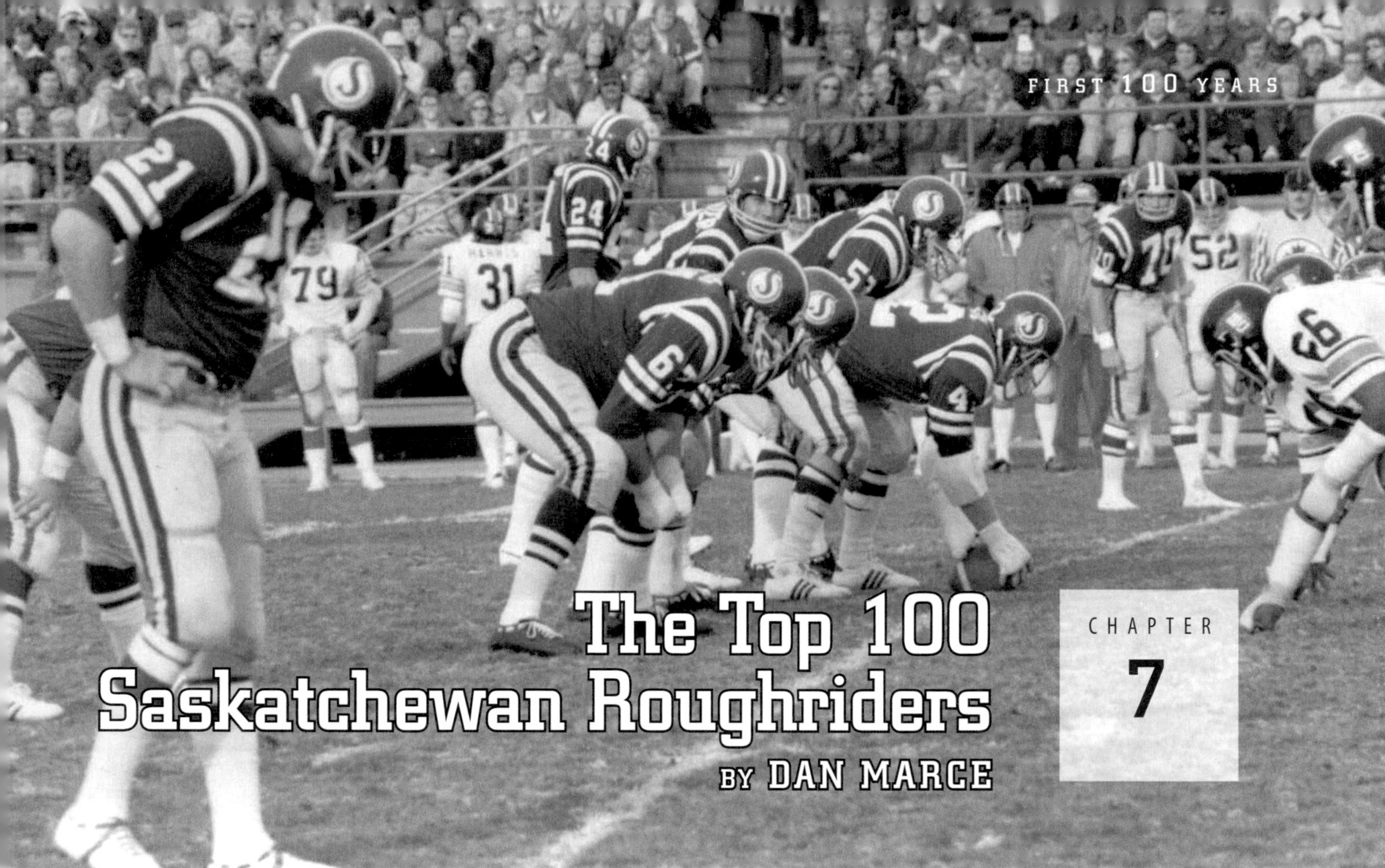

The Top 100 Saskatchewan Roughriders

BY DAN MARCE

CHAPTER 7

Photo courtesy of SSHFM

Ron Lancaster audibles while Al Ford (21), Tom Campana (24) and Steve Mazurak (70) listen attentively. (Top Photo)

Our listing of the 100 key players in Saskatchewan Roughriders history does not just include those who played on the field. This is a poll with a twist, being that players and builders have all been appraised by our panel of 54 ardent followers of the Roughriders.

One hundred points were given to each number one selection, ninety-nine points to the number two selection and on down to one point for the one-hundredth selection. The top 100 was compiled after ballots were returned by:

Govind Achyuthan, Paul Barnby, Gary Benson, Norm Benson, Larry Bird, Mitchell Blair, Jim Blevins, Vern Byrne, Bob Calder, Carm Carteri, Willy Cole, Darrell Davis, Al Driver, Betty Lou Gaudette, John Gormley, Ian Hamilton, Lorne Harasen, Heather Hodgson, Jim Hopson, Ken Howland, John Hudson, Mal Isaac, Harvey Johnson, Graham Kelly, Wendy Kelly, Paul Klinger, John Lipp, John Lynch, Dan Marce, Jason Matity, Steve Mazurak, Don McDougall, Jill McDougall, Kevin Mitchell, Wray Morrison, Dennis Mulvihill, Rod Pedersen, Ron Petrie, Tony Playter, Ned Powers, Doug Rogers, Bernie Schmidt, Larry Schneider, Bill Selnes, Tom Shepherd, Gordon Staseson, Brian Towriss, Rob Vanstone, Hugh Vassos, Brian Williams, Don Wilson, Cory Wolfe, Murray Wood and Bill Wright (the latter of whom tabulated the results).

All who participated said that it was one of the toughest and most emotionally time-consuming exercises of which they have been a part.

To all who participated – a most sincere THANK YOU!

TOP 100 RIDERS **1**

RON LANCASTER; PLAYER 1963-78, ASSISTANT COACH 1977-78, HEAD COACH 1979-80

Born in Fairchance, Pennsylvania but moved to Clairton, Pennsylvania as a young boy...was a high school sensation as a quarterback at Clairton High School but due to his small stature most college scouts did not pay attention to him...went to tiny Wittenberg University in Springfield, Ohio and had an outstanding career, but once again his size was against him as he was ignored by the NFL scouts...signed with Ottawa in the CFL in 1960...came to Saskatchewan in 1963 and 'the rest, they say, is history'...in the 16 years he played for the Riders they won 170 games...named the Roughriders Outstanding Player six times...Lancaster was a finalist for the Schenley Award as the CFL Outstanding Player in 1966, 1968, 1969, 1970 and 1976 and was the winner of the award in 1970 and 1976...CFL All-Star four times in 1970, 1973, 1975 and 1976 and a Western All-Star in 1966, 1968, 1969, 1970, 1973, 1975 and 1976...member of the Riders' 1966 Grey Cup championship team...and also played in the Grey Cup game in 1967, 1969, 1972 and 1976...played in the Western final in 1963 and a remarkable 11 straight Western finals,1966 through to 1976...Riders were in the playoffs for an amazing 14 consecutive years under Lancaster making it to the Western final on 12 occasions... in November 2006, Lancaster was voted the seventh best player in CFL history by TSN...third in CFL history in career touchdown passes thrown at 333...fourth in CFL history in pass completions at 3,384, pass attempts at 6,233 and passing yardage at 50,535...was a player-coach in 1977 and 1978, serving as the offensive co-ordinator...became Roughrider head coach immediately after his retirement in early 1979 for two years, resigning after the 1980 season...became a CBC football color commentator from 1980-90 with Don Wittman and was a member of the CBC broadcast team at the 1988 Summer Olympics in Seoul as the play-by-play broadcaster for basketball...became Eskimo head coach in 1991 through 1997 and had a record of 83-42 which made him the winningest coach in Eskimo history...under his coaching the Eskimos won the 1993 Grey Cup and played in the 1996 Grey Cup final and were in the playoffs every year...coached the Hamilton Tiger-Cats from 1998-2003 and again as interim coach in 2006...led Hamilton to the Grey Cup in 1998 and 1999 winning it in 1999...Lancaster's 142 regular season wins as a head coach put him in fifth place on the All-Time CFL career regular season list...his number 23 is one of the eight numbers retired by the club...inducted into the Plaza of Honor in 1987 and Canadian Football Hall of Fame as a player in 1982...Tom Pate Memorial Award winner in 1977...elected to Riders' 75th Silver Anniversary All-Star team in 1985... passed away on Sept 18, 2008 from a heart attack, and at the CFL awards ceremony for the 2008 season was posthumously awarded the Commissioner's Award for his outstanding contributions to the CFL by Commissioner Mark Cohon.

Ron Lancaster came to Saskatchewan in 1963 and "the rest, they say, is history." In the 16 years he played for the Riders they won 170 games.

Celebrating the 1966 Grey Cup win

At Mosaic Stadium, Hamilton head coach, 2006

Ron and Bev Lancaster

GEORGE REED, 1963-75

George Robert Reed was born in Vicksburg, Mississippi in October 1939...played his college football at Washington State University in Pullman, Washington for the Cougars of the Pac 8 Conference from 1959-62 where he played both running back on offence and outside linebacker on defence...signed with Saskatchewan in 1963 and played fullback until 1975...in 13 seasons he played in 203 games and rushed for 16,116 yards (2nd All-Time in CFL history)...holds the CFL record for rushing touchdowns at 134...led the West in rushing in 1965, 1966, 1967, 1968, 1969 and 1974...rushed for 1,000 yards in 11 of his 13 seasons...CFL All-Star fullback nine times (1965, 1966, 1967, 1968, 1969, 1971, 1972, 1973 and 1974)...Western All-Star in 1965, 1966, 1967, 1968, 1969, 1971, 1972, 1973, 1974 and 1975...won the Schenley Award as the league's Outstanding Player in 1965...named the Riders' Outstanding Player five times...4th in Rider history in total points with 823...Riders All-Time leader in rushing attempts at 3,243...7th in receptions with 300 for 2,772 yards...Riders were in the playoffs every year he played for them, including 11 Western finals and four Grey Cup games (1966, 1967, 1969, 1972)... member of 1966 Grey Cup team... inducted into Plaza of Honor in 1987 and the Canadian Football Hall of Fame in 1979...named to the Riders' 75th Silver Anniversary All-Star team in 1985...won the Tom Pate Award in 1976...his number 34 is one of eight that have been retired by the club...between 1972 and 1981 was the president of the CFL Players' Association...in 1978 Reed was honoured with Canada's highest civilian honour, being made a Member of the Order of Canada... in November of 2006 TSN voted Reed the number two player in the modern era of the CFL.

Reed scoring in 1966 Grey Cup

In 13 seasons George Reed played in 203 games and rushed for 16,116 yards (2nd All-Time in CFL history).

Early in his career

Records recognized by Lt. Gov. Dinny Hanbidge (1973)

Mosaic Stadium, 2008

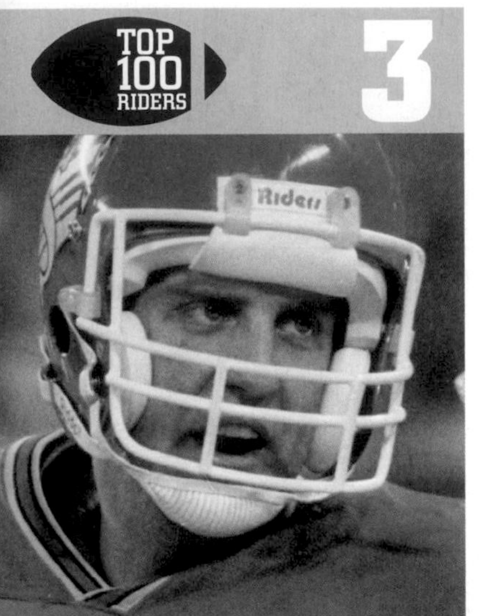

KENT AUSTIN; PLAYER 1987-93, HEAD COACH 2007

Born in Natick, Massachusetts...played high school football in Tennessee...led high school team at Brentwood Academy to a 14-0 season in his senior year, including league, county and state championships...attended University of Mississippi (Ole Miss) setting numerous school and college records for pass attempts, completions, touchdown passes, yardage gained and completion percentage...named Academic All-American...drafted by NFL's St. Louis Cardinals along with future Rider Don Narcisse...joined Riders in 1987...101 games played...34 touchdowns scored (10th All-Time Riders), 2,859 passing attempts (2nd), 1,964 completions (2nd), 20,872 yards passing (2nd), 151 touchdown passes (2nd)...Western All-Star 1990...CFL All-Star 1990...member Western Conference champions 1989 and quarterbacked Riders to their second Grey Cup win in what has been hailed as the best Grey Cup ever, 1989's 43-40 victory over the Hamilton Tiger-Cats...returned to Riders in 2007 as head coach leading Riders to their third Grey Cup with a 23-19 victory over Winnipeg...following 2007 season returned to his college, Ole Miss, as offensive co-ordinator...inducted into Plaza of Honor in 1999.

ROGER ALDAG; 1976-92

Born in Gull Lake, Saskatchewan where he played six-and eight man high school football before joining the Regina Rams in 1972...as a Ram was All-Star centre four times and the league's Most Outstanding Lineman and MVP his last two seasons...participated in three training camps before joining the Riders in 1976...during his 17 seasons played in 271 games (1st All-Time Riders)... Western All-Star eight times (1982, 1983, 1986-91)...CFL All-Star five times (1986-90)...Rider nominee for Most Outstanding Lineman nine times (1980, 1983-90)...CFL Most Outstanding Lineman winner twice (1986 and 1988)...four-time winner of Mack Truck Award for top offensive lineman as voted on by league players...inducted into Canadian Football Hall of Fame in 2002, Saskatchewan Sports Hall of Fame in 2006 and the Plaza of Honor in 1993.

RAY ELGAARD; 1983-96

Born in Alberta...the Elgaards moved to Vancouver when Ray was 11...active in all sports, his first love was rugby which he played in high school and in a men's league...turned to football in Grade 11...MVP as a tailback...played junior college and rugby in Huntington Beach, California... transferred to University of Utah as a tight end where he was heralded as a punishing blocker and clutch receiver...and also won the Decleater Award as team's hardest hitter, a rarity for an offensive player...Riders number two pick in 1983 CFL Draft...220 games (7th All-Time Riders), 830 catches (2nd Riders, 5th CFL), 13,198 yards receiving (1st Riders, 5th CFL), eight seasons 1,000 yards or more receiving (1st Riders, 5th CFL)...selected Riders nominee for Outstanding Canadian seven times... winner CFL Outstanding Canadian (1988, 1990, 1992)...named Riders Most Outstanding Player 1988...Western All-Star six times (1985, 1987, 1988, 1990, 1992, 1993)...CFL All-Star four times (1985, 1988, 1992, 1993)...voted CFLPA Most Outstanding Receiver 1992...won Molson Cup voted on by Rider fans as Most Popular Player 1992...Rider Player Rep six years...member Western Division champions 1989...member 1989 Grey Cup team...inducted into Plaza of Honor in 1999...Canadian Football Hall of Fame in 2002.

ALAN FORD; PLAYER 1965-76, COACH 1979, GENERAL MANAGER 1989-1999

Born July 1943...raised in Regina, Saskatchewan...attended Central Collegiate, starring in football, basketball and baseball...attended University of the Pacific in Stockton, California before returning home to play 12 great seasons with his hometown Roughriders...known for his versatility to line up just about anywhere on the field, Ford played running back, defensive back, tight end and kick returner and was the team's full-time punter for 10 seasons...182 games played (17th All-Time Riders)...also scored 22 touchdowns (23rd) and compiled 1,086 rushing yards (32nd)...259 receptions (11th) 3,819 receiving yards (11th), and 14 receiving touchdowns (22nd)...Mr. Versatility also shone as a punter, with1,041 punts (2nd) for 41,880 yards (2nd)...was part of Grey Cup champions as a player 1966 and general manager 1989...inducted into Plaza of Honor in 1992 and Regina Sports Hall of Fame in 2003.

HUGH CAMPBELL; 1963-67, 1969

Born in May 1941 in Bellingham, Washington...played his college football at Washington State University in Pullman, Washington for the Cougars in the Pac 8 Conference from 1959-62...three of his teammates were George Reed, Garner Ekstran and Wally Dempsey...had a sensational college career, being named All-American in 1961 and 1962, and played in the Hula Bowl, the College All-Star game, the Coaches All-America game and the East-West Shrine Game upon graduating in 1962... drafted by the San Francisco 49ers in the fourth round of the 1963 NFL Draft with the 50th pick... joined the Riders in mid-September of 1963...in six seasons caught 321 passes, averaging 16.9 yards every time he caught a pass, and he scored 60 touchdowns (4th All-Time Riders)...scored a league-record 17 touchdowns on receptions in 1966...CFL All-Star in 1965 and 1966...Western All-Star in 1964, 1965, 1966 and 1969...caught TD passes in six consecutive games in 1969...played on Riders Grey Cup championship team in 1966 and in the Grey Cup in 1967 and 1969...played in the 1963 Western final and the Western semi-finals in 1964 and 1965...his spectacular receiving ability earned him the name 'Gluey Hughie'...named to the Riders' 75th Silver Anniversary All-Star team in 1985... inducted into the Plaza of Honor 1988...upon retiring became head coach at Whitworth College... in 1977 he became head coach of the Edmonton Eskimos and in the next six years won 70 games, finished first six times and went to six consecutive Grey Cup games, winning a record five in a row from 1978-82...his 77% winning percentage is the best ever with the same team...went to the USFL in 1983 as head coach of the Los Angeles Express and then on to the Houston Oilers of the NFL for the 1984 and 1985 seasons...returned to Edmonton in 1986 as general manager and later team president for the next 21 years...in that period the Eskimos were Grey Cup champions four times (1987, 1993, 2003 and 2005)...retired at the end of the 2006 season after being directly involved as the head coach, general manager and team president in nine of the Eskimos' Grey Cup victories.

DON NARCISSE; 1987-99

Born in February 1965 in Port Arthur, Texas...in high school achieved All-District honours as a receiver and was team MVP...attended Texas Southern University where he won the receiving crown as a senior...named first district All-American and All-Southwest Conference...played in Freedom Bowl... joined Riders in 1987 following a tryout with the NFL's St. Louis Cardinals...played 216 games as a Rider (8th All-Time Riders)...919 receptions (1st)...75 receiving touchdowns (2nd)...caught at least one reception in all 216 games...Riders leading receiver three times...CFL leader twice...Western All-Star five times (1989, 1990, 1993, 1995, 1998) and CFL All-Star four times (1989, 1990, 1995, 1998)... member of 1989 Grey Cup champions and 1997 Grey Cup finalist...only three-time winner of Molson Cup as Most Popular Player voted on by fans...inducted in to Plaza of Honor in 2003.

KEN PRESTON; PLAYER 1940, PLAYER-COACH 1946-48, GENERAL MANAGER 1958-77

Considered the 'Dean of General Managers' in the CFL, Ken Preston was a player, coach, game official as well as general manager, in a football career in Canada which spanned more than 40 years between 1936 and 1978...born in Smith Falls, Ontario...played football at Queen's University 1936-39 and first joined the Regina Roughriders in 1940...in 1941 he was a fullback with the Winnipeg Blue Bombers when they won the Grey Cup...played for the Bombers in 1942...after serving in the Armed Forces he played for the Ottawa Rough Riders in 1945...in 1946 returned to the Regina Roughriders as a player/coach and part-time general manager, for 10 years...in 1958 he was engaged as general manager of the Saskatchewan Roughriders, a position he held for 20 years until his retirement in 1977...organized a minor football program in the province of Saskatchewan and arranged for Canadian players to attend American colleges on scholarships...adept at recruiting talent on a tight budget...under Ken's management, the Saskatchewan Roughriders compiled the best record of any team in the CFL – 15 playoffs, five times a Grey Cup finalist with a win in 1966, the best win-loss record...installed in the Saskatchewan Sports Hall of Fame in 1980, the Plaza of Honor in 1987 and the Canadian Football Hall of Fame in 1990...died in 1991

EAGLE KEYS; ASSISTANT COACH 1964, HEAD COACH 1965-1970

Born in Tompkinsville, Kentucky in 1924, was an outstanding centre and linebacker for the Western Kentucky Hilltoppers football team in 1942 and, after a stint in the Marine Corps in the Second World War, again in 1946 and 1947...also lettered as a baseball pitcher-outfielder three straight years (1946-48)...was inducted into the Western Kentucky University Athletic Hall of Fame in 1994... played in Montreal from 1949-51, Edmonton 1952-54...as a player, selected to three All-Star teams in the Eastern Conference and three All-Star teams in the Western Conference...played in three Grey Cup games, winning in 1949 and 1954...often remembered for his outstanding performance in his final Grey Cup game in 1954 because he played with a broken leg. ...became assistant coach with the Riders in 1964 and head coach in 1965...selected CFL coach-of-the-year in 1968...under his leadership the team played in three Grey Cup games, winning the Riders first-ever Grey Cup in 1966...in 1970, the Riders finished the season with 14 wins and 2 losses, a CFL record that stood until 1989...retired from coaching after the 1975 season...144 wins as a coach (6th All-Time CFL, 1st Riders)...selected head coach of the Riders' 75th Silver Anniversary All-Star Team in 1985...inducted into the Plaza of Honor in 1987 and the Canadian Football Hall of Fame in 1990.

ED McQUARTERS, 1966-74

Born in Tulsa, Oklahoma in April 1943...attended the University of Oklahoma from 1961-1964 where he excelled at wrestling, track and field and, of course, football...was a Big Eight All-Star and All-American in his senior year as a defensive end and tackle...was noted for his speed, strength and ability to rush quarterbacks and being able to beat the double-team blocking that he consistently faced...selected in the 18th round of the 1965 NFL Draft (the 250th player drafted) by St. Louis Cardinals... played for the Cardinals for one year before being released and waived through the NFL...came to Saskatchewan in September of 1966...played for the Roughriders from 1966-1974... member of the 1966 Grey Cup team and Grey Cup finalists in 1967, 1969 and 1972...was a CFL and Western All-Star in 1967, 1968 and 1969...recorded two touchdowns off fumble recoveries during the playoffs in his career...stayed in Saskatchewan after his retirement from football and was employed in the Public Relations Department of SaskPower...winner of the DeMarco-Becket Trophy (1968, 1969) and Schenley Award for CFL's Outstanding Lineman in 1967...named to the Riders' 75th Silver Anniversary All-Star team in 1985, the Canadian Football Hall of Fame in 1988 and the Plaza of Honor in 1989.

RON ATCHISON, 1952-68

Played his junior football with the Saskatoon Hilltops from 1947-49 where he played both ways as an offensive centre and middle guard on defence...joined the Roughriders in 1952...tied with Roger Aldag for the most seasons as a Roughrider at 17...initially played middle guard on a five-man defensive line...known as 'Big Atch' he was an intimidating force on the Roughrider defensive line...in his early years wore a protective cast on his right arm which he used as a weapon, and made many offensive linemen very aware of his presence...he had to be constantly double-teamed...a big, rough and tough mauler who knew all the tricks and, along with fellow Canadian defensive lineman Bill Clarke, anchored the Rider defensive line from 1954 until 1965...in 1963 Atchison was one of the key reasons the Riders defence did not give up a touchdown in five games...named a Western All-Star middle guard in 1956, 1960, 1961, 1962 and 1963... switched to defensive tackle in 1964 on a four-man defensive line and was again named an All-Star that year ...played 237 games (5th All-Time Riders)...member of the Roughriders 1966 Grey Cup championship team...also played in the Grey Cup game in 1967...Western finals in 1956, 1963, 1968 and Western semi-finals in 1953, 1954, 1955, 1958, 1962, 1964, 1965...inducted into the Canadian Football Hall of Fame in 1980...named to the Riders' 75th Anniversary All-Star team in 1985 and the Plaza of Honor in 1987.

BILL BAKER, 'THE UNDERTAKER', 1968-73, 1977-78, GENERAL MANAGER 1987-88

Born in August 1944 in Kindersley, Saskatchewan...played junior football for the Regina Rams in 1963...College football at Otterbein College in Ohio where he was an All-Star for four years and his motto was "your opponents are only as tough as you let them be"...Western All-Star (1971, 1972, 1973) and CFL All-Star in 1972 and 1973 while with Saskatchewan and Western All-Star and CFL All-Star with B.C. Lions in 1975 and 1976...named CFL Outstanding Defensive Player in 1976...became Rider general manager in 1987 before becoming commissioner of the CFL in 1989...played in 1969 and 1972 Grey Cup games against Ottawa and Hamilton...in 2006 in a poll, Baker was listed at #43 on the TSN Top 50 CFL Players of All-Time...notorious for his forearm shiver and according to the Canadian Football Hall of Fame "a Baker forearm to the head was greatly respected by opposing quarterbacks who came within his range"...ranks 24th on the Rider All-Time list for quarterback sacks...played virtually all of his career as a defensive end and had to be consistently double teamed...knocked out three Eskimo quarterbacks, Tom Wilkinson, Bruce Lemmerman and Dave Syme, in one unforgettable game at Taylor Field...named to the Riders' 75th Silver Anniversary All-Star team in 1985...inducted into the Plaza of Honor in 1990 and the Canadian Football Hall of Fame in 1994.

DAVE RIDGWAY; 1982-95

Born in Stockport England in 1959, emigrated to Canada at 15...played high school in Burlington, Ontario...received a scholarship to University of Toledo as a placekicker...drafted by Montreal, was released and was also released from Winnipeg a week later...joined Riders in 1982...played 14 years and in 238 games (6th place All-Time Riders)...2,374 points (1st), 574 field goals (1st), 541 converts (1st)...made 574 of 736 field goals, a phenomenal 78 per cent success rate...nicknamed 'Robokicker'...seven-time Western All-Star (1982, 1987, 1988, 1989, 1990, 1991, 1993)...six-time CFL All-Star in (1982, 1987, 1988, 1989, 1990, 1993)...twice kicked eight field goals in a game (CFL record) and set a CFL record with a 60-yard field goal in 1987...forever remembered for last-second field goal – 'The Kick' - in 1989's 43-40 Grey Cup victory over the Hamilton Tiger-Cats...inducted into the Plaza of Honor in 2000 and Canadian Football Hall of Fame in 2003.

BOBBY JURASIN; 1986-97

Born in Wakefield, Michigan in 1964...attended Northern Michigan University...one of the most popular players in Saskatchewan Roughrider history...terrorized opposing quarterbacks from 1986-1997...six-time Western All-Star (1987, 1988, 1989, 1992, 1994, 1997) and four-time CFL All-Star (1987, 1988, 1992, 1997)...Riders All-Time leader in quarterback sacks with 142... during his remarkable career in Saskatchewan, played in 197 games (11th All-Time Riders), registering 411 defensive tackles...in 1987, set a team record with 22 quarterback sacks...for his tireless efforts and on-field leadership, selected the Riders' Most Outstanding Defensive Player three times (1987, 1996 and 1997)...also won the Molson Cup Most Popular Player in 1987 and 1997 as well as the Club's Most Outstanding Player in 1997...in 12 seasons with the Roughriders, was instrumental in leading the Green and White to two Western finals, two West Division championships, two Grey Cup appearances and a Grey Cup championship in 1989...inducted into the Plaza of Honor in 2002 and the Canadian Football Hall of Fame in 2006.

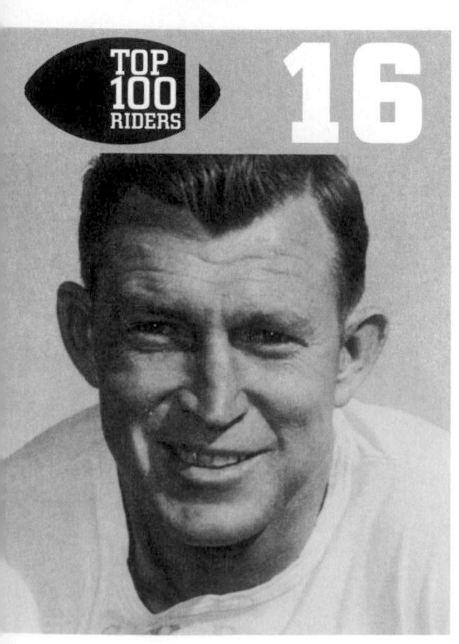

GLENN DOBBS; PLAYER 1951-53, PLAYER-COACH 1952

Was the most celebrated player to wear the Green and White in his era and a phenomenally popular figure in Saskatchewan...only played or coached the Roughriders for three years but left a lasting impression...although a Texan by birth, Dobbs went to high school in Frederick, Oklahoma, where he was a tailback and a punter... continued in football at the University of Tulsa where he led his team to victory in the Sun Bowl in 1942..that year Glenn was selected to the Associated Press All-America team, the first back from the Missouri Conference so honoured...drafted by the Chicago Cardinals in 1943 but did not sign an NFL contract, instead joining the U.S. Air Force...playing for his service team, his performance led to him being selected to AP's All-Service team during his hitch...in 1946 he signed with the Brooklyn Dodgers in the newly formed All-America Football Conference and instantly became a star in the new league...in 1951 Rider president Bob Kramer lured him out of retirement and his sportscasting job to play for the Roughriders...his arrival in Regina produced a frenzy by rabid Rider fans...a Texas gentleman with great personality and tremendous football talent... performed well for the Roughriders and led the team to play in the 1951 Grey Cup...that year, he led the Western Interprovincial Football Union in punting and was chosen Western All-Star quarterback...also won the Jeff Nicklin Memorial Trophy as MVP in the West...held the best lifetime punting average in the history of pro football until surpassed by Edmonton's Hank Ilesic in 1979...was inducted into the College Football Hall of Fame in 1980 and the Plaza of Honor in 1988...died in 2002.

RICHIE HALL, PLAYER 1988-1991, ASSISTANT COACH 1994-2008

Born in San Antonio, Texas in October, 1960...played college at Colorado State...played four seasons with the Roughriders and quickly became a fan favourite...153 CFL games played, including 72 as a Roughrider...in four seasons with the Green and White, Hall tallied 13 interceptions and eight quarterback sacks, as well as one fumble returned for a touchdown...four-time West Division All-Star, (1983 and 1986 with the Calgary Stampeders; 1988, 1990 in Saskatchewan)...named CFL All-Star for outstanding rookie performance in 1983 with the Stampeders...Rider fans voted him Most Popular Player in 1990...the club's nominee for Outstanding Defensive Player in 1988...recognized by the CFLPA in 1990 by winning the Tom Pate Award for his outstanding dedication to the CFL, the community and his performance on the field...following his playing career with the Riders, became a member of the Roughrider coaching staff...served 15 years as a defensive coach, including the last eight seasons as defensive co-ordinator...in December of 2008, Hall was named head coach of the Edmonton Eskimos.

GENE MAKOWSKY, 1995-PRESENT

Born in Saskatoon, Saskatchewan in April 1973...four-year University of Saskatchewan Huskie, ... starter since rookie season at the UofS...never missed a game...played in 32 consecutive regular-season games...member of 1991 and 1994 Hardy Cup champions...named to Canada West All-Star team in 1994...chosen as CIS Lineman of the Year in 1993...selected by Roughriders in second round (23rd overall) in 1995 CFL draft...in 15th season in Saskatchewan... after 2008 season he played in 237 career games for Saskatchewan (tied for 4th) and has been a model of consistency...has played all five positions on the offensive line for the Green and White...a five-time Western All-Star (2004-2008) as well as four-time CFL All-Star (2004, 2005, 2006, 2008) and a two-time winner of the CFL Most Outstanding Offensive Lineman Award (2004, 2005) and runner-up in 2008.

TED URNESS, 1961-70

Born in Regina in 1939...played high school football at Scott Collegiate and one year of junior football with the Regina Rams...played university football at the University of Arizona in Tuscon, Arizona where he was a standout centre for the Arizona Wildcats...played with the Roughriders from 1961-70...named West's Outstanding Lineman in 1968...Western and CFL All-Star centre (1965, 1966, 1967, 1968, 1969 and 1970)...inducted into Canadian Football Hall of Fame in 1989...Bud Grant, former Winnipeg Blue Bombers and Minnesota Vikings head coach, said that Ted Urness was in his mind the best centre to ever play the game on either side of the border...Ted's father Al, uncle Harold, brother Jack and son Mark were also members of the Roughriders, leaving a family football legacy unmatched...after retiring he served on the Rider board of directors...played in the Western finals in 1963, 1966, 1967, 1968, 1969 and 1970 and was a member of the Riders' first Grey Cup championship team in 1966...named to Riders' 75th Silver Anniversary All-Star team in 1985...also played in 1967 and 1969 Grey Cup games...inducted into the Plaza of Honor along with his father Al in 1989.

JOEY WALTERS; 1977-79, 1980-82

Born in Florence, South Carolina in October 1954...played his college football at Clemson University for the Tigers from 1971-74...led his team in receiving in 1973 and 1974 and was named Atlantic Coast Conference All-Star receiver...in 1977 came to the CFL to Winnipeg...joined Saskatchewan later in 1977 and played through to 1982...played wide receiver, slotback, cornerback, and kick returner...named CFL and Western All-Star in 1981 and 1982...Molson Cup winner in 1981 and 1982 as the Riders' Most Popular Player...also named the Roughriders' Outstanding Player in 1981 and 1982...set Rider receiving record for yardage gained in a season at 1,751 in 1981 and followed that with 1,692 receiving yards in 1982...had over 100 yards receiving in 11 of the Rider games in 1981...290 receptions (8th), 5,181 yards receiving (5th)...averaged 17.9 yards per reception...had 14 receiving touchdowns in 1981 (3rd)... returned 80 punts for 860 yards and one touchdown, averaging 10.8 yards per return...named to the Riders' 75th Silver Anniversary All-Star team in 1985...was one of the most exciting players to ever play in Saskatchewan because of his ability to make the spectacular reception and dazzling broken-field running...he was almost impossible to cover one-on-one...played with the Washington Federals of the USFL in 1983 and 1984 and the Orlando Renegades of the USFL in 1985...Houston Oilers in 1987... inducted into the Plaza of Honor in 1990.

JACK ABENDSCHAN; 1965-1975

Born in 1943...played his college football with the University of New Mexico Lobos from 1961 to 1964...won two All-American awards in his senior year...standout offensive guard and placekicker... one of the last of the old-time straight ahead, non-soccer-style placement kickers who played a regular position as well as handling kickoffs...Abendschan and Al Benecick gave the Riders the best pair of guards in the league from 1966 to 1968...twice led the CFL in scoring (1969 and 1970) with identical 100-point seasons...five time All-Canadian guard (1967, 1969, 1971, 1972, 1973) and seven-time Western All-Star (1966, 1967 and 1969-73)...is the Riders third All-Time leading scorer with 863 points...312 converts (3rd)...159 field goals (3rd)...member of the 1966 Grey Cup championship team...played in four Grey Cup games (1966, 1967, 1969 and 1972)...member of the Riders' 75th Silver Anniversary All-Star team selected in 1985...inducted into Plaza of Honor in 1992.

JEFF FAIRHOLM; 1988-1993

Born in 1965 and raised in Montreal...played college ball at the University of Arizona...first-round pick (2nd overall) by the Roughriders in 1988 Canadian College Draft...played six seasons with the Roughriders...received Jackie Parker Trophy as the West Division rookie-of-the-year...member of the 1989 Grey Cup champion Roughriders...had two catches for 97 yards and a touchdown in Grey Cup victory...named to the Western All-Star team in 1989...named the Most Outstanding Canadian in the West Division in 1989...led the Riders in receiving in 1991 with 1,239 yards and 13 touchdowns... set a career high with 1,391 yards receiving in 1993...sixth on Roughriders All-Time touchdown list with 53...fourth on Roughriders' All-Time receptions list with 358...third on Roughriders All-Time receiving yards list with 6,171...inducted into the Plaza of Honor in 2005.

FRANK TRIPUCKA; 1953-58, 1959, 1963, HEAD COACH, 1958-59

Born on December 8,1927 in Bloomfield, New Jersey...played his college football at Notre Dame...was backup to Heisman Trophy-winning quarterback Johnny Lujack in 1946 and 1947. When Lujack graduated, Tripucka became the starter in 1948 and led the team to a 9-0-1 record. Notre Dame finished number two nationally and Tripucka was named All- American...first-round draft choice of the Philadelphia Eagles in 1949 and was the ninth player taken in the draft...traded to Detroit before the season started...1950-1952, played for the Chicago Cardinals...played with the Riders from 1953-57, after playing in Ottawa for the first half of the 1958 season, returned to the Saskatchewan Roughriders for the second half as player/head coach (1958-59) and again in 1963 as the backup quarterback after playing in Denver from 1960 until halfway through the 1963 season...the Roughriders were in the playoffs under his direction at quarterback from 1953-1956 and again in 1958...Riders were in the Western final against Edmonton in 1956...50 years later he still ranks 3rd in all major passing categories with the Riders, behind only Ron Lancaster and Kent Austin...1,785 passes attempted (3rd All-Time Riders), 1,011 completions (3rd), 56.6 completion percentage...14,387 yards passing (3rd), 83 touchdown passes (3rd),...Western All-Star quarterback in 1954...he is the father of former Notre Dame and Detroit Pistons basketball star Kelly Tripucka...inducted into the Plaza of Honor in 1989.

TOM SHEPHERD; PRESIDENT 1987-89

Born and raised in Regina in 1943...played for Balfour Tech and won a provincial high school championship under legendary coach Gord Currie in 1960...joined board of directors of Regina Rams junior club in 1968...driving fundraising force which helped expand Ram clubhouse, which at the time was the envy of junior football clubs in Canada...commenced fundraising involvement with the Riders in 1966 on the annual fundraising dinner...joined Rider executive committee in 1979 as treasurer, a position he held for 23 years...club vice-president 1985-86...president 1987-1989...past president 1990, 1991, 1992 and again in 1994, 1995...served as CFL governor 1987-89...chaired search for CFL commissioner in 1989...in 1992 won CFL Commissioner's Award for outstanding contribution to CFL...founder Rider Green and White Corporate Lounge...co-founder enclosed Club Seating with Paul Hill...remains as top seller of Rider Plaza of Honor Dinner tickets ($350 each) to this day...for the past 22 years has single-handedly managed a province-wide lottery for the Riders and has raised close to $11.5 million...in the spring of 2005 the Province of Saskatchewan recognized his efforts with the Saskatchewan Order of Merit for volunteerism...inducted into the Plaza of Honor in 1995, Regina Sports Hall of Fame in 2007, the Canadian Football Hall of Fame in 2008 and the Saskatchewan Sports Hall of Fame in 2009.

AL BENECICK; 1959-68

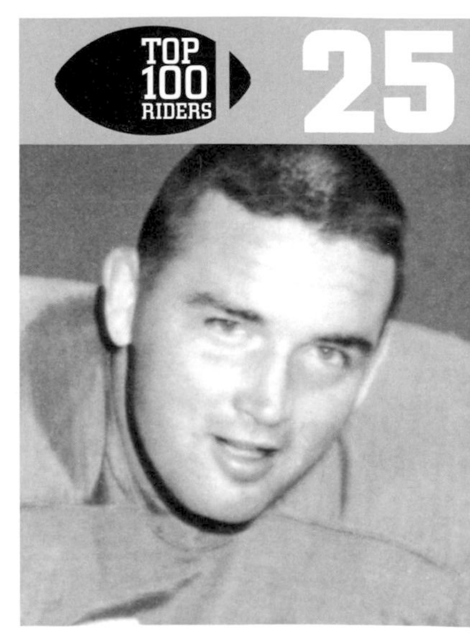

Born in Bristol, Connecticut in 1935...played his college football at Syracuse University for the Orangemen in the Big East Conference from 1955 until 1958...selected by the Philadelphia Eagles of the NFL in 1959 in the 6th round of the NFL draft...was the final cut of the Eagles in 1959 and came to Saskatchewan after being recruited by legendary Rider general manager Ken Preston...played offensive guard and tackle with Saskatchewan from 1959 until 1968...Western All-Star in 1963, 1964, 1965, 1966 and CFL All-Star in 1964, 1965, 1966...named the Riders' Outstanding Offensive Lineman in 1964, 1965 and 1966...member of the 1966 Grey Cup championship team...played in the Grey Cup in 1967...inducted into the Rider Plaza of Honor in 1991 and the Canadian Football Hall of Fame in 1996...only man in football history to have blocked for NFL legend Jim Brown (at Syracuse) and George Reed (with Saskatchewan)...many consider Brown and Reed two of the greatest of all time...named to the Riders' 75th Silver Anniversary All-Star team in 1985.

KEN McEACHERN; 1974-82, 1984

Born and raised in Regina...outstanding all-around athlete in baseball, hockey and football at O'Neill High School...accepted a baseball scholarship to Weber State...switched to football, playing defensive halfback and safety...named Conference Outstanding Defensive player-of-the-week five times and Big Sky Conference All-Star twice...earned starting position with the Riders immediately upon joining the team in 1974...38 interceptions (2nd All-Time Riders), 799 return yards (1st), four interceptions returned for touchdowns (tied for 1st)...led the league in interceptions in 1980 with 10...Western All-Star three times (1976, 1980, 1981)...CFL All-Star in 1980 and Eastern All-Star in 1983 while playing for the Toronto Argonauts...won a Grey Cup with Toronto...named to the Riders' 75th Silver Anniversary Team in 1985...inducted into Plaza of Honor in 1993.

CLYDE BROCK; 1964-75

Born in Los Angeles, California in 1940 where he played his high school football...played college football at Utah State...drafted by and had a brief sojourn with the Dallas Cowboys and the San Francisco 49ers...joined the Riders in 1964 and soon became a key piece to the puzzle of building a championship team...owned the right tackle position his entire 159-game career (27th All-Time Riders)...joined the likes of Al Benecick, Ted Urness, Reg Whitehouse, Jim Worden and later Jack Abendschan, forming an offensive line that dominated defences for many years...his first year was the first 1,000-yard rushing season for George Reed and Ed Buchanan. It was Buchanan's only 1,000-yard season...played in four Grey Cups (1966, 1967, 1969, 1972), winning one in 1966...five-time Western All-Star (1965, 1966, 1967, 1968, 1969)...four-time CFL All-Star (1966, 1967, 1968, 1969)... named to Riders' 75th Silver Anniversary team in 1985...inducted into Plaza of Honor in 1995.

GLEN SUITOR; 1984-94

Born in Prince George, British Columbia in 1962...played quarterback and cornerback in high school...attended Simon Fraser University...started four years at cornerback and was NAIA All-American his last three years...as a senior, led conference in punt returns...selected 10th overall by the Riders in 1984 CFL college draft...starting safety for Riders all 11 years, never missing a game...51 interceptions (1st All-Time Riders), 667 return yards on interceptions (2nd) and tied for third with two TDs on returns...had 348 tackles and did the placement holding for Dave Ridgway's field goals begining in 1985...including the most famous one – 'The Kick' - a last-second field goal that gave Saskatchewan its second-ever Grey Cup in 1989 with a thrilling 43-40 victory over the Hamilton Tiger-Cats...four-time Western All-Star (1989, 1991, 1992, 1993) and three-time All-Canadian (1991, 1992, 1993)...has been a colour analyst on TSN's CFL broadcasts since 1995... inducted into the Plaza of Honor in 1998.

MARTIN RUBY; PLAYER 1951-57, PLAYER-COACH 1952

Born in June 1922 in Lubbock, Texas ...played his college football at Texas A & M in College Station, Texas where he played both offensive and defensive tackle...named the Outstanding Lineman in the Southwest Conference in 1941...selected as captain of the College All-Stars for their game against the Washington Redskins...an All-American choice in both 1941 and 1942, was drafted in the fifth round by the Chicago Bears in 1943...spent the next three years in the army...returned to pro football in 1946 and played for the Brooklyn Dodgers of the All-America Football Conference from 1946 to 1948 and the New York Yankees of the same conference in 1949...in 1950 he played with the New York Yanks of the National Football League...came to Saskatchewan in 1951...played both offensive and defensive tackle...Western All-Star as an offensive tackle in 1951, 1954 and 1956, and a Western All-Star as a defensive tackle in 1953, 1954 and 1956...two-way All-Star in 1954 and 1956...named Roughriders Outstanding Player in 1954...named to the Riders' 75th Silver Anniversary All-Star team in 1985...named Rider offensive line coach in 1952 under head coach Glenn Dobbs...played in the 1951 Grey Cup game against Ottawa...inducted into the Canadian Football Hall of Fame in 1974 and the Plaza of Honor in 1988...died on January 3, 2002 at age 79 in Salmon Arm, British Columbia.

EDDIE LOWE; 1983-91

Born in Columbus, Georgia in 1960...raised in Phenix City, Alabama...following one year at University of Tennessee, Chattanooga, transferred to University of Alabama and played under the legendary Bear Bryant and his Crimson Tide...brother Woodrow also played at Alabama and spent 12 years in the NFL... Eddie was All-Southwest Conference as a senior...following a brief stint with Birmingham of the fledgling USFL, joined Riders as the mainstay on Rider defence for the next nine years at middle linebacker...played in 151 games (27th All-Time Riders)...662 tackles for an average of 73.5 per year...16 interceptions (18th) and 10 fumble recoveries (10th)...33 quarterback sacks (7th)... Rider nominee for Outstanding Defensive Player Award in 1985, 1991...named Western and CFL All-Star in 1989...known as a tenacious hitter who was a silent leader who had the total respect of his teammates, coaches, opponents, fans and media alike...his hit on Edmonton's Tracy Ham caused a fumble that teammate David Albright returned for a touchdown and provided the impetus to upset the heavily favoured Eskimos, putting the Riders in the 1989 Grey Cup...member of 1989 Grey Cup Championship team...voted winner of Molson Cup as fans' Most Popular Player in 1985...inducted into Plaza of Honor in 1995.

NEIL (PIFFLES) TAYLOR; PLAYER, BUILDER

Born in Ontario and raised in Regina, he started playing football with the Regina Intermediates, the forerunner to junior football in Regina...was pressed into service with the Regina Rugby Club when the club found itself without a quarterback...led the team to Western rugby championships in 1913, 1914, 1915...in 1916 he joined the war efforts as a fighter pilot...shot down and became a prisoner of war...following the war returned home and in 1919 rejoined the club as quarterback and also practised law...his size, strength, quickness and leadership allowed him to excel at quarterback... became Rider president in 1934 during difficult economic times...President of the Western Interprovincial Football Union for three years in the 1930s...president of the Canadian Rugby Union in 1946...instrumental in revitalizing interest in football in Western Canada following the war...active as a player and member of the Rider executive for close to 30 years...inducted posthumously into Canadian Football Hall of Fame in 1963...Inducted into Saskatchewan Sports Hall of Fame in 1987 and Plaza of Honor in 1993...Rider playing field, Taylor Field, was named in his honour in 1947, the year he died.

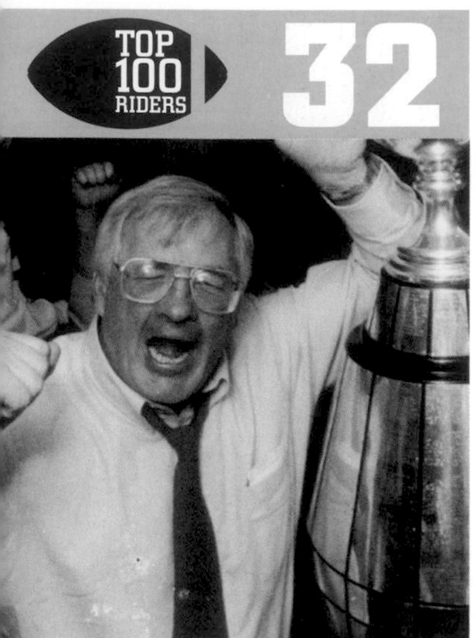

JOHN GREGORY; HEAD COACH 1987-91

Born in Webster City, Iowa in 1938...starred in high school and, was team captain, MVP and first-team All-State...played college ball at the University of Northern Iowa, winning the North Central championship and Mineral Bowl in 1960...following six years of coaching high school and three years of coaching junior college, he became defensive co-ordinator at South Dakota State for two years, followed by 10 more as head coach, turning around a program that had a losing record for eight straight years...in 1981 he joined Ray Jauch's, then Cal Murphy's coaching staff in Winnipeg the next year...Winnipeg won Grey Cup in 1984...joined Riders as head coach in 1987, joining a program that had a 10-year playoff drought...led Riders to a second place finish in 1988...in 1989, following a rollercoaster season, the Riders finished third only to knock off the heavily favoured Alberta teams in Calgary and Edmonton on their way to winning what is heralded as the best Grey Cup ever–a 43-40 victory over the Hamilton Tiger-Cats...after a coaching stint in Hamilton, coached in the Arena Football League for many years, with his most notable protégé being Super Bowl winner and Pro Bowl quarterback Kurt Warner...inducted into the Plaza of Honor in 1996.

VINCE GOLDSMITH; 1981-83, 1988-90

Born in 1959 in Tacoma, Washington where he played his high school football...joined the Riders after a stellar college career with the University of Oregon Ducks, earning All-Pac 10 honours three times as a defensive lineman...second-team All-American...inducted into University of Oregon Hall of Fame in 1982...overlooked by the NFL, Vince's size, quickness and tremendous strength were tailor-made for the then-newly defined position of rush end...in his rookie year he recorded 18.5 sacks, setting a then Rider record...this earned him the CFL's rookie-of-the-year award, the first Rider in history to do so...also earned him the first of three Western All-Star awards (1981, 1983, 1988) and one CFL All-Star award in 1983 by virtue of his 20.5 sacks that year...89 sacks (2nd All-Time Riders)... inducted into Plaza of Honor in 1994.

ROBERT (BOB) KRAMER; PRESIDENT 1951-53, 1961-1965

Born in California...became a Canadian citizen in 1922...his family farmed near Lethbridge and he taught school in rural Alberta before entering the construction industry...came to Regina from Calgary in 1944 to take over the Caterpillar Tractor dealership...was a strong community leader, and an astute businessman with a strong entrepreneurial spirit... Kramer Tractor expanded and flourished under his leadership...was president of the Saskatchewan Roughriders on two occasions...in 1951, Kramer lured All-America Conference All-Star quarterback Glenn Dobbs to come out of retirement, gained notice for travelling to New York to pull off some of the greatest recruiting coups of all time, securing the services of several import star players including Martin Ruby...under Kramer's guidance the Roughriders played in the Grey Cup in 1951...in 1961, Kramer along with general manager Ken Preston brought in a new coaching staff and many excellent players including Ron Lancaster and George Reed both in 1963...provided the team with stability on and off the field that enabled the Roughriders to not only stay in the league but also to appear in the playoffs 15 consecutive years, and win their first Grey Cup championship in 1966...was also active in many other community endeavours including St. Michaels's Retreat House in Lumsden...The Kramer Imax Theatre in the Saskatchewan Science Centre was provided by his family as a legacy to the community in his honour...inducted into both the Canadian Football Hall of Fame and the Plaza of Honor the same year, 1987...died in 1991.

KEN CARPENTER; PLAYER 1954-59, HEAD COACH 1960

Born February in 1926 in Seaside, Oregon...played his college football at Oregon State in Corvallis, Oregon at both halfback and fullback...selected in the first round of the 1950 NFL draft by the Cleveland Browns where he played from 1950-1953...started in the same backfield with the legendary Otto Graham at quarterback and Marion Motley at fullback...came to Saskatchewan in 1954...played halfback, fullback and receiver...punted and placekicked on occasion...scored 55 rushing touchdowns (5th All-Time Riders) and rushed for 2,128 yards (13th)...had 195 career receptions (17th) for 3,157 yards (15th) and 27 touchdowns (19th)...scored 303 points (12th)...still holds the Rider record for touchdowns in a season at 18, set in 1955 when he was named the West's Outstanding Player as he led the West in scoring with 90 points (touchdowns were worth five points at the time)...named the Roughriders' Outstanding Player in 1955 and 1956...won the Jeff Nicklin Memorial Trophy in 1955 and the Dave Dryburgh Memorial Trophy in 1956...Western All-Star as a running back in 1955 and 1956 and as a receiver in 1958...led the Riders in receiving in 1954, 1955 and 1956...played in Western semi-finals in 1954, 1955, 1956, 1958 and Western final in 1956...Rider head coach for one season, 1960...inducted into the Plaza of Honor in 1989.

GARNER EKSTRAN; 1961-67

Born in 1939, son of a dairy farmer from Bow, Washington...attended Burlington-Madison High School in neighbouring Burlington where he learned to play football...scouts noticed his talent and he was offered a football scholarship to Washington State where he received several team and league player awards...because of his size NFL scouts did not offer him the opportunity of a tryout... uncertain of his future, he made contact with Rider coach Steve Owen through a college teammate who had already signed a contract with the Riders...although he had no idea where Regina was and who the Roughriders were, he accepted an invitation from Owen to attend training camp in 1961... immediately became a starter...four-time Western All-Star (1962, 1963, 1966, 1967) and three-time CFL All-Star (1962, 1963, 1967)...one of the most punishing defensive linemen in the CFL...member of the 1966 Grey Cup team...teammates say that was the best game he ever played...named to the Riders' 75th Silver Anniversary All-Star team in 1985...in 1968 Garner was traded to the B.C. Lions so he could be closer to his dairy farm in Washington...inducted into the Plaza of Honor in 1990.

BRUCE BENNETT; 1966-72

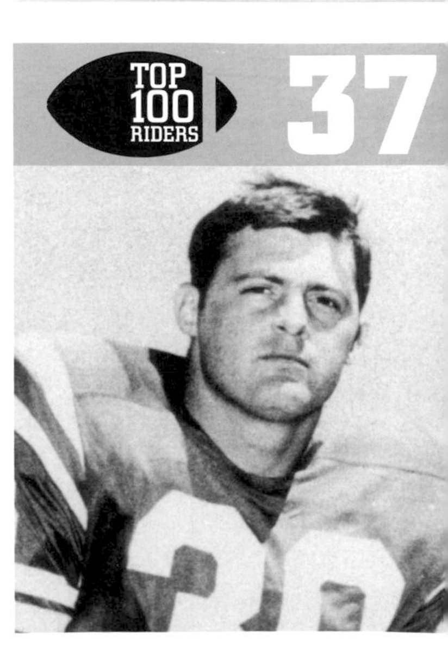

Played his college football in Gainesville, Florida for the University of Florida Gators of the Southeastern Conference from 1962 to 1965...was chosen All-Conference and All-American defensive halfback by UPI in1965...had been an All-Star quarterback in high school and played some quarterback for the Gators...was not drafted by an NFL team because of his small stature so he came to the CFL...played safety and backup quarterback for the Roughriders from 1966 to 1972...Western All-Star six consecutive years (1966-72), and CFL All-Star in 1969...has longest interception return for a touchdown in Rider history at 112 yards against Calgary in 1972...returned 35 interceptions for 606 yards which is third in both categories in Rider history...led Riders in interceptions in 1967, 1969 and 1971...played in Grey Cup game in 1966 as Saskatchewan defeated Ottawa...played in Grey Cup games in 1967, 1969 and 1972...member of the Roughriders' 75th Silver Anniversary All-Star team chosen in 1985...inducted into the Plaza of Honor in 1991.

DEAN GRIFFING; COACH, PLAYER, BUILDER

Came to Regina from Kansas in 1936 to coach the Roughriders...due to an injury to the team's centre, it was necessary for Griffing to play as well...known as 'bad man' throughout his career because of his hard-hitting, rugged playing style...was a colourful performer and extremely popular with the fans... was Western All-Star with the Riders in 1937, 1938 and 1940 and is credited for keeping football alive in Regina in the war years...moved to Calgary while still active on the field...he and other investors reorganized the Calgary football club after the Second World War...after retiring from football for several years he served as general manager of the Roughriders from 1954 to 1957...was flamboyant and controversial and had many contacts in Regina from his earlier years here and quickly developed a plan to put a strong team on the field...coached like he played...gave no quarter...didn't ask for any quarter...inducted into the Canadian Football Hall of Fame in 1965 and the Plaza of Honor in 1987.

BILL CLARKE; 1951-65

Born in Regina in November 1932...played high school football at Scott Collegiate and one year of junior football with the Regina Dales...was only 19 when he joined the Roughriders in 1951 and played defensive tackle for the next 14 years...Riders defensive captain for eight years...named the Riders Most Outstanding Canadian in 1959 and 1961 and awarded the Stack Tibbits Trophy...Western Conference All-Star in 1961 and 1963...a key member of the 1963 Riders' defence which went five games without yielding a touchdown...played in the Grey Cup game in 1951 against Ottawa, in the Western semi-finals in 1953, 1954, 1955, 1958, 1962 and 1964, and in the Western final in 1956 and 1963...inducted into the Saskatchewan Sports Hall of Fame in 1979, the Plaza of Honor in 1988 and the Canadian Football Hall of Fame in 1996...received an honourary Doctorate of Law from the University of Regina in 1995...served on the Rider executive after his retirement and because of his overall long-time dedication to the club received a life membership...died, December 2000.

BOBBY MARLOW; 1953-59

Born in Bessemer, Alabama...played his university football for the Crimson Tide of Alabama in Tuscaloosa, Alabama in the tough Southeastern Conference...in college he was referred to as 'Bama's Blazin' Bobby' going both ways as a running back on offence and outside linebacker on defence... rushed for 233 yards against Auburn in 1952 which was an all-time Alabama record which stood until 1986...Southeastern Conference All-Star running back in1951 and 1952...unanimous All-American in 1952...he and Oklahoma's Billy Vessels, who later came to Edmonton, were considered as the top two running backs in American college football in 1952...selected in the first round of the 1953 NFL draft by the New York Giants but decided to come to Saskatchewan where he played from 1953 until 1959...played fullback and linebacker for the Riders and rushed for a career total of 4,291 yards (3rd All-Time Riders)...24 touchdowns (8th) 189 points scored (22nd)...scored 10 touchdowns in 1957... Western All-Star as a running back in 1953, 1954 and 1955 and as a linebacker in 1956 and 1957... known here as the 'Alabama Basher' for his tough, bruising style of play...played in the Western semi-finals in 1953, 1954 , 1955 and 1958 and the Western final in 1956...inducted posthumously into the Plaza of Honor in 1989...died in 1985.

WAYNE SHAW; 1961-72

Born in Bladworth, Saskatchewan in 1939...introduction to football was at Notre Dame College in Wilcox...played two years with the junior Saskatoon Hilltops, appearing in two national finals, winning one in 1959...joined Riders in 1961...played 186 games (14th All-Time Riders), 16 fumble recoveries (3rd), 100 return yards (12th), 21 interceptions (tied for 11th), 198 return yards (25th)... Western All-Star six times (1963, 1964, 1966, 1967, 1969, 1971)...CFL All-Star, 1967...made the playoffs 11 years...played on Western Conference championship teams four times and in four Grey Cups (1966, 1967, 1969, 1972) - winning one in 1966...had the innate ability to get to the ball carrier as if blockers were not present and once near the ball carrier his strength would not allow him to escape...his teammates called him 'Clamps'...named to the Riders' 75th Silver Anniversary Team in 1985...inducted into the Plaza of Honor in 1994 and the Saskatchewan Sports Hall of Fame in 1995.

SANDY ARCHER; TRAINER 1951-80

Born in Moose Jaw in 1921...was working as a physiotherapist at the Regina Medical Arts Building when he was invited to become the Roughrider trainer in 1951...the position was his exclusively until 1978 when he was sidelined by a heart attack that forced the first of two bypass surgeries... the following two years, 1978 and 1979, he shared trainer duties with Ivan Gutfriend, who ultimately replaced him in 1980 when Sandy retired...Ivan remains as the club's physical therapist as of 2009... Sandy tended to the injuries of hundreds of Rider players in his 30 seasons and was highly praised for his ability to mend players so they could return to the field...players and coaches considered Sandy the club psychologist as well as the trainer...the Roughriders gave Sandy credit for their success through the 1950s, '60s and '70s, which included six Grey Cup appearances...Gutfriend says that many of the taping procedures taught by 'the Sandman' are those he still uses today...in the off-season Sandy served as trainer for the Regina Pats and was trainer for 16 seasons with the Regina Caps senior hockey team...was an active member of the National Athletic Trainers Association and a founding member of the Canadian Athletic Therapists Association...was inducted into the Plaza of Honor in 1988 and the Saskatchewan Sports Hall of Fame and Museum in 2003...died in 2007.

AL RITCHIE; COACH

Alvin Horace (Al) Ritchie was born in Cobden, Ontario in 1890...moved to Regina with his family prior to the First World War in which he served as an artilleryman and was a prisoner of war for one year...returned to Regina after the war and became actively involved in coaching hockey and football...known as the Silver Fox, he was just as comfortable coaching on the football field as in the hockey rink...coached the Regina Pats junior hockey and football teams and is the only person in history to have won national championships in both sports...as coach of the Regina Roughriders, Ritchie led his teams to 56 consecutive regular season wins and nine Western championships – but he never won the Grey Cup, despite four straight appearances in the final (1929-1932)... although he lost each one, he was proud of the fact that he initiated, and made traditional, the concept of a western team playing an eastern team for the national championship...his persistence and fighting spirit laid the groundwork for the present day east-west rivalry...it was Ritchie who began to call the Regina football club the Saskatchewan Roughriders...devoted himself to the pigskin in the summer and fall, but coached the Regina Pats junior hockey team in winter with equal success, leading the team to a Memorial Cup in 1925 and repeating as national junior champions in 1928 and 1930...western scout for the New York Rangers of the NHL for many years...continued to coach football in 1935 and 1936 before retiring. Despite never having won the Grey Cup, he left his mark by way of the rules committee... negotiated for western football to reduce the number of men on the field from 14 to 12, a move the east later adopted...also had the west using forward passes two years before the east adopted a similar rule...was inducted in to the Canadian Football Hall of Fame in 1963, Canada's Sports Hall of Fame in 1964, the Saskatchewan Sports Hall of Fame in 1966 and the Plaza of Honor in 1987....died in 1966.

KERRY JOSEPH; 2006-07

Born in New Iberia, Louisiana in October 1973...played QB for McNeese State for four seasons (1992 -95)...led the team to a 42-11 record and two Southland Conference championships...was both team MVP and Conference player-of-the-year in 1995...selected first overall by Saskatchewan in the Ottawa dispersal draft in April, 2006 and played two memorable years, using both his intelligence and athleticism led them to a Grey Cup victory over Winnipeg in 2007...his career passing totals in two seasons as a Roughrider are 922 attempts (10th All-Time), 534 completions (10th), 7,491 yards (9th) and 46 touchdowns (8th)...also a threat to run, Kerry ran for 1,320 yards (27th) on 181 attempts (a 7.3-yard average) and 17 touchdowns (12th), all in just two seasons...capped off his 2007 season by winning the league Most Outstanding Player award two days prior to the Grey Cup victory.

EDDIE DAVIS; 2001-PRESENT

Born in St. Louis, Missouri in 1973...four-year letterman at Northern Illinois...where he started 19 of 20 games, registering; 129 defensive tackles, four interceptions, 16 pass deflections and two fumble recoveries...originally signed by the CFL's Birmingham Barracudas in May, 1995... selected by Calgary Stampeders in third round (26th overall) of 1996 CFL Dispersal Draft...ninth year with the Riders...signed free agent contract with Saskatchewan in March 2001...in 15 years in the CFL, Eddie has totalled 745 tackles, 107 special teams tackles, 14 quarterback sacks and 34 interceptions...19 interceptions as a Rider (13th All-Time), nine fumble recoveries and two touchdowns...four-time Western All-Star (2001, 2004, 2005 and 2006)...also a four time CFL All- Star (2000, 2004, 2005, and 2006)...member 2007 Grey Cup champion Rider team.

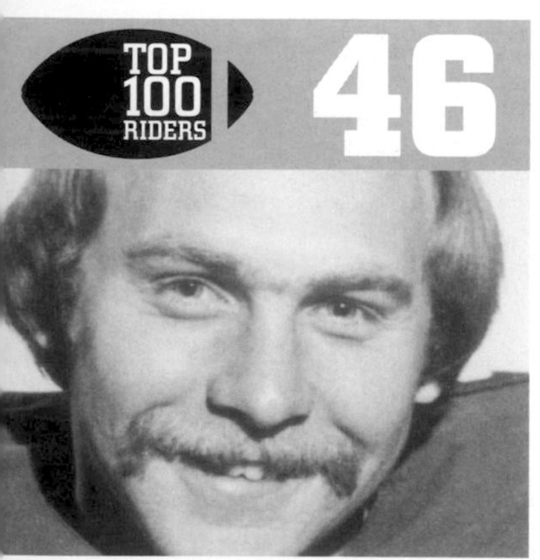

TOM CAMPANA; ASSISTANT COACH 1979

Born in Youngstown, Ohio in 1950...raised in Kent, Ohio...attended Kent City High School...lettered in football, basketball and track...high school All-American...high school player-of-the-year... attended Ohio State University where he played for the legendary Woody Hayes...played both offensive halfback and defensive back...played in 1970 Rose Bowl...named Outstanding Senior Player at OSU...drafted by NFL's St. Louis Cardinals but Rider head coach John Payne convinced him to come to Saskatchewan...Western Conference rookie-of-the-year in 1972...89 games as a Rider...263 receptions (10th All-Time Riders)...4,040 yards receiving (10th)...28 touchdowns (8th)... extremely fast—great kickoff and punt returner...87 kickoff returns (5th) for 1,963 yards (4th) and 1,394 punt return yards (12th) ...Western All-Star in 1972...assistant coach to Ron Lancaster following retirement...inducted into the Plaza of Honor in 2008.

COREY HOLMES; 2001-2005, 2007

Born in Greensville, Mississippi in November 1976...attended Mississippi Valley State...played eight games in senior season with the Delta Devils...named SWAC all-Conference and SWAC player-of-the-year...rushed 189 times for 1,167 yards and 10 touchdowns...led team in scoring with 60 points...averaged 6.2 yards per rush...originally signed a free agent contract in June, 2001...traded to Hamilton in 2006, and reacquired midway through the 2007 season...played six of his seven years with the Roughriders and was a fan favourite in Saskatchewan...rewrote the Riders return yardage records...4,077 kick return yards (1st All-Time Riders)...3,440 punt return yards (1st)...five punt returns for touchdowns (1st)...one kickoff return for touchdown (tied for 2nd All-Time)...3,455 combined yards in 2005 place him 3rd All-Time in the CFL for a single season...2,136 rushing yards (12th)...1,664 receiving yards (35th)...winner of CFL Most Outstanding Special Teams Player (2002, 2005)...winner of Molson Cup as Riders' Most Popular Player as voted on by fans in 2005.

LORNE RICHARDSON; 1973-76

Born in Moose Jaw in 1950...led his high school Central Cyclones to Moose Jaw's first-ever provincial football championship...led league in passing, rushing and punting...named Moose Jaw High School athlete-of-the-year...Riders helped him obtain a scholarship to the University of Colorado... as a senior named Big 8 Defensive player-of-the-week...Rider territorial exemption...led Western Conference in 1973 with seven interceptions...Western Conference rookie-of-the-year in 1973...in four years as a Rider had 21 picks (11th All-Time Riders)...409 return yards (9th)...Western All-Star four times (1973-76)...CFL All-Star four times (1973-76)...played in four Western finals and one Grey Cup...named to 1985 Riders' 75th Silver Anniversary All-Star team...inducted into the Plaza of Honor in 1997.

ANDREW GREENE; 1997, 1999-2006

Born in Kingston, Jamaica in September 1969... a four-year letterman at Indiana and a three-year starter. He was twice named Indiana's Outstanding Offensive Lineman...as a senior, also won first-team All-Big Ten Conference honours and was a second-team All-American...originally selected by the Roughriders in the second round of the CFL Draft in 1994...was also selected by the Miami Dolphins in the second round (53rd overall) of the 1995 NFL Draft. ..NFL career included stops at Miami, New York, Atlanta, Seattle and Jacksonville...signed a free-agent deal with Saskatchewan, and returned to the CFL in 1999... five-time Western All-Star (2000, 2001, 2003, 2004, 2005)... four-time CFL All-Star (2000, 2003, 2004, 2005)...two-time winner of the DeMarco-Becket Memorial Trophy (2000, 2003) which is awarded to the outstanding lineman in the West Division...CFL's Most Outstanding Offensive Lineman in 2003.

CHRIS DeFRANCE; 1981-85

Born in Waldo, Arkansas in 1956...played college football at Arizona State...drafted in the sixth round by the Dallas Cowboys...after brief stints with the NFL's Dallas Cowboys, Washington Redskins and Chicago Bears, joined the Riders in 1981...fit in right away with three consecutive 1,000-plus-yards receiving seasons...solid reputation as a control receiver with soft hands and the ability to get open... known to make seemingly impossible catches with the ease and grace of an acrobat...played 71 games, catching 328 passes (4th All-Time Riders) for 5,035 yards (7th) while averaging 15.4 yards per catch...longest reception was 100 yards and on Aug 5, 1983 he caught nine passes for a team-record 260 yards...two-time recipient of the Molson Cup voted on by fans as Most Popular Rider Player (in 1983, 1984)...Western All-Star (1983, 1984) and named to the Riders' 75th Silver Anniversary team in 1985 while still an active player...inducted into Plaza of Honor in 1994.

BOB POLEY; 1978-84, 1988-92

Born in 1955 in Prairie River, Saskatchewan and raised in nearby Hudson Bay where he played nine-man football...played five years and won three national championships with the Regina Rams under legendary coach Gord Currie...All-Star defensive end four times...joined Riders under head coach Ron Lancaster who turned him into a centre...a move that gave 'The Polecat' a 15-year career in the CFL...played all interior offensive line positions and played them all well...recognized as the premier long snapper in his day...snapped for the winning field goal in the 43-40 Grey Cup victory over Hamilton in 1989...played 236 games, 183 as a Rider (15th All-Time Riders)...Western and CFL All-Star in 1986...inducted into the Plaza of Honor in 1996.

JEREMY O'DAY; 1999-PRESENT

Born in Buffalo, New York in August 1974...spent college career at Edinboro University in Pennsylvania...played from 1992-1996 with Fighting Scots...was a three-time All-American Division II player...chosen by Toronto in the second round of the 1997 supplemental draft...signed a free agent contract with Saskatchewan in February, 1999...four-time West Division All-Star (2003, 2005, 2006, 2007) and a two-time CFL All-Star (2006, 2007)...won two Grey Cup championships, 1997 with Toronto, and 2007 in Saskatchewan...after the 2008 season O'Day had played in 166 games as a Rider, which placed him 21st All-Time in Rider history...has been a mainstay on a consistently strong offensive line as a Rider.

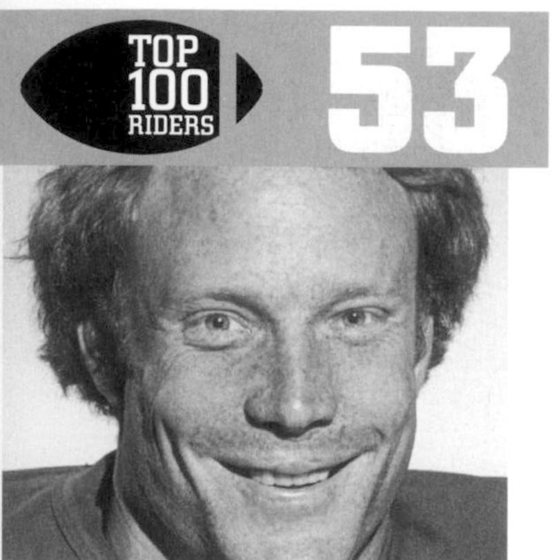

RHETT DAWSON; 1974-76

Born in Valdosta, Georgia in 1948...played his college ball at Florida State University...drafted by Houston Oilers in 1972...played with Minnesota Vikings in 1973...played three seasons with the Roughriders...started 37 games for the Riders at wide receiver...finished Rider career with 148 receptions (26th All-Time Riders) for 2,419 yards (20th)...recorded 23 touchdowns (10th) with the Green and White...Western All-Star in 1975 and 1976...CFL All-Star in 1976...played in 1976 Grey Cup game...had a league-high 85-yard touchdown reception in 1975...named to Riders' 75th Silver Anniversary All-Star Rider team in 1985...selected to Florida State Hall of Fame in 2006...inducted into the Plaza of Honor in 2006.

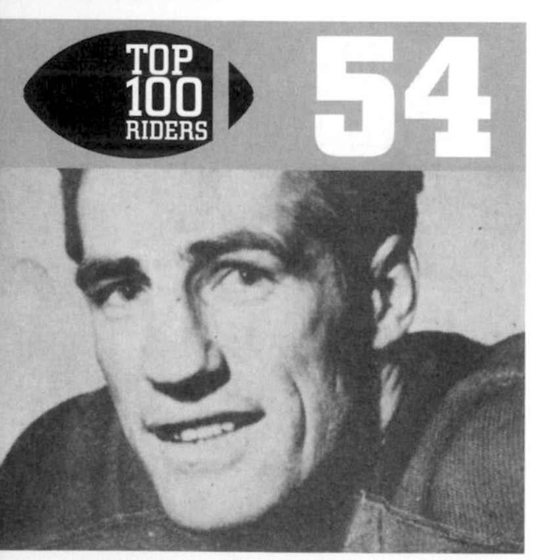

KEN CHARLTON; 1941, 1943, 1948-54

Like his long-time teammate Sully Glasser, Ken Charlton was born in Regina and excelled in hockey and baseball as well as football...played junior football for the Regina Dales and first became a Roughrider in 1941...with the commencement of the Second World War, Ken joined the RCAF and was stationed in Winnipeg where he played football for the RCAF Bombers and was a member of the 1942 Bomber Grey Cup team...returned to the Riders in 1943 but did not play football in 1944 because of RCAF commitments...from 1945-47 played with the Ottawa Rough Riders and was named team captain...selected to the CFL All-Star team in 1946...returned to play for the Riders in 1948 through 1954 as a running back, punter and both a kickoff and punt returner and finished his career as a defensive back...was a Rider All-Star in 1941, 1948 and 1949 and played for the Roughriders in the Grey Cup in 1951...after retirement, Ken's company transferred him to Winnipeg and was the president of the St. James Senior Football Club when it won the Canadian championship in 1963...was inducted into the Saskatchewan Sports Hall of Fame in 1986, the Plaza of Honor in 1988 and the Canadian Football Hall of Fame in 1992...died at the age of 84 in 2004.

REG WHITEHOUSE; 1952-66

Was lured by Glenn Dobbs from his Montreal junior football team at the age of 17 to try out for the Roughriders...the main attraction of Regina for him was that if he failed to make the team, he could at least join the RCMP...over the next 15 years, Whitehouse was an integral part of the offensive line, first as guard and then as tackle...was also a talented kicker and became one of the most colourful characters ever to wear the green and white uniform...played on defence in the East-West-All-Star Shrine game in Vancouver in 1956...was the team's leading scorer in 1959, 1961 and 1963 and ranks third in total games played as a Roughrider with 238...often played injured...married Joanne Baird, who was winner of Miss Roughrider and Miss Grey Cup in 1953...Reg's greatest thrill as a Roughrider was being a captain on the team when it won the Grey Cup in 1966...inducted into the Plaza of Honor in 1992...died in 2008.

PAUL McCALLUM; 1994-95, 1996-2005

Born in Vancouver, British Columbia in January 1970...played with the Surrey Rams of the Canadian Junior Football League...then travelled to Scotland to play professional soccer in the Scottish Third Division...in 1993 returned to Canada and signed as a free agent with the CFL's Hamilton Tiger-Cats...after being released, he had short stints with the Ottawa Rough Riders, B.C. Lions and Saskatchewan Roughriders until 1996, when he departed for Scotland again, this time as the punter/placekicker for the Scottish Claymores of the World League, and was with the team when it won World Bowl in 1996...returned to the Roughriders and played 10 consecutive seasons...during his tenure placed his name at, or near the top of, every Rider punting or placekicking list...had 387 converts (2nd All-Time) 339 field goals (2nd) 1,116 punts (1st), 45,670 punting yards (1st), 105 singles (2nd), 679 kickoffs (2nd), 39,544 kickoff yards (2nd) and 1,503 points (2nd) as a kicker...Western All-Star in 2003... played in 1997 Grey Cup loss to Toronto Argonauts...currently the punter/placekicker for his hometown B.C. Lions.

MIKE SAUNDERS; 1992-94, 1997-99

Born in Milton, Wisconsin in October 1969...was one of the top running backs in the CFL in a career that spanned from 1992-99...played for five CFL teams (Saskatchewan, San Antonio, Hamilton, Montreal and Toronto), having his best success as a Rider...was a true dual-threat running back, adept at both rushing and catching the ball out of the backfield...his career began with the Roughriders in 1992, playing with the Green and White for three seasons, and he would later return in 1997...career numbers as a Rider of 48 touchdowns (7th All-Time), 294 points (13th), 872 rushing attempts (2nd), 4,396 rushing yards (2nd All-Time), 28 rushing touchdowns (4th), 239 receptions (14th), 2,678 receiving yards (17th, 20 receiving touchdowns (13th)...Divisional All-Star with Riders in 1994 and San Antonio in 1995...CFL All-Star with Antonio in 1995...led the Riders in rushing in 1993, 1994, 1997, 1998 and 1999 as well as kickoff return yards in 1993...played in 1997 Grey Cup loss to Toronto Argonauts.

TOM BURGESS; 1987-89, 1994-95

Born in Newark, New York in March 1964...a graduate of Colgate University, played from 1982 to 1985, and was inducted into the Colgate University Athletic Hall of Honor in 1986...came to the Riders from Ottawa in 1987...passing numbers in just five years as a Roughrider still rank him among the best —1,634 attempts (4th All-Time), 827 completions (4th), 11,852 yards (4th), and 74 touchdown passes (4th)...won back-to-back Grey Cups, winning one in 1989 with the Riders, and in 1990 he led the Winnipeg Blue Bombers to victory in the 78th Grey Cup, capturing the Most Valuable Player award...rarely does a team win a championship in the CFL without a quality tandem—Tom Burgess and Kent Austin provided solid, timely leadership in their three years together as Riders... inducted into the Plaza of Honor in 2009.

BOB KOSID; 1964-72

Born in Brandon, Manitoba in 1942...family moved to Minneapolis, then Chicago where he starred in high school as a running back and defensive back...team MVP...All-Conference...All-Chicago Area team...chose University of Kentucky, again playing two ways...named Kentucky's Outstanding Defensive Back...recruited by Riders' Ken Preston...32 career interceptions (6th All-Time Riders), 1,151 return yards (15th)...returned two interceptions for touchdowns (5th)...had five picks in 1967 and eight in 1968 (4th)...Riders made playoffs every year of his career...four first-place finishes... played in seven Western finals and four Grey Cups (1966, 1967, 1969, 1972) - winning in 1966... Western All-Star in 1966 and 1968, CFL All-Star in 1968...legendary trainer Sandy Archer labelled Kosid "a 100 per-center"...inducted into the Plaza of Honor in 1997.

GORDON BARWELL; 1964-73

Born in 1944 and raised in Saskatoon...legendary star high school athlete at City Park High excelling at track, hockey, baseball, curling and, of course, football...played only one year with the Saskatoon Hilltops before being called up to the Riders in 1964 at the tender age of 19...great hands, blazing speed...played 150 games (28th All-Time Riders)...242 receptions (13th), and 4,314 yards (8th) for an impressive average of 17.8 yards per catch...32 touchdowns receiving (14th)...longest reception was for 102 yards from Ron Lancaster in 1965...Eagle Keys stated that of all the players he coached, Barwell was given the least amount of credit due to him...Barwell never missed playoffs...won four Western Conference titles (1966, 1967, 1969, 1972)...played in four Grey Cups (1966, 1967, 1969, 1972) winning one in 1966...CFL teams of any era would have loved to have a non-import play the wideout position as well as Barwell...inducted posthumously into Plaza of Honor in 1994...died in 1988.

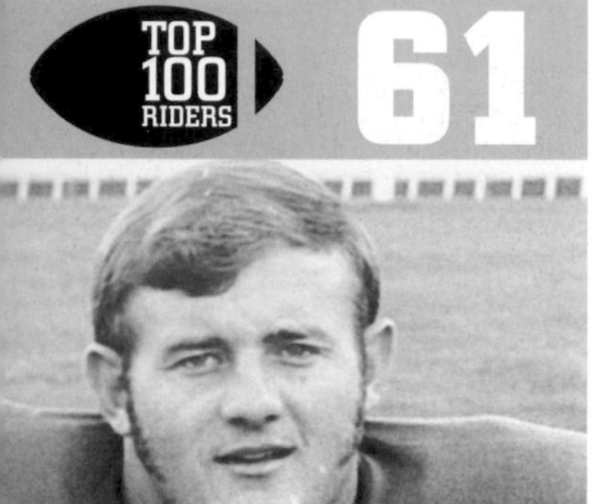

RALPH GALLOWAY; 1969-79

Born in 1946 and raised in Illinois...started his athletic career at East Aurora High...started on both offence and defence...named All-Conference and Honorable Mention All-State...at Southern Illinois University played on both offence and defence and placekicked...named All-State in senior year... attended NFL training camps with the Minnesota Vikings and St. Louis Cardinals...one year in Continental League...joined Riders in 1969, starting at tackle before being moved to guard position where he was five-time Western Conference All-Star (1973-77) and two-time CFL All-Star (1976, 1977)...Rider nominee as Most Outstanding Lineman in 1974 and 1977...played in eight straight Western semifinals and eight finals...three Grey Cup games (1969, 1972, 1976)...member of best regular-season team in Rider history in 1970 when the Riders were 14-2...inducted into Plaza of Honor in 1996.

ED BUCHANAN; 1963-67

Born in April 1940 in San Diego, California and was a legendary high school football and basketball star in San Diego...attended San Diego Junior College from 1958 to 1960...joined the Calgary Stampeders in 1961...came to the Riders in 1963 ...was a CFL and Western Conference All-Star in 1964 as he led the league in rushing with 1,390 yards, averaging 7.8 yards per carry...also excelled as a receiver and on returns...defences were bedazzled in 1964 with the inside running of George Reed and Ed's outside speed...played on the 1966 Rider Grey Cup-winning team...on Aug 3, 1964 he ran 93 yards for a touchdown against Calgary, which is the second-longest touchdown run in Rider history...compiled 2,799 yards rushing (8th All-Time Riders list), along with 1,832 receiving yards (31st), and 1,530 kickoff return yards (11th) and scored 11 touchdowns...died of Lou Gehrig's disease in San Diego on August 31, 1991at the young age of 51.

ROGER GOREE; 1975-80

Born in 1951 and raised in Baton Rouge, Louisiana...dad was All-American lineman at Louisiana State University...mom was a star softball player...played tight end and linebacker in high school...first athlete named to his high school Hall of Fame...attended Baylor University in Texas...Conference MVP...Consensus All-American...MVP in Hula Bowl...inducted into Baylor Hall of Fame in 1983... All-Southwest Team of Decade...in 1989 named to Texas 75-Year Diamond Jubilee Team...played for Calgary in 1973-74...Western All-Star four times (1973, 1974, 1976, 1977)...CFL All-Star twice (1974, 1976)...played in two Western finals...one Grey Cup appearance in 1976...averaged 80 tackles per season (five per game over his eight-year career)...Rider Schenley nominee for Outstanding Defensive Player in 1977...named to the Riders' 75th Silver Anniversary team...inducted into the Plaza of Honor in 1998.

MIKE ANDERSON; 1984-1995

Another Rider territorial exemption who came home to play for the Riders, just as his father, Paul, did before him...born in Regina in 1961, raised in Saskatoon, starred for the Evan Hardy Souls and after one season with the Saskatoon Hilltops accepted a scholarship in California with the College of Sequoias where he was player-of-the-year, All-Conference and second Team All-State, before transferring to San Diego State University to join the Aztecs...joined the Riders in 1984, playing on special teams and as backup centre and guard before soon taking over at the starting centre position, which was his until his retirement in 1995...played 12 seasons and 205 games (9th All-Time Riders)... chosen as Western Conference All-Star twice (1988 and 1994)...CFL All-Star in 1994...integral part of the offensive line on 1989 Grey Cup championship team...inducted into the Plaza of Honor in 2004.

JIM HOPSON; PLAYER 1973-76, PRESIDENT AND CEO 2005-PRESENT

Born in Regina in 1951, played three years of high school football at Thom Collegiate as an All-Star offensive guard and tackle...played four years with Regina Rams...All-Star three times (1970, 1971, 1972)...national champions twice (1970, 1971)...joined Riders in 1973...started at guard and tackle... retired after 1976 to concentrate on career in education...spent 30 years as a teacher, principal and Director of Education in Saskatchewan...joined Rider organization again in 2001 as special advisor at the request of the Rider alumni...appointed the Riders' first-ever full-time president and CEO in 2005, hired to streamline the organization and manage the day-to-day affairs of the team on both a local business and league level...heading into the 2009 season, Riders had made the playoffs each year under his leadership...hosted two home playoff games and won one Grey Cup 2007...the team had a club record of 18 consecutive sellouts in 2007 and 2008...as a result the club is in the best financial position in its history.

TED DUSHINSKI; 1965-75

Native of Saskatoon...legendary high school athlete at Nutana...continued as a star with the Saskatoon Hilltops...joined Riders in 1965 where he played right corner and right defensive half through 1975...known for aggressive tackling and his ability to cover man-to-man...innate sense and ability for timely interceptions...played 153 games as a Rider (23rd All-Time Riders), 38 interceptions (4th), 491 return yards (7th), two touchdowns on interceptions (tied for 6th), 10 fumble recoveries (10th), 491 return yards (1st)...won four Western finals (1966, 1967, 1969, 1972)...played in four Grey Cups (1966, 1967, 1969, 1972), winning one in 1966...Western All-Star twice (1970, 1975)... named to Riders' 75th Silver Anniversary team in 1985...inducted into Plaza of Honor in 1993...died on October 24, 2005.

NEIL HABIG; 1958-64

Played his college football at Purdue in West Lafayette, Indiana...started in his final two years as both a centre and middle linebacker...was named the Purdue Boilermakers MVP in 1957 and All-Big Ten centre...drafted by the Green Bay Packers in 1958 but was lured north to the CFL with Saskatchewan where he played from 1958-64...was chosen CFL All-Star centre in 1962 and Western All-Star centre in 1959, 1960, 1961, 1962 and Western All-Star middle linebacker in 1963 and 1964...as a middle linebacker in 1963 had seven interceptions and overall had 10 interceptions in his entire career... played in the Western semi-finals in 1958, 1962 , and 1964 and Western final in 1963...inducted into the Plaza of Honor in 1992 and just weeks after his induction, he and his wife Myrna were tragically killed in a car accident in Philadelphia.

CLAIR WARNER; PLAYER 1928-33, PRESIDENT 1945, GENERAL MANAGER 1946-49, 1951-52

Began his football career in 1919, two years after his family moved to Regina from South Dakota...was a member of the Regina Rugby Club that later became the Regina Roughriders and played in four Grey Cups coached by the 'Silver Fox', Al Ritchie, in the years 1928 through 1931...continued to play for the Roughriders until 1933 after which he became the club's general manager, serving for a total of six years in the 1940s and 1950s...was club president in 1945 and was instrumental in the reorganization of the team at the end of the war...assembled a management committee that included former teammate Jack Rowand, Stack Tibbits, Don MacDonald and later Don McPherson. They became known as 'The Big Five'...served on the management committee for 21 years...was a player and executive with the Roughriders for five decades...as manager of his own company he offered employment to many football players who were attracted to Regina to play for the Roughriders...was president of the Western Interprovincial Football Union in 1948 and a member of the rules committee of the Canadian Football Union for several years...was awarded the Canadian Rugby Union Plaque in 1956 for outstanding contributions to the game and inducted into the Canadian Football Hall of Fame in 1965, Saskatchewan Sports Hall of Fame and Museum in 1971 and the Plaza of Honor in 1989...died in 1970.

CLEVELAND VANN; 1976-1980

Born in 1951 in Seguin, Texas where he starred as a linebacker and fullback in high school...named All-District, All-State and High School All-American at fullback...school retired his jersey...offered 75 college scholarships...chose Oklahoma State where he played exclusively at linebacker...named All Big 8 and All-American...played in East-West Shrine Bowl and Blue-Grey game...drafted by Miami Dolphins and California Sun, chose to play with the Sun in the soon-to-be-defunct World Football League...joined Riders in 1976...in rookie season with Green and White made 109 defensive tackles and had two interceptions...helped lead Roughriders to 11-5 regular-season record and first place in the West...Riders defeated Edmonton 23-13 in the Western final...known for incredible performance in 1976 Grey Cup game...named defensive player-of-the-game...also named Saskatchewan's nominee as Outstanding Defensive Player in 1976 and 1978...Cleveland Vann, Roger Goree and Bill Manchuk played together as a linebacking corps for five years - many believe it was the steadiest, most dependable linebacking corps unit in Rider history...continues to live in Regina...works at SaskEnergy...excellent ambassador for the Roughriders...inducted into the Plaza of Honor in 2000.

BOBBY THOMPSON; 1969-74, 1977

Born in Raleigh, North Carolina in 1948...raised in Providence, Rhode Island...All-American Junior College halfback at Western Arizona at Yuma...attended University of Oklahoma at Norman one year before signing with Riders by then-Rider assistant coach Jim Spavital...had outstanding rookie season...891 receiving yards, 467 rushing yards and 600 kickoff return yards...over seven seasons played 90 games...2,961 rushing yards (5th All-Time Riders), 4,207 receiving yards (9th), and 1,472 return yards (13th)...holds the Rider record for the longest kickoff return of 115 yards which he achieved in 1971...Riders' leading receiver in 1969, 1971, 1972 and 1974...played with the NFL's Detroit Lions in 1975 and 1976 before completing his career with Riders in 1977...spent 30 years teaching and coaching special needs children in Michigan...inducted into the Plaza of Honor in 2007.

IVAN GUTFRIEND; ATHLETIC THERAPIST 1978-PRESENT

Born in Moose Jaw, Saskatchewan...the 2009 season is his 23rd as the team's athletic therapist... has been with the Roughriders since 1978 and named head athletic therapist in 1981, taking over from his legendary predecessor, Sandy Archer...responsible for the day-to-day treatment and rehabilitation needs of all Roughrider players and coaches...also oversees programs designed to maintain the team's health and welfare...has received undergraduate degrees from the University of Saskatchewan and completed a master's degree in Athletic Training from Indiana University...is a certified athletic therapist through the Canadian Athletic Therapists' Association.

GENE (GENO) WLASUIK; 1959-67

Born in 1936, raised in Winnipeg...played high school football at Isaac Newton High before joining the Winnipeg Junior Rods...two-way player who led the Rods to two national junior championships...played for Blue Bombers for two years on offence...joined Riders in September 1959...switched to defensive backfield and punt returner...549 punt returns (1st All-Time Riders, 10th All-Time CFL) and 3,296 returning yards (2nd)...his return prowess was all achieved before blocking was allowed on punt returns...sure hands, rarely fumbled a punt...27 career interceptions (8th) and 287 return yards (15th)...led Riders in interceptions 1960, 1961, 1962...led CFL with five interceptions in 1962...12 fumble recoveries (8th)...played in 132 games as a Rider...member of two Western Conference champions...played in two Grey Cups (1966, 1967), winning one in 1966... lighthearted personality was a major catalyst for team morale...inducted into Plaza of Honor in 1995.

DAN FARTHING; 1991-2001

Born in Regina in 1969, moved to Saskatoon at an early age...led his high school team, the Holy Cross Crusaders, to provincial high school championships in 1985, 1986...also excelled in track and field... awarded Don Powell Memorial Scholarship as Outstanding High School Football Player in Saskatchewan... played college football for University of Saskatchewan Huskies...CIS rookie-of-the-Year in 1987...led nation in receiving yardage at 17 years of age...Western nominee for Hec Crighton Award as Top Player in CIS... member of 1989 Vanier Cup champions...drafted in first round by Riders (2nd pick overall) in 1991... played 169 games (21st All-Time Riders), 384 receptions (3rd), 5,108 yards receiving (6th), 19 touchdowns receiving (tied 15th)...best year was 1997, led team in receiving yardage (959)...three-time nominee as Riders' Outstanding Canadian...great moves, great hands, 'go-to' possession receiver...played in 1997 Grey Cup loss to Toronto Argonauts who were led by Doug Flutie...inducted into Plaza of Honor in 2009.

JACK HILL; 1957-61

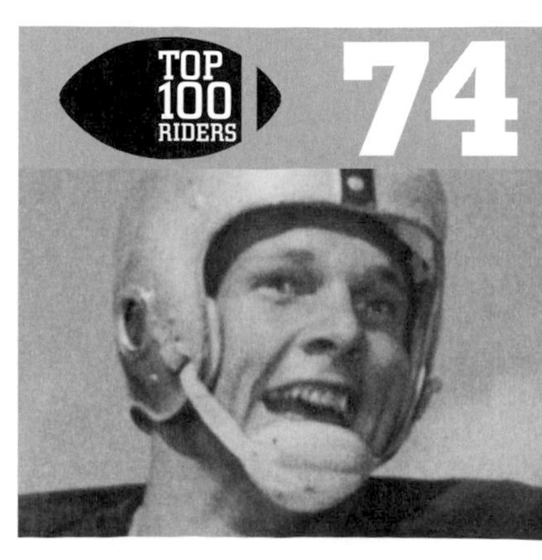

Played his college football at Utah State University in Logan, Utah where he played halfback and wide receiver for the Aggies...led the nation in scoring in 1956 and was named a Western Athletic Conference first-team All-Star as well being named an All-American by UPI...selected in the 1957 NFL draft by the Baltimore Colts but elected instead to come to Saskatchewan where he played until 1961...very versatile player...played running back, wide receiver, kick returner and was the placement kicker for the Riders as well as handling kickoff duties...was named Western All-Star in 1958 as he led the West in scoring with 145 points, a Rider record until kicker Dave Ridgway broke it in 1982...scored 16 touchdowns in 1958 including 14 receiving...first Rider with over 1,000 receiving yards...1,065 in 1958...1,860 career receiving yards (29th All-Time)...122 career receptions...216 scoring points (15th)...kicked off 43 times for 2,501 yards (13th)...inducted into the Plaza of Honor in 1989...died in 2005.

NORM FONG, EQUIPMENT MANAGER 1979-2008

Born and raised in Regina in 1951...graduated from Balfour Tech where he began learning the secrets of being a good equipment man...after high school, Fong stepped into the equipment room of the Regina Rams for a number of years and then in 1972, he joined the Los Angeles Sharks of the World Hockey Association...in 1973, Fong became equipment manager and trainer of the Regina Pats where he remained for five seasons and was part of their last Memorial Cup win in 1974...has travelled throughout the province promoting the importance of proper-quality equipment at the amateur ranks, which also included producing a video through Football Saskatchewan highlighting the proper use and fitting of football equipment...was a member of the Saskatchewan Roughrider Football Club for more than three decades...2008 marked his 34th and final season with the team which made him the longest-serving head equipment manager in the CFL...served as an assistant at four training camps, beginning in 1975, before accepting the head equipment position in 1979... inducted into the Plaza of Honor in 2009.

ERIC TILLMAN; GENERAL MANAGER 2006-PRESENT

Born in Jackson, Mississippi in 1957...graduated with a journalism degree in 1979 from the University of Mississippi...began his football career in 1981 when he joined the public relations department of the Houston Oilers of the NFL...moved to the CFL in 1982 as director of player personnel with the Montreal Concordes...in 1984 he became director of the United States College Senior Bowl, held annually in Mobile, Alabama...in 1993 he accepted the position as general manager of the B.C. Lions, winning a Grey Cup his second year in 1994...in 1995 and 1996 he was employed as director of football operations for NFL Europe...returned to the CFL in 1997 as general manager of the Toronto Argonauts and the Argos won the Grey Cup that year...from 2002-04 he was the general manager of the expansion Ottawa Renegades...in 2005 joined CBC and Sportsnet as a CFL television analyst... joined the Saskatchewan Roughriders on Aug 23, 2006 as general manager...in his first two years the Roughriders' record was 27-13 which included a Grey Cup victory in 2007...this was the best record in the CFL over that period of time.

GARY LEWIS; 1985-94

Born in Oklahoma City, Oklahoma in 1961...was high school All-American at offensive guard and defensive tackle...played his college football at Oklahoma State...team captain and consensus All-American two years running...drafted by the New Orleans Saints in the fourth round in 1983... originally signed with the Ottawa Rough Riders in 1985...traded to Saskatchewan in 1985...played 10 seasons in Saskatchewan...his 152 games played places him 24th on the All-Time Rider list... Western All-Star twice (1988, 1991)...was a member of the 1989 Grey Cup champions...had a quarterback sack in Grey Cup game...had 70 career regular season quarterback sacks (3rd)...had 242 career defensive tackles and also had eight career fumble recoveries (tied 8th) and one touchdown... had 11 career tackles for losses...inducted into the Plaza of Honor in 2006.

WALLY DEMPSEY; 1965-72

Born in Reseda, California...starred at Cleveland High in Reseda...played at Pierce Junior College where he was named All-Conference and Junior College All-American...transferred to Washington State...named to All-Pacific team...teammate of George Reed and Hugh Campbell at WSU...joined Riders in 1965 when he started as middle linebacker...hard-hitting leader...strong and great instinct to get to and punish ball carriers, which was his idea of fun...played on four Western champion Rider teams...played in four Grey Cups (1966, 1967, 1969, 1972), winning one in 1966...Western All-Star in 1968, 1969...CFL All-Star in 1968...named to the Riders' 75th Anniversary All-Star team in 1985... his Rider teams never had a losing season or missed the playoffs...member of the 1970 team with best-ever Rider record (14-2)...inducted into Plaza of Honor in 1995.

SULLIVAN JOHN (SULLY) GLASSER; 1942, 1946-57

Born in Regina in 1922...an outstanding athlete who excelled at hockey and baseball as well as football...played junior football for the Regina Dales and Bombers and became a Regina Roughrider in 1942...like so many young Canadians of that era, Sully interrupted his career to serve his country in the Canadian Navy from 1942 to 1945...returning after the Second World War, Sully found that the Riders still had a place for him on the roster...this local product was invaluable to the team, playing both the halfback and fullback positions on offence and defence where needed...also ran back kicks on special teams...had a very distinguished career including an outstanding performance in the 1951 Grey Cup game in which he scored a touchdown for the Riders...that touchdown was the last scored by a Saskatchewan Roughrider in a Grey Cup game until 1966 when the Riders won their first Grey Cup...has been recognized as one of the great Canadians playing in the CFL...was named to the Western All-Star team in 1946...fondly remembered by football fans who watched the team in the 1940s and 1950s...retired in 1958 after a heart attack on the practice field...Sully was later chosen by the Kiwanis Club of Regina as the first 'Dad of the Year' and inducted into the Plaza of Honor posthumously in 1991...died in 1986.

STEVE MAZURAK; 1973-80, V.P. OF MARKETING 2005-PRESENT

Born in Regina in 1951, this Regina Rams graduate has lived his childhood dream from the sandlot pee wee and midget leagues through high school in Regina to the Riders...starred with the Sheldon-Williams Spartans before playing one season with the University of North Dakota Fighting Sioux on a scholarship...returned home for two all-star seasons as a Regina Ram under the legendary Gordon Currie...joined the Riders in 1973, playing eight seasons, catching 237 passes (15th All-Time Riders) for 3,714 yards (13th), and an impressive 15.7 average gain per catch...also scored 17 touchdowns (18th)...was twice voted by his peers to play in all-star games...was a Rider captain from 1977-80, team player rep and the club's Schenley nominee for Most Outstanding Canadian in 1977...spent five years as executive director of the CFLPA...currently vice-president of marketing for the Riders... inducted into the Plaza of Honor in 2004.

DALE WEST; 1962-68

Born in Cabri, Saskatchewan in 1941, raised in Saskatoon...high school football and track star... gained 1,000 yards rushing as a senior (10-yard average per carry)...holds high school provincial record in 100-yard dash at 9.8 seconds...played at University of Arizona at Tucson for two years with future Rider teammates Ted Urness and Larry Dumelie...finished college eligibility at University of Saskatchewan and was named MVP of the Western Intercollegiate Conference...also led conference in rushing...joined Riders in 1962 and saw duty as a wide receiver, punter and defensive back... in 1963 became full-time defensive back...had 10 interceptions (2nd All-Time Riders) for 226 yards (1st) and one touchdown...named Western Outstanding Canadian for his 1963 efforts, losing out on the CFL award to the legendary Russ Jackson...17 career interceptions (16th) and 263 return yards (18th)...Western All-Star three times (1963, 1964 and 1965)...played in four Western finals...played in two Grey Cups, winning once in 1966...inducted into the Saskatchewan Sports Hall of Fame in 1989 and the Plaza of Honor in 1997.

LARRY ISBELL; 1954-58

A much-revered native of Texas...earned high school All-City status in Houston both in football as a quarterback and in baseball as a catcher...in his junior and senior years as quarterback at Baylor, the Bears won 15 of 20 games with his leadership, passing, running and kicking abilities...in 1951 he was voted All-American and placed 7th in voting for the Heisman trophy...also named All-American in baseball...was number one pick of both the NFL's Washington Redskins and baseball's Boston Red Sox...after two years in the Red Sox minor system, Riders' player and fellow Texan Stan Williams talked him into joining the Riders...played offensive and defensive back, backup quarterback and punter...led Western Conference in punting from 1954-58...42.7-yard career punting average...50 singles (6th All-Time Riders)...caught 92 passes for 1,528 yards and 12 touchdowns...12 career interceptions (tied 23rd) and 172 yards (29th)...in 1954 set a punting record of a then-unheard-of average of 46.3 yards...Western All-Star three times as a defensive back (1956, 1957 and 1958)...was equally adept on offence as a prime target of quarterback Frank Tripucka...member of Texas Sports Hall of Fame, Baylor Sports Hall of Fame and was inducted posthumously into the Plaza of Honor in 1999...died in 1978.

DON MCPHERSON; PRESIDENT 1956-57

Born in Regina in 1918...was president of the Saskatchewan Roughriders in 1957 and the Canadian Football League in 1959...was also president of the Canadian Rugby Union in 1963 and the Western Football Conference in 1965...made major contributions to football at the local, regional and national levels...was appointed director of the Roughriders in 1949 and served on the Clubs' management committee, known as the 'Big Five', until his death in 1973...in 1962 Don McPherson accepted an invitation by the B.C. Lions to chair a committee to reorganize their management structure...was awarded a Life Membership in the B.C. club for his tireless efforts on their behalf... was inducted into the Canadian Football Hall of Fame in 1983 and the Plaza of Honor in 1988... was an ardent sportsman and prominent Regina business entrepreneur...served as an alderman on Regina City Council and was a member of the government in the Saskatchewan Legislature, deeply involved in the improvement of health care facilities throughout Saskatchewan...the McPherson Wing of the Regina General Hospital was named in his honour in 1966.

REGGIE HUNT; 2002-2007

Born in Denison, Texas in October 1977...spent four seasons at Texas Christian University... earned All-WAC honors as safety and kick returner in senior season...ended TCU career with 271 defensive tackles, three interceptions, and seven forced fumbles...holds TCU single-season record with kickoff return average of 34.1 yards in senior season...signed a free agent contract with the NFL's San Diego Chargers in 2000...joined the WFL's Scottish Claymores in 2001...signed with the Saskatchewan Roughriders as a free agent in 2002. As a Rider amassed 453 tackles, 45 special teams tackles, 27 quarterback sacks (10th All-Time), 5 interceptions and 8 fumble recoveries (8th)...was a Western All-Star four times (2003, 2004, 2006, 2007) and a CFL All-Star in 2003...set the CFL record for most tackles in a game with 16 in a 2003 game against Winnipeg...played an integral role in Saskatchewan's 2007 Grey Cup victory over Winnipeg.

VIC STEVENSON; 1983-92, 1998

Born in New Westminster, British Columbia in 1960...grew up in Calgary...played 4 years in the CIAU (new called CIS) with the University of Calgary Dinos...drafted by the Roughriders as a tight end, a position he played for his first three years as a Dino...Riders switched him to the interior offensive line and sent him back to Dinos for his fourth year...played 11 seasons and 172 games for Riders (17th All-Time Riders)...two-time Rider Western All-Star (1991, 1992)...CFL All-Star in 1992 and was named West Division's Most Outstanding Offensive Lineman in 1992...member of 1989 Rider Grey Cup champions...played with B.C. Lions and Toronto Argos, winning two more Grey Cups...played one season with Eskimos before finishing his career with Riders in 1998...inducted into the Plaza of Honor in 2007.

GORDON STASESON; PRESIDENT 1978-81

Born in 1926 and raised in Regina...attended Strathcona Elementary and Central Collegiate...as an athlete was accomplished as a hockey player...played with junior Regina Abbotts (1942, 1945, 1946), Boston Olympics (1943, 1944) and the Regina Capitals of the old Western Hockey League (1947-54)... began involvement with the Roughriders as a fan in the 1930s and has continued being a fan and volunteer ever since...joined Rider management committee in 1974...heavily involved in the 1978 Taylor Field expansion...became club president in 1979...Chair of CFL board of governors in 1982... remained on Riders management committee until 1984...producer of Riders' 75th Silver Anniversary celebration...co-founder and original producer of Plaza of Honor Induction and Dinner ceremonies in 1987...original chair of Plaza of Honor selection committee 1986-92...member 1995 Grey Cup committee...received Saskatchewan Order of Merit, Honorary Doctorate from the University of Regina...also received the prestigious Order of Canada...inducted into the Regina Sports Hall of Fame in 2004 as a builder for seven sports...inducted into Plaza of Honor in 1993.

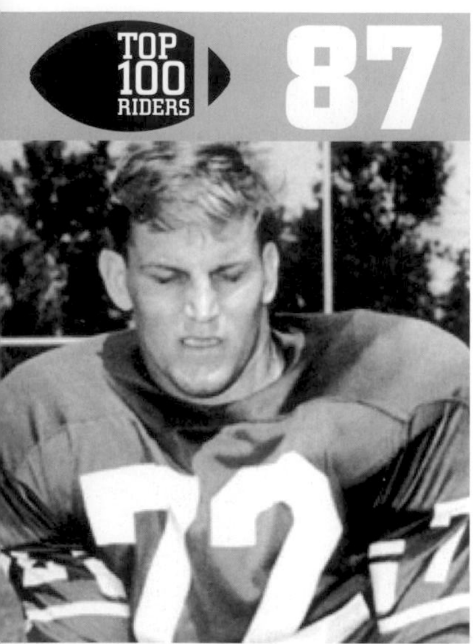

JIM WORDEN; 1964-69

Born and raised in Ohio in 1942...played tight end and linebacker at Wittenberg College...played in prestigious Senior Bowl...named to Wittenberg's Hall of Honor in 1964...drafted by NFL's Dallas Cowboys but chose to join the Riders...one of the best tight ends ever seen on the Canadian gridiron...had knack of making the big catch in key situations...his savage blocking added a new dimension to Rider running game...was a character and a great team player when loyalty was the strength of the Riders' mid-1960s teams...instrumental in George Reed and Ed Buchanan's 1,000-yard rushing seasons...member of 1966 Grey Cup team...Western All-Star and CFL All-Star, 1966... big block against Winnipeg in 1966 Western final sent Buchanan on a 73-yard touchdown run...97 receptions for 1,789 yards (33rd All-Time Riders)...18.4 yards per catch which is outstanding for a tight end of any era...11 touchdowns...best season was 1966—28 catches for 469 yards...caught touchdown pass from Lancaster, also a Wittenberg grad, in 1966 Grey Cup...inducted into Plaza of Honor in 1996...died in 2007.

JACK GOTTA; PLAYER 1960-64, ASSISTANT COACH 1965-67, HEAD COACH 1985-86

Born in 1930 in Ironwood, Michigan where he played his minor and high school football...played college football at Oregon State in Corvallis, Oregon from 1953-1955...joined the Cleveland Browns in 1956...played in Calgary from 1957-1959...joined the Roughriders in 1960...led the Riders in receiving in 1961 and 1963 and has 131 career receptions as a Rider, good for 2,412 yards (21st All-Time Riders) and 13 touchdowns...rejoined Riders in 1965 as assistant coach through1967 under Eagle Keys and was with the Riders' 1966 Grey Cup champions and Grey Cup finalists in 1967...in 1968 he left Saskatchewan and went to Ottawa as an assistant and took over as head coach in 1970... had a 30-26 record in Ottawa, winning the Grey Cup in 1973 and the Annis Stukus Trophy for coach-of-the-year in 1972,1973 and 1978...was head coach of the World Football League's Birmingham Americans in 1974 and 1975...head coach of Calgary from 1976-1983...became Saskatchewan's head coach in 1985 and had a 11-22-1 record (for 1985 and 1986).

OMARR MORGAN; 2000-2006, 2008-PRESENT

Born in Hollywood, California in 1976...spent two seasons at Brigham Young University...teammate of former Rider Steve Sarkisian...was All-WAC First Team All-Star in 1996, 1997...and honourable mention All-American in 1997...played in 23 career games at BYU...was a starter in final season... also played on kickoff and punt coverage teams...played two seasons at El Camino Junior College... played one year with Sarkisian at El Camino...signed by the St. Louis Rams in 1998...signed by the Roughriders in June, 1999...spent the 2007 season with the Edmonton Eskimos before re-signing with the Riders in 2008...going into the 2009 season Morgan had appeared in 154 career CFL games, has compiled 503 tackles, 34 special teams tackles, 23 interceptions (9th All-Time Riders)...also returned three of those for touchdowns (3rd)...four-time Western All-Star (2001, 2002, 2003, 2005)... three-time CFL All-Star (2002, 2003 and 2005).

HENRY (HANK) DORSCH; PLAYER 1964-71, GENERAL MANAGER 1978-79

Born in Glaslyn, Saskatchewan and raised in Weyburn...had two star seasons with the Regina Rams, with whom he led league in rushing both years...accepted a scholarship at Tulsa University...at Tulsa, led the Golden Hurricanes in rushing both seasons...he also played defence and intercepted Joe Namath in a game versus Alabama...following graduation returned home to play for the Green and White as a territorial exemption...as a Rider, played defensive back, cornerback and blocking fullback for the great George Reed...played in three Grey Cups (1966, 1967, 1969), winning once, that being the Riders' first-ever Grey Cup win—29-14 over the Ottawa Rough Riders in 1966...played eight seasons, 119 regular-season games, and his Rider teams made the playoffs every one of his seasons... strength, quickness, desire and hard hitting were attributes that typified his contributions during his career...following his retirement in 1971, worked for the Regina General Hospital and served on the Rider executive committee before being general manager of the Riders for two years (1978, 1979)... inducted into the Plaza of Honor in 2004.

MATT DOMINGUEZ; 2003-2008

Born in Georgetown, Texas in June 1978...played in 44 games at Sam Houston State...was the school's first NCAA Div. I-AA All-American...caught 211 passes for 3,272 yards and 27 touchdowns... caught a career-high 67 passes for 1,155 yards and 13 touchdowns as a junior...was the team MVP in 1998 and 1999...originally signed with the NFL's Denver Broncos in 2001...signed free agent contract with Saskatchewan in May, 2003...signed free-agent contract with the New York Jets in 2004, but was among the Jets' final cuts despite catching the game winning touchdown in his final game with the Jets...soon thereafter rejoined the Riders...was a West Division All-Star in 2006 when he had 72 catches of 1,169 yards and five touchdowns...in six years as a Rider he compiled 250 catches (12th All-Time Riders) for 3,741 yards (12th) and 20 touchdowns receiving (15th)...was leading the league in receiving yardage when he suffered a knee injury in 2007...exceeded 1,000 yards receiving in both 2003 and 2006...extremely popular member of the community. Matt has stayed in Regina following his career as a Rider, working as a realtor.

STEVE DENNIS; 1977-84

Born in Shreveport, Louisiana in 1951...raised in the nearby town of Sanepta...two-time All-State in high school basketball and once in football...played college football at Grambling under legendary coach Eddie Robinson...played in the World Football League with the New York Stars and two seasons with Toronto Argos before being awarded to the Riders as compensation after Lorne Richardson and James Marshall left the Riders as free agents...traded to Ottawa for Tom Clements and came back to Riders the same year...Eastern All-Star once, Western Conference All-Star once... "Stickman" as he was known by his teammates...played eight seasons and 86 games for Riders...33 career interceptions (tied 4th All-Time Riders)...named to Riders' 75th Silver Anniversary All-Star team as cornerback...teaches high school in Shreveport and also coaches football...inducted into the Plaza of Honor in 2007.

MIKE SAMPLES; PLAYER 1978-83, ASSISTANT COACH 1983-87

Born in Boone Terre, Missouri in 1950...raised in nearby St. Charles, Missouri...played high school at St. Charles High as a fullback and defensive lineman...varsity letterman three years in both baseball and football...All-Conference in football his senior year...attended Drake University from 1969-73... First-team All-Missouri Valley Conference defensive tackle and Kodak All-American in 1972...played in the 1972 Pioneer Bowl...drafted by the Atlanta Falcons in 1973 as a linebacker and defensive end...upon his release was picked up by the B.C. Lions...then joined Hamilton in early 1974 and was named Eastern All-Star in 1976...traded to Saskatchewan in 1978 for George Wells...Western All-Star twice (1981, 1982)...CFL All-Star once (1982)...assistant coach with the Riders from 1983-87...resides in Hamilton where he works in television sales and marketing...inducted into the Plaza of Honor in 1991.

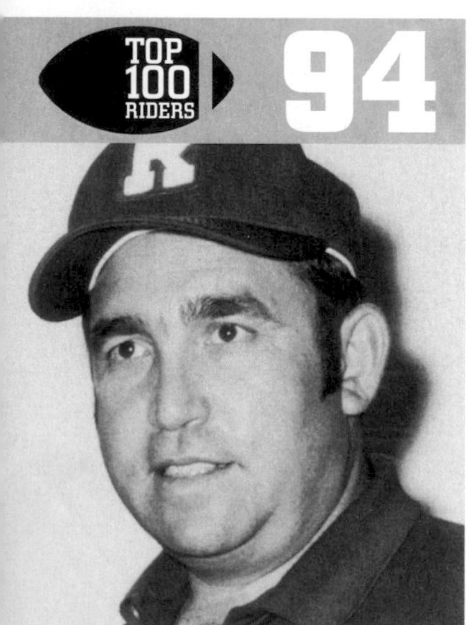

JOHN PAYNE; ASSISTANT COACH 1971-72, HEAD COACH 1973-76

Native of Wewoka, Oklahoma...played college ball as a lineman at Oklahoma State University... Missouri Valley Conference All-Star in 1953...selected to play in Blue Grey Classic as a guard...named coach of OSU's freshman team in 1956...athletic director and coach at Tulsa's McLean High from 1959-62...coach-of-the-year in 1962...defensive coach at Oklahoma Central State College, 1963-64...1965-67 at Brigham Young as assistant coach...made CFL debut as assistant coach in Edmonton 1968...Winnipeg in 1970 and over to the Riders in 1971 under head coach Dave Skrien...named Roughrider head coach in December 1972...44-27-1 overall record (4th All-Time in Rider coaching wins)...went to four Western finals, winning once in 1976...lost 1976 Grey Cup 23-20 to Ottawa...had two 10-win seasons (1973 and 1975)...had one 11-win season in 1976...finished second in Western Conference three times and first once (1976)...resigned as Roughrider head coach in February 1977 to accept an assistant coaching position with the Detroit Lions...inducted into the Plaza of Honor in 2001.

SCOTT SCHULTZ; 2001-2009

Born in Moose Jaw, Saskatchewan in April, 1978...spent college career with North Dakota Fighting Sioux...four-year starter at nose guard...team captain in 2000...played in 39 regular-season games...registered 146 career defensive stops...added 11.5 quarterback sacks...five pass knockdowns and two fumble recoveries...chosen by the Riders in the first round (1st overall) in the 2001 CFL Draft...signed with the NFL's San Diego Chargers in 2001...Scott had played in 128 regular season and 11 playoff games...by the end of his career he had numbers of 178 tackles, 35 quarterback sacks (5th All-Time) and four fumble recoveries...Western All-Star and CFL All-Star in 2005...was a member of the 2007 Grey Cup champion Rider team...retired in 2009 after five games to pursue a business career in Regina.

RICHARD (DICK) RENDEK; PRESIDENT 1982-84

TOP 100 RIDERS 96

Born in June, 1931 in Middle Lake, Saskatchewan...involvement in sport began as an athlete and then moved into sports administration...started sporting career in high school at Bedford Road Collegiate...continued career at University of Saskatchewan...played quarterback for the Huskies in 1950s...served as vice-president of the Riders from 1979-81, president from 1982-84...was on Rider executive from 1977-86...was also a member of the CFL board of governors from 1982-84...also chairman of the fundraising committee that helped raise more than $1 million during the expansion of Taylor Field in the late 1970s which at the time was an extremely significant success...chaired the 1995 Grey Cup bid committee...entered Saskatchewan Sports Hall of Fame in 1997...was on the board of directors of the Saskatchewan Sports Hall of Fame from 1976-79...member of the Canadian Olympic Association...president of Canada Summer Games Society in 1974 and 1975...chairman of first-ever Western Canada Summer Games held in Regina in 1975...chaired the Regina committee for the 1989 Canada Summer Games...also chaired 1997 Word Pioneer International Gymnastics Classic held in Regina in 1977...served on Board of Directors of Regina Exhibition from 1970-96...appointed to Queen's Counsel in 1981...inducted into the Plaza of Honor in 1997.

ROY SHIVERS; GENERAL MANAGER 2000-2006

Born in July 1941 in Hally, Arkansas...star running back at Utah State in 1964 and 1965...chosen in the first round of the 1966 supplemental draft by the NFL's St. Louis Cardinals where he played until the 1972 season...excelled at kickoff returns...coached running backs at Meritt Junior College upon his retirement as a player...coached at the University of Nevada, University of Hawaii and University of Las Vegas...in 1983 he became assistant coach with the B.C. Lions and stayed for six years while also doing some player personnel work which many believe to be his forte...in 1989 became the United Sates scout for the Calgary Stampeders...in 1991 became Calgary's assistant general manager...named general manager of the CFL's Birmingham Barracudas in 1995...when the team folded after one year, Shivers returned to Calgary again as an assistant GM to Wally Buono...named general manager of the Roughriders on Dec. 24, 1999 and would remain until Aug. 21, 2006...overall record with the Riders was 52 wins, 64 losses and one tie...after two rebuilding seasons as general manager, the Riders made the playoffs from 2002 to 2005 and were Western finalists twice (2003, 2004)...following a two-year retirement from football, rejoined the B.C. Lions in 2008 as director of player personnel.

JEARLD BAYLIS; 1992-1993

Born in Jackson, Mississippi in August 1962...a star in college at Southern Mississippi...had an impressive 10-year career in the CFL, including two seasons as a Saskatchewan Roughrider...entered the league in 1986...joined the Riders for the 1992, 1993 seasons...four-time divisional and CFL All-Star (1987, 1992, 1993, and 1995)...earned divisional and All-Canadian awards in both years as a Rider...compiled 19 quarterback sacks in his two seasons with Saskatchewan (16th All-Time Riders) and earned the CFL Most Outstanding Defensive Player award in 1993 while with the Riders...was a member of the 1995 Grey Cup champion Baltimore Stallions.

GORDON STURTRIDGE; 1953-56

After being cut from the Winnipeg Blue Bombers in 1950, Sturtridge played two years of intermediate football in Winnipeg before making the Roughrider team in 1953, immediately shining as a defensive end...was named Western Conference rookie-of-the-year in 1953...two years later he won the Stack Tibbits Award for Outstanding Canadian with the Riders...was a Western Conference All-Star in 1955 and 1956...a hard-nosed defensive end whose career ended abruptly in 1956 as a result of an airplane crash after the East-West Shrine All-Star Game in Vancouver...with Gordon and his wife were teammates Mel Becket, Mario DeMarco and Ray Syrnyk...the North Star aircraft experienced engine trouble and crashed into Mount Slesse in the Rocky Mountains and was not located for several months...Gord and his wife Mildred left behind three children who were raised by their grandparents...the uniforms of the four players–Becket (40), DeMarco (55), Syrnyk (56) and Sturtridge (73)–were retired...the Gordon Sturtridge Minor Football League was established at Northgate Park in North Vancouver in his honour in September of 1957.

GREG GRASSICK; PLAYER, COACH, BUILDER

Was the son of Regina pioneer James Grassick who was Mayor of Regina...first played football for the Regina Rugby Club in the early 1920s and then played for McGill University...returned to Regina to continue his football career with the renamed Regina Roughriders...played in four Grey Cups for Al Ritchie from 1929 to 1932 and was a player-coach in 1934...after his playing career, he became team manager and in 1945 was instrumental with fellow teammates Jack Rowand and Clair Warner in the reorganization of the Roughriders...was travel and accommodations manager for the Roughriders from 1948 to 1950...credited with being instrumental in the introduction of the forward pass to Canadian football...was associated in football with the Roughriders for more than 20 years as a player, coach and executive...was inducted into the Saskatchewan Sports Hall of Fame in 1982 and the Plaza of Honor in 1988...died in 1985.

BOOKS PRODUCED THROUGH THE SPORT HISTORY PROJECT

Andrews, Gary. *Fifty Years of Athletics in Saskatchewan: A History of the Saskatchewan High Schools Athletic Association*. Regina: Saskatchewan High School Athletics Association and the Saskatchewan Sports Hall of Fame and Museum, 1999

Argan, William. *Saskatchewan Curling: Heartland Tradition (1882-1990)*. Regina: Saskatchewan Curling Association and the Saskatchewan Sports Hall of Fame and Museum, 1992. OUT OF PRINT

Bingaman, Sandra. *Breaking 100: A Century of Women's Golf in Saskatchewan*. Saskatchewan Ladies' Golf Association and the Saskatchewan Sports Hall of Fame and Museum, 1997.

Bingaman, Sandra. *Spinning Into the Spotlight: Figure Skating in Saskatchewan 1883-1996*. Regina, Saskatchewan Figure Skating Association and the Saskatchewan Sports Hall of Fame and Museum, 2000

Bingaman, Sandra. *For the Love of the Game: Tennis in Saskatchewan 1883-2001*. Regina: Tennis Saskatchewan and the Saskatchewan Sports Hall of Fame and Museum, 2004

Bingaman, Sandra. *Courts, Killshots, and Conquests: Saskatchewan Racquetball's First 46 Years*. Regina: Saskatchewan Racquetball Association and the Saskatchewan Sports Hall of Fame and Museum, 2007

Boyle, Mickey. *Ninety Years of Golf: An Illustrated History of Golf in Saskatchewan*. Regina: Saskatchewan Golf Association, 1987. OUT OF PRINT

Brass, Dana. *Twisting and Tumbling Through Saskatchewan: A History of Gymnastics*. Regina: Saskatchewan Gymnastics Association and the Saskatchewan Sports Hall of Fame and Museum, 1992.

Brown, David W. *Saskatchewan Rugby: A History*. Regina: Saskatchewan Rugby Union and the Saskatchewan Sports Hall of Fame and Museum, 1992.

Conrad, Peter. *In the Winning Lane: A History of Competitive Swimming in Saskatchewan*. Regina: Swim Saskatchewan, Inc., 1990. OUT OF PRINT

DeRyk, Dick. *The Highest Skill: The Story of Karate in Saskatchewan*. Regina: Saskatchewan Karate Association, 1987. OUT OF PRINT

Dewar, John D. *Basketball, Saskatchewan's Story: 1891-1989*. Regina: Basketball Saskatchewan Inc., 1989.

Dewar, John M. *Saskatchewan Soccer: A History*. Saskatoon: Saskatchewan Soccer Association, 1986.

Elasser, Douglas. *Magic Boards: A History of Skiing in Saskatchewan*. Regina: Saskatchewan Ski Association and the Saskatchewan Sports Hall of Fame and Museum, 1995.

Goplen, Henrietta. *Saskatoon Lion's Speed Skating Club, 1942-1987: 45 Years of History*. 1987

Hack, Paul and Shury, Dave. *Wheat Province Diamonds: a Story of Saskatchewan Baseball*. Saskatchewan Baseball Association and Saskatchewan Sports Hall of Fame and Museum, 1997.

Hughes, Bob. *Regina Rams: A Winning Tradition*. Regina: University of Regina Rams Football Club and the Saskatchewan Sports Hall of Fame and Museum. 2003.

Kennedy, Michael P.J. *Dogs on Ice: A History of Hockey at University of Saskatchewan*. Saskatchewan Sports Hall of Fame and Museum and Friends of the Huskies, 2006.

Mortin, Jenni. *Safe at Home: A History of Softball in Saskatchewan*. Softball Saskatchewan and the Saskatchewan Sports Hall of Fame and Museum, Regina 1997

Nixon, Elva. *Fifty Years to Gold: Synchronized Swimming in Saskatchewan (1941-1991)*. Regina: Canadian Amateur Synchronized Swimming Association, Saskatchewan Section, Inc. and the Saskatchewan Sports Hall of Fame and Museum, 1993.

Powers, Ned. *Strikes 'n' Spares: A History of Bowling in Saskatchewan*. Regina: Bowling Federation of Saskatchewan and the Saskatchewan Sports Hall of Fame and Museum, 1993.

Powers, Ned. *Personal Best: The History of Track and Field in Saskatchewan*. Saskatoon: Saskatchewan Athletics and the Saskatchewan Sports Hall of Fame and Museum, 1997.

Powers, Ned. *The Hilltops: A Canadian Junior Football Legacy*. Saskatoon. Saskatoon Hilltop Junior Football Club and the Saskatchewan Sports hall of fame and Museum, 2006 OUT OF PRINT

Pugh, Terry. *Prevailing Westerlies: A History of Sailing in Saskatchewan*. St Peter's Press, Meunster, SK, Saskatchewan Sailing Clubs Association (Saskatchewan Sports Hall of Fame and Museum – Omitted in the credits), 1999.

Rediger, Pat. *Blades of Glory: The History of Speed Skating in Saskatchewan*. Mississagua: Saskatchewan Amateur Speed Skating Association and the Saskatchewan Sports Hall of Fame and Museum, 1999.

Rediger, Pat. *Riding With the Wind: The History of Cycling in Saskatchewan*. Regina: Saskatchewan Cycling Association and the Saskatchewan Sports Hall of Fame and Museum, 2001.

Riches, Stefan. *Moving Forward ... Looking Back: Saskatchewan Rowing in the 20th Century*. Regina: Saskatchewan Rowing Association and the Saskatchewan Sports Hall of Fame and Museum, 2000.

Schneider, Anne. *With This Ring: The History of Ringette in Saskatchewan*. Regina: Ringette Association of Saskatchewan and the Saskatchewan Sports Hall of Fame and Museum, 1998.

Vanstone, Rob. *West Riders Best – 1966: Before, Then & After*. Regina: Leader-Post Foundation and the Saskatchewan Sports Hall of Fame and Museum. 2009.

Zeman, Brenda. *88 Years of Puck Chasing in Saskatchewan*. Regina: WDS Associates and the Saskatchewan Sports Hall of Fame, 1983.

For further information on the Sport History Project Grant or to enquire about purchasing these publications, please contact:

The Executive Director
Saskatchewan Sports Hall of Fame and Museum
2205 Victoria Ave.
Regina, Saskatchewan S4P 0S4
Telephone (306) 780-9232 Fax (306) 780-9427